Computational Methods and Application in Machine Learning

Computational Methods and Application in Machine Learning

Guest Editors

Chunwei Tian
Huawen Liu
Chengyuan Zhang
Weiren Yu

Basel • Beijing • Wuhan • Barcelona • Belgrade • Novi Sad • Cluj • Manchester

Guest Editors

Chunwei Tian
Northwestern Polytechnical University
Xi'an
China

Huawen Liu
Zhejiang Normal University
Jinhua
China

Chengyuan Zhang
Hunan University
Changsha
China

Weiren Yu
University of Warwick
Coventry
UK

Editorial Office
MDPI AG
Grosspeteranlage 5
4052 Basel, Switzerland

This is a reprint of the Special Issue, published open access by the journal *Mathematics* (ISSN 2227-7390), freely accessible at: https://www.mdpi.com/journal/mathematics/special_issues/Computational_Methods_and_Application_in_Machine_Learning.

For citation purposes, cite each article independently as indicated on the article page online and as indicated below:

Lastname, A.A.; Lastname, B.B. Article Title. *Journal Name* **Year**, *Volume Number*, Page Range.

ISBN 978-3-7258-2819-7 (Hbk)
ISBN 978-3-7258-2820-3 (PDF)
https://doi.org/10.3390/books978-3-7258-2820-3

© 2024 by the authors. Articles in this book are Open Access and distributed under the Creative Commons Attribution (CC BY) license. The book as a whole is distributed by MDPI under the terms and conditions of the Creative Commons Attribution-NonCommercial-NoDerivs (CC BY-NC-ND) license (https://creativecommons.org/licenses/by-nc-nd/4.0/).

Contents

About the Editors vii

Preface ix

Xinghui Zhu, Liewu Cai, Zhuoyang Zou and Lei Zhu
Deep Multi-Semantic Fusion-Based Cross-Modal Hashing
Reprinted from: *Mathematics* 2022, 10, 430, https://doi.org/10.3390/math10030430 1

Yingxin Xiang, Chengyuan Zhang, Zhichao Han, Hao Yu, Jiaye Li, Lei Zhu
Path-Wise Attention Memory Network for Visual Question Answering
Reprinted from: *Mathematics* 2022, 10, 3244, https://doi.org/10.3390/math10183244 21

Feng Jiang, Yang Cao, Huan Wu, Xibin Wang, Yuqi Song and Min Gao
Social Recommendation Based on Multi-Auxiliary Information Constrastive Learning
Reprinted from: *Mathematics* 2022, 10, 4130, https://doi.org/10.3390/math10214130 40

Lixiang Zhang, Yian Zhu, Jiang Su, Wei Lu, Jiayu Li and Ye Yao
A Hybrid Prediction Model Based on KNN-LSTM for Vessel Trajectory
Reprinted from: *Mathematics* 2022, 10, 4493, https://doi.org/10.3390/math10234493 56

Liang She, Jianyuan Wang, Yifan Bo and Yangyan Zeng
MACA: Multi-Agent with Credit Assignment for Computation Offloading in Smart Parks Monitoring
Reprinted from: *Mathematics* 2022, 10, 4616, https://doi.org/10.3390/math10234616 76

Hongbo Chen, Zhenwei Ma, Jinbo Wang and Linfeng Su
Online Trajectory Optimization Method for Large Attitude Flip Vertical Landing of The Starship-like Vehicle
Reprinted from: *Mathematics* 2023, 11, 288, https://doi.org/10.3390/math11020288 94

Ziyan Zhao, Li Zhang, Xiaoli Lian, Xiaoyun Gao, Heyang Lv and Lin Shi
ReqGen: Keywords-Driven Software Requirements Generation
Reprinted from: *Mathematics* 2023, 11, 332, https://doi.org/10.3390/math11020332 111

Jingyi Qu, Shixing Wu and Jinjie Zhang
Flight Delay Propagation Prediction Based on Deep Learning
Reprinted from: *Mathematics* 2023, 11, 494, https://doi.org/10.3390/math11030494 133

Jing Cheng, Jiayi Zhao, Weidong Xu, Tao Zhang, Feng Xue and Shaoying Liu
Semantic Similarity-Based Mobile Application Isomorphic Graphical User Interface Identification
Reprinted from: *Mathematics* 2023, 11, 527, https://doi.org/10.3390/math11030527 157

Quantao Wang, Ziming He, Jialiang Zou, Haobin Shi and Kao-Shing Hwang
Behavior Cloning and Replay of Humanoid Robot via a Depth Camera
Reprinted from: *Mathematics* 2023, 11, 678, https://doi.org/10.3390/math11030678 174

Yishun Liu, Chunhua Yang, Keke Huang and Weiping Liu
A Multi-Factor Selection and Fusion Method through the CNN-LSTM Network for Dynamic Price Forecasting
Reprinted from: *Mathematics* 2023, 11, 1132, https://doi.org/10.3390/math11051132 191

Huawen Liu, Minhao Yin, Zongda Wu, Liping Zhao, Qi Li, Xinzhong Zhu and Zhonglong Zheng
PLDH: Pseudo-Labels Based Deep Hashing
Reprinted from: *Mathematics* 2023, *11*, 2175, https://doi.org/10.3390/math11092175 211

Zhongli Ma, Yi Wan, Jiajia Liu, Ruojin An and Lili Wu
A Kind of Water Surface Multi-Scale Object Detection Method Based on Improved YOLOv5 Network
Reprinted from: *Mathematics* 2023, *11*, 2936, https://doi.org/10.3390/math11132936 224

Huan Chen, Farong Gao and Qizhong Zhang
FDDS: Feature Disentangling and Domain Shifting for Domain Adaptation
Reprinted from: *Mathematics* 2023, *11*, 2995, https://doi.org/10.3390/math11132995 242

Hang Yin, Zeyu Wu, Junchao Wu, Junjie Jiang, Yalin Chen, Mingxuan Chen, et al.
A Hybrid Medium and Long-Term Relative Humidity Point and Interval Prediction Method for Intensive Poultry Farming
Reprinted from: *Mathematics* 2023, *11*, 3247, https://doi.org/10.3390/math11143247 261

Xuanyu Zhang, Chunwei Tian, Qi Zhang, Hong-Seng Gan, Tongtong Cheng and Mohd Asrul Hery Ibrahim
Lightweight Image Denoising Network for Multimedia Teaching System
Reprinted from: *Mathematics* 2023, *11*, 3678, https://doi.org/10.3390/math11173678 283

About the Editors

Chunwei Tian

Dr. Chunwei Tian is an Associate Professor at the School of Software, Northwestern Polytechnical University, and a member of the National Engineering Laboratory for Integrated Big Data Application Technologies in Air, Space, Earth, and Sea, holds a Ph.D. in Computer Application Technology from Harbin Institute of Technology. His achievements include being listed among the top 2% scientists worldwide in 2022/2023, recognized as a provincial-level talent, a municipal-level talent. He has also received numerous accolades, such as the 2022 Excellent Doctoral Dissertation Award from the Provincial Artificial Intelligence Society, the 2021 Shenzhen CCF Outstanding Doctoral Dissertation Award, the 2022 Harbin Institute of Technology Outstanding Doctoral Dissertation Award, and a special invitation for the Huawei Global Genius Program Interview in 2021. My research interests lie in video/image restoration and recognition, image generation, and deep learning. He has published over 70 papers in prestigious international journals and conferences such as IEEE TNNLS, IEEE TMM, IEEE TSMC, IEEE TGRS, IEEE TCSVT, IEEE TIV, Pattern Recognition, Neural Networks, Information Sciences, Information Fusion, and ICASSP. Among these, six are ESI highly cited papers, three are ESI hot papers, four are cover papers in top journals, and five are included in the Benchmark List of the international super-resolution field. Notably, the technology described in one of my papers has been purchased for commercial use by an American medical imaging company, and the technology in another paper has been applied to Apple phones by Japanese engineers. Furthermore, He serves as an editorial board member for several SCI journals, including CAAI Transaction on Intelligence Technology and Dense Technology. He is also a reviewer for the National Natural Science Foundation of China, a technology expert in Shanghai, and an expert in the National Graduate Education Evaluation and Monitoring Expert Database.

Huawen Liu

Prof. Huawen Liu is a professor with the College of Mathematics and Computer Sciences of Zhejiang Normal University, P.R.China since July, 2010. He received his Ph.D. and Ms.D. of Computer Science from Jilin University, P.R.China. He was a post-doctor at University of South Australia from 2012 to 2013, and a visiting fellow at University of Texas at San Antonio from 2018 to 2019. His research interests are in the fields of multimedia systems, feature selection, data mining, machine learning and their applications in image processing and multimedia data. He has published above 30 refereed papers in international journals and conference proceedings, including IEEE Trans Neural Netw & Learning Syst., IEEE Trans. on Cybernetics, IEEE Trans. on Multimedia, IEEE Trans. on Syst. Man and Cybern., Pattern Recognition, Information Sciences, and so on. He has served as an editor of J. Fuzzy and Intelligent Systems from 2016. He served a lead guest editor of two international journals including Neural Computing and Applications (NCAA) and Computing and Informatics (CAI), and served as the organising chair of the 2015 National Conf. of Theoretical Computer Science, the 2014 China Conference on Data Mining, and a PC member for several conferences such as ADMA, ICBK and KSEM.

Chengyuan Zhang

Dr. Chengyuan Zhang is an Associate Professor in College of Computer Science and Electronic Engineering, Hunan University. He successively acquired his Master's and Doctoral degrees from the School of Computer Science and Engineering at the University of New South Wales in 2011 and 2015, respectively. From April 2015 to April 2016, he served as a Research Assistant in the Database Group of the School of Information Science and Engineering at the University of New South Wales. From 2016 to 2020, he worked as a lecturer at Central South University. In 2020, he was introduced as a talent (with the title of Associate Professor) to the School of Information Science and Engineering at Hunan University. His main research areas include querying and processing spatiotemporal multimedia data, data mining, machine learning, graph data analysis, and missing data handling. He has presided over one National Natural Science Foundation of China (NSFC) Young Scientists Fund project and one Hunan Provincial Natural Science Foundation for Youth project, and participated in two NSFC projects. He has published nearly 30 papers in related fields, with nearly 20 papers as the first/corresponding author in international authoritative journals or conferences such as IEEE TKDE, IEEE ICDE, EDBT, Neurocomputing, Pattern Recognition Letters, Multimedia Tools and Applications, among which there are 4 highly cited papers in ESI 1%. He has applied for 2 national invention patents and published one monograph. He has served as a member of the program committee for IJCAI-2020 and a reviewer for PVLDB2020, as well as a reviewer for SCI journals including ACM TOIS, IEEE TKDE, VLDBJ, ACM TOMM, IEEE TNNLS, ACM TKDD, Neurocomputing, Pattern Recognition Letters, Multimedia Tools and Applications, Applied Intelligence, and IEEE Multimedia. Also, he has served as a guest editor for Multimedia Tools and Applications.

Weiren Yu

Dr. Weiren is an Associate Professor in the Department of Computer Science at the University of Warwick. He is the Data Science Course Director and a member of the Zeeman Institute for Systems Biology and Infectious Disease Epidemiology Research (SBIDER). He was awarded an Honorary Visiting Fellow by the Department of Computing at Imperial College. He received his Ph.D. degree from the School of Computer Science and Engineering at the University of New South Wales (UNSW, Sydney). During his years at UNSW, he was also a Research Assistant at the Commonwealth Scientific and Industrial Research Organisation (CSIRO), and National ICT Australia (NICTA). After that, he spent two years as a Postdoctoral Researcher at the Adaptive Embedded Systems Engineering (AESE) Laboratory in the Department of Computing at Imperial College. He collaborated with NEC Europe Ltd and the Department of Civil and Environmental Engineering at Imperial, working on an IoT project "Big Data Technologies for Smart Water Systems". He is a recipient of seven Best Paper Awards, including one Best Research Paper Award for ECSA 2016, two CiSRA (Canon Information Systems Research Australia) Best Research Paper Awards for ICDE 2014 and VLDB 2013 respectively, one of the Best Papers of ICDE in 2013, and three Best (Student) Paper Awards for APWEB 2010, WAIM 2010 and WAIM 2011, respectively. He is a member of the IEEE and the ACM.

Preface

Dear Colleagues,

Machine learning is an interdisciplinary subject involving probability theory, statistics, approximation theory, convex analysis, optimization, algorithm complexity theory, etc. It focuses on how computers simulate or realize human learning behaviors to obtain new knowledge or skills. It is the core of artificial intelligence. In essence, the aim of machine learning is to enable computers to simulate human learning behaviors, automatically acquire knowledge and skills through learning, continuously improve performance, and realize artificial intelligence.

The main focus of this Special Issue is the progress of machine learning methods and applications, as well as emerging intelligent applications and models in topics of interest, and they include but are not limited to the following: information retrieval, expert systems, automatic reasoning, natural language understanding, pattern recognition, computer vision, intelligent robot, and deep learning.

Chunwei Tian, Huawen Liu, Chengyuan Zhang, and Weiren Yu
Guest Editors

Article

Deep Multi-Semantic Fusion-Based Cross-Modal Hashing

Xinghui Zhu, Liewu Cai, Zhuoyang Zou and Lei Zhu *

College of Information and Intelligence, Hunan Agricultural University, Changsha 410128, China; zhuxh@hunau.edu.cn (X.Z.); liewucai@stu.hunau.edu.cn (L.C.); zzy@stu.hunau.edu.cn (Z.Z.)
* Correspondence: leizhu@hunau.edu.cn

Abstract: Due to the low costs of its storage and search, the cross-modal retrieval hashing method has received much research interest in the big data era. Due to the application of deep learning, the cross-modal representation capabilities have risen markedly. However, the existing deep hashing methods cannot consider multi-label semantic learning and cross-modal similarity learning simultaneously. That means potential semantic correlations among multimedia data are not fully excavated from multi-category labels, which also affects the original similarity preserving of cross-modal hash codes. To this end, this paper proposes deep multi-semantic fusion-based cross-modal hashing (DMSFH), which uses two deep neural networks to extract cross-modal features, and uses a multi-label semantic fusion method to improve cross-modal consistent semantic discrimination learning. Moreover, a graph regularization method is combined with inter-modal and intra-modal pairwise loss to preserve the nearest neighbor relationship between data in Hamming subspace. Thus, DMSFH not only retains semantic similarity between multi-modal data, but integrates multi-label information into modal learning as well. Extensive experimental results on two commonly used benchmark datasets show that our DMSFH is competitive with the state-of-the-art methods.

Keywords: cross-modal hashing; semantic label information; multi-label semantic fusion; graph regularization; deep neural network

Citation: Zhu, X.; Cai, L.; Zou, Z.; Zhu, L. Deep Multi-Semantic Fusion-Based Cross-Modal Hashing. *Mathematics* 2022, 10, 430. https://doi.org/10.3390/math10030430

Academic Editor: Alfredo Milani

Received: 21 November 2021
Accepted: 12 January 2022
Published: 29 January 2022

Publisher's Note: MDPI stays neutral with regard to jurisdictional claims in published maps and institutional affiliations.

Copyright: © 2022 by the authors. Licensee MDPI, Basel, Switzerland. This article is an open access article distributed under the terms and conditions of the Creative Commons Attribution (CC BY) license (https://creativecommons.org/licenses/by/4.0/).

1. Introduction

In recent years, with the rapid development of information technology, massive amounts of multi-modal data (i.e., text [1], image [2], audio [3], video [4], and 3D models [5]) have been collected and stored on the Internet. How to utilize the extensive multi-modal data to improve cross-modal retrieval performance has attracted increasing attention [6,7]. Cross-modal retrieval, a hot issue in the multimedia community, is the use of queries from one modality to retrieve all semantically relevant instances from another modality [8–10]. In general, the structuring of data in different modalities is heterogeneous, but there are strong semantic correlations between these structures. Therefore, the main tasks of cross-modal retrieval are discovering how to narrow the semantic gap and exploring the common representations of multi-modal data, the former being the most challenging problem faced by researchers in this field [11–14].

Most of existing cross-modal retrieval methods, including traditional statistical correlation analysis [15], graph regularization [16], and dictionary learning [17], learn a common subspace [18–21] for multi-modal samples, in which the semantic similarity between different modalities can be measured easily. For example, based on canonical correlation analysis (CCA) [22], several cross-modal retrieval methods [23–25] have been proposed to learn a common subspace in which the correlations between different modalities are easily measured. Besides, graph regularization has been applied in many studies [16,26–28] to preserve the semantic similarity between cross-modal representations in the common subspace. The methods in [17,29,30] draw support from dictionary learning to learn consistent representations for multi-modal data. However, these methods usually have high computational costs and low retrieval efficiency [31]. In order to overcome these shortcomings, hashing-based cross-modal retrieval techniques are gradually replacing the traditional ones. A practical way to speed up similarity searching is with binary representation learning, referred to as hashing learning, which projects a high-dimensional feature representation from each modality as a compact hash code and preserves similar instances with similar hash codes. In this paper, we focus on the cross-modal binary representation learning task, which can be applied to large-scale multimedia searches in the cloud [32–34].

In general, most of the existing traditional cross-modal hashing methods can be roughly divided into two groups: unsupervised [35–39] and supervised methods [40–44]. Unlike unsupervised methods, supervised methods can excavate similarity relationships between data through semantic labels to achieve better performance. However, these methods rely on shallow features that cannot provide sufficient semantic discrimination information. Recently, deep models [45–48] have been widely adopted to perform feature learning from scratch with very promising performance. This powerful representation learning technique boosts the non-linear correlation learning capabilities of cross-modal hashing models. Thus, lots of deep hashing method [28,49–58] have been developed, which can effectively learn more discriminative semantic representations from multi-modal samples and are gradually replacing the traditional hashing approaches.

Motivation. Although deep hashing algorithms have made remarkable progress in cross-modal retrieval, the semantic gap and heterogeneity gap between different modalities need to be further narrowed. On the one hand, most methods lack mining of ample semantic information from multiple category labels. That means these methods cannot completely retain multi-label semantic information during cross-modal representation learning. Taking [28] as an example, graph regularization is used to support intra-modal and inter-modal similarity learning, but the multi-label semantics are not mined fully during the cross-modal representation learning, which affect the semantic discrimination of hash codes. On the other hand, after the features learned from normal networks are quantized into binary representations, some semantic correlations may be lost in Hamming subspace. For instance, [59] studies the effective distance measurement of cross-modal binary representations in Hamming subspace. However, multi-label semantics learning is ignored, which leads to insufficient semantic discriminability of the hash code. Therefore, to further improve the quality of cross-modal hash codes, two particularly important problems cannot be overlooked during the hashing learning: (1) *how to capture more semantic discriminative features*, and (2) *how to efficiently preserve cross-modal semantic similarity in common Hamming subspaces*. In this work, we consider these two key issues simultaneously during the cross-modal hashing learning to generate more semantically discriminative hash codes.

Our Method. To this end, we propose a novel end-to-end cross-modal hashing learning approach, named deep multi-semantic fusion-based cross-modal hashing (**DMSFH** for short) to efficiently capture multi-label semantics and generate high-quality cross-modal hash codes. Firstly, two deep neural networks are used to learn cross-modal representations. Then, intra-modal loss and inter-modal loss are utilized by generating a semantic similarity matrix to preserve semantic similarity. To further capture the rich semantic information, a multi-label semantic fusion module is used following the feature learning module, which fuses the multiple label semantics into cross-modal representations to preserve the semantic consistency across different modalities. In addition, we introduce a graph regularization method to preserve semantic similarity among cross-modal hash codes in Hamming subspace.

Contributions. The main contributions of this paper are summarized as follows:

- We propose a novel deep learning-based cross-modal hashing method, termed DMSFH, which integrates cross-modal feature learning, multi-label semantic fusion, and hash code learning into an end-to-end architecture.
- We combine the graph regularization method with inter-modal and intra-modal pairwise loss to enhance cross-modal similarity learning in Hamming subspace. Addition-

ally, a multi-label semantic fusion module was developed to enhance the cross-modal consistent semantics learning.
- Extensive experiments conducted on two well-known multimedia datasets demonstrate the outstanding performance of our methods compared to other state-of-the-art cross-modal hashing methods.

Roadmap. The rest of this paper is organized as follows. The related work is summarized in Section 2. The problem definition and the details of the proposed method DMSFH are presented in Section 3. The experimental results and evaluations are reported in Section 4. We discuss the main contributions and characteristics of our research in Section 5. Finally, we conclude this paper in Section 6.

2. Related Work

According to learning manner, the existing cross-modal hashing techniques fall into two categories: unsupervised approaches and supervised approaches. Due to the vigorous development of deep learning, cross-modal deep hashing approaches sprang up in the last decade. This section reviews the works that are related to our paper.

Unsupervised Methods. To learn a hash function, the unsupervised hashing methods aim to mine the unlabeled samples to discover the relationship between multi-modal data. One of the most typical technique is collective matrix factorization hashing (CMFH) [60], which utilizes matrix decomposition to learn two view-specific hash functions, and then different modal data can be mapped into unified hash codes. The latent semantic sparse hashing (LSSH) method [35] uses sparse coding to find the salient structures of images, and matrix factorization to learn the latent concepts from text. Then, the learned latent semantic features are mapped to a joint common subspace. Semantic topic multimodal hashing (STMH) [37], which discovers clustering patterns of texts and factorizes the matrix of images, to acquire multiple semantic of texts and concepts of images in order to learn multimodal semantic features, into a common subspace by their correlations. Multi-modal graph regularized smooth matrix factorization hashing (MSFH) [61] utilizes a multi-modal graph regularization term which includes an intra-modal similarity graph and an inter-modal similarity graph to preserve the topology of the original instances. The latent structure discrete hashing factorization (LSDHF) [62] approach uses the Hadamard matrix to align all eigenvalues of the similarity matrix to generate a hash dictionary, and then straightforwardly distills the shared hash codes from the intrinsic structure of modalities.

Supervised Methods. Supervised cross-modal hashing methods improve the search performance by using supervised information, such as training data labels. Typical supervised approaches include cross-modal similarity sensitive hashing (CMSSH) [40], semantic preserving hashing for cross-view retrieval (SEPH) [41], semantic correlation maximization (SCM) [42], and discrete cross-modal hashing (DCH) [43]. CMSSH applies boosting techniques to preserve the intra-modal similarity. SEPH transforms the semantic similarity of training data into an affinity matrix by using a label as supervised information, and minimizes the Kullback–Leibler divergence to learn hash codes. SCM utilizes all the supervised information for training with linear-time complexity by avoiding explicitly computing the pairwise similarity matrix. DCH learns discriminative binary codes without relaxation, and label information is used to elevate the discriminability of binary codes through linear classifiers. Nevertheless, these cross-modal hashing methods are established on hand-crafted features [43,63]. It is hard to explore the semantic relationships among multi-modal data. Therefore, it is difficult to obtain satisfying retrieval results.

Deep Methods. In recent years, deep learning, as a powerful representation learning technique, has been widely used in cross-modal retrieval tasks. A number of methods integrating deep neural networks and cross-modal hashing have been developed. For example, deep cross-modal hashing (DCMH) [64] firstly applies the end-to-end deep learning architecture for cross-modal hashing retrieval and utilizes the negative logistic likelihood loss to achieve great performance. Pairwise relationship-guided deep hashing (PRDH) [65] uses pairwise label constraints to supervise the similarity learning of inter-modal and intra-modal data. A correlation hashing network (CHN) [66] adapts the triplet loss measured by cosine distance to find the semantic relationship between pairwise instances. Cross-modal hamming hashing (CMHH) [59] learns high-quality hash representations to significantly penalize similar cross-modal pairs with Hamming distances larger than the Hamming radius threshold. The ranking-based deep cross-modal hashing approach (RDCMH) [49] integrates the semantic ranking information into a deep cross-modal hashing model and jointly optimizes the compatible parameters of deep feature representations and hashing functions. In fusion-supervised deep cross-modal hashing (FDCH) [67], both pair-wise similarity information and classification information are embedded in the hash model, which simultaneously preserves cross-modal similarity and reduces semantic inconsistency. Despite the above-mentioned benefits, most of these methods only use binary similarity to constrain the generation of different instances of hash codes. This causes low correlations between retrieval results and the inputs, as the semantic label information cannot be expressed adequately. Besides, most methods only concentrate on hash code learning, but ignore the deep mining of semantic features. Thus, it is essential to keep sufficient semantic information in the modal structure and generate discriminative hash codes to enhance the cross-modal hashing learning.

To overcome the above challenges, this paper proposes a novel approach to excavate multi-label semantic information to improve the semantic discrimination of cross-modal hash codes. This approach not only uses the negative logistic likelihood loss, but also exploits multiple semantic labels' prediction losses based on cross entropy to enhance semantic information mining. Apart from this, we introduce graph regularization to preserve the semantic similarity of hash codes in Hamming subspace. Therefore, the proposed method is designed to generate high-quality hash codes that better reflect high-level cross-modal semantic correlations.

3. The Proposed Approach

In this section, we propose our method DMSFH, including the model's formulation and the learning algorithm. The framework of the proposed DMSFH is shown in Figure 1, which mainly consists of three parts. The first part is the feature learning module, in which multimedia samples are transformed into high-dimensional feature representations by corresponding deep neural networks. The second part is the multi-label semantic fusion part. This part aims to embed rich multi-label semantic information into feature learning. The third part is the hashing learning module, which retains the semantic similarity of the cross-modal data in the hash codes using a carefully designed loss function. In the following, we introduce the problem definition first, and then discuss DMSFH method in detail.

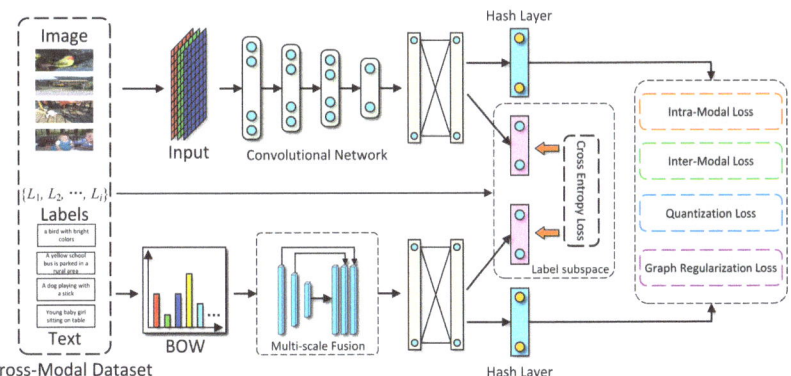

Figure 1. The framework of DMSFH. It contains three main components: (1) the feature learning module, which contains a classical convolutional neural network for image-modality feature learning, and a multi-scale fusion-based convolutional neural network for text-modality feature learning; (2) a multi-label semantic information learning module that is realized by deep neural networks, which is to fuse rich semantic information from multiple labels to generate consistent semantic representations in label subspace; (3) a hash function module that is trained by inter-modal and intra-modal pairwise loss, quantization loss, and graph regularization loss to generate cross-modal hash codes.

3.1. Problem Definition

Without loss of generality, bold uppercase letters, such as W, represent matrices. Bold lowercase letters, such as w, represent vectors. Moreover, the ij-th element of W is denoted as W_{ij}, the i-th row of W is denoted as W_{i*}, and the j-th column of W is denoted as W_{*j}. W^T is the transpose of W. We use I for the identity matrix. $tr(\cdot)$ and $||\cdot||_F$ denote the trace of the matrix and the Frobenius norm of a matrix, respectively. $sign(\cdot)$ is the sign function, shown as follows:

$$sign(x) = \begin{cases} 1, & x \geq 0 \\ -1, & x < 0 \end{cases}. \tag{1}$$

To facilitate easier reading, the frequently used mathematical notation is summarized in Table 1.

Table 1. A summary of frequently-used notation.

Notation	Definition
n	the number of training instances
k	length of hash codes
c	the number of categories
v_i	the ith image sample
t_i	the ith text sample
O	multimedia datasets
L	semantic label matrix of instances
$\hat{L}^v$	predicted semantic label matrix of instances in image network
$\hat{L}^t$	predicted semantic label matrix of instances in text network
S	binary similarity matrix
F	image modality continuous hash code
G	textual modality continuous hash code
B	the unified binary hash codes

This paper focuses on two common modalities: texts and images. Assume that a cross-modal training dataset consists of n instances, i.e., $O = \{o_1, o_2, \ldots, o_n\}$, where $o_i = (v_i, t_i, L_i)$ denotes the i-th training instances, and v_i and t_i are the i-th image and text, respectively. $L_i = [L_{i1}, L_{i2}, \ldots, L_{ic}]$ is the multi-label annotation assigned to o_i, where c is the number of categories. If o_i belongs to the jth class, $L_{ij} = 1$; otherwise, $L_{ij} = 0$. In addition, a cross-modal similarity matrix $S = \{S^{vt}, S^{vv}, S^{tt}\}$ is given. If image v_i and text t_j are similar, $S_{ij} = 1$; otherwise, $S_{ij} = 0$.

Given a set of training data O, the goal of cross-modal hashing is to learn two hashing functions, i.e., $h^v(v)$ and $h^t(t)$ for image modality and textual modality, respectively, where $h^v(v) \in \{-1,1\}^k$, $h^t(t) \in \{-1,1\}^k$, k is the length of the hash code. In addition, the hash codes preserve the similarities in similarity matrix S. If the Hamming distance between the codes $b_i^{(v)} = h^v(v_i)$ and $b_i^{(t)} = h^t(t_i)$ is small, $S_{ij} = 1$; otherwise $S_{ij} = 0$. To easily calculate the similarity between two binary codes b_i and b_j, we use the inner product $\langle b_i, b_j \rangle$ to measure the Hamming distance as follows:

$$dis_H(b_i, b_j) = \frac{1}{2}(K - \langle b_i, b_j \rangle), \tag{2}$$

where K is the length of the hash code.

3.2. Feature Learning Networks

For cross-modal feature learning, deep neural networks are used to extract semantic features from each modality individually. Specifically, for image modality, ResNet34 [46], a well-known deep convolutional network, is used to extract image data features. The original ResNet was pre-trained on imagenet datasets; in addition, excellent results have been achieved on image recognition issues. We replaced the last layer with a network that has $(k + c)$ hidden nodes, which is followed by a hash layer and a tag layer. The hash layer has k hidden nodes for generating binary representations. The label layer has c hidden nodes for generating predictive labels.

For text modality, a deep model named TxtNet is used to generate textual feature representations, which is a three-layer network followed by a multi-scale (MS) fusion model ($T \to MS \to 4096 \to 512 \to k + c$). The last layer of TxtNet is a fully-connected layer with $(k + c)$ hidden nodes, which outputs deep textual features and prediction labels. The input of TxtNet is the Bag-of-Words (BoW) representation of each text sample. The BoW vector is too sparse, but the features extracted by the multi-scale fusion model are more abundant. Firstly, the BoW vectors are evenly pooled at different scales; then, the semantic information is extracted by nonlinear mapping through a convolution operation and an activation function. Finally, the representations from different scales are fused to obtain richer semantic information. The M_s fusion model contains 5 interpretation blocks. Each block contains a 1×1 convolutional layer and an average pooling layer. The filter sizes of the average pooling layer are set to 50×50, 30×30, 15×15, 10×10 and 5×5, respectively.

3.3. Hash Function Learning

In the network of image modality, let $f_1^v(v_{i*}; \theta_v, \theta_{vh}) \in \mathbb{R}^{1 \times k}$ denote the learned image feature of the i-th sample v_i, where θ_v is all network parameters before the last layer of the deep neural network, and θ_{vh} is the network parameter of the hash layer. Furthermore, let $f_2^v(v_{i*}; \theta_v, \theta_{vl}) \in \mathbb{R}^{1 \times c}$ denote the output of the label layer for sample v_i, where θ_{vl} is the network parameter of the label layer. In the network of text modality, let $f_1^t(t_{i*}; \theta_t, \theta_{th}) \in \mathbb{R}^{1 \times k}$ denote the learned text feature of the i-th sample t_i, where θ_t is all network parameters before the last layer of deep neural network, and θ_{th} is the network parameter of the hash layer. Furthermore, let $f_2^t(t_{i*}; \theta_t, \theta_{tl}) \in \mathbb{R}^{1 \times c}$ denote the output of the label layer for sample t_i, where θ_{tl} is the network parameter of the label layer.

To capture the semantic consistency between different modalities, the inter-modal negative log likelihood function is used in our approach, which is formulated as:

$$\mathcal{L}_1 = -\sum_{i,j=1}^{n}(S_{ij}^{vt}\phi_{ij}^{vt} - \log(1 + e^{\phi_{ij}^{vt}})), \tag{3}$$

where $\phi_{ij}^{vt} = \frac{1}{2} F_{i*} G_{j*}^T$ is the inner product of two instances, $F \in \mathbb{R}^{n \times k}$ with $F_{i*} = f_1^v(v_{i*}; \theta_v, \theta_{vh})$, and $G \in \mathbb{R}^{n \times k}$ with $G_{i*} = f_1^t(t_{i*}; \theta_t, \theta_{th})$. The likelihood function composed of text feature F and image feature G is as follows:

$$p(S_{ij}|F_{i*}, G_{j*}) = \begin{cases} \sigma(\phi_{ij}), & S_{ij} = 1 \\ 1 - \sigma(\phi_{ij}), & S_{ij} = 0 \end{cases}, \quad (4)$$

where $\sigma(\phi_{ij}) = \frac{1}{1+e^{-\phi_{ij}}}$ is a sigmoid function, and $\phi_{ij} = \frac{1}{2} F_{i*} G_{j*}^T$.

To generate the hash codes with rich semantic discrimination, two essential factors need to be considered: (1) the semantic similarity between different modes should be preserved, and (2) the high-level semantics within each mode should be preserved, which can raise the accuracy of cross-modal retrieval effectively. To realize this strategy, we define the intra-modal pair-wise loss as follows:

$$\mathcal{L}_2 = \mathcal{L}_2^v + \mathcal{L}_2^t, \quad (5)$$

where $\mathcal{L}_2^v$ is the intra-modal pair-wise loss for image-to-image and $\mathcal{L}_2^t$ is the intra-modal pair-wise loss for text-to-text, and $\mathcal{L}_2^v$ and $\mathcal{L}_2^t$ are defined as:

$$\mathcal{L}_2^v = -\sum_{i,j=1}^n (S_{ij}^{vv} \phi_{ij}^{vv} - \log(1 + e^{\phi_{ij}^{vv}})), \quad (6)$$

$$\mathcal{L}_2^t = -\sum_{i,j=1}^n (S_{ij}^{tt} \phi_{ij}^{tt} - \log(1 + e^{\phi_{ij}^{tt}})), \quad (7)$$

where $\phi_{ij}^{vv} = \frac{1}{2} F_{i*} F_{j*}^T$ is the inner product of image data, and $\phi_{ij}^{tt} = \frac{1}{2} G_{i*} G_{j*}^T$ is the inner product of text data.

Based on the negative log likelihood, the loss function can be used to distinguish identical and completely dissimilar instances. However, for more fine-grained hash features, we can extract higher-level semantic information by adding a tag prediction layer, so that the network can learn hash features with deep semantics. The semantic label cross-entropy loss is:

$$\mathcal{L}_3 = \mathcal{L}_3^{v\_label} + \mathcal{L}_3^{t\_label}, \quad (8)$$

where $\mathcal{L}_3^{v\_label}$ is the cross entropy loss for image modalities and $\mathcal{L}_3^{t\_label}$ is the cross entropy loss for text modalities. $\mathcal{L}_3^{v\_label}$ and $\mathcal{L}_3^{t\_label}$ are defined as:

$$\mathcal{L}_3^{v\_label} = \sum_{i}^n \sum_{j}^c (-L_{ij} \hat{L}_{ij}^v + \log(1 + e^{\hat{L}_{ij}^v})), \quad (9)$$

$$\mathcal{L}_3^{t\_label} = \sum_{i}^n \sum_{j}^c (-L_{ij} \hat{L}_{ij}^t + \log(1 + e^{\hat{L}_{ij}^t})), \quad (10)$$

where L_{i*} is the original semantic label information, for instance, o_i; and $\hat{L}_{i*}^v = f_2^v(v_{i*}; \theta_v, \theta_{vl})$ and $\hat{L}_{i*}^t = f_2^t(t_{i*}; \theta_t, \theta_{tl})$ represent the prediction labels of instance o_i in the image network and text network, respectively.

In order to enhance the correlation between the same hash code in Hamming subspace, we introduce graph regularization to establish the degree of correlation between multi-modal datasets. We formulate a spectral graph learning loss from the label similarity matrix S as follows:

$$\mathcal{L}_4 = \frac{1}{2} \sum_{i,j=1}^n ||b_i - b_j||_F^2 S_{ij}^{vt} = tr(B^T L B), \quad (11)$$

where S^{vt} is the similarity matrix, and $B = \{b_i\}_{i=1}^{n}$ represents the unified hash codes. we define diagonal matrix $D = diag(d_1, \ldots, d_n)$, and $L = D - S^{vt}$ is the graph Laplacian matrix.

We regard F and G as the continuous substitution of the image network hash code B^v and the text network hash code B^t to reduce quantization loss. According to the empirical analysis, the training effect will be better if the same hash code is used for different modes of the same training data, so we set $B^v = B^t = B$. Therefore, quantization loss can be defined as:

$$\mathcal{L}_5 = ||B - F||_F^2 + ||B - G||_F^2. \tag{12}$$

The overall objective function, combining the inter-modality pair-wise loss $\mathcal{L}_1$, the intra-modal pair-wise loss $\mathcal{L}_2$, the cross entropy loss $\mathcal{L}_3$ for the predicted label, graph regularization loss $\mathcal{L}_4$ and quantization loss $\mathcal{L}_5$, is written as below:

$$\min_{B, \theta_v, \theta_{vh}, \theta_{vl}, \theta_t, \theta_{th}, \theta_{tl}} \mathcal{L} = \mathcal{L}_1 + \mathcal{L}_2 + \mathcal{L}_3 + \gamma \mathcal{L}_4 + \beta \mathcal{L}_5 \tag{13}$$
$$\text{s.t.} \quad B \in \{-1, +1\}^{n \times k},$$

where γ and β are hyper-parameters to control the weight of each part.

3.4. Optimization

The objective in Equation (13) can be solved by using an alternative optimization iteratively. We adopt the mini-batch stochastic gradient descent (SGD) method to learn parameter $\vartheta_v = \{\theta_v, \theta_{vh}, \theta_{vl}\}$ in an image network and parameter $\vartheta_t = \{\theta_t, \theta_{th}, \theta_{tl}\}$ in a text network, and B. Each time we optimize one network with the other parameters fixed. The whole alternating learning algorithm for DMSFH is briefly outlined in Algorithm 1, and a detailed derivation is described in the following subsections.

3.4.1. Optimize ϑ_v

When ϑ_t and B are fixed, we can learn the deep network parameter ϑ_v for the image modality by using SGD with back-propagation(BP). For the i-th image F_{i*}, we first calculate the following gradient:

$$\frac{\partial \mathcal{L}}{\partial F_{i*}} = \frac{\partial \mathcal{L}_1}{\partial F_{i*}} + \frac{\partial \mathcal{L}_2^v}{\partial F_{i*}} + \frac{\partial \mathcal{L}_5}{\partial F_{i*}}$$
$$= \frac{1}{2} \sum_{j=1}^{n} (\sigma(\phi_{ij}^{vt}) G_{j*} - S_{ij}^{vt} G_{j*}) + \frac{1}{2} \sum_{j=1}^{n} (\sigma(\phi_{ij}^{vv}) F_{j*} - S_{ij}^{vv} F_{j*}) \tag{14}$$
$$+ 2\beta (F_{i*} - B_{i*}),$$

$$\frac{\partial \mathcal{L}}{\partial \hat{L}_{ij}^{v}} = \frac{\partial \mathcal{L}_3^{v\_label}}{\partial \hat{L}_{ij}^{v}} = (-L_{ij} + \sigma(\hat{L}_{ij}^{v})). \tag{15}$$

Then we can compute $\frac{\partial \mathcal{L}}{\partial \theta_v}$, $\frac{\partial \mathcal{L}}{\partial \theta_{vh}}$, and $\frac{\partial \mathcal{L}}{\partial \theta_{vl}}$ by utilizing the chain rule, based on which BP can be used to update the parameters ϑ_v.

3.4.2. Optimize ϑ_t

Similarly, when ϑ_v and $\boldsymbol{B}$ are fixed, we also learn the network parameter ϑ_t of the text modality by using SGD and the BP algorithm. For the i-th text $\boldsymbol{G}_{i*}$, we calculate the following gradient:

$$\begin{aligned}\frac{\partial \mathcal{L}}{\partial \boldsymbol{G}_{i*}} &= \frac{\partial \mathcal{L}_1}{\partial \boldsymbol{G}_{i*}} + \frac{\partial \mathcal{L}_2^t}{\partial \boldsymbol{G}_{i*}} + \frac{\partial \mathcal{L}_5}{\partial \boldsymbol{G}_{i*}} \\ &= \frac{1}{2}\sum_{j=1}^n (\sigma(\boldsymbol{\phi}_{ij}^{vt})\boldsymbol{F}_{j*} - \boldsymbol{S}_{ij}^{vt}\boldsymbol{F}_{j*}) + \frac{1}{2}\sum_{j=1}^n(\sigma(\boldsymbol{\phi}_{ij}^{tt})\boldsymbol{G}_{j*} - \boldsymbol{S}_{ij}^{vv}\boldsymbol{G}_{j*}) \\ &\quad + 2\beta(\boldsymbol{G}_{i*} - \boldsymbol{B}_{i*}),\end{aligned} \quad (16)$$

$$\frac{\partial \mathcal{L}}{\partial \hat{\boldsymbol{L}}_{ij}^t} = \frac{\partial \mathcal{L}_3^{t\_label}}{\partial \hat{\boldsymbol{L}}_{ij}^t} = (-L_{ij} + \sigma(\hat{L}_{ij}^t)). \quad (17)$$

Then we can compute $\frac{\partial \mathcal{L}}{\partial \theta_t}$, $\frac{\partial \mathcal{L}}{\partial \theta_{th}}$, and $\frac{\partial \mathcal{L}}{\partial \theta_{tl}}$ by utilizing the chain rule, based on which BP can be used to update the parameters ϑ_t.

3.4.3. Optimize $\boldsymbol{B}$

When ϑ_v and ϑ_t are fixed, the objective in Equation (13) can be reformulated as follows:

$$\min_{\boldsymbol{B}} \mathcal{L} = \gamma(||\boldsymbol{B}-\boldsymbol{F}||_F^2 + ||\boldsymbol{B}-\boldsymbol{G}||_F^2) + \beta tr(\boldsymbol{B}^T\boldsymbol{L}\boldsymbol{B}) \\ s.t. \quad \boldsymbol{B} \in \{-1, +1\}^{n\times k}. \quad (18)$$

We compute the derivation of Equation (18) with respect to $\boldsymbol{B}$ and infer that $\boldsymbol{B}$ should be defined as follows:

$$\boldsymbol{B} = sign((\boldsymbol{F}+\boldsymbol{G})(2\boldsymbol{I} + \frac{\beta}{\gamma}\boldsymbol{L}^{-1})), \quad (19)$$

where γ and β are hyper-parameters, and $\boldsymbol{I}$ denotes the identity matrix.

3.4.4. The Optimization Algorithm

As shown in Algorithm 1, DMSFH's learning algorithm takes raw input training data, including images, text, and labels: $O = \{o_1, o_2, \ldots, o_n\}$, with $o_i = (v_i, t_i, L_i)$. Before the training, parameters ϑ_v and ϑ_t of image network and text network were initialized; mini-batch size $N_v = N_t = 128$; the maximal number of epochs $max\_epoch = 500$; iteration times in each epoch was $iter_v = n/N_v$; $iter_t = n/N_t$, where n is the total number of training data. The training of each epoch consisted of three steps. Step 1: Randomly selecting N_v images from O and setting them as a mini-batch. For each datum in the mini-batch, we calculated $\boldsymbol{F}_{i*} = f_1^v(v_i; \theta_v; \theta_{vh})$ and $\hat{L}_{i*}^v = f_2^v(v_i; \theta_v; \theta_{vl})$ by forward propagation. After the gradient was calculated, the network parameters θ_v, θ_{vh} and θ_{vl} were updated using SGD and back propagation. Step 2: Randomly selecting N_t texts from O and setting them as a mini-batch. For each datum in the mini-batch, we calculated $\boldsymbol{G}_{i*} = f_1^t(t_i; \theta_t; \theta_{th})$ and $\hat{L}_{i*}^t = f_2^t(t_i; \theta_t; \theta_{tl})$ by forward propagation. After the gradient is calculated, the network parameters θ_t, θ_{th} and θ_{tl} were updated using SGD and back propagation. Step 3: Updating $\boldsymbol{B}$ by Equation (19). The above three steps were repeatedly iterated to realize the alternating training of image hash network and text hash network until the maximum epoch number of iterations was reached.

Algorithm 1 The learning algorithm for DMSFH

Require: Training data includes images, text, and labels: $O = \{o_1, o_2, \ldots, o_n\}$, with $o_i = (v_i, t_i, L_i)$.
Ensure: Parameters ϑ_v and ϑ_t of deep neural networks, and binary code matrix B.
  Initialization
  initialize parameters ϑ_v and ϑ_t, mini-batch size $N_v = N_t = 128$, the maximal number of epochs $max\_epoch = 500$, and iteration number $iter_v = n/N_v$, $iter_t = n/N_t$.
  repeat
   for $iter = 1, 2, \ldots, iter_v$ **do**
    Randomly sample N_v images from O to construct a mini-batch of images.
    For each instance v_i in the mini-batch, calculate $F_{i*} = f_1^v(v_i; \theta_v; \theta_{vh})$ and $\hat{L}_{i*}^v = f_2^v(v_i; \theta_v; \theta_{vl})$ by forward propagation.
    Updata F.
    Calculate the derivatives according to Equations (14) and (15)
    Update the network parameters θ_v, θ_{vh} and θ_{vl} by applying backpropagation.
   end for
   for $iter = 1, 2, \ldots, iter_t$ **do**
    Randomly sample N_t texts from O to construct a mini-batch of texts.
    For each instance t_i in the mini-batch, calculate $G_{i*} = f_1^t(t_i; \theta_t; \theta_{th})$ and $\hat{L}_{i*}^t = f_2^t(t_i; \theta_t; \theta_{tl})$ by forward propagation.
    Updata G.
    Calculate the derivatives according to Equations (16) and (17)
    Update the network parameters θ_t, θ_{th} and θ_{tl} by applying backpropagation.
   end for
   Update B using Equation (19)
  until the max epoch number max_epoch

4. Experiment

We conducted extensive experiments on two commonly used benchmark datasets, i.e., MIRFLICKR-25K [68] and NUS-WIDE [69], to evaluate the performance of our method, DMSFH. Firstly, we introduce the datasets, evaluation metrics, and implementation details, and then discuss performance comparisons of DMSFH and 6 state-of-the-art methods.

4.1. Datasets

MIRFLICKR-25K: The original MIRFLICKR-25K [68] dataset contains 25,000 image–text pairs, which were collected from the well-known photo sharing website Flickr. Each of these images has several textual tags. We selected those instances that have at least 20 textual tags for our experiments. The textual tags for each of the selected instances were transformed into a 1386-dimensional BoW vector. In addition, each instance was manually annotated with at least one of the 24 unique labels. We selected 20,015 instances for our experiments.

NUS-WIDE: The NUS-WIDE [69] dataset is a large real-world Web image dataset comprising over 269,000 images with over 5000 user-provided tags, and 81 concepts for the entire dataset. The text of each instance is represented as a 1000-dimensional BoW vector. In our experiment, we removed the instances without labels, and selected instances labeled by the 21 most-frequent categories. This gave 190,421 image–text pairs.

Table 2 presents the statistics of the above two datasets. Figure 2 shows some samples of these two datasets.

Figure 2. Some examples from the MIRFLICKR-25K and NUS-WIDE datasets.

Table 2. Statistics of the datasets in our experiments.

Dataset	Total	Train/Query/Retrieval	Labels	Text Feature
MIRFLICKR-25K	20,015	10,000/2000/18,015	24	1386d
NUS-WIDE	190,421	10,500/2100/188,321	21	1000d

4.2. Evaluation

Two widely used evaluation methods, i.e., Hamming ranking and hash lookup, were utilized for cross-modal hash retrieval evaluations. Based on the query data and the Hamming distance of the retrieved samples as the sorting criteria, Hamming sorting sorts the retrieved data one by one according to the increasing order of the Hamming distance. In Hamming sorting, mean average precision (MAP) is one of the performance metrics that is commonly used to measure the accuracy of the query results. The larger the MAP value, the better the method retrieval performance. The topN precision curve reflects the changes in precision according to the number of retrieved instances. Besides, a hash search is also based on the criteria of the query data and the Hamming distance of the retrieved samples. However, it only returns the data to be retrieved within the specified Hamming distance as the final result. This can be measured by a precision recall (PR) curve. The larger the area enclosed by the curve and the coordinate axis, the better the retrieval performance of the method.

The value of MAP is defined as:

$$MAP = \frac{1}{M} \sum_{i=1}^{M} AP(q_i), \qquad (20)$$

where M is the query dataset and $AP(q_i)$ is the average accuracy of query data q_i. The average value of accuracy is calculated as shown in Equation (21):

$$AP(q_i) = \frac{1}{N} \sum_{r=1}^{R} p(r)d(r), \qquad (21)$$

where N is the number of relevant instances in the retrieved set, and R represents the total amount of data. $p(r)$ denotes the precision of the top r retrieved instances, and $d(r) = 1$ if the r-th retrieved result is relevant to the query instances; otherwise, $d(r) = 0$.

To comprehensively measure the retrieval performance, we utilize another important evaluation metric, i.e., F-score. It is an important evaluation metrics that comprehensively considers precision and recall, which are defined as:

$$F\text{-}score = (1 + \beta^2) \frac{Precision * Recall}{\beta^2 * Precision + Recall}; \qquad (22)$$

if $\beta = 1$, this measurement is called F1-score. At this time, the accuracy rate and recall rate have the same weight. That means they are same important. In our experiments, we used F1-score to evaluate the cross-modal retrieval performance.

4.3. Baselines and Implementation Detail

Baselines. In this paper, the proposed SFDCH method is compared with several baselines, including SCM [42], SEPH [41], PRDH [65], CMHH [59], CHN [66], and DCMH [64]. SCM and SEPH use manual features, and the other approaches extract features through deep neural networks. Here is a brief introduction to these competitors:

- **SCM** integrates semantic labels into the process of hash learning to conduct large-scale data modeling, which not only maintains the correlation between models, but also achieves good performance in accuracy.
- **SEPH** transforms the semantic similarity of training data into affinity matrix by using a label as supervised information, and minimizes the Kullback–Leibler divergence to learn hash codes.
- **PRDH** integrates two types of pairwise constraints from inter-modality and intra-modality to enhance the similarities of the hash codes.
- **CMHH** learns high-quality hash representations to significantly penalize similar cross-modal pairs with Hamming distances larger than the Hamming radius threshold.
- **CHN** is a hybrid deep architecture that jointly optimizes the new cosine max-margin loss in semantic similarity pairs and the new quantization max-margin loss in compact hash codes.
- **DCMH** integrates features and hash codes learning into a general learning framework. The cross-modal similarities are preserved by using a negative log-likelihood loss.

Implementation Details. Our SFDCH approach was implemented by Pytorch framework. All the experiments were performed on a workstation with Intel(R) Xeon E5-2680_v3 2.5 GHz, 128 GB RAM, 1 TB SSD, and 3TB HDD storage; and 2 NVIDIA GeForce RTX 2080Ti GPUs with Windows 10 64-bit operating system. We set the $max\_epoch = 500$; the learning rate was initialized to $10^{-1.5}$ and gradually lowered to 10^{-6} in 500 epochs. We set the batch size of the mini-batch to 128 and the iteration number of the outer-loop in Algorithm 1 to 500, and the hyper-parameters $\gamma = \beta = 1$. For whole experiment, we used $I \rightarrow T$ to denote using a querying image while returning text, and $T \rightarrow I$ to denote using a querying text while returning an image.

4.4. Performance Comparisons

To evaluate the performance of the proposed method, we compare DMSFH with the six baselines in terms of MAP and PR curves on MIRFLICKR-25K and NUS-WIDE, respectively. Two query tasks, i.e., image-query-text and text-query-image, are considered. Tables 3 and 4 illustrate the MAP results of DMSFH and other methods on different lengths (16, 32, 64 bits) of hash codes on MIRFlickr-25K and NUS-WIDE, respectively. Figures 3–5 demonstrate the PR curves of different coding lengths on MIRFlickr-25K and NUS-WIDE, respectively. Table 5 reports the F1-measure with hash code length 32 bits on the MIRFLICKR-25K dataset.

Hamming Ranking: Tables 3 and 4 report the MAP scores of the proposed method and its competitors for image-query-text and text-query-image on MIRFLICKR-25K and NUS-WIDE, where $I \rightarrow T$ and $T \rightarrow I$ represent image retrieval by text and text retrieval by image, respectively. It is clear from the Tables 3 and 4 that the deep hashing methods perform better than the non-deep methods. Specifically, on MIRFLICKR-25K, we can see in Table 3 that the proposed method DMSFH achieved the highest MAP score for both queries ($I \rightarrow T$: 16 bits MAP = 79.12%, 32 bits MAP = 79.60%, 64 bits MAP = 80.45%; $T \rightarrow I$: 16 bits MAP = 78.22%, 32 bits MAP = 78.62%, 64 bits MAP = 79.50%). It defeated the two most competitive deep learning-based baselines, CNH and DCMH, due to the multiple label semantic fusion. Similarly, we can find from Table 4 that DMSFH won the competition again on NUS-WIDE by $I \rightarrow T$ MAP = 64.08% (16 bits), 65.12% (32 bits), 66.43% (64 bits);

and $T \rightarrow I$ MAP = 63.89% (16 bits), 65.31% (32 bits), 66.08% (64 bits), respectively. This superiority of DMSFH due to the fact that it incorporates richer semantic information than other techniques. In addition, DMSFH leverages graph regularization to measure the semantic correlation of the unified hash codes. That means it can capture more semantic consistent features between different modalities than other deep hashing models, such as CHN and DCMH. Therefore, the above results confirm that the hash codes generated by DMSFH have better semantic discrimination and can better adapt to the task of mutual retrieval of multi-modal data.

Table 3. Mean average precision (MAP) comparison on MIRFLICKR-25K. The best results are in bold font.

Methods	MIRFLICKR-25K					
	Image-Query-Text			Text-Quary-Image		
	16 bits	32 bits	64 bits	16 bits	32 bits	64 bits
SCM [42]	0.6410	0.6478	0.6608	0.6450	0.6532	0.6623
SEPH [41]	0.6785	0.6853	0.6884	0.7168	0.7298	0.7325
PRDH [65]	0.7016	0.7101	0.7184	0.7663	0.7764	0.7811
CMHH [59]	0.7374	0.7328	0.7510	0.7388	0.7241	0.7326
CHN [66]	0.7543	0.7533	0.7512	0.7724	0.7782	0.7810
DCMH [64]	0.7406	0.7415	0.7434	0.7617	0.7716	0.7748
DMSFH	**0.7912**	**0.7960**	**0.8045**	**0.7822**	**0.7862**	**0.7950**

Table 4. Mean average precision (MAP) comparison on NUS-WIDE. The best results are in bold font.

Methods	NUS-WIDE					
	Image-Query-Text			Text-Quary-Image		
	16 bits	32 bits	64 bits	16 bits	32 bits	64 bits
SCM [42]	0.4642	0.4825	0.4910	0.4308	0.4414	0.4536
SEPH [41]	0.4831	0.4898	0.4953	0.6117	0.6322	0.6342
PRDH [65]	0.6002	0.6118	0.6180	0.6214	0.6302	0.6357
CMHH [59]	0.5574	0.5720	0.6021	0.5798	0.5834	0.5935
CHN [66]	0.5802	0.6024	0.6086	0.5878	0.6034	0.6045
DCMH [64]	0.5512	0.5638	0.5940	0.5878	0.6011	0.6106
DMSFH	**0.6408**	**0.6512**	**0.6643**	**0.6389**	**0.6531**	**0.6608**

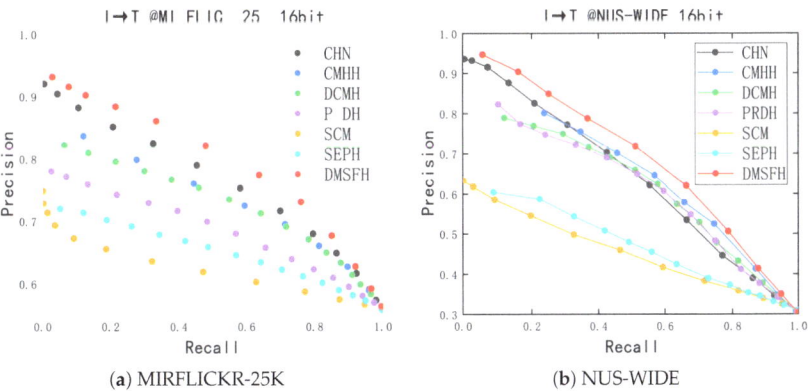

(a) MIRFLICKR-25K (b) NUS-WIDE

Figure 3. Cont.

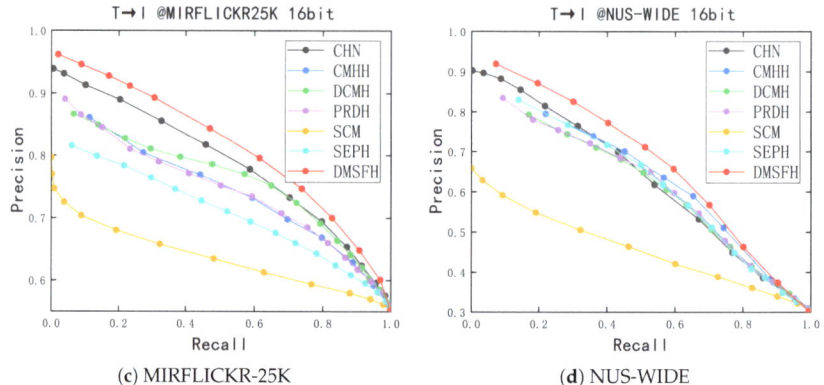

(c) MIRFLICKR-25K (d) NUS-WIDE

Figure 3. Precision–recall curves on MIRFLICKR-25K and NUS-WIDE. I→T query: (**a**,**b**); T→I query: (**c**,**d**). The code length was 16 bits.

Table 5. F1-measures of our method and the competitors on MIRFLICKR-25K. The code length was 32 bit. The best results are in bold font.

Methods	MIRFLICKR-25K					
	Image-Query-Text			Text-Quary-Image		
	Precision	Recall	F1-Measure	Precision	Recall	F1-Measure
DMSFH	0.9135	0.0616	**0.1154**	0.9046	0.0562	**0.1058**
CHN	0.8852	0.0376	0.0721	0.8741	0.0321	0.0619
DCMH	0.8682	0.0525	0.0990	0.8556	0.0428	0.0815
CMHH	0.8373	0.0412	0.0785	0.8216	0.0308	0.0694
PRDH	0.8586	0.0206	0.0402	0.8742	0.0326	0.0628

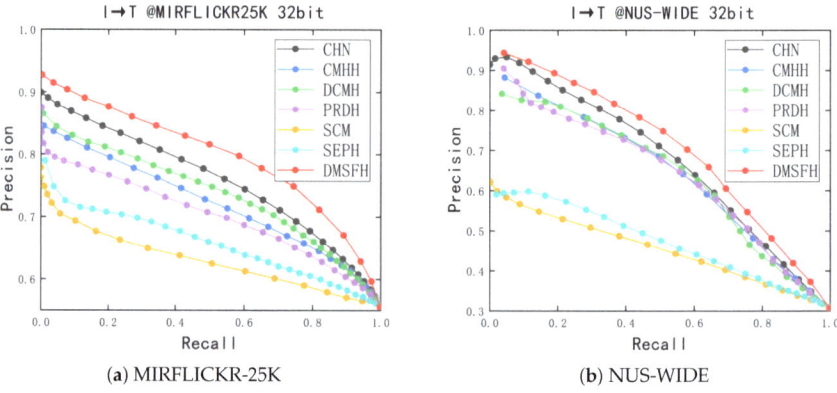

(a) MIRFLICKR-25K (b) NUS-WIDE

Figure 4. *Cont.*

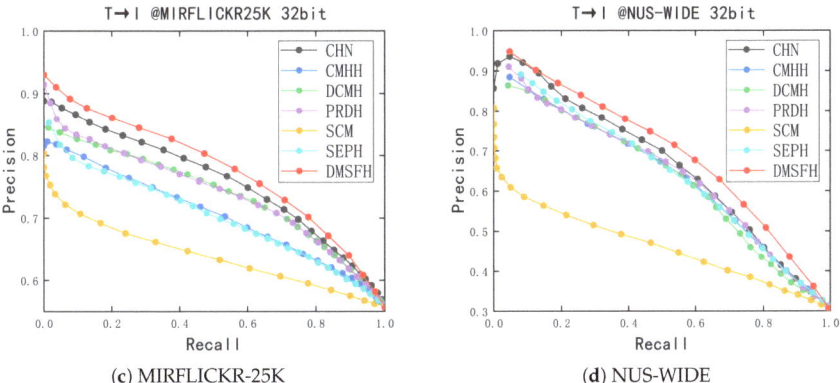

(c) MIRFLICKR-25K (d) NUS-WIDE

Figure 4. Precision-Recall curves on MIRFLICKR-25K and NUS-WIDE dataset. I→T query: (**a**,**b**); T→I query: (**c**,**d**). The code length was 32 bits.

Hash Lookup: To further demonstrate the comparison of the proposed model with these baselines, we used PR curves to evaluate their retrieval performances. Figures 3–5 show the PR curves with different coding lengths (16 bits, 32 bits, and 64 bits) on MIRFLICKR-25K and NUS-WIDE datasets, respectively. As expected, the deep learning-based models had better performances than the manual features-based models, mainly due to the powerful representation capabilities of deep neural networks. Besides, no matter what the length of the hash code was, our method performed better, obviously, on the PR curve than the other deep based competitors. That happened mainly because DMSFH has stronger cross-modal consistent semantic learning capabilities by not only considering both the intra-modal and inter-modal semantic discriminative information, but integrating graph regularization into hashing learning as well. Besides, we selected the best five methods, and report their average precision, average recall, and average F1-measure with Hamming radius $r = 0, 1, 2$ in Table 5 on MIRFLICKR-25K for when the code length was 32. We found that in all cases our DMSFH can achieve the best F1-measure.

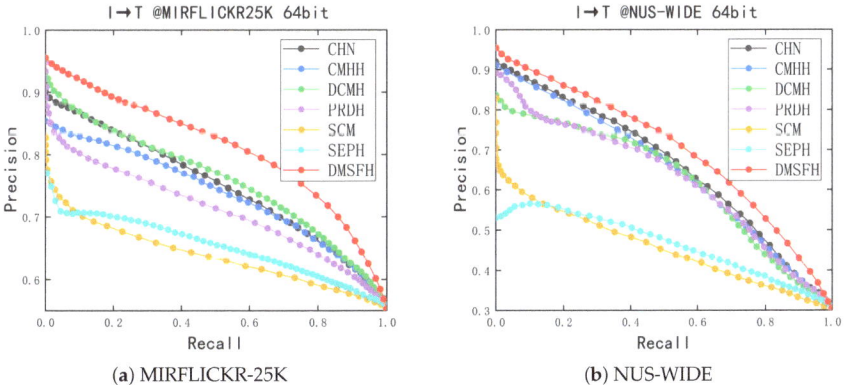

(a) MIRFLICKR-25K (b) NUS-WIDE

Figure 5. *Cont.*

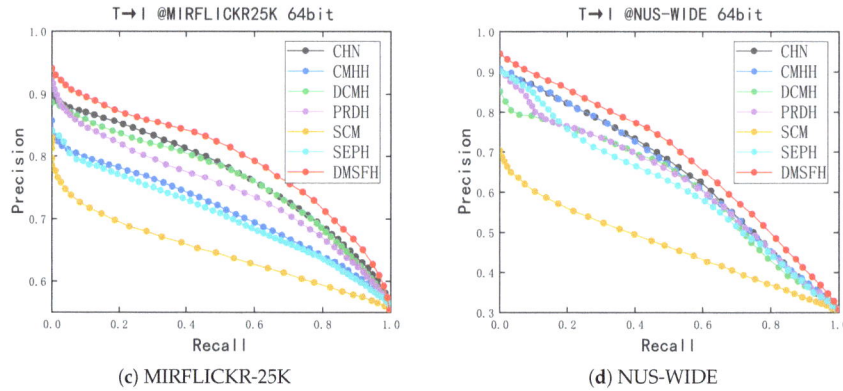

Figure 5. Precision–recall curves on MIRFLICKR-25K and NUS-WIDE datasets. I→T query: (**a**,**b**); T→I query: (**c**,**d**). The code length was 64 bits.

4.5. Ablation Experiments of DMSFH

To verify the validity of the DMSFH components, we conducted ablation experiments on the MIRFLICKR-25K dataset, and the experimental results are shown in Table 6. We define DMSFH-P as employing only intra-modal pairwise loss and inter-modal pairwise loss, and DMSFH-S removed the graph regularization loss. From Table 6, we can see that both the semantic prediction discriminant loss and graph regularization loss employed by DMSFH can effectively improve the retrieval accuracy. From the results, it can be seen that DMSFH can obtain better performance when using the designed modules.

Table 6. Ablation experiments of DMSFH on the MIRFLICKR-25K dataset. The best results are in bold font.

Methods	MIRFLICKR-25K					
	Image-Query-Text			Text-Quary-Image		
	16 bits	32 bits	64 bits	16 bits	32 bits	64 bits
DMSFH-P	0.7708	0.7812	0.7904	0.7690	0.7728	0.7802
DMSFH-S	0.7876	0.7926	0.8012	0.7786	0.7836	0.7918
DMSFH	**0.7912**	**0.7960**	**0.8045**	**0.7822**	**0.7862**	**0.7950**

5. Discussion

This paper proposes deep multi-semantic fusion-based cross-modal hashing (DMSFH) for cross-modal retrieval tasks. Firstly, it preserves the semantic similarity between data through intra-modal loss and inter-modal loss, and then introduces a multi-label semantic fusion module to further capture more semantic discriminative features. In addition, semantic similarity in Hamming space is preserved by graph regularization loss.

We compared DMSFH with other methods. We used the cross-modal multi-label datasets MIRFLICKR-25K and NUS-WIDE, which have 24 and 21 label attributes, respectively. According to Tables 3 and 4, it can be seen that the map scores of DMSFH are better than those of the other methods. As for DCMH and PRDH, DMSFH outperformed these two deep learning methods based on the same inter-modal and intra-modal pairwise loss, precisely because it captured more semantic information with the addition of new losses. Therefore, DMSFH is able to optimize the semantic heterogeneity problem to a certain extent and improve the accuracy. In addition, the computational cost of the model is measured using floating point operations (FLOPs), with an approximate number of FLOPs of 3.67 billion for DMSFH. Compared with real-valued cross-modal retrieval methods, the computational and retrieval cost of our method is quite low due to the shorter binary cross-modal representations (i.e., 64 bits hash codes) and Hamming distance measurements. As they generate higher dimensional feature representations (i.e., 1000 dimensional feature map), the real-valued cross-modal representation learning models always have higher complexity.

Although our study achieved some degree of performance improvement, there are limitations. First, when constructing the sample similarity matrix, our method in this paper does not fully extract the fine-grained labeling information between data, and there is still a higher performance improvement in fine-grained semantic information extraction. Second, our method mainly focuses on the construction and optimization of the loss function, but how to improve the cross-modal semantic feature representation learning is also an important issue. Therefore, deeper semantic mining in the semantic feature learning part is also a direction for our future research. Third, our method was tested on a specific dataset, and common cross-modal hash retrieval methods use data of known categories, but in practical applications, the rapid emergence of new unlabeled things often affects the accuracy of cross-modal data retrieval. How to achieve high precision cross-modal retrieval in the absence of annotation information is also an important research problem.

6. Conclusions

In this paper, we proposed an effective hashing approach dubbed deep multi-semantic fusion-based cross-modal hashing (DMSFH) to improve semantic discriminative feature learning and similarity preserving of hash codes in common Hamming subspace. This method learns an end-to-end framework to integrate feature learning and hash code learning. A multi-label semantic fusion method is used to realize cross-modal consistent semantic learning to enhance the semantic discriminability of hash codes. Moreover, we designed the loss function with graph regularization from inter-modal and intra-modal perspectives to enhance the similarity learning of hash codes in Hamming subspace. Extensive experiments on two cross-modal datasets demonstrated that our proposed approach can effectively improve cross-modal retrieval performance, which is significantly superior to other baselines.

In future work, we will consider the heterogeneous semantic correlations between multi-modal samples in both aspects of high-level semantics and fine-grained semantics, which can be formulated as heterogeneous information networks (HIN) to capture more semantic information and realize cross-modal semantic alignment in a more effective manner. In addition, how to measure the distance of the relation distribution of semantic details between different modalities will be studied. An essential problem will be enhancing the cross-modal semantic representation learning.

Author Contributions: Conceptualization, X.Z. and L.C.; methodology, L.C. and L.Z.; software, L.C.; validation, L.C., L.Z. and Z.Z.; formal analysis, L.Z.; investigation, X.Z. and L.C.; resources, X.Z. and L.Z.; data curation, Z.Z.; writing—original draft preparation, L.C.; writing—review and editing, L.Z.; visualization, Z.Z.; supervision, X.Z. and L.Z.; project administration, X.Z.; funding acquisition, X.Z. All authors have read and agreed to the published version of the manuscript.

Funding: This research was funded by the Key Research and Development Program of Hunan Province (2020NK2033), and the National Natural Science Foundation of China (62072166).

Institutional Review Board Statement: Not applicable.

Informed Consent Statement: Not applicable.

Acknowledgments: This work was supported in part by the Key Research and Development Program of Hunan Province (2020NK2033) and the National Natural Science Foundation of China (62072166).

Conflicts of Interest: The authors declare no conflict of interest.

References

1. Wang, Y. Survey on deep multi-modal data analytics: Collaboration, rivalry, and fusion. *ACM Trans. Multimed. Comput. Commun. Appl. (TOMM)* **2021**, *17*, 1–25. [CrossRef]
2. Zhu, L.; Zhang, C.; Song, J.; Liu, L.; Zhang, S.; Li, Y. Multi-Graph Based Hierarchical Semantic Fusion for Cross-Modal Representation. In Proceedings of the 2021 IEEE International Conference on Multimedia and Expo (ICME), Virtual, 5–9 July 2021; pp. 1–6.
3. Morgado, P.; Vasconcelos, N.; Misra, I. Audio-visual instance discrimination with cross-modal agreement. In Proceedings of the IEEE/CVF Conference on Computer Vision and Pattern Recognition, Virtual, 19–25 June 2021; pp. 12475–12486.
4. Zhang, B.; Hu, H.; Sha, F. Cross-modal and hierarchical modeling of video and text. In Proceedings of the European Conference on Computer Vision (ECCV), Munich, Germany, 8–14 September 2018; pp. 374–390.
5. Jing, L.; Vahdani, E.; Tan, J.; Tian, Y. Cross-Modal Center Loss for 3D Cross-Modal Retrieval. In Proceedings of the IEEE/CVF Conference on Computer Vision and Pattern Recognition, Virtual, 19–25 June 2021; pp. 3142–3151.
6. Liu, R.; Wei, S.; Zhao, Y.; Zhu, Z.; Wang, J. Multiview Cross-Media Hashing with Semantic Consistency. *IEEE Multimed.* **2018**, *25*, 71–86. [CrossRef]
7. Zhang, D.; Wu, X.J.; Yu, J. Label consistent flexible matrix factorization hashing for efficient cross-modal retrieval. *ACM Trans. Multimed. Comput. Commun. Appl. (TOMM)* **2021**, *17*, 1–18. [CrossRef]
8. Zhu, L.; Song, J.; Zhu, X.; Zhang, C.; Zhang, S.; Yuan, X. Adversarial Learning-Based Semantic Correlation Representation for Cross-Modal Retrieval. *IEEE Multimed.* **2020**, *27*, 79–90. [CrossRef]
9. Wu, L.; Wang, Y.; Shao, L. Cycle-consistent deep generative hashing for cross-modal retrieval. *IEEE Trans. Image Process.* **2018**, *28*, 1602–1612. [CrossRef] [PubMed]
10. Wang, Y.; Zhang, W.; Wu, L.; Lin, X.; Fang, M.; Pan, S. Iterative views agreement: An iterative low-rank based structured optimization method to multi-view spectral clustering. *arXiv* **2016**, arXiv:1608.05560.
11. Zhao, M.; Liu, Y.; Li, X.; Zhang, Z.; Zhang, Y. An end-to-end framework for clothing collocation based on semantic feature fusion. *IEEE Multimed.* **2020**, *27*, 122–132. [CrossRef]
12. Shen, H.T.; Liu, L.; Yang, Y.; Xu, X.; Huang, Z.; Shen, F.; Hong, R. Exploiting subspace relation in semantic labels for cross-modal hashing. *IEEE Trans. Knowl. Data Eng.* **2020**, *33*, 3351–3365. [CrossRef]
13. Zhang, C.; Song, J.; Zhu, X.; Zhu, L.; Zhang, S. HCMSL: Hybrid Cross-modal Similarity Learning for Cross-modal Retrieval. *ACM Trans. Multimed. Comput. Commun. Appl. (TOMM)* **2021**, *17*, 1–22. [CrossRef]
14. Zhao, S.; Xu, M.; Huang, Q.; Schuller, B.W. Introduction to the special issue on MMAC: Multimodal affective computing of large-scale multimedia data. *IEEE Multimed.* **2021**, *28*, 8–10. [CrossRef]
15. Sharma, A.; Kumar, A.; Daume, H.; Jacobs, D.W. Generalized multiview analysis: A discriminative latent space. In Proceedings of the 2012 IEEE Conference on Computer Vision and Pattern Recognition, Providence, RI, USA, 16–21 June 2012; pp. 2160–2167.
16. Wang, K.; He, R.; Wang, L.; Wang, W.; Tan, T. Joint feature selection and subspace learning for cross-modal retrieval. *IEEE Trans. Pattern Anal. Mach. Intell.* **2015**, *38*, 2010–2023. [CrossRef] [PubMed]
17. Deng, C.; Tang, X.; Yan, J.; Liu, W.; Gao, X. Discriminative dictionary learning with common label alignment for cross-modal retrieval. *IEEE Trans. Multimed.* **2015**, *18*, 208–218. [CrossRef]
18. Li, K.; Qi, G.J.; Ye, J.; Hua, K.A. Linear subspace ranking hashing for cross-modal retrieval. *IEEE Trans. Pattern Anal. Mach. Intell.* **2016**, *39*, 1825–1838. [CrossRef] [PubMed]
19. Zhu, L.; Song, J.; Wei, X.; Yu, H.; Long, J. CAESAR: Concept augmentation based semantic representation for cross-modal retrieval. *Multimed. Tools Appl.* **2020**, 1–31. [CrossRef]
20. Chen, Y.; Wang, Y.; Ren, P.; Wang, M.; de Rijke, M. Bayesian feature interaction selection for factorization machines. *Artif. Intell.* **2022**, *302*, 103589. [CrossRef]
21. Wei, Y.; Zhao, Y.; Lu, C.; Wei, S.; Liu, L.; Zhu, Z.; Yan, S. Cross-modal retrieval with CNN visual features: A new baseline. *IEEE Trans. Cybern.* **2016**, *47*, 449–460. [CrossRef]
22. Hotelling, H. Relations between Two Sets of Variates. In *Breakthroughs in Statistics*; Springer: New York, NY, USA, 1992; pp. 162–190.
23. Gong, Y.; Ke, Q.; Isard, M.; Lazebnik, S. A multi-view embedding space for modeling internet images, tags, and their semantics. *Int. J. Comput. Vis.* **2014**, *106*, 210–233. [CrossRef]
24. Zu, C.; Zhang, D. Canonical sparse cross-view correlation analysis. *Neurocomputing* **2016**, *191*, 263–272. [CrossRef]
25. Ballan, L.; Uricchio, T.; Seidenari, L.; Del Bimbo, A. A cross-media model for automatic image annotation. In Proceedings of the International Conference on Multimedia Retrieval, Glasgow, UK, 1–4 April 2014; pp. 73–80.
26. Wang, L.; Zhu, L.; Dong, X.; Liu, L.; Sun, J.; Zhang, H. Joint feature selection and graph regularization for modality-dependent cross-modal retrieval. *J. Vis. Commun. Image Represent.* **2018**, *54*, 213–222. [CrossRef]
27. Zhang, C.; Liu, M.; Liu, Z.; Yang, C.; Zhang, L.; Han, J. Spatiotemporal activity modeling under data scarcity: A graph-regularized cross-modal embedding approach. In Proceedings of the Thirty-Second AAAI Conference on Artificial Intelligence, New Orleans, LA, USA, 2–7 February 2018; pp. 531–538.
28. Deng, C.; Chen, Z.; Liu, X.; Gao, X.; Tao, D. Triplet-based deep hashing network for cross-modal retrieval. *IEEE Trans. Image Process.* **2018**, *27*, 3893–3903. [CrossRef]

29. Xu, X.; Shimada, A.; Taniguchi, R.I.; He, L. Coupled dictionary learning and feature mapping for cross-modal retrieval. In Proceedings of the 2015 IEEE International Conference on Multimedia and Expo (ICME), Turin, Italy, 29 June–3 July 2015; pp. 1–6.
30. Xu, X.; Yang, Y.; Shimada, A.; Taniguchi, R.I.; He, L. Semi-supervised coupled dictionary learning for cross-modal retrieval in internet images and texts. In Proceedings of the 23rd ACM international conference on Multimedia, Brisbane, Australia, 26–30 October 2015; pp. 847–850.
31. Zhang, C.; Zhong, Z.; Zhu, L.; Zhang, S.; Cao, D.; Zhang, J. M2GUDA: Multi-Metrics Graph-Based Unsupervised Domain Adaptation for Cross-Modal Hashing. In Proceedings of the 2021 International Conference on Multimedia Retrieval, Taipei, Taiwan, 16–19 November 2021; pp. 674–681.
32. Zhu, L.; Song, J.; Yang, Z.; Huang, W.; Zhang, C.; Yu, W. DAP^{2}2 CMH: Deep Adversarial Privacy-Preserving Cross-Modal Hashing. *Neural Process. Lett.* **2021**, 1–21. [CrossRef]
33. Mithun, N.C.; Sikka, K.; Chiu, H.P.; Samarasekera, S.; Kumar, R. Rgb2lidar: Towards solving large-scale cross-modal visual localization. In Proceedings of the 28th ACM International Conference on Multimedia, Seattle, WA, USA, 12–16 October 2020; pp. 934–954.
34. Zhan, Y.W.; Wang, Y.; Sun, Y.; Wu, X.M.; Luo, X.; Xu, X.S. Discrete online cross-modal hashing. *Pattern Recognit.* **2022**, *122*, 108262. [CrossRef]
35. Zhou, J.; Ding, G.; Guo, Y. Latent semantic sparse hashing for cross-modal similarity search. In Proceedings of the 37th International ACM SIGIR Conference on Research & Development in Information Retrieval, Gold Coast, QLD, Australia, 6–11 July 2014; pp. 415–424.
36. Song, J.; Yang, Y.; Yang, Y.; Huang, Z.; Shen, H.T. Inter-media hashing for large-scale retrieval from heterogeneous data sources. In Proceedings of the 2013 ACM SIGMOD International Conference on Management of Data, New York, NY, USA, 22–27 June 2013; pp. 785–796.
37. Wang, D.; Gao, X.; Wang, X.; He, L. Semantic topic multimodal hashing for cross-media retrieval. In Proceedings of the Twenty-fourth International Joint Conference on Artificial Intelligence, Buenos Aires, Argentina, 25–31 July 2015; pp. 3890–3896.
38. Hu, M.; Yang, Y.; Shen, F.; Xie, N.; Hong, R.; Shen, H.T. Collective reconstructive embeddings for cross-modal hashing. *IEEE Trans. Image Process.* **2018**, *28*, 2770–2784. [CrossRef]
39. Zhang, J.; Peng, Y.; Yuan, M. Unsupervised generative adversarial cross-modal hashing. In Proceedings of the Thirty-Second AAAI Conference on Artificial Intelligence, New Orleans, LA, USA, 2–7 February 2018; pp. 539–546.
40. Bronstein, M.M.; Bronstein, A.M.; Michel, F.; Paragios, N. Data fusion through cross-modality metric learning using similarity-sensitive hashing. In Proceedings of the 2010 IEEE Computer Society Conference on Computer Vision and Pattern Recognition, San Francisco, CA, USA, 13–18 June 2010; pp. 3594–3601.
41. Lin, Z.; Ding, G.; Hu, M.; Wang, J. Semantics-preserving hashing for cross-view retrieval. In Proceedings of the IEEE Conference on Computer Vision and Pattern Recognition, Boston, MA, USA, 7–12 June 2015; pp. 3864–3872.
42. Zhang, D.; Li, W.J. Large-scale supervised multimodal hashing with semantic correlation maximization. In Proceedings of the AAAI Conference on Artificial Intelligence, Québec City, QC, Canada, 27–31 July 2014; Volume 28, pp. 2177–2183.
43. Xu, X.; Shen, F.; Yang, Y.; Shen, H.T.; Li, X. Learning discriminative binary codes for large-scale cross-modal retrieval. *IEEE Trans. Image Process.* **2017**, *26*, 2494–2507. [CrossRef] [PubMed]
44. Mandal, D.; Chaudhury, K.N.; Biswas, S. Generalized semantic preserving hashing for cross-modal retrieval. *IEEE Trans. Image Process.* **2018**, *28*, 102–112. [CrossRef] [PubMed]
45. Krizhevsky, A.; Sutskever, I.; Hinton, G.E. Imagenet classification with deep convolutional neural networks. *Adv. Neural Inf. Process. Syst.* **2012**, *25*, 1097–1105. [CrossRef]
46. He, K.; Zhang, X.; Ren, S.; Sun, J. Deep residual learning for image recognition. In Proceedings of the IEEE Conference on Computer Vision and Pattern Recognition, Las Vegas, NV, USA, 27–30 June 2016; pp. 770–778.
47. Chatfield, K.; Simonyan, K.; Vedaldi, A.; Zisserman, A. Return of the devil in the details: Delving deep into convolutional nets. *arXiv* **2014**, arXiv:1405.3531.
48. Yang, W.; Peng, J.; Wang, H.; Wang, M. Progressive Learning with Multi-scale Attention Network for Cross-domain Vehicle Re-identification. *Sci. China Inf. Sci.* **2021**. [CrossRef]
49. Liu, X.; Yu, G.; Domeniconi, C.; Wang, J.; Ren, Y.; Guo, M. Ranking-based deep cross-modal hashing. In Proceedings of the AAAI Conference on Artificial Intelligence, Honolulu, HI, USA, 27 January–1 February 2019; Volume 33, pp. 4400–4407.
50. Zhen, L.; Hu, P.; Wang, X.; Peng, D. Deep supervised cross-modal retrieval. In Proceedings of the IEEE/CVF Conference on Computer Vision and Pattern Recognition, Long Beach, CA, USA, 16–20 June 2019; pp. 10394–10403.
51. Jiang, Q.Y.; Li, W.J. Discrete latent factor model for cross-modal hashing. *IEEE Trans. Image Process.* **2019**, *28*, 3490–3501. [CrossRef]
52. Wei, J.; Xu, X.; Yang, Y.; Ji, Y.; Wang, Z.; Shen, H.T. Universal weighting metric learning for cross-modal matching. In Proceedings of the IEEE/CVF Conference on Computer Vision and Pattern Recognition, Seattle, WA, USA, 13–19 June 2020; pp. 13005–13014.
53. Zhang, M.; Li, J.; Zhang, H.; Liu, L. Deep semantic cross modal hashing with correlation alignment. *Neurocomputing* **2020**, *381*, 240–251. [CrossRef]
54. Li, C.; Deng, C.; Li, N.; Liu, W.; Gao, X.; Tao, D. Self-supervised adversarial hashing networks for cross-modal retrieval. In Proceedings of the IEEE Conference on Computer Vision and Pattern Recognition, Salt Lake City, UT, USA, 18–22 June 2018; pp. 4242–4251.

55. Xie, D.; Deng, C.; Li, C.; Liu, X.; Tao, D. Multi-task consistency-preserving adversarial hashing for cross-modal retrieval. *IEEE Trans. Image Process.* **2020**, *29*, 3626–3637. [CrossRef] [PubMed]
56. Wang, X.; Shi, Y.; Kitani, K.M. Deep Supervised Hashing with Triplet Labels. In *Asian Conference on Computer Vision*; Springer: Cham, Switzerland, 2016; pp. 70–84.
57. Chen, S.; Wu, S.; Wang, L. Hierarchical semantic interaction-based deep hashing network for cross-modal retrieval. *PeerJ Comput. Sci.* **2021**, *7*, e552. [CrossRef] [PubMed]
58. Zou, X.; Wang, X.; Bakker, E.M.; Wu, S. Multi-label semantics preserving based deep cross-modal hashing. *Signal Process. Image Commun.* **2021**, *93*, 116131. [CrossRef]
59. Cao, Y.; Liu, B.; Long, M.; Wang, J. Cross-modal hamming hashing. In Proceedings of the European Conference on Computer Vision (ECCV), Munich, Germany, 8–14 September 2018; pp. 202–218.
60. Ding, G.; Guo, Y.; Zhou, J. Collective matrix factorization hashing for multimodal data. In Proceedings of the IEEE Conference on Computer Vision and Pattern Recognition, Columbus, OH, USA, 23–28 June 2014; pp. 2075–2082.
61. Fang, Y.; Zhang, H.; Ren, Y. Unsupervised cross-modal retrieval via multi-modal graph regularized smooth matrix factorization hashing. *Knowl.-Based Syst.* **2019**, *171*, 69–80. [CrossRef]
62. Fang, Y.; Li, B.; Li, X.; Ren, Y. Unsupervised cross-modal similarity via Latent Structure Discrete Hashing Factorization. *Knowl.-Based Syst.* **2021**, *218*, 106857. [CrossRef]
63. Kumar, S.; Udupa, R. Learning hash functions for cross-view similarity search. In Proceedings of the Twenty-Second International Joint Conference on Artificial Intelligence, Barcelona, Spain, 16–22 July 2011; pp. 1360–1365.
64. Jiang, Q.Y.; Li, W.J. Deep cross-modal hashing. In Proceedings of the IEEE Conference on Computer Vision and Pattern Recognition, Honolulu, HI, USA, 21–26 July 2017; pp. 3232–3240.
65. Yang, E.; Deng, C.; Liu, W.; Liu, X.; Tao, D.; Gao, X. Pairwise relationship guided deep hashing for cross-modal retrieval. In Proceedings of the AAAI Conference on Artificial Intelligence, San Francisco, CA, USA, 4–9 February 2017; Volume 31, pp. 1618–1625.
66. Cao, Y.; Long, M.; Wang, J.; Yu, P.S. Correlation hashing network for efficient cross-modal retrieval. *arXiv* **2016**, arXiv:1602.06697.
67. Wang, L.; Zhu, L.; Yu, E.; Sun, J.; Zhang, H. Fusion-supervised deep cross-modal hashing. In Proceedings of the 2019 IEEE International Conference on Multimedia and Expo (ICME), Shanghai, China, 8–12 July 2019; pp. 37–42.
68. Huiskes, M.J.; Lew, M.S. The mir flickr retrieval evaluation. In Proceedings of the 1st ACM International Conference on Multimedia Information Retrieval, Vancouver, BC, Canada, 30–31 October 2008; pp. 39–43.
69. Chua, T.S.; Tang, J.; Hong, R.; Li, H.; Luo, Z.; Zheng, Y. Nus-wide: A real-world web image database from national university of singapore. In Proceedings of the ACM International Conference on Image and Video Retrieval, Santorini Island, Greece, 8–10 July 2009; pp. 1–9.

Article

Path-Wise Attention Memory Network for Visual Question Answering

Yingxin Xiang [1], Chengyuan Zhang [2,*], Zhichao Han [3], Hao Yu [2], Jiaye Li [2] and Lei Zhu [4,*]

1 School of Computer Science and Engineering, Central South University, Changsha 410083, China
2 College of Computer Science and Electronic Engineering, Hunan University, Changsha 410083, China
3 College of Science and Technology, Xiangsihu College Guangxi University for Nationalities, Nanning 530008, China
4 College of Information and Intelligence, Hunan Agricultural University, Changsha 410128, China
* Correspondence: cyzhangcse@hnu.edu.cn (C.Z.); leizhu@hunau.edu.cn (L.Z.)

Abstract: Visual question answering (VQA) is regarded as a multi-modal fine-grained feature fusion task, which requires the construction of multi-level and omnidirectional relations between nodes. One main solution is the composite attention model which is composed of co-attention (CA) and self-attention (SA). However, the existing composite models only consider the stack of single attention blocks, lack of path-wise historical memory, and overall adjustments. We propose a path attention memory network (PAM) to construct a more robust composite attention model. After each single-hop attention block (SA or CA), the importance of the cumulative nodes is used to calibrate the signal strength of nodes' features. Four memoried single-hop attention matrices are used to obtain the path-wise co-attention matrix of path-wise attention (PA); therefore, the PA block is capable of synthesizing and strengthening the learning effect on the whole path. Moreover, we use guard gates of the target modal to check the source modal values in CA and conditioning gates of another modal to guide the query and key of the current modal in SA. The proposed PAM is beneficial to construct a robust multi-hop neighborhood relationship between visual and language and achieves excellent performance on both VQA2.0 and VQA-CP V2 datasets.

Keywords: attention mechanism; path-wise attention; attention memory; memory network

MSC: 68T04

1. Introduction

Traditionally, computer vision and natural language processing are two important but mutually independent research fields of Artificial Intelligence. Both fields have made significant progress toward their goals and have gradually been driven to mutual convergence by the explosion of visual and textual data and the requirements of complex real-world tasks. At present, multi-modal learning has bridged the gap between visual and language and has been widely concerned [1–5]. Remarkable progress has been made in many multi-modal learning tasks, e.g., image captioning [6–9], video captioning [10–12], cross-modal retrieval [13–22], and visual question answering(VQA) [7,23–31].

The VQA task is more challenging than other multi-modal learning tasks because it requires a full understanding of textual information in the question and visual information in the image and finding out the key information to solve the problem for comprehensive reasoning.

Inchoate methods coarsely learn joint embedding representation with global features [32–34], which contains more noise and has difficulty answering the fine-grained questions. To address the problem, two lines of work have made major contributions and shown effective improvement in accuracy. Firstly, on data representations, global features are replaced by image regions features [27,29,35,36] and words features [29,37], which enable the model to fuse modal information at a finer level. Secondly, different variants of attention mechanisms are applied to enhance the interaction between fine-grained visual features and language features. The underlying motivation is to selectively focus on important parts and ignore irrelevant information. We combine fine-grained representation and attention mechanism and further improve the multi-step joint reasoning ability of the model; then we propose a Path Attention Memory network (PAM). By recording and tracking the attention distribution pattern, the path-wise memory attention block is constructed to strengthen the effective signal and weaken the invalid noise.

The application of the attention mechanism in VQA is very extensive, and various types of attention have been proposed. REGAT [27] uses question self-attention to aggregate words embedding into a global sentence feature. MCAN [36] uses self-attention on attended word features and attended regions features in the fusion stage so that an answer vector is obtained by adding the learned global question vector and global visual vector. The attention mechanism mentioned above fuses information from a sequence of features into a single feature vector, while graph-based attention similar to graph attention network(GAT) [38] does not change the length of the input feature sequence. Graph-based self-attention can be used to establish region-to-region relations on the visual channels and word-to-word relations on the textual channels. Co-attention is able to learn fine-grained correlations between two feature sequences [25,37], so region-to-word and word-to-region relations can be acquired when applied to the VQA task. Compared with single-stream early fusion and dual-stream late fusion, the introduction of co-attention can flexibly adjust the hidden values according to the context of the other modal and learn the inter-modal relations.

Many existing works use self-attention [23,27,35]; only a few works use co-attention and self-attention simultaneously [29,36]. Existing models aggregate important information in multi-hop neighborhoods by stacking several layers of attention modules. An encoder–decoder architecture similar to Transformer is also proposed in MCAN [36] to stack self-attention and co-attention. However, visual features and linguistic features are in different feature spaces, and some deviations may exist even if transformation matrices are used for feature projection. Inspired by the channel-wise conditioning gates used in DFAF [29], we used channel-wise guard gates to check and reshape the projected values from another modal in co-attention.

In addition, we believe that the multi-hop neighborhood relationship constructed by stacking attention modules needs a path-wise module to summarize the previous learning effects and correct some learning biases. This path-wise module needs to be directly connected to the previous attention modules and play a role of centralized control to instruct and constrain the learning of single-hop modules. We refer to the idea of a memory network to memorize four attention matrices that represent pairs' relationships in a set of regions and words. These attention matrices are regarded as the direct link between the single-hop module and the path-wise module. In short, we propose the path-wise attention block(PA) which is designed as a special co-attention block. The PA takes four attention matrices and two modality features as inputs to calculate a path-wise attention matrix with the adjusted features as output, so it can directly guide the attention matrix learning of the single-hop attention module along the entire path in the backpropagation. The attention matrix of the general attention module is calculated by query and key and is directly related to the current input features, while the attention matrix of PA is not directly related to the input features but to the updated history of features.

The contributions of our work are four-fold:

(1) We propose a novel framework Path-wise Attention Memory (PAM) Network to construct a robust multi-hop neighborhood relationship between visual and language.

(2) We design a central governor for attention-based models, namely Path-wise Attention, to instruct and constrain the learning of single-hop attention blocks in the path.

(3) We use the cumulative nodes' importance to calibrate the signal strength of regions and words after each single-hop attention block. This strategy is simple, inexpensive but effective.

(4) We adaptively adopt a new gate mechanism in self-attention and co-attention, to make the information interaction between modalities tight and useful.

Roadmap. The rest of this paper is organized as follows. The related work is summarized in Section 2. The details of the proposed method PAM are presented in Section 3. The experimental results and evaluations are reported in Section 4. Finally, we conclude this paper in Section 5.

2. Related Work
2.1. Visual Question Answering

Visual question answering requires a comprehensive and fine-grained understanding of both visual information and text information. One line of work focuses on designing vector fusion functions to capture a high-level correlation between the global visual vector space and the global text vector space [32,33,39]. Some approaches on this line achieve excellent results. However, the direct use of coarse-grained global features in this way may lead to the loss of local details, and inter-modal relations are highly abstract and poorly interpretable. Therefore, research began to shift from coarse-grained to fine-grained, and many methods gradually use image regions features to replace global image vectors and words features to replace global sentence vectors [25,40]. Moreover, the attention mechanism was also introduced to aggregate fine-grained node information and has become the most mainstream inference framework. Ref. [27] takes the question as a global sentence vector to be concrete after each visual region feature. Three types of visual relationships are considered, and their relations matrices are pre-trained and applied to mask the soft attention of a bidirectional graph attention network. Fine-grained representations of both visual and language features are adopted by [29]. They use intra-modal apply self-attention, and inter-modal apply cross-modal feature gate vector to guide self-attention; that is, the query and key in inter-modal self-attention need an element-wise product with the average pooling aggregate cross-modal features [36]. The stack question self-attention module and question guided visual self-attention module are instituted through the proposed encoder–decoder stacking form.

2.2. Attention Mechanisms

By selectively focusing on important parts and ignoring irrelevant information, an attention mechanism can effectively solve the problem of long-term dependencies in model training and improve the interpretability of neural networks and has been widely applied to many unimodal tasks(e.g., machine translation [41,42], visual detection [43], image classification) and multimodal tasks(e.g., multimedia retrieval, visual question answering [23]).

A typical attention module uses a query and key to calculate the weight of each item in the input sequence then sums the weighted values to obtain the output sequence. The attention mechanism is not restricted to the length of the input sequence suitable for an inductive learning problem. Different varieties of attention modules are produced in different application scenarios.

The attention mechanism is usually combined with an RNN for machine translation tasks in the early stage. The attention model was first introduced for Machine Translation by Bahdanau et al. [41] with sequence input but non-sequence output. Similarly, Yang et al. use an RNN and attention mechanism to capture document information gradually at word level and statement level and finally construct a document level feature vector. In such a scenario, attention is used to weight the tokens in the input sequence and aggregate the representation of those tokens to form a holistic vector. An RNN's recurrent architectures are nonparallel which result in computational inefficiency. To address this, Vaswani et al. proposed eminent Transformer architecture which only relies on a self-attention mechanism to calculate the relationship between each word and all the other words [44].

In the VQA task, self-attention is extensively used to model word-to-word relationships for questions and region-to-region relationships for images in the VQA task. Question-guided attention on image regions or video frames is generally explored for visual question answering [27,36,45,46], video question answering [47–49], image captioning [6], etc. In order to capture more intensive correlation between cross-modal nodes, co-attention-based approaches [25,29,36,37] use bi-direction attention to learn the relationships between word–region pairs.

2.3. Graph Attention Network

When processing graph structure data, graph convolution networks (GCNs) use the Laplacian matrix to aggregate node information leading to fixed-size neighborhoods and allocate non-parametric node weight according to node degree. However, graph attention networks(GATs) use the attention mechanism to aggregate node information, which guarantees that more important nodes receive higher weight. The parallelism, flexibility, and interpretability of the attention mechanism make it overcome such problems and perform well. Presented by Smith et al. [38], graph attention networks aggregate multi-hop neighborhood information as the number of layers deepens. Meanwhile, each layer applies the multi-head attention to stabilize the learning process, K hidden states are computed by K independent mechanisms and can be interpreted as observing features from different K perspectives.

When GAT applies to the VQA task, visual regions nodes and language words nodes jointly compose a fully connected graph, whose edges weights can be learned from associative node features by attention alone or constrained by calculating relative spatial positions between nodes or additional relational label data [27,50]. Our model represents both visual features and language features as graph structure, simultaneously learning the inter-relation and intra-relation of two types of nodes by attention mechanism. The fine-grained aggregation at the node level makes the reasoning process of the model more meticulous and precise. For the sequence of the nodes processed by multiple graph attention, we retrace its importance on the meta-path to construct meta-path-based cross-modal attention, thereby reinforcing and verifying the previous reasoning.

3. The Proposed Approach

According to the input visual information and question information, a solver of VQA extracts features from a singular modality, fusions feature between the visual and language modalities, finally predicting the answer based on the learned joint representation. The VQA model can be divided into three steps: feature extraction, feature fusion, and answer prediction.

Our proposed Path-wise Attention Memory Network (PAM) also follows this structure, as shown in Figure 1. In feature fusion, we use a composite attention network composed of co-attention, self-attention, and path-wise attention. The node impact factor is used to self-reinforce the signal. In the following paragraphs, we introduce the problem definition first and then discuss PAM in that order.

3.1. Problem Definition

As most existing approaches do, we regard the visual question answering task as a multi-class problem rather than a generation problem. Let (X,Y,Z) denote the training set, where X is the space of grounded images, Y is the space of questions, and Z is the space of labels. Following previous VQA methods, we consider the multi-class classification problem with binary cross-entropy (BCE) loss.

$$P = \text{Sigmoid}(f(X, Y; \theta)) \quad (1)$$

$$L(P, Z) = -\sum_{i=1}^{C} z_i \log(p_i) + (1 - z_i)\log(1 - p_i) \quad (2)$$

C denotes the number of categories, and f(.) represents the VQA model that fuses the visual and language information to a C dim predictive vector.

Our model takes fine-grained visual features and question features as input to divide the image into multiple regions according to the different objects identified in the image and divide the text of the question into consecutive words. The image regions and question words are collectively called nodes.

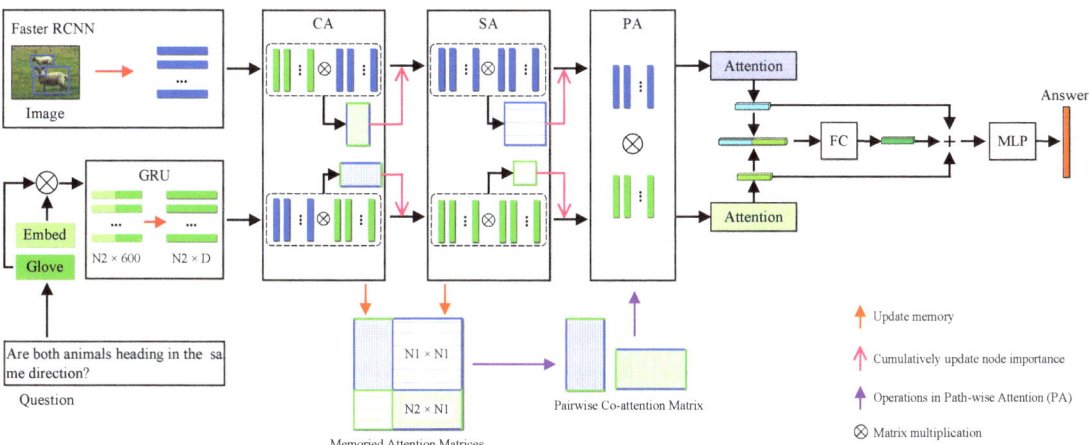

Figure 1. Illustration of the proposed Path-wise Memory Network(PAM) for visual question answering. It contains three main parts: (1) feature extraction, which contains a Faster-RCNN for image regions feature extraction, and a gated recurrent unit for question words feature learning; (2) a composite attention network composed of co-attention, self-attention, and path-wise attention, which is to dynamically swap and fuse information between the visual modality and the text modality; (3) an answer predictor which computes the final fused multi-modal feature and map features to the answer vector space.

3.2. Build Fine-Grained Feature Vectors

The visual information used in our model is fine-grained image region information. A Faster-RCNN [51] model is pre-trained on a visual genome dataset to detect objects in origin images. Then the image regions feature is extracted. Each image is represented as a feature vector $R \in \Re^{m \times 2048}$ with at most m = 100 regions.

The input question is first tokenized into a word sequence and padded or truncated to the maximum length of $n = 14$; each word has 600 dimensions. Then the words sequence is further transformed into feature vector $W \in \Re^{n \times 1024}$ by a bidirectional RNN with a gated recurrent unit (GRU) [52]. In order to better capture the overall information in the language modality, we use the simple self-attention mechanism [41] to fuse the information of the entire words sequence feature vector to obtain a global information node of the question with the same dimension of 1024, which is concatenated after the words feature vector, and the final language feature vector is 15×1024.

To facilitate the subsequent processing of cross-modal and self-modal graph attention information, two linear layers with an ReLU activation function and 0.1 dropout is used to map the visual feature vector and language feature vector to the same dimension D. That is, the visual feature vector is represented as $R \in \Re^{N1 \times D}$ and the language feature vector is represented as $W \in \Re^{N2 \times D}$. For the feature with less than N1 or N2 nodes, zero-padding is used to add a fake empty node, and the attention logits of an empty node are filled with negative infinity by using nodes masks in the following several attention modules.

3.3. Attention Blocks with Memory

Taking the input sequences of regions R and words W, we use a composite attention network composed of three types of attention blocks to fuse the dual-modal information.

In this subsection, we first introduce the standard attention block and then introduce our memory improved attention blocks, that is co-attention with guard gates, self-attention with conditioning gates, and path-wise attention block. Then we introduce the details of the node impact factor used in co-attention and self-attention.

3.3.1. Standard Attention Block

For the standard Transformer attention [44], given the input features $I \in \Re^{N \times D}$, three linear layers project it to the query, key, and value matrices and divide it into multiple heads, $Q \in \Re^{H \times N \times D_h}$, $K \in \Re^{H \times N \times D_h}$, $V \in \Re^{H \times N \times D_h}$,

$$Q, K, V = \text{Linear}(I), \tag{3}$$

$$\text{Att} = \text{Softmax}(\frac{QK^T}{\sqrt{D_h}}), \tag{4}$$

where "Linear" denotes a fully-connected layer, D_h is the dimension of heads, and K^T denotes the transpose of K. Query feature Q and key feature K are used to calculate the attention matrix Att which is regarded as the weight of value feature V, so then the sum of the weighted value feature is fed to the Feed Forward Network(FFN) to obtain the updated feature I^*,

$$I^* = \text{FFN}(\text{AttV}), \tag{5}$$

$$\text{FFN}(x) = \text{Linear}(\text{ReLU}(\text{Linear}(x))). \tag{6}$$

"ReLU" is used to filter positive values; that is, $\text{ReLU}(x) = \max(0, x)$.

Nowadays, many works follow the attention mechanism in Transformer which brings huge computing and memory overhead. Our work introduce gates to it and pruned it. To simultaneously gain a simpler network and good performance, we trimmed the single attention module of Transformer appropriately to delete the Feed Forward Network and some projection linear layers. Details are covered separately in specific attention blocks.

3.3.2. Co-Attention with Guard Gates

The co-attention block as shown in Figure 2 learns to capture the attention score between each pair of regions and word feature. This information flow structure is able to learn cross-modal relations and facilitate cross-modal information interaction.

Given the visual regions feature and words feature, we first transformed the input feature into query, key, and value features.

$$Q = \text{Linear}(R), K = W \tag{7}$$

$$V_r = Q, V_w = W \tag{8}$$

For the co-attention block, query and value of visual are the heads divided visual regions feature with linear projection; key and value of language are the heads divided words feature without linear projection.

By calculating the matrix multiplication between query and key, then applying the Softmax function on different dimensions, we obtain two inter-modality attention matrices.

$$\text{Att}_{r2w} = \text{Softmax}(\frac{QK^T}{\sqrt{D_h}}, -1) \tag{9}$$

$$\text{Att}_{w2r} = \text{Softmax}(\frac{QK^T}{\sqrt{D_h}}, -2)^T \tag{10}$$

where $\text{Att}_{r2w} \in \Re^{H \times N1 \times N2}$ represent regions' attention to words, and $\text{Att}_{w2r} \in \Re^{H \times N2 \times N1}$ represent words' attention to regions.

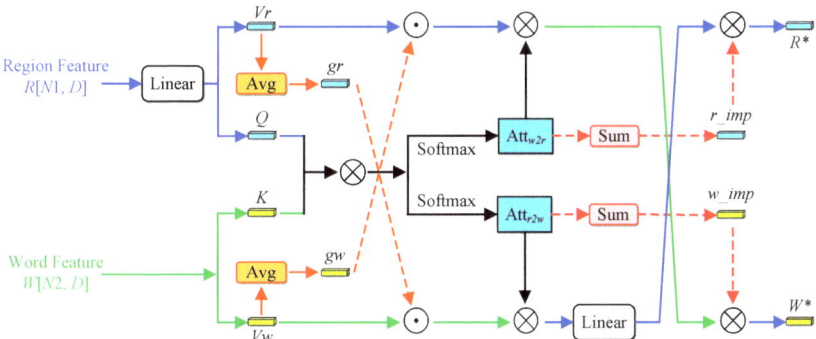

Figure 2. The co-attention (CA) block used in PAM, with the guard gates (orange marked) and importance rectification (red marked).

Then, the two attention matrices are used to gather the cross-modal information from the value of regions or words. To reduce the noise caused by the difference between two modal feature spaces, we use the guard gates to check and filter the noise info in cross-modal values. The guard gates are computed by average pooling of target modal values and used in the element-wise product with the source modal values to reduce the noise of cross-modal message passing, defined as g_r and g_w.

$$g_r = \mathrm{Avg}(V_r), g_r \in \Re^{H \times D_h} \tag{11}$$

$$g_w = \mathrm{Avg}(V_w), g_w \in \Re^{H \times D_h} \tag{12}$$

$$\mathrm{Avg}(Y) = \frac{1}{N} \sum_i^N y_i, Y \in \Re^{H \times N \times D_h} \tag{13}$$

We denote the updated information flows as updated regions feature R^* and updated words feature W^*, respectively,

$$R^* = \mathrm{Linear}(\mathrm{Att}_{r2w}(V_w \times g_r)) \times r_{\mathrm{imp}} \tag{14}$$

$$W^* = \mathrm{Att}_{w2r}(V_r \times g_w) \times w_{\mathrm{imp}} \tag{15}$$

Here r_{imp} is the accumulated regions importance, and w_{imp} is the accumulated words importance. See details in Section 3.3.5.

The updated regions feature and words feature would then be fed into the following self-attention block to learn the mutual relations between the same modal nodes.

3.3.3. Self-Attention with Conditioning Gates

Co-attention promotes the fusion of relevant information between visuals and language, while self-attention facilitates the accurate location of important nodes through multi-hop relations. For example, for the question, "What is the man doing under the tree?", the self-attention block helps the model focus on the right man by recognizing the relation between the man and the tree.

Two symmetrical self-attention (SA) blocks are used respectively for regions and words; the SA for regions is shown in Figure 3. We pruned the network and introduce conditioning gates to standard transformer attention which is the base of our proposed self-attention.

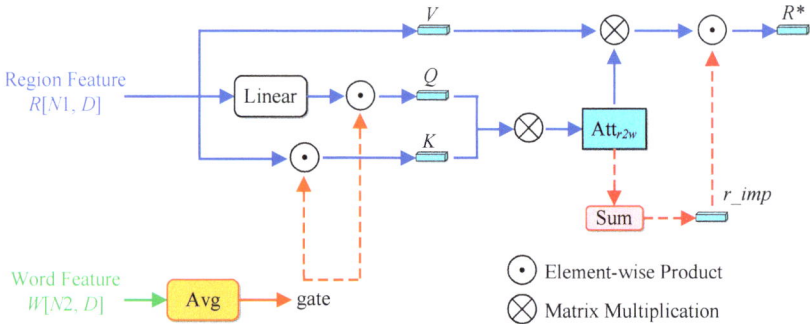

Figure 3. The self-attention (SA) block used in PAM for regions, with the conditioning gate (orange marked) and importance rectification (red marked). Similarly, an SA for words and Att$_{w2w}$ exist.

The conditioning gate from the other modal is an element-wise product with the query and key to building the context-appropriate relations between nodes. Then, we obtain a pair of different attention matrices by the gated query and key. Att$_{r2r} \in \Re^{H \times N1 \times N1}$ represent regions' attention to regions, Att$_{w2w} \in \Re^{H \times N2 \times N2}$ represent words' attention to words.

$$\text{Att}_{r2r} = \text{Softmax}(\frac{(\text{Linear}(R) \times \text{Avg}(W))(R \times \text{Avg}(W))^T}{\sqrt{D_h}}) \quad (16)$$

$$\text{Att}_{w2w} = \text{Softmax}(\frac{(\text{Linear}(W) \times \text{Avg}(R))(W \times \text{Avg}(R))^T}{\sqrt{D_h}}) \quad (17)$$

In the self-attention blocks, the image regions feature and words feature are finally updated as follows,

$$R^* = (\text{Att}_{r2r} R) \times r_{\text{imp}} \quad (18)$$

$$W^* = (\text{Att}_{w2w} W) \times w_{\text{imp}} \quad (19)$$

The details of accumulated importance are described in Section 3.3.5.

3.3.4. Path-Wise Attention Block

A co-attention block and two self-attention blocks have been used previously; hence four attention matrices have been memorized. These memorized attention matrices are good for exactly two things. One is used to calculate the importance of global nodes which will be declared in Section 3.3.5, and the other important usage is to calculate a path-wise attention matrix.

Path-wise attention block is a special co-attention block without the linear projection from features to query and key. Instead of that, the memoried four attention matrices are used to calculate its attention matrix which could influence all the single-hop attention blocks along the entire path in the backpropagation. Adding a PAM after the stack of single-hop attention modules enables the model not only to gradually transmit information in the single-hop neighborhood, but also to adjust the signal strength along the multi-hop constructed path.

To be clear, four memorized matrices from previous attention blocks are region-to-region attention Att$_{r2r}$, word-to-word attention Att$_{w2w}$, region-to-word attention Att$_{r2w}$, and word-to-region attention Att$_{w2r}$. To calculate the path-wise attention matrix, we first use the sum of the attention matrix to calculate the four importance scores with the multi-head structure remaining. For example,

$$S_{r2w} = \sum_{i}^{N1} Att_{r2w}^{i}, S_{r2w} \in \Re^{H \times N2 \times 1} \tag{20}$$

$$S_{w2w} = \sum_{i}^{N1} Att_{w2w}^{i}, S_{w2w} \in \Re^{H \times N2 \times 1} \tag{21}$$

S_{r2w} represents the word's importance scores which are rated by visual regions, and S_{w2w} represents the word's importance scores which are rated by language words. The importance score rated by two different modalities can be combined into a unified rating score; we perform the matrix multiplication with a tanh activation function to obtain both regions unified rating score and words unified rating score. Then we can calculate the PAM attention matrix score,

$$S = \tanh(S_{w2r}S_{r2r}^T)Att_{r2w} \times (\tanh(S_{r2w}S_{w2w}^T)Att_{w2r})^T, \tag{22}$$

$$scores = Conv1d(S), \tag{23}$$

where S comprehensively considers the importance of the previous attention module to each node, and final PAM attention matrix scores are further fused by one-dimensional convolution, $scores \in \Re^{H \times N1 \times N2}$. Such a calculation helps each attention block of the model construct the same-level interdependence in the backpropagation. The interactivity between attention blocks is stronger, so that the PAM has the ability to directly regulate the blocks along the entire attention path.

As shown in Figure 4, the rest part of PA block is similar to CA block. we calculate the cross-modal path-wise attention matrix by Softmax on different dimensions of the same attention scores,

$$Att_{r2w}^{P} = Softmax(scores, -1), \tag{24}$$

$$Att_{w2r}^{P} = Softmax(scores, -2)^T. \tag{25}$$

Then the two path-wise attention matrices are used to update values and output the updated R^* and W^*. The guard gates of values mentioned in Equations (11) and (12) are also adopted in PA.

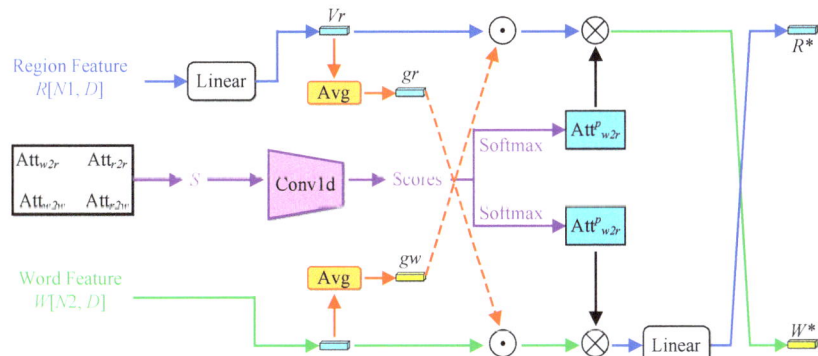

Figure 4. The path-wise attention (PA) block with the guard gate (orange marked). The specific calculation method of score is given by the formula.

3.3.5. Node Impact Factor

The node impact factor measures the relative importance of a node according to how much attention has been received in the attention network. It is declared as global node importance in our paper. This concept is introduced to amplify the signal of important nodes and reduce the signal of irrelevant nodes after each attention operation.

$$\text{imp}* = \text{Sigmoid}((1-\alpha)\text{imp} + \alpha \sum_i^H \sum_j^N \text{Att}). \tag{26}$$

Global nodes importance updates after each attention block and are obtained by the sum in another dimension and activated with a sigmoid function, $\text{imp} \in \Re^N$. In order to remember the importance of nodes along the whole attention path, a cumulative strategy is adopted to update the importance of nodes. H is the number of heads, and α is the cumulative coefficient, ranging from 0 to 1. Experiments show that the value of α between 0.9 and 0.96 will have better performance. Each region or word feature multiplies by its global node importance to adjust the signal strength of node.

3.4. Answer Prediction

After several blocks of feature updating by CA, SA, and PA, we obtain the final visual regions and language words features by gathering nodes information via robust multi-hop bi-modality neighborhood relationships. As described in Figure 1, two attention blocks are used to turn regions and words features into global visual feature $r \in \Re^D$ and global language feature $w \in \Re^D$. The attention block uses multi-layer perceptron to compress the input's dimension from D to 1, then uses the Softmax function to obtain each item's contribution to global representation, $a \in \Re^{N1 \times 1}$, and finally, computes a matrix multiplication between input and a.

$$a_r = \text{Softmax}(\text{MLP}(R), -2), a_r \in \Re^{N1 \times 1}, \tag{27}$$

$$r = R^T a_r, \tag{28}$$

$$a_w = \text{Softmax}(\text{MLP}(W), -2), a_w \in \Re^{N2 \times 1}, \tag{29}$$

$$w = W^T a_w. \tag{30}$$

The global features r and w are eventually fused to generate the last answer prediction,

$$\text{answer} = \text{MLP}(\text{FC}([r, w])) + r + w, \tag{31}$$

$$\text{FC}(x) = \text{ReLU}(xW_x + b), \tag{32}$$

$$\text{MLP}(x) = \text{ReLU}(xW_1 + b_1)W_2 + b_2. \tag{33}$$

FC is a linear layer with ReLU and 0.1 dropout. Its MLP maps the hidden dimension H of the fused feature vector to C, where C is the number of the most frequent answers in the training set. So the binary cross-entropy (BCE) loss is calculated with the prediction and data labels by Equation (2).

4. Experiment

4.1. Datasets

We conduct our experiments mainly on VQA2.0 [53], but also test out-of-distribution generalization on VQA-CP [54].

VQA2.0 [53] is the most commonly used VQA benchmark dataset. It is composed of human-annotated question–answer pairs for the real images from the Microsoft COCO dataset [55]. Compared with previous VQA 1.0 [56], VQA 2.0 has many more annotations and less dataset bias. The entire dataset is split into training (82,783 images and 443,757 QA pairs), validation (40,504 images and 214,354 QA pairs) and test-standard sets (81,434 images and 447,793 QA pairs). Additionally, the test-dev set is a 25% subset of the size of the test-standard set. An average of 3 questions are generated for each image; 10 answers are collected for each image–question pair by human annotations, and the most frequent answer is treated as the ground truth. The results are divided into three per-type accuracies(yes/no, number, and other) and an overall accuracy according to question type.

VQA-CP v2 [54] dataset was constructed by reorganizing VQA2.0, which is called visual question answering under changing priors, such that the distribution of answers for each question type differs in the training set and the testing set to avoid the model's over-reliance on the prior knowledge of potential relationships between questions and answers.

4.2. Implementation Details

Our model is implemented with PyTorch. All initialization is the Pytorch's default initialization; that is, the initial weights of linear layers and conv1d layers are sampled from the uniform distribution. We use cross-validation to evaluate the accuracy under different hyperparameters and select the group with the best performance. We declare the final hyperparameters setting in Table 1. The batch size is set to 64. We adopted 8 heads (H = 8) of attention in CA/SA/PA, hidden dimension is 2048 (D = 2048), and the dimension of each head is 256 (HD = 2048/8).

The dropout rate of fully connected layers is set as 0.1. We use binary cross entropy as the loss function with the Adamax optimizer. The basic learning rate is set as 0.001, and the hot start strategy is adopted. The learning rates of the first three epochs are 0.0005, 0.001, and 0.0015, and then the learning rate remains unchanged at 0.002 until the 10th epoch begins to decay with a step length of 2 epochs and a decay rate of 0.5. The cumulative coefficient of global nodes importance is set as 0.95.

Table 1. Setting of hyperparameters.

Hyperparameters	Value
Hidden dimension	2048
Number of attention heads	8
Learning rate (lr)	0.001
Decay start epoch of lr	10
Decay interval of lr	2
Decay factor of lr	0.5
Dropout factor	0.1
Batch size	64
Epochs	15

4.3. Baselines

In this paper, the proposed PAM method is compared with several baselines which can be divided into two categories based on the dataset they are focused on.

One is mainly concerned with the performance on VQA2.0, including Teney et al., 2018 [57], DCN [25], DRAU [58], BLOCK [26], Zhang et al., 2020 [59], MuRel [28], RA-MEN [60], and ReGAT-implicit [27].

The other is mainly concerned with VQA-CP to verify its generalization performance, including AReg [24], Grand et al., 2019 [61], CSS-UpDn [30], Teney et al., 2021 [31], and Whitehead et al., 2021 [62].

To reflect the improvements in the model structure, we select their models with similar feature extraction methods and without extra annotations, without ensembling or tuning. Here is a brief introduction to these baselines.

- Teney et al., 2018 [57] adopts the question/image early joint embedding and the single-layer question-guided image self-attention mechanism.
- DCN [25] designs a bi-directional interactions hierarchy network stacked by several dense co-attention maps to fuse visual and language features.
- DRAU [58] combines convolutional attention and recurrent attention to promote bi-modal fusion reasoning.
- BLOCK [26] is a multi-modal fusion method based on the tensor composition which can perform fine-grained inter-modal representation while maintaining strong single-modal representation ability.
- Zhang et al., 2020 [59] designs a question-guided top-down visual attention block and a question-guided convolutional relational reasoning block.

- MuRel [28] adopts a method similar to the graph attention mechanism to learn the inter-regional relations of the image and updates the regions hidden representation under the guidance of questions and image geometric information.
- RAMEN [60] performs an early fusion of fine-grained image regions' feature and global question feature and then processes the fused feature by bi-directional gated recurrent unit(bi-GRU) but without an attention or a bi-linear pooling mechanism [63].
- ReGAT-implicit [27] models implicit relations between visual regions via graph attention network.
- AReg [24] prevents the VQA model from capturing language bias by introducing the question-only adversary to encourage visual grounding.
- Grand et al., 2019 [61] research how to alleviate linguistically biased by introducing adversarial regularization.
- CSS-UpDn [30] forces the model to reason correctly by adding custom counterfactual samples to the training data; then the model could achieve better performance on VQA-CP.
- Teney et al., 2021 [31] adopts a new multiple environment training scheme to improve the out-of-distributed generalization. We choose its best non-ensemble model to compare with our PAM in Table 2.
- Whitehead et al., 2021 [62] utilize both labeled and unlabeled image–question pairs and try to separate skills and concepts for the model to improve its generalization.

Table 2. Model accuracy on the VQA 2.0 and VQA-CP benchmark.

Model	VQA2.0			VQA-CP
	Test-Dev	Test-Std	val	Test
Teney et al., 2018 [57]	65.32	65.67	63.15	-
DCN [25]	66.60	67.00	-	-
DRAU [58]	66.45	66.85	-	-
BLOCK [26]	66.41	67.92	-	-
Zhang et al., 2020 [59]	67.20	67.34	-	-
MuRel [28]	68.03	68.41	65.14	39.54
RAMEN [60]	65.96	-	-	39.21
ReGAT-implicit [27]	67.6	67.81	65.93	40.13
Our PAM	69.01	69.24	66.20	41.60
AReg [24]	-	-	62.75	41.17
Grand et al., 2019 [61]	-	-	51.92	42.33
CSS-UpDn [30]	-	-	59.21	41.16
Teney et al., 2021 [31]	-	-	61.08	42.39
whitehead et al., 2021 [62]	-	-	61.08	41.71

4.4. Results and Analysis

The PAM is trained on the training set of VQA2.0 [53]. Table 2 shows its overall performance on VQA2.0 test-dev, test-std, and val splits using the accuracy metric [56] in comparison to the baselines and evaluated on the VQA-CP v2 [54] dataset to demonstrate its generalizability. Our PAM has already achieved the state-of-the-art overall accuracy on VQA2.0 (69.24% vs. 68.41% in test-std split, 66.20% vs. 65.93% in val split), and 41.60% overall accuracy on the test set of VQA-CP. It states that the PAM is not only the best performing among the baselines focused on VQA2.0, but also very competitive in VQA-CP focused baselines, which means our PAM can rely less on prior knowledge and more on correct inference understanding and can be generalized to the VQA-CP dataset as well.

To be more specific about PAM's generalizability comparison, the bottom five other models focus on VQA out-of-distribution generalization which leads them to achieve higher accuracy on the VQA-CP dataset, but obviously at the cost of huge performance degradation on the VQA2.0 dataset. Take Grand et al., 2019 [61] for example, compared with ReGAT-implicit it gained a 2.2% performance improvement on the VQA-CP test, but a 14.01% performance degradation on the VQA2.0 val.

Our PAM did not specifically optimize performance on VQA-CP v2 like the models in the bottom five rows in Table 2; however, without adversarial regularization or optimized training data, our PAM can achieve competitive performance on the VQA-CP dataset and avoid the obvious degradation on VQA2.0. PAM outperforms other popular models by ±0.8% on the VQA-CP test set, and obtains an improvement of at least 3.45% on the VQA2.0 val set. This shows that our model achieves a more suitable balance between generalization ability and fitting ability.

4.5. Ablation Study

Ablation studies are performed on the VQA2.0 [53] validation dataset to evaluate the effectiveness of our proposed actions. The results are shown in Table 3.

The "PAM" model in the first row is our complete model involving all actions. The next few rows progressively remove blocks based on PAM. "-PA" indicates that path attention is removed, which is the block marked in purple in Figure 1, while "-PA+CA" means to replace PA with CA. The "-imp" indicates the importance of the global nodes after each SA and CA block is removed; that is, the operations marked in red at the end of the SA (Figure 3) and CA (Figure 2) are deleted. We remove guard gates marked in orange in CA (Figure 2); it shows as "-gates in CA" in Table 3 and "-gate in CA/SA" if gates in SA are also removed.

Table 3. Ablation studies of our proposed actions on the VQA2.0 validation dataset. "-" is the operation to delete trick based on complete model PAM.

Model	VQA v2 val
PAM	66.20
-PA	65.69
-PA+CA	65.32
-PA-imp	65.01
-gate in SA	66.11
-gates in CA/SA/PA	65.85
-PA-imp-gates in CA/PA	64.66
-PA-imp-gates in SA	65.58
-PA-imp-gates in CA/SA/PA	65.34

Comparing "PAM" with "-PA", we achieved a 0.51% performance improvement by adding the path-wise attention. To eliminate the influence of the change of parameters number, we also experimented with replacing a PA with CA in "-PA+CA", as PA is designed as a special CA, and their parameters are mainly derived from two linear layers. Results in Table 3 show that "-PA+CA" does not achieve a similar performance as PAM and even has a performance decrease compared to "-PA". We believe that the reason is that CA is only a single-hop attention module and cannot summarize and strengthen the multi-hop neighborhood formed by multiple attention modules along the whole path like PA.

Comparing "-PA" with "-PA-imp", we achieved a 0.68% performance improvement by applying the importance of the global nodes. The "imp" trick is universal and easy to operate for all the popular attention blocks with almost no extra overhead. Moreover, the importance of accumulation is very suitable for concatenating multiple models in boosting-based ensemble learning. Due to the limitation of computing resources, we only tried concatenating two PAM on small dimensions, and it shows performance improvement compared with one PAM. The gates vector is inspired by the conditioning gating vector mentioned in DFAF. Some adaptive changes have been made in the calculation method and applied to both SA and CA for different purposes, while the gating vector in DFAF is only used to guide SA learning. The improved guard gates in CA are effective, as removing them from "-PA-imp" decreases accuracy from 65.01 to 64.66.

From Table 3, removing gates in SA from "-PA-imp" brings performance improvement, while removing gates from PAM brings performance decrement. We believe the reason is that SA can perfect and supplement other proposed strategies in PAM, which is beneficial to the overall performance.

Figure 5 shows the validation accuracy versus epochs of different ablations of our model, and our PAM model keeps the advantage of accuracy in the whole training process.

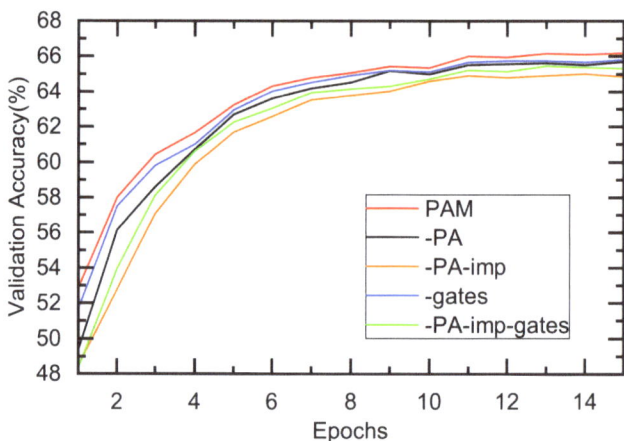

Figure 5. Validation accuracy versus epochs for the proposed VQA model.

4.6. Distribution of Attention and Prediction

In Figure 6, we analyzed the distribution of eight attention heads. Each colored line represents a head in the attention block. Its calculation formula is similar to Equation (20). The PAM successfully focuses on the important words and regions compared with the model without path-wise attention block.

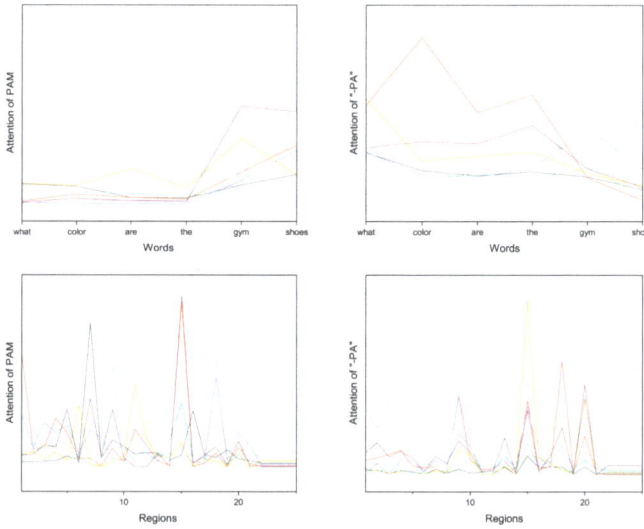

Figure 6. An example of attention distribution by 8 heads, the left two from PAM and the right two from "-PA". The path-wise attention block helps the model focus on useful information to answer the question.

In Figures 7 and 8, our PAM gave a higher degree of confidence in correct answers compared to the model without path-wise attention block.

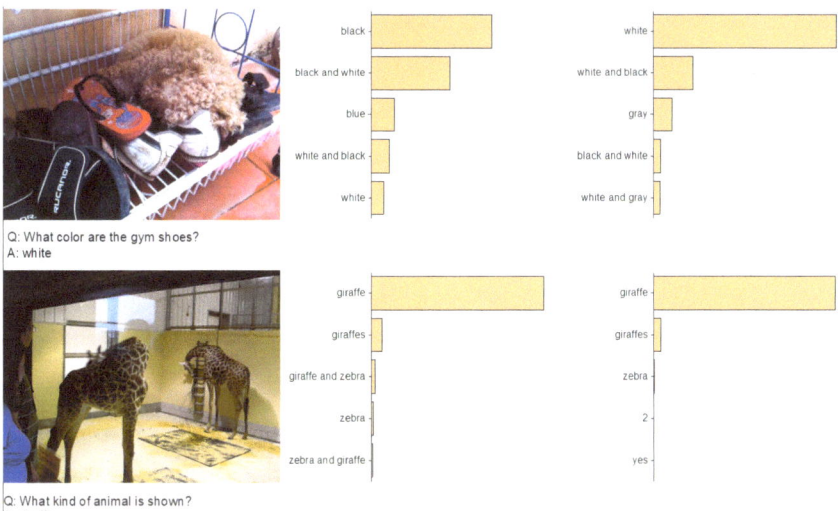

Figure 7. Examples of model prediction. The second column is the TOP5 prediction of the "-PA" model, and the third column is the TOP5 prediction of PAM.

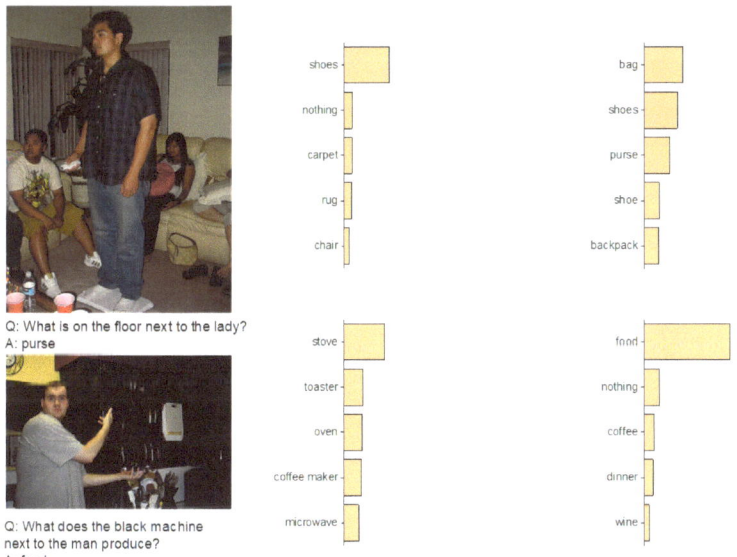

Figure 8. Examples of model prediction for complicated questions. The second column is the TOP5 prediction of the "-PA" model, and the third column is the TOP5 prediction of PAM.

5. Conclusions

In this paper, we proposed a novel path-wise attention memory(PAM) network framework for visual question answering. Four attention matrices of self-attention and co-attention are memorized by the network. They benefit to calculate global nodes importance and a new attention matrix of path-wise attention. The cumulative nodes importance could calibrate the signal strength of regions and words after each single-hop attention block. The path-wise attention could directly guide the attention matrix learning of a single-hop attention module as a central governor. The gates vectors in SA/CA/PA are used to enhance the interaction between the visual and the language modal. These actions bring model effectiveness improvement, and PAM shows good accuracy and generalization performance in experiments.

Author Contributions: Conceptualization, C.Z.; Methodology, Z.H. and J.L.; Resources, H.Y.; Software, Y.X.; Visualization, Y.X. and L.Z.; Writing—original draft, Y.X.; Writing—review & editing, C.Z. and L.Z. All authors have read and agreed to the published version of the manuscript.

Funding: This research was funded by the National Natural Science Foundation of China (62072166, 61836016) and the Natural Science Foundation of Hunan Province (2022JJ40190).

Institutional Review Board Statement: Not applicable.

Informed Consent Statement: Not applicable.

Data Availability Statement: Our Code is available at https://github.com/bluehat999/PAM-for-VQA (accessed on 21 July 2022). VQA2.0 and VQA1.0 download at: https://visualqa.org/download.html (accessed on 21 July 2022), and VQA-CP download at: https://computing.ece.vt.edu/~aish/vqacp (accessed on 21 July 2022).

Conflicts of Interest: The authors declare no conflict of interest.

Notations

The following notations are used in this manuscript:

r	Final global visual vector
w	Final global question vector
α	Cumulative coefficient of nodes impact factor
R	Image regions feature
W	Question words feature
C	Number of categories
D	Hidden dimension
N_1	Number of image regions
N_2	Number of question words
H	Number of attention heads
D_h	Dimension of attention heads
$W_{1,2,R,\ldots}$	Weights of linear layer
$b_{1,2,R,\ldots}$	Bias of linear layer
Avg	Average pooling layer
Linear	Linear layer

References

1. Kim, J.; Koh, J.; Kim, Y.; Choi, J.; Hwang, Y.; Choi, J.W. Robust Deep Multi-Modal Learning Based on Gated Information Fusion Network. In Proceedings of the Asian Conference on Computer Vision, Perth, Australia, 2–6 December 2018; Springer: Berlin/Heidelberg, Germany, 2018; pp. 90–106.
2. Dou, Q.; Liu, Q.; Heng, P.A.; Glocker, B. Unpaired multi-modal segmentation via knowledge distillation. *IEEE Trans. Med. Imaging* **2020**, *39*, 2415–2425. [CrossRef]
3. Feng, D.; Haase-Schütz, C.; Rosenbaum, L.; Hertlein, H.; Glaeser, C.; Timm, F.; Wiesbeck, W.; Dietmayer, K. Deep multi-modal object detection and semantic segmentation for autonomous driving: Datasets, methods, and challenges. *IEEE Trans. Intell. Transp. Syst.* **2020**, *22*, 1341–1360. [CrossRef]
4. Kamath, A.; Singh, M.; LeCun, Y.; Synnaeve, G.; Misra, I.; Carion, N. MDETR-modulated detection for end-to-end multi-modal understanding. In Proceedings of the IEEE/CVF International Conference on Computer Vision, Montreal, BC, Canada, 11–17 October 2021; pp. 1780–1790.
5. Yu, H.; Zhang, C.; Li, J.; Zhang, S. Robust sparse weighted classification For crowdsourcing. *IEEE Trans. Knowl. Data Eng.* **2022**, 1–13. [CrossRef]
6. Mun, J.; Cho, M.; Han, B. Text-guided attention model for image captioning. In Proceedings of the AAAI Conference on Artificial Intelligence, San Francisco, CA, USA, 4–9 February 2017; Volume 31.

7. Anderson, P.; He, X.; Buehler, C.; Teney, D.; Johnson, M.; Gould, S.; Zhang, L. Bottom-up and top-down attention for image captioning and visual question answering. In Proceedings of the IEEE Conference on Computer Vision and Pattern Recognition, Salt Lake City, UT, USA, 18–22 June 2018; pp. 6077–6086.
8. Jiang, M.; Huang, Q.; Zhang, L.; Wang, X.; Zhang, P.; Gan, Z.; Diesner, J.; Gao, J. Tiger: Text-to-image grounding for image caption evaluation. *arXiv* **2019**, arXiv:1909.02050.
9. Ding, S.; Qu, S.; Xi, Y.; Wan, S. Stimulus-driven and concept-driven analysis for image caption generation. *Neurocomputing* **2020**, *398*, 520–530. [CrossRef]
10. Rohrbach, M.; Qiu, W.; Titov, I.; Thater, S.; Pinkal, M.; Schiele, B. Translating video content to natural language descriptions. In Proceedings of the IEEE International Conference on Computer Vision, Sydney, Australia, 1–8 December 2013; pp. 433–440.
11. Dong, J.; Li, X.; Snoek, C.G. Predicting visual features from text for image and video caption retrieval. *IEEE Trans. Multimed.* **2018**, *20*, 3377–3388. [CrossRef]
12. Ding, S.; Qu, S.; Xi, Y.; Wan, S. A long video caption generation algorithm for big video data retrieval. *Future Gener. Comput. Syst.* **2019**, *93*, 583–595. [CrossRef]
13. Wang, L.; Zhu, L.; Dong, X.; Liu, L.; Sun, J.; Zhang, H. Joint feature selection and graph regularization for modality-dependent cross-modal retrieval. *J. Vis. Commun. Image Represent.* **2018**, *54*, 213–222. [CrossRef]
14. Zhang, C.; Liu, M.; Liu, Z.; Yang, C.; Zhang, L.; Han, J. Spatiotemporal activity modeling under data scarcity: A graph-regularized cross-modal embedding approach. In Proceedings of the AAAI Conference on Artificial Intelligence, New Orleans, LA, USA, 2–7 February 2018; Volume 32.
15. Gao, D.; Jin, L.; Chen, B.; Qiu, M.; Li, P.; Wei, Y.; Hu, Y.; Wang, H. Fashionbert: Text and image matching with adaptive loss for cross-modal retrieval. In Proceedings of the 43rd International ACM SIGIR Conference on Research and Development in Information Retrieval, Xi'an, China, 25–30 July 2020; pp. 2251–2260.
16. Xie, D.; Deng, C.; Li, C.; Liu, X.; Tao, D. Multi-task consistency-preserving adversarial hashing for cross-modal retrieval. *IEEE Trans. Image Process.* **2020**, *29*, 3626–3637. [CrossRef] [PubMed]
17. Mithun, N.C.; Sikka, K.; Chiu, H.P.; Samarasekera, S.; Kumar, R. Rgb2lidar: Towards solving large-scale cross-modal visual localization. In Proceedings of the 28th ACM International Conference on Multimedia, Seattle, WA, USA, 12–16 October 2020; pp. 934–954.
18. Zhang, C.; Song, J.; Zhu, X.; Zhu, L.; Zhang, S. Hcmsl: Hybrid cross-modal similarity learning for cross-modal retrieval. *ACM Trans. Multimed. Comput. Commun. Appl.* **2021**, *17*, 1–22. [CrossRef]
19. Zhang, C.; Xie, F.; Yu, H.; Zhang, J.; Zhu, L.; Li, Y. PPIS-JOIN: A novel privacy-preserving image similarity join method. *Neural Process. Lett.* **2021**, *54*, 2783–2801. [CrossRef]
20. Zhang, C.; Zhong, Z.; Zhu, L.; Zhang, S.; Cao, D.; Zhang, J. M2guda: Multi-metrics graph-based unsupervised domain adaptation for cross-modal Hashing. In Proceedings of the 2021 International Conference on Multimedia Retrieval, Taipei, Taiwan, 21–24 August 2021; pp. 674–681.
21. Zhu, L.; Zhang, C.; Song, J.; Liu, L.; Zhang, S.; Li, Y. Multi-graph based hierarchical semantic fusion for cross-modal representation. In Proceedings of the 2021 IEEE International Conference on Multimedia and Expo (ICME), Shenzhen, China, 5–9 July 2021; pp. 1–6.
22. Zhu, L.; Zhang, C.; Song, J.; Zhang, S.; Tian, C.; Zhu, X. Deep Multi-Graph Hierarchical Enhanced Semantic Representation for Cross-Modal Retrieval. *IEEE Multimed.* **2022**. [CrossRef]
23. Zhu, C.; Zhao, Y.; Huang, S.; Tu, K.; Ma, Y. Structured attentions for visual question answering. In Proceedings of the IEEE International Conference on Computer Vision, Venice, Italy, 22–29 October 2017; pp. 1291–1300.
24. Ramakrishnan, S.; Agrawal, A.; Lee, S. Overcoming language priors in visual question answering with adversarial regularization. *arXiv* **2018**, arXiv:1810.03649.
25. Nguyen, D.K.; Okatani, T. Improved fusion of visual and language representations by dense symmetric co-attention for visual question answering. In Proceedings of the IEEE Conference on Computer Vision and Pattern Recognition, Salt Lake City, UT, USA, 18–22 June 2018; pp. 6087–6096.
26. Ben-Younes, H.; Cadene, R.; Thome, N.; Cord, M. Block: Bilinear superdiagonal fusion for visual question answering and visual relationship detection. In Proceedings of the AAAI Conference on Artificial Intelligence, Honolulu, HI, USA, 27 January–1 February 2019; Volume 33, pp. 8102–8109.
27. Li, L.; Gan, Z.; Cheng, Y.; Liu, J. Relation-aware graph attention network for visual question answering. In Proceedings of the IEEE/CVF International Conference on Computer Vision, Seoul, Korea, 27 October–2 November 2019; pp. 10313–10322.
28. Cadene, R.; Ben-Younes, H.; Cord, M.; Thome, N. Murel: Multimodal relational reasoning for visual question answering. In Proceedings of the IEEE/CVF Conference on Computer Vision and Pattern Recognition, Long Beach, CA, USA, 15–20 June 2019; pp. 1989–1998.
29. Gao, P.; Jiang, Z.; You, H.; Lu, P.; Hoi, S.C.; Wang, X.; Li, H. Dynamic fusion with intra-and inter-modality attention flow for visual question answering. In Proceedings of the IEEE/CVF Conference on Computer Vision and Pattern Recognition, Long Beach, CA, USA, 15–20 June 2019; pp. 6639–6648.
30. Chen, L.; Yan, X.; Xiao, J.; Zhang, H.; Pu, S.; Zhuang, Y. Counterfactual samples synthesizing for robust visual question answering. In Proceedings of the IEEE/CVF Conference on Computer Vision and Pattern Recognition, Seattle, WA, USA, 14–19 June 2020; pp. 10800–10809.

31. Teney, D.; Abbasnejad, E.; van den Hengel, A. Unshuffling data for improved generalization in visual question answering. In Proceedings of the IEEE/CVF International Conference on Computer Vision, Montreal, BC, Canada, 11–17 October 2021; pp. 1417–1427.
32. Zhou, B.; Tian, Y.; Sukhbaatar, S.; Szlam, A.; Fergus, R. Simple baseline for visual question answering. *arXiv* **2015**, arXiv:1512.02167.
33. Chen, K.; Wang, J.; Chen, L.C.; Gao, H.; Xu, W.; Nevatia, R. Abc-cnn: An attention based convolutional neural network for visual question answering. *arXiv* **2015**, arXiv:1511.05960.
34. Ren, M.; Kiros, R.; Zemel, R. Exploring models and data for image question answering. *Adv. Neural Inf. Process. Syst.* **2015**, 28.
35. Shih, K.J.; Singh, S.; Hoiem, D. Where to look: Focus regions for visual question answering. In Proceedings of the IEEE Conference on Computer Vision and Pattern Recognition, Las Vegas, NV, USA, 27–30 June 2016; pp. 4613–4621.
36. Yu, Z.; Yu, J.; Cui, Y.; Tao, D.; Tian, Q. Deep modular co-attention networks for visual question answering. In Proceedings of the IEEE/CVF Conference on Computer Vision and Pattern Recognition, Long Beach, CA, USA, 15–20 June 2019; pp. 6281–6290.
37. Lu, J.; Yang, J.; Batra, D.; Parikh, D. Hierarchical question-image co-attention for visual question answering. *Adv. Neural Inf. Process. Syst.* **2016**, 29, 289–297.
38. Veličković, P.; Cucurull, G.; Casanova, A.; Romero, A.; Lio, P.; Bengio, Y. Graph attention networks. *arXiv* **2017**, arXiv:1710.10903.
39. Santoro, A.; Raposo, D.; Barrett, D.G.; Malinowski, M.; Pascanu, R.; Battaglia, P.; Lillicrap, T. A simple neural network module for relational reasoning. *Adv. Neural Inf. Process. Syst.* **2017**, 30.
40. Ghosh, S.; Burachas, G.; Ray, A.; Ziskind, A. Generating natural language explanations for visual question answering using scene graphs and visual attention. *arXiv* **2019**, arXiv:1902.05715.
41. Bahdanau, D.; Cho, K.; Bengio, Y. Neural machine translation by jointly learning to align and translate. *arXiv* **2014**, arXiv:1409.0473.
42. Bapna, A.; Chen, M.X.; Firat, O.; Cao, Y.; Wu, Y. Training deeper neural machine translation models with transparent attention. *arXiv* **2018**, arXiv:1808.07561.
43. Zhang, H.; Kyaw, Z.; Chang, S.F.; Chua, T.S. Visual translation embedding network for visual relation detection. In Proceedings of the IEEE Conference on Computer Vision and Pattern Recognition, Honolulu, HI, USA, 21–26 July 2017; pp. 5532–5540.
44. Vaswani, A.; Shazeer, N.; Parmar, N.; Uszkoreit, J.; Jones, L.; Gomez, A.N.; Kaiser, Ł.; Polosukhin, I. Attention is all you need. *Adv. Neural Inf. Process. Syst.* **2017**, 30, 5998–6008.
45. Xu, H.; Saenko, K. Ask, Attend and Answer: Exploring Question-Guided Spatial Attention for Visual Question Answering. In Proceedings of the European Conference on Computer Vision, Amsterdam, The Netherlands, 11–14 October 2016; Springer: Berlin/Heidelberg, Germany, 2016; pp. 451–466.
46. Guo, W.; Zhang, Y.; Yang, J.; Yuan, X. Re-attention for visual question answering. *IEEE Trans. Image Process.* **2021**, 30, 6730–6743. [CrossRef]
47. Yu, T.; Yu, J.; Yu, Z.; Tao, D. Compositional attention networks with two-stream fusion for video question answering. *IEEE Trans. Image Process.* **2019**, 29, 1204–1218. [CrossRef]
48. Jiang, J.; Chen, Z.; Lin, H.; Zhao, X.; Gao, Y. Divide and conquer: Question-guided spatio-temporal contextual attention for video question answering. In Proceedings of the AAAI Conference on Artificial Intelligence, New York, NY, USA, 7–12 February 2020; Volume 34, pp. 11101–11108.
49. Kim, N.; Ha, S.J.; Kang, J.W. Video Question Answering Using Language-Guided Deep Compressed-Domain Video Feature. In Proceedings of the IEEE/CVF International Conference on Computer Vision, Montreal, BC, Canada, 11–17 October 2021; pp. 1708–1717.
50. Teney, D.; Liu, L.; van Den Hengel, A. Graph-structured representations for visual question answering. In Proceedings of the IEEE Conference on Computer Vision and Pattern Recognition, Honolulu, HI, USA, 21–26 July 2017; pp. 1–9.
51. Ren, S.; He, K.; Girshick, R.; Sun, J. Faster r-cnn: Towards real-time object detection with region proposal networks. *Adv. Neural Inf. Process. Syst.* **2015**, 28. [CrossRef]
52. Chung, J.; Gulcehre, C.; Cho, K.; Bengio, Y. Empirical evaluation of gated recurrent neural networks on sequence modeling. *arXiv* **2014**, arXiv:1412.3555.
53. Goyal, Y.; Khot, T.; Summers-Stay, D.; Batra, D.; Parikh, D. Making the v in vqa matter: Elevating the role of image understanding in visual question answering. In Proceedings of the IEEE Conference on Computer Vision and Pattern Recognition, Honolulu, HI, USA, 21–26 July 2017; pp. 6904–6913.
54. Agrawal, A.; Batra, D.; Parikh, D.; Kembhavi, A. Don't just assume; look and answer: Overcoming priors for visual question answering. In Proceedings of the IEEE Conference on Computer Vision and Pattern Recognition, Salt Lake City, UT, USA, 18–22 June 2018; pp. 4971–4980.
55. Lin, T.Y.; Maire, M.; Belongie, S.; Hays, J.; Perona, P.; Ramanan, D.; Dollár, P.; Zitnick, C.L. Microsoft coco: Common Objects in Context. In Proceedings of the European Conference on Computer Vision, Zurich, Switzerland, 6–12 September 2014; Springer: Berlin/Heidelberg, Germany, 2014; pp. 740–755.
56. Antol, S.; Agrawal, A.; Lu, J.; Mitchell, M.; Batra, D.; Zitnick, C.L.; Parikh, D. Vqa: Visual question answering. In Proceedings of the IEEE International Conference on Computer Vision, Santiago, Chile, 7–13 December 2015; pp. 2425–2433.
57. Teney, D.; Anderson, P.; He, X.; Van Den Hengel, A. Tips and tricks for visual question answering: Learnings from the 2017 challenge. In Proceedings of the IEEE Conference on Computer Vision and Pattern Recognition, Salt Lake City, UT, USA, 18–22 June 2018; pp. 4223–4232.

58. Osman, A.; Samek, W. DRAU: Dual recurrent attention units for visual question answering. *Comput. Vis. Image Underst.* **2019**, *185*, 24–30. [CrossRef]
59. Zhang, W.; Yu, J.; Hu, H.; Hu, H.; Qin, Z. Multimodal feature fusion by relational reasoning and attention for visual question answering. *Inf. Fusion* **2020**, *55*, 116–126. [CrossRef]
60. Shrestha, R.; Kafle, K.; Kanan, C. Answer them all! toward universal visual question answering models. In Proceedings of the IEEE/CVF Conference on Computer Vision and Pattern Recognition, Long Beach, CA, USA, 15–20 June 2019; pp. 10472–10481.
61. Grand, G.; Belinkov, Y. Adversarial regularization for visual question answering: Strengths, shortcomings, and side effects. *arXiv* **2019**, arXiv:1906.08430.
62. Whitehead, S.; Wu, H.; Ji, H.; Feris, R.; Saenko, K. Separating Skills and Concepts for Novel Visual Question Answering. In Proceedings of the IEEE/CVF Conference on Computer Vision and Pattern Recognition, Nashville, TN, USA, 20–25 June 2021; pp. 5632–5641.
63. Kim, J.H.; Jun, J.; Zhang, B.T. Bilinear attention networks. *arXiv* **2018**, arXiv:1805.07932.

Article

Social Recommendation Based on Multi-Auxiliary Information Constrastive Learning

Feng Jiang [1], Yang Cao [2,*], Huan Wu [3], Xibin Wang [4], Yuqi Song [5] and Min Gao [2]

[1] School of Finance and Management, Chongqing Business Vocational College, Chongqing 401331, China
[2] School of Big Data and Software Engineering, Chongqing University, Chongqing 401331, China
[3] College of Environmental Science and Engineering, Tongji University, Shanghai 200092, China
[4] School of Data Science, Guizhou Institute of Technology, Guiyang 550003, China
[5] Department of Computer Science and Engineering, University of South Carolina, Columbia, SC 29201, USA
* Correspondence: caoyang@cqu.edu.cn

Abstract: Social recommendation can effectively alleviate the problems of data sparseness and the cold start of recommendation systems, attracting widespread attention from researchers and industry. Current social recommendation models use social relations to alleviate the problem of data sparsity and improve recommendation performance. Although self-supervised learning based on user–item interaction can enhance the performance of such models, multi-auxiliary information is neglected in the learning process. Therefore, we propose a model based on self-supervision and multi-auxiliary information using multi-auxiliary information, such as user social relationships and item association relationships, to make recommendations. Specifically, the user social relationship and item association relationship are combined to form a multi-auxiliary information graph. The user–item interaction relationship is also integrated into the same heterogeneous graph so that multiple pieces of information can be spread in the same graph. In addition, we utilize the graph convolution method to learn user and item embeddings, whereby the user embeddings reflect both user–item interaction and user social relationships, and the item embeddings reflect user–item interaction and item association relationships. We also design multi-view self-supervising auxiliary tasks based on the constructed multi-auxiliary views. Signals generated by self-supervised auxiliary tasks can alleviate the problem of data sparsity, further improving user/item embedding quality and recommendation performance. Extensive experiments on two public datasets verify the superiority of the proposed model.

Keywords: social relations; auxiliary information; self-supervised learning; graph convolutional neural network

MSC: 68T01

1. Introduction

The rapid development of the Internet has made life more convenient and produced a large amount of information, causing the problem of information overload. It is difficult for users to select a target product that matches their preferences among hundreds of millions of products. The recommendation system significantly alleviates information overload and improves user experience. However, it is difficult to mitigate the problems of data sparsity and the cold start problem [1–4] in recommendation systems. In recommendation scenarios, user preferences are influenced by the preferences of friends [5,6]. Based on this hypothesis, researchers have integrated users' social information into the recommendation system as auxiliary information, which can alleviate the problems of data sparseness and cold start problems, thus forming social recommendations.

Some researchers have attempted to make social recommendations based on graph embedding learning of heterogeneous networks [7–9]. Implicit friends with similar preferences do not have explicit links, but they can be indirectly linked based on what they have

interacted with. Implicit friends can be used to mine more reliable information from sparse data, specifically learning node embeddings that can accurately express user preferences. Mainstream social recommendation models use heterogeneous networks to describe user social relations and user–item interaction relations and then use the graph embedding learning method to obtain user/item node representation. Node embedding can express node attributes or relationships between nodes (such as user preferences). For example, IF-BPR [8] designed "user–item–user", "user–user–user", and other multi-meta paths based on domain knowledge to guide a random walk in a heterogeneous network, thus learning high-quality node embedding. MoHINRec [9] used the meta-path of a variety of motif structures (triangular structures that reflect strong connections between nodes) to guide the random walk and obtain more accurate node embedding. In recent years, graph neural networks (GNNs) have achieved considerable success in node classification and link prediction. Owing to their powerful modeling ability in graph relation, GNNs are also applied in the field of recommendation systems. However, there are three challenges in social recommendation based on GNNs: (1) information is not fully mined from existing data as auxiliary information; (2) users' social relationships have limited ability to alleviate data sparsity; and (3) information is transmitted independently in the user–item interaction graph, and the user social network graph and node embedding are formed independently, whereas user–item interactions and user social relationships do not affect user preference simultaneously. To tackle these challenges, we design a social recommendation model based on self-supervision and multi-auxiliary information.

The main contributions of this paper are as follows:

- We mine item association relationships, user social relationships, and user–item interaction relationships as auxiliary information to alleviate the problem of data sparsity. Unlike the existing social recommendation models of graph neural networks that independently carry out interactive information and social information dissemination, we design a dissemination mode to make multiple auxiliary information affect the formation of user/item embedding simultaneously.
- We design self-supervised auxiliary tasks for the social recommendation scenario to improve the node embedding quality and alleviate data sparsity, construct several views according to different combinations of auxiliary information, and maximize the mutual information of node embedding under different perspectives based on contrastive self-supervised learning.
- We conduct extensive experiments on two public datasets to demonstrate the effectiveness of the proposed model and analyze the benefits of auxiliary information and self-supervised tasks.

2. Related Work

In this section, we introduce graph neural networks and contrastive self-supervised learning.

2.1. Graph Neural Networks (GNNs)

In recent years, GNNs have attracted increasing attention because, owing to their excellent performance on various tasks. Inspired by the success of other fields, such as node classification and link prediction, the applicability of GNNs in recommendation tasks was investigated. In particular, GCN [10] has driven a large number of graph-based neural network recommendation models, such as GCMC [11], NGCF [12], and LightGCN [13]. The basic idea of these GCN-based models is to improve the representation of the target node by aggregating the node representation of the neighbor [14] to obtain higher-order neighbor information in the user–item interaction graph. In addition to these generic models, GNNs support other recommendation methods for specific graphs, such as session and social graphs.

GNNs are often used for information transmission in social networks because information is transmitted in social networks the same was as in GNNs. Researchers naturally transplanted GNN into social recommendation work. GraphRec is the first model to introduce GNN into social recommendation [15]. It learns target node embedding by aggregating first-order neighbor information in the user–item interaction graph and the social network graph. User embedding of DiffNet [10] comes from the social network graph and the user–item interaction graph. It carries out more profound information dissemination in the social network through a multi-layer GNN. Moreover, node embedding in the user–item interaction graph only comes from the first-order neighbor. DiffNet uses a multi-layer GNN structure to realize the dynamic propagation of social influence in the social network. Wu et al. [16] proposed a dual-graph attention network for collaborative learning of node embedding influenced by two layers of society. DGRec uses two circulating neural networks to dynamically simulate user behavior and social influence [17]. Yu et al. [18] enhanced social recommendation with adversarial graph convolutional networks to process complicated high-order interactions among users. Later, they [19] improve social recommendation with a multi-channel hypergraph convolutional network to leverage high-order user relations. Huang et al. [20] proposed a knowledge-aware coupled GNN that injects knowledge across items and users into the recommendation. Yang et al. [21] proposed the ConsisRec model to calculate the consistency score between neighbors as the probability of sampling neighbors and further handle the problem of relationship inconsistency through an attention mechanism.

2.2. Contrastive Self-Supervised Learning

Self-supervised learning was first proposed in the field of robotics, whereby training data are automatically generated from data of two or more sensors. The principle of self-supervised learning can be explained a description of complete data based on observation of different aspects or different parts of data. Self-supervised learning enhances data by deforming, intercepting, and disturbing the original data and generates data as pseudo-labels of the original data to make up for the data deficiency. Self-supervised learning can be divided into two types: generative self-supervised learning and contrastive self-supervised learning. In this paper, the comparative self-supervised learning method is used to provide more auxiliary information to alleviate the problem of data sparsity and realize a recommendation algorithm.

Contrast learning is a discriminant method with the aim of making the embeddings of similar samples (positive samples) closer to each other in the representation space and the embeddings of different samples (negative samples) farther apart. This method uses a similarity measure to quantify the distance between two inserts (commonly known as cosine similarity). Studies based on contrastive self-supervision have made significant progress, such as SwAV [22], MoCo [23], and SimCLR [24], and their extensions, with performances comparable to those of related models based on supervised learning.

Pseudo-label construction is an essential strategy for embedded learning based on contrastive self-supervised learning. Positive samples and negative samples are essentially pseudo-labels of data to expand training data. The original samples are based on positive/negative samples for supervised learning. The proposed goal of self-supervised learning is to reduce the cost of manual labeling, so the generation of false labels (the selection of positive/negative samples) is an automatic process.

Based on contrastive self-supervised learning, the model needs to design auxiliary tasks to complete contrastive learning and assist with the main tasks of specific scenes to train the model. The training process is as follows:

- The auxiliary task performs data enhancement based on the original sample. The original and positive/negative samples generate corresponding low-dimensional embedding through the encoder and construct the loss function through contrast learning.
- The main task generates the corresponding low-dimensional embedding of the original sample through the encoder and constructs the principal loss function through the main task. Finally, by comparing the loss function with the main loss function, higher quality embedding can be obtained.

Contrastive self-supervised learning is also applied flexibly in graph embedding learning (graph contrast learning for short). This work mainly constructs self-supervised signals from graph structures of different perspectives to explore higher-quality graph structure embedding [25,26]. Generally, a new perspective can be obtained through random data enhancement of the same graph. Common data enhancement methods include but are not limited to the random deletion of nodes, random deletion of edges, the random transformation of features or attributes, random walk-based pattern graphs, etc. Inspired by such work, some researchers began to apply graph contrast learning to recommendation tasks [27–30]. Zhou et al. [30] designed self-supervised auxiliary tasks, specifically adding random embedding masks for item embedding and randomly skipping given items and sub-sequences to carry out pre-training for sequence recommendation. Yao et al. [29] proposed a two-tower network structure based on DNNs (deep neural networks), on which random feature mask and random feature discarding operations were carried out for self-supervised item recommendations. Ma et al. [28] reconstructed short-term future sequences by observing long-term sequences, which essentially mined more self-supervised signals using feature masks. Wu et al. [27] summarized the above random data enhancement operations (random node/edge deletion and random walk) and integrated them into a recommendation framework based on self-supervised graph learning. Long et al. [31] proposed a heterogeneous graph neural network based on meta-relation and used self-supervised learning to guide the interaction between users and items under different views, incorporating the knowledge information of the item and the high-level semantic relationship between users and items into the user representation. Liu et al. [32] designed two new information augmentation methods. Furthermore, they proposed a contrastive self-supervised learning framework, CoSeRec, for sequence recommendation, which alleviates the problems of data sparsity and noisy interaction issues. Wu et al. [33] proposed a social recommendation model that disentangles the collaborative domain and social domain to learn user representations separately and uses cross-domain contrastive learning to further improve the recommendation performance.

Unlike these models, we use item-association-aware contrastive learning in self-supervised learning. We maximize the mutual information of node embedding in two item-association-aware views in self-supervised learning; view 1 is constructed by the user–item interaction relationship and the item association relationship, and view 2 is formed by the user–item interaction relationship and the user social relationship. Although the model proposed in [33] also uses cross-domain contrastive learning, the domains are the user–item interaction domain and the social relationship domain, not taking item association into consideration. Our model is designed to utilize more auxiliary information to improve recommendation performance, and self-supervised learning can finetune the embeddings from different kinds of auxiliary information. There are two main differences between our model and SEPT [34]. First, we use item-association-aware contrastive learning in self-supervised learning, whereas SEPT does not take item association into consideration. Second, SEPT focuses more on finding positive samples for contrastive learning and uses tri-training to determine which samples are positive; however, our model does not attempt to identify additional positive samples and treat the same node in different views as a positive sample.

3. Problem Analysis

Accurately capturing user preferences is the key to improving the recommendation quality of recommendation systems. The recommendation algorithm is committed to learning more accurate user embedding to improve the recommendation performance. The current social recommendation algorithm based on a graph neural network believes that user preference is jointly determined by items that have interacted historically, was well as the influence of social friends. The process of learning user/item embedding in this kind of algorithm is summarized as follows: In the first step, by default, user–item interaction influence and social influence are spread in an independent scope, and information is spread and embedded in the user–item interaction graph and user social network graph. In the second step, there are two different embeddings of user nodes in the two graphs. The two embeddings representing user–item interaction information and social influence are aggregated to form the final embeddings.

Social recommendations based on graph neural networks are subject to the following problems:

- They carry out user–item interaction information and social information dissemination in two graphs instead of being affected by both simultaneously (more realistic).
- As auxiliary information, social relationship alleviates the problem of data sparsity in the recommendation system, but its role is limited, and more auxiliary information is needed.

4. Methodology

To alleviate the above problems, we propose a social recommendation model based on self-supervised and multi-auxiliary information (SlightGCN). We combine user social relationships, item association relationships, and self-supervised auxiliary signals as auxiliary information to carry out social recommendations. First, the model SlightGCN mines item association relationships based on user–item interaction records and item attributes. Then, a heterogeneous network is constructed, including user social relationships, item association relationships, and user–item interaction relationships. In the heterogeneous network graph containing multi-auxiliary information, information is transmitted and output-embedded through a GCN. The user/item embedding containing rich information is used to recommend the main task. In addition, two heterogeneous networks with different perspectives are constructed according to different combinations of existing auxiliary information, and self-supervised auxiliary tasks are constructed to maximize the mutual information of nodes under different perspectives to obtain higher quality node embedding. Finally, the model is trained through the combination of primary task (recommendation task) loss and auxiliary task (contrastive self-supervised learning).

SlightGCN can be generally divided into three parts: the heterogeneous network construction, main recommendation task, and self-supervision auxiliary task (See Figure 1).

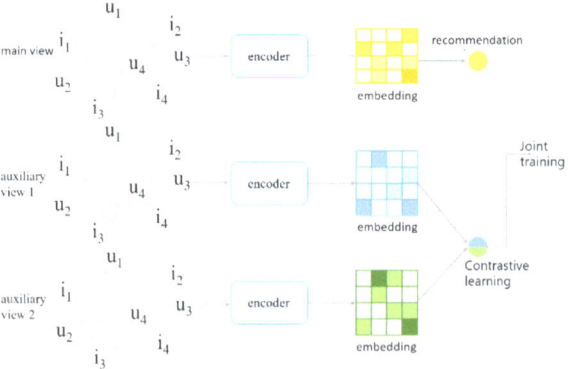

Figure 1. The overall framework of SlightGCN.

4.1. Heterogeneous Network Construction

First, the association relationship is mined from the user–item interaction relationship and item attribute through the meta-path rule to alleviate the data sparsity problem. Secondly, three types of information (user social relationship, user–item interaction relationship, and item association relationship) are integrated into the same heterogeneous network in the form of edges. The construction process of a heterogeneous network is shown in Figure 2.

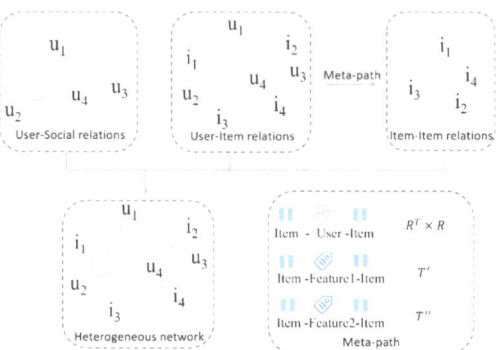

Figure 2. The heterogeneous network construction process.

In the process of information dissemination of the recommendation scenario, the user node is influenced by friends and items that have been interacted with, and the item node is influenced by items that are closely connected and users that have been interacted with to learn user/item embedding of higher quality. To realize this information transmission mode, user–item interaction relationship, user social relationship, and item association relationship need to be integrated into the same heterogeneous network in the form of an edge. The user node receives information from friends and historical interaction records through user–item interaction relationships and user social relationships, and the item node receives information from closely related items and users who have interacted with each other through user–item interaction relationships and item association relationships.

4.2. Main Tasks

A recommendation algorithm is based on the main task of supervised learning to optimize model parameters. The prediction is established on user embedded (e_u) and item-embedded (e_i). Generally, the inner product of the embedded $e_u^T e_i$ is used to predict user's (u) preference degree ($\hat{y}_{ui}$) for item i, as in (1):

$$\hat{y}_{ui} = e_u^T e_i. \tag{1}$$

Specifically, it assumes the observed interactions as monitoring signals and makes the predicted preference ($\hat{y}_{ui}$) as close as possible to the real preference (y_{ui}). It takes the unobserved data as a negative sample. We take the generally used Bayesian personalized recommendation [35] (BPR) as the loss function for the ranking recommendation task. The core idea is that the target user (u) prefers interactive item i (observable data) to uninteractive item j (unobserved data). The specific loss function is shown in (2):

$$\mathcal{L}_{main} = \sum_{(u,i,j) \in \mathcal{D}} -log(\hat{y}_{ui} - \hat{y}_{uj}), \tag{2}$$

where $\mathcal{D} = \{(u,i,j) | (u,i) \in \mathcal{D}^+, (u,j) \in \mathcal{D}^-\}$ is all training data, $\mathcal{D}^+$ is the set of observable interactions, and $\mathcal{D}^-$ is the set of unobserved interactions.

The basis of the recommendable task is to learn user/item embedding. Heterogeneous networks can output user/item embedding through a graph encoder. Inspired by the excellent graph convolution neural network recommendation model LightGCN [13], feature transformation, nonlinear transformation, and self-connection operation are redundant for the collaborative filtering recommendation model. We integrate user social relations and item associations to realize that user nodes are affected by social friends and interactive items simultaneously, and item nodes are affected by interactive users and closely connected items simultaneously.

In graph convolution mode, simple weighted aggregation is sampled in the convolution process and feature transformation. The specific convolution operation is shown in (3):

$$e_u^{(k+1)} = \sum_{q \in N_u} \frac{1}{\sqrt{|N_u||N_p|}} e_p^{(k)}, \quad e_i^{(k+1)} = \sum_{q \in N_i} \frac{1}{\sqrt{|N_i||N_q|}} e_q^{(k)}, \tag{3}$$

where $e_u^{(k+1)}$ and $e_i^{(k+1)}$ represent the embedment of user u and item i at the $(k + 1)$ layer, respectively; and the $(k + 1)$ layer embedment is aggregated from the k layer embedment. Taking the formation of $e_u^{(k+1)}$ as an example, user u's neighbor, N_u, contains the user's neighbor and item neighbor, and $e_u^{(k+1)}$ is aggregated by embedding the k layer of user u's neighbor, N_u. $e_i^{(k+1)}$ Similarly, the neighbor N_i of item i contains user neighbors and item neighbors. $e_i^{(k+1)}$ is aggregated by embedding the k layer of item i's neighbor, N_i.

After the multi-layer convolution, the final node embedding is obtained by average aggregation of each layer embedding of the node, as shown in (4):

$$e_u = \frac{e_u^{(0)} + e_u^{(1)} + \cdots + e_u^{(k)}}{k+1}, \quad e_i = \frac{e_i^{(0)} + e_i^{(1)} + \cdots + e_i^{(k)}}{k+1}. \tag{4}$$

In the graph matrix representation of the convolution process, the heterogeneous network adjacency matrix ($A \in \mathbb{R}^{(N+M) \times (N+M)}$) is composed of the user–item interaction matrix (R) and its transpose (R^T), the user social matrix (S), and the item association matrix (T). The specific expression of adjacency matrix A is shown in (5):

$$A = \begin{pmatrix} S & R \\ R^T & T \end{pmatrix}, \tag{5}$$

User embedding and item embedding constitute the 0-layer embedding matrix, $E^{(0)} \in \mathbb{R}^{(N+M) \times d}$, where d is the embedding dimension, and $E^{(0)}$ is randomly initialized. The matrix form of the convolution operation is shown in (6),

$$E^{(k+1)} = \left(D^{-1/2} A D^{-1/2} \right) E^{(k)}, \tag{6}$$

where $D \in \mathbb{R}^{(N+M) \times (N+M)}$ is a diagonal matrix, and the value of D_{ii} is the number of non-zero elements in the ith row of matrix A.

Finally, the embedding matrix ($E \in \mathbb{R}^{(N+M) \times d}$) is evenly aggregated by each embedding matrix, as shown in (7).

$$E = \frac{E^{(0)} + E^{(1)} + \cdots + E^{(k)}}{k+1}. \tag{7}$$

4.3. Self-Supervised Auxiliary Tasks

The main view composed of three types of relationships (user–item interaction relationship, user social relationship, and item association relationship) introduced in the previous section helps to recommend the embedding of main task learning nodes. When a designer models a character, it is necessary to observe the character information from different aspects and combine the information from multiple perspectives to build a more accurate character model. In the recommendation scenario, the recommendation algorithm needs to model the user and the item before recommending the user to build a more accurate portrait of the person/item (user/item embedding). The graph neural network plays the role of a model and can generate more accurate node embedding by combining node information from different perspectives.

Based on the main view, we remove the user's social relationship and item association relationship and generate auxiliary view 1 and auxiliary view 2, respectively. In the process of information transmission, the two auxiliary views correspond to the adjacency matrices

A_1 and A_2, respectively, as shown in (8). The convolution of the two auxiliary views is to generate two groups of different embedded nodes (E_1 and E_2), as shown in (9).

$$A_1 = \begin{pmatrix} 0 & R \\ R^T & T \end{pmatrix}, \quad A_2 = \begin{pmatrix} S & R \\ R^T & 0 \end{pmatrix}, \quad (8)$$

$$E_1^{(k+1)} = \left(D_1^{-1/2} A_1 D_1^{-1/2}\right) E_1^{(k)}, \quad E_2^{(k+1)} = \left(D_2^{-1/2} A_2 D_2^{-1/2}\right) E_2^{(k)}. \quad (9)$$

Contrastive self-supervised learning is used to maximize the mutual information of node embedding in different views to learn node embedding of higher quality. Specifically, the node embedding of the same node in different views is a positive sample pair (i.e., $\{(e'_u, e''_u) | u \in U\}$), and the node embedding of different nodes in different views is a negative sample pair (i.e., $\{(e'_u, e''_v) | u, v \in U, u \neq v\}$). Auxiliary tasks make similar nodes as similar as possible, whereas different sample nodes are embedded as far away as possible. The self-supervised loss function is formed according to the comparative loss, InfoNCE, as shown in (10):

$$\mathcal{L}_{ssl}^{user} = \sum_{u \in U} -\log \frac{exp(s(e'_u, e''_u)/\tau)}{\sum_{v \in U} exp(s(e'_u, e''_v)/\tau)}, \quad \mathcal{L}_{ssl}^{item} = \sum_{i \in I} -\log \frac{exp(s(e'_i, e''_i)/\tau)}{\sum_{j \in I} exp(s(e'_i, e''_j)/\tau)}, \quad (10)$$

$$\mathcal{L}_{ssl} = \mathcal{L}_{ssl}^{user} + \mathcal{L}_{ssl}^{item}, \quad (11)$$

where the function $s(\cdot)$ is cosine similarity, which is used to measure the distance between two embeddings, and the hyperparameter τ is the temperature index, which can reduce or amplify the effect of distance between nodes. Finally, as shown in (11), the loss function ($\mathcal{L}_{ssl}$) of the self-supervision auxiliary task is the sum of the loss function ($\mathcal{L}_{ssl}^{user}$) of the user node and the loss function ($\mathcal{L}_{ssl}^{item}$) of the item node.

To improve the recommendation performance, the main recommendation task and self-supervised auxiliary task are combined for training. The loss function of the combined training is shown in (12), where λ_1 and λ_2 are the hyperparameters, and θ is the model parameter.

$$\mathcal{L} = \mathcal{L}_{main} + \lambda_1 \mathcal{L}_{ssl} + \lambda_2 ||\theta||_2^2. \quad (12)$$

5. Experiments

In this study, extensive experiments were carried out on two public datasets to verify the following points: (1) the advantages of SlightGCN in terms of recommendation performance, (2) that SlightGCN effectively alleviates data sparsity and cold start problems; (3) that multi-auxiliary information (users' social relationship, item association relationship, and self-supervised learning signal) plays an essential role in improving the recommendation performance, and (4) the influence of hyperparameters on SlightGCN.

5.1. The Datasets

We conducted extensive experiments on two public datasets: DoubanMovie and DoubanBook. Detailed information on the datasets is shown in Table 1, including the number of users, the number of items, the number of user–item interactions, the number of user social relationships, and the density of user–item interactions.

Table 1. Dataset statistics.

The Dataset	Number of Users	Number of Items	Number of User–Item Interactions	Number of Social Connections	Density of Interactions
DoubanMovie	13,367	12,677	1,067,278	4085	0.63%
DoubanBook	13,024	22,347	792,062	84,575	0.27%

DoubanMovie is a movie dataset of the Douban platform, which contains 13,367 users' 1,067,278 viewing behaviors on 12,677 movies and 4085 users' social friend relationships. We select two crucial attributes of film type and director in DoubanMovie to excavate the social relations of objects. DoubanBook is a book dataset of the Douban platform, which contains 792,062 interactions between 13,024 users and 22,347 books and 169,150 social friend relationships between users. Two important attributes of DoubanBook (publisher and author) are selected to mine the social relations. In this study, the dataset is divided into a training set, a validation set, and a test set (70%, 10%, and 20%, respectively). The model was cross-verified ten times, and the average value was taken as the result.

5.2. Baselines and Metrics

To verify the recommendation performance of SlightGCN, we select six baseline algorithms, as shown below:

- BPR: Bayesian personalized ranking [35], a classical sorting recommendation algorithm. Based on user–item interaction information, it is assumed that the target user prefers interactive items rather than non-interactive items.
- SBPR: A classic social recommendation algorithm [36] that integrates social relations to optimize the item preference priority of target users based on BPR.
- DiffNet: A social recommendation algorithm based on a graph neural network [37] that simulates the social influence of dynamic propagation in user social networks.
- LightGCN: A recommendation algorithm based on a graph convolutional neural network [13] that learns node embedding in a simple convolution mode suitable for collaborative filtering.
- SGL: A recommendation algorithm based on self-supervised learning and a graph convolution neural network [27] that creates multiple views by randomly changing the graph structure to improve the embedding quality.
- SEPT: A graph convolution neural network recommendation algorithm based on self-supervised learning and collaborative training [34] that finds more suitable positive/negative samples for self-supervised learning through collaborative training to learn more accurate embedding.

Evaluation metrics are precision, recall, F1, and NDCG (normalized impairment cumulative gain).

$$Prec@k = \frac{\sum u \in U |R(u) \cap T(u)|}{k}, \quad (13)$$

$$Rec@k = \frac{\sum u \in U |R(u) \cap T(u)|}{|T(u)|}, \quad (14)$$

$$F1 = \frac{2 * Prec * Rec}{Prec + Rec}, \quad (15)$$

$$NDCG@k = \frac{DCG}{iDCG}, \quad (16)$$

$$DCG = \sum_{i}^{k} \frac{2^{rel_i} - 1}{\log_2(i+1)}, \quad (17)$$

where u is a user; U is the set of all users; $R(u)$ denotes recommended items for user u; $T(u)$ is user u's real liked items; rel_i represents item i's relevance score, which can be predefined; and $iDCG$ is the DCG of the ideal order for the recommendation set.

In the experiments, the depth of LightGCN, SGL, and SlightGCN for information propagation is three, and that of SEPT is two because SEPT can achieve the best performance in that case [34].

5.3. Results

5.3.1. Overall Comparison

We compare the proposed model, SlightGCN, with six baselines on DoubanMovie and DoubanBook. The advantages and disadvantages of each model are shown by comparing the four metrics in top-10 and top-20 recommendations. Based on the experimental results in Tables 2 and 3 (the bold numbers mean the best performance), the following conclusions can be drawn:

1. SlightGCN's recommendation performance is significantly better than that of the other five baseline models on the two datasets. Specifically, the evaluation metrics of Slight-GCN on DoubanMovie and DoubanBook improved by 1.84–4.26% and 2.08–3.30%, respectively, compared with the suboptimal model. In addition, the interactive data density of the DoubanMovie dataset is higher than that of DoubanBook. Thus, the recommendation performance of all models on the DoubanMovie dataset is significantly better than that of DoubanBook.

2. The results show that SBPR is superior to BPR in some indicators, indicating that SBPR can alleviate data sparsity to a certain extent by integrating users' social relationships based on BPR. SBPR's simple approach of integrating users' social relationships by directly optimizing the order of items does not accurately simulate the impact of social relationships on users' preferences. DiffNet enables the influence of friends' preferences on users to propagate dynamically in social networks through multi-layer graph neural network simulation. The performance of DiffNet is better than that of SBPR owing to the ability of the graph neural network to capture graph relation and the dynamic propagation of social influence. LightGCN's simple convolution mode makes it more suitable for collaborative filtering, and its recommendation performance is significantly higher than that of the previous recommendation model. Based on LightGCN as a graph encoder, collaborative training is used to find more suitable positive and negative samples for self-supervised learning, and SEPT improves the recommendation performance based on LightGCN. Using LightGCN as the graph encoder and designing the self-supervised auxiliary task based on random graph structural disturbance, the SGL recommendation performance was considerably improved.

3. SlightGCN performs best on both datasets. SlightGCN has the following advantages over other models. First, it not only uses user–item interaction relationships and user-social relationships but also mines item association relationships from existing information to form multi-auxiliary information. Second, a more appropriate convolution mode is designed so that users are affected by both user–item interaction relationships and user-social relationships, and objects are affected by both user–item interaction relationships and item association relationships. Third, multi-view self-supervised auxiliary tasks are designed to learn more accurate user/item embedding.

Table 2. Comparison of recommendation performances on DoubanMovie.

	BPR	SBPR	DiffNet	SEPT	LightGCN	SGL	SlightGCN	Ascension
Prec@10	0.1243	0.1175	0.1311	0.1617	0.1602	0.1642	**0.1712**	4.26%
Prec@20	0.1049	0.0994	0.1119	0.1343	0.1331	0.1352	**0.1407**	4.07%
Rec@10	0.0784	0.0903	0.1012	0.1218	0.1186	0.1252	**0.1281**	2.32%
Rec@20	0.1281	0.1426	0.1647	0.1862	0.1833	0.1890	**0.1931**	2.17%
F1@10	0.0962	0.1021	0.1142	0.1389	0.1363	0.1421	**0.1465**	3.10%
F1@20	0.1153	0.1171	0.1333	0.1560	0.1542	0.1576	**0.1628**	3.30%
NDCG@10	0.1493	0.1480	0.1642	0.2061	0.2034	0.2110	**0.2166**	2.65%
NDCG@20	0.1498	0.1517	0.1706	0.2070	0.2043	0.2122	**0.2161**	1.84%

Table 3. Comparison of recommendation performances on DoubanBook.

	BPR	SBPR	DiffNet	SEPT	LightGCN	SGL	SlightGCN	Ascension
Prec@10	0.0715	0.0664	0.0727	0.0942	0.0876	0.1061	**0.1096**	3.30%
Prec@20	0.0561	0.0539	0.0583	0.0743	0.0702	0.0826	**0.0850**	2.91%
Rec@10	0.0696	0.0725	0.0830	0.1008	0.0909	0.1079	**0.1104**	2.32%
Rec@20	0.1027	0.1093	0.1239	0.1480	0.1372	0.1587	**0.1620**	2.08%
F1@10	0.0705	0.0693	0.0775	0.0974	0.0892	0.1070	**0.1100**	2.80%
F1@20	0.0726	0.0722	0.0793	0.0989	0.0929	0.1086	**0.1115**	2.67%
NDCG@10	0.0956	0.0921	0.1019	0.1320	0.1195	0.1496	**0.1541**	3.01%
NDCG@20	0.0980	0.0980	0.1090	0.1371	0.1261	0.1532	**0.1577**	2.94%

5.3.2. Cold-Start User Experiment

Cold-start users have few or no interactions, and extremely sparse data make it difficult to generate recommend for such users. In this section, users with fewer than 10 interactions are selected as cold-start users; the recommendation results for these users are shown in Figures 3 and 4.

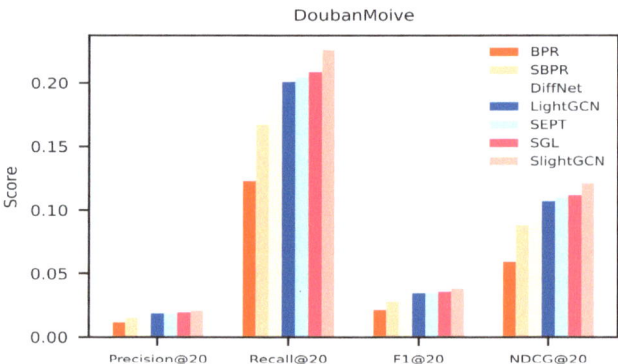

Figure 3. Comparison of the cold-start user recommendation performances on DoubanMovie.

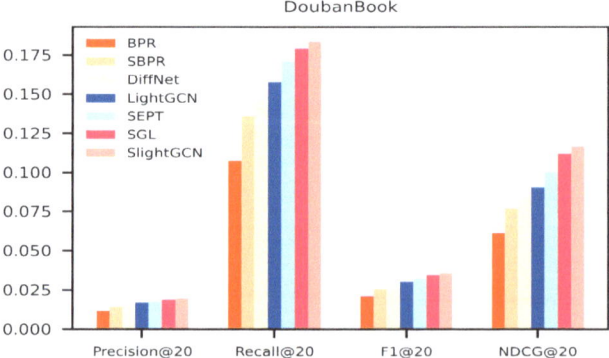

Figure 4. Comparison of the cold-start user recommendation performances on DoubanBook.

The recommendation performance of SBPR is better than that of BPR, indicating that users' social relationships alleviate the problem of data sparsity to some extent. For the other four recommendation models based on GNN, the recommendation performance increases in the order of DiffNet, LightGCN, SEPT, SGL, and SlightGCN. LightGCN, which only uses user–item interaction relationships, achieves a better recommendation performance than DiffNet, which uses the social relationship as auxiliary information. Its simple and efficient convolution structure is more suitable for collaborative filtering. SEPT uses collaborative training to find positive and negative samples for self-supervised learning. SGL is based on the structure of a random disturbance graph for data enhancement, and the generated self-supervised signal alleviates data sparsity and improves the embedding quality. The proposed SlightGCN model incorporates multiple pieces of auxiliary information, such as user social relationship and item association relationship, as well as various perspectives of self-supervised auxiliary task construction, all of which alleviate the problem of data sparsity to a certain extent. In addition, user/item embedding is influenced by multiple relationships simultaneously, improving the capture of user preferences.

5.3.3. The Benefit of Self-Supervised Auxiliary Tasks

To verify that user social relationship, item association relationship, and self-supervised auxiliary tasks can help improve the recommendation performance of SlightGCN, we designed an ablation experiment as follows.

To verify the effectiveness of self-supervised auxiliary tasks, the self-supervised auxiliary tasks were removed to form the UI model variant. In addition, to verify the benefits of user social relationship and item association relationship to improve the model performance, user–item interaction relationship and user social relationship are reserved to form the U model variant, and user–item interaction relationship and item association relationship) are reserved to form the I model variant. The experimental results of SlightGCN and its three deformation models on the two datasets are shown in Tables 4 and 5 (the bold numbers mean the best performance).

Table 4. SlightGCN ablation experimental results on DoubanMovie.

Metrics	LightGCN	Variant-U	Variant-I	Variant-UI	SlightGCN
Prec@10	0.1602	0.1635	0.1630	0.1637	**0.1712**
Prec@20	0.1331	0.1348	0.1343	0.1350	**0.1407**
Rec@10	0.1186	0.1217	0.1223	0.1226	**0.1281**
Rec@20	0.1833	0.1876	0.1869	0.1881	**0.1931**
F1@10	0.1363	0.1395	0.1397	0.1402	**0.1465**
F1@20	0.1542	0.1569	0.1563	0.1572	**0.1628**
NDCG@10	0.2034	0.2091	0.2082	0.2095	**0.2166**
NDCG@20	0.2043	0.2101	0.2096	0.2104	**0.2161**

Table 5. SlightGCN ablation experimental results on DoubanBook.

Evaluation Index	LightGCN	Variant U	Variant I	Variant UI	SlightGCN
Prec@10	0.0876	0.0890	0.0893	0.0897	**0.1096**
Prec@20	0.0702	0.0712	0.0719	0.0726	**0.0850**
Rec@10	0.0909	0.0927	0.0934	0.0941	**0.1104**
Rec@20	0.1372	0.1386	0.1390	0.1389	**0.1620**
F1@10	0.0892	0.0908	0.0913	0.0918	**0.1100**
F1@20	0.0929	0.0941	0.0948	0.0954	**0.1115**
NDCG@10	0.1195	0.1223	0.1226	0.1238	**0.1541**
NDCG@20	0.1261	0.1285	0.1290	0.1296	**0.1577**

Compared with LightGCN, variant UI, variant U, and variant I, the three deformation models all improved to a certain extent, indicating that user social relationship and item association relationship can improve the recommendation performance by alleviating data sparsity. However, there is no significant difference in the recommendation performance between variant UI containing two auxiliary relationships and variant U and variant I, containing only one auxiliary relationship, indicating that the user social relationship and item association relationship cannot be well-integrated. SlightGCN removes the user social relationship and the item social relationship to construct different auxiliary views. Contrastive self-supervised learning maximizes the mutual information of the two views and promotes the integration of user social relationships and item association relationships. SlightGCN's recommendation performance is superior to that of variant UI, which does not include self-supervised assistance tasks.

5.3.4. Parameter Sensitive Analysis

In the training process of the model, it is constrained by the main recommendation task and the self-supervised auxiliary task. The self-supervised task assists the recommendation task to guide the updating direction of model parameters. In the loss function of the joint training, the hyperparameter λ_1 is the weight coefficient of the loss of the self-supervised auxiliary task, and λ_1 can control the influence of the self-supervised auxiliary task on the overall recommendation performance of the model. The training process of the parameter λ_1 ambassador model is more dependent on the information of the self-supervised auxiliary task and less dependent on the information of the self-supervised auxiliary task. The experiments of hyperparameter λ_1 on dataset DoubanMovie and dataset DoubanBook are shown in Figures 5 and 6, respectively.

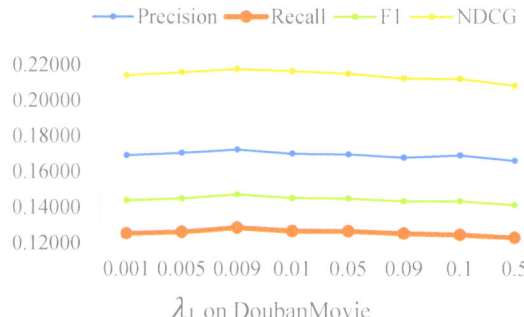

Figure 5. Parameter λ_1 sensitivity analysis on DoubanMovie.

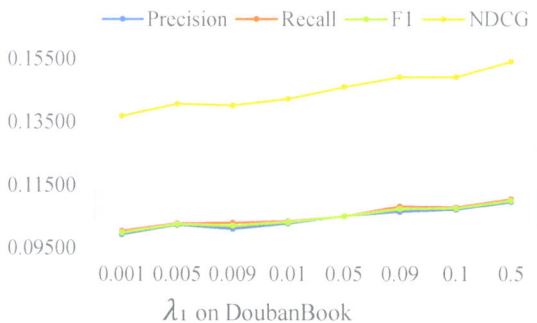

Figure 6. Parameter λ_1 sensitivity analysis on DoubanBook.

In DoubanMovie, the overall trend of the values of the four metrics is consistent, increasing first and then decreasing with increased λ_1, with the recommendation performance reaching its peak at $\lambda_1 = 0.009$. In DoubanBook, the overall variation trend of the four metrics is consistent, increasing with increased in λ_1, with the recommendation performance reaching its peak at $\lambda_1 = 0.05$. Two conclusions can be drawn from observations:

- The optimal $\lambda_1 = 0.009$ on DoubanMovie is far less than the optimal $\lambda_1 = 0.05$ on DoubanBook, indicating that the model relies much more on self-supervised auxiliary

tasks on DoubanBook than on DoubanMovie. The reasons for the above phenomenon are as follows: the user–item interaction density on DoubanBook is lower than that on DoubanMovie. To learn higher-quality node embedding and improve recommendation performance, the model in the DoubanBook environment needs to obtain more information from self-supervised auxiliary tasks.
- The improvement of the four metrics in DoubanBook with sparse data is much more significant than that in DoubanMovie, indicating the effectiveness of self-supervised auxiliary tasks in alleviating the data sparsity problem.

6. Conclusions

In this paper, we propose a social recommendation model based on self-supervision and multi-auxiliary information (SlightGCN). The social relationships between users and the related relationships between items are mined from user–item interaction data and item attribute information. The relationships between items and users can be used as multiple auxiliary information to alleviate data sparsity. The user–item interaction relationship, user social relationship, and item associate relationship are integrated into the same heterogeneous network in the form of an edge. A heterogeneous network is used as the input of a graph convolutional neural network to carry out the main recommendation task, and an appropriate convolutional mode is designed; user embedding is simultaneously affected by user social relationship and user–item interaction relationship, and item embedding is simultaneously affected by item association relationship and user–item interaction relationship. Auxiliary views are constructed according to different combinations of information, and self-supervised auxiliary tasks of multi-auxiliary views are designed to improve the embedding quality of nodes and recommendation performance. Extensive experiments were conducted on two public datasets to verify the superiority of SlightGCN in terms of recommendation performance, the effectiveness of multi-auxiliary information, and self-supervised auxiliary tasks.

Many data argumentation methods for comparative self-supervised learning are available in the GNN-based method, such as randomly removing edges or nodes, randomly adding edges or nodes, removing/adding edges or nodes on purpose, and even rewiring the graph. Further research is required with deep analysis of the effectiveness of these data argumentation methods within the framework the proposed SlightGCN model.

Author Contributions: Conceptualization, F.J. and Y.C.; methodology, M.G. and Y.C.; software, Y.C.; validation, H.W. and X.W.; formal analysis, Y.S.; writing—original draft preparation, F.J.; writing—review and editing, Y.S.; supervision, M.G. All authors have read and agreed to the published version of the manuscript.

Funding: This study was supported by the National Natural Science Foundation (72161005), the Research Program of Chongqing Technology Innovation and Application Development (cstc2020kqjscx-phxm1301), Chongqing Technology Innovation and Application Development Project (cstc2020jscx-lyjsAX0010), and Scientific and Technological Research Program of Chongqing Municipal Education Commission (KJZD-K202204402).

Data Availability Statement: DoubanMovie: http://shichuan.org/dataset/Semantic Path.zip (accessed on 12 January 2022).; DoubanBook: http://shichuan.org/dataset/Recommendation.zip (accessed on 12 January 2022).

Conflicts of Interest: The authors declare no conflict of interest.

References

1. Aljunid, M.F.; Huchaiah, M.D. An efficient hybrid recommendation model based on collaborative filtering recommender systems. *CAAI Trans. Intell. Technol.* **2021**, *6*, 13.
2. Meng, X.W.; Liu, S.D.; Zhang, Y.J.; Hu, X. Research on Social Recommender Systems. *J. Softw.* **2015**, *26*, 1356–1372.
3. Zhang, Y.J.; Dong, Z.; Meng, X.W. Research on personalized advertising recommendation systems and their applications. *J. Comput.* **2021**, *44*, 531–563.
4. Shang, M.; Luo, X.; Liu, Z.; Chen, J.; Yuan, Y.; Zhou, M. Randomized latent factor model for high-dimensional and sparse matrices from industrial applications. *IEEE/CAA J. Autom. Sin.* **2018**, *6*, 131–141. [CrossRef]
5. Sinha, R.R.; Swearingen, K. Comparing recommendations made by online systems and friends. *DELOS* **2001**, *106*. Available online: https://www.researchgate.net/publication/2394806_Comparing_Recommendations_Made_by_Online_Systems_and_Friends (accessed on 28 April 2022).
6. Iyengar, R.; Han, S.; Gupta, S. *Do Friends Influence Purchases in a Social Network?* Harvard Business School Marketing Unit Working Paper No. 09-123; Harvard Business School: Boston, MA, USA, 2009.
7. Kang, M.; Bi, Y.; Wu, Z.; Wang, J.; Xiao, J. A heterogeneous conversational recommender system for financial products. In Proceedings of the 28th ACM International Conference on Information and Knowledge Management, Beijing, China, 3–7 November 2019; pp. 26–30.
8. Yu, J.; Gao, M.; Li, J.; Yin, H.; Liu, H. Adaptive implicit friends identification over heterogeneous network for social recommendation. In Proceedings of the 27th ACM International Conference on Information and Knowledge Management, Torino, Italy, 22–26 October 2018; pp. 357–366.
9. Zhao, H.; Zhou, Y.; Song, Y.; Lee, D.L. Motif enhanced recommendation over heterogeneous information network. In Proceedings of the 28th ACM International Conference on Information and Knowledge Management, Beijing, China, 3–7 November 2019.
10. Kipf, T.N.; Welling, M. Semi-supervised classification with graph convolutional networks. In Proceedings of the 5th International Conference on Learning Representations (ICLR 2017), Toulon, France, 24–26 April 2017.
11. Berg, R.; Kipf, T.N.; Welling, M. Graph convolutional matrix completion. In Proceedings of the 24th ACM SIGKDD Conference on Knowledge Discovery and Data Mining (KDD 2018), London, UK, 19–23 August 2018.
12. Wang, X.; He, X.; Wang, M.; Feng, F.; Chua, T.-S. Neural graph collaborative filtering. In Proceedings of the 42nd international ACM SIGIR Conference on Research and Development in Information Retrieval, Paris, France, 21–25 July 2019; pp. 165–174.
13. He, X.; Deng, K.; Wang, X.; Li, Y.; Zhang, Y.; Wang, M. Lightgcn: Simplifying and powering graph convolution network for recommendation. In Proceedings of the 43rd International ACM SIGIR Conference on Research and Development in Information Retrieval, Virtual Event, China, 25–30 July 2020; pp. 639–648.
14. Wu, S.; Sun, F.; Zhang, W.; Xie, X.; Cui, B. Graph neural networks in recommender systems: A survey. *arXiv* **2011**, arXiv:2011.02260. [CrossRef]
15. Fan, W.; Ma, Y.; Li, Q.; He, Y.; Zhao, E.; Tang, J.; Yin, D. Graph neural networks for social recommendation. In Proceedings of the World Wide Web Conference, San Francisco, CA, USA, 13–17 May 2019; pp. 417–426.
16. Wu, Q.; Zhang, H.; Gao, X.; He, P.; Weng, P.; Gao, H.; Chen, G. Dual graph attention networks for deep latent representation of multifaceted social effects in recommender systems. In Proceedings of the World Wide Web Conference, San Francisco, CA, USA, 13–17 May 2019; pp. 2091–2102.
17. Song, W.; Xiao, Z.; Wang, Y.; Charlin, L.; Zhang, M.; Tang, J. Session-based social recommendation via dynamic graph attention networks. In Proceedings of the Twelfth ACM International Conference on Web Search and Data Mining, Melbourne, VIC, Australia, 11–15 February 2019; pp. 555–563.
18. Yu, J.; Yin, H.; Li, J.; Gao, M.; Huang, Z.; Cui, L. Enhance social recommendation with adversarial graph convolutional networks. *IEEE Trans. Knowl. Data Eng.* **2020**, *34*, 3727–3739. [CrossRef]
19. Yu, J.; Yin, H.; Li, J.; Wang, Q.; Hung, N.Q.; Zhang, X. Self-supervised multi-channel hypergraph convolutional network for social recommendation. In Proceedings of the Web Conference 2021, Ljubljana, Slovenia, 19–23 April 2021; pp. 413–424.
20. Huang, C.; Xu, H.; Xu, Y.; Dai, P.; Xia, L.; Lu, M.; Bo, L.; Xing, H.; Lai, X.; Ye, Y. Knowledge-aware coupled graph neural network for social recommendation. In Proceedings of the AAAI Conference on Artificial Intelligence, Virtual Conference, 2–9 February 2021; Volume 35, pp. 4115–4122.
21. Yang, L.; Liu, Z.; Dou, Y.; Ma, J.; Yu, P.S. Consisrec: Enhancing GNN for social recommendation via consistent neighbor aggregation. In Proceedings of the 44th International ACM SIGIR Conference on Research and Development in Information Retrieval, Virtual Event, Canada, 11–15 July 2021; pp. 2141–2145.
22. Blau, Y.; Michaeli, T. Rethinking lossy compression: The rate-distortion-perception tradeoff. In Proceedings of the International Conference on Machine Learning, PMLR, Long Beach, CA, USA, 10–15 June 2019; pp. 675–685.
23. Bojanowski, P.; Grave, E.; Joulin, A.; Mikolov, T. Enriching word vectors with subword information. *Trans. Assoc. Comput. Linguist.* **2017**, *5*, 135–146. [CrossRef]
24. Brock, A.; Donahue, J.; Simonyan, K. Large Scale GAN Training for High Fidelity Natural Image Synthesis. ICLR2019. Available online: https://openreview.net/forum?id=B1xsqj09Fm (accessed on 28 April 2022).
25. Qiu, J.; Chen, Q.; Dong, Y.; Zhang, J.; Yang, H.; Ding, M.; Wang, K.; Tang, J. Gcc: Graph contrastive coding for graph neural network pre-training. In Proceedings of the 26th ACM SIGKDD International Conference on Knowledge Discovery & Data Mining, Virtual Event, CA, USA, 6–10 July 2020; pp. 1150–1160.

26. Velickovic, P.; Fedus, W.; Hamilton, W.L.; Liò, P.; Bengio, Y.; Hjelm, R.D. Deep Graph Infomax. *ICLR (Poster)* **2019**, *2*, 4.
27. Wu, J.; Wang, X.; Feng, F.; He, X.; Chen, L.; Lian, J.; Xie, X. Self-supervised graph learning for recommendation. In Proceedings of the 44th International ACM SIGIR Conference on Research and Development in Information Retrieval, Virtual Event, Canada, 11–15 July 2021; pp. 726–735.
28. Ma, J.; Zhou, C.; Yang, H.; Cui, P.; Wang, X.; Zhu, W. Disentangled self-supervision in sequential recommenders. In Proceedings of the 26th ACM SIGKDD International Conference on Knowledge Discovery & Data Mining, Virtual Event, CA, USA, 6–10 July 2020; pp. 483–491.
29. Yao, T.; Yi, X.; Cheng, D.Z.; Felix, X.Y.; Menon, A.K.; Hong, L.; Chi, E.H.; Tjoa, S.; Kang, J.; Ettinger, E. Self-Supervised Learning for Deep Models in Recommendations. 2020. Available online: https://openreview.net/forum?id=BCHN5z8nMRW (accessed on 13 May 2022).
30. Zhou, K.; Wang, H.; Zhao, W.X.; Zhu, Y.; Wang, S.; Zhang, F.; Wang, Z.; Wen, J.R. S3-rec: Self-supervised learning for sequential recommendation with mutual information maximization. In Proceedings of the 29th ACM International Conference on Information & Knowledge Management, Galway, Ireland, 19–23 October 2020; pp. 1893–1902.
31. Long, X.; Huang, C.; Xu, Y.; Xu, H.; Dai, P.; Xia, L.; Bo, L. Social recommendation with self-supervised metagraph informax network. In Proceedings of the 30th ACM International Conference on Information & Knowledge Management, Gold Coast, QID, Australia, 1–5 November 2021; pp. 1160–1169.
32. Liu, Z.; Chen, Y.; Li, J.; Yu, P.S.; McAuley, J.; Xiong, C. Contrastive self-supervised sequential recommendation with robust augmentation. *arXiv* **2021**, arXiv:2108.06479.
33. Wu, J.; Fan, W.; Chen, J.; Liu, S.; Li, Q.; Tang, K. Disentangled contrastive learning for social recommendation. In Proceedings of the 31st ACM International Conference on Information & Knowledge Management, Atlanta, GA, USA, 17–21 October 2022; pp. 4570–4574.
34. Yu, J.; Yin, H.; Gao, M.; Xia, X.; Zhang, X.; Viet Hung, N.Q. Socially-aware self-supervised tri-training for recommendation. In Proceedings of the 27th ACM SIGKDD Conference on Knowledge Discovery & Data Mining, Singapore, 14–18 August 2021; pp. 2084–2092.
35. Rendle, S.; Freudenthaler, C.; Gantner, Z.; Schmidt-Thieme, L. BPR: Bayesian personalized ranking from implicit feedback. In Proceedings of the Twenty-Fifth Conference on Uncertainty in Artificial Intelligence, Montreal, QC, Canada, 18–21 June 2009; pp. 452–461.
36. Zhao, T.; McAuley, J.; King, I. Leveraging social connections to improve personalized ranking for collaborative filtering. In Proceedings of the 23rd ACM International Conference on Information and Knowledge Management, Shanghai, China, 3–7 November 2014; pp. 261–270.
37. Wu, L.; Sun, P.; Fu, Y.; Hong, R.; Wang, X.; Wang, M. A neural influence diffusion model for social recommendation. In Proceedings of the 42nd International ACM SIGIR Conference on Research and Development in Information Retrieval, Paris, France, 21–25 July 2019; pp. 235–244.

Article

A Hybrid Prediction Model Based on KNN-LSTM for Vessel Trajectory

Lixiang Zhang [1], Yian Zhu [1,*], Jiang Su [2], Wei Lu [3], Jiayu Li [4] and Ye Yao [1]

1. School of Computer Science, Northwestern Polytechnical University, Xi'an 710072, China
2. School of Software, Northwestern Polytechnical University, Xi'an 710072, China
3. School of Information, Xi'an University of Finance and Economics, Xi'an 710100, China
4. Queen Mary University of London Engineering School, Northwestern Polytechnical University, Xi'an 710072, China
* Correspondence: zhuya@nwpu.edu.cn

Abstract: Trajectory prediction technology uses the trajectory data of historical ships to predict future ship trajectory, which has significant application value in the field of ship driving and ship management. With the popularization of Automatic Identification System (AIS) equipment in-stalled on ships, many ship trajectory data are collected and stored, providing a data basis for ship trajectory prediction. Currently, most of the ship trajectory prediction methods do not fully consider the influence of ship density in different sea areas, leading to a large difference in the prediction effect in different sea areas. This paper proposes a hybrid trajectory prediction model based on K-Nearest Neighbor (KNN) and Long Short-Term Memory (LSTM) methods. In this model, different methods are used to predict trajectory based on trajectory density. For offshore waters with a high density of trajectory, an optimized K-Nearest Neighbor algorithm is used for prediction. For open sea waters with low density of trajectory, the Long Short-Term Memory model is used for prediction. To further improve the prediction effect, the spatio-temporal characteristics of the trajectory are fully considered in the prediction process of the model. The experimental results for the dataset of historical data show that the mean square error of the proposed method is less than 2.92×10^{-9}. Compared to the prediction methods based on the Kalman filter, the mean square error decreases by two orders of magnitude. Compared to the prediction methods based on recurrent neural network, the mean square error decreases by 82%. The advantage of the proposed model is that it can always obtain a better prediction result under different conditions of trajectory density available for different sea areas.

Keywords: LSTM neural network; KNN; trajectory prediction; automatic recognition system; sea area division

MSC: 68T01

1. Introduction

To help maritime supervisors track ships and ensure navigation safety, the Interna-tional Maritime Organization (IMO) requires that ships with a gross tonnage of more than 300, or ships with a cargo capacity of more than 500 gross tons and non-international voyage cargo ships to be equipped with automatic identification system (AIS) [1,2]. Meanwhile, with the increase of the AIS data scale and the continuous development of artificial intelligence technology in recent years [3,4], ships' intelligence and behavioral autonomy have been significantly improved [5,6]. However, the level of intelligence of the existing AISs is far from meeting the maritime management requirements. The ship trajectory prediction is vital to the intelligence of an AIS, and the higher the accuracy of ship trajectory prediction using AIS data, the more sufficient the response space and time to avoid accidents of ship collision [7,8].

This paper focuses on the ship trajectory prediction problem. In the past, ship path prediction relied on mathematical models such as the one proposed by Sutulo [9], the structure of the generic maneuvering mathematical model leads naturally to two basic approaches based on dynamic and purely kinematic prediction models. An analytical scheme for the short-term kinematic prediction accounting for current values of accelerations is proposed. However, the mathematical model requires a large amount of input parameters, such as ship shape, current, wind direction, maneuvering, etc. It is difficult to obtain all the input parameters data needed. On the other hand, the inference-based trajectory prediction methods, such as Markov Chain [10], based on the hidden Markov model (HMM), a spatio-temporal predictor, and a next-place predictor are proposed. Living habits are analyzed in terms of entropy, upon which users are clustered into distinct groups. They are subjected to unbiased statistics, resulting in poor scalability. Recently, neural network technologies, such as Recurrent Neural Network (RNN) [11] and Long Short-Term Memory Networks [12], based on the route data, a prediction algorithm such as LSTM (Long Short-Term Memory) recurrent neural network used to realize the prediction of the ship's navigation trajectory showed good performance in trajectory prediction in cases where sufficient samples are available. However, most of these techniques focus only on the optimization of the methods, the density of ships and the density of ship routes are not considered. According to the distribution of real-time ship trajectory data, not only there is a great difference in ship density between offshore areas with high vessel density and open sea with low ship density [13], the human factors also increased the complexity of the ship trajectory prediction, especially in offshore areas. The traditional machine learning algorithm can be used to predict the ship's navigation trajectory. However, there are limitations in both accuracy and flexibility, as ship trajectory prediction is quite different in the offshore sea and open seas.

This paper proposed a new ship trajectory prediction method based on a neural network. The main innovation is to embed the optimized algorithm into the discriminant learning method, which combined the optimized KNN algorithm with neural network and LSTM neural network (Long Short-Term Memory network) to predict the ship trajectory in the open sea area when ship density is low. However, in offshore areas where ship density is high, current methods based on distance-trajectory similarity do not fully consider the speed characteristics of ship trajectories. Existing methods do not measure distance for the spherical characteristics of the nautical domain, resulting in less accurate measurement results, this paper used a new similarity distance formula in the KNN algorithm to predict ship tracks. As a result, the influence caused by different characteristics of trajectory data in trajectory prediction can be eliminated effectively.

The main contributions of this paper are as follows: (1) In view of the poor performance of the traditional KNN algorithm in low-density areas, the sea areas where the ships travel are divided according to the density of ships, and different trajectory prediction methods are adopted in sea areas with different vessel densities to avoid the influence of different trajectory data characteristics on prediction accuracy as far as possible. (2) The similarity distance formula in the traditional KNN algorithm is optimized to solve the problem that the effect of the KNN algorithm is not good because the Euclidean distance is not applicable to the similarity measurement between ship tracks, and further improves the prediction results in the sea area with large ship density. (3) The improved KNN algorithm and LSTM neural network are used to predict different ship density areas, respectively, to solve the problem of LSTM's reduced prediction effect caused by insufficient data.

The remainder of the paper is organized as follows. In Section 2 we discuss related work, in Section 3 we describe our algorithm, in Section 4 we illustrate the experiments we did to test the algorithm. Finally, in Section 5 we give our conclusions and future work.

2. Related Works

The study of the transportation system model has been classical research content, and the method of big data analysis has the advantages of good experimental effect and portability compared with the transport system model, but it cannot make accurate estimation of the influence produced by the intervention of infrastructures and transport services [14]. This paper predicts the trajectory of ships sailing at sea, and the ships are rarely interfered with by infrastructure and traffic service during the long voyage, so the method of big data analysis is more suitable for the trajectory prediction of ships at sea. Moreover, for the ship trajectory prediction, the most commonly used prediction methods in previous literature predict the ship movement using historical trajectory information of the ship to predict the future ship trajectory accurately and efficiently. In the discussion of related works, the mainstream of the existing work was classified, according to the implementation mechanism of ship trajectory prediction methods into three categories: methods based on the physical (mathematical) models, methods based on the learning models, and methods using a mixture of multiple models.

2.1. Methods Based on the Physical (Mathematical) Models

This kind of method attempts to explicitly consider all influencing factors in the modeling process. Abdelaal et al. [15] took impact force and yaw moment into consideration to build a prediction model and applied it to the anti-collision system. However, the use scenarios are limited since detailed ship information is required by this method. Vijverberg et al. [16] used a linear extrapolation model to predict the future position of the ships. This method did not consider environmental factors, which affect the prediction accuracy. Zhang et al. [17] used pneumatic parameters to design a set of maneuvering modes using aerodynamic parameters, and realized trajectory prediction using Markov chain Monte Carlo and Bayesian decision theory. Compared with the traditional extrapolation theory, the accuracy was higher, but it needed more comprehensive maneuvering modes, which were difficult to obtain in reality. Virjonen et al. [18] used the KNN algorithm to predict ship trajectories, and the performance of the method as well as the hyperparameters of the proposed model was optimized using a nested leave-one-out crossvalidation approach. Based on the traditional Kalman filter theory, Liang et al. [19] constructs a polynomial Kalman filter to fit a non-linear system and predict the ship's trajectory based on latitude and longitude information. The results show that the method is simple to implement and converges quickly, and can effectively solve the problem of predicting ship trajectories in practical processes, meeting basic timeliness and accuracy. Xie et al. [20] proposed a short-term trajectory prediction method based on a movement model and a long-distance trajectory prediction method based on maneuvering intention, and applied two interacting multiple models for trajectory prediction. The dynamic model prediction in this method achieves better real-time performance, but it needed to establish a more accurate dynamic model for the target, and this is difficult to achieve in real situations. Therefore, this method often leads to serious prediction errors.

2.2. Methods Based on the Machine Learning Model

The ship movement is often modeled using a learning model in this type of method, which learns the movement characteristics from the historical movement data to implicitly integrate all possible influencing factors. According to the existing research results in this field, Burger et al. [21] compared DKF (Discrete Kalman Filter) and LRM (Linear Regression Model) under the learning model based on statistics. When these two methods were used to predict linear trajectories, DKF was much higher than LRM in parameter complexity, but the results showed no significant improvement in performance. Moreover, the error distribution of DKF was more dispersed than that of LRM, which was unfavorable for the observation of outliers. Hexeberg et al. [22] proposed a data-driven Single Point Neighbor Search (SPNS) method based on AIS ship trajectory prediction. This method recursively used historical AIS data to predict the next position and time near the predicted location, but the time accuracy of this algorithm was within 30 min, and it could not deal with the sea branch conditions. In addition, for the model based on machine learning, Liu et al. proposed an online multiple outputs Least Squares Support Vector Machine (LS-SVM) based on a selection mechanism. The LS-SVM model [23] was used for ship trajectory prediction. Murray et al. [24] evaluated a data-driven method, which used historical data to predict ship track within the time range of 5–30 min, and proposed a single point neighbor search based on clustering. The method of trajectory extraction was used to evaluate the predicted ship route. The disadvantage is that the speed is constant, which reduces the result of prediction iteration. Bao [25] proposes a high-precision ship track prediction model based on a combination of a multi-head attention mechanism, and bidirectional gate recurrent unit (MHA-BiGRU). Last et al. [26] proposed a new method for ship movement prediction based on movement data. By compressing AIS data, a background trajectory model was proposed, but it can only predict local clustering for a given region. Volkova [27] uses a neural network of the previous coordinates of the vessel's trajectory to predict the estimated next coordinates of the vessel during river navigation. Wang et al. [28] proposed a sequence-to-sequence Deep Long Short-Term Memory network (SS-DLSTM) for trajectory prediction, which increased the prediction accuracy and robustness. However, it was only applied to the Terminal Airspace. The trajectories in Terminal Airspace were relatively stable. In the case of complex trajectories, the prediction accuracy would be greatly reduced. Han et al. [29] used a gated recurrent unit (GRU) to predict flight trajectory, selected the optimal GRU network by comparing the number of network layers and neuron number, and compared it with the BP network. The prediction error was reduced, but it needed too much data in the offline training process. Liu et al. [30] proposed an end-to-end Convolutional Neural Network (CNN) to predict the trajectory, which used an encoder to encode flight information as a hidden state variable and a decoder to learn the temporal and spatial relevance of historical tracks. However, when the trajectory changed dramatically, the prediction error will grow large. The above research showed that the machine learning methods are easy to implement and can achieve high accuracy in the case of sufficient data, but the training process requires too much data and have strong data dependence.

2.3. Methods Based on the Hybrid Model

The main goal of a hybrid model approach is to combine the advantages of its constituent models, which either explicitly consider some of the influencing factors and train with historical movement data, or combine different learning methods to form a model to achieve better performance. Lin et al. [31] proposed a prediction method in which the Hidden Markov Model (HMM) was used to model the flight movement trend based on the historical trajectory and the Gaussian Mixture Model was used to predict the aircraft speed vector, but the prediction error was large in the case of high-speed maneuvering. Yang et al. [32] proposed a high-precision trajectory prediction model under multi-dimensional factors. In this algorithm, the Douglas–Peucker algorithm is used to compress track data, the DBSCAN algorithm is used to perform track clustering, and trajectory is predicted by LRCN (Long-term Recurrent Convolutional Networks) prediction model. Wang et al. [33] proposed a gray dynamic filtering method for trajectory prediction. Compared with the traditional KALMAN FILTER and the original gray method, the prediction accuracy was greatly improved. However, it used Minimum Variance Estimation to replace the actual value and introduced differential equations, therefore parameters could not be accurately estimated. Inaccurate parameters would reduce the accuracy of prediction. Qiao et al. [34] proposed a trajectory prediction method based on the Hidden Markov Model (HMM), in which adaptive parameters were added to the Hidden Markov process to improve the prediction efficiency and the trajectory prediction length could be adjusted adaptively, but the prediction accuracy must be enhanced. Ma et al. [35] designed an integrated model for the simultaneous prediction of multiple trajectories using the proposed features and employed the Long Short-Term Memory-based neural network and Recurrent Neural Network to pursue this time series task. Wang X et al. [36] designed a trajectory prediction framework on the spark platform based on the second-order Hidden Markov Model. Compared with the hidden Markov model, the robustness of the algorithm was higher, but the prediction accuracy of the algorithm needed to be improved. The above methods showed that the hybrid theory method is widely applied, but the algorithm is too complex, and the prediction accuracy and real-time prediction performance are not outstanding.

Through the study of relevant literature, it can be seen that AIS data are very important for ship trajectory prediction results. However, the density of ships in the offshore and far-sea areas is very different. The density of ships in offshore waters is high, and the trajectories of ships are easily affected by other ships or human influences. The density of ships in the open seas is relatively low, the ship trajectories are mostly single-vessel trajectories, and are less influenced by the trajectory data of other ships around. At the same time, the trajectory of the ship to be predicted cannot be filled with the future trajectory of the surrounding similar ships, Therefore, it is necessary to adopt different targeted trajectory prediction methods for sea areas with different ship densities. This paper proposes a new prediction method based on neural network. Its core idea is to embed the optimization algorithm into the discriminant learning method, analyze the characteristics of data existing in different ship density regions, and adopt targeted prediction methods for different ship density regions.

3. The Proposed Method

The model's architecture in this paper is divided into two layers according to various ship densities, ship trajectory prediction in the offshore area, and ship trajectory prediction in the open sea area. From the observations of the offshore area, the data on single ships are small in size, but the overall number of ships is high. Furthermore, the ships influence each other in their trajectories. Thus, the classification method can be used for this prediction. When the ship enters the open sea, due to the change in the density of ships in the sea and the density of routes, the previous forecasting methods can no longer achieve the desired results all the time. Therefore, a new trajectory prediction method is proposed.

The overall structure of the model in this paper is shown in Figure 1. The first step is to preprocess AIS data to remove null values inside, and divide the data according to the sea areas [37]. Then, the optimized KNN algorithm is used to separate sea areas into offshore sea areas, and distant sea area by ship density, the details of the sea area division are described in Section 3.2. After selecting the label and characteristic data, the final optimal hyperparameters are obtained by the retention method. The KNN algorithms obtain the classification of ships, the KNN algorithm is described in detail in Section 3.2. For far seas, it is necessary to serialize the preprocessed data and divide the dataset first, before training and predicting the LSTM neural network. The LSTM neural network is described in detail in Section 3.3.

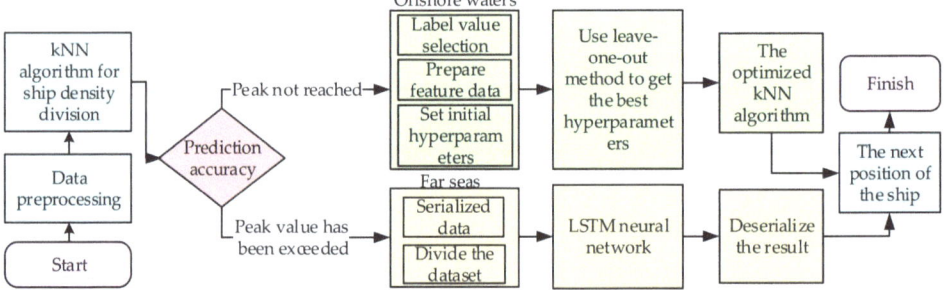

Figure 1. The ship trajectory prediction method flow chart.

3.1. Trajectory Prediction Method for the Offshore Areas

Due to the high concentration of ships in an offshore area, the classification approach is to classify ships using their characteristics, predicting the ship's following positions according to the ships' positions of the same type. While the traditional KNN algorithm is to classify the trajectory points of the ship, this paper uses the KNN algorithm to classify the characteristics of ships, which can reduce the influence of other factors on the ship's navigation trajectory.

The main idea of the KNN algorithm is that if most K closest samples in the feature space belong to a certain category, the samples also belong to that category, and have the same characteristics as samples in this category [38–40]. The KNN method mainly depends on the surrounding limited adjacent samples to determine the category, rather than the method of discriminating the class domain. Therefore, the KNN method is more suitable than the other methods for classifying sample sets with overlapping class domains.

The KNN algorithm that predicts the ship trajectory uses Euclidean distance as similarity distance and classification standard. However, many features were included dur-ing the classification of ship trajectory, such as latitude and longitude, velocity to earth, etc. Since the calculation of the ship distance is not the calculation of the straight-line distance on the plane, but the calculation of the spherical distance, the calculation of the Euclidean distance is prone to overfitting, so Euclidean distance, Frechet distance, Manhattan distance, etc., are no longer applicable. Therefore, the similarity distance in the KNN algorithm needs to be optimized, the relationships between ship position and speed are integrated, and the dynamic weights are allocated, so that the optimized KNN algorithm can be better applied to the ship trajectory classification.

Based on the above ideas, the KNN algorithm is obtained and the input training data set is given as the Formula (1).

$$T = x_1, y_1, (x_2, y_2), \ldots \ldots, (x_n, y_n) \text{ where } x_i \in X \subseteq R^n \tag{1}$$

The instance eigenvector of n dimension as the Formula (2).

$$y_i \in Y = c_1, c_2, \ldots \ldots c_k \tag{2}$$

This formula is the category of instances, where $i = 1, 2, 3 \ldots n$, prediction instance x. Output category Y to which prediction instance X belongs.

Distance equation: The Euclidean distance adopted by the KNN algorithm cannot measure the similarity between ship tracks and the actual movement of ships, its earth-moving velocity has a great influence on ship tracks, and Euclidean distance does not involve this factor.

The distance measurement adopted in this paper is as the Formula (3)

$$D = a * D_1 + (1 - a) * D_2 \tag{3}$$

In Formula (3), a is the weight value. In the new similarity distance, a is used as the hyperparameter value and the new similarity distance uses the idea of weighted voting, so a more reasonable weight value can lead to better prediction results.

Assume that the latitude of point A is lat_1, and the longitude is lon_1. The latitude of point B is lat_2, the longitude is lon_2, and the radius of the Earth is R. Before finding this angle, first convert the coordinates to a point in the Cartesian space coordinate system, and let the center of the Earth be the coordinate center point, The coordinates of points A and B after the transformation are shown in Formulas (4) and (5).

$$A\ Rcos(lat_1)cos(lon_1),\ Rcos(lat_1)sin(lon_1),\ Rsin(lat_1) \tag{4}$$

$$B\ Rcos(lat_2)cos(lon_2),\ Rcos(lat_2)sin(lon_2),\ Rsin(lat_2) \tag{5}$$

Then, calculate the angle and use the vector angle calculation method to find the cosine value of the angle, let A be (x_1, y_1, z_1), B (x_2, y_2, z_2), and the formula is as the Formula (6).

$$COS = (x_1 * y_2 + y_1 * y_2 + z_1 * z_2) / \left(\sqrt{x_1^2 + y_1^2 + z_1^2} + \sqrt{x_2^2 + y_2^2 + z_2^2} \right) \tag{6}$$

Substitute the latitude and longitude coordinates as the Formula (7)

$$COS = cos(lat_2) * cos(lat_1) * cos(lon_1 - lon_2) + sin(lat_2) * sin(lat_1) \tag{7}$$

Let D_1 be the actual distance between two ships, and further find the arc length (distance between ships), the formula is as the Formulas (8) and (9).

$$D_1 = 2\pi R * \left(\frac{arccos(COS)}{2\pi}\right) \tag{8}$$

$$D_1 = R * arccos(COS) \tag{9}$$

the specific calculation formula is as the Formula (10).

$$D_1 = R * arccos[sin(\lambda_1)sin(\lambda_2) + cos(\lambda_1)cos(\lambda_2)cos(l_1 - l_2)] \tag{10}$$

Let D_2 be the difference in ground speed between two ships, which is computed as the Formula (11).

$$D_2 = v_1 - v_2 \tag{11}$$

The parameter description is shown in Table 1.

Table 1. Information of KNN algorithm parameters.

Parameters	Describes
a	The weight
R	The average radius of the Earth
λ_1	Latitude of node 1
φ_1	Longitude of node 1
λ_2	Latitude of node 2
φ_2	Longitude of node 2
v_1	Speed of node 1 to ground
v_2	Speed of node 2 to ground

The steps of the method to predict the ship trajectory based on the KNN algorithm are as follows.

Step 1: prepare and preprocess data;

Step 2: calculate the similarity distance between the test sample point and every other sample point;

Step 3: sort all distances and select k points with the smallest similarity distance;

Step 4: compare the categories in which K track points belong, and classify the test sample points into the category with the highest proportion among k points according to classification decision rules;

Step 5: replace the next position of the ship to be predicted with the track point of a similar ship;

3.2. Division of the Sea Areas

In a traditional trajectory prediction model, for the coastal area with a high density of ships, the trajectory of one ship is affected by other ships. For example, the mutual blocking and collision avoidance between ships will affect the trajectory of the ship's navigation. Therefore, the trajectory prediction error can be large if only the ship is considered. Furthermore, in offshore waters, the initial amount of ship data (such as latitude and longitude information, etc.) may also be insufficient to support the training part of the neural network model. Therefore, in offshore waters, using the LSTM neural network method for prediction may not achieve good results.

Due to the limitation of the number of relevant samples in the classification, the prediction accuracy will decrease as the ship density decreases. In addition, the ship track with low ship density is less affected by other ships. In open sea area with low ship density, the continuous use of the offshore area trajectory prediction method for ship track domain measurement will lead to poor classification effects. Therefore, according to the density of ship distribution, the method in this paper needs to choose the KNN algorithm to predict the peak time as the point at which the sea borders ship prior to this point in time, defined as the offshore waters, is optimized by KNN algorithm.

The steps of the method to predict the ship trajectory based on the KNN algorithm are as follows.

Step 1: Prepare and preprocess data;

Step 2: Select the trajectory data of the ship sailing from offshore to offshore in the experimental data set, and get the trajectory data of the surrounding ships in different time intervals corresponding to the trajectory.

Step 3: Experiment with the data of different time intervals obtained in the first step separately using the KNN algorithm, and optimize them using the leave-one-out method, and finally obtain the classification accuracy.

Step 4: analyze the results obtained in the second step and select the peak point of KNN classification accuracy as the dividing point of offshore and distant sea areas.

According to the actual environment and ship type factors in the offshore area, the reference data of a single ship is rich, which is suitable for trajectory prediction based on the machine learning classification method. For a ship in the open sea, its track can be regarded as the single ship track in the region. There is little that can be predicted on the influences among the trajectories of other ships, As the other ships have little influence on the predicted ship's trajectory, the accuracy of the trajectory prediction method in the offshore area decreases. Moreover, the amount of track data of a single ship in the open sea is large, and the fluctuation of the ship's track is small. Thus, it is suitable for adopting deep learning methods to predict the position based on historical track data.

3.3. Trajectory Prediction Method for the Open Sea Area

It can be regarded that the track of a ship in the open sea will not be affected by the track of other ships. The neural network method can implicitly consider the weather and sea area influence factors of the ship track in the open sea area. On the other hand, the ship track strongly correlates with time.

LSTM is usually suitable for dealing with issues sensitive to time series [41]. LSTM can learn long-term dependence and has the form of a repeat module chain of a neural network, but it has a different structure in Recurrent Neural Network from other neural networks [42,43]. LSTM has a four-layer structure in which the layers uniquely interact with each other, and its selective memory-forget mechanism design makes it a powerful tool for sequence generation and prediction [44]. As shown in Figure 2, the key to LSTM is the cell state, the line running horizontally through the top of Figure 2B represents the cell state.

The LSTM can delete and add information to the cell state, which is enabled by a structure called a gate. As shown in Figure 2C, a gate is an optional way to let information through. It consists of a sigmoid neural network layer and a dot multiplication operation.

The ship trajectory prediction method for the open sea area based on LSTM performs the following steps.

Step 1: determine what information should be discarded from the cell state, which is implemented by the Sigmoid layer called "forget gate" (f_t). It looks at h_{t-1} (the previous output) and x_t (the current input), and outputs the number between 0 and 1 for each number in the cell state C_{t-1} (the previous state) as Formula (12). Here, 1 represents complete retention and 0 represents complete deletion.

$$f_t = \sigma\left(W_f * [h_{t-1}, x_t] + b_f\right) \tag{12}$$

where $\sigma(z) = \frac{1}{1+e^{-z}}$.

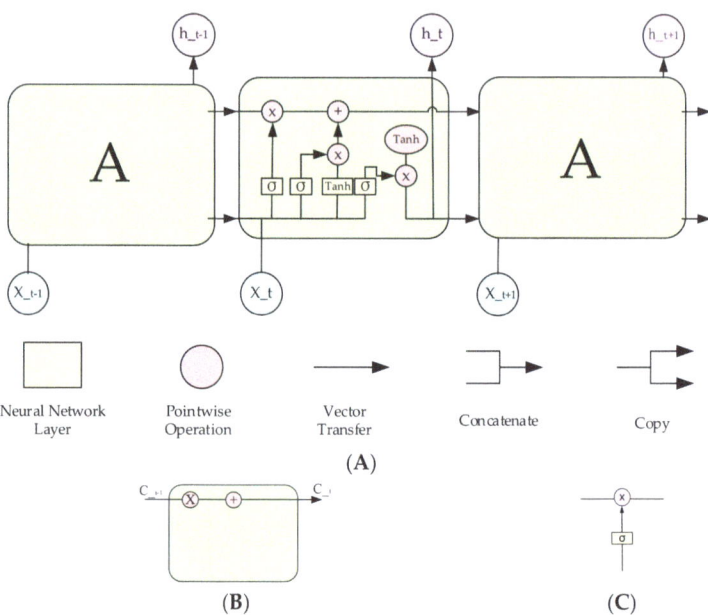

Figure 2. LSTM neural network structure diagram. (**A**) Repeated modules in LSTM contain four layers of interactive neural network. (**B**) Cell status. (**C**) Repeated modules in LSTM contain four layers.

Step 2: decide what information is to be stored in the cell state. The Sigmoid layer, called the Input Gate layer i_t, determines which values will be updated. The TANH layer then creates candidate vector C_t, which will be added to the state of the cell as the Formulas (13) and (14).

$$i_t = \sigma(W_i * [h_{t-1}, x_t] + b_i) \quad (13)$$

$$\widetilde{C}_t = tanh(W_c * [h_{t-1}, x_t] + b_C) \quad (14)$$

where $tanh(z) = \frac{e^x - e^{-x}}{e^x + e^{-x}}$.

Step 3: update the previous state value, C_{t-1}, and update it to C_t. Multiply the previous state value to express the part expected to be forgotten. All these values are then added to $i_t \widetilde{C}_t$ to create new candidate values as the Formula (15).

$$C_t = f_t * C_{t-1} + i_t * \widetilde{C}_t \quad (15)$$

Step 4: run a Sigmoid layer that determines which parts of the cell state to output. The cell state is then passed through tanh (normalizing the value to between -1 and 1) and multiplied by the output of the Sigmoid gate as the Formula (16).

$$O_t = \sigma(W_o * [h_{t-1}, x_t] + b_o) \quad (16)$$

where $h_t = o_t * tanh(C_t)$.

The tunable elements of the LSTM model can be divided into two broad categories, parameters, and hyperparameters. Although parameters are model elements learned directly from training data, there is no available analysis formula to calculate appropriate values, therefore, it is not possible to estimate the hyperparameters directly from training data, and they are usually specified manually based on heuristic methods [45].

The main hyperparameters that affect the performance of neural networks are the number of hidden layer layers, the number of nodes in each layer, the Activation Function in each layer, the Batch size, and the Dropout rate in each layer. Dropout rates apply to deep artificial neural networks by randomly deleting nodes (and their connections) from nodes to reduce model over-fitting during training. Dropout rates control for the likelihood of such a random effect occurring at each node.

These layers control the depth of the neural network. Increasing the depth of the network will increase its ability to learn features at different levels of abstraction. Excessive increasing depth will lead to over-fitting of the model. The number of nodes in each layer controls its width. Increasing the width will increase its memory capacity, and if the propagation depth is excessively increased, the gradient amplitude will be sharply reduced, which will lead to slow weight update of shallow neurons, and result in gradient dispersion.

Given a neural network with input layer X, a hidden layer of Z_m with M nodes and a regressor of the output layer composed of a single node, the form of each node is as the Formulas (17) and (18).

$$Z_m = \sigma\left(\alpha_{0m} + a_m^T x\right) \tag{17}$$

$$Y = f(X) = g\left(w_0 + w^T Z\right) \tag{18}$$

where $Z = (Z_1, Z_2......, Z_m)$, $\sigma(*)$ is the activation function, and $g(*)$ is the optional output function. The sigmoID, TANH, or Relu functions are the main activation functions.

The batch size specifies the number of training instances entered into the model before updating the model parameters. Larger batches reduce the computational cost required, which may result in local optimality.

To sum up, when it comes to the trajectory prediction of ships in the open sea, it is necessary to preprocess the trajectory data of ships first, screen the data sensitive to time series as characteristic values, then convert these characteristic values into time series, and train the model by adjusting the hyperparameters of the neural network. The prediction of ship trajectory can then be realized after the training.

3.3.1. Parameter Settings

Hyperparameter selection of KNN algorithm: the value of weight a is 0.7, 0.8, 0.9, and the value range of k is [11,24], parameters are mainly used for tuning hyperparameters using grid search methods, parameter settings are shown in Table 2.

Table 2. Information of KNN parameters.

Hyperparameter	Value
A	0.7, 0.8, 0.9
K	11–24

LSTM network parameters are set as follows: the neural network layer is set to 3 layers, the LSTM network width of layer 1 is set to 64, the Dropout rate is set to 0.3, and the activation function is set to ReLU. The LSTM network width of layer 2 is set to 128, the Dropout rate is set to 0.3, and the activation function is set to ReLU. The width of the output gate is set to 2, the activation function is set to ReLU, the Optimizer of the neural network is set to Adam, and the number of samples contained in each batch in gradient Descent is 64. The epoch value of training model iteration times was 100 when training terminated. The structure of the LSTM neural network is shown in Table 3.

Table 3. Information of neural network parameters.

Hyperparameter	Value
Network depth	3
LSTM_1 width	64
LSTM_2 width	128
Dense width	2
Layer 1 Dropout rate	0.3
Layer 2 Dropout rate	0.3
Layer 1 Activation function	ReLU
Layer 2 Activation function	ReLU
Layer 3 Activation function	ReLU
Optimizer	Adam
Batch size	64
Epochs	100

3.3.2. Evaluation Criteria

In this paper, three evaluation criteria are used to evaluate the effect of the method on ship trajectory prediction: accuracy, mean square error, and coefficient of determination. Accuracy ACC refers to the degree to which the average value measured several times is consistent with the actual value under certain experimental conditions. It is expressed by error and used to indicate the size of systematic error.

Mean-square error (MSE) can be used to evaluate the degree of data change. The smaller the MSE value is, the better accuracy the prediction model has in describing experimental data. The real value-predicted value is adopted, and then the square is followed by the sum and average. The calculation formula is as the Formula (19).

$$MSE = \frac{1}{m}\sum_{i=1}^{m}(y_i - \hat{y}_i)^2 \qquad (19)$$

The R2 coefficient, also known as the coefficient of determination, measures the overall fitting degree of the regression equation and expresses the overall relationship between the dependent variable and all independent variables. The closer R2_score is to 1, the better the regression fitting effect is. Its calculation formula is as the Formula (20).

$$R2 = 1 - \frac{\sum_{i=1}^{m}(y_i - \hat{y}_i)^2}{\sum_{i=1}^{m}(y_i - \bar{y}_i)^2} \qquad (20)$$

4. Experiment and Verification

4.1. Preparation for Experiment

4.1.1. Dataset

In the sea area division experiment, the data used in this experiment are from the AIS data of the sea area near Xiamen Port, Fujian Province, China [46], The dataset covers the period from 1 January 2018, to 3 January 2019, The latitude range covered by the dataset is 24.16° N to 24.61° N, and the longitude range covered by the dataset is 117.84° E to 118.63° E. The data used in the experiments are parsed AIS data and do not require the use of a GIS tool.

The data used in this experiment is a random sample of 30 ships in the dataset and divided into 8 time periods. The 30 ships contain a total of 2,915,683 trajectory data. A total of 200 track points were selected for each ship in each time period, and a total of 48,000 data samples were used for the KNN algorithm experiment. The time span was from 12:52:54 on 25 November 2018, to 14:40:25 on 21 December 2018. The latitude and longitude were selected from 118.02–118.15° and 24.33–24.5°.

In the experiment of trajectory prediction in offshore waters, 30 ships near Xiamen port were randomly selected with their corresponding 200 trajectory point data, and a total of 6000 pieces of data samples were selected for the KNN algorithm experiment. The time span was from 11:46:46 on 21 December 2018, to 12:05:54 on 21 December 2018. Its latitude and longitude were $118° \pm 1°$ and $24° \pm 1°$, respectively.

In the open sea area trajectory prediction experiment, the track data of a ship near Xiamen port were selected, and the MMSI value of the ship was 41,369 ****, a total of 9571 data samples were used for the experiment. The time span was from 11:46 min 41 s on 21 December 2018 to 7:30 min 22 s on 3 January 2019, with latitude and longitude of 118.06–118.07° and 24.483–24.484°.

The data fields are shown as in Table 4.

Table 4. Data field description.

Field	Instructions
MMSI	Ship's identity
Longitude	Longitude
Latitude	Latitude
SOG	Ground speed

4.1.2. Experimental Environment

The experimental hardware environment in this paper is Intel(R) Core(TM) i7-8700 octa-core CPU (3.20 GHz), 8 GB RAM; the software experimental environment is Windows10 (Microsoft, Redmond, Washington, DC, USA), Pycharm2020 (JetBrains, Prague, Czech Republic), Python3.8, Scikit-learn 0.20 and TensorFlow2.0.

4.2. Sea Area Division Experiment

Aiming at the problem of how to divide sea areas, the AIS data in different time stamps (Unix Timestamp) were used for the experimental test of the optimized KNN algorithm. The experimental results showed that the Timestamp of 1,545,371,999 (Unix Timestamp) should be selected for the threshold of division between offshore sea area and open sea area. The data of ships with a time stamp less than 1,545,371,999 is regarded as data in the offshore sea, and data of ships with a timestamp greater than 1,545,371,999 is regarded as data in the open sea. According to the nuclear density graph, the density of ships decreases with the increase of time stamps.

The Unix timestamp, which was defined as the total number of seconds from 00:00:00, 01, 01, 1970 GMT to the present, was added to the original AIS data, and the timestamp node was selected to conduct an experiment every 200 data pieces.

Experimental results show that when the optimized KNN algorithm is used for ship trajectory prediction, the timestamp reaches 154,537,199 (Unix timestamp), and the prediction accuracy of the KNN algorithm reaches the peak of 99.1%, after which, the accuracy of the KNN algorithm in trajectory prediction begins to decline. Experimental results are shown in Figure 3.

Shown in Figures 4 and 5 A–D are the four moments during the voyage of the ship, the Maritime Mobile Service Identify (MMSI) number of the ship is 15,453 ****, Figure 4 shows the prediction accuracy of the KNN algorithm at four different times, The horizontal and vertical coordinates in Figure 5 represent the latitude and longitude, and the change in color depth represents the change in the density of ships. The darker the color in Figure 5, the higher the density of the ships. As can be seen from Figures 4 and 5, as the ship density increases, the prediction accuracy of the KNN algorithm also increases, both the prediction accuracy and the ship density peaked at time c, but as the ship density decreases, the accuracy of the KNN algorithm's prediction also decreases.

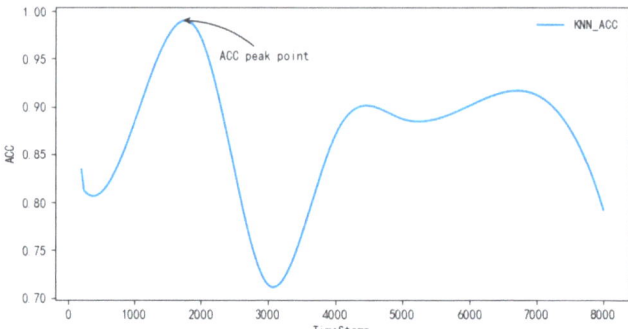

Figure 3. KNN_ACC prediction accuracy diagram.

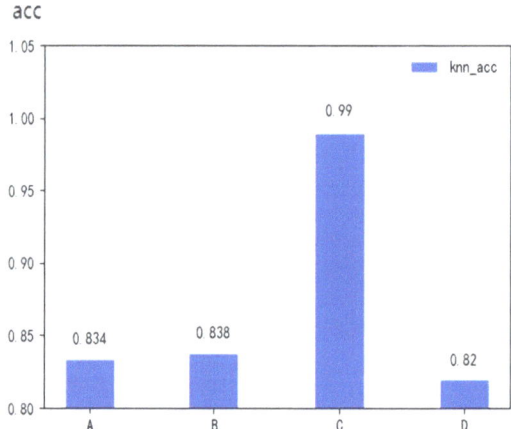

Figure 4. The prediction accuracy of KNN in each density diagram.

4.3. Trajectory Prediction in the Offshore Sea

4.3.1. Experiment Content and Results

Due to the small amount of trajectory data of a single ship in the offshore area, there is insufficient training data for neural network training. The KNN algorithm is used to classify ship trajectories, and ship trajectories belonging to the same class are regarded as the same trajectory. That is, according to the trajectory data within a certain time interval, the longitude and latitude values of ships of the same category at the next moment are regarded as the ones of ships to be predicted.

After optimizing the similarity distance formula of the KNN algorithm, adding longitude and latitude and ground speed (SOG) as parameters, and setting weights as hyperparameters, AIS data were allocated into training sets and test sets in a ratio of 8:2 for the experiments. The Leave-One-Out (LOO) method was used to obtain the best hyperparameter values. The optimal hyperparameter is substituted into the KNN algorithm to verify its classification results.

The first 10 predicted results (MMSI values) are shown as examples: ['41,369 ****', '41,245 ****', '41,370 ****', '41,275 ****', '41,370 ****', '22,180 ****', '41,275 ****', '41,233 ****', '41,370 ****', '11,133 ****'].

Experimental results show that the optimal hyperparameter of the algorithm is K = 22. A = 0.9. The experimental accuracy was 0.947. To verify the accuracy of the prediction of the KNN algorithm. The confusion matrix of the classification results of the KNN algorithm is plotted. The total number of experimental samples is 440 data, which are divided into 11 classes, and the horizontal coordinates are the predicted values and the vertical coordinates are the actual values, the diagonal line in the figure is TP (True Position), and the test results are shown in Figure 6.

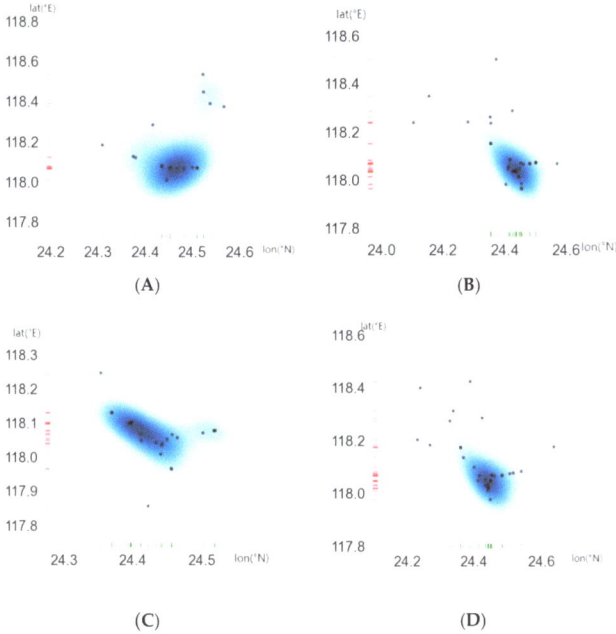

Figure 5. The ship density distribution diagram. (**A**) Schematic of ship density at moment A, (**B**) Schematic of ship density at moment B, (**C**) Schematic of ship density at moment C, (**D**) Schematic of ship density at moment D.

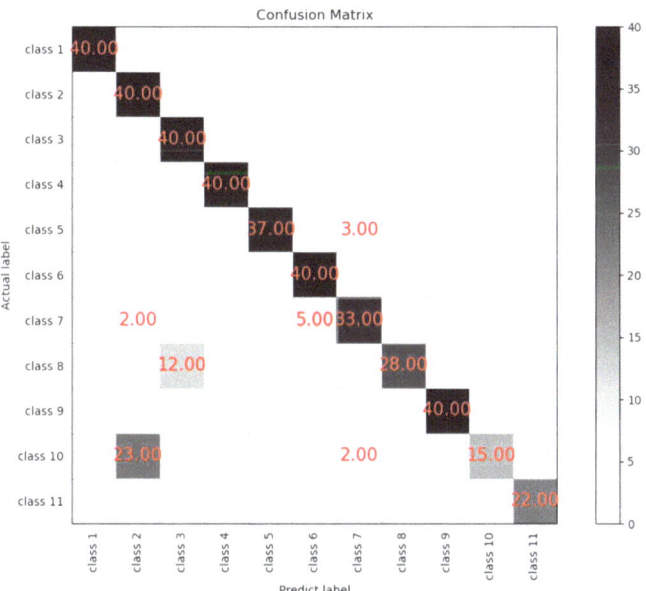

Figure 6. Confusion matrix plot of the KNN algorithm.

4.3.2. Experiment Comparison

The Leave-One-Out (LOO) method is to divide a large dataset into K small datasets, among which K-1 is used as the training set and the remaining one as the test set, and then select the next one as the test set and the remaining K-1 as the training set. The accuracy of classification is adopted as the evaluation standard. Experimental results show that, when the hyperparameter K is 22 and a is 0.9, the algorithm achieves the best effect and the accuracy is 83.1% in the test set. The comparison effect is shown in Figure 7.

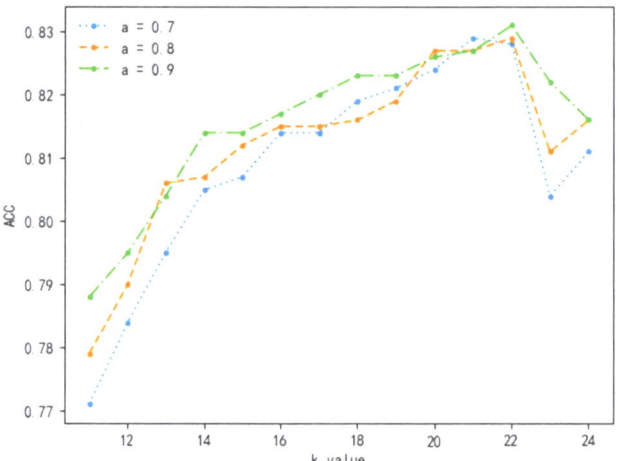

Figure 7. Comparison of KNN prediction results under different parameters.

The comparison results are shown in Table 5.

Table 5. Experimental results of leaving-one method.

k \ a	0.7	0.8	0.9
11	0.771	0.779	0.788
12	0.784	0.790	0.795
13	0.795	0.806	0.804
14	0.805	0.807	0.814
15	0.807	0.812	0.814
16	0.814	0.815	0.817
17	0.814	0.815	0.820
18	0.819	0.816	0.823
19	0.821	0.819	0.823
20	0.824	0.827	0.826
21	0.829	0.827	0.827
22	0.828	0.829	0.831
23	0.804	0.811	0.822
24	0.811	0.816	0.816

4.4. Trajectory Prediction in the Open Sea
Experiment Content and Results

Since AIS initial data cannot be put directly into the LSTM model for training, it needs to be processed as the serialized data first, turning it into temporal data as the input of the neural network and deleting AIS null values in the original data, the neural network input for the first 15 timestamp vessel position information, outputting the ship position information for the next time stamp, and then normalizing the data. The experiment divided the data into three parts according to the ratio of 8:1:1 for the train, validation, and test sets. The training set is used for neural network training, and the verification set is used to verify the loss value in neural network training and display the model's performance on the verification set. Finally, the model completed by training is predicted on the test set.

The LSTM network uses a 5-layer network structure and dropout layer to prevent overfitting in the network structure except for the output input layer, with a dropout rate of 0.3. The Relu function is used as the activation function of the neural network, the optimizer is Adam, and the MSE is used to measure the training loss of the neural network. 100 iterations are used to train the neural network. The experimental results show that the neural network Loss values tend to be smooth after 40–50 epochs.

Experimental results show that the R2 value of longitude and latitude prediction by this method is 99% and the mean square error is only 2.92×10^{-9}. The ship trajectory prediction results are shown in Figure 8.

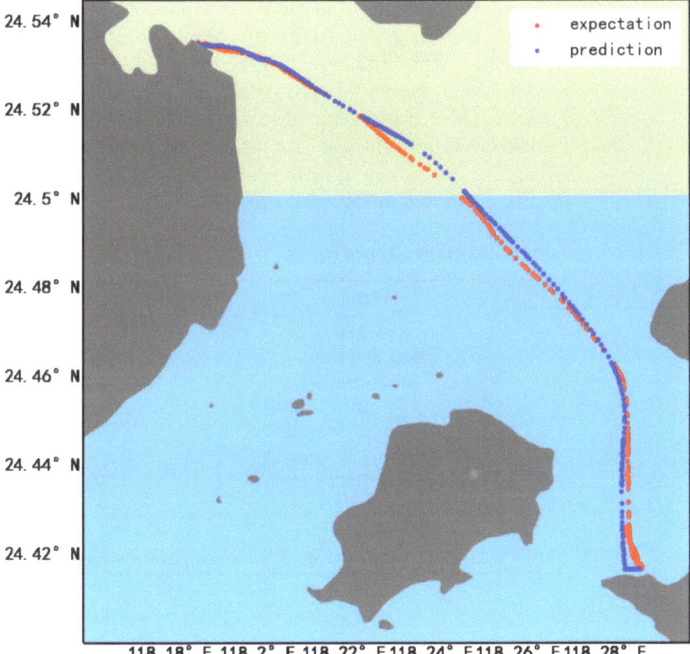

Figure 8. AIS trajectory prediction effect diagram.

To achieve better prediction of ship trajectories using neural networks, the longitude and latitude values predicted by the different number of previous timestamps were compared, the experiment was conducted five times in total with the results averaged. The results show that the neural network achieved better prediction results when the number of previous timestamps using prediction was greater than 10. The results were compared from five aspects: loss value, accuracy, running time, mean square error, and R2 value, after the number of predicted timestamps reaches 10, the loss values and the accuracy of the predictions achieve better results, as shown in Table 6.

Table 6. Comparison of prediction effects with the different number of timestamps.

Number of AIS Data Evaluation Standard	5	10	15	20	30
Loss	0.07516	0.00028	0.0005	0.0005	0.00048
Accuracy	99.45%	99.62%	99.73%	99.73%	99.72%
Running time	0.67 s	0.66 s	0.68 s	0.68 s	0.67 s
MSE	9.46×10^{-5}	3.69×10^{-9}	7.52×10^{-9}	7.52×10^{-9}	8.19×10^{-10}
R2	0.95	0.98	0.98	0.98	0.99

4.5. Verification of Experimental Results

4.5.1. The Experimental Results

Methods proposed in top papers in recent years are selected, and the experimental methods in these papers were reproduced. Nine trajectory prediction methods are selected, which are HMM, Seq2Seq-single, Seq2Seq-multi, BP(back propagation), Kalman filtering model, Linear kernel function SVM, Polynomial kernel function SVM, Recurrent Neural Network (RNN), and Gated Recurrent Unit (GRU), the same AIS data used for this paper are used in the experiment, and mean square error (MSE) is used to evaluate the prediction effect. The experimental methods in these papers were reproduced and the experimental results are shown in Table 7.

Table 7. Experimental results.

Method	Mean-Square Error
HMM	0.0074
Seq2Seq-single	0.0079
Seq2Seq-multi	0.0062
BP	5.766×10^{-5}
Kalman filter model	1.27×10^{-6}
Linear kernel function SVM	0.98
Polynomial kernel function SVM	1.003
RNN	2.40×10^{-7}
GRU	0.004
KNN-LSTM	2.92×10^{-9}

From the experimental results, the MSE of the KNN-LSTM hybrid method proposed in this paper is far lower than other methods and has better performance in ship trajectory prediction.

In order to reflect the difference of the prediction accuracy before and after the division of the sea area, the error value of the prediction of the offshore sea area and the open sea area was counted, and good prediction results were achieved in both the offshore sea area and the open sea area by this method, and the experimental results are shown in Table 8.

Table 8. Comparison of predicted results for offshore area and open sea area.

Description	Error Value
Minimum longitude error of offshore area prediction results	0.005126
Maximum longitude error of offshore area prediction results	0.008338
Minimum latitude error of offshore area prediction results	0.003233
Maximum latitude error of offshore area prediction results	0.003403
Minimum longitude error of open sea area prediction results	0.000184
Maximum longitude error of open sea area prediction results	0.001337
Minimum latitude error of open sea area prediction results	0.000436
Maximum latitude error of open sea area prediction results	0.007026

4.5.2. Comparison of Experimental Results

The BP neural network method proposed by Zhang Z et al. [47] and the Kalman filtering algorithm mentioned by Jiang et al. [19] were selected to reproduce AIS data using the same method as in this paper, and mean square error was selected as the evaluation standard. The experimental results show that the MSE value of the BP neural network is 7.482, while the MSE value of the Kalman filter algorithm is 2.25×10^{-6}.

From the experimental results, the MSE of the KNN-LSTM hybrid method proposed in this paper is far lower than other methods and has better performance in ship trajectory prediction. The model prediction time is controlled within 0.86 s and meets the needs of ship position prediction for a long time interval. The experimental results are shown in Table 9.

Table 9. Results contrast.

Method	Mean-Square Error
BP neural network	7.482
Kalman filtering algorithm	2.25×10^{-6}
KNN-LSTM	2.92×10^{-9}

5. Conclusions

This paper proposed a new vessel trajectory prediction method based on the trajecto-ry prediction of different ship densities in different sea areas. In the offshore sea area, the accuracy of the improved KNN algorithm for ship category judgment reaches 94.7%, which makes up for the poor prediction effect of the neural network due to the lack of training data. Our future work is mainly to cluster ship trajectories, and the result of ship clustering is used as the label value to predict the trajectory of the offshore sea. In the open sea area, the R2 value of the LSTM neural network for ship trajectory prediction reaches about 99%, and the mean square error value is in the order of 10^{-9}. According to the ex-perimental comparison results, this method's effectiveness is significantly superior to other methods. The next research step is to predict the ship's trajectory based on weather factors and sea conditions.

Author Contributions: Conceptualization, L.Z. and Y.Z.; methodology, L.Z.; software, L.Z., J.S. and W.L.; validation, L.Z., J.S. and W.L.; formal analysis, W.L., J.L. and Y.Y.; investigation, L.Z., J.S. and W.L.; resources, Y.Z., W.L. and Y.Y.; data curation, L.Z. and J.S.; writing—original draft preparation, L.Z. and J.S.; writing—review and editing, L.Z., J.S. and W.L.; visualization, J.S. and J.L.; supervision, Y.Z., W.L. and Y.Y.; project administration, Y.Z., W.L. and Y.Y.; funding acquisition, Y.Z. All authors have read and agreed to the published version of the manuscript.

Funding: This research was funded by Key Research and Development Program of China, grant number 2020YFB1712201 and 2021YFC2802503; Key Research and Development Program of Shaanxi Province, grant number 2021ZDLGY05-05.

Data Availability Statement: The data presented in this study are available from https://www.vtexplorer.com (accessed on 10 December 2018).

Acknowledgments: We would like to thank the reviewers for their helpful comments.

Conflicts of Interest: The authors declare no conflict of interest.

References

1. Liu, C.; Wang, J.; Liu, A.; Cai, Y.; Ai, B. An Asynchronous Trajectory Matching Method Based on Piecewise Space-Time Constraints. *IEEE Access* **2020**, *8*, 224712–224728. [CrossRef]
2. Iphar, C.; Napoli, A.; Ray, C. Detection of false AIS messages for the improvement of maritime situational awareness. In Proceedings of the OCEANS 2015—MTS/IEEE, Washington, DC, USA, 19–22 October 2015; pp. 1–7. [CrossRef]
3. Gasparin, A.; Lukovic, S.; Alippi, C. Deep learning for time series forecasting: The electric load case. *CAAI Trans. Intell. Technol.* **2022**, *7*, 1–25. [CrossRef]
4. Mukherjee, S.; Sadhukhan, B.; Sarkar, N.; Roy, D.; De, S. Stock market prediction using deep learning algorithms. *CAAI Trans. Intell. Technol.* **2021**, 8–31. [CrossRef]

5. Yang, C.-H.; Lin, G.-C.; Wu, C.-H.; Liu, Y.-H.; Wang, Y.-C.; Chen, K.-C. Deep Learning for Vessel Trajectory Prediction Using Clustered AIS Data. *Mathematics* **2022**, *10*, 2936. [CrossRef]
6. Graser, A.; Dragaschnig, M.; Widhalm, P.; Koller, H.; Brändle, N. Exploratory Trajectory Analysis for Massive Historical AIS Datasets. In Proceedings of the 2020 21st IEEE International Conference on Mobile Data Management (MDM), Versailles, France, 30 June 2020–3 July 2020; IEEE: Piscataway, NJ, USA.
7. Cui, H.; Zhang, F.; Li, M.; Cui, Y.; Wang, R. A Novel Driving-Strategy Generating Method of Collision Avoidance for Unmanned Ships Based on Extensive-Form Game Model with Fuzzy Credibility Numbers. *Mathematics* **2022**, *10*, 3316. [CrossRef]
8. Yuan, X.; Zhang, D.; Zhang, J.; Zhang, M.; Soares, C.G. A novel real-time collision risk awareness method based on velocity obstacle considering uncertainties in ship dynamics. *Ocean. Eng.* **2020**, *220*, 108436. [CrossRef]
9. Sutulo, S.; Moreira, L.; Soares, C.G. Mathematical models for ship path prediction in manoeuvring simulation systems. *Ocean. Eng.* **2002**, *29*, 1–19. [CrossRef]
10. Lv, Q.; Qiao, Y.; Ansari, N.; Liu, J.; Yang, J. Big Data Driven Hidden Markov Model Based Individual Mobility Prediction at Points of Interest. *IEEE Trans. Veh. Technol.* **2017**, *66*, 5204–5216. [CrossRef]
11. Feng, J.; Li, Y.; Zhang, C.; Sun, F.; Meng, F.; Guo, A.; Jin, D. DeepMove: Predicting Human Mobility with Attentional Recurrent Networks. In Proceedings of the 2018 World Wide Web Conference, Lyon, France, 23–27 April 2018.
12. Zhang, Z.; Ni, G.; Xu, Y. Ship Trajectory Prediction based on LSTM Neural Network. In Proceedings of the 2020 IEEE 5th Information Technology and Mechatronics Engineering Conference (ITOEC), Chongqing, China, 12–14 June 2020; IEEE: Piscataway, NJ, USA.
13. Available online: https://ais.msa.gov.cn/ (accessed on 1 May 2020).
14. Birgillito, G.; Rindone, C.; Vitetta, A. Passenger mobility in a discontinuous space: Modelling Access/Egress to maritime barrier in a case study. *J. Adv. Transp.* **2018**, *2018*, 1–13. [CrossRef]
15. Abdelaal, M.; Fränzle, M.; Hahn, A. Nonlinear Model Predictive Control for trajectory tracking and collision avoidance of underactuated vessels with disturbances. *Ocean. Eng.* **2018**, *160*, 168–180. [CrossRef]
16. Vijverberg, K. Radboud University Object Localization and Path Prediction Using Radar and Other Sources Towards Autonomous Shipping. *Radboud Univ.* **2018**.
17. Zhang, K.; Xiong, J.J.; Li, F.; Fu, T.T. Bayesian Trajectory Prediction for a Hypersonic Gliding Reentry Vehicle Based on Intent Inference. *Yuhang Xuebao/J. Astronaut.* **2018**, *39*, 1258–1265.
18. Virjonen, P.; Nevalainen, P.; Pahikkala, T.; Heikkonen, J. Ship Movement Prediction Using k-NN Method. In Proceedings of the 2022 8th International Conference on Energy Efficiency and Agricultural Engineering (EE&AE), Olsztyn, Poland, 21–23 June 2018; pp. 304–309.
19. Jiang, B.; Guan, J.; Zhou, W.; Chen, X. Vessel Trajectory Prediction Algorithm Based on Polynomial Fitting Kalman Filtering. *J. Signal Process.* **2019**, *5*, 74I–746. [CrossRef]
20. Xie, G.; Gao, H.; Qian, L.; Huang, B.; Li, K.; Wang, J. Vehicle Trajectory Prediction by Integrating Physics- and Maneuver-Based Approaches Using Interactive Multiple Models. *IEEE Trans. Ind. Electron.* **2017**, *65*, 5999–6008. [CrossRef]
21. Burger, C.N.; Grobler, T.L.; Kleynhans, W. Discrete Kalman Filter and Linear Regression Comparison for Vessel Coordinate Prediction. In Proceedings of the 2020 21st IEEE International Conference on Mobile Data Management (MDM), Versailles, France, 30 June 2020–3 July 2020; IEEE: Piscataway, NJ, USA.
22. Hexeberg, S.; Flåten, A.L.; Eriksen, B.H.; Brekke, E.F. AIS-based vessel trajectory prediction. In Proceedings of the 2017 20th International Conference on Information Fusion (Fusion), Xi'an, China, 10–13 July 2017; pp. 1–8. [CrossRef]
23. Liu, J.; Shi, G.; Zhu, K. Online multiple outputs least-squares support vector regression model of ship trajectory prediction based on automatic information system data and selection mechanism. *IEEE Access* **2020**, *8*, 154727–154745. [CrossRef]
24. Murray, B.; Perera, L.P. A Data-Driven Approach to Vessel Trajectory Prediction for Safe Autonomous Ship Operations. In Proceedings of the the 13th International Conference on Digital Information Management (ICDIM 2018), Berlin, Germany, 24–26 September 2018.
25. Bao, K.; Bi, J.; Gao, M.; Sun, Y.; Zhang, X.; Zhang, W. An Improved Ship Trajectory Prediction Based on AIS Data Using MHA-BiGRU. *J. Mar. Sci. Eng.* **2022**, *10*, 804. [CrossRef]
26. Last, P.; Hering-Bertram, M.; Linsen, L. Interactive history-based vessel movement prediction. *IEEE Intell. Syst.* **2019**, *34*, 3–13. [CrossRef]
27. Volkova, T.A.; Balykina, Y.E.; Bespalov, A. Predicting Ship Trajectory Based on Neural Networks Using AIS Data. *J. Mar. Sci. Eng.* **2021**, *9*, 254. [CrossRef]
28. Zeng, W.; Quan, Z.; Zhao, Z.; Xie, C.; Lu, X. A Deep Learning Approach for Aircraft Trajectory Prediction in Terminal Airspace. *IEEE Access* **2020**, *8*, 151250–151266. [CrossRef]
29. Han, P.; Wang, W.; Shi, Q.; Yang, J. Real-time Short-Term Trajectory Prediction Based on GRU Neural Network. In Proceedings of the 2019 IEEE/AIAA 38th Digital Avionics Systems Conference (DASC), San Diego, CA, USA, 8–12 September 2019; pp. 1–8.
30. Liu, Y.; Hansen, M. Predicting Aircraft Trajectories: A Deep Generative Convolutional Recurrent Neural Networks Approach. *arXiv* **2018**, arXiv:1812.11670.
31. Lin, Y.; Zhang, J.W.; Liu, H. An algorithm for trajectory prediction of flight plan based on relative motion between positions. *Front. Inf. Technol. Electron. Eng.* **2018**, *19*, 95–106. [CrossRef]
32. Yang, Y.; Zhu, Q.; Hu, Q.; Wen, X. High-precision intelligent track prediction under multi-dimensional conditions. In Proceedings of the 2020 39th Chinese Control Conference (CCC), Shenyang, China, 27–30 July 2020.

33. Wang, Q.; Zhang, Z.; Wang, Z.; Wang, Y.; Zhou, W. The trajectory prediction of spacecraft by grey method. *Meas. Sci. Technol.* **2016**, *27*, 085011. [CrossRef]
34. Qiao, S.; Shen, D.; Wang, X.; Han, N.; Zhu, W. A Self-Adaptive Parameter Selection Trajectory Prediction Approach via Hidden Markov Models. *IEEE Trans. Intell. Transp. Syst.* **2015**, *16*, 284–296. [CrossRef]
35. Ma, H.; Zuo, Y.; Li, T. Vessel Navigation Behavior Analysis and Multiple-Trajectory Prediction Model Based on AIS Data. *J. Adv. Transp.* **2022**, *2022*, 1–10. [CrossRef]
36. Wang, X.; Jiang, X.; Wu, Y.; Lin, M. A Second-Order HMM Trajectory Prediction Method based on the Spark Platform. *J. Inf. Hiding Multim. Signal Process* **2019**, *10*, 346–358.
37. Zhang, L.; Zhu, Y.; Lu, W.; Wen, J.; Cui, J. A detection and restoration approach for vessel trajectory anomalies based on AIS. *J. Northwestern Polytech. Univ.* **2021**, *39*, 119–125. [CrossRef]
38. Wang, L.; Khan, L.; Thuraisingham, B. An Effective Evidence Theory Based K-Nearest Neighbor (KNN) Classification. In Proceedings of the 2008 IEEE/WIC/ACM International Conference on Web Intelligence and Intelligent Agent Technology, Sydney, Australia, 9–12 December 2008; Volume 1, pp. 797–801.
39. Xiang, Y.; Cao, Z.; Yao, S.; He, J. CW-KNN: An efficient KNN-based model for imbalanced dataset classification. In Proceedings of the ICCIP '18: The 4th International Conference on Communication and Information Processing, Qingdao, China, 2–4 November 2018.
40. Altman, N. An Introduction to Kernel and Nearest-Neighbor Nonparametric Regression. *Am. Stat.* **1992**, *46*, 175–185.
41. Lecun, Y.; Bengio, Y. Convolutional Networks for Images, Speech, and Time-Series. In *The Handbook of Brain Theory and Neural Networks*; The MIT Press: Cambridge, MA, USA, 1995.
42. Xu, X. Context-based Trajectory Prediction with LSTM Networks. In Proceedings of the 2020 the 3rd International Conference on Computational Intelligence and Intelligent Systems, Tokyo, Japan, 13–15 November 2020.
43. Xue, H.; Huynh, D.; Reynolds, M. PoPPL: Pedestrian Trajectory Prediction by LSTM with Automatic Route Class Clustering. *IEEE Trans. Neural Netw. Learn. Syst.* **2021**, *32*, 77–90. [CrossRef]
44. Xue, P.; Liu, J.; Chen, S.; Zhou, Z.; Huo, Y.; Zheng, N. Crossing-Road Pedestrian Trajectory Prediction via Encoder-Decoder LSTM. In Proceedings of the 2019 IEEE Intelligent Transportation Systems Conference (ITSC), Auckland, New Zealand, 27–30 October 2019; pp. 2027–2033. [CrossRef]
45. Gkerekos, C.; Lazakis, I. A novel, data-driven heuristic framework for vessel weather routing. *Ocean. Eng.* **2020**, *197*, 106887. [CrossRef]
46. Historical AIS Data Services [DB/OL]. Available online: http://www.vtexplorer.com/ (accessed on 10 December 2018).
47. Zhang, Z.; Ni, G.; Xu, Y. Trajectory prediction based on AIS and BP neural network. In Proceedings of the 2020 IEEE 9th Joint International Information Technology and Artificial Intelligence Conference (ITAIC), Chongqing, China, 11–13 December 2020; Volume 9, pp. 601–605.

Article

MACA: Multi-Agent with Credit Assignment for Computation Offloading in Smart Parks Monitoring

Liang She [1,2], **Jianyuan Wang** [3,*], **Yifan Bo** [4] **and Yangyan Zeng** [5,*]

1. School of Computer Science and Engineering, Central South University, Changsha 410083, China
2. School of Computer Science, Hunan University of Technology and Business, Changsha 410205, China
3. School of Automation Science and Electrical Engineering, Beihang University, Beijing 100191, China
4. School of Computer Science and Engineering, Beihang University, Beijing 100191, China
5. School of Frontier Crossover Studies, Hunan University of Technology and Business, Changsha 410205, China
* Correspondence: wangjy90@buaa.edu.cn (J.W.); yangyanz@csu.edu.cn (Y.Z.)

Abstract: Video monitoring has a wide range of applications in a variety of scenarios, especially in smart parks. How to improve the efficiency of video data processing and reduce resource consumption have become of increasing concern. The high complexity of traditional computation offloading algorithms makes it difficult to apply them to real-time decision-making scenarios. Thus, we propose a multi-agent deep reinforcement learning algorithm with credit assignment (MACA) for computation offloading in smart park monitoring. By making online decisions after offline training, the agent can give consideration to both decision time and accuracy in effectively solving the problem of the curse of dimensionality. Via simulation, we compare the performance of MACA with traditional deep Q-network reinforcement learning algorithm and other methods. Our results show that MACA performs better in scenarios where there are a higher number of agents and can minimize request delay and reduce task energy consumption. In addition, we also provide results from a generalization capability verified experiment and ablation study, which demonstrate the contribution of MACA algorithm to each component.

Keywords: computation offloading; deep reinforcement learning; credit assignment; multi-agent; video monitoring

MSC: 68T42

1. Introduction

Video monitoring systems represent the momentous application of the Internet of Things while also playing an important role in urban security, traffic management, building security, and other fields [1]. According to data statistics, the number of global Internet video monitoring system has multiplied several fold in recent years [2], and the masses of data are bringing new challenges to video data processing. With the rise of mobile internet, it has become a new trend to offload computing tasks to the cloud center or the edge computing node of the network. Mobile edge computing (MEC) technology [3] is a distributed computing architecture and an intermediate layer connecting a traditional cloud center and devices. It was deployed as close as possible to the users and only sends necessary results to the cloud data center, which greatly reduces the time delay of the data transmission process. MEC technology aims at offloading computing tasks to mobile edge servers, which are always connected to the user device. Thus, computing intensive and delay critical tasks can be well supported because of the short distance between user devices and the mobile edge server.

This paper will focus on the computation offloading approach in smart park monitoring. In Figure 1, the video analysis data are first collected by the camera sensor and then transmitted to the MEC server for further computation. For high complexity and delay critical image processing tasks, the bottleneck to solve the delay problem is the limitation of computing capability and communication resources between the channels. The existing MEC based on video data analysis computation offloading task approaches usually tends to allocate all computing tasks to local video devices or mobile edge servers. However, both of the approaches have their own inherent problems [4]. Due to the unacceptable level of energy consumption, it is impractical to allocate sufficient computation resources to the local video device to satisfy the video analysis task. On the other extreme, offloading the entire task to the MEC consumes excessive bandwidth resources for transmitting the raw video data, which is also unrealistic because of the limitation of bandwidth resources. In order to resolve the abovementioned problems, an MEC based on computation offloading approach is proposed, in which assignment of the computing task is balanced between the local device and MEC server. However, the NP hard problem gives rise to a new issue, namely that traditional approaches often fail to provide the allocation scheme of computational offloading in time [5]. At the same time, the transmission order of multiple local devices and the time-varying communication channel raise new challenges for the computation offloading strategy.

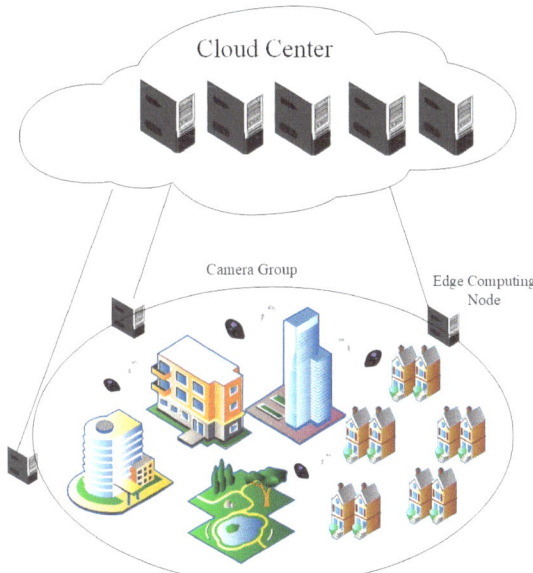

Figure 1. Computation offloading scenario comprising multiple video monitoring devices, multiple edge computing nodes, and a cloud data center. The video analysis data can be offloaded from local monitoring devices to an edge computing node and thereafter to the cloud data center.

In this paper, we aim to establish a computation offloading approach to minimize the request delay while reducing the task energy consumption. We model the computation offloading task as a cooperative multi-agent reinforcement learning (MARL) problem. We proposed a multi-agent deep reinforcement learning algorithm with credit assignment (MACA) and introduce a centralized training with decentralized execution framework. In addition, we focus on the online decision-making ability speed and the accuracy after offline training. The contributions of this paper are as follows:

(1) In order to solve the video monitoring analysis task in smart parks, the edge computing node and cloud data center are introduced to satisfy the computation offloading requirements. The system model includes multiple devices and multiple edge computing nodes, taking into account the dynamically changing communication channel states and task characteristics. We introduce reinforcement learning to overcome the

ultra-high computation time of traditional methods through offline training and online decision-making, which makes the computation offloading utilizable in real-time scenes.

(2) To deal with the curse of dimensionality caused by the expansion of the decision feasible region, we introduce a credit assignment method into value-based reinforcement learning, which is converted from being a single-agent scenario to a multi-agent scenario. The credit assignment method decomposes the global Q-value Q_{tot} to each individual Q-value Q_a, which enforces the monotonous constraint between global and individual Q-values. Meanwhile, the centralized training and decentralized execution framework makes use of the global statue information when training agents, which makes agents work more cooperatively and accelerates the training process.

(3) In addition, we introduce a double Q-network, dueling Q-network, and priority experience replay method into our proposed multi-agent reinforcement learning algorithm and analyze the contribution of each component via an ablation study. Through numerical simulation, we demonstrate that our proposed MACA algorithm can achieve better performance compared with traditional DQN algorithms and other approaches, especially when the number of agents increases. Furthermore, we also verify the generalization capability of our proposed MACA algorithm.

The rest of this paper is organized as follows: In Section 2, we introduce relevant research results of computation offloading and deep reinforcement learning algorithms. In Section 3, we introduce the system model of the computation offloading scenario and our proposed MACA multi-agent reinforcement learning algorithm, in which credit assignment is applied in the training process. Section 4 introduces the simulation experiment. Finally, Section 5 concludes this article.

2. Related Works

2.1. Computation Offloading Task

Edge computation offloading, which deploys multiple edge devices with computational capability as nodes of providing services [6], extends the concept of cloud computing. It can reduce the request delay, but the timing-vary bandwidth and resources required for users give rise to a crucial problem regarding to which server node the computational task can be offloaded such that the requirements of computational resource and delay are satisfactory. Computation offloading is one of the important research directions of edge computing. Computation offloading generally includes two aspects: one is the offload decision, which mainly concerns determining whether a computation offloading process is required and the selection of computation offloading nodes; the second is resource allocation, which aims to solve how to allocate resources for global nodes, or how to allocate communication resources in the process of offloading and transmission. The application of edge computation multi-level offloading technology in real-time video monitoring networks has important research significance. Real-time video monitoring networks need to satisfy the characteristics of low delay requirement. At the same time, due to the wide application of video monitoring networks, it is also necessary to consider reducing energy consumption in resource-constrained scenarios.

2.2. Reinforcement Learning

Reinforcement learning [7] can be seen as the process of interaction between agents and the environment in addition to the constant exploration of strategies for learning to obtain the maximum cumulative reward in experiments. In reinforce learning [8], the agent performs actions in the environment, and the environment is transformed to a new state while the agent can obtain a certain reward. The interaction process can be described as follows: at time t, the agent executes action according to the probability distribution of strategy π_t, and at the next time $t + 1$, the state of the environment changes from S_t to S_{t+1}, and propagates the agent with a certain reward R_t. The Markov process can be described as follows: at the next time $t + 1$, the state S_{t+1} of the environment is only related to S_t, and has nothing to do with the time of the past environment. Reinforcement learning is usually described using five tuples (S, A, P, R, γ), where P is the action to environment mapping and γ is the discount factor.

The reinforcement learning algorithm can be classified into different categories: according to the algorithm update mechanism, where it can be divided into a round update Monte Carlo algorithm and one-step update temporary difference algorithm; according to the consistency of policy execution and policy evaluation, where it is divided into an on-policy and an off-policy algorithm; according to whether to build a model, where it is divided into model-free algorithm and model-based algorithm; according to the way of action selection, where reinforcement learning is divided into value-based, policy-based, and actor–critic reinforcement learning algorithms. Using deep reinforcement learning, end-to-end learning from perception to decision-making is realized.

Among the value-based reinforcement learning algorithms, the traditional reinforcement learning algorithms include the Q-learning and SARSA [9] algorithm. The deep Q-network [10] algorithm is based on experience replay and estimation of the value function of the target network and surpasses human players in Atari games. Since then, there has been various variants of the DQN algorithm [11], which effectively solves the overfitting problem in the DQN algorithm and has higher learning efficiency, value function evaluation, and search ability [12].

In the model-based reinforcement learning algorithm, the strategy parameters are updated by directly searching the best strategy to maximize the return. The classic REINFORCE [13] algorithm uses the Monte Carlo method to estimate the gradient strategy. In the estimation process, the information of the whole trajectory is considered, and it has a large strategy gradient variance. By introducing the value baseline, it can effectively reduce the variance. In order to improve the stability and convergence speed of the algorithm, avoid excessive update step size, and obtain returns monotonically and incrementally to continuously obtain the optimal policy, there are trust region policy optimization algorithms (TRPO) [14], proximate policy optimization algorithms (PPO) [15] and distributed proximate policy optimization algorithms (DPPO) [16].

In the reinforcement learning algorithm based on combined value strategy, strategy and value are learned at the same time. The actor–critic algorithm [17] is used as the benchmark of the strategy gradient. The actor network trains the strategy according to the value function fed back by critic network, and the critic network trains the value function, and uses the time series difference method for one-step update. The actor–critic algorithm has the characteristics of small variance of value function estimation, high sample utilization, and fast training speed. Subsequently, a series of reinforcement learning algorithms that are improvements of the actor–critical algorithm have appeared, such as deep deterministic policy gradient algorithm (DDPG) [18], asynchronous advanced actor–critical algorithm (A3C) [19], twin delayed deep deterministic policy gradient algorithm (TD3) [20], and soft actor–critical algorithm (SAC) [21].

At present, there are many excellent algorithms to complete the control of a single agent, among which DDPG, PPO, and other deep reinforcement learning algorithms are the most effective. Strategically, a multi-agent system composed of multiple independent agents lacks flexibility, due to the complexity and dynamic characteristics of the environment. The MADDPG [22] algorithm proposed in an article published by OpenAI on nips in 2017 is an extension of the DDPG [18] algorithm, which enables an actor to learn decision-making ability through interaction with complex environments and provides a good idea for multi-agent collaborative control.

Based on reinforcement learning algorithm to solve computation offloading problem, Lee et al. [23] proposed a reinforcement learning method based on an auction mechanism to solve the problem of computation offloading using the real secondary price auction as the baseline, in which the requirements of personal rationality and incentive compatibility are met. The experimental simulation showed that the proposed method can meet the above characteristics and increase the overall income of the seller. Pradhan et al. [24] used reinforcement learning to solve the problem of computation offloading of IOT applications in multiple input and output cloud wireless access networks. A computation offloading algorithm was proposed to minimize the total transmission power of the Internet of Things, and a low complexity supervised deep learning method was used to solve the problem. The effectiveness of the method was demonstrated using comparative experiments. Zhang et al. [25] proposed a method to alleviate the heavy burden of equipment through mobile edge computing and adopted a reinforcement learning method to design different states of multiple different edge servers and offloading modes of various vehicles. The experiments show that the proposed computation offloading scheme has great advantages in optimizing system utility and improving offloading reliability. Ren et al. [26] solved the problem of fog computing access node in the industrial Internet of Things through deep reinforcement learning. The created environment has multiple IIOT devices and multiple access nodes. The multi-agent reinforcement learning method was compared with a greedy algorithm and genetic algorithm. It was shown that the proposed algorithm can overcome the dimensional curse caused by the increase of access nodes and is competitive among the many algorithms in use. Yu et al. [27] proposed a new deep simulation learning-driven MEC network edge cloud computing offload framework. By optimizing behavior cloning to minimize the offloading cost in time-varying networks, the direction and advantages of applying the deep learning method to multiple MEC research fields are discussed, including edge data analysis, dynamic resource allocation, security, and privacy.

3. The Proposed Approach

In this section, we will first establish the task model, delay model, energy consumption model, and transmission model in computation offloading and determine the goal of computation offloading tasks, namely minimizing calculation delay and energy consumption, which will play an important role in subsequent simulation experiments. The main notation in our model is listed in Abbreviations. We will then introduce the multi-agent reinforce learning framework and our proposed MACA algorithm.

3.1. Problem Definition

We consider a computation offloading scenario where a large number of video monitoring cameras are set up in the smart park, and multiple cameras transmit monitoring video data to a relay node, which can complete some computational tasks. The camera that transfers computational tasks to the same node is called a camera group. There are N camera groups that generate computationally intensive tasks. In this paper, a camera group denotes the minimum unit device for computation task offloading. We assume that the decision-making time is slotted as $t = 0, 1, \ldots$, which is called a computation offloading cycle. In a computation offloading cycle, each device generates only one computationally intensive task (if a device generates multiple tasks, the device can be decomposed into multiple devices). The task characteristics are (O_t, B_t), where O_t denotes the amount of data that needs to be uploaded to complete the task, and B_t denotes the number of CPU cycles for computing tasks (in this paper, it is assumed that the number of CPU cycles required to complete a task is unchanged no matter where the task is executed). Above the relay node, multiple edge computing access nodes are deployed in the smart park to process the computing tasks offloaded by the camera group. If the edge computing node remains busy, it can choose to further offload the computing task to the cloud data center for executing. In a computation offloading cycle, the relay node can select to execute computing task locally or offload the task to the edge computing node, the edge computing node can directly calculate the task or further offload the task to the cloud computing service center. In this way, a three-level cloud-edge-segment computation offloading scenario from camera groups to edge computing nodes to a cloud computing center is built.

Due to the limited number of edge computing nodes, it may not be enough to meet the needs of computing all tasks at the same time in one computation offloading cycle. We define the channel bandwidth between the device n and the edge computing node f as

$W_{n,f}$. Since the available bandwidth resources between device and edge computing node is time-varying, we assume that the bandwidth variation conforms to a Markov process. There are three states of original bandwidth, 0.6 times bandwidth and 0.2 times bandwidth. The transition probability between each state is shown in Figure 2.

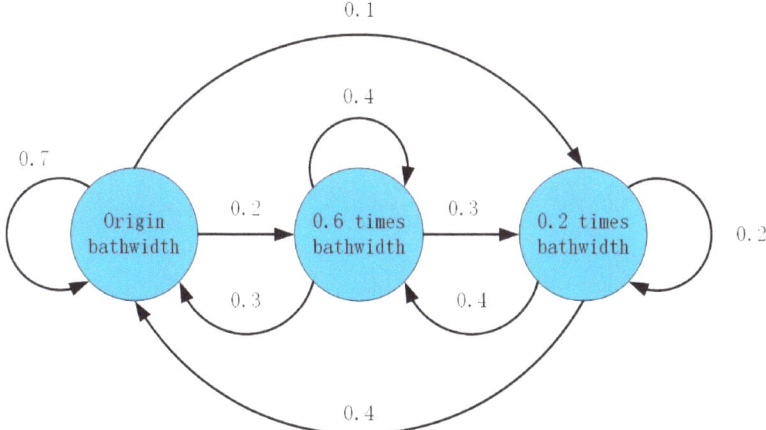

Figure 2. The transition probability between three bandwidth status, where the origin state remains unchanged with a probability of 0.7, transitions to the 0.6 times bandwidth status state with a probability of 0.2, then transitions to the 0.2 times bandwidth status with a probability of 0.1. The 0.6 times bandwidth state remains unchanged with a probability of 0.4, transitions to the 0.2 times bandwidth status state with a probability of 0.3, and then transitions to the origin bandwidth status with a probability of 0.3. The 0.2 times bandwidth state remains unchanged with a probability of 0.2, and then transitions to the 0.6 times bandwidth status state with a probability of 0.4, and then transitions to the origin bandwidth status with a probability of 0.4.

If multiple devices simultaneously select one edge computing node to offload the task, the channel bandwidth will be equally allocated to all devices to offload data. Therefore, the data offload rate of the device can be expressed as Formula (1):

$$r_{c,f} = \frac{W_{n,f}}{N} log(1 + \frac{P \cdot h}{\frac{W}{N} \cdot noise}) \tag{1}$$

where N denotes the number of devices offloading tasks at the same time, P denotes the offload power of the computation offloading task, h denotes the gain of the communication channel when the task is transmitted, and $noise$ is the variance of the complex Gaussian white channel noise. Next, we will introduce the time delay and energy consumption model of local computation.

If device n determines that the computing task R_n should be executed locally, we define the local request time delay as T_n^l. The local computing request delay only includes the CPU processing delay during the local computing of tasks. The computing capacity (CPU cycles per second) of each relay node may be different, which is expressed in F_n^l. Then, the time delay of the local calculation can be defined as Formula (2):

$$T_n^l = \frac{B_n}{F_n^l} \tag{2}$$

We define the energy consumption of tasks as E_n^l, which can be expressed as Formula (3):

$$E_n^l = B_u \cdot (F_n^l)^2 \cdot \delta_f \tag{3}$$

where B_u denotes the number of CPU cycles required by the task, δ_f denotes the calculation factor, set as 10^{-27}, and F_n^l denotes the computing capacity of the local relay node.

If device n chooses to offload task R_n in the computation process, the task needs to go through three stages: task data uploading, task calculation, and result data downloading. Due to the fact that, when computing tasks are uploaded, there is often a large amount of raw data, the data can be ignored when the results are being downloaded in contrast to when they are being uploaded, and the downlink communication capability is often strong, the delay when the task results are downloaded is not considered in this paper. Moreover, since the edge computing nodes can choose whether to further offload tasks to the cloud center via the greedy algorithm, we integrate the computing capabilities of the cloud computing center into the edge computing nodes and then only consider the computation offloading process from the device to the edge computing node.

According to the above analysis, the delay of task uploading can be expressed as:

$$T_{n,t}^o = \frac{O_n}{r_n} \tag{4}$$

where r_n denotes the data upload rate when device n is connected to the edge access node through the communication channel. Similarly, the calculation delay in the task calculation can be expressed as:

$$T_{n,p}^o = \frac{B_n}{F_f} \tag{5}$$

where F_f denotes the computing capacity of the edge computing node (CPU cycles per second). A requirement is that the sum of computing resources allocated to each task does not exceed the overall computing capacity of the current node $\sum_{n=1}^{N} \alpha_n f_n \leq F$.

The calculation delay in the whole computation offloading process can be expressed as:

$$T_n^o = T_{n,t}^o + T_{n,p}^o \tag{6}$$

Correspondingly, the energy consumption in the offloading process is calculated as:

$$E_{n,t}^o = P_n T_{n,t}^o = \frac{P_n O_n}{r_n} \tag{7}$$

where P_n denotes the energy gain in the transmission process, and the energy consumption in the calculation task can be expressed as:

$$E_{n,p}^o = B_n \cdot (F_F)^2 \cdot \delta_f \tag{8}$$

Then, the energy consumption after offloading can be expressed as:

$$E_n^o = \frac{P_n O_n}{R_n} + B_n \cdot (F_F)^2 \cdot \delta_f \tag{9}$$

3.2. Multi-Agent Reinforcement Learning Scenario

In this subsection, we first provide some necessary background on reinforcement learning as a basis for deriving our proposed algorithm. Then, we model computation offloading scenario as a multi-agent reinforcement learning process and introduce the four key elements in reinforcement learning: action, state, observation, and reward.

Differently from the reinforcement learning algorithm of a single agent, the multi-agent cooperative algorithm can be described as $\Gamma = \langle S, A, P, r, Z, O, N, \gamma \rangle$, where Γ denotes a stochastic Markov decision process. S_t denotes the global state at time step t, and the action of each agent u is $a_t^u \in A$, which generate the joint action $a_t \in A$. The mapping of action change state of the environment is $P(S_{t+1} \mid S_t, a_t) : S \times A \times S$. Since the problem is modeled as a cooperative task, all agents share a global reward function $r(S_t, a_t)$. In addition, O denotes the global observation of agents. N denotes the number of agent participate in the game. In particular, Z denotes a partial observation in which each agent draws individual observations $z \in Z$ according to the observation function $O(s) : S \to Z$.

The reward discount function is γ, which denotes the total return as $R_t = \sum_{k=0}^{\infty} \gamma^k r_{t+k}$. An agent trains its own policy $\pi^u(a_t^u \mid z_t^u)$ to maximize the expected reward. There are three standard definitions to describe a joint action policy, the state-action value function Q^π, the state value function V^π, and the advantage function A^π:

$$Q^\pi(s_t, a_t) = \mathbb{E}_{s_{t+1}, a_{t+1}}[R_t \mid s_t, a_t] \tag{10}$$

$$V^\pi(s_t) = \mathbb{E}_{s_{t+1}, a_t}[R_t \mid s_t] \tag{11}$$

$$A^\pi(s_t, a_t) = Q^\pi(s_t, a_t) - V^\pi(s_t) \tag{12}$$

All the agents work together to maximize the total reward and generate a joint policy as:

$$\pi = \arg\max_\pi \eta(\pi) \tag{13}$$

Next, we will introduce four key elements of reinforcement learning settings in the computation offloading experiment.

Action: In the video monitoring computation offloading scenario of the smart parks, each device (camera group) is set as an agent with its own individual environment observation. In each computation offloading cycle, agents make action decisions by observing the partial state of the environment. Agents can choose local computing or to offload tasks to an edge computing node.

Suppose there are N devices, each of which acts as an agent. After receiving the offloading request from a device, the agent n observes the local status Z_n. Then, the offloading decision is generated by back-propagation of the Q-network reward. In this process, due to the limitation of computing capability, we set the maximum number of CPU cycles that each edge computing node can allocate. The maximum allocatable task number that the agent can assign on each edge computing node is F_n^u, and agent n executes operation a_n, which can be expressed as:

$$a_n \in \{0, 1, 2, \ldots, f_n\} \tag{14}$$

where $a_n = 0, 1, 2, \ldots, f_{n-1}$ means that the agent chooses to offload the task, and $a_n = f_n$ means the agent chooses to complete the task locally.

State and Observation: When making offloading decisions, the agent's local observation of the environment Z_n can be defined as:

$$Z_n = \{b_l^n, O_n^t, B_n^t\} \tag{15}$$

where b_n^t denotes the channel gain state between device n and edge computing nodes, O_n^t denotes the number of bits required for the task to upload, and B_n^t denotes the CPU cycle required for the task to complete the calculation. The global observation S_n is composed of all agents' partial observations, which can be expressed as:

$$S_n = \{b^t, O^t, B^t\} \tag{16}$$

After the agent makes a decision to offload, it propagates the action to the environment and gains rewards R_t, and it then enters the next stage S_{t+1}, so as to constantly interact with the environment. Next, the obtained information is placed in the experience buffer D.

Reward: In this paper, the task of computation offloading process is set to minimize request delay and energy consumption. It is obvious that the request delay of computation offloading process is lower than the local computing because of the higher computing capability of edge computing nodes. Thus, we can define relative increments of request delay as:

$$C_t = \sum_{n=1}^{N} \frac{T_n^l - Tn_o}{T_n^l} \quad (17)$$

The smaller the value of T_l, the larger the reward value, which is consistent with our target. In the same way, we can define the relative increments of energy consumption as:

$$C_e = \sum_{n=1}^{N} \frac{E_n^l - En_o}{E_n^l} \quad (18)$$

Combined with the above time delay and energy consumption formula, the reward can be expressed as:

$$Reward = \varepsilon_t C_t + \varepsilon_e C_e \quad (19)$$

where ε_t and ε_e denote the proportion weight of request delay and energy consumption in the computation offloading task R_n, which needs to meet the constraints of $0 \leq \varepsilon_t \leq 1$, $0 \leq \varepsilon_e \leq 1$, and $\varepsilon_t + \varepsilon_e = 1$. The proportion weight may change with different task scenarios. After estimation, we take $\varepsilon_t = \varepsilon_e = 0.5$ as remaining unchanged during the entire computation offloading process in this paper.

3.3. MACA Algorithm Design for Computation Offloading

In the real computation offloading scene, monitoring devices' cooperation in making decisions in a decentralized manner. However, in the experimental environment, we can train the agents using a centralized function [28]. Thus, there is a question of how to represent and use the action-value function defined in Formula (10). On the one hand, some approaches forgo the use of centralized information and estimate the Q_a of each agent, which cannot explicitly reflect the communication between a cooperative agent and the confounded contribution of each agent in the total reward. At the other extreme, having a training processing that is fully centralized makes it impractical to train agents with mass information, and it becomes impossible to support the global observation hypothesis in some application scenarios [29].

Thus, the multi-agent reinforcement learning algorithm with credit assignment (MACA) for computation offloading is proposed by us, in which we introduce centralized training and decentralized execution thinking. We assume that the agents jointly interact with the environment and receive a global reward, denoted as Q_{tot}. Each agent holds an individual Q function Q_a, and the global reward Q_{tot} can be decomposed into individual rewards Q_a for each agent. The relationship between Q_n and Q_{tot} is much more than simple factorization and involves a complex nonlinear combination in which a neural network, called a mixing network, is implemented and can distinguish the contribution between each agent with credit assignment process.

We focus on the consistency of partial reward and global reward, namely the monotonicity constraint of Q_n and Q_{tot}. Therefore, we rule that the weight of the mixing network must be non-negative; that is, there is a requirement to satisfy the relationship between the individual reward and the global reward:

$$\frac{\partial Q_{tot}}{\partial Q_n} \geq 0, \forall n \in N \quad (20)$$

We add global observation information S to the mixing network while imposing the limitation that the weight of the mixing network must remain non-negative. The addition of global information allows the mixing network to more explicitly determine the contribution of each agent. In addition, when building the Q-network, we introduced some existing tricks for Q-networks, such as the double Q-network and dueling Q-network, which can improve the training effect. The double Q-network requires the construction of two action-value functions, one for estimating the action and one for estimating the value of that action.

In the application of the MACA algorithm, the evaluation network is used to determine the action, and the target network is used to determine the action value. This double Q-network architecture can effectively solve the overestimation problem generated by the Q-network.

Similarly, considering that the reward obtained from the computation offloading scenario is less related to the environment state but more related to the joint action selected by the agent, we introduce the dueling Q-network architecture during training. Dueling Q-network changes the output value to two branches, which are the scalar state value V of the state and the advantage value A of each action. The advantage value A is a vector of the same dimension as the action space. Under this framework, Q-network is more inclined to change each advantage value A of each action instead of changing the state value V, and this architecture can better distinguish the pros and cons of each action of the agent, speeding up training. The overall architecture of our proposed MACA algorithm is shown in Figure 3.

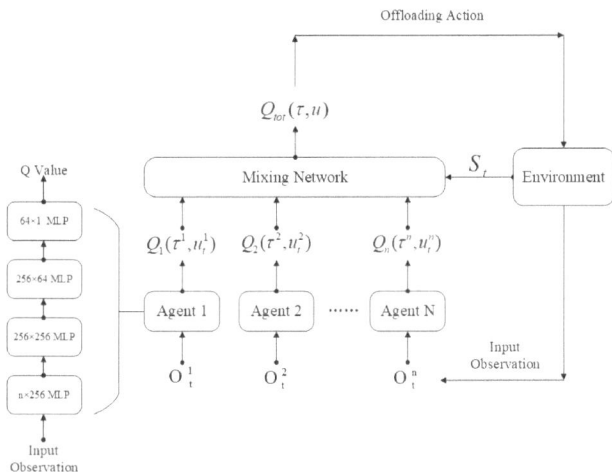

Figure 3. Schematic diagram of MACA network architecture. The Q-network of each agent contains [256, 256, 64] hidden layers, introducing a double Q-network and dueling Q-network. The global state information is added to the mixing network, and the global reward is monotonically decomposed into the local reward of each agent.

At the beginning of each offloading decision cycle, each agent n obtains part of the current environment state through interaction with the environment, that is, the observation Z_n of the agent is used as the input of the Q-network. The Q-network generates the estimated Q value for further rewards. The Q value generated by multiple agent networks is jointly input to the credit assignment mixing network. All weight items in the network are non-negative, so the output result is positively related to the Q value generated by the agent Q-network. The credit assignment network back-propagates the action space to generate and select the maximum reward actions that react to the environment. Then, the environment changes from S_t to S_{t+1} state. Before the next round of computing offloading decisions, the experience storage $(S_t, S_{t+1}, action, reward)$ enters the buffer. After interactions with the environment, the agent takes a small batch of experience values from the buffer to learn and update the Q-network and the mixing network. The loss function is defined as follows:

$$L(\theta) = \sum_{i=1}^{b} \left[(y_i^{tot} - Q_{tot}(\tau, action, S_t, \theta))^2 \right] \tag{21}$$

where b is the batch size of experience sampled form the replay buffer, and y^{tot} represents the real future reward. θ represents the parameters for the Q-network. Then, we can obtain the corresponding agent's policy of maximizing the Q value through the following formula traversal enumeration, naturally avoiding the curse of dimensionality. The whole process of MACA algorithm can be represented by Algorithm 1.

$$\pi(s) = arg\max Q^{\pi}(s,a) \tag{22}$$

Algorithm 1: Multi-Agent Deep Reinforcement Learning Algorithm with Credit Assignment.

1 **for** *agent* $n = 1, 2, \cdots, N$ **do**
2 | Initialize the Q-network with random weight and bias parameter
3 **end**
4 Initialize mixing network with non-negative weight parameter
5 Initialize replay buffer D
6 **for** *epoch* $= 0, 1, \cdots, M$ **do**
7 | Initialize state S_0 and observation O_0 for each agent i
8 | **for** $t = 0, 1, \cdots, T$ **do**
9 | | Select an action randomly with probability ε
10 | | choose $u_i^t = arg\max_{u_i^t} Q_i(\tau_i^t, u_i^t)$ for each agent i
11 | | Take action u_i^t and get next observation S_{t+1} and reward R_t
12 | | Store tuple (S_t, u_t, R_t, S_{t+1}) in buffer D
13 | | sample a random minibatch of tuple (S_t, u_t, R_t, S_{t+1}) from D
14 | | Decomposition Q_{tot} value and get the Q_n for each agent. Update θ by minimizing total loss:
15 | | $L(\theta) = \sum_{i=1}^{b} \left[(y_i^{tot} - Q_{tot}(\tau, action, S_t, \theta))^2\right]$
16 | | Update target network parameter θ' with θ
17 | **end**
18 **end**

---

4. Experiment

In this section, we will first outline the simulation experiment settings. Then, we will compare our proposed MACA algorithm with other traditional algorithms through discussion and analysis.

4.1. Simulation Settings

In the simulation experiment, we simulate smart park video monitoring computation offloading of video data processing tasks by considering scenarios consisting of multiple edge computing nodes and multiple camera groups where tasks are to be assigned to devices. The simulation process goes through a total of five computation offloading cycles. During this process, the communication transmission channels of all tasks are shared and time-varying. The computational capacity of each local relay node is 5×10^8 Hz per second.

For actual computation offloading scenarios, the size of task data and the number of required CPU cycles will not be fixed. Therefore, we assume that a task model within the scope is randomly generated during the offloading process. In addition, considering the cumulative cost of computing delay and energy consumption in each computation offloading cycle, the discounter factor γ is set to 1. In addition, other parameters are summarized as follows in Table 1.

Table 1. Main parameters.

Parameter	Value	Description
O_n	$[1000, 1600]$	The data of the task to be uploaded
B_n	$[900, 1200]$	The CPU cycles required for the task
F_f	$[21 \times 10^8, 25 \times 10^8, 23 \times 10^8]$	The computational capacity of the edge computing node
δ_f	1×10^{-27}	The computing constant factor of the edge computing node
δ_l	5×10^{-26}	The computing constant factor of the local device
$W_{f,n}$	$[1, 0.6, 0.2] \times 4 \times 10^7$	Time-varying bandwidth channel
h	$0.1W$	The channel gain
P	10^{-3}	The transmit power
lr	10^{-4}	The learning rate
batchsize	128	The size sample from buffer
F_f	$[21 \times 10^8, 25 \times 10^8, 23 \times 10^8]$ bit per second	Computing capacity of the edge computing node
f_l	5×10^8 bit per second	Local computing capacity
B	20^6 Hz	Channel bandwidth
noise	10^{-3} W	Communication channel noise

4.2. Simulation Results

In this subsection, we will introduce the simulation results of the MACA algorithm experiment from the aspects of the training process, agent number comparison experiment, and ablation experiment. Through comparison with numerous existing algorithms, we demonstrate the superiority of our proposed MACA algorithm.

4.2.1. Training Process

In the process of the computation offloading experiment, we set up seven agents to conduct computation offloading decisions. Tasks can be offloaded to three edge computing nodes or executed locally by agents. In the experiment, the observation space of each agent is $[b_t^n, O_n^t, B_n^t]$, 5 in total. The action space is 4, meaning there are three edge computing nodes and one local device. Every ten generations of data are collected, and the agent loads the data with a batch size of 128 from the buffer for learning. The learning rate is 10^{-4}, and the size of the hidden layer of the neural network is $[256, 256, 64]$. Since computation offloading is a continuous process, we set the discounted factor γ as 1. At the same time, in order to encourage agents to explore more actions, we adopted the ε-*greedy* method, with ε decaying from 1 to 0.05 during the training process. We gave the iteration curve of Q-loss value and reward value in the training process, as shown in Figure 4.

It can be seen from Figure 4 that the network loss value has been declining and finally approaches zero near the 1.5×10^4th generation. The reward function has a significant improvement in this process and tends to be stable around 1.5 in the 2×10^4th generation. This shows that the agent is increasingly accurate in estimating the environment Q-value in the continuous interaction of the environment and has learned the method to improve the target reward value.

In order to more clearly illustrate the results of agent training, we select 10,000 and 30,000 generations of agent training models to evaluate in one round of computing offloading scenarios. The results are shown in Figures 5 and 6.

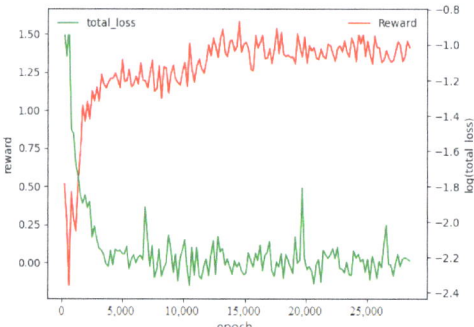

Figure 4. Iteration curve of loss value and reward value. The data are smoothed for five generations. In order to better observe the trend of data changes, the *total_loss* data are logarithmically processed. Each evaluation of the agent goes through five interactions with the environment, and the final reward is stable at around 1.5, which is equivalent to an average reward value of 0.3 per interaction with the environment. That is, after the computation offloading plan, the current consumption is only 0.7 times of the local computation.

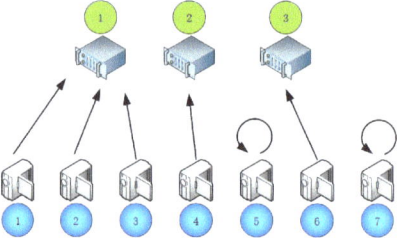

Figure 5. Agent joint-action of 10,000 epoch training. In the above experimental settings, an optimal situation for two devices would be to select an edge computing node for computation offloading at the same time. In this scenario, three devices simultaneously select an edge node for offloading, which will cause channel congestion and increase the request delay. Nodes 2 and 3 are selected by only one device in computation offloading, which will lead to a waste of resources, while one device is chosen for local computation. The desired optimal effect was obviously not achieved in this action situation.

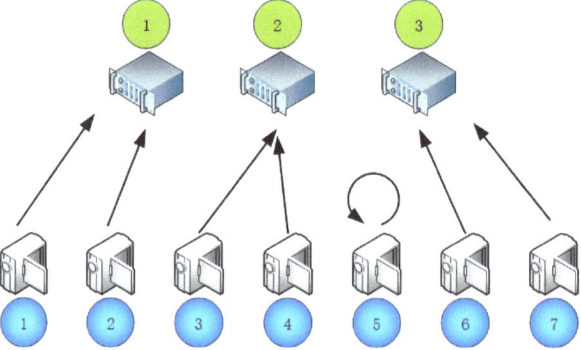

Figure 6. Agent joint-action of 30,000 epoch training. In this scenario, each edge computing node is selected by two devices for computation offload, which achieves the best utilization of resources. At the same time, the device No. 5, with the worst channel state, is selected for local computing. It can be seen that, after 30,000 generations of training, the agent has learned how to make optimal decisions.

In addition, to demonstrate the rationality of our parameter selection, we conduct experiments comparing learning rate *lr* and *batchsize*. The result is shown as Figure 7.

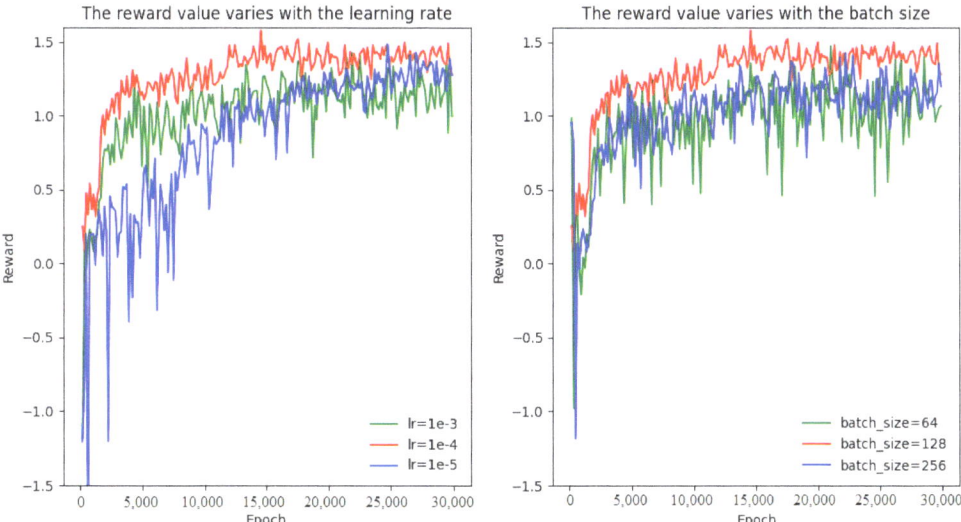

Figure 7. Reward curse change with learning rate and batch size.

It can be seen that, when a higher learning rate is selected, the learning effect is not good, and the reward function cannot converge due to oscillation back and forth. When a lower learning rate is selected, the reward value function converges slowly and cannot reach the optimal value. Similarly, when a large batch size is selected, convergence of the reward value function is difficult, and it is difficult to reach the optimal value. When a small batch size is selected, it is difficult for the agent to effectively learn knowledge, resulting in non-convergence of the training curve.

4.2.2. Agent Number Comparison Experiment

In order to demonstrate that our proposed MACA algorithm is superior to traditional methods, we compare the performance of the MACA algorithm with a deep Q-learning algorithm, random offloading approach, and local computation approach. To ensure fairness in comparison, we use the same training trick of double Q-network and dueling Q-network in DQN. It can be seen that the reinforcement learning algorithm is more effective than the random approach and local computation approach. Moreover, when the number of devices as independent agents increases, the performance of DQN decreases significantly, while the performance of our proposed algorithm remains relatively stable. This is obvious because, as the number of agents increases, the action space of the DQN algorithm will increase in geometric multiples, while the multi-agent algorithm will combine the rewards of each agent into an overall reward, which only increases the action space linearly, thus allowing it to easily avoid this problem, and the specific results are shown in Figure 8.

As the number of agents increases, the reward value obtained by interacting with the environment is increasingly diminished because the computing resources available to edge computing nodes also continually decrease, and so to does the reduced value relative to local computing. It can be seen that the performance of our proposed MACA algorithm is more stable and higher than the corresponding DQN algorithm, and this phenomenon is especially obvious when the number of agents increases. However, when the number of agents is 7, the effect of random assignment approach is even worse than that of local computation, which further illustrates the importance of planning computing offloading. More results are shown in Table 2.

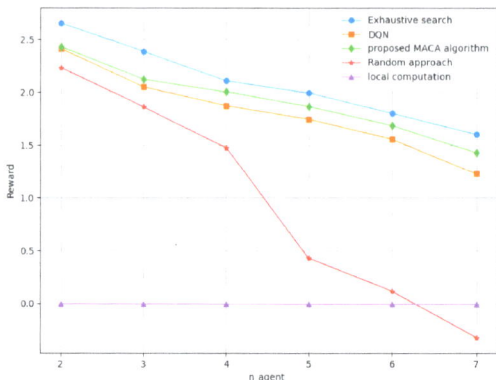

Figure 8. Algorithm performance varies with the number of agents.

Table 2. The reward value varies with devices and computing nodes.

Reward		Edge Computing Nodes Number					
		f = 2			f = 3		
Method		Exhaustive Search	DQN	MACA	Exhaustive Search	DQN	MACA
edge computing node number	n = 2	2.537	2.273	2.176	2.655	2.412	2.432
	n = 3	1.906	1.583	1.764	2.387	2.053	2.124
	n = 4	1.387	1.215	1.22	2.109	1.875	2.005
	n = 5	1.138	0.965	1.104	1.995	1.748	1.869
	n = 6	0.406	0.351	0.362	1.803	1.558	1.687
	n = 7	0.319	0.257	0.297	1.604	1.232	1.432

We also evaluate the time taken to solve the computation offloading schedule for different methods. Solving a problem of the same size and parameters on the same computer configuration, the DQN method takes 0.902 s, our proposed MACA method takes 0.971 s, and the method using exhaustive search takes 184.985 s. It can be seen that our method reduces the computation time to about 1/200 of the original.

4.2.3. Ablation Experiment

In this subsection, we ablate each component in the MACA algorithm and compare the contribution of each component in the algorithm.

We compared the original MACA algorithm, the MACA algorithm without a mixing network, the MACA algorithm without a double Q-network, and the MACA algorithm without dueling Q-network, corresponding to a total of four curves. In the ablation experiment, seven local device and three edge computing nodes are set. In addition, all experiments were carried out under the optimal experimental conditions selected above. The results of the ablation experiment are shown as Figure 9.

As can be seen in Figure 9, compared with the original MACA algorithm, if the mixing network is removed, the training curve will fluctuate greatly, which results in difficulties for achieving convergence, and it is difficult to obtain the optimal effect. Removing the double Q-network or dueling Q-network will lead to slower training and worse final results. The results of the ablation experiments show that our proposed value decomposition method based on credit assignment can avoid the problem of the dimensional curse and allow the agent to more effectively learn the cooperative strategy. At the same time, the addition of the double Q-network and dueling Q-network to the architecture can effectively alleviate the overestimation of the Q network and help the agent reduce the interference caused by the dynamic environment, effectively promoting the learning process of the agent.

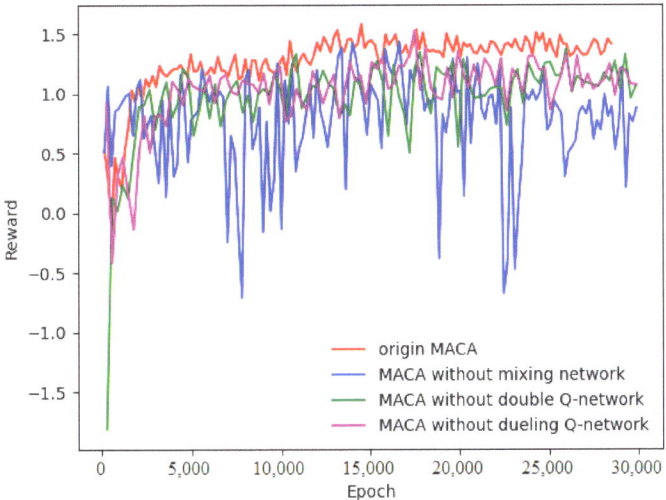

Figure 9. Ablation experiment results.

4.3. Discussion

In this paper, a multi-agent reinforcement learning algorithm is proposed for computation offloading in smart park monitoring. By training the agent offline and making decisions online, the reinforcement learning method solves the shortcomings of high computing delay in the traditional method and can effectively reduce the delay and energy consumption in the process of computation offloading. In the experimental part, we demonstrated the effectiveness of our proposed algorithm by presenting the training process and training results of the MACA algorithm. Then, through generalization experiments on the number of agents and devices, we show that, compared with the DQN algorithm, random allocation, and local computation approaches, our proposed MACA algorithm achieves the highest performance in most cases. Finally, the contribution of each component of the MACA algorithm to the overall algorithm is verified through the ablation experiment for the Q-network architecture.

Although, to a certain extent, some progress has been made in our research in terms of performance, there are still some limitations. First, more complex challenges are often faced in real computation offloading environments. On the one hand, the impact of edge computing node deployment location on offloading efficiency should be considered and, on the other hand, the queuing theory model between tasks should be considered. Second, the performance comparison between our proposed value-based multi-agent reinforcement learning method and some existing policy-based reinforcement learning methods remains to be conducted. Finally, the safety and interpretability of artificial intelligence algorithms, such as reinforcement learning, have always been an issue, and further work on the interpretation of models needs to be conducted.

5. Conclusions

This paper studies the problem of computation offloading for multiple video monitoring in smart parks and introduces deep reinforcement learning as a solution, in which offline training and online decision-making are introduced to resolve unbearable computational delays, which represent the problem of traditional methods. Credit assignment is used to extend the single-agent scenario to a multi-agent scenario and solve the problem of cooperation between agents. As an agent, each device chooses to deal with computing-intensive tasks locally or through computation offloading. We evaluated the algorithm effect with different numbers of devices and edge computing nodes, thus demonstrating that our proposed MACA algorithm is more stable than many existing algorithms and can more effectively identify the computation offloading scheme in the search space with geometric multiple growth. On this basis, the random arrival of tasks and time-varying bandwidth channel is simulated, and offline training and online decision-making are carried out according to the task size and CPU cycles within a certain range to better formulate resource allocation strategies. With the introduction of the Q-network tricks, agents can optimize themselves more clearly based on the double Q-network and dueling Q-network. A large number of simulation experiments and ablation experiments were used to verify the validity of the model. This model can meet the requirements of the real-time offloading of computing-intensive tasks and reduce the request delays and computing energy consumption of tasks.

Author Contributions: Methodology, L.S.; Investigation, J.W. and Y.B.; Data curation, L.S.; Writing — original draft, L.S. and Y.B.; Writing — review and editing, J.W.; Supervision, J.W. and Y.Z.; Funding acquisition, Y.Z. All authors have read and agreed to the published version of the manuscript.

Funding: This work was supported by the National Natural Science Foundation of China (Grant No. 72274058).

Data Availability Statement: Not applicable.

Conflicts of Interest: The authors declare no conflict of interest.

Abbreviations

The following abbreviations are used in this manuscript:

Notation	Definition
N	The set of camera device group
f	Edge computing node
T	The computation offloading cycle
O_t	The amount of data that needs to be uploaded to complete the task
B_t	The number of CPU cycles required for computing tasks
$W_{n,f}$	The channel bandwidth between the device n and the edge computing node f
P	The power of the computational offloading task
h	The gain of the communication channel when the task is transmitted
$noise$	The variance of the complex Gaussian white channel noise
T_n^l	Time delay of execute task locally
F_n^l	Local computational capability
F_f	Edge computing node computational capability
E_n^l	Energy consumption for executing task locally
$T_{n,t}^o$	Time delay of transmission when executing task with edge node
$T_{n,p}^o$	Time delay of computation when executing task with edge node
$E_{n,t}^o$	Energy consumption of transmission when executing task with edge node
$E_{n,p}^o$	Energy consumption of computation when executing task with edge node
$Cost$	The cost of computation offloading process

References

1. Kim, J.B.; Kim, H.J. Efficient region-based motion segmentation for a video monitoring system. *Pattern Recognit. Lett.* **2003**, *24*, 113–128. [CrossRef]
2. Li, C.; Pourtaherian, A.; van Onzenoort, L.; a Ten, W.T.; de With, P. Infant facial expression analysis: Towards a real-time video monitoring system using R-CNN and HMM. *IEEE J. Biomed. Health Inform.* **2020**, *25*, 1429–1440. [CrossRef] [PubMed]
3. Kekki, S.; Featherstone, W.; Fang, Y.; Kuure, P.; Li, A.; Ranjan, A.; Purkayastha, D.; Jiangping, F.; Frydman, D.; Verin, G.; et al. Mec in 5G networks. *ETSI White Pap.* **2018**, *28*, 1–28.
4. Zeng, F.; Tang, J.; Liu, C.; Deng, X.; Li, W. Task-offloading strategy based on performance prediction in vehicular edge computing. *Mathematics* **2022**, *10*, 1010. [CrossRef]
5. Mach, P.; Becvar, Z. Mobile edge computing: A survey on architecture and computation offloading. *IEEE Commun. Surv. Tutor.* **2017**, *19*, 1628–1656. [CrossRef]
6. Lin, L.; Liao, X.; Jin, H.; Li, P. Computation offloading toward edge computing. *Proc. IEEE* **2019**, *107*, 1584–1607. [CrossRef]
7. Henderson, P.; Islam, R.; Bachman, P.; Pineau, J.; Precup, D.; Meger, D. Deep reinforcement learning that matters. In Proceedings of the AAAI Conference on Artificial Intelligence, New Orleans, LA, USA, 2–7 February 2018; Volume 32.

8. Nosratabadi, S.; Mosavi, A.; Duan, P.; Ghamisi, P.; Filip, F.; Band, S.S.; Reuter, U.; Gama, J.; Gandomi, A.H. Data science in economics: Comprehensive review of advanced machine learning and deep learning methods. *Mathematics* **2020**, *8*, 1799. [CrossRef]
9. Sutton, R.S.; Barto, A.G. *Reinforcement Learning: An Introduction*; MIT Press: Cambridge, MA, USA, 2018.
10. Mnih, V.; Kavukcuoglu, K.; Silver, D.; Graves, A.; Antonoglou, I.; Wierstra, D.; Riedmiller, M. Playing atari with deep reinforcement learning. *arXiv* **2013**, arXiv:1312.5602.
11. François-Lavet, V.; Henderson, P.; Islam, R.; Bellemare, M.G.; Pineau, J. An introduction to deep reinforcement learning. *Found. Trends Mach. Learn.* **2018**, *11*, 219–354. [CrossRef]
12. Hou, Y.; Liu, L.; Wei, Q.; Xu, X.; Chen, C. A novel DDPG method with prioritized experience replay. In Proceedings of the 2017 IEEE International Conference on Systems, Man, and Cybernetics (SMC), Banff, AB, Canada, 5–8 October 2017; pp. 316–321.
13. Thomas, P.S.; Brunskill, E. Policy gradient methods for reinforcement learning with function approximation and action-dependent baselines. *arXiv* **2017**, arXiv:1706.06643.
14. Schulman, J.; Levine, S.; Abbeel, P.; Jordan, M.; Moritz, P. Trust region policy optimization. In Proceedings of the International Conference on Machine Learning, Lille, France, 6–11 July 2015; pp. 1889–1897.
15. Schulman, J.; Wolski, F.; Dhariwal, P.; Radford, A.; Klimov, O. Proximal policy optimization algorithms. *arXiv* **2017**, arXiv:1707.06347.
16. Heess, N.; TB, D.; Sriram, S.; Lemmon, J.; Merel, J.; Wayne, G.; Tassa, Y.; Erez, T.; Wang, Z.; Eslami, S.; et al. Emergence of locomotion behaviours in rich environments. *arXiv* **2017**, arXiv:1707.02286.
17. Konda, V.; Tsitsiklis, J. Actor-critic algorithms. *Adv. Neural Inf. Process. Syst.* **1999**, *12*, 1008–1014.
18. Lillicrap, T.P.; Hunt, J.J.; Pritzel, A.; Heess, N.; Erez, T.; Tassa, Y.; Silver, D.; Wierstra, D. Continuous control with deep reinforcement learning. *arXiv* **2015**, arXiv:1509.02971.
19. Mnih, V.; Badia, A.P.; Mirza, M.; Graves, A.; Lillicrap, T.; Harley, T.; Silver, D.; Kavukcuoglu, K. Asynchronous methods for deep reinforcement learning. In Proceedings of the International Conference on Machine Learning, New York, NY, USA, 19–24 June 2016; pp. 1928–1937.
20. Fujimoto, S.; Hoof, H.; Meger, D. Addressing function approximation error in actor-critic methods. In Proceedings of the International Conference on Machine Learning, Stockholm, Sweden, 10–15 July 2018; pp. 1587–1596.
21. Haarnoja, T.; Zhou, A.; Abbeel, P.; Levine, S. Soft actor-critic: Off-policy maximum entropy deep reinforcement learning with a stochastic actor. In Proceedings of the International Conference on Machine Learning, Stockholm, Sweden, 10–15 July 2018; pp. 1861–1870.
22. Lowe, R.; Wu, Y.I.; Tamar, A.; Harb, J.; Abbeel, O.P.; Mordatch, I. Multi-agent actor-critic for mixed cooperative-competitive environments. *Adv. Neural Inf. Process. Syst.* **2017**, *30*, 6382–6393.
23. Lee, H.; Park, S.; Kim, J.; Kim, J. Auction-based deep learning computation offloading for truthful edge computing: A myerson auction approach. In Proceedings of the 2021 International Conference on Information Networking (ICOIN), Jeju Island, Republic of Korea, 13–16 January 2021; pp. 457–459.
24. Pradhan, C.; Li, A.; She, C.; Li, Y.; Vucetic, B. Computation offloading for iot in C-RAN: Optimization and deep learning. *IEEE Trans. Commun.* **2020**, *68*, 4565–4579. [CrossRef]
25. Zhang, K.; Zhu, Y.; Leng, S.; He, Y.; Maharjan, S.; Zhang, Y. Deep learning empowered task offloading for mobile edge computing in urban informatics. *IEEE Internet Things J.* **2019**, *6*, 7635–7647. [CrossRef]
26. Ren, Y.; Sun, Y.; Peng, M. Deep reinforcement learning based computation offloading in fog enabled industrial internet of things. *IEEE Trans. Ind. Inform.* **2020**, *17*, 4978–4987. [CrossRef]
27. Yu, S.; Chen, X.; Yang, L.; Wu, D.; Bennis, M.; Zhang, J. Intelligent edge: Leveraging deep imitation learning for mobile edge computation offloading. *IEEE Wirel. Commun.* **2020**, *27*, 92–99. [CrossRef]
28. Rashid, T.; Samvelyan, M.; Schroeder, C.; Farquhar, G.; Foerster, J.; Whiteson, S. Qmix: Monotonic value function factorisation for deep multi-agent reinforcement learning. In Proceedings of the International Conference on Machine Learning, Stockholm, Sweden, 10–15 July 2018; pp. 4295–4304.
29. Bušoniu, L.; Babuxsxka, R.; Schutter, B.D. Multi-agent reinforcement learning: An overview. In *Innovations in Multi-Agent Systems and Applications—1*; Springer: Berlin/Heidelberg, Germany, 2010; pp. 183–221.

Article

Online Trajectory Optimization Method for Large Attitude Flip Vertical Landing of The Starship-like Vehicle [†]

Hongbo Chen *, Zhenwei Ma, Jinbo Wang and Linfeng Su

School of Systems Science and Engineering, Sun Yat-sen University, Guangzhou 510006, China
* Correspondence: chenhongbo@mail.sysu.edu.cn
[†] This paper is an extended version of our paper published in the 2022 IEEE International Conference on Unmanned Systems (ICUS), Guangzhou, China, 28–30 October 2022.

Abstract: A high-precision online trajectory optimization method combining convex optimization and Radau pseudospectral method is presented for the large attitude flip vertical landing problem of a starship-like vehicle. During the landing process, the aerodynamic influence on the starship-like vehicle is significant and non-negligible. A planar landing dynamics model with pitching motion is developed considering that there is no extensive lateral motion modulation during the whole flight. Combining the constraints of its powered descent landing process, a model of the fuel optimal trajectory optimization problem in the landing point coordinate system is given. The nonconvex properties of the trajectory optimization problem model are analyzed and discussed, and the advantages of fast solution and convergence certainty of convex optimization, and high discretization precision of the pseudospectral method, are fully utilized to transform the strongly nonconvex optimization problem into a series of finite-dimensional convex subproblems, which are solved quickly by the interior point method solver. Hardware-in-the-loop simulation experiments verify the effectiveness of the online trajectory optimization method. This method has the potential to be an online guidance method for the powered descent landing problem of starship-like vehicles.

Keywords: starship-like vehicle; large attitude flip vertical landing; online trajectory optimization; convex optimization; Radau pseudospectral method

MSC: 37M10

Citation: Chen, H.; Ma, Z.; Wang, J.; Su, L. Online Trajectory Optimization Method for Large Attitude Flip Vertical Landing of The Starship-like Vehicle. *Mathematics* 2023, 11, 288. https://doi.org/10.3390/math11020288

Academic Editors: Huawen Liu, Chengyuan Zhang, Weiren Yu and Chunwei Tian

Received: 12 December 2022
Revised: 28 December 2022
Accepted: 31 December 2022
Published: 5 January 2023
Corrected: 10 April 2024

Copyright: © 2023 by the authors. Licensee MDPI, Basel, Switzerland. This article is an open access article distributed under the terms and conditions of the Creative Commons Attribution (CC BY) license (https:// creativecommons.org/licenses/by/ 4.0/).

1. Introduction

As the demand for human space exploration continues to expand, providing more reliable, economical, and fast spacecraft launch services is a significant development direction, and one of the main challenges for the aerospace launch industry [1–3]. Reusable launch vehicles (RLV) are an essential technological approach to meet this challenge, and have been a research hotspot for the world's major spacefaring nations [4,5]. Starting from the 1960s, the United States has presented a variety of reusable launcher programs, and carried out a large number of technology verification tests, the successful development and application of the Space Shuttle being one of the high points [6]. Since entering the 21st century, SpaceX has made a breakthrough in vertical takeoff and vertical landing (VTVL) technology. Based on the continuous research and verification of many key technologies such as advanced reusable liquid rocket motors and landing guidance control, a sub-stage of its Falcon 9 rocket has taken the lead in achieving sea/land fixed-point soft landing and multiple reuses. The feasibility and reliability of relevant technologies were verified, and marking the entry of VTVL reuse technology into the large-scale engineering application stage [7].

On this basis, for Mars one and other large-scale interplanetary exploration missions, SpaceX proposed a fully reusable "Starship + Super Heavy" launch vehicle program [8]. Among them, the starship as the upper stage returns to re-entry at orbital velocity after completing the delivery mission, resulting in more significant deceleration requirements, and more complex aerodynamic [9]. Therefore, the flight profile of the starship return landing process can be considered as a "combination" of the lifting body glide re-entry and the Falcon 9 sub-stage landing. During the high-speed phase, the glide re-entry deceleration is performed at a relatively small ballistic inclination, and this phase is controlled by a combination of multiple aerodynamic rudders and a reaction control system (RCS), which restarts the engine above the landing point, and performs an attitude flip close to 90 degrees, followed by a vertical soft landing based on thrust vector control (TVC) technology [10]. After a series of flight test explorations, in May 2021, the starship technology prototype SN15 achieved the above large attitude flip vertical landing (LAFVL) for the first time, verifying the relevant guidance and control technologies, and laying the foundation for the subsequent starship and super heavy combination tests [11].

The return-landing flight profile of Starship, and the new GNC technology towed by it, are of high reference value for high-speed return and vertical landing flights such as the upper stage recovery missions of reusable launch vehicles. In particular, the online trajectory optimization problem of its unique "Belly Flop" LAFVL flight segment is of high academic exploration and engineering application value. In this paper, we propose a high-precision online trajectory optimization algorithm combining convex optimization and Radau pseudospectral method (RPM) to provide methodological and technical support for the research of related space exploration projects.

The vertical landing onboard real-time trajectory optimization problem must be solved quickly, accurately and with high precision. Considering the in-flight deviations, especially unexpected situations such as wind disturbances, the algorithm needs to converge without good initial guesses, which is not satisfied by most conventional optimization methods. The interior point method (IPM) can solve convex problems in polynomial time, without initial guesses from the user, which is attractive for aerospace applications [12]. However, most practical aerospace problems are not convex optimization problems, and cannot be solved directly by IPM. Therefore, most researchers focus on formulating nonconvex optimization problems within a convex framework, called convexification [13]. Ideally, the nonconvex trajectory optimization problem should be equivalently transformed into a convex optimization problem, called lossless convexification (LCvx). In recent years, LCvx has been successfully achieved by equivalence transformation of control variables and constraint relaxation [14–16]. According to the optimal control theory, the equivalence of the transformations can be proved rigorously. LCvx technology has been successfully applied to powered Mars landings [17], launch vehicle ascent flights [18], and missiles [19]. However, most path and terminal constraints as well as nonlinear dynamic constraints cannot be convexized by LCvx, then the method of successive convexification (SCvx) subsequently emerged to convexify complex nonconvex and nonlinear constraints [20]. This is an iterative procedure for solving the linearization convex subproblem until it converges to an optimal solution [21,22]. At the same time, discretization techniques [23,24], linearization strategies [21], and trust region constraints [25] need to be considered to ensure the convergence of the method [26]. Convex optimization has been successfully applied to UAVs [27], spacecraft [28], and high-speed atmospheric vehicles [29]. In summary, the convex optimization algorithm has good computational efficiency and robustness.

In this paper, we present a SCvx-RPM algorithm for online trajectory optimization and autonomous guidance of LAFVL of the starship-like vehicle (SLV). At the same time, the following studies are conducted to improve the optimization problem modeling, discretization and convexification algorithm techniques:

(1) The coupling relationship between pitch angle and engine nozzle swing angle of a SLV, and the effect of nonlinear aerodynamic forces on the motion of the vehicle are considered. Combining the characteristics of the LAFVL trajectory optimization problem, a planar landing trajectory optimization model considering the pitch attitude is developed. The model can describe the landing motion process of the SLV with high granularity compared with 3-DOF problem [30,31], it significantly improves the computational efficiency compared with 6-DOF problem [32,33].

(2) Based on the above planning model, the research of the low-loss convexification method is carried out to avoid direct linearization leading to large errors [19,20]. We maximize the use of the LCvx method to pre-process nonconvex motion models in order to improve the convergence efficiency and reliability of the subsequently proposed SCvx algorithm. Based on the original SCvx method, an online update strategy of the trust region is used to improve the speed of convergence of the SCvx algorithm.

(3) Using RPM to discretize the continuous optimal control problem, and designing the landing terminal moment as a special control variable to optimize together, which improves the optimality of the moment value and the optimization precision of the trajectory compared with the methods of fixed terminal moment and additional search for the optimal moment [34–36].

The paper is organized as follows: a model of the fuel-optimal trajectory optimization problem in the landing site coordinate system (LSCS) is given in Section 2; the nonconvex trajectory optimization model is convexized and discretized, and a suitable SCvx algorithm is designed in Section 3; an ANSI-C trajectory optimization algorithm is developed in Section 4 to verify the relevant modeling and analytical conclusions; and conclusions are drawn in Section 5.

2. LAFAL Trajectory Optimization Problem for The SLV

Firstly, the dynamics model of the SLV is discussed. A 3-DOF rocket motion model is commonly used to study the powered descent landing (PDL) problem. However, the 3-DOF rocket motion model assumes that the rocket itself is a mass point, and focuses only on the translational aspect of the PDL problem, which cannot describe the large attitude flip process of a SLV. The 6-DOF rocket motion model is a more accurate problem formulation, and can better characterize the rocket translational and center-of-mass motion during the vertical landing of a SLV. However, there are no explicit structural properties of the solution to the 6-DOF rocket motion model for the fuel-optimal trajectory optimization problem (e.g., Bang-Bang thrust properties for the 3-DOF problem). In addition, the nonlinear complexity of the 6-DOF model and a large number of variables leads to a long computational time for its trajectory optimization, which is not conducive to online implementation.

In this study, considering that there is no large-scale lateral motion modulation in the final PDL phase of the SLV, in order to reduce the complexity of the model, a planar landing flight motion model that considers the pitch attitude motion can describe the motion characteristics of the LAFVL process of the SLV. Unlike the 3-DOF or 6-DOF motion models, the planar landing motion model considering pitch attitude introduces pitch attitude and angular velocity variables, and restricts the translational motion to the fixed x-z plane of the LSCS, which can better characterize the large attitude flip motion process of the SLV than the 3-DOF model, and has higher computational efficiency than the 6-DOF motion model.

As shown in Figure 1, the origin of the LSCS is located at the landing point, the z-axis direction is pointed upward from the center of the earth, and the x-axis is perpendicular to the z-axis, so that the initial position and velocity vectors in the LSCS are located in the plane containing the landing point. Then, the equations of motion describing the planar landing of the SLV are shown as follows:

$$\begin{aligned}
\dot{x} &= V_x, \\
\dot{z} &= V_z, \\
\dot{V}_x &= \frac{-T\sin(\theta+\delta)+D_x}{m}, \\
\dot{V}_z &= \frac{T\cos(\theta+\delta)+D_z}{m} - g_0, \\
\dot{\theta} &= w, \\
\dot{w} &= \frac{(M_T+M_D)}{J}, \\
\dot{m} &= -\frac{T}{I_{sp}g_0}
\end{aligned} \qquad (1)$$

where $r = [x,z]^T$ is the position vector, $V = [V_x, V_z]^T$ is the velocity vector, θ is the pitch angle, δ is the engine nozzle swing angle, w is the pitch angle rate, m is the SLV mass, T is the engine thrust, I_{sp} is the engine specific impulse, and g_0 is the Earth's gravitational acceleration. D_x and D_z are the total aerodynamic drag in the x and z directions, respectively, described as

$$D_x = -C_{LD} \cdot \sqrt{V_x^2 + V_z^2} \cdot V_x,$$
$$D_z = -C_{LD} \cdot \sqrt{V_x^2 + V_z^2} \cdot V_z \quad (2)$$

where C_{LD} is the total drag coefficient generated by aerodynamic drag and lift. M_T and M_D are the moments generated by engine thrust and aerodynamic forces, respectively, and J is the rotational inertia estimated from engineering experience about the position of the vehicle's center of mass, which is expressed as

$$J = \frac{1}{12} m \left(6 r_s^2 + l_s^2 \right),$$
$$M_T = -l_{cg} \cdot T \cdot \sin \delta,$$
$$M_D = -\left(l_{cp} - l_{cg}\right) \cdot (D_x \cdot \cos\theta + D_z \cdot \sin\theta) \quad (3)$$

where r_s is the body radius, l_s is the body height, l_{cg} is the position of the vehicle center of mass, and l_{cp} is the position of the vehicle center of pressure. For this motion model, the state variables are defined as $x = [x, z, V_x, V_z, \theta, w, m]^T \in \mathbb{R}^7$ and the control variables are $u = [T, \delta]^T \in \mathbb{R}^2$.

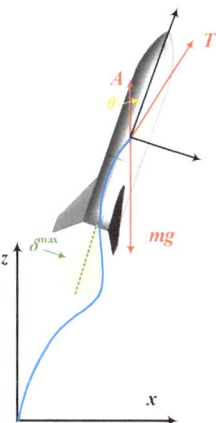

Figure 1. Planar landing model considering pitch attitude motion.

The state and control constraints involved in the planar landing problem of the SLV in the LSCS are discussed below. Although the landing mode of the SLV is vertical, the deceleration mode is the same as that of the lift-type re-entry vehicle, which is mainly aerodynamic until the large attitude flip maneuver is performed. After the large attitude flip maneuver, the thrust of the SLV reaches its peak and decelerates under the combined effect of thrust and aerodynamic force. The optimization model built in the LSCS has a more definite dynamic pressure and heat flow density trajectory pattern and change pattern as the powered descent phase begins, and is almost monotonically decreasing to zero. Therefore, the model established in this section does not consider the dynamic pressure and heat flow constraints, and only considers the initial state constraints and the terminal state constraints that satisfy the fixed-point vertical soft landing as follows.

$$x(t_0) = x_0, \quad x|_{1:6}(t_f) = x_f, \quad m(t_f) \geq m_{dry} \tag{4}$$

where t_0 and t_f are the initial and terminal moments, respectively, x_0 is the initial state navigation and sensor sampling value, and x_f is the terminal state. m_{dry} is the dry weight of the rocket, $x|_{1:6}(t_f) \triangleq [x_f, z_f, V_{xf}, V_{zf}, \theta_f, w_f]^T \in \mathbb{R}^6$. Since the landing point is the origin of the LSCS, there are generally zero rocket states except for the rocket mass, which is greater than the rocket dry weight. In order to characterize the large attitude flip maneuver of the vehicle, $\theta_0 = \pi/2$ is taken.

For the control constraints, there are thrust amplitude constraints and engine nozzle swing angle amplitude constraints.

$$\begin{aligned} T_{min} \leq T \leq T_{max}, \\ -\delta_{max} \leq \delta \leq \delta_{max} \end{aligned} \tag{5}$$

The objective function of the optimal control problem is defined as the fuel-optimal, and its performance index can be expressed as

$$J = -m(t_f) \tag{6}$$

The nonconvex fuel-optimal trajectory optimization problem P_1 under the continuous system is given by combining the above-mentioned SLV motion model and constraints as follows.

$$\begin{aligned} \min \quad & J = -m(t_f) \\ \text{s.t.} \quad & \text{Dynamics : Equation (1)} \\ & \text{Constraints : Equations (4) and (5)} \end{aligned} \tag{7}$$

where the optimization variables are $X_{opt} = [x, z, V_x, V_z, \theta, w, m, T, \delta, t_f]^T$, containing state variables, control variables, and terminal time variable t_f. It can be seen that the larger nonconvexity of the optimization problem lies in the SLV motion model. Therefore, the focus in the next section is on convexification and discretization methods for nonconvex system dynamics.

3. Convexization and Discretization of P_1 Problem

3.1. LCvx of P_1 Problem

In this subsection, the nonconvex trajectory optimization model is initially convexified. Firstly, to improve the landing precision, the engine nozzle swing angle command is made smoother, and the coupling of the state quantity pitch angle and the control quantity engine nozzle swing angle is uncoupled. The engine nozzle swing angle rate is used as the control quantity instead of engine nozzle swing angle, and an augmented SLV motion model is proposed.

$$\begin{aligned} \dot{x} = V_x, \quad \dot{z} = V_z, \quad \dot{V}_x = \frac{-T\sin(\theta+\delta) + D_x}{m}, \quad \dot{V}_z = \frac{T\cos(\theta+\delta) + D_z}{m} - g_0, \\ \dot{\theta} = w, \quad \dot{w} = \frac{(M_T + M_D)}{J}, \quad \dot{m} = -\frac{T}{I_{sp}g_0}, \quad \dot{\delta} = \chi \end{aligned} \tag{8}$$

For this motion model, the state variables are defined as $x = [x, z, V_x, V_z, \theta, w, m, \delta]^T \in \mathbb{R}^8$ and the control variables are $u = [T, \chi]^T \in \mathbb{R}^2$. Additionally, increasing the augmented control quantity constraint on the angular rate of the engine nozzle swing angle.

$$-\chi_{max} \leq \chi \leq \chi_{max} \tag{9}$$

where χ_{max} is the upper limit of the angular rate of the engine nozzle swing angle. The augmented nonconvex fuel-optimal trajectory optimization problem P_2 is obtained as follows.

$$\begin{aligned}\min \quad & J = -m(t_f) \\ \text{s.t.} \quad & \text{Dynamics : Equation (8)} \\ & \text{Constraints : Equations (4), (5) and (9)}\end{aligned} \qquad (10)$$

Then, in order to reduce the degree of nonlinearity in the augmented dynamics, the component of the engine thrust in the LSCS is introduced as a new control variable.

$$T_x = T\sin(\theta+\delta), \quad T_z = T\cos(\theta+\delta) \qquad (11)$$

In turn, the trigonometric function term is substituted out of the system dynamics. Before and after the transformation, the degrees of freedom of the system control variables are two, but the variable substitution introduces new process constraints as follows.

$$T_x^2 + T_y^2 = T^2 \qquad (12)$$

$$\arctan\left(\frac{T_x}{T_z}\right) - (\theta+\delta) = 0 \qquad (13)$$

Equation (12) is a natural derivation of the trigonometric relationship. The thrust component trigonometric function is determined by two parameters, namely the pitch angle and the engine nozzle swing angle, and the effect of applying the constraint Equation (13) is to make its two relations equivalent to the original constraint form.

For the new nonconvex constraint introduced by the variable substitution, Equation (12) can be handled by borrowing the LCvx method, i.e., directly relaxing the equation constraint to the inequality constraint.

$$T_x^2 + T_z^2 \leq T^2 \qquad (14)$$

That is, the constraint is convexized by taking the form of a convex package, and the equivalence of the two can be proved by the principle of maximal value. Equation (13), however, still contains trigonometric terms, which are difficult to perform LCvx. In the subsequent design, it will be sequential linearization.

The thrust-acceleration term in the velocity dynamics is still nonlinear due to the time-varying mass of the SLV during the landing process. To convexify this nonlinear term, a new variable is further introduced to substitute it.

$$\sigma \triangleq \frac{T}{m}, \quad T_{xm} \triangleq \frac{T_x}{m}, \quad T_{zm} \triangleq \frac{T_z}{m}, \quad \omega \triangleq \ln m \qquad (15)$$

Then, the mass dynamics transformation is given by

$$\dot{\omega} = \alpha\sigma \qquad (16)$$

where $\alpha = -1/(I_{sp}g_0)$. The mass terminal constraint transformation is given by

$$\omega(t_f) \geq \ln(m_{dry}) \qquad (17)$$

The nonconvex constraint (13) transforms as

$$\arctan\left(\frac{T_{xm}}{T_{zm}}\right) - (\theta+\delta) = 0 \qquad (18)$$

The convex constraint (14) and the first equation of (5) transform, respectively, as

$$\sqrt{T_{xm}^2 + T_{zm}^2} \leq \sigma \qquad (19)$$

$$T_{\min} \cdot e^{-\varpi} \leq \sigma \leq T_{\max} \cdot e^{-\varpi} \tag{20}$$

Then, the system dynamics is transformed as

$$\begin{aligned}
\dot{x} &= V_x, \\
\dot{z} &= V_z, \\
\dot{V}_x &= -T_{xm} + D_{xm}, \\
\dot{V}_z &= T_{zm} + D_{zm} - g_0, \\
\dot{\theta} &= w, \\
\dot{w} &= L_T \cdot \sigma \cdot \sin\delta + L_D \cdot (D_{xm} \cdot \cos\theta + D_{zm} \cdot \sin\theta), \\
\dot{\varpi} &= \alpha\sigma, \\
\dot{\delta} &= \chi
\end{aligned} \tag{21}$$

where

$$\begin{aligned}
D_{xm} &= e^{-\varpi} \cdot D_x, \\
D_{zm} &= e^{-\varpi} \cdot D_z, \\
L_T &= -12 l_{cg} / \left(6 r_s^2 + l_s^2\right), \\
L_D &= -12 (l_{cp} - l_{cg}) / \left(6 r_s^2 + l_s^2\right)
\end{aligned} \tag{22}$$

For this motion model, the state variables are defined as $x = [x, z, V_x, V_z, \theta, w, \varpi, \delta]^T \in \mathbb{R}^8$ and the control variables are $u = [T_{xm}, T_{zm}, \sigma, \chi]^T \in \mathbb{R}^4$. Thereby, the fuel-optimal trajectory optimization problem P_3 after LCvx is obtained as follows.

$$\begin{aligned}
\min \quad & J = -m(t_f) \\
\text{s.t.} \quad & \text{Dynamics}: \text{Equation (21)} \\
& \text{Constraints}: x(t_0) = x_0, \quad x|_{1:6}(t_f) = x_f, \quad \varpi(t_f) \geq \ln(m_{\text{dry}}) \\
& -\delta_{\max} \leq \delta \leq \delta_{\max}, \quad -\chi_{\max} \leq \chi \leq \chi_{\max} \\
& \arctan(T_{xm}/T_{zm}) - (\theta + \delta) = 0 \\
& \sqrt{T_{xm}^2 + T_{zm}^2} \leq \sigma, \quad T_{\min} \cdot e^{-\varpi} \leq \sigma \leq T_{\max} \cdot e^{-\varpi}
\end{aligned} \tag{23}$$

3.2. Discretization of Problem P_3

The significance of using RPM to discretize the system dynamics is mainly reflected in two aspects: high discretization precision and facilitation of handling the free time problem. The technical details of the RPM and its precision and convergence speed are discussed in detail in the literature [23–25]. Using the unique form of discretization time domain of RPM, the terminal moment t_f of the LAFVL process of the SLV is designed as a special control variable for optimization, which is an important feature of this paper, and an effective means to improve the optimality and precision of the results. In many similar problems, in order to reduce the complexity of the optimization model, and ensure the convexity of the problem, the terminal moment is determined offline or fixed, which may not be the optimal shutdown point [34–36], and thus the optimality of the whole trajectory is not guaranteed and the fuel consumption is not optimal.

The pseudospectral discretization of the system dynamics equations takes the following form.

$$\sum_{j=1}^{N+1} D_{ij} x(\tau_i) - \frac{t_f}{2} f(x(\tau_i), u(\tau_i)) = 0 \tag{24}$$

The terminal moments are regarded as special control variables and the above discrete algebraic equation constraints are expressed as follows.

$$2\sum_{j=1}^{N+1} D_{ij}x(\tau_i) + f_{\text{aug}}(y_i) = 0 \qquad (25)$$

where $f_{\text{aug}}(y_i) = f(x(\tau_i), u_{\text{aug}}(\tau_i))$, $y_i = \{x(\tau_i), u_{\text{aug}}(\tau_i)\}$, $u_{\text{aug}} = [u, t_f]^{\text{T}}$, $f_{\text{aug}}(y)$ as a function of the right-hand side of the augmented dynamics equation treating the terminal moment as a special control variable.

3.3. SCvx of Discretization Optimization Problem

The preliminary convexification of the nonconvex trajectory optimization model is performed in Section 3.1, and the nonconvex trajectory optimization model is completely lossless by LCvx. The reason for giving the discretization model of the system dynamics equations in Section 3.2 before the treatment of the SCvx method in this subsection is that the discretization introduces the multiplication of the free time with the right-hand side function of the system dynamics, which generates new nonlinear terms, requiring the convexification method to transform them approximately. In this subsection, the discretization free-time problem system dynamics equations and process constraints are approximated linearly, the trust region constraints required by the SCvx algorithm are designed, and the specific form of the discretization matrix required by the IPM solver format is given in conjunction with other constraint models.

The dynamics constraints are first studied. In Equation (25), the nonlinear correlation terms are concentrated in the function $f_{\text{aug}}(y_i)$ at the right end of the augmented dynamics equation. The first-order Taylor expansion of $f_{\text{aug}}(y_i)$ takes the following form.

$$f_{\text{aug}}(y_i) = A_i(x^k, u_{\text{aug}}^k)x(\tau_i) + B_i(x^k, u_{\text{aug}}^k)u_{\text{aug}}(\tau_i) + w_i(x^k, u_{\text{aug}}^k) \qquad (26)$$

where $A = \frac{\partial f_{\text{aug}}}{\partial x}$, $B = \frac{\partial f_{\text{aug}}}{\partial u_{\text{aug}}}$, and $w_i(x^k, u_{\text{aug}}^k) = f_{\text{aug-}i}(x^k, u_{\text{aug}}^k) - A_i(x^k, u_{\text{aug}}^k)x^k(\tau_i) - B_i(x^k, u_{\text{aug}}^k)u_{\text{aug}}^k(\tau_i)$. x^k and u_{aug}^k are the reference points of the Taylor expansion in the k-th iteration, and $f_{\text{aug-}i}(x^k, u_{\text{aug}}^k)$ denotes the value of the right-hand side function of the augmented dynamics equation at the i-th discretization point out in the k-th iteration.

Secondly, for the nonlinear terms in the process constraints (18) and (20) of the trajectory optimization problem, there is no LCvx methods for the time being, and their nonlinearity is strong, so the above process constraints are similarly approximated by sequential linearization, and the linearized expressions correspond to (27) and (28), respectively, as follows.

$$k_{Tx}^i T_{xm} + k_{Tz}^i T_{zm} - \theta - \delta = b_T^i \qquad (27)$$

$$T_{\min}e^{-\omega_0}\cdot(1-(\omega-\omega_0)) \leq \sigma \leq T_{\max}e^{-\omega_0}\cdot(1-(\omega-\omega_0)) \qquad (28)$$

An important part of the above linearization process is the selection of the Taylor expansion reference point. In the SCvx algorithm, the reference point for the 1st iteration is provided by the coarse selection of the initial value, and the reference point in the subsequent iterations is taken to be the optimal solution obtained in the previous iteration. According to the characteristics of Taylor expansion, the linearized dynamics and state constraints are a good approximation to the original nonlinear form only when the optimization variables are taken near the reference point during the iterative process of SCvx. Therefore, the following trust region constraints are added to the SCvx algorithm.

$$|x^{k+1} - x^k| \leq \varepsilon_x, \quad |u_{\text{aug}}^{k+1} - u_{\text{aug}}^k| \leq \varepsilon_{u_{\text{aug}}} \qquad (29)$$

where ε_x and $\varepsilon_{u_{\text{aug}}}$ are the trust region values designed for each state and control variable, respectively, and become smaller as the number of iterations increases to improve the convergence speed of the algorithm.

Ultimately, the linearization convex subproblem P_4 is obtained as follows.

$$
\begin{aligned}
\min \quad & J = -m(t_f) \\
\text{s.t.} \quad & \text{Dynamics}: \text{Equation (26)} \\
& \text{Constraints}: \quad x(t_0) = x_0, \quad x|_{1:6}(t_f) = x_f, \quad \omega(t_f) \geq \ln(m_{\text{dry}}) \\
& -\delta_{\max} \leq \delta \leq \delta_{\max}, \quad -\chi_{\max} \leq \chi \leq \chi_{\max} \\
& k_{Tx}^i T_{xm} + k_{Tz}^i T_{zm} - \theta - \delta = b_T^i, \quad \sqrt{T_{xm}^2 + T_{zm}^2} \leq \sigma \\
& T_{\min} e^{-\omega_0} \cdot (1 - (\omega - \omega_0)) \leq \sigma \leq T_{\max} e^{-\omega_0} \cdot (1 - (\omega - \omega_0))
\end{aligned}
\tag{30}
$$

3.4. SCvx Algorithm

For the convenience of programming the trajectory optimization algorithm, the equation constraints and inequality constraints for each iteration of the optimization problem input to the IPM solver are transcribed as $A - X_{\text{opt}} = b$ and $G - X_{\text{opt}} \leq h$ standard forms, respectively, to facilitate the implementation of the SCvx algorithm. Based on the above discussion, the SCvx algorithm for LAFVL of a SLV is given in this subsection as follows.

Input: set the number of collocation points N; set the initial reference trajectory X_{opt}^0; set the initial value of the trust region constraint $\varepsilon_x, \varepsilon_{u_{\text{aug}}}$; set the iteration termination criterion parameter $\varepsilon > 0$; set the maximum number of iterations $k_{\max}$; set the number of iterations $k = 1$, $\triangle X_{\text{opt}}^1 = 1$.

Step 1: Solve the linearization convex subproblem P_4 using the IPM solver and compute the updates of the optimal variables X_{opt}^k.

Step 2: Check the convergence condition $|X_{\text{opt}}^k - X_{\text{opt}}^{k-1}| < \varepsilon$, if the convergence condition is satisfied, go to Step 3. Otherwise, set $k = k + 1$, and return to Step 1.

Step 3: The optimization problem is solved, $X_{\text{opt}}^* = X_{\text{opt}}^k$.

4. Numerical Experiments

The numerical optimization simulation session is an important part of validating the LAFVL guidance algorithm for the SLV. In this section, GPOPS validation programs for the aforementioned P_1, P_2, and P_3 trajectory optimization problems for vertical landing, and the C language program for the SCvx algorithm are developed. The IPM solution of the subproblems in the C program can be called from the open source or commercial packages such as ECOS, MOSEK, etc., and GPOPS is used as a benchmark for calibration and verification of the algorithm. In this section, numerical simulation experiments are conducted based on the above algorithm programs to verify the correctness, effectiveness, and efficiency of the programs.

Section 4.1 prepares a trajectory optimization program based on the GPOPS-II package for problems with different optimization contexts, followed by numerical optimization simulation experiments on the Windows 10 operating system to verify the correctness of the model and convexification methods.

In Section 4.2, a C-language program for optimizing the LAFVL trajectory of the SLV based on the ECOS open source software package is developed for the P_4 trajectory optimization problem under the premise that the GPOPS-II validation modeling and lossless convexification methods are correct. At the same time, the C program is run on the embedded guidance computer of the hardware-in-the-loop simulation system to simulate the test operation conditions under the onboard computing platform. The correctness and real-time performance of the SCvx guidance algorithm are effectively verified under the Linux operating system.

To perform a SLV large attitude flip maneuver, the spacecraft speed needs to be reduced by exposing the greater aerodynamic drag created by the wider surface. At an altitude of about 600 m, the vehicle starts a large maneuver to change its attitude from horizontal to vertical to perform a precision landing maneuver. The model parameters of the SLV are shown in Table 1.

Table 1. SLV model parameters.

Variable Symbols	Variable Name	Numerical Value
m_0	Initial Mass	120,000 kg
m_{dry}	Dry Weight of The Vehicle	85,000 kg
l_s	Vehicle Altitude	50 m
r_s	Vehicle Radius	4.5 m
l_{cg}	Center of Mass Position	20 m
l_{cp}	Center of Pressure Position	22.5 m
δ_{max}	Maximum Engine Nozzle Swing Angle	20 deg
χ_{max}	Maximum Engine Nozzle Swing Angle Rate	20 deg/s
T_{max}	Maximum Engine Thrust	2210 kN
T_{min}	Minimum Engine Thrust	880 kN
I_{sp}	Engine Ratio Impulse	330 s

The boundary conditions to be satisfied are as follows.

$$x(t_0) = 100 \text{ m}, \ z(t_0) = 600 \text{ m}, \ V_x(t_0) = 0 \text{ m/s}, \ V_z(t_0) = -85 \text{ m/s}$$

$$\theta(t_0) = \frac{\pi}{2} \text{ rad}, \ w(t_0) = 0 \text{ rad/s}, \ m(t_0) = 120{,}000 \text{ kg}, \ x(t_f) = 0 \text{ m}$$

$$z(t_f) = 0 \text{ m}, \ V_x(t_f) = 0 \text{ m/s}, \ V_z(t_f) = 0 \text{ m/s}, \ \theta(t_f) = 0 \text{ rad}$$

$$w(t_f) = 0 \text{ rad/s}, \ m(t_f) \geq 85{,}000 \text{ kg}$$

4.1. GPOPS Numerical Optimization Simulation Analysis

The main purpose of this subsection is to verify the correctness of the developed and partially convexified models of the SLV planar landing trajectory optimization problem. Based on the GPOPS-II software package, the trajectory optimization procedures for the above P_1, P_2, and P_3 problems are prepared, and the analysis of the model characteristics and the correctness of the convexification method is carried out based on numerical experiments. The operating system environment of numerical simulation in this subsection is Windows 10, intel i7-10710U CPU@1.1 GHz, and 16 GB RAM.

The free terminal time problem is considered, i.e., the terminal time is the discrete optimization variable. Forty Radau collocation points are used in the preliminary optimization experiments, i.e., a total of 41 discretization points. For this problem size, GPOPS-II is invoked to solve the nonconvex fuel optimal trajectory optimization problem P_1, the augmented nonconvex fuel optimal trajectory optimization problem P_2, and the nonconvex fuel optimal augmented trajectory optimization problem P_3 after lossless convexification in the above computer environment for comparison experiments. The optimization results of the three problems are given below, as shown in Figure 2, and the position precision and velocity precision of the vehicle landing by using the trajectory integration precision comparison method are shown in Table 2.

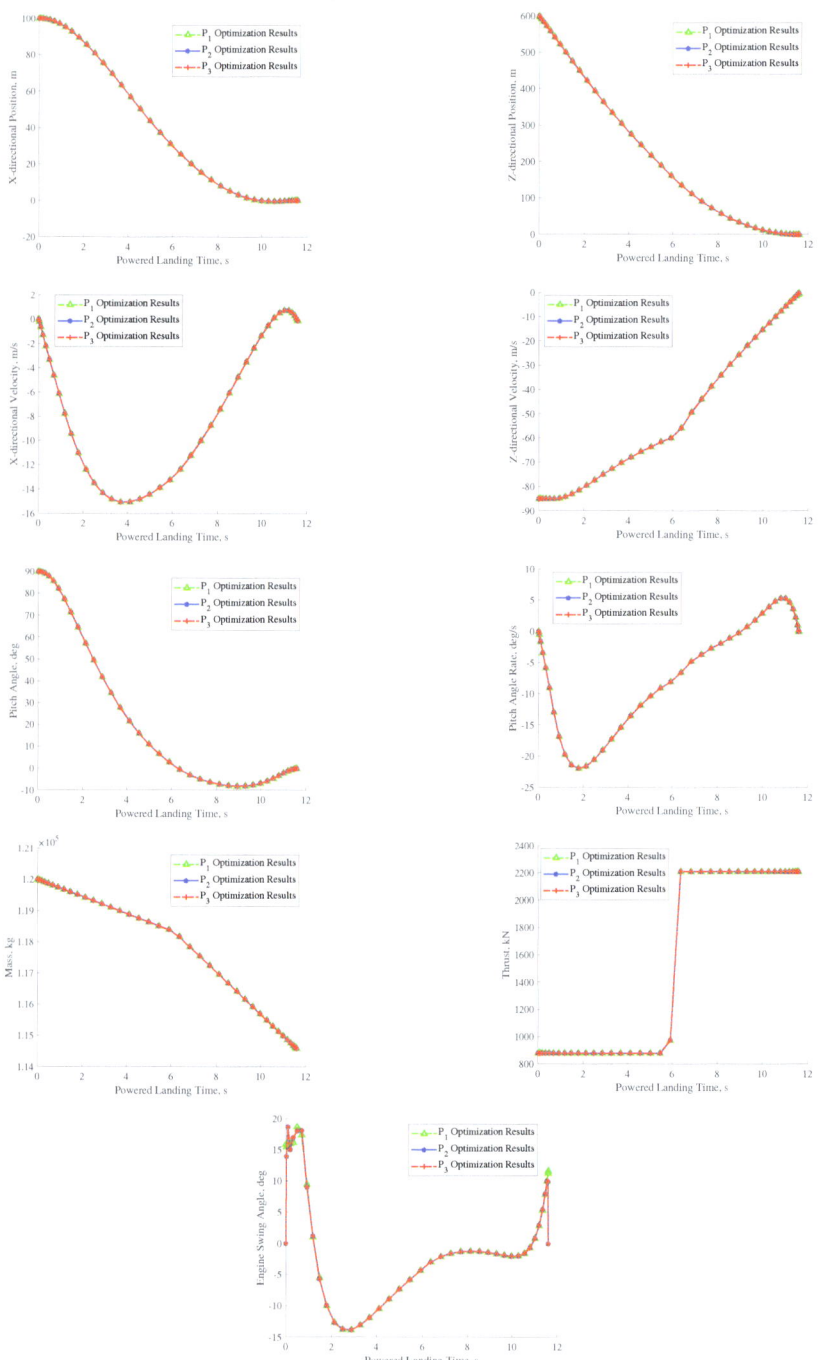

Figure 2. Comparison of optimization results for P_1, P_2 and P_3.

Table 2. Comparison of landing precision.

Optimization Problem	Positional Precision	Velocity Precision
P_1	2.8273 m	0.42003 m/s
P_2	0.42707 m	0.099739 m/s
P_3	0.42708 m	0.09974 m/s

In summary, the preliminary analysis can be concluded as follows.

(1) By invoking the GPOPS-II software package to solve the nonconvex fuel optimal trajectory optimization problem P_1, the augmented nonconvex fuel optimal trajectory optimization problem P_2 and the nonconvex fuel optimal augmented trajectory optimization problem P_3 after lossless convexification, the correctness of the current trajectory optimization model design, transformation, and partial convexification is initially verified.

(2) The comparison of the optimization results of P_2 and P_3 problems shows that using the engine nozzle swing angle rate instead of engine nozzle swing angle as the control quantity uncouples the state quantity pitch angle and the control quantity engine nozzle swing angle, makes the engine nozzle swing angle smoother, and effectively improves the landing precision.

(3) A comparison of the optimization results of the P_2 and P_3 problems shows that the nonconvex constraint Equation (18) is equivalent to the original nonconvex constraint Equation (11), which does not reduce its nonconvexity, but effectively reduces the constraint dimension without losing the additive characteristic relationship characterizing the pitch angle of the vehicle and the swing angle of the engine nozzle.

The above conclusions indicate that the P_3 problem is the lowest nonconvex problem representation before the pseudospectral discretization operation, and also has the conditions to form a C program by discretization and sequential convexification processing in the subsequent study.

4.2. Hardware in the Loop Simulation Analysis

In this subsection, the performance of the proposed SCvx algorithm is verified by a hardware-in-the-loop simulation. The hardware-in-the-loop simulation system built based on the Speedgoat real-time target computer also includes the real-time simulation host computer, the onboard flight control computer, the simulated onboard guidance computer and the nozzle actuation simulator, and the main equipment components, etc, in which the GNC computers are analogous to those onboard the vehicle or at ground stations, the navigation computer collects the current vehicle status, the guidance computer runs the guidance algorithm and generates guidance commands based on the current vehicle status, and the control computer generates control commands based on the guidance information. The system architecture is shown in Figure 3. The test experiment uses a self-developed dedicated guidance and control computer, which is based on the NVIDIA Jetson Xavier NX motherboard as the core computing unit, the operating system is Ubuntu 18.04.5 LTS, the Visual Studio Code integrated development environment, using standard C programming language, the CPU is NVIDIA Carmel Arm v8.2 64-bit CPU with 1.4 GHz, 6 cores and 16 GB RAM.

This subsection compares the SCvx algorithm proposed in this paper with the Matlab GPOPS-II package, a RPM package that has been tested in a wide range of problem solving and is a typical representative of software based on pseudospectral method and nonlinear programming. Therefore, GPOPS-II is used in this paper to verify the correctness of the algorithm. In this calculation example, the number of collocation points are set to 20. The convex optimization procedure formed by the SCvx algorithm through C programming uses the trajectory generated by linear interpolation after concatenating the initial and terminal points as the initial trajectory, which is solved by the IPM solver ECOS.

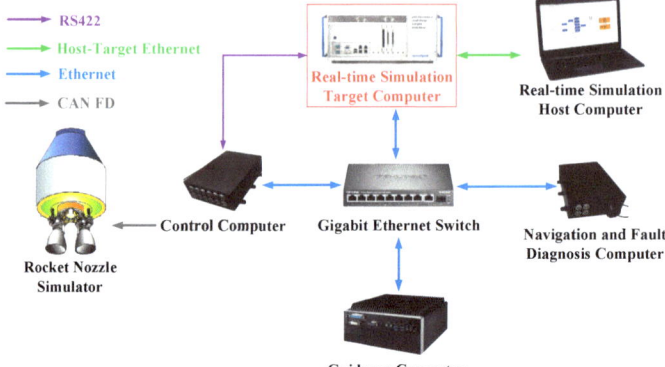

Figure 3. Hardware-in-the-loop simulation system framework.

From the results in Figure 4 and Table 3, it can be seen that the results obtained from the optimization of the SCvx algorithm procedure are in basic agreement with Matlab GPOPS-II. In terms of computational speed, the computational time consumed by the SCvx algorithm procedure is 0.286 s, which satisfies the requirement of computational efficiency for online trajectory optimization for powered landing. The number of iterations at the end of the SCvx algorithm procedure is 5, which indicates that the proposed SCvx algorithm can obtain the optimal solution by iteration without exact initial values. The large attitude flip planar landing trajectory of the SLV is shown in Figure 5, which can more visually reflect the vertical landing process of the vehicle under the SCvx guidance algorithm.

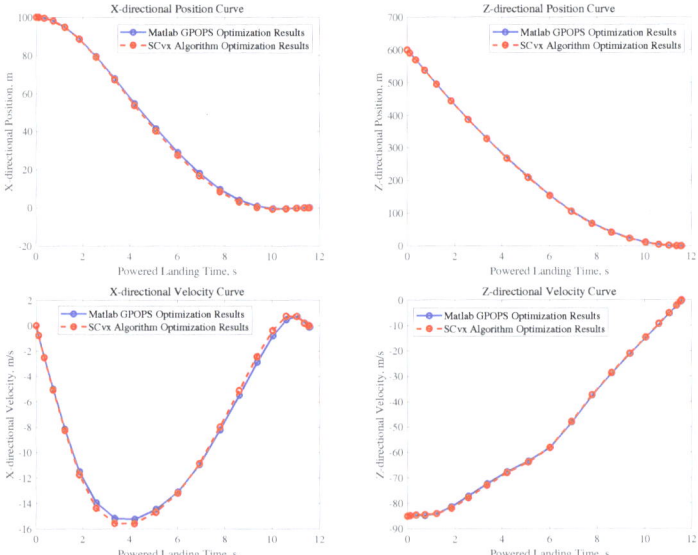

Figure 4. *Cont.*

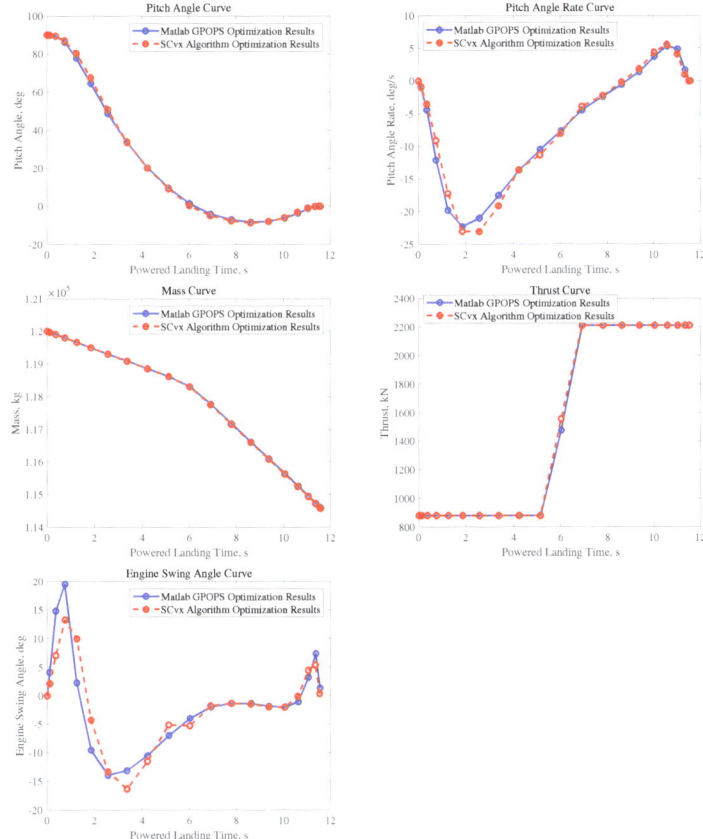

Figure 4. Comparison of optimization trajectories.

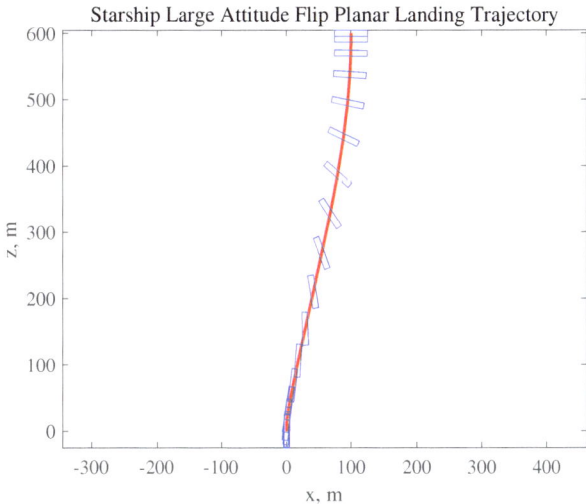

Figure 5. Starship large attitude flip planar landing trajectory.

Table 3. Optimization results.

Optimization Procedure	Terminal Moment	Terminal Mass	CPU Time Consumption
SCvx Algorithm	11.5666 s	114,568.6 kg	0.286 s
Matlab GPOPS	11.5666 s	114,580.7 kg	/

The landing precision of the optimization results of the SCvx algorithm and Matlab GPOPS-II are shown in Table 4. The two are comparable in magnitude, and the precision differs for different simulation conditions (e.g., number of discretization points, see Table 5), i.e., the SCvx algorithm proposed in this paper achieves the precision of a general RPM-based nonlinear programming algorithm. When the number of discretization points increases, the landing precision also increases, but the computational efficiency decreases. By comparing the above optimization results, the correctness of the SCvx algorithm can be verified. Meanwhile, the advantage of the SCvx algorithm in computational efficiency makes it possible for onboard operation.

Table 4. Comparison of SCvx algorithm and Matlab GPOPS-II integration precision.

Optimization Procedure	Positional Precision	Velocity Precision
SCvx Algorithm	0.77127 m	0.30135 m/s
Matlab GPOPS	0.62173 m	0.33001 m/s

Table 5. Precision Comparison with Different Number of Collocation Points.

Optimization Procedure	Number of Collocation Points	Positional Precision	Velocity Precision
SCvx Algorithm	15	1.1597 m	0.29861 m/s
	20	0.77127 m	0.30135 m/s
	30	0.7097 m	0.23689 m/s
Matlab GPOPS	15	1.1636 m	0.39594 m/s
	20	0.62173 m	0.33001 m/s
	30	0.42617 m	0.1531 m/s

5. Conclusions

For the online trajectory optimization problem of LAFVL problem of SLV, a SCvx algorithm combining RPM and convex optimization techniques is proposed, which has high optimization precision and fast solving speed without exact initial values. The main research work and conclusions obtained in this paper are as follows. (1) The problem is discretized by the RPM with high precision, and the unique time-domain mapping of the RPM is used to transform the powered soft-landing terminal moments into special control variables, which is different from the fixed terminal moments method used in similar literature, and improves the optimization precision and optimality of the trajectory optimization results. (2) The nonconvex optimization model was convexified by combining LCvx and SCvx techniques to obtain a sequential convex optimization problem equivalent to the original problem. (3) The proposed SCvx algorithm is experimentally verified by a hardware-in-the-loop simulation platform to verify the correctness, high precision and fast convergence of the algorithm. In the future, we will further investigate the online guidance problem of the 6DOF dynamics model of SLV and design solution algorithms with faster computational efficiency in specific problems with more optimization variables and larger dimensionality.

Author Contributions: Methodology, Z.M.; Validation, L.S.; Data curation, H.C.; Writing—original draft, Z.M.; Writing—review & editing, Z.M.; Supervision, H.C.; Project administration, J.W.; Funding acquisition, J.W. All authors have read and agreed to the published version of the manuscript.

Funding: This research received no external funding.

Data Availability Statement: All data used during the study appear in the submitted article.

Conflicts of Interest: The authors certify that there are no conflict of interest with any individual/organization for the present work.

References

1. Chen, S.Q.; Huang, H.; Shao, Y.T.; Huang, B. Study on the requirement trend and development suggestion for China space propulsion system. *Astronaut. Syst. Eng. Technol.* **2019**, *3*, 62–70.
2. Chen, S.Q.; Huang, H.; Zhang, Q.S.; Qin, X.D.; Rong, Y. Research on the development directions of Chinese launch vehicle liquid propulsion system. *Astronaut. Syst. Eng. Technol.* **2020**, *4*, 1–12.
3. Luo, M.; Chen, S.Q.; Li, D.P.; Pan, H. Characteristics of starship propulsion system and numerical simulation of propellant flow during reentry. *J. Nanjing Univ. Aeronaut. Astronaut.* **2021**, *53*, 9–16.
4. Song, Z.Y.; Wang, C. Development of online trajectory planning technology for launch vehicle return and landing. *Astronaut. Syst. Eng. Technol.* **2019**, *3*, 1–12.
5. Chen, Z.H.; Ning, L.; Wang, P. The development of launch vehicle booster recovery technology. *Astronaut. Syst. Eng. Technol.* **2021**, *5*, 66–74.
6. Hu, D.S.; Liu, N.; Liu, B.L.; Yan, N. Analysis on the development of reusable launch vehicles in the United States. *Space Int.* **2020**, *12*, 38–45.
7. Yang, K.; Mi, X. Analysis of the development of SpaceX's reusable launch vehicle. *Space Int.* **2020**, *9*, 13–17.
8. Yan, N.; Hu, D.S.; Hao, Y.X. Analysis of SpaceX's "Super HeavyStarship" transportation system scheme. *Space Int.* **2020**, *11*, 11–17.
9. Long, X.D. A brief analysis of the super-heavy-starship transport system and its future impact. *Aerosp. Technol.* **2021**, *8*, 32–35.
10. Cantou, T.; Merlinge, N.; Wuilbercq, R. 3DoF simulation model and specific aerodynamic control capabilities for a SpaceX's Starship-like atmospheric reentry vehicle. In Proceedings of the 8nd European Conference for Aeronautics and Space Sciences, Madrid, Spain, 1–5 July 2019.
11. Palmer, C. SpaceX starship lands on Earth, But manned missions to Mars will require more. *Engineering* **2021**, *7*, 1345–1347. [CrossRef]
12. Liu, X. *Autonomous Trajectory Planning by Convex Optimization*; Iowa State University: Ames, IA, USA, 2013.
13. Liu, X.; Lu, P.; Pan, B. Survey of convex optimization for aerospace applications. *Astrodynamics* **2017**, *1*, 23–40. [CrossRef]
14. Açıkmeşe, B.; Blackmore, L. Lossless convexification of a class of optimal control problems with non-convex control constraints. *Automatica* **2011**, *47*, 341–347. [CrossRef]
15. Blackmore, L.; Açıkmeşe, B.; Carson, J.M. Lossless convexification of control constraints for a class of nonlinear optimal control problems. *Syst. Control. Lett.* **2012**, *61*, 863–870. [CrossRef]
16. Harris, M.W.; Açıkmeşe, B. Lossless convexification of non-convex optimal control problems for state constrained linear systems. *Automatica* **2014**, *50*, 2304–2311. [CrossRef]
17. Acikmese, B.; Ploen, S.R. Convex programming approach to powered descent guidance for mars landing. *J. Guid. Control Dyn.* **2007**, *30*, 1353–1366. [CrossRef]
18. Cheng, X.; Li, H.; Zhang, R. Efficient ascent trajectory optimization using convex models based on the Newton–Kantorovich/Pseudospectral approach. *Aerosp. Sci. Technol.* **2017**, *66*, 140–151. [CrossRef]
19. Zhang, K.; Yang, S.; Xiong, F. Rapid ascent trajectory optimization for guided rockets via sequential convex programming. *Proc. Inst. Mech. Eng. Part G J. Aerosp. Eng.* **2019**, *233*, 4800–4809. [CrossRef]
20. Zhang, Z.; Li, J.; Wang, J. Sequential convex programming for nonlinear optimal control problems in UAV path planning. *Aerosp. Sci. Technol.* **2018**, *76*, 280–290. [CrossRef]
21. Reynolds, T.P. *Computational Guidance and Control for Aerospace Systems*; University of Washington: Seattle, WA, USA, 2020.
22. Malyuta, D. *Convex Optimization in a Nonconvex World: Applications for Aerospace Systems*; University of Washington: Seattle, WA, USA, 2021.
23. Garg, D. *Advances in Global Pseudospectral Methods for Optimal Control*; Massachusetts Institute of Technology: Cambridge, MA, USA, 2011.
24. Darby, C.L. *hp-Pseudospectral Method for Solving Continuous-Time Nonlinear Optimal Control Problems*; University of Florida: Gainesville, FL, USA, 2011.
25. Wang, J.B.; Cui, N.G.; Guo, J.F.; Xu, D.F. High precision rapid trajectory optimization algorithm for launch vehicle landing. *Control Theory Appl.* **2018**, *35*, 389–398.
26. Wang, J.B.; Cui, N.G. A pseudospectral-convex optimization algorithm for rocket landing guidance. In Proceedings of the 2018 AIAA Guidance, Navigation, and Control Conference, Kissimmee, FL, USA, 8–12 January 2018; p. 1871.
27. Szmuk, M.; Pascucci, C.A.; Dueri, D. Convexification and real-time on-board optimization for agile quad-rotor maneuvering and obstacle avoidance. In Proceedings of the 2017 IEEE/RSJ International Conference on Intelligent Robots and Systems (IROS), Vancouver, BC, Canada, 24–28 September 2017; pp. 4862–4868.
28. Zhou, D.; Zhang, Y.; Li, S. Receding horizon guidance and control using sequential convex programming for spacecraft 6-DOF close proximity. *Aerosp. Sci. Technol.* **2019**, *87*, 459–477. [CrossRef]

29. Wang, Z.B. Optimal trajectories and normal load analysis of hypersonic glide vehicles via convex optimization. *Aerosp. Sci. Technol.* **2019**, *87*, 357–368. [CrossRef]
30. Wang, J.B.; Ma, H.J.; Li, H.X.; Chen, H.B. Real-time guidance for powered landing of reusable rockets via deep learning. *Neural Comput. Appl.* **2022**, 1–22. [CrossRef]
31. Furfaro, R.; Scorsoglio, A.; Linares, R. Adaptive generalized ZEM-ZEV feedback guidance for planetary landing via a deep reinforcement learning approach. *Acta Astronaut.* **2020**, *171*, 156–171. [CrossRef]
32. Gaudet, B.; Linares, R.; Furfaro, R. Deep reinforcement learning for six degree-of-freedom planetary landing. *Adv. Space Res.* **2020**, *65*, 1723–1741. [CrossRef]
33. Xu, X.; Chen, Y.; Bai, C. Deep Reinforcement Learning-Based Accurate Control of Planetary Soft Landing. *Sensors* **2021**, *21*, 8161. [CrossRef]
34. Dueri, D.; Açıkmeşe, B.; Scharf, D.P.; Harris, M.W. Customized real-time interior-point methods for onboard powered-descent guidance. *J. Guid. Control Dyn.* **2017**, *40*, 197–212. [CrossRef]
35. Dueri, D.; Zhang, J.; Açikmese, B. Automated custom code generation for embedded, real-time second order cone programming. *IFAC Proc. Vol.* **2014**, *47*, 1605–1612. [CrossRef]
36. Ren, G.F.; Gao, A.; Cui, P.Y.; Luan, E.J. A rapid power descent phase trajectory optimization method with minimum fuel consumption for Mars pinpoint landing. *J. Astronaut.* **2014**, *35*, 1350–1358.

Disclaimer/Publisher's Note: The statements, opinions and data contained in all publications are solely those of the individual author(s) and contributor(s) and not of MDPI and/or the editor(s). MDPI and/or the editor(s) disclaim responsibility for any injury to people or property resulting from any ideas, methods, instructions or products referred to in the content.

Article

ReqGen: Keywords-Driven Software Requirements Generation

Ziyan Zhao [1], Li Zhang [1], Xiaoli Lian [1,*], Xiaoyun Gao [1], Heyang Lv [1] and Lin Shi [2]

[1] The State Key Laboratory of Software Development Environment (SKLSDE), Beihang University, Beijing 100191, China
[2] Institute of Software, Chinese Academy of Sciences, Beijing 100190, China
* Correspondence: lianxiaoli@buaa.edu.cn

Abstract: Software requirements specification is undoubtedly critical for the whole software life-cycle. Currently, writing software requirements specifications primarily depends on human work. Although massive studies have been proposed to speed up the process via proposing advanced elicitation and analysis techniques, it is still a time-consuming and error-prone task, which needs to take domain knowledge and business information into consideration. In this paper, we propose an approach, named *ReqGen*, which can provide further assistance by automatically generating natural language requirements specifications based on certain given keywords. Specifically, *ReqGen* consists of three critical steps. First, keywords-oriented knowledge is selected from the domain ontology and is injected into the basic Unified pre-trained Language Model (UniLM) for domain fine-tuning. Second, a copy mechanism is integrated to ensure the occurrence of keywords in the generated statements. Finally, a requirements-syntax-constrained decoding is designed to close the semantic and syntax distance between the candidate and reference specifications. Experiments on two public datasets from different groups and domains show that *ReqGen* outperforms six popular natural language generation approaches with respect to the hard constraint of keywords' (phrases') inclusion, BLEU, ROUGE, and syntax compliance. We believe that *ReqGen* can promote the efficiency and intelligence of specifying software requirements.

Keywords: software requirements generation; knowledge injection; requirements syntax

MSC: 68N01; 46-04

1. Introduction

There is no doubt about the importance of software requirements to the whole software life-cycle [1–3]. As the vital product of requirements analysis, software requirements specifications act as the essential bridge between the requirements analysis stage and the following development and testing. Currently, writing software requirements specifications primarily relies on human work, and this work is complex and time-consuming due to the following factors:

- Enough domain knowledge is required to state the right content, as well as to select appropriate words and expressions. However, domain analysis typically requires non-trivial human effort [4].
- Writing the specifications word-by-word is time-consuming, let alone that many expressions are repeated, especially in similar or related requirements. Writing or locating, copying, and then pasting the repeated content is a waste of human effort.
- Generally accepted requirements syntax, such as EARS [5], is suggested for writing well-formed specifications. Learning and carefully applying non-business-related knowledge is also a burden on requirements analysts.

Intuitively, it would be quite helpful to automatically recommend requirements specifications as long as the analysts can provide some simple related information almost

effortlessly. To the best of our knowledge, most of the automated requirements specifications generation work focus on transforming software engineering models (e.g., the i* framework [6,7], KAOS [8–10], UML models [11–13]) or other semi-structured inputs (e.g., security goals in specific syntactic patterns [14]) into natural language requirements specifications based on pre-defined rules, which are usually brittle and restrict the usability of these approaches. What is more, constructing expressive and precise models is another complex work as well.

Besides, much research has been conducted to speed up the requirements analysis process by identifying and analyzing requirements information from, for example, domain documents [4,15–17], developers' online chats [18], and product descriptions [19,20]. The primary results of these studies are features [19–25], requirements-related sentences [4,15,16,18,26–29], and requirements classifications [22,30,31]. Although these resources are relevant and helpful for requirements acquisition and generation, they are only *separate pieces of information*. Requirements analysts still need to spend significant efforts to understand them, to integrate them with the project background, and then, to specify the final requirements by following at least one requirements syntax [16].

In this work, we aim to automatically generate the requirements statement draft once the analyst has an intuitive idea and can provide two or more keywords (phrases) of the desired requirements. Optionally, the analyst can also suggest the syntax roles of part of or all keywords. We hope to recommend the requirements specifications, although requirements analysts probably need to revise our generation for the final acceptance.

In this paper, we propose an approach, named *ReqGen*, to generate requirements specifications from the keywords (phrases) provided by requirements analysts. In particular, three critical designs are proposed based on the basic Unified pre-trained Language Model (UniLM) [32], which was selected as the backbone of our framework because of its promising performance in natural language generation (NLG) tasks [32–34]. Like other pre-trained language models, UniLM can adapt to downstream tasks smoothly through light fine-tuning [35]. What is more, its parameter sharing design makes the learned text representations more general since the corpus context is utilized in different ways during the pre-training procedure, which helps mitigate overfitting to any single LM task [32]. First, we injected domain knowledge in the format of pseudo-sentences created from domain ontologies into several selected layers of UniLM. Second, we used a copy mechanism in the training phase and set the given keywords as a hard constraint to ensure that they occur in the final statements. Last but not least, we designed a requirements-syntax-constrained decoding approach to accommodate the requirements syntax constraints of the generated statements, given that well-formed requirements should follow a certain syntax [5,36,37].

To illustrate our approach, we contrived one example from a requirements instance of ISO/IEC/IEEE 29148:2018(E) [37], shown in Figure 1. Given that analysts can provide three keywords (i.e., *landing, internal simulator, and ground*) and their syntax roles (i.e., *event, agent, and input*, respectively), our *ReqGen* will firstly retrieve the keywords-related knowledge from the domain ontology and convert them into pseudo-sentences in the first stage. Then, these pseudo-sentences will be injected into UniLM, and the candidate requirements sentences will be produced in the second stage. In the third stage, *ReqGen* sorts the candidate sentences based on the default scoring in UniLM and our syntax-constrained measure in decoding and selects the final requirements draft. Finally, requirements analysts can edit the draft to obtain the final requirements statement.

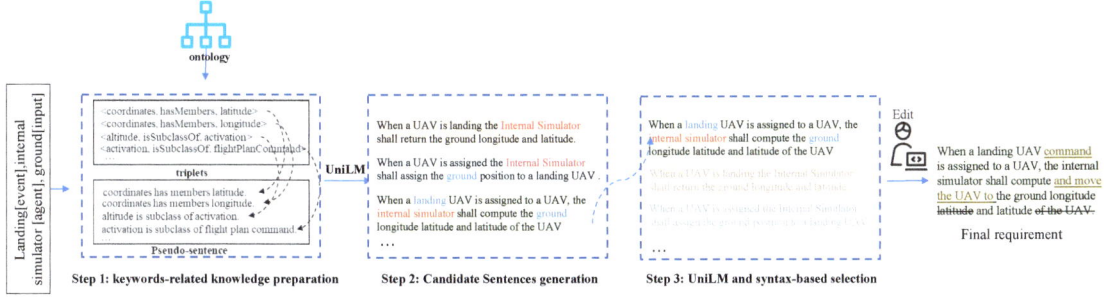

Figure 1. One example showing the target of this work.

To evaluate our approach, we conducted experiments on public datasets consisting of two domains, which were collected from previous work [38]. The results demonstrate the promising performance of *ReqGen*, especially on the dataset with a larger knowledge scale. The comparisons with six popular NLG approaches show that *ReqGen* obtains better Bilingual Evaluation Understudy (BLEU), Recall-Oriented Understudy for Gisting Evaluation (ROUGE), and requirements syntax compliance. We also show the effectiveness of the three proposed components in *ReqGen* using an ablation experiment. The major contributions of this work are as follows.

- An approach, *ReqGen*, for automatically generating software requirements statements based on two or more keywords and their syntax roles.
- The evaluation of *ReqGen* on two public datasets from different domains with promising results and suggestions for knowledge injection into pre-trained models.
- The source code and experimental data made publicly available on Github https://github.com/ZacharyZhao55/ReqGen, accessed on 1 September 2022.

Significance: Requirements recommendation is a major concern in RE. Comparing with the traditional approaches, we took a step forward by recommending the requirements specification draft rather than only identifying the useful, but indirect information.

2. Background

This section describes three key techniques: UniLM, attention mechanisms, and bidirectional long short-term memory (Bi-LSTM).

2.1. UniLM

We used UniLM [32] as the backbone of our approach because of its good NLG performance [33,39]. UniLM is a multi-layer Transformer network with 786 hidden dimensions and 16 attention heads. Its parameter size is 340M, and the activation function is the Gaussian error linear unit (GeLU), the same as those of the Bidirectional Encoder Representation from Transformers (BERT) [40]. It is pre-trained using two unidirectional language models (LM), one bidirectional LM, and one seq2seq LM. For our requirements generation task, we configured it using seq2seq LM (also known as the encoder–decoder model). UniLM uses the 12-layer bidirectional Transformer encoder like BERT. Each encoder layer includes a multi-head attention and a feed-forward neural network. During decoding, UniLM uses beam search (the beam size is five in our implementation) to select the candidate tokens of top-k scores in each step.

2.2. Attention Mechanism

The model with conventional encoders cannot pay attention to information outside the input sequence. Our aim was to make the model able to pay more attention to the injected knowledge, in other words to let the model change the weights of the original hidden state so that higher weights can be assigned to the injected knowledge.

Many attention methods exist, including the dot product model, scaled dot product model, additive model, and bi-linear model. Moreover, the steps of these methods are almost the same, including: (1) the calculation of the similarity between a *Query* and *Key* and obtaining the weights; (2) normalization of the weights; and (3) summation of the weights with a *Value*. The scaled dot product is the most-common, fastest, and most-space-efficient attention mechanism [41], and we used it. This model has an input consisting of a *Query* and *Key* with d_k dimensions and a *Value* with d_v dimensions. We first calculated the dot product of the *Query* and *Key* (MatMul), then divided every *Key* by $\sqrt{d_k}$ (Scale). Finally, we fed it to a *softmax* layer to obtain the weights corresponding to the *Value*s.

2.3. Bi-LSTM

To better understand the injected knowledge, contextual information should be considered in the model. Before injection, we need to encode the knowledge. In our case, we selected the ontology as the source of the supplemented knowledge for keywords. The domain ontology is a graph structure, and most entities have both parent and child nodes. In other words, the contextual information of the injected knowledge from the ontology is bidirectional, not sequential. Therefore, in the method proposed in this paper, to obtain a more comprehensive bidirectional representation of the injected knowledge, we used Bi-LSTM [42] to perform the encoding, where the knowledge is embedded by BERT.

Bi-LSTM is a variant of the recurrent neural network, which combines two standard LSTM [43] layers in opposite directions to learn the two-way representation. An LSTM cell has three gates: the input, forget, and output gates. These three gates have different functions, acting as filters that decide which information to keep and which to forget. This increases the accessible information of the Bi-LSTM network, and hence, the model can better understand the context of the knowledge.

3. Related Work

We first review the requirements generation research. Then, we describe the related work on common NLG.

3.1. Automated Requirements Generation

The existing studies on automated requirements generation mainly focus on transforming the (semi-)structured models (e.g., business process model in [44,45], i* framework in [6,7], KAOS and Ojectiver in [8–10], UML models in [11–13]) or other representations (e.g., security goals in [14]) into specific syntactic pattern-oriented natural language requirements specifications, based on a set of pre-defined rules. They usually require precise representation of the critical elements, such as the roles, inputs, outputs, and their relationships in the business process model [44] or the security goals expressed as clauses with the main verb + several security criteria + several target assets [14]. Both the (semi-) structured inputs and the pre-defined rules restrict the application scope of these approaches.

Mohamed et al. [46] proposed to generate *non-quality* requirements based on grammatical rules and a supplied dictionary, to resolve small-scale requirements sets for current requirements quality checking work.

There are very few studies on requirements specification generation from a few simple keywords. Most available research on software requirements capturing and generation concerns automatically collecting and/or analyzing requirements-related information with the purpose of *assisting* requirements analysts to *manually* acquire, interpret, and specify the final requirements statements. This information can be requirements-relevant sentences obtained from domain documents [4,15–17,26,30], features and their relationships mined from developer online chats [18], online reviews [23,24] and product descriptions [19,20], or the classifications of types of user statements [22,31] and of obligation or non-obligation statements in contracts [30]. Besides, better product descriptions can be automatically generated with the techniques of summarization from user reviews [47,48] and website information [49]. Although these sources of information are definitely essential for requirements specification, analysts still need to invest significant time and effort in interpreting this information and specifying the requirements clearly under the premise of knowing the basic requirements syntax and the domain phrases involved in the requirements.

3.2. Automated NLG with Lexical Constraints

In an early work on lexical constraints generation, Mou et al. [50] proposed the backward and forward language model (B/F-LM) and used the recurrent neural network to generate previous and subsequent words conditioned on the given word. Liu et al. [51] extended the B/F-LM by introducing a discriminator, but these two methods can generate sentences with only one lexical constraint. To overcome this limitation, Hokamp et al. [52] incorporated constraints by performing a grid beam search in the sentence space. The CGMH framework [53] models local transitions (e.g., deletion and insertion) to achieve better fluency, but it is slow to converge. Sha et al. [54] proposed an unsupervised lexical constraint generation method, in which a series of differentiable loss functions was used to calculate the fluency of the generated sentences and to determine whether they satisfy the constraints. Ding et al. [55] proposed a framework to customize the message content for appealing to different individuals.

Recently, the fine-tuning of pre-trained language models has provided more research opportunities for small datasets in many domains. BERT [40] and RoBERTa [56] use masked language modeling pre-training objectives for deep bidirectional representations by jointly conditioning on both the left and right contexts in all layers. GPT-2/3 [57,58] and CTRL [59] are causal language models, which use the auto-regressive language to model the target. UniLM [32] and GLM [60] combine the advantages of the first two models and use a special mask mechanism so that the tokens in the input sequence can focus on each other, whereas the tokens in the output sequence can focus only on the tokens to the left. MASS [61], T5 [62], and BART [63] are encoder–decoder models and adopt the standard Transformer structure [41].

4. Our Approach: *ReqGen*

As shown in Figure 2, we selected UniLM as the backbone of *ReqGen*, because of its advantages in natural language understanding and NLG [32]. On the basis of UniLM, four components were designed and implemented to improve the compliance of the generated statements with domain knowledge and software requirements syntax (as indicated by the light blue rectangles in Figure 2):

- A knowledge preparation module that retrieves keywords-related information from the domain ontology (in terms of triples consisting of entity pairs and their relationships), transforms all related information into pseudo-sentences, and selects the knowledge to be injected into the different layers of UniLM.
- A knowledge-injection model to inject the knowledge produced by the knowledge preparation module into UniLM. The injected knowledge sequence is encoded by a Bi-LSTM structure using a BERT-based sentence embedding and is injected through the attention mechanism.
- A keywords copy mechanism was added in the original UniLM, which enables it to perform a copied-word classification task in the UniLM training. Moreover, a prediction method was added to the UniLM inference model to decide whether the next token is a copied word.
- A requirements-syntax-constrained decoding module that includes a semantics-related metric used in the inference model with the original beam search to optimize the final statements towards a specific syntax.

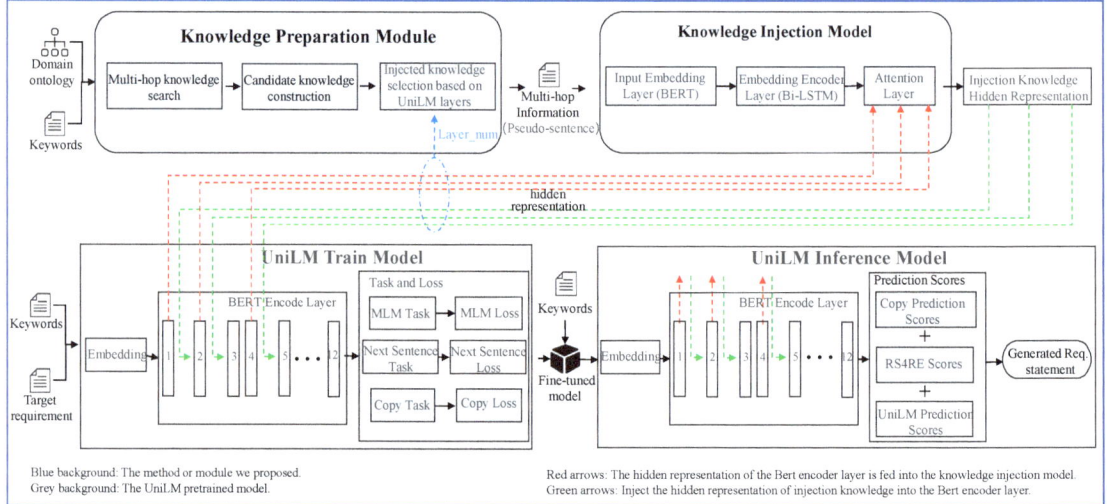

Figure 2. The procedure of our *ReqGen*.

4.1. Knowledge Preparation Module

The purpose of this module is to produce the knowledge to be injected into the backbone UniLM according to the input keywords from the domain ontology. It consists of three steps: multi-hop knowledge search, pseudo-sentence construction, and knowledge selection for the UniLM layers.

4.1.1. Multi-Hop Knowledge Search

This step aims to obtain the keywords-related concepts and their relationships from a domain ontology. We would like to increase the probability of the co-occurrence of these concepts and the input keywords by managing the attention in the knowledge injection model.

We obtained knowledge from the domain ontology, which is a collection of all of the relevant concepts and their relationships in a single domain. It is represented as a graph structure composed of triples $\langle Entity_1, Relation, Entity_2 \rangle$, built based on the OWL ontology language rules [64].

To obtain the context information of the keywords, we first performed a multi-hop graph search to acquire as much useful information as possible (five hops in this work), starting from the keywords, and collecting all types of entities in the retrieved paths.

Because all of the input keywords are regarded as start nodes, there must be repeated retrieved paths. We believe the concepts in the repeated paths are important; that is, the more often they are retrieved, the more important they are. Following this principle, we filtered some concepts according to the retrieval times to avoid noise.

4.1.2. Pseudo-Sentence Construction

We converted the extracted multi-hops $\langle Entity_1, Relation, Entity_2 \rangle$ into pseudo-sentences for the following injection task. In the OWL ontology language, entity types include *Classes*, *Object Properties*, and *Named Individuals*. There are two types of relations between these entities: the *subclass relation* and *constraint relation*. We set pseudo-sentence generation rules for these two relation types as follows:

(1) The *subclass* type includes *subClassOf* and *subPropertyOf* relations:

- *subClassOf* or *hasSuperClasses*: For the triple of $\langle a, \text{subClassOf}, b \rangle$, we created a sentence of "a is subclass of b". We converted the triple of $\langle a, \text{hasSuperClasses}, b \rangle$ into "a has super class b."

- *subPropertyOf*: For the triple of ⟨a, subPropertyOf, b⟩, we created a sentence like "a is subproperty of b".

  (2) The *Constraint* type includes *has domain* and *has range* relations:
- *has domain*: specifies the domain of a property *P*, indicating that any resource with a given property is an instance of the domain class (e.g., ⟨teaching, hasdomain, teacher⟩).
- *has range*: specifies the range of a property *P*, indicating that the value of a property is an instance of the range class (e.g., ⟨teaching, hasrange, lesson⟩).

Generally, the relationships of *has domain* and *has range* are paired. If the property has a *has domain* triple, there must be a corresponding *has range* triple simultaneously. Hence, we produced sentences for the relationship pairs. Taking the triples of ⟨teaching, hasdomain, teacher⟩ and ⟨teaching, hasrange, lesson⟩ as examples, we can create the pseudo-sentence "Teacher is teaching lesson".

Note that the grammar of the pseudo-sentences generated automatically may be wrong. However, it can provide an important context for the concepts in sentences that is required by the Bi-LSTM encoder.

4.1.3. Knowledge Selection towards the UniLM Layers

In the human learning process, when learning new things, we typically learn relatively broad knowledge first and, then, pay more attention to the essential parts, which is a repeated and gradual process. Inspired by this, we injected different keywords-related knowledge three times into the UniLM encoder, and the injected knowledge was more refined every time, rather than the common one-time knowledge injection into the pre-trained model [39].

Following the traditional one-time knowledge injection into the first layer of the pre-trained BERT model [39], we observed that the injected knowledge cannot be reflected in the decoder of BERT. We believe the primary reason is the strong fitting ability of BERT on training data, i.e., too small weights of the external knowledge injected once compared to those of the training data.

Therefore, we designed a knowledge injection mechanism by increasing the number of injections and selecting different knowledge for different layers of UniLM. In this work, we injected the knowledge into the 1st, 2nd, and 4th layer of the UniLM encoder, as shown in Figure 2. Moreover, we injected more valuable information into the higher layers. In particular, we selected all 5-hop keywords-related information for the first layer, 2-hop information for the second layer, and only 1-hop information for the fourth layer. This gradual refinement of the injected knowledge should enhance the ability of UniLM to absorb externally injected information. The evaluation and analysis of these three layers' selection (i.e., 1, 2, 4) are shown in Section 5.2.2.

4.2. Knowledge Injection Model

As Figure 2 shows, the knowledge injection model is composed of three layers. The multi-hop information in the format of pseudo-sentences is first embedded using BERT and, then, encoded using Bi-LSTM. Finally, an attention layer is used to increase the weights of the injected knowledge in the hidden representation layer of the UniLM encoder.

4.2.1. Pseudo-Sentence Embedding and Encoding

The basic unit of BERT embedding is a token. Thus, during the embedding phase, a pseudo-sentence set (knowledge) is first given to the BERT tokenizer. The [CLS] and [SEP] labels are added at the beginning and end of each sentence, respectively. Moreover, the tokenizer separates words into sub-words including the root of the words (e.g., "flying" is divided into ["fly","##ing"]).

There are three parts of the BERT embedding process: token embedding, position embedding, and segment embedding. Token embedding converts the tokens into vector representations in 768 dimensions ($[1, n, 768]$, where n is the length of a sequence). Segment embedding is used to distinguish between the keywords and target requirements in each input pair ([1, n, 768]). Position embedding converts the position information in the sequence into a vector representation of 768 dimensions ([1, n, 768]). Then, we summed these three embeddings and used this representation as the output of the BERT embedding.

We sent the embedding to the Bi-LSTM encoder [42] to obtain the pseudo-sentence encodings. The shape of the encoded hidden representation is [b, n, 768], where b is the batch size of UniLM and n is the sequence length.

4.2.2. Attention Mechanism

We used an attention mechanism to emphasize the importance of the injected knowledge. An attention mechanism is formally defined as follows:

$$\begin{aligned} A &= softmax(QK^T/\sqrt{d} + M) \\ H_{ctxt} &= A \cdot V \\ H_{knowledge} &= LayerNorm(W^T \cdot H_{ctxt} + H_{UniLM}) \end{aligned} \quad (1)$$

Here, Q is a Query, which represents the hidden representation of the UniLM encoder layer; K and V are the Key and Value, respectively representing the hidden representations of the pseudo-sentences (knowledge) encoding. To obtain the attention weights of Q and K, we used the scaled dot product method. M is the joint mask of the pseudo-sentence and the original input of UniLM (i.e., source keywords and target specifications), and d represents the length of the last dimension of K. According to experience, the use of $\sqrt{d}$ reduces the sensitivity of the method to the length of K and improves the stability of network training. Then, we calculated the dot product between A and V to update V and obtain the context representation of the attention. Finally, we summed the updated values H_{ctxt} and H_{UniLM} and fed them into *LayerNorm* (i.e., the normalization layer) to obtain the hidden representation of the knowledge.

4.3. UniLM Module

We modified UniLM in three ways, by adding multi-layer knowledge injection, a copy mechanism in the training model, and a requirements-syntax-constrained decoding in the inference model. The knowledge injection was discussed in Sections 4.1 and 4.2. Here, we focus on the other two modifications.

4.3.1. Copy Mechanism

The copy mechanism is very popular in NLG tasks such as translation and conversation generation [65]. Its aim is to resolve the "hard-constraint" problem, which requires the tokens or fragments of the source sequence to occur in the target sequence. However, most copy mechanisms can only guarantee the copy of a single word, not continuous fragments [66]. However, in our scenario, the input keywords (phrases), even the single-term words, can be multi-term words after tokenization, making it a challenge to ensure the integrity of words in the generated statements.

We adopted a simple, but novel copy mechanism [66]. In our implementation, this mechanism first marks the copied fragments in the target requirements according to the source keywords. Then, we added a new copied label prediction task in the training phase of our seq2seq model to predict whether a token has been copied from the source keywords or not. In the decoder prediction stage, the original next token prediction probability is changed to a mixed probability model of the next token prediction probability and copied token prediction probability.

4.3.2. Requirement-Syntax-Constrained Decoding

Well-formed requirements specifications should follow a certain syntax, and there are several related guidelines or models, such as EARS [5], IEEE 29148:2018 [37] and M-FRDL [36]. They all define the fine-grained elements of single requirements specifications, and each indicates one semantic role.

The requirements generated by *ReqGen* should attempt to follow at least one existing syntax so that they can accurately capture stakeholder needs [37]. Hence, if requirements analysts follow a specific requirements syntax when writing requirements specifications and they could give the semantic roles that the keywords belong to (the content in brackets of Figure 1), we would like to use this information to improve the generated sentence further. We designed an indicator called *RS4RE* to evaluate the overlap of the semantic constitution of the generated requirements with those set by engineers. The *RS4RE* value of each generated candidate statement is used to help select the final statement by adding it to the original probability score during beam search.

RS4RE is defined formally as follows. We measured the closeness of agreement of each semantic element in the generated statement and the input of an analyst.

$$RS4RE = \sum \alpha_i \frac{|E_i(R_{aut}) \cap E_{i\_ref}|}{|E_{i\_ref}|} \quad where\ 1 \leq i \leq N \quad (2)$$

Let N be the number of semantic elements in the syntax requirements analysts have selected and E_i be the i_{th} element. Here, E_{i_ref} is used to indicate the word set of the element E_i given by the requirements analysts, and $E_i(R_{aut})$ indicates the set of words of the element E_i in the automatically generated sentence. The agreement on element i is calculated as the ratio of the scale of overlapping words to the size of the manually given set. Moreover, α_i is a hyper-parameter that indicates the weight of element i, and the sum of all α_i is 1.

In this work, we used M-FRDL [36] as the syntax because they shared the source code with us. This enabled us to automatically identify the fine-grained elements in the natural language requirements, which is required by the automated calculation of *RS4RE*.

5. Experimental Evaluation

We evaluated *ReqGen* by addressing the following research questions:

- **RQ1**: How well does *ReqGen* perform in comparison with existing NLG approaches on requirements specification generation based on keywords?
- **RQ2**: To what extent does the multi-layer knowledge injection contribute to the requirements specification generation?
- **RQ3**: To what extent does the knowledge frequency filtering contribute to the requirements specification generation?
- **RQ4**: To what extent does each proposed design component contribute to the requirements specification generation?

5.1. Experimental Design

5.1.1. Data Preparation

To evaluate our *ReqGen*, we used two datasets of open-source requirements specifications and two domain ontologies, i.e., the unmanned aerial vehicle (UAV) and building automation system (BAS) domains, following previous work [38].

The UAV requirements are from the University of Notre Dame (https://dronology.info/, accessed on 23 May 2018) including 99 requirements [67]. The public ontology for the UAV domain (http://www.dronetology.net/, accessed on 2 February 2021) includes 400 entities. The BAS requirements are from the Standard BAS Specification (2015) [68] and consist of 456 requirements, involving functional, performance, and security requirements. The open-domain model of BAS (https://gitlab.fi.muni.cz/xkucer16/semanticBMS, accessed on 1 December 2017) includes 484 entities.

The requirements are represented using natural language sentences, and we required the related keywords before the model training and testing. Thus, we performed a reverse extraction process. To be specific, we automatically extracted the noun words or phrases based on the parts-of-speech tagged by Stanford CoreNLP [69]. We extracted the noun and noun phrases with a series of linguistic filters for the nested noun selection, such as

$Noun^{+}Noun$. For each requirements, we randomly selected n noun phrases ($n \in [2, N]$, where N is the total number of noun and noun phrases in one requirement) as the keywords.

To evaluate the effectiveness of the requirements-syntax-constrained decoding described in Section 4.3.2, we implemented the M-FRDL constraint [36] and manually assigned the semantic roles to the randomly selected keywords according to their context in the requirements statements. To ensure correctness, we invited one author of the work [36] to check and revise them.

Another problem with the data is that the domain ontology may be unable to cover all the content of the requirements because these datasets were generated by different groups who have different concerns. Only if the keywords are contained in the domain ontology will the ontology be helpful for the keywords-driven requirements generation. Thus, we performed automated domain ontology completion using an approach of [70]. This approach first aligns the requirements and domain ontology using TransE [71]. Then, it selects the requirements concepts that are related to the entities in the domain ontology and adds them, as well as their corresponding relationships to the ontology.

Given the limited data, we performed 10-fold and 5-fold cross-validation on the UAV and BAS requirements, respectively. In addition, we performed a batch knowledge injection and injected the knowledge for all of the random keywords of the testing requirements, considering the potential association of the requirements. In particular, 17,681 pseudo-sentences were created for the 10 test requirements of the UAV and 139,494 pseudo-sentences for the 93 test requirements of the BAS.

5.1.2. Baselines

We selected six popular constrained text generation approaches as the baseline methods, including four pre-trained models and two other NLG models (i.e., POINTER [72] and CGMH [53]). Similarly, we trained these models using the UAV and BAS datasets separately (10-fold and 5-fold cross-validation, respectively):

- BERT [40] jointly conditions on contextual information, which enables pre-training and deep bidirectional representation from unlabeled text. We fine-tuned the BERT base model on our task, and the number of parameters was 110 M.
- Generative Pre-trained Transformer 3 (GPT3) [58] uses the one-way language model training of GPT2. The model size was increased to 175 billion, and 45 terabytes of data were used for training. GPT3 can perform downstream tasks without fine-tuning in a zero-shot setting. We also did not perform fine-tuning.
- Bidirectional and Auto-Regressive Transformers (BART) [63] is a denoising autoencoder built with a sequence-to-sequence model suitable for various tasks. It uses a standard Transformer-based neural machine translation architecture. It is trained using text corrupted with an arbitrary noising function and by learning to reconstruct the original text. We used the BART-large model on our task, and the number of parameters was 400 M.
- UniLM [32] uses three types of language modeling tasks for pre-training, which is achieved by employing a shared Transformer network and using specific self-attention masks to control the context of the prediction conditions. We used the UniLM base model, whose parameter amount is 340 M.
- Zhang et al. [72] proposed POINTER, which is based on the inserted non-autoregressive pre-training method. A beam search method was proposed to achieve log-level non-autoregressive generation.
- The constrained generation by Metropolis–Hastings sampling (CGMH) method [53] can cope with both hard and soft constraints during sentence generation. Different from the traditional latent space usage, it directly samples from the sentence space using the Metropolis–Hastings sampling.

5.1.3. Metrics

We selected *BLEU* [73] as the first metric, which is commonly used in machine translation, NLG, and source code generation. It measures the degree of overlap between the generated and reference sentences using n-grams. The higher the degree of overlap, the higher the quality of the generated text. Here, *BLEU1* measures word-level accuracy and *BLEU2* measures sentence fluency to a specific degree. In addition, we employed the *ROUGE* metric [74]. ROUGE-N calculates the total sum of the number of n-grams occurring in both the generated and target sentences, and *ROUGE-L* calculates the longest common subsequence. We calculated the recall, precision, and F-measure for each kind of ROUGE rather than the simple n-gram recall [74].

Besides, we used the *RS4RE* metric to evaluate the agreement of syntax compliance between the generated and target sentences, as described in Section 4.3.2. Here, E_{i_ref} refers to the set of words in the i_{th} semantic element of the target requirement. We also recorded the time used by each model (except GPT-3) for training and testing, considering its practical value.

5.2. Experimental Results and Analysis

5.2.1. RQ1 Effectiveness of Our Approach

We illustrate the experimental results for the UAV and BAS cases in Table 1. The average and standard deviation are given for each metric on the 5 and 10 runs on the UAV and BAS, respectively. For better illustration, we highlight the cells with the best results for each metric with grey background, and the second best results with yellow background. Table 2 presents an example of the requirements generated by each baseline and *ReqGen*, from which we can draw three conclusions:

(1) **Our method achieves the best or second-best results for all metrics.** In the UAV case, our method yields the best results for five metrics and the second-best results for the remaining eight metrics. BART achieves good performance with six best and five second-best results, which demonstrates the benefits of its hard constraint design. However, it can only embed a single input word and loses the complete semantic meaning of phrases (i.e., it obtains better BLEU1 and ROUGE-1 results, but weaker BLEU2 and ROUGE-2 results), which can also be seen in the example in Table 2. Moreover, *ReqGen* obtains a better RS4RE result than BART, indicating that it has a better semantic-oriented text generation ability.

On the BAS domain, our *ReqGen* achieves seven best and four second-best results, outperforming all baselines. The basic UniLM performs moderately well because it considers both the input and its context during the next token prediction. This is the reason that we select it as the backbone of *ReqGen*.

(2) **The four pre-trained models perform better than the other two baselines.** Among the four pre-trained models in the UAV domain, BART obtains the best ROUGE-1, ROUGE-2, and ROUGE-L results. It even outperforms *ReqGen* in ROUGE-1, which is possible because BART forces all keywords to be included in the output during decoding. However, because it only sees the input, it performs worse in ROUGE-2. UniLM obtains good BLEU1 and BLEU2 results and the best ROUGE-2 results in the BAS case, indicating its better ability to generate relatively fluent statements.

CGMH performs worst according to the two BLEU metrics and the F-measure of the three ROUGE metrics, as shown in Tables 1 and 2. POINTER also has a weak performance, and a possible reason for this performance could be that it places the entire generation burden on the decoder, which means that the sentences it generates are very long, but the correlation with the target is weak (see the example in Table 2).

From the standard derivation values, we can observe that the stability of the four pre-trained models is weaker than the other two baselines on the UAV. However, for the bigger BAS case, all of the pre-trained models achieve more stable results. This indicates that more domain knowledge is helpful for the stable results' generation for the pre-trained models.

(3) **Our method is slightly slower than UniLM and BART.** As shown in the last column of Table 1, we recorded the average time consumed by each method (in hours) to perform the 10-fold cross-validation on the UAV and the 5-fold cross-validation on the BAS data. We did not record the time used by GPT3 because it does not need extra fine-tuning [58]. We observed that *ReqGen* needs slightly more time than UniLM and BART, but less time than the other approaches, even though it uses extra knowledge injection, a copy mechanism, and requirements-syntax-constrained decoding.

Table 1. Results of the baselines and our *ReqGen* (%).

	Method	BLEU1	BLEU2	ROUGE-1			ROUGE-2			ROUGE-L			RS4RE	Time (HRS)
				R.	P.	F.	R.	P.	F.	R.	P.	F.		
UAV	Bert_base	37.92 ±3.3	23.53 ±2.54	54.33 ±2.29	42.04 ±3.61	47.40 ±2.33	31.32 ±2.37	24.88 ±3.25	27.73 ±2.57	51.29 ±2.77	39.90 ±3.38	44.88 ±2.68	8.00 [2] ±1.27	1.5
	GPT3	34.20 ±6.64	18.28 ±5.41	34.51 ±8.66	59.42 [1] ±11.39	43.66 ±9.39	16.49 ±6.77	14.82 ±8.05	15.61 ±7.12	31.02 ±8.39	56.22 ±10.64	39.98 ±8.89	1.31 ±0.26	-
	UniLM	34.27 ±8.95	17.83 ±5.69	55.15 ±10.99	41.53 ±13.26	47.38 ±11.68	18.21 ±6.71	14.44 ±8.42	16.11 ±7.19	49.73 ±10.27	37.71 ±12.42	42.89 ±10.92	2.54 ±0.14	1
	BART	42.66 ±7.90	23.99 ±9.17	71.75 ±6.23	52.12 ±6.16	60.38 ±4.85	37.86 ±8.95	26.90 ±7.70	31.45 ±8.16	66.07 ±7.20	47.79 ±6.56	55.47 ±5.89	5.76 ±1.45	1
	CGMH	12.07 ±2.63	1.84 ±0.56	35.06 ±4.45	17.86 ±9.99	23.66 ±6.06	5.48 ±0.92	2.47 ±2.95	3.41 ±1.39	32.42 ±4.24	16.52 ±9.34	21.89 ±5.75	0.00 ±0.00	22
	POINTER	17.26 ±3.63	2.46 ±0.98	24.15 ±3.86	38.66 ±3.58	29.73 ±3.72	2.83 ±1.61	5.20 ±1.09	3.67 ±1.26	19.92 ±2.60	32.07 ±2.76	24.58 ±2.80	4.60 ±1.87	1
	ReqGen	42.15 ±6.55	25.04 ±6.19	69.93 ±5.44	49.91 ±6.13	58.25 ±5.66	39.03 ±6.04	28.21 ±8.27	32.75 ±6.87	65.12 ±5.96	46.47 ±6.92	54.23 ±6.27	8.89 ±1.18	1.2
BAS	Bert_base	29.08 ±2.23	9.28 ±1.63	46.69 ±2.58	35.90 ±3.31	40.59 ±2.54	12.84 ±1.73	10.57 ±1.86	11.60 ±1.66	40.79 ±2.51	31.64 ±2.98	35.64 ±2.45	12.48 ±2.05	1
	GPT3	28.34 ±2.47	7.87 ±1.21	37.17 ±2.56	41.07 ±4.25	33.56 ±3.18	10.02 ±1.15	9.64 ±1.56	9.30 ±1.28	31.98 ±1.85	35.74 ±3.12	30.53 ±2.33	7.08 ±1.33	-
	UniLM	30.08 ±2.15	13.31 ±1.06	42.44 ±1.36	33.58 ±1.98	37.49 ±1.29	24.42 ±1.14	18.86 ±0.99	21.28 ±1.01	39.58 ±1.41	31.47 ±1.22	35.06 ±1.16	13.56 ±2.43	0.8
	BART	27.05 ±1.63	10.60 ±0.55	63.67 ±0.36	37.37 ±3.93	47.10 ±1.38	20.59 ±0.56	12.43 ±1.64	15.50 ±0.77	58.78 ±0.34	34.14 ±3.73	43.19 ±1.39	14.58 ±1.79	0.7
	CGMH	10.58 ±2.25	1.85 ±0.32	57.69 ±4.33	20.94 ±11.21	30.73 ±5.99	4.23 ±0.55	1.64 ±1.41	2.36 ±0.77	44.70 ±3.06	16.41 ±8.05	24.01 ±4.26	3.26 ±0.84	72
	POINTER	21.34 ±3.74	2.34 ±0.75	25.34 ±5.05	43.82 ±3.36	32.11 ±4.02	1.93 ±1.43	3.69 ±0.74	2.53 ±0.96	21.01 ±3.74	36.53 ±2.59	26.68 ±3.07	5.72 ±0.57	1
	ReqGen	38.07 ±1.62	15.62 ±0.87	58.96 ±1.33	44.63 ±3.21	50.80 ±1.95	20.35 ±1.35	16.45 ±2.11	18.19 ±1.62	52.82 ±1.16	40.17 ±2.76	45.63 ±1.65	17.42 ±2.83	0.9

[1] Grey background: Best results for each metric. [2] Yellow background: Second-best results for each metric.

Table 2. Examples showing the requirements generated by the baselines and our method from three keywords.

Keywords: landing, internal simulator, ground
Target: When given a **landing** [1] command the **internal simulator** shall move the UAV from to the **ground** altitude corresponding to its current longitude and latitude.

Alg.	Generated Sentence	Required Modifications
Bert_base	when a flight **simulator** is activated the flight **simulator** shall compute the location of the UAV.	Useless: no semantic overlap with the target.
GPT3	When a UAV lands the **Internal Simulator** shall record the time of **landing**.	Useless: no semantic overlap with the target.
UniLM	When a UAV is loaded the **internal simulator** shall display the location of the UAV.	Useless: no semantic overlap with the target.
BART	**landing internal** flight **simulator** shall compute the **ground** position of a UAV.	The trigger is missing, and the main clause is partially right: when given a landing command [2], the internal flight simulator shall compute the ground position of a UAV and move the UAV to ground latitude.
CGMH	**simulator** owners for takeoff at a corresponding latitude.	Useless: syntax errors and no semantic overlap with the target.
POINTER	in which a single point **landing** system, when a single point that is assigned a separate GPS system or for an active navigation system has to orient at its current position and to display the current **ground** coordinates.	Useless: syntax errors and no semantic overlap with the target.
ReqGen	When a **landing** UAV is assigned to a UAV, the **internal simulator** shall compute the **ground** longitude latitude and latitude of the UAV.	The trigger is right, and the main clause is partially right: when a **landing** UAV command is assigned to a UAV, the **internal simulator** shall compute the **ground** longitude latitude and latitude of the UAV and move the UAV to ground latitude.

[1] Bold font: Keywords in the sentences generated by the all automated approaches. [2] Blue font: The parts added by analysts manually.

5.2.2. RQ2 Effectiveness of Multi-Layer Knowledge Injection

We also evaluated the effectiveness of the multi-layer knowledge injection in the two domains. To implement and evaluate *ReqGen*, given that we collected five-hop keywords-related information and there are 12 layers in UniLM, we had to determine (1) *which levels should have knowledge injected* and (2) *what kind of knowledge should be injected into the different layers*. Because of the uncertainty in the injected layers and the injected knowledge for one specific layer (i.e., which hop in the five hops), there are many combinations that could have been used in our experiments. Thus, we pruned the candidate combinations for the experiments.

As for the injected layers, Li et al. [39] injected knowledge into the first layer. Jawahar et al. [75] experimented with different layers of BERT on 10 sentence-level detection tasks. They observed that the 1st and 2nd layers learn surface information such as word detection in sentences. Layers 4 to 7 learn syntactic information such as word order sensitivity. Layers 8 to 12 learn semantic-level information such as subject–verb agreement. Inspired by these two studies, we focused on three combinations of shallow layers, shallow + syntactic layers, and shallow + syntactic + semantic layers, with layer combinations of (1,2), (1, 2, 4), and (1, 2, 4,8), respectively. Moreover, considering the five hops in our collected information, we made an extra evaluation on the combination (1, 2, 4,8,11), and each layer was assigned one-hop information.

For the injected knowledge, we followed the cognitive process of human learning, in which humans usually start from general and overview knowledge and, then, pay close attention to the critical parts. Similarly, we assigned more keyword knowledge to the lower layers. For example, for the layer combination (1,2), we assigned all 5-hop knowledge to the first layer and the most-related 1-hop knowledge to the second layer. The injected knowledge details of different layer combinations can be found in the *layer (hop)* of Table 3, which presents the results of this experiment.

For the UAV case, we observed that the best BLEU1 and BLEU2 scores are achieved by the (1, 2, 4) combination. For ROUGE-1, the best recall is achieved by injecting knowledge into Layers 1, 2, 4 and 8, the best precision is achieved by the (1,2) combination, and the best of F-measure is achieved by the (1, 2, 4) combination. Similar phenomena were observed for the ROUGE-2 and ROUGE-L metrics. In the BAS case, the best BLEU1 and BLEU2 results are also achieved by the (1, 2, 4) combination. For ROUGE-1, the best F-value is achieved by the (1,2) combination; however, for ROUGE-2 and ROUGE-L, the best performance is achieved by the (1, 2, 4) combination. Besides, the stability of this configuration has no obvious change.

In summary, the (1, 2, 4) combination with the 5-, 2-, and 1-hop knowledge injection achieves seven best results in the UAV case and nine best results in the BAS case, out of all 11 metrics. Hence, we suggest three knowledge injections by injecting all 5-hop knowledge into the first layer, 2-hop knowledge into the second layer, and the most-critical 1-hop knowledge into the fourth layer.

Table 3. The effectiveness of different injection times (%).

	Layer (Hop)	BLEU1	BLEU2	ROUGE-1			ROUGE-2			ROUGE-L		
				R.	P.	F.	R.	P.	F.	R.	P.	F.
UAV	1(5), 2(1)	43.23 ±5.76	24.63 ±6.18	63.21 ±5.44	50.51[1] ±4.69	56.15 ±4.18	34.90 ±7.02	27.61 ±6.00	29.86 ±6.15	58.83 ±5.25	47.04 ±5.80	51.12 ±4.96
	1(5), 2(2), 4(1)	43.87 ±6.07	25.05 ±6.89	65.69 ±6.82	50.34 ±6.54	57.00 ±6.15	35.59 ±9.57	27.18 ±7.04	30.82 ±7.98	61.13 ±7.60	46.86 ±6.95	53.05 ±6.91
	1(5), 2(3), 4(2), 8(1)	42.57 ±3.29	23.63 ±4.65	66.22 ±7.59	49.96 ±3.98	56.95 ±4.35	35.14 ±9.76	26.10 ±5.86	29.95 ±6.52	61.39 ±7.77	46.57 ±4.72	52.95 ±5.02
	1(5), 2(4), 4(3), 8(2), 11(1)	40.2 ±5.82	21.64 ±5.97	63.04 ±6.08	47.37 ±5.91	54.09 ±5.05	32.40 ±8.58	24.17 ±6.44	26.89 ±7.04	58.65 ±6.15	44.17 ±7.07	49.42 ±6.17
BAS	1(5), 2(1)	34.51 ±2.69	13.25 ±1.77	55.54 ±3.00	41.74 ±2.20	47.66 ±2.36	17.86 ±1.94	14.13 ±1.82	15.78 ±1.84	49.87 ±2.38	37.66 ±1.92	42.91 ±1.96
	1(5), 2(2), 4(1)	34.55 ±2.28	13.73 ±0.69	55.02 ±2.97	41.76 ±2.07	47.48 ±2.38	18.30 ±1.22	14.68 ±0.99	16.29 ±1.01	49.83 ±2.54	38.03 ±1.66	43.14 ±1.95
	1(5), 2(3), 4(2), 8(1)	33.26 ±2.37	12.92 ±1.20	54.51 ±1.72	40.64 ±2.53	46.56 ±2.14	18.13 ±0.99	14.19 ±1.24	15.92 ±1.14	49.21 ±1.31	36.92 ±2.08	42.19 ±1.80
	1(5), 2(4), 4(3), 8(2), 11(1)	32.33 ±2.05	12.31 ±1.12	54.27 ±2.99	40.16 ±2.43	46.16 ±2.55	17.38 ±1.49	13.77 ±1.23	15.37 ±1.30	49.02 ±2.57	36.55 ±2.14	41.88 ±2.23

[1] Grey background: Best results for each metric for each case.

5.2.3. RQ3 Effectiveness of Frequency Filtering in the Knowledge Search

We further evaluated the impact of different frequency sets in the knowledge search on the final requirements generation (as described in Section 4.1.1). We regarded more-frequent knowledge as more important, and our aim was to inject only important information into *ReqGen* to reduce noise pollution in the data.

To evaluate the impact of a frequency filter (a single dependent variable), we set the injected layer as a constant. We experimented with frequency thresholds of 0, 10, and 50 on all five-hop knowledge injected into the first layer. In other words, we injected all traversed entities, entities occurring more than 10 times, or those occurring more than 50 times in the ontology graph traversal. The results are shown in Table 4, and the best result of each metric is highlighted with bold font and grey background.

We observed different results for the two cases. For the UAV, no frequency filtering is best, followed by 10 and 50 frequency filters, whereas, for the BAS, the best performance is achieved with 10 frequency filters and with 50 frequency filters is the second best. There is no obvious difference between the stability of their results. This result led us to the following two observations. (1) Intuitively, the frequency set is strongly correlated with the scale of injected knowledge. In our case, the five-hop knowledge of the UAV domain includes 17,681 pseudo-sentences, and the BAS includes 139,494 sentences (approximately 7.9 times). (2) When there is a massive amount of information, less- and more-refined knowledge is more valuable. For example, 50 frequency filters are better than no filter in the BAS domain. However, when the information is small, all related knowledge is valuable (e.g., in the UAV case, no filter is better than the 10 frequency filters, which is better than the 50 frequency filters). However, because of the limited available cases, we cannot give a criterion for frequency filter selection temporarily in this initial study.

Table 4. The effectiveness of knowledge frequency filtering (%).

	Frequency Filtering	BLEU1	BLEU2	ROUGE-1			ROUGE-2			ROUGE-L		
				R.	P.	F.	R.	P.	F.	R.	P.	F.
UAV	no	42.78 ±3.84	24.14 [1] ±5.23	66.54 ±6.54	49.85 ±4.57	57.00 ±4.25	35.51 ±7.55	26.59 ±5.37	30.41 ±5.87	61.76 ±6.55	46.45 ±5.08	53.02 ±4.79
	10	43.50 ±5.07	23.97 ±5.04	65.80 ±7.59	49.92 ±5.27	56.77 ±5.20	34.99 ±8.68	26.22 ±5.58	29.24 ±6.14	61.75 ±7.30	47.04 ±6.11	52.46 ±5.79
	50	40.47 ±5.80	21.39 ±6.09	61.87 ±4.00	46.58 ±4.71	53.15 ±4.27	32.05 ±7.58	23.63 ±6.10	27.21 ±6.60	57.90 ±4.34	43.70 ±4.94	49.80 ±4.58
BAS	no	34.15 ±1.90	13.37 ±1.03	54.75 ±1.99	41.30 ±1.10	47.08 ±1.28	18.01 ±1.22	14.49 ±1.05	16.06 ±1.03	49.41 ±2.02	37.52 ±1.34	42.65 ±1.48
	10	34.43 ±1.80	13.65 ±1.38	55.93 ±2.41	41.76 ±0.98	47.82 ±1.10	18.84 ±1.29	14.80 ±0.92	16.58 ±0.97	50.29 ±2.22	37.76 ±0.77	43.13 ±0.96
	50	34.33 ±1.83	13.45 ±1.31	55.68 ±1.64	41.69 ±0.96	47.68 ±1.22	18.65 ±1.59	14.66 ±1.07	16.41 ±1.28	50.28 ±1.87	37.83 ±1.09	43.18 ±1.39

[1] Grey background: Best results for each metric for each case.

5.2.4. RQ4 Ablation Experiment

The ablation experiment was designed to verify the effectiveness of each critical proposed component in our *ReqGen*: multi-layer injection (including frequency filtering), copy mechanism, and syntax-constrained decoding. Table 5 shows the results of *ReqGen* and its four variants. For the convenience of comparison, we indicate the values that are better than those in the previous row with an up-arrow.

Table 5. The ablation experiment (%).

	Settings	BLEU1	BLEU2	ROUGE-1			ROUGE-2			ROUGE-L		
				R.	P.	F.	R.	P.	F.	R.	P.	F.
UAV	Layer 1	42.78 ±3.84	24.14 ±5.23	66.54 ±6.54	49.85 ±4.57	57.00 ±4.25	35.51 ±7.55	26.59 ±5.37	30.41 ±5.87	61.76 ±6.55	46.45 ±5.08	53.02 ±4.79
	Layer 1, 2, 4	43.87 ↑[1] ±6.07	25.05 ↑ ±6.89	65.69 ±6.82	50.34 ↑ ±6.54	57.00 ±6.15	35.59 ↑ ±9.57	27.18 ↑ ±7.04	30.82 ↑ ±7.98	61.13 ±7.60	46.86 ↑ ±6.95	53.05 ↑ ±6.91
	Layer 1, 2, 4 + 10 Fre.	44.80 [2] ↑ ±4.00	25.12 ↑ ±5.23	65.35 ±6.64	52.18 ↑ ±4.26	58.03 ↑ ±4.22	35.48 ±8.98	28.11 ↑ ±5.62	31.37 ↑ ±6.66	60.95 ±7.35	48.93 ↑ ±5.94	54.28 ↑ ±5.56
	Layer 1, 2, 4 + 10 Fre. + Copy	42.15 ±6.55	25.04 ±6.19	69.93 ↑ ±5.44	49.91 ±6.13	58.25 ↑ ±5.66	39.03 ↑ ±6.04	28.21 ↑ ±8.27	32.75 ↑ ±6.87	65.12 ↑ ±5.96	46.47 ±6.92	54.23 ±6.27
	Layer 1, 2, 4 + 10 Fre. + Copy + Syntax cons. (*ReqGen*)	42.15 ±6.55	25.04 ±6.19	69.93 ±5.44	49.91 ±6.13	58.25 ±5.66	39.03 ±6.04	28.21 ±8.27	32.75 ±6.87	65.12 ±5.96	46.47 ±6.92	54.23 ±6.27
BAS	Layer 1	34.15 ±1.90	13.37 ±1.03	54.75 ±1.99	41.30 ±1.10	47.08 ±1.28	18.01 ±1.22	14.49 ±1.05	16.06 ±1.03	49.41 ±2.02	37.52 ±1.34	42.65 ±1.48
	Layer 1, 2, 4	34.55 ↑ ±2.28	13.73 ↑ ±0.69	55.02 ↑ ±2.97	41.76 ↑ ±2.07	47.48 ↑ ±2.38	18.30 ↑ ±1.22	14.68 ↑ ±0.99	16.29 ↑ ±1.01	49.83 ↑ ±2.54	38.03 ↑ ±1.66	43.14 ↑ ±1.95
	Layer 1, 2, 4 + 10 Fre.	37.99 ↑ ±1.61	15.57 ↑ ±0.07	56.30 ↑ ±2.27	45.05 ↑ ±1.60	50.05 ↑ ±1.67	19.58 ↑ ±1.29	16.57 ↑ ±0.85	17.95 ↑ ±0.99	50.60 ↑ ±2.14	40.68 ↑ ±1.27	45.10 ↑ ±1.38
	Layer 1, 2, 4 + 10 Fre. + Copy	38.41 ↑ ±2.51	15.06 ±1.13	59.47 ↑ ±3.23	44.93 ±2.34	51.18 ↑ ±2.82	19.46 ±1.83	15.75 ±1.00	17.41 ±1.38	53.30 ↑ ±2.70	40.48 ±2.00	46.01 ↑ ±2.40
	Layer 1, 2, 4 + 10 Fre. + Copy + Syntax cons. (*ReqGen*)	38.07 ±1.62	15.62 ↑ ±0.87	58.96 ±1.33	44.63 ±3.21	50.80 ±1.95	20.35 ↑ ±1.35	16.45 ↑ ±2.11	18.19 ↑ ±1.62	52.82 ±1.16	40.17 ±2.76	45.63 ±1.65

[1] Up-arrow: The value in one cell is better than that of the previous row for the same metric. [2] Grey background: Best results for each metric for each case.

In the UAV case, compared with the one-layer knowledge injection, the three injections into Layers 1, 2, and 4 yield an approximately 1% increase in BLEU1 and BLEU2. For the

ROUGE results, the improvement is primarily in the three precision scores, which are increased by 0.5%. However, the recall in ROUGE is slightly decreased, possibly due to some related knowledge loss in Layers 2 and 4. However, the F-measure values remain unchanged or become better with respect to the values obtained for the single-layer injection. In the BAS case, all metrics, including the BLEU and three ROUGE metrics, are improved by three-layer knowledge injection. This observation shows that the multi-layer injection design mainly improves the BLEU metric and the precision of ROUGE, indicating that this mechanism enhances the ratio of valid words in the final statements. In other words, although the single-layer injection can help the model obtain the knowledge, *the multi-layer injection is further helpful for knowledge absorption.*

The comparisons between the second and third rows in both the UAV and BAS domains show the impact of 10 frequency filters on Layers 1, 2, and 4. We can see that the two BLEU values in both cases are better with this frequency setting. For the UAV, the precision and F-measure of the three ROUGE metrics increase further. However, the recall values are weaker. This is expected because the filtering operation on a relatively small set of knowledge would probably lessen the number of useful clues, whereas, for the BAS, due to its larger scale, all metrics improve even after filtering. We note that *the 10 frequency filters indeed effectively reduce the noise.*

Figure 3 shows one example of the effects of frequency filtering. In this example, when no frequency filtering is used, the terms "loses" and "routing" in the domain ontology are injected into *ReqGen* and reflected in the generated requirement, showing that noise words are reflected in the lexical constitutions of the generated requirements, which then determine the semantic meaning. By contrast, the example with 10 frequency filters shows that our frequency filtering method helps reduce the noise in the injected knowledge.

Source: GCS, connected UAV, middleware

Target: The **GCS** shall report newly **connected UAVs** to the **GCS middleware.**

No frequency filtering: When the **GCS** loses the **connection** to a **UAV** the **UAV Middleware** shall transmit the routing to an **UAV**.

10 frequency filtering: When a **UAV** is **connected** via the **GCS middleware** shall transmit the **connection** to **UAV**.

Blue background: Keywords of the original input.
Pink background: The target requirement statement.
Yellow background: The sentence generated by our approach with no frequency filtering.
Green background: The sentence generated by our approach with 10 frequency filtering.
Bold font: Keywords in the target and generated sentences.

Figure 3. An example with or without frequency filtering.

The comparisons between the fourth and fifth rows of Table 5 for both domains show the influence of the copy mechanism. From the results for the UAV domain, we observed that six results, mainly ROUGE scores, improve and achieve the best values with this design, whereas the two BLEU scores fall approximately 2%. Similarly, the results for five metrics increase, and the remaining six decrease for the BAS domain. This shows that the copy mechanism is helpful for the *recall of the overlapping n-grams* in the generated sentences. However, because it was designed to guarantee that the given keywords must appear in the generated sentence, this actually increases the length of the generated sentences. In other words, it is highly likely to dilute the ratio of the overlapping n-grams in the whole statements, which decreases the BLEU scores.

We also show the influence of the copy mechanism with an example in Figure 4, and we can see that all keywords, including the multi-term phrases, can occur in the final sentence. Without this mechanism, some keywords are abandoned, in favor of the *more important injected knowledge* and the syntax learned during the pre-training process of UniLM.

Source: operator, trend log, setup information

Target: **Operator** shall be able to change **trend log setup information.**

No copy mechanism: **Operator** shall be able to use a **trend log** to share **trend logs** with other **operators**.

Copy mechanism: **Operator** shall be able to use a **trend log** for quick **trend log setup information.**

Blue background: Keywords of the original input.
Pink background: The target requirement statement.
Yellow background: The sentence generated by our approach with no copy mechanism.
Green background: The sentence generated by our approach with copy mechanism.
Bold font: Keywords in the target and generated sentences.

Figure 4. An example with or without the copy mechanism.

Finally, we added syntax-constrained decoding into the settings, and the results are listed in the fifth row of each case in Table 5. We can see consistent enhancements of the ROUGE-2 results for both cases and a positive effect on the BLEU2 in the BAS domain and no change to the BLEU2 result of the UAV domain. This indicates that *our syntax decoding is helpful for valid two-gram generation*, the semantic units with a larger granularity than single-term words.

6. Discussion

6.1. Threats to Validity

Construct validity mainly concerns the evaluation metrics. We used BLEU1, BLEU2, and the precision, recall, and F-measure of ROUGE-1, ROUGE-2, and ROUGE-L, which are the most-common metrics of NLG [33,39,54]. Moreover, to consider the special syntax constraints of well-formed software requirements [5,36,37], we designed the RS4RE metric, which measures the syntax distance between the automated generated and target requirements. We also recorded the training and testing time of the automated approaches for practical consideration.

Besides, the UAV and BAS ontologies were collected online by [38]. Their quality will impact the construct validity. However, both ontologies have been peer-reviewed, and there are series of follow-up peer-reviewed works (i.e., 3 for UAV [76–78] and 40 for BAS [79]). We believe the quality of the two ontologies can be guaranteed.

Internal validity concerns the validity of the causal relations between the results and our approaches. We reused the open-source code of UniLM, the backbone of our *ReqGen* and the six baselines, to ensure the accuracy of experiments. Another threat comes from the measure of RS4RE, which involves the manual annotation of the semantic elements of M-FRDL [36] for the case requirements. In the two sets of requirements, the UAV requirements were annotated by the work of [36], and we used their original annotations directly. For the BAS domain, our authors performed pair annotations, which were then carefully checked individually by the first author of [36]. We believe the annotations are trustworthy.

External validity concerns the generalization of the experimental results to other cases. In this initial study, we experimented with two public datasets from different domains with different scales. All of the requirements and ontologies were from different groups, reflecting different writing styles. However, because of the data limitations, we only performed 10- and 5-fold cross-validation on the UAV and BAS cases. Although the results are promising, more diverse data for further experiments will be needed in the future.

6.2. Implications

Based on our results, the primary implication is that, like traditional large-scale text-based fine-tuning, concept-net knowledge injection is beneficial for pre-trained models performing downstream tasks. This means that our approach is potentially helpful for other document generation, such as the description of software design. In addition, multiple knowledge injections into the pre-trained model are better than once, and the knowledge injected into higher layers should be more refined than that injected into the lower layers, just as in the human learning process. Our experiments show that injection of all 5-hop knowledge into the first layer, 2-hop knowledge into the second layer, and only the most-relevant 1-hop knowledge into the fourth layer achieves the best results on both domains in our task (as shown in Table 3).

The second implication suggested by our study is that automated requirements generation requires related domain knowledge, but "more" does not always mean "better". In the BAS case, 10 frequency filters were better than no filtering. However, the injected knowledge is also critical because the general UniLM has to learn the domain knowledge for the valid requirements generation. Thus, for the small UAV case, no filtering is the best (as shown in Table 4).

Besides, our study has two practical impacts. First, *ReqGen* can assist analysts in generating the final correct requirements quickly since it can automatically generate the keywords-driven, domain-knowledge-restricted, and syntax-compliant requirements draft. As show in Figure 5, we used the example in Table 2 to illustrate the usefulness. The analyst only needs to make two modifications by adding "command" and "add move the UAV to ground latitude", to obtain the target synonymous statement.

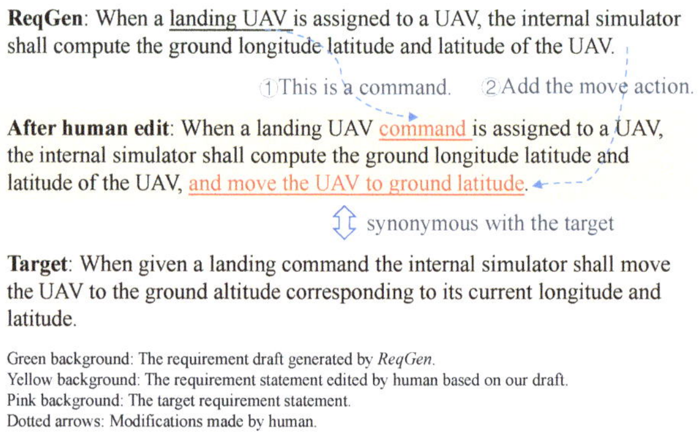

ReqGen: When a landing UAV is assigned to a UAV, the internal simulator shall compute the ground longitude latitude and latitude of the UAV.
① This is a command. ② Add the move action.

After human edit: When a landing UAV command is assigned to a UAV, the internal simulator shall compute the ground longitude latitude and latitude of the UAV, and move the UAV to ground latitude.

⇕ synonymous with the target

Target: When given a landing command the internal simulator shall move the UAV to the ground altitude corresponding to its current longitude and latitude.

Green background: The requirement draft generated by *ReqGen*.
Yellow background: The requirement statement edited by human based on our draft.
Pink background: The target requirement statement.
Dotted arrows: Modifications made by human.

Figure 5. One example showing the usefulness of *ReqGen*.

Second, people may use different terms to represent the same concept, causing ambiguity and difficulty for understandability and automation of follow-up tasks, e.g., traceability. *ReqGen* generates the drafts based on the domain ontology and it can provide domain terms, making the analyst start from the draft, rather than starting from scratch. After human editing, some domain terms still remain. Thus, our approach is helpful for consistent usage of domain terms.

6.3. Limitations

Temporarily, we only randomly selected a few keywords as the seeds of *ReqGen* for the requirements statement generation and did not restrict their roles (e.g., specifying that the subject is mandatory). We plan to explore the impact of syntax role configurations, that the given keywords belong to, on the specifications generation.

Our method cannot replace the elicitation and analysis of users' requirements. In other words, our aim was only to assist engineers to quickly produce the requirements that they already roughly know (i.e., the keywords). Meanwhile, we cannot guarantee that all the specifications are generated with professional domain words and clear formal expressions.

We did not perform an empirical study of the practical usefulness of *ReqGen* in real-world practice. In this initial study, we only evaluated its effectiveness by comparing it with six popular NLG approaches on the common indicators of BLEU, ROUGE, and our proposed RS4RE.

7. Conclusions

This study aimed to automatically generate requirements statements based on pre-defined keywords. We proposed an approach called *ReqGen*, which fine-tunes UniLM by injecting keywords-related knowledge with repeated emphasis on the most-relevant ones, integrates a copy mechanism to ensure the hard constraint of keyword inclusion, and uses syntax-constrained decoding to cater to syntax requirements. Compared with six popular baselines, we showed that *ReqGen* obtains superior performance on the requirements specification generation task.

Author Contributions: Conceptualization: Z.Z., L.Z. and X.L.; methodology and software: Z.Z., X.G. and H.L.; validation: Z.Z., X.L. and X.G.; formal analysis: Z.Z. and X.L.; resources: Z.Z.; data curation: Z.Z.; writing—original draft: Z.Z.; writing—review and editing: X.L. and L.S.; visualization: Z.Z.; supervision: L.Z. and X.L.; project administration: X.L.; funding acquisition: X.L. and L.Z. All authors have read and agreed to the published version of the manuscript.

Funding: This work was funded by the National Science Foundation of China Grant Nos. 62102014 and 62177003. It is also partially supported by the State Key Laboratory of Software Development Environment No. SKLSDE-2021ZX-10.

Institutional Review Board Statement: Not applicable.

Informed Consent Statement: Not applicable.

Data Availability Statement: The data that support the findings of this study are available within the article.

Conflicts of Interest: The authors declare no conflict of interest.

References

1. Terzakis, J. The impact of requirements on software quality across three product generations. In Proceedings of the 2013 21st IEEE International Requirements Engineering Conference (RE), Rio de Janeiro, Brazil, 15–19 July 2013; pp. 284–289.
2. Aurum, A.; Wohlin, C. *Engineering and Managing Software Requirements*; Springer: Berlin/Heidelberg, Germany, 2005. [CrossRef]
3. Wiegers, K. *Software Requirements*; Microsoft Press: Redmond, WA, USA, 2013.
4. Lian, X.; Rahimi, M.; Cleland-Huang, J.; Zhang, L.; Ferrai, R.; Smith, M. Mining Requirements Knowledge from Collections of Domain Documents. In Proceedings of the 24th IEEE International Requirements Engineering Conference (RE), Beijing, China, 12–16 September 2016; IEEE Computer Society: New York, NY, USA, 2016; pp. 156–165. [CrossRef]
5. Mavin, A.; Wilkinson, P.; Harwood, A.; Novak, M. Easy Approach to Requirements Syntax (EARS). In Proceedings of the 17th IEEE International Requirements Engineering Conference, Atlanta, GA, USA, 31 August 2009–4 September 2009; pp. 317–322. [CrossRef]
6. Maiden, N.A.M.; Manning, S.; Jones, S.; Greenwood, J. Generating requirements from systems models using patterns: A case study. *Requir. Eng.* **2005**, *10*, 276–288. [CrossRef]
7. Yu, E.S.K.; Bois, P.D.; Dubois, E.; Mylopoulos, J. From Organization Models to System Requirements: A 'Cooperating Agents' Approach. In Proceedings of the Third International Conference on Cooperative Information Systems (CoopIS-95), Vienna, Austria, 9–12 May 1995; pp. 194–204.
8. Letier, E.; van Lamsweerde, A. Deriving operational software specifications from system goals. In Proceedings of the Tenth ACM SIGSOFT Symposium on Foundations of Software Engineering 2002, Charleston, SC, USA, 18–22 November 2002; pp. 119–128.
9. Landtsheer, R.D.; Letier, E.; van Lamsweerde, A. Deriving tabular event-based specifications from goal-oriented requirements models. *Requir. Eng.* **2004**, *9*, 104–120. [CrossRef]
10. Van Lamsweerde, A. Goal-oriented requirements engineering: A roundtrip from research to practice [enginering read engineering]. In Proceedings of the 12th IEEE International Requirements Engineering Conference, Kyoto, Japan, 6–10 September 2004; pp. 4–7.
11. van Lamsweerde, A.; Willemet, L. Inferring Declarative Requirements Specifications from Operational Scenarios. *IEEE Trans. Softw. Eng.* **1998**, *24*, 1089–1114. [CrossRef]
12. Meziane, F.; Athanasakis, N.; Ananiadou, S. Generating Natural Language specifications from UML class diagrams. *Requir. Eng.* **2008**, *13*, 1–18. [CrossRef]
13. Berenbach, B. The Automated Extraction of Requirements from UML Models. In Proceedings of the 11th IEEE International Conference on Requirements Engineering (RE 2003), Monterey Bay, CA, USA, 8–12 September 2003; IEEE Computer Society: New York, NY, USA, 2003; p. 287.
14. Souag, A.; Mazo, R.; Salinesi, C.; Comyn-Wattiau, I. Using the AMAN-DA Method to Generate Security Requirements: A Case Study in the Maritime Domain. *Requir. Eng.* **2018**, *23*, 557–580. [CrossRef]

15. Lian, X.; Cleland-Huang, J.; Zhang, L. Mining Associations Between Quality Concerns and Functional Requirements. In Proceedings of the 25th IEEE International Requirements Engineering Conference, RE 2017, Lisbon, Portugal, 4–8 September 2017; Moreira, A., Araújo, J., Hayes, J., Paech, B., Eds.; IEEE Computer Society: New York, NY, USA, 2017; pp. 292–301. [CrossRef]
16. Lian, X.; Liu, W.; Zhang, L. Assisting engineers extracting requirements on components from domain documents. *Inf. Softw. Technol.* **2020**, *118*, 106196. [CrossRef]
17. Li, Y.; Guzman, E.; Tsiamoura, K.; Schneider, F.; Bruegge, B. Automated Requirements Extraction for Scientific Software. *Procedia Comput. Sci.* **2015**, *51*, 582–591. [CrossRef]
18. Shi, L.; Xing, M.; Li, M.; Wang, Y.; Li, S.; Wang, Q. Detection of Hidden Feature Requests from Massive Chat Messages via Deep Siamese Network. In Proceedings of the 2020 IEEE/ACM 42nd International Conference on Software Engineering (ICSE), Seoul, Republic of Korea, 5–11 October 2020; pp. 641–653.
19. Dumitru, H.; Gibiec, M.; Hariri, N.; Cleland-Huang, J.; Mobasher, B.; Castro-Herrera, C.; Mirakhorli, M. On-demand feature recommendations derived from mining public product descriptions. In Proceedings of the 33rd International Conference on Software Engineering, ICSE, Honolulu, HI, USA, 21–28 May 2011; pp. 181–190.
20. Sree-Kumar, A.; Planas, E.; Clarisó, R. Extracting software product line feature models from natural language specifications. In Proceedings of the 22nd International Systems and Software Product Line Conference—Volume 1, SPLC 2018, Gothenburg, Sweden, 10–14 September 2018; ACM: New York, NY, USA, 2018; pp. 43–53.
21. Zhou, J.; Hänninen, K.; Lundqvist, K.; Lu, Y.; Provenzano, L.; Forsberg, K. An environment-driven ontological approach to requirements elicitation for safety-critical systems. In Proceedings of the 23rd IEEE International Requirements Engineering Conference, RE 2015, Ottawa, ON, Canada, 24–28 August 2015; IEEE Computer Society: New York, NY, USA, 2015; pp. 247–251.
22. Khan, J.A.; Xie, Y.; Liu, L.; Wen, L. Analysis of Requirements-Related Arguments in User Forums. In Proceedings of the 27th IEEE International Requirements Engineering Conference, RE 2019, Jeju, Republic of Korea, 23–27 September 2019; pp. 63–74.
23. Astegher, M.; Busetta, P.; Perini, A.; Susi, A. Requirements for Online User Feedback Management in RE Tasks. In Proceedings of the 29th IEEE International Requirements Engineering Conference Workshops, RE 2021 Workshops, Notre Dame, IN, USA, 20–24 September 2021; p. 336.
24. Johann, T.; Stanik, C.; Alizadeh, B.A.M.; Maalej, W. SAFE: A Simple Approach for Feature Extraction from App Descriptions and App Reviews. In Proceedings of the 25th IEEE International Requirements Engineering Conference, RE 2017, Lisbon, Portugal, 4–8 September 2017; IEEE Computer Society: New York, NY, USA, 2017; pp. 21–30.
25. Dąbrowski, J.; Kifetew, F.M.; Muñante, D.; Letier, E.; Siena, A.; Susi, A. Discovering Requirements through Goal-Driven Process Mining. In Proceedings of the 2017 IEEE 25th International Requirements Engineering Conference Workshops (REW), Lisbon, Portugal, 4–8 September 2017; pp. 199–203. [CrossRef]
26. Sleimi, A.; Ceci, M.; Sannier, N.; Sabetzadeh, M.; Bri, L.; Dann, J. A Query System for Extracting Requirements-Related Information from Legal Texts. In Proceedings of the 27th IEEE International Requirements Engineering Conference, RE 2019, Jeju, Republic of Korea, 23–27 September 2019; pp. 319–329.
27. Falkner, A.; Palomares, C.; Franch, X.; Schenner, G.; Aznar, P.; Schoerghuber, A. Identifying Requirements in Requests for Proposal: A Research Preview. In Proceedings of the Requirements Engineering: Foundation for Software Quality—25th International Working Conference, REFSQ 2019, Essen, Germany, 18–21 March 2019; Knauss, E., Goedicke, M., Eds.; Lecture Notes in Computer Science; Springer: Berlin/Heidelberg, Germany, 2019; Volume 11412, pp. 176–182.
28. Devine, P.; Koh, Y.S.; Blincoe, K. Evaluating Unsupervised Text Embeddings on Software User Feedback. In Proceedings of the 29th IEEE International Requirements Engineering Conference Workshops, RE 2021 Workshops, Notre Dame, IN, USA, 20–24 September 2021; pp. 87–95.
29. Henao, P.R.; Fischbach, J.; Spies, D.; Frattini, J.; Vogelsang, A. Transfer Learning for Mining Feature Requests and Bug Reports from Tweets and App Store Reviews. In Proceedings of the 29th IEEE International Requirements Engineering Conference Workshops, RE 2021 Workshops, Notre Dame, IN, USA, 20–24 September 2021; pp. 80–86.
30. Sainani, A.; Anish, P.R.; Joshi, V.; Ghaisas, S. Extracting and Classifying Requirements from Software Engineering Contracts. In Proceedings of the 28th IEEE International Requirements Engineering Conference, RE 2020, Zurich, Switzerland, 31 August–4 September 2020; pp. 147–157.
31. Tizard, J. Requirement Mining in Software Product Forums. In Proceedings of the 27th IEEE International Requirements Engineering Conference, RE 2019, Jeju, Republic of Korea, 23–27 September 2019; pp. 428–433.
32. Dong, L.; Yang, N.; Wang, W.; Wei, F.; Liu, X.; Wang, Y.; Gao, J.; Zhou, M.; Hon, H.W. Unified Language Model Pre-training for Natural Language Understanding and Generation. In Proceedings of the Advances in Neural Information Processing Systems 32: Annual Conference on Neural Information Processing Systems 2019, NeurIPS 2019, Vancouver, BC, Canada, 8–14 December 2019; pp. 13042–13054.
33. Lin, B.Y.; Zhou, W.; Shen, M.; Zhou, P.; Bhagavatula, C.; Choi, Y.; Ren, X. CommonGen: A Constrained Text Generation Challenge for Generative Commonsense Reasoning. In Proceedings of the Findings of the Association for Computational Linguistics: EMNLP 2020, Online Event, 16–20 November 2020; Findings of ACL; Association for Computational Linguistics: Stroudsburg, PA, USA, 2020; Volume EMNLP 2020, pp. 1823–1840.
34. Rothe, S.; Narayan, S.; Severyn, A. Leveraging pre-trained checkpoints for sequence generation tasks. *Trans. Assoc. Comput. Linguist.* **2020**, *8*, 264–280. [CrossRef]

35. Wu, C.; Wu, F.; Qi, T.; Huang, Y. Empowering news recommendation with pre-trained language models. In Proceedings of the 44th International ACM SIGIR Conference on Research and Development in Information Retrieval, Virtual, 11–15 July 2021; pp. 1652–1656.
36. Guo, W.; Zhang, L.; Lian, X. Putting software requirements under the microscope: Automated extraction of their semantic elements. In Proceedings of the 29th IEEE International Requirements Engineering Conference, RE, Notre Dame, IN, USA, 20–24 September 2021; pp. 416–417.
37. *ISO/IEC/IEEE 29148:2018(E)*; ISO/IEC/IEEE International Standard—Systems and Software Engineering—Life Cycle Processes—Requirements Engineering. IEEE: New York, NY, USA, 2018; pp. 1–104. [CrossRef]
38. Zhao, Z.; Zhang, L.; Lian, X. What can Open Domain Model Tell Us about the Missing Software Requirements: A Preliminary Study. In Proceedings of the 29th IEEE International Requirements Engineering Conference, RE, Notre Dame, IN, USA, 20–24 September 2021; pp. 24–34.
39. Li, Y.; Goel, P.; Rajendra, V.K.; Singh, H.S.; Francis, J.; Ma, K.; Nyberg, E.; Oltramari, A. Lexically-constrained Text Generation through Commonsense Knowledge Extraction and Injection. *arXiv* **2020**, arXiv:2012.10813.
40. Devlin, J.; Chang, M.W.; Lee, K.; Toutanova, K. Bert: Pre-training of deep bidirectional transformers for language understanding. *arXiv* **2018**, arXiv:1810.04805.
41. Vaswani, A.; Shazeer, N.; Parmar, N.; Uszkoreit, J.; Jones, L.; Gomez, A.N.; Kaiser, L.; Polosukhin, I. Attention is All you Need. In Proceedings of the Advances in Neural Information Processing Systems 30: Annual Conference on Neural Information Processing Systems 2017, Long Beach, CA, USA, 4–9 December 2017; pp. 5998–6008.
42. Graves, A.; Mohamed, A.; Hinton, G.E. Speech recognition with deep recurrent neural networks. In Proceedings of the IEEE International Conference on Acoustics, Speech and Signal Processing, ICASSP 2013, Vancouver, BC, Canada, 26–31 May 2013; pp. 6645–6649.
43. Hochreiter, S.; Schmidhuber, J. Long Short-Term Memory. *Neural Comput.* **1997**, *9*, 1735–1780. [CrossRef] [PubMed]
44. Türetken, O.; Su, O.; Demirörs, O. Automating software requirements generation from business process models. In Proceedings of the 1st Conference on the Principles of Software Eng.(PRISE'04), Buenos Aires, Argentina, 22–26 November 2004.
45. Cox, K.; Phalp, K.; Bleistein, S.J.; Verner, J.M. Deriving requirements from process models via the problem frames approach. *Inf. Softw. Technol.* **2005**, *47*, 319–337. [CrossRef]
46. Osama, M.; Zaki-Ismail, A.; Abdelrazek, M.; Grundy, J.; Ibrahim, A. DBRG: Description-Based Non-Quality Requirements Generator. In Proceedings of the IEEE 29th International Requirements Engineering Conference (RE), Notre Dame, IN, USA, 20–24 September 2021; pp. 424–425.
47. Novgorodov, S.; Elad, G.; Guy, I.; Radinsky, K. Generating Product Descriptions from User Reviews. In Proceedings of the World Wide Web Conference, WWW 2019, San Francisco, CA, USA, 13–17 May 2019; pp. 1354–1364.
48. Novgorodov, S.; Guy, I.; Elad, G.; Radinsky, K. Descriptions from the Customers: Comparative Analysis of Review-based Product Description Generation Methods. *ACM Trans. Internet Technol.* **2020**, *20*, 44:1–44:31. [CrossRef]
49. Elad, G.; Guy, I.; Novgorodov, S.; Kimelfeld, B.; Radinsky, K. Learning to Generate Personalized Product Descriptions. In Proceedings of the 28th ACM International Conference on Information and Knowledge Management, CIKM 2019, Beijing, China, 3–7 November 2019; pp. 389–398.
50. Mou, L.; Yan, R.; Li, G.; Zhang, L.; Jin, Z. Backward and forward language modeling for constrained sentence generation. *arXiv* **2015**, arXiv:1512.06612.
51. Liu, D.; Fu, J.; Qu, Q.; Lv, J. BFGAN: Backward and Forward Generative Adversarial Networks for Lexically Constrained Sentence Generation. *IEEE ACM Trans. Audio Speech Lang. Process.* **2019**, *27*, 2350–2361. [CrossRef]
52. Hokamp, C.; Liu, Q. Lexically Constrained Decoding for Sequence Generation Using Grid Beam Search. In Proceedings of the 55th Annual Meeting of the Association for Computational Linguistics, ACL 2017, Volume 1: Long Papers, Vancouver, BC, Canada, 30 July–4 August 2017; Association for Computational Linguistics: Stroudsburg, PA, USA, 2017; pp. 1535–1546.
53. Miao, N.; Zhou, H.; Mou, L.; Yan, R.; Li, L. CGMH: Constrained Sentence Generation by Metropolis-Hastings Sampling. In Proceedings of the AAAI Conference on Artificial Intelligence, Honolulu, HI, USA, 27 January–1 February 2019; Volume 33, pp. 6834–6842. [CrossRef]
54. Sha, L. Gradient-guided Unsupervised Lexically Constrained Text Generation. In Proceedings of the 2020 Conference on Empirical Methods in Natural Language Processing, EMNLP 2020, Online, 16–20 November 2020; Association for Computational Linguistics: Stroudsburg, PA, USA, 2020; pp. 8692–8703.
55. Ding, T.; Pan, S. Personalized Emphasis Framing for Persuasive Message Generation. In Proceedings of the 2016 Conference on Empirical Methods in Natural Language Processing, EMNLP 2016, Austin, TX, USA, 1–4 November 2016; The Association for Computational Linguistics: Stroudsburg, PA, USA, 2016; pp. 1432–1441.
56. Liu, Y.; Ott, M.; Goyal, N.; Du, J.; Joshi, M.; Chen, D.; Levy, O.; Lewis, M.; Zettlemoyer, L.; Stoyanov, V. Roberta: A robustly optimized bert pretraining approach. *arXiv* **2019**, arXiv:1907.11692.
57. Radford, A.; Wu, J.; Child, R.; Luan, D.; Amodei, D.; Sutskever, I. Language models are unsupervised multitask learners. *OpenAI Blog* **2019**, *1*, 9.
58. Brown, T.; Mann, B.; Ryder, N.; Subbiah, M.; Kaplan, J.D.; Dhariwal, P.; Neelakantan, A.; Shyam, P.; Sastry, G.; Askell, A.; et al. Language models are few-shot learners. *Adv. Neural Inf. Process. Syst.* **2020**, *33*, 1877–1901.

59. Keskar, N.S.; McCann, B.; Varshney, L.R.; Xiong, C.; Socher, R. CTRL: A Conditional Transformer Language Model for Controllable Generation. *arXiv* **2019**, arXiv:1909.05858.
60. Du, Z.; Qian, Y.; Liu, X.; Ding, M.; Qiu, J.; Yang, Z.; Tang, J. GLM: General Language Model Pretraining with Autoregressive Blank Infilling. In Proceedings of the 60th Annual Meeting of the Association for Computational Linguistics (Volume 1: Long Papers), ACL 2022, Dublin, Ireland, 22–27 May 2022; Association for Computational Linguistics: Stroudsburg, PA, USA, 2022; pp. 320–335.
61. Song, K.; Tan, X.; Qin, T.; Lu, J.; Liu, T. MASS: Masked Sequence to Sequence Pre-training for Language Generation. In Proceedings of the 36th International Conference on Machine Learning, ICML 2019, Long Beach, CA, USA, 9–15 June 2019; Volume 97, pp. 5926–5936.
62. Raffel, C.; Shazeer, N.; Roberts, A.; Lee, K.; Narang, S.; Matena, M.; Zhou, Y.; Li, W.; Liu, P.J. Exploring the Limits of Transfer Learning with a Unified Text-to-Text Transformer. *J. Mach. Learn. Res.* **2020**, *21*, 140:1–140:67.
63. Lewis, M.; Liu, Y.; Goyal, N.; Ghazvininejad, M.; Mohamed, A.; Levy, O.; Stoyanov, V.; Zettlemoyer, L. BART: Denoising Sequence-to-Sequence Pre-training for Natural Language Generation, Translation, and Comprehension. *arXiv* **2019**, arXiv:1910.13461.
64. Bechhofer, S.; Van Harmelen, F.; Hendler, J.; Horrocks, I.; McGuinness, D.L.; Patel-Schneider, P.F.; Stein, L.A. OWL web ontology language reference. *W3C Recomm.* **2004**, *10*, 1–53.
65. Gu, J.; Lu, Z.; Li, H.; Li, V.O.K. Incorporating Copying Mechanism in Sequence-to-Sequence Learning. In Proceedings of the 54th Annual Meeting of the Association for Computational Linguistics, ACL 2016, Volume 1: Long Papers, Berlin, Germany, 7–12 August 2016; The Association for Computer Linguistics: Stroudsburg, PA, USA, 2016.
66. Su, J. SPACES: Extract Generate Long Text Summaries. Available online: https://spaces.ac.cn/archives/8046/comment-page-1 (accessed on 1 January 2021).
67. Cleland-Huang, J.; Vierhauser, M.; Bayley, S. Dronology: An incubator for cyber-physical systems research. In Proceedings of the 40th International Conference on Software Engineering: New Ideas and Emerging Results, ICSE (NIER), Gothenburg, Sweden, 27 May–3 June 2018; pp. 109–112.
68. *Standard Building Automation System (BAS) Specification*; Technical Report; City of Toronto, Standard Specifications. Available online: https://www.toronto.ca/wp-content/uploads/2017/10/918d-Standard-Building-Automation-System-BAS-Specification-for-City-Buildings-2015.pdf (accessed on 1 October 2017).
69. Manning, C.D.; Surdeanu, M.; Bauer, J.; Finkel, J.R.; Bethard, S.; McClosky, D. The Stanford CoreNLP Natural Language Processing Toolkit. In Proceedings of the 52nd Annual Meeting of the Association for Computational Linguistics, ACL 2014, Baltimore, MD, USA, 22–27 June 2014; The Association for Computer Linguistics: Stroudsburg, PA, USA, 2014; pp. 55–60.
70. Zhao, Z.; Zhang, L.; Lian, X. A Preliminary Study on the Potential Usefulness of Open Domain Model for Missing Software Requirements Recommendation. *arXiv* **2022**, arXiv:2208.06757.
71. Zhong, H.; Zhang, J.; Wang, Z.; Wan, H.; Chen, Z. Aligning knowledge and text embeddings by entity descriptions. In Proceedings of the 2015 Conference on Empirical Methods in Natural Language Processing, Lisbon, Portugal, 17–21 September 2015; pp. 267–272.
72. Zhang, Y.; Wang, G.; Li, C.; Gan, Z.; Brockett, C.; Dolan, B. POINTER: Constrained progressive text generation via insertion-based generative pre-training. *arXiv* **2020**, arXiv:2005.00558.
73. Papineni, K.; Roukos, S.; Ward, T.; Zhu, W.J. Bleu: A method for automatic evaluation of machine translation. In Proceedings of the 40th Annual Meeting of the Association for Computational Linguistics, Philadelphia, PA, USA, 6–12 July 2002; pp. 311–318.
74. Lin, C.Y. Rouge: A package for automatic evaluation of summaries. In Proceedings of the Text Summarization Branches Out, Barcelona, Spain, 25–26 July 2004; pp. 74–81.
75. Jawahar, G.; Sagot, B.; Seddah, D. What Does BERT Learn about the Structure of Language? In Proceedings of the 57th Conference of the Association for Computational Linguistics, ACL 2019, Volume 1: Long Papers, Florence, Italy, 28 July–2 August 2019; Association for Computational Linguistics: Stroudsburg, PA, USA, 2019; pp. 3651–3657.
76. Martín-Lammerding, D.; Astrain, J.J.; Córdoba, A.; Villadangos, J. An ontology-based system to avoid UAS flight conflicts and collisions in dense traffic scenarios. *Expert Syst. Appl.* **2022**, *215*, 119027. [CrossRef]
77. Martın-Lammerding, D.; Astrain, J.J.; Córdoba, A. A Reference Ontology for Collision Avoidance Systems and Accountability. In Proceedings of the Fifteenth International Conference on Advances in Semantic Processing, Barcelona, Spain, 3–7 October 2021.
78. Martín-Lammerding, D.; Astrain, J.J.; Córdoba, A.; Villadangos, J. A Multi-UAS Simulator for High Density Air Traffic Scenarios. In Proceedings of the VEHICULAR 2022, The Eleventh International Conference on Advances in Vehicular Systems, Technologies and Applications, Venice, Italy, 22–26 May 2022; pp. 32–37.
79. Kučera, A.; Pitner, T. Semantic BMS: Allowing usage of building automation data in facility benchmarking. *Adv. Eng. Inform.* **2018**, *35*, 69–84. [CrossRef]

Disclaimer/Publisher's Note: The statements, opinions and data contained in all publications are solely those of the individual author(s) and contributor(s) and not of MDPI and/or the editor(s). MDPI and/or the editor(s) disclaim responsibility for any injury to people or property resulting from any ideas, methods, instructions or products referred to in the content.

Article

Flight Delay Propagation Prediction Based on Deep Learning

Jingyi Qu *, Shixing Wu and Jinjie Zhang

Tianjin Key Laboratory of Advanced Signal Processing, Civil Aviation University of China, Tianjin 300300, China
* Correspondence: jyqu@cauc.edu.cn

Abstract: The current flight delay not only affects the normal operation of the current flight, but also spreads to the downstream flights through the flights schedule, resulting in a wide range of flight delays. The analysis and prediction of flight delay propagation in advance can help civil aviation departments control the flight delay rate and reduce the economic loss caused by flight delays. Due to the small number of data samples that can constitute flight chains, it is difficult to construct flight chain data. In recent years, the analysis of the flight delay propagation problem is generally based on traditional machine learning methods with a small sample size. After obtaining a large amount of raw data from the China Air Traffic Management Bureau, we have constructed 36,287 pieces of three-level flight chain data. Based on these data, we tried to use a deep learning method to analyze and forecast flight delays. In the field of deep learning, there are CNN models and RNN models that deal with classification problems well. Based on these two classes of models, we modify and innovate the study of the problem of flight delay propagation and prediction. Firstly, the CNN-based CondenseNet algorithm is used to predict the delay level of the three-level flight chain data. Based on this, the CondenseNet network is improved by inserting CBAM modules and named CBAM-CondenseNet. The experimental results show that the improved algorithm can effectively improve the network performance, and the prediction accuracy can reach 89.8%. Compared with the traditional machine learning method, the average prediction accuracy increased by 8.7 percentage points. On the basis of the CNN model, we also considered the superiority of the LSTM (Long Short-Term Memory network) considering the processing time sequence information, and then constructed the CNN-MLSTM network and injected the SimAM module to enhance the attention of flight chain data. In the experiment of flight delay propagation prediction, the accuracy rate is 91.36%, which is a significant improvement compared to using the CNN or LSTM alone.

Keywords: flight delay propagation; deep learning; CBAM-CondenseNet; CNN-MLSTM

MSC: 68T07

1. Introduction

As the same aircraft performs multiple flights in one day, there are close connections between the upstream and downstream flights, so delays in upstream flights may affect many other downstream flights, causing massive propagation of flight delays. It is necessary to deeply study the propagation path of flight delays in the airline network and predict the delay level of downstream flights. Therefore, it can provide a theoretical basis and data support for civil aviation departments to prevent and control delay propagation.

Many studies have been conducted by scholars on the prediction of flight delay propagation. Earlier, starting from the characteristics of delay propagation, they built flight delay propagation models to analyze the delay propagation impact [1–7]. Some researchers constructed a colored-time Petri net model for multiple flights at airports [1]. The model predicts whether flight delay will also occur at the downstream airport when the initial airports experience flight delays. Other researchers [2] proposed a flight delay propagation prediction model based on a Bayesian network. From the aspect of complex air transport networks, the delay propagation phenomenon of hub airports in large-scale networks has been studied. Based on the queuing theory mechanism, researchers [3] proposed an analytical queuing and network decomposition model, and constructed an approximate network delay model to study the delay of 34 busy airports in the United States. The authors [4] proposed the analysis and prediction method of flight delay propagation based on complex network theory, and showed the specific classification of delay propagation. All the above methods are used to study the development of flight delay propagation by analyzing and modeling the existing historical data. Most of them use small sample data to study the causes of flight delay propagation problems. Traditional flight delay propagation analysis methods are easily influenced by model selection and subjective factors. As the volume of data in the civil aviation industry accumulates, more and more machine learning methods [8,9] are used for civil aviation delay prediction. Researchers [8] have proposed the use of machine learning to predict air traffic delay, and the use of shallow artificial neural networks to predict flight delay. Based on the problem of controllable delay in air traffic control, some researchers [9] used machine learning methods to predict the delay of individual aircrafts, taking into account the influencing factors such as weather, aircraft navigation, and control.

At present, the feature extraction ability of the CNN (Convolutional Neural Networks) is obviously more excellent than the traditional methods, and the practical application effect is remarkable [10–12]. Compared with the general CNN, CondenseNet proposed previously [10] can effectively solve the phenomenon of gradient disappearance during deep network training, with higher computational efficiency and less parameter storage. Researchers [11] have proposed a new Convolutional Block Attention Mechanism Module (CBAM) to improve the network accuracy by double feature weight calibration from spatial dimension and feature dimension. In this essay, the deep learning methods are used to study the flight delay propagation problem and prediction. The CBAM-CondenseNet algorithm is proposed by combining CondenseNet and the design ideas of CBAM. It is able to predict other flight departure delays caused by the spread of upstream flight delays.

In aviation networks, the data that make up the flight chain contain both rich spatial information and rich temporal information [13,14]. Although we use the deep learning method to build a model based on the convolutional neural network to predict the impact of flight delays, this model only extracts the spatial features of flight data and lacks the consideration of temporal information. Therefore, this paper combines the CNN network and Mogrifier LSTM (Mogrifier Long Short-Term Memory) to predict the problem of flight delay propagation. The Long Short-Term Memory (LSTM) network can remember the previous temporal information more profoundly in the time dimension, but the input x in the LSTM and the previous state h_{prev} are independent of each other before being input into the cell. The MLSTM makes these two inputs from completely independent to autonomic interaction, which greatly improves network performance. The SimAM proposed in literature [15] is different from the existing channel spatial attention module. The module deduces the 3D attention weight for the feature graph without additional parameters, which can better extract the feature of the flight chain data structure. Therefore, we fuse the attention module SimAM on the basis of CNN-MLSTM to improve the prediction accuracy. The final model is named SimAM-CNN-MLSTM.

According to the spatial and temporal characteristics of flight chains, in this paper, the method of flight delay propagation prediction based on deep learning [16–38] is proposed. This method not only uses the advantages of the CNN in spatial feature extraction, but also considers the advantages of the LSTM network in processing temporal information, and uses the attention mechanism module to enhance the feature matrix with important neurons. When the same aircraft performs multiple flight missions, it can predict the delay level of subsequent flights according to the propagation pattern of flight delays, and provide corresponding suggestions for the relevant civil aviation departments to control the delay propagation.

2. Flight Delay Propagation Prediction

The flight delay propagation prediction based on deep learning mainly includes the following parts: data preprocessing and flight chain data set construction, feature extraction, and classification prediction. Feature extraction is mainly introduced in the third and fourth parts of this paper. The following mainly introduces data preprocessing, flight chain data set construction, classification, and prediction.

2.1. Data Preprocessing

The flight data used in this project are the flight data of China from March 2018 to May 2019 provided by the Civil Aviation Administration of the China East China Regional Administration (ECRA). Among them, the key sample attributes include flight number, aircraft number, actual departure/arrival airport, flight path, planned departure/arrival time, actual departure/arrival time, planned departure/arrival airport, planned aircraft type, cruise altitude, cruise speed, military batch number, coverage type, and a total of 38 attributes. These characteristics are closely related to whether the flight is delayed or not, which not only contains important spatial features but also contains abundant time information. Since there are some abnormal values and null values in the flight data provided by the ECRA, the mainstream data analysis library Pandas is selected to clean the original flight data set. The characteristic attributes required by the model are defined as follows.

Definition 1. *Flight data F_f, including 38 characteristic attributes such as flight number, aircraft number, actual departure/arrival airport, flight path, planned departure/arrival time, actual departure/arrival time, etc.*

Definition 2. *Flight chain data F_c, within a certain time range, the same aircraft respectively performs different flight tasks from class 1 airport to class 2 airport and then to class 3 airport, and the time sequence is related. This is a flight chain. Multiple flight chain data constitute the flight chain data set.*

2.2. Construction of the Flight Chain Data Set

Flight delay has the characteristics of temporal and spatial distribution. When the same aircraft performs different flight missions in succession, it is common for subsequent flights to be delayed due to the previous flight delay. After the delay of the previous flight is passed along the flight plan step by step, it will lead to a large area of flight delays. The airport where the same aircraft takes off for the first time within a certain time range is defined as the class 1 airport. The airport where the aircraft arrives from the class 1 departure airport for flight task 1 is called the class 2 airport, also known as the class 1 arrival airport or the class 2 departure airport. By analogy, the same aircraft Z continuously performs flight tasks between multiple airports, which are connected in chronological order to form a flight chain relationship, as shown in Figure 1. Taking "Beijing-Tianjin-Shanghai" as an example, Beijing is defined as a class 1 airport. The same aircraft performs flight task 1 from Beijing to Tianjin. Tianjin is the class 2 airport in the flight chain, also known as the class 1 arrival airport or the class 2 departure airport. The plane starts from Tianjin and performs flight task 2. It flies from Tianjin to Shanghai. Shanghai is the class 3 airport in the flight chain, also known as the class 2 arrival airport or the class 3 departure airport.

Based on the above characteristic attributes, the flight chain data set is constructed. Firstly, a hub airport is selected as the class 1 airport. The airports with the number of flights from this class 1 airport are ranked from high to low, and the top 20 airports are selected as class 2 airports. Then, we directly select the airport with flights from each class 2 airport as class 3 airports. Thus, the air transport network is determined with the class 1 airport as the center and radiating outward. Secondly, taking the time and the flight tail number as key values, each flight chain is extracted from the aviation network to form a flight chain data set. Thirdly, the discrete data and continuous data in the original data are encoded by different methods to avoid misleading the training process of the network. Lastly, the processed data are converted into a suitable characteristic matrix that feed into the network. In order to more clearly describe the flight chain data set, the i-th flight chain data in Definition 2 are represented by $f_i = (f_{i1}, f_{i2}, f_{i3})$, where f_{i1}, f_{i2}, and f_{i3}, respectively, represent the flight chain data f_i containing the information of three single flights that perform flight tasks before and after in the time dimension. The F_c dataset can be further represented by $F_c = \{(f_{11}, f_{12}, f_{13}), (f_{21}, f_{22}, f_{23}), \ldots, (f_{n1}, f_{n2}, f_{n3})\}$. The flight chain dataset description is shown in Figure 2.

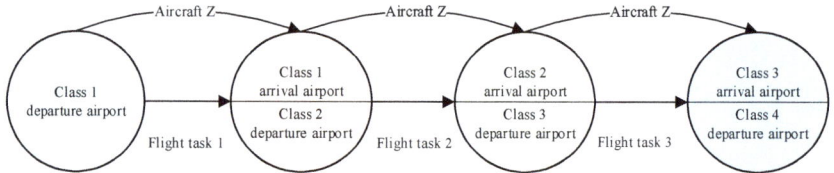

Figure 1. Flight chain model.

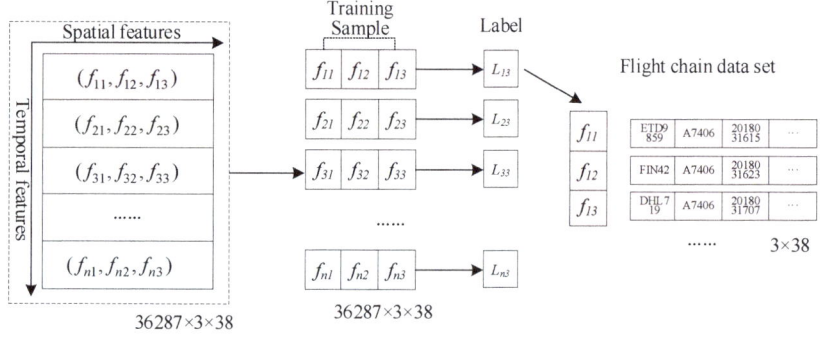

Figure 2. Flight chain data set description.

The flight data of three consecutive flights of the same aircraft within a certain time range constitute the flight chain data. There are 1,048,576 pieces of data in the original single flight. After data cleaning and construction of the flight chain data set, the data volume of the flight chain data used in the flight delay propagation prediction experiment are 36,287 pieces. The data set construction steps are as follows:

According to Definition 2, an aircraft performs continuous flight missions. In this paper, a three-class flight chain data set is formed according to the change of the same aircraft within 24 h. Firstly, select the four attributes of the aircraft number, flight execution date, class 1 arrival airport, and class 2 departure airport as the key values of data fusion; conduct the first data fusion on the cleaned flight data set; and remove the abnormal flight chain whose departure time of the secondary airport is earlier than that of the primary airport. At this time, in the flight chain data set, the aircraft performed two flight missions and turned around three airports in space.

The generation of the delayed propagation phenomenon has the characteristic of passing from one class to another, so we continue to fuse the flight chain data set for the second time. The aircraft number and flight execution date remain unchanged, and the class 2 arrival airport and class 3 departure airport are selected for the second data fusion. The abnormal flight chain whose departure time from the class 3 airport is earlier than the arrival time at the class 2 airport is removed. The flight chain data set of two consecutive flight tasks is obtained.

By analogy, the data are fused three times in this paper to form the final flight chain dataset. The aircraft in each data chain performed three consecutive flight missions, and the spatial dimension involved the transit situation in four airports. A total of four airports including the first-class airport, second-class airport, third-class airport, and fourth-class airport are affected by flight delays. The delay label of the flight chain is the delay level of the class 3 flight mission. Most aircrafts fly one mission and do not fly another that day. As more flights are performed on the same day, the available data in the flight chain data set become smaller and smaller. Therefore, we focus on the delayed propagation of flight chains consisting of three consecutive flight missions. Finally, the characteristic attributes in the flight chain data set are divided into the numerical type and discrete type. The numerical type features are coded by Min-Max normalization, and the discrete type features are coded by CatBoost.

2.3. Classification and Prediction

Based on the relevant meaning of "flight delay" in the regulations on normal flight management, the flight delay is subdivided into five delay levels, and the number of delay levels is divided into different levels. The judging standard is shown in Table 1. Grade labels are calculated based on the difference value between the flight planned arrival time and the flight actual arrival time in the data set, and finally obtains the flight delay prediction grade with the Softmax classifier.

Table 1. Classification of flight delays.

Delay Level	Delay Time T/min	Delay Level Classification
No delay	$T \leq 15$	0
Minor delay	$15 < T \leq 60$	1
Moderate delay	$60 < T \leq 120$	2
High delay	$120 < T \leq 240$	3
Significant delay	$T > 240$	4

3. CBAM-CondenseNet

CondenseNet [10] is a densely connected network based on the convolutional neural network. Based on the excellent feature extraction ability and higher computational efficiency of the CondenseNet network, we insert the CBAM [11] module on the CondenseNet network to improve the base network. The CBAM module adopts channel and spatial attention mechanisms to enhance the information transfer of the deep network structure. The CBAM-CondenseNet algorithm proposed in this paper combines the advantages of CondenseNet and CBAM. The improved CBAM-CondenseNet algorithm is used to extract features from the fused flight chain data to make it more adaptable to the task of flight delay propagation prediction. The experimental results show that the improved algorithm effectively improves the network performance.

3.1. Model Description

The traditional CondenseNet network structure is given in Figure 3a. Each network layer in each structural block is linked to all the following layers in a dense connection, and different structural blocks are also connected in a dense connection. The CBAM-CondenseNet proposed in this paper is to add a CBAM block after the convolutional layers (3×3) of each structural block, as shown in Figure 3b. After the integration of the CondenseNet and CBAM modules, the network can improve useful features and suppress useless features according to the different importance of channels and spaces, owing to which the model's ability of feature expression has been enhanced.

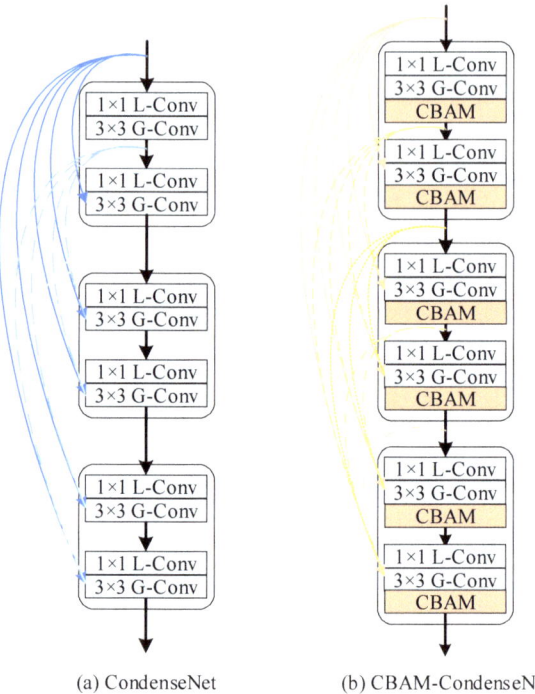

Figure 3. Network structure diagram. (**a**) CondenseNet network structure. (**b**) CBAM-CondenseNet network structure.

3.2. CBAM Convolution Module

CBAM mainly consists of two steps: first, the information is compressed into a channel descriptor using global max pooling and global average pooling in the spatial dimension, and the weight array of the aggregation in the compression operation is calibrated. Secondly, the importance degree between pixels is modeled based on the above operations. Two different channel descriptors are obtained by using global max pooling and global average pooling in the channel dimension, and the two channel descriptions are combined according to their channel dimension. Then, a hidden layer containing a single convolution kernel is used to carry out the convolution operation on the feature mapping to generate the final calibration of weights.

The CBAM module structure diagram is shown in Figure 4. For an input feature array $F \in R^{C \times H \times W}$ of an intermediate layer (F represents the input characteristic array of the CBAM, whose dimension is $C \times H \times W$. In general, C represents the number of channels, H represents the height, and W represents the width), the CBAM first undergoes a compression manipulation on a 1-dimensional channel. Then, the CBAM is multiplied with the feature array of inputs to obtain F'. Finally, the spatial weight array of $F' \in R^{C \times H \times W}$ is calculated by the 2-dimensional space compression operation to obtain F'', where $\odot$ indicates element-wise multiplication that the array elements in the corresponding positions are multiplied one by one.

$$F' = M_c(F) \odot F \quad (1)$$

$$F'' = M_S(F') \odot F' \quad (2)$$

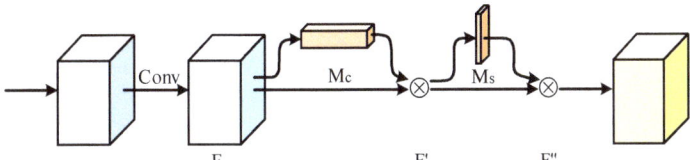

Figure 4. CBAM structure diagram.

Among them, $F \in R^{C \times H \times W}$, $F' \in R^{C \times H \times W}$, and $F'' \in R^{C \times H \times W}$ indicate the feature array of the input, the feature mapping via channel attention selection, and the feature mapping via spatial attention selection, respectively. Feature mapping $M_C \in R^{C \times 1 \times 1}$ is the channel compression weight array, and $M_S \in R^{1 \times H \times W}$ is the space compression weight array. $M_c(F)$ is used to represent the formula for calculating the channel attention characteristic array, and $M_s(F')$ is the formula for calculating the spatial attention characteristic array [11].

3.3. CBAM-CondenseNet Single Building Block

The computational unit structure of a single structural block in the CBAM-CondenseNet network is shown in Figure 5. Among them, X_1 is the array eigenvalue of the input of the corresponding layer, which means the nonlinear feature mapping after convolution transformation, X_2 represents the output array of the current layer, and M', H', C', M, H, and C in the figure represent three dimensions information of the array eigenvalue X_1, X_2.

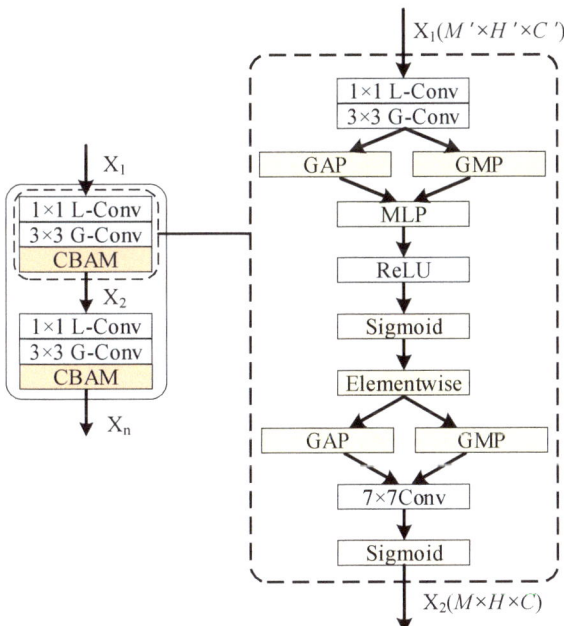

Figure 5. Network structure diagram.

In the CBAM-CondenseNet network structure, the feature mapping U after the convolution transformation of the L-th layer network is shown in formula (3).

$$U = W^L \otimes f(BN(W^{(L-1)} \otimes f(BN([X_0 X_1 \ldots X_{L-1}])))) \tag{3}$$

The outputs of all previous layers are first densely concatenated, and the outputs are obtained after batch normalization and activation function and then convolution operation with the weight array. Among them, $[X_0, X_1, \ldots, X_{L-1}]$ indicates that the feature mappings of all previous layers are took as input of the next layer network in the way of dense connection [10]; $W^{(L-1)}$ and W^L denote the $1 \times 1, 3 \times 3$ convolutional weight matrix in turn; $BN(\cdot)$ represents batch normalization of the output data for each hidden layer; $f(\cdot)$ is the ReLU activation function; And $\otimes$ represents the convolution operation.

3.4. Back Propagation

The CBAM-CondenseNet model training process is mainly implemented by the Back Propagation (BP) algorithm. BP passes the error messages of the training samples back to the hidden layers to realize the continuous iterative update of the weight array between the hidden layers until the network converges. According to the BP algorithm, taking the first two network structure blocks of CBAM-CondenseNet as an example, the gradient value between each hidden layer is deduced. It is assumed that each structural block contains two groups of nonlinear transformations, and each group of transformations of the first structural block has one convolution layer and one CBAM. The second structure block has two convolution layers and one CBAM for each set of transformations, as shown in Figure 6.

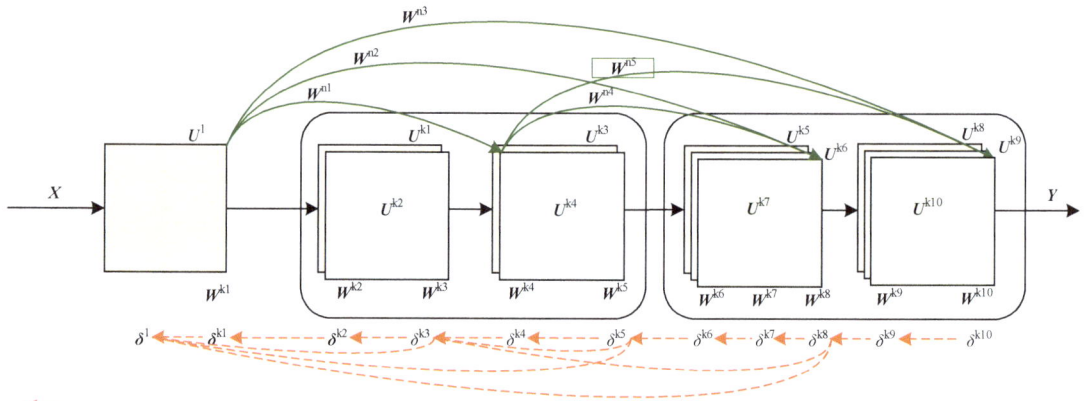

Figure 6. CBAM backpropagation.

Then, the calculation of the error term of each hidden layer in the structure block is shown in formulas (4)–(13).

$$\delta^{k10} = \partial J / \partial U^{k10} \tag{4}$$

$$\delta^{k9} = \delta^{k10} * W^{k10} \otimes f'(U^{k9}) \tag{5}$$

$$\delta^{k8} = \delta^{k9} * W^{k9} \otimes f'(U^{k8}) \tag{6}$$

$$\delta^{k7} = \delta^{k8} * W^{k8} \tag{7}$$

$$\delta^{k6} = \delta^{k7} * W^{k7} \otimes f'(U^{k6}) \tag{8}$$

$$\delta^{k5} = \delta^{k6} * W^{k6} \otimes f'(U^{k5}) \tag{9}$$

$$\delta^{k4} = \delta^{k5} * W^{k5} \tag{10}$$

$$\delta^{k3} = \delta^{k4} * W^{k4} + \delta^{k8} * W^{n5} + \delta^{k5} * W^{n4} \tag{11}$$

$$\delta^{k2} = \delta^{k3} * W^{k3} \otimes f\prime(U^{k2}) \tag{12}$$

$$\delta^{k1} = \delta^{k2} * W^{k2} \otimes f\prime(U^{k1}) \tag{13}$$

Among them, $\delta^{k1}, \delta^{k2}, \ldots, \delta^{k10}$ are the error terms corresponding to each layer in the two structural blocks, respectively. $U^{k1}, U^{k2}, \ldots, U^{k10}$ represent the output feature mappings of each layer. W^{n5} represents the weight array between the $k3$ and the $k5$ layers. $\partial J/\partial U^{k10}$ represents the derivative of loss function J with respect to the last layer of network output characteristic mapping. * indicates flipping the convolution kernel in the convolution operation $\otimes$. The error terms of the remaining structural blocks can also be derived from Equations (4)–(13). The gradient value of the 1st hidden layer of the CBAM-CondenseNet network can be expressed as shown in formula (14).

$$\begin{aligned}\partial J/\partial W^1 = (\delta^{k1} * W^{k1} + \delta^{k3} * W^{n1} + \delta^{k5} * W^{n2} + \\ \delta^{k8} * W^{n3} + \delta^{k5} * W^{n4} + \delta^{k8} * W^{n5}) \otimes A^0\end{aligned} \quad (14)$$

Among them, W^{n1}, W^{n2}, and W^{n3} represent the weight array between the $k3$ layer, the $k5$ layer, the $k8$ layer, and the first layer, respectively, and A^0 represents the feature array of the input. From the above equation, the gradient information of the 1st hidden layer contains not only the gradient weights of the backpropagation of the next layer, but also the gradient information of each set of nonlinear transformations in the 1st structural block and the 2nd structural block. As a result, the gradient value of the hidden layer has been maintained in a stable range. Therefore, the CBAM-CondenseNet network can not only make efficient use of information features through dual attention mechanism strategy, but also reduce the decay of the error term in each hidden layer by its own backward conduction mechanism. It can also enhance the ability of learning and expression in deep networks, and improve the robustness of the network.

4. SimAM-CNN-MLSTM

Considering the temporal and spatial characteristics of flight delay propagation, we introduce the Mogrifier LSTM method on the basis of the CNN. The CNN has significant advantages in feature extraction, while the Mogrifier LSTM network is better at processing time sequence information. The SimAM-CNN-MLSTM integrating attention mechanism SimAM not only considers the spatial characteristics of flight tasks but also pays attention to the temporal relationship between flight chain data. The model also uses the attention mechanism module to enhance important neurons in the feature matrix. The improved model has great advantages in dealing with the task of flight delay and prediction.

4.1. Model Description

The CNN network model has achieved great success in the field of feature extraction. The key to feature extraction is the use of convolution kernel. It makes the network model have local receptive field, which can avoid the defect that the traditional feature extraction model is difficult to correlate the whole data. Therefore, the CNN convolutional layer is first used to extract the spatial features of the flight chain data set. However, the CNN has difficulty in learning the correlation between time-series data in prediction. Due to the time-series character of flight chain data, the prediction of the flight chain delay propagation problem requires the enhancement of recurrent neural network series methods. The traditional CNN-LSTM network structure diagram is shown in Figure 7a.

The key features enhanced by the attention mechanism make the prediction results more accurate. The proposed SimAM fusion convolutional layer in this paper adopts the addition of the SimAM attention module after each convolutional layer to carry out channel and space synchronization weighting for the extracted key feature information. The Mogrifier LSTM model is selected in the extraction part of time sequence features to better enable the interaction between the previous state and the input data before the cell input. The CNN-Mogrifier LSTM network model of the fusion attention mechanism SimAM proposed in this paper is shown in Figure 7b.

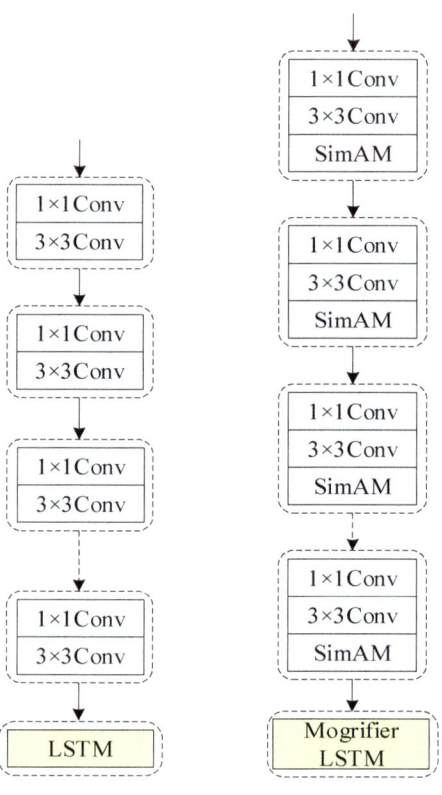

(a) CNN-LSTM   (b) SimAM-CNN-MLSTM

Figure 7. Network structure diagram. (**a**) CNN-LSTM network structure. (**b**) SimAM-CNN-MLSTM network structure.

4.2. SimAM Attention Mechanism Module

At present, the commonly used attention mechanism CBAM usually carries out channel attention first and then spatial attention. It is impossible to pay attention to space and channel at the same time. Channel attention is shown in Figure 8a, and spatial attention is shown in Figure 8b.

However, the two types of attention in the human brain tend to work together. In neuroscience, information-rich neurons usually show different firing patterns from those of the surrounding neurons. Moreover, activating neurons usually suppresses surrounding neurons, i.e., spatial inhibition. Furthermore, neurons with spatial inhibition effects should be assigned higher importance. In order to better realize the attention, SimAM realizes an attention module with unified weights based on the neuroscience theory, and the structure diagram of SimAM is shown in Figure 8c. Taking the first feature extraction module in Figure 7b as an example, the single structural block of the CNN convolutional layer fused with SimAM is shown in Figure 9.

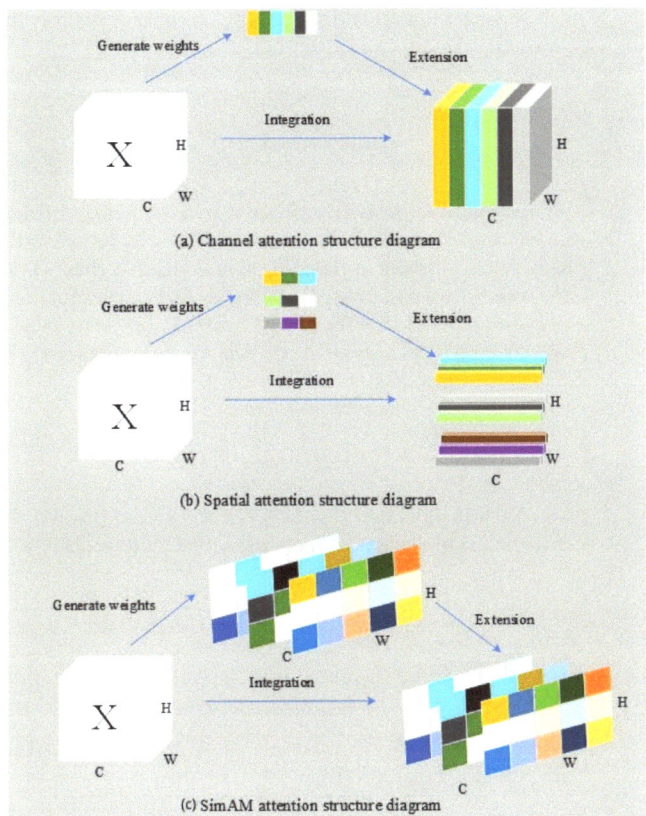

Figure 8. Attention comparison diagram. (**a**) Channel attention structure. (**b**) Spatial attention structure. (**c**) SimAM attention structure.

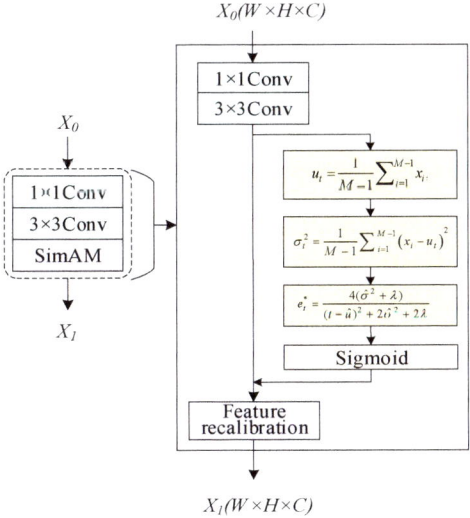

Figure 9. Integration of SimAM individual building blocks.

In order to evaluate the importance of each neuron, the easiest way is to distinguish the target neuron from other neurons. The energy function of SimAM [15] is defined as shown in formula (15).

$$e_t(w_t, b_t, y, x_i) = (y_t - \hat{t})^2 + \frac{1}{M-1}\sum_{i=1}^{M-1}(y_o - \hat{x}_i)^2 \tag{15}$$

where $\hat{t}$ and x_i represent the target neurons and other neurons of the input three-dimensional eigenvector x, and $\hat{t} = w_t t + b_t$, $\hat{x}_i = w_t x_i + b_t$, i represent the index in the spatial dimension, M denotes the number of all neurons in a channel, w_t and b_t, respectively, refer to the weight and paranoia of neurons during transformation. To facilitate the computation of the minimization of the energy formula, the binary label method is adopted. Let $y_t = 1$, $y_0 = -1$, and add regular items. λ is a super parameter. The energy function is shown in Equation (16).

$$e_t(w_t, b_t, y, x_i) = \frac{1}{M-1}\sum_{i=1}^{M-1}(-1 - (w_t x_i + b_t))^2 + (1 - (w_t t + b_t))^2 + \lambda w_t^2 \tag{16}$$

Each channel has $M = H \times W$ energy functions. We then find the analytical solution to formula (16). w_t and b_t are represented by formulas (17) and (18), respectively.

$$w_t = -\frac{2(t - u_t)}{(t - u_t)^2 + 2\sigma_t^2 + 2\lambda} \tag{17}$$

$$b_t = -\frac{1}{2}(t + u_t)w_t \tag{18}$$

where $u_t = \frac{1}{M-1}\sum_{i=1}^{M-1} x_i$, $\sigma_t^2 = \frac{1}{M-1}\sum_{i=1}^{M-1}(x_i - u_t)^2$. Therefore, the energy formula is simplified to Equation (19).

$$e_t^* = \frac{4(\hat{\sigma}^2 + \lambda)}{(t - \hat{u})^2 + 2\hat{\sigma}^2 + 2\lambda} \tag{19}$$

Equation (19) indicates that the greater the distinction between t neurons and peripheral neurons, the higher the importance, and the neuron importance can be calculated through $1/e^*$. Finally, after judging the importance of neurons according to formula (19), the feature matrix is enhanced according to the definition of the attention mechanism, as shown in formula (20).

$$X = \text{sigmoid}(\frac{1}{E}) \otimes X \tag{20}$$

4.3. Mogrifier LSTM Module

Since the increasing use of deep learning, the LSTM has been widely used in various time-series related tasks. The LSTM is a kind of RNN. The LSTM can relieve the gradient disappearance and information forgetting issues. However, in the LSTM, the current input is independent of the previous hidden layer state h_{prev}, and they only interact in the gate. The lack of previous interaction may lead to missing context information. The Mogrifier LSTM [14] allows the input and state to interact first without changing the structure of the LSTM itself, hoping to enhance the context modeling ability.

The unit structure of the Mogrifier LSTM is shown in Figure 10. The main approach of the Mogrifier LSTM is to alternately let x and h_{prev} interact for QR decomposition before ordinary LSTM computation. Let the input x and state h_{prev} first conduct multiple rounds of interaction, and then send them into the LSTM to participate in calculation. This simple modification achieves remarkable results, and its formula is shown in (7).

$$Mogrify(x, C_{prev}, h_{prev}) = Lstm\left(x^\uparrow, C_{prev}, h_{prev}^\uparrow\right) \tag{21}$$

where C_{prev} represents the previous Mogrifier LSTM unit cell state and h_{prev} represents the hidden layer state. $x^{\uparrow}$ and $h_{prev}^{\uparrow}$ are defined as the value with the largest superscript in x^i and h_{prev}^i, as shown in formulas (22) and (23). The number of alternating rounds r in the formula is a hyperparameter; if $r = 0$, then this is an ordinary LSTM.

$$x^i = 2\sigma\left(Q^i h_{prev}^{i-1}\right) \odot x^{i-2}, \text{ odd } i \in [1 \ldots r] \tag{22}$$

$$h_{prev}^i = 2\sigma\left(R^i x^{i-1}\right) \odot h_{prev}^{i-2}, \text{ even } i \in [1 \ldots r] \tag{23}$$

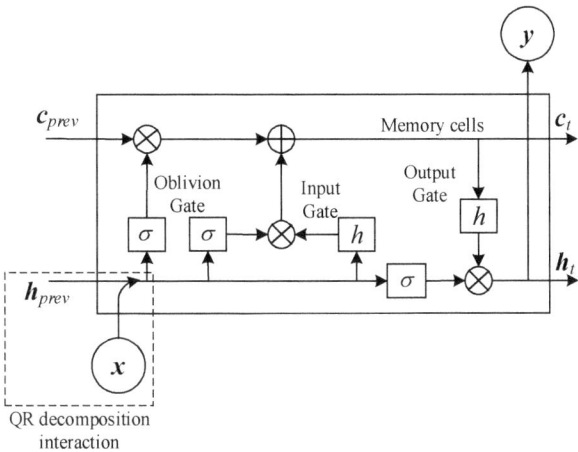

Figure 10. The Mogrifier LSTM cell structure.

The SimAM-CNN-Mogrifier LSTM model in this paper integrating the attention mechanism is compared and tested, and the number of alternating rounds $r = 6$ has the best effect. When $r = 6$, the interaction process of the Mogrifier LSTM is further shown in Figure 11.

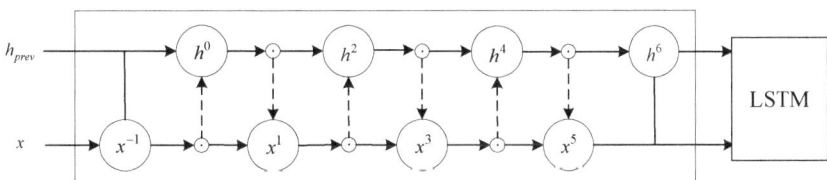

Figure 11. The Mogrifier LSTM interaction process.

The interaction between x and h_{prev} in this paper before entering the LSTM network is shown in formulas (24)–(29), where $x^{-1} = x$, $h_{prev}^0 = h_{prev}$.

$$h_{prev}^6 = 2\sigma\left(R^6 x^5\right) \odot h_{prev}^4 \tag{24}$$

$$x^5 = 2\sigma\left(Q^5 h^4\right) \odot x^3 \tag{25}$$

$$h_{prev}^4 = 2\sigma\left(R^4 x^3\right) \odot h_{prev}^2 \tag{26}$$

$$x^3 = 2\sigma\left(Q^3 h^2\right) \odot x^1 \tag{27}$$

$$h_{prev}^2 = 2\sigma\left(R^2 x^1\right) \odot h_{prev}^0 \tag{28}$$

$$x^1 = 2\sigma\left(Q^1 h^0\right) \odot x^{-1} \tag{29}$$

The final result after the interaction is input into LSTM cells, and its unit structure formula is expressed as formulas (30)–(35).

$$f = \sigma\left(W^{fx} x^5 + W^{fh} h^6_{prev} + b^f\right) \tag{30}$$

$$i = \sigma\left(W^{ix} x^5 + W^{ih} h^6_{prev} + b^i\right) \tag{31}$$

$$j = \tanh\left(W^{jx} x^5 + W^{jh} h^6_{prev} + b^j\right) \tag{32}$$

$$o = \sigma\left(W^{ox} x^5 + W^{oh} h^6_{prev} + b^o\right) \tag{33}$$

$$c = f \odot c_{prev} + i \odot j \tag{34}$$

$$h = o \odot \tanh(c) \tag{35}$$

where f is the forget gate, it is set to manage how much the previous memory cell C_{prev} retains. i is the input gate used to manage how much the current information should be input. O is the output gate to manage how much the current memory cell should output.

4.4. Backpropagation

The backpropagation process of the network is iterated layer by layer through a gradient descent algorithm, and parameters are updated according to the error term until the network converges. The CNN-MLSTM fused with the attention mechanism SimAM is divided into the Mogrifier LSTM module and the CNN module fused with SimAM in the process of backpropagation. The backpropagation process is shown in Figure 12.

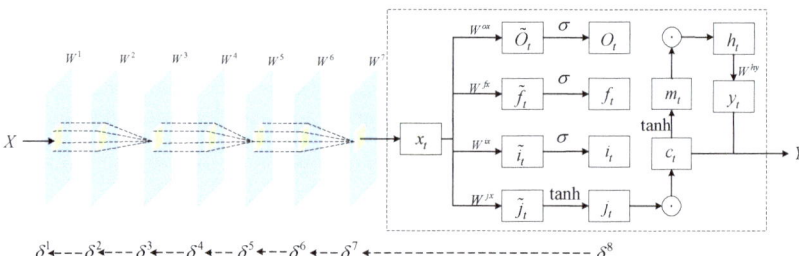

Figure 12. Network reverse propagation map.

According to the gradient descent algorithm, the error term in the backpropagation process of the Mogrifier LSTM network is first deduced. According to the principle of error backpropagation, it is derived that the backpropagation process of the error along the number of network layers is shown in formula (36).

$$\delta_t^8 = \delta_{i,t}^l W^{ix} + \delta_{f,t}^l W^{fx} + \delta_{\tilde{j},t}^l W^{jx} + \delta_{o,t}^l W^{ox} \tag{36}$$

where $\delta_{i,t}^l, \delta_{f,t}^l, \delta_{\tilde{j},t}^l, \delta_{o,t}^l$, respectively, represent the error terms of each gate in each memory cell as shown in Equations (37)–(40). It represents the weight matrix of the input gate, forget gate, and output gate in turn.

$$\delta_{i,t}^l = \delta_t^l o_t^l f\left(j_t^l\right) \tilde{j}_t^l i_t^l \left(1 - i_t^l\right) \tag{37}$$

$$\delta_{f,t}^l = \delta_t^l o_t^l f\left(j_t^l\right) j_{t-1}^l f_t^l \left(1 - f_t^l\right) \tag{38}$$

$$\delta_{j,t}^{l} = \delta_{t}^{l} o_{t}^{l} f\left(j_{t}^{l}\right) i_{t}^{l}\left(1-\left(\tilde{j}_{t}^{l}\right)^{2}\right) \quad (39)$$

$$\delta_{o,t}^{l} = \delta_{t}^{l} f\left(c_{t}^{l}\right) o_{t}^{l}\left(1-o_{t}^{l}\right) \quad (40)$$

where $f(\cdot)$ is the activation function and $f(\cdot)$ is the derivative of the activation function. The superscript l represents the current layer, and the subscript t represents the current moment. The error calculation of each hidden layer in the convolution module is shown in Equations (41)–(47).

$$\delta^{7} = \delta_{t}^{8} * f\left(U^{6}\right) \quad (41)$$

$$\delta^{6} = \delta^{7} * W^{6} \otimes f\left(U^{5}\right) \quad (42)$$

$$\delta^{5} = \delta^{6} * W^{5} \otimes f\left(U^{4}\right) \quad (43)$$

$$\delta^{4} = \delta^{5} * W^{4} \otimes f\left(U^{3}\right) \quad (44)$$

$$\delta^{3} = \delta^{4} * W^{3} \otimes f\left(U^{2}\right) \quad (45)$$

$$\delta^{2} = \delta^{3} * W^{2} \otimes f\left(U^{1}\right) \quad (46)$$

$$\delta^{1} = \delta^{2} * W^{1} \otimes f\left(U^{1}\right) \quad (47)$$

Among them, $\delta^1, \delta^2 \ldots \delta^7$ represent the error term of the corresponding layer, respectively; $U^1, U^2, \ldots U^6$ is the output feature mapping of each layer; and W represents the mapping matrix between each layer.

5. The Discussion about Simulation Results

In this paper, the improved CBAM-CondenseNet network based on the CNN, and the improved SimAM-CNN-MLSTM network, are constructed respectively. The prediction experiments are conducted separately for the departure flight delay levels of class 3 airports affected by the propagation of preceding flight delay. The experiment shows the result of predicting the departure delay level of class 3 airports affected by the departure delay of class 1 and class 2 airports. Therefore, flight delay levels of class 3 airports are used as labels for training on the training set, and flight delay level predictions are performed on the test set. Next, the data, experimental environment, and parameter configuration are introduced, and then, the performance of the model before and after improvement is compared using various indicators.

5.1. Dataset Description

The dataset used for the experiments in this paper is the national flight data from March 2018 to May 2019 provided by the ECRA. Flight chain data are formed by the flight data of an aircraft flying three times in a certain time range. The original flight data used in the experiments are 1,048,576 items. In the original data, five levels of delay are divided according to the delay time, among which the proportion of no delay, minor delay, moderate delay, high delay, and significant delay is 65:20:8:4:3. After data cleaning and flight chain dataset construction, the final flight chain dataset used in the flight delay propagation includes 36,287 data items. Subsequent experiments are conducted and verified on this flight chain dataset. The training set and validation set are divided in a ratio of 5:1. The experimental environment is a Dell PoweredgeR370 rackmount server with 16G video memory, double Intel XeonE5-2630 CPUs with 2.20 GHz CPU frequency, and NVIDIA P100 GPU accelerated graphics card. The model is run on the Pytorch deep learning framework built on the Ubuntu 16.04 operating system.

5.2. Parameters Selection

After several experiments and parameter adjustments, the parameter selection information for the CBAM-CondenseNet network and the SimAM-CNN-MLSTM network is shown in Table 2. The CBAM-CondenseNet network is initialized with weight orthogonality. The optimizer introduces the Momentum's Stochastic Gradient Descent method, where the momentum factor is set to 0.9. The coalescence factor in the grouped convolution is set to 4. The learning rate is set to 0.1, and the learning rate is adjusted by cosine annealing. The number of batches during training is 128, and the maximum number of iterations is 69,000.

Table 2. Experimental environment parameters.

Parameter Name	CBAM-CondenseNet	SimAM-CNN-MLSTM
Loss function	Cross entropy loss function	Cross entropy loss function
Learning rate	0.1	0.001
Optimizer	SGD	Adam
Regular term λ	-	1×10^{-5}
Alternate rounds r	-	6
Dropout	0	0.2
Number of training rounds	100	100

The CNN-MLSTM fused with SimAM uses four-layer convolution in the convolution layer. The convolution layer is configured as (3 × 3, 64), indicating that the size of the convolution kernel is set to 3 × 3, the number of convolution filters is set to 64, and the step size is the default value of 1. At the same time, padding 0 is performed on the boundary to ensure that the output size does not change after the input of the convolution layer. The pooling layer is averaged pooling with a pooling dimension of 2 × 2, and the step size is also set to 1. Then, the next layer is the Mogrifier LSTM network with hidden layer dimension 256.

5.3. Evaluation Metrics

The experiment in this paper is a typical multi-classification task. The main common evaluation metrics are accuracy, precision, recall, and F1 value. Each evaluation metric is explained below using a confusion matrix, as shown in Figure 13.

Confusion Matrix		True Value	
		Positive	Negative
Predicted Value	Positive	TP	FP
	Negative	FN	TN

Figure 13. Confusion matrix.

TP: True Positive, indicates that the prediction value is a positive case and the true value is a positive case.

TN: True Negative, indicates that the prediction value is a negative case and the true value is a negative case.

FP: False Positive, indicates that the prediction value is a positive case and the true value is a negative case.

FN: False Negative, indicates that the prediction value is a negative case and the true value is a positive case.

The accuracy rate represents the proportion of the number of samples with correct classification to the total number of samples, which reflects the overall performance of the model. However, when the number of positive samples and negative samples are extremely unbalanced, the accuracy rate is not a good evaluation of the model's performance. The calculation formula is shown in Equation (48)

$$Accuracy = \frac{n_{correct}}{N} \qquad (48)$$

The precision rate is the proportion of true positive classes among all results predicted to be positive classes. The accuracy rate is calculated as shown in Equation (49).

$$P = \frac{TP}{TP + FP} \qquad (49)$$

Recall indicates the proportion of the number of correctly predicted positive samples to the total number of true positive samples. The recall's calculation method is shown as follows:

$$R = \frac{TP}{TP + FN} \qquad (50)$$

The F1 value is the result of a combination of considerations, and is the summed average of the precision and recall rates. Since P and R can easily go up and down, the numerator of F1 is P * R. This makes that blindly increasing either P or R will not improve the F1 index. F1 will only be high when both are high. Equation (51) following the second equal sign also suggests that the F1 index is designed to lower both FP and FN (false positives and false negatives).

$$F1 = \frac{2 * P * R}{P + R} = \frac{TP}{TP + (FP + FN)/2} \qquad (51)$$

5.4. Analysis of Experimental Results

Before training the neural network, the data set needs to be divided into two categories: the training set and test set. The training set data are used for neural network learning. The generalization ability of the trained model is examined by using the test set. Table 3 shows the loss values, accuracy, precision, recall, and F1 value of the CBAM-CondenseNet and SimAM-CNN-MLSTM models in the data set.

Table 3. Experimental indicators.

Indicators	CBAM-CondenseNet	SimAM-CNN-MLSTM
Loss value	0.3	0.2
Accuracy	0.898	0.9136
Precision	0.913	0.825
Recall	0.892	0.874
F1	0.904	0.849

The performance of model prediction is measured by the loss value of the training set. The smaller the loss value, the more the model converges. It also means that the prediction result is closer to the true value and the robustness of the model is better. With the same training dataset, the faster the model converges, the better the learning ability of the model is. Figure 14 shows the changes of the loss values of the CBAM-CondenseNet and SimAM-CNN-MLSTM with the number of iterations. The SimAM-CNN-MLSTM model converges after 20 rounds of training, and the CBAM-CondenseNet model converges after 40 rounds of training. The SimAM-CNN-MLSTM network performs better in terms of the model learning capability.

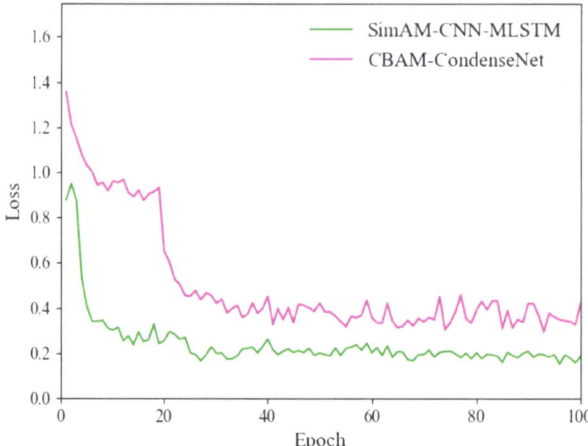

Figure 14. Variations of loss values of the CBAM-CondenseNet and SimAM-CNN-MLSTM with the number of iterations.

The accuracy rate represents the overall performance of the model and evaluates the generalization capability of the model classification. The CBAM-CondenseNet is able to achieve an accuracy of 89.8%, while the SimAM-CNN-MLSTM performs even better, with an accuracy that is 1.56 percentage points higher than that of the CBAM-CondenseNet network. The flight delay prediction in this paper is a typical multiple classification task. However, the number of flights of each delay level in the flight data set is not evenly distributed. Therefore, accuracy is not the only indicator of the overall performance of the model. Precision represents the degree of accuracy in predicting the positive sample results. Recall indicates how many of the positive cases in the sample are predicted correctly. Precision and recall reflect the assessment of the classification ability for each category in a multiclassification problem. The F1 value is the summed average of the precision and recall. From Table 3, the SimAM-CNN-MLSTM outperforms CBAM-CondenseNet in the evaluation of model accuracy, but the CBAM-CondenseNet network performs better in terms of precision and recall, which represented classification capabilities of each category. This means that CBAM-CondenseNet has a more balanced prediction performance in multiple categories.

5.5. Effect of Network Layers on CBAM-CondenseNet

In order to compare the effect of model improvement before and after, the influence of different number of network layers on the accuracy of the model is explored. Table 4 shows the accuracy of the improved CBAM-CondenseNet and CondenseNet models with different number of layers on the dataset. The experimental results show that the improved CBAM-CondenseNet model has a higher model accuracy than the CondenseNet model for the same number of layers. When the network reaches 44 layers, the accuracy rate is 89.81%. To further verify the stability of the improved model and the trainable depth, the network is tested with deeper training. When the number of layers of the network is 70, 102, and 126, the experimental results show that the CBAM-CondenseNet network could maintain good stability, and the accuracy rate is maintained stable at about 89.8% as the network deepened.

Table 4. Comparison of classification accuracy (%).

Number of Network Layers	CondenseNet	CBAM-CondenseNet
18	83.13	87.52
28	85.72	89.36
36	86.66	89.75
44	86.68	89.81
70	85.56	89.82
102	86.66	89.82
126	86.65	89.82

To verify that the CBAM-CondenseNet model is more advantageous in terms of data processing and prediction accuracy, the accuracy of the CBAM-CondenseNet and CondenseNet algorithms with different layers is analyzed and compared with the algorithm model proposed previously [39] on the flights chain dataset, as shown in Table 5. When the network has 18, 36, and 44 layers, the accuracy of the CondenseNet algorithm is higher than that of the DenseNet, SE-DenseNet, and CBAM-CondenseNet algorithm models. When the network reaches 44 layers, the CBAM-CondenseNet model is 4.25% more accurate than the CondenseNet model. It indicates that the CBAM-CondenseNet network has better performance and higher classification accuracy.

Table 5. Comparison of classification accuracy of different models (%).

Number of Network Layers	DenseNet	SE-DenseNet	CondenseNet	CBAM-CondenseNet
18	80.81	82.03	83.93	89.19
36	81.28	82.37	86.52	91.31
44	82.57	83.28	87.11	91.36

5.6. Effect of Alternate Rounds on SimAM-CNN-MLSTM

The number of alternating rounds r value is an important hyperparameter in the Mogrifier LSTM network. The larger the r value, the more fully the input x of the LSTM network interacts with the state of the previous cells, and the better the network can explore the correlation between the temporal information. However, when r value increases by 1, each update of the LSTM cell state requires one more QR matrix decomposition, and the amount of network calculation and training time will greatly increase. Due to the limited arithmetic power of the experimental hardware facilities, the experimental r is set to 6 at most. Table 6 shows the experimental results of the prediction accuracy of flight delay propagation and the training time per round when the number of alternating rounds r increases. The experiments in this paper are not very demanding in terms of time consumption, and priority is given to the impact on accuracy, so the r value is set to 6.

Table 6. Comparison of alternating rounds r accuracy and training time.

Alternate Rounds	Accuracy	Training Time per Round
1	88.45%	26.22 s
2	88.91%	28.41 s
3	90.42%	32.47 s
4	90.28%	40.86 s
5	90.97%	56.53 s
6	91.31%	71.34 s

5.7. Comparison of Model Complexity

Space complexity and time complexity are two important metrics to indicate the complexity of an algorithm. Space complexity is used to calculate the degree of resource consumption. The model parameters are measured by Params, and the more complex the algorithm is, the more parameters are involved. The time complexity is measured by the number of floating-point operations (FLOPs), and the higher the complexity of the model, the longer the model training and prediction time will be. To test the performance of the improved model, Table 7 shows the complexity of the model in this paper compared with several other models, where Mogrifier LSTM is abbreviated as MLSTM.

Table 7. Comparison of model complexity of different network models.

Model	FLOPs (M)	Params (M)
CNN	3.23	0.32
LSTM	1.56	0.64
MLSTM	1.57	0.68
CNN-LSTM	4.80	0.98
CNN-MLSTM	4.82	1.05
SimAM-CNN-MLSTM	4.82	1.05
CondenseNet	20.55	1.39
CBAM-CondenseNet	20.77	1.46

The comparison shows that, with the same amount of data input, the computation amount of the CBAM-CondenseNet network increased slightly compared with the model before the improvement. The growth of the improved network model parameters is not significant compared to the improved network model. Therefore, the embedding of CBAM brings about a negligible growth in the overall parameters and computation of the model, and the algorithm complexity is basically the same as before the improvement.

As can be seen in Table 7, the MLSTM does not have a great increase in complexity compared to the LSTM algorithm. The parametric increase basically does not change after incorporating the attention mechanism SimAM module in the CNN-MLSTM, which further verifies the parametric-free property of the SimAM module.

5.8. Comparison with Traditional Models

To test the performance of the CBAM-CondenseNet network and SimAM-CNN-MLSTM network, this section uses CNN, LSTM, MLSTM, CNN-LSTM, CNN-MLSTM, and CBAM-CondenseNet network models on the flight chain dataset to conduct accuracy and loss value comparison experiments. For the same flight chain data set, the comparative experimental results of different models are shown in Figures 15 and 16. Figure 15 is the comparison of loss values, and Figure 16 is the comparison of accuracy.

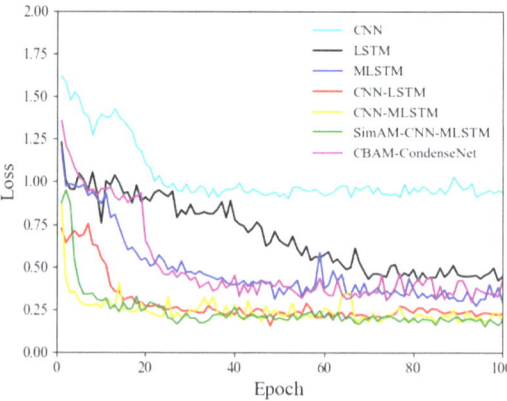

Figure 15. Comparison of the loss values of different network models.

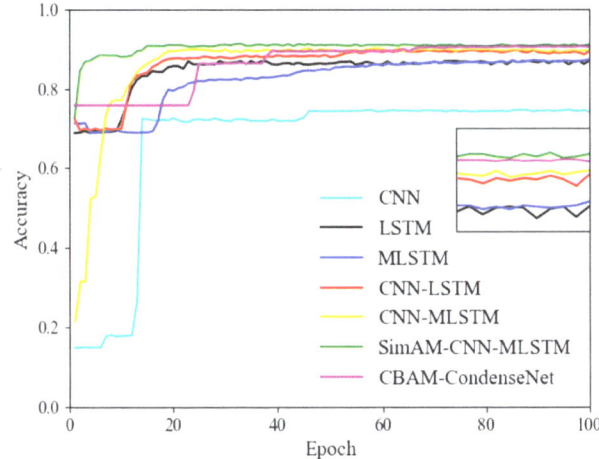

Figure 16. Comparison of the accuracy of different network models.

From the experimental results, we can see that the CNN-MLSTM network with the addition of the convolutional idea has a significant improvement in the accuracy on the flight chain dataset compared to the CNN network alone or the LSTM network, with an improvement of 16.46% and 3.16%, respectively. In this paper, the addition of the SimAM attention mechanism module to CNN-MLSTM improves 1.56% to 91.36% on the flight chain dataset, which is significantly higher than the accuracy of other networks and has the lowest loss function value.

It is comprehensively shown that when performing flight delay propagation prediction, the SimAM-CNN-MLSTM network with fused attention mechanism proposed in this paper predicts the closest flight delay propagation classification results to the actual ones, and the network performance is the best in terms of accuracy prediction.

In order to further verify that the accuracy prediction of flight delay propagation based on big data using the deep learning methods is greatly enhanced compared with the traditional algorithms, this experiment uses several different flight delay propagation prediction models [8,40,41] to compare with the models in this paper on the same flight chain data set. The experimental results are shown in Table 8. The experimental results demonstrate that the deep learning models have better performance in handling the task of flight delay propagation prediction compared with the traditional models. In particular, the improved CBAM-CondenseNet network and SimAM-CNN-MLSTM network achieve the best prediction performance.

Table 8. Comparison of accuracy of traditional models.

Network Model	Accuracy (%)
C4.5 Decision tree	78.05
Support vector machine	80.00
ATD Bayesian network	80.00
Artificial Neural Network	86.30
CBAM-CondenseNet	89.80
SimAM-CNN-MLSTM	91.36

6. Conclusions

In this paper, the chain spread model of flight delay propagation is established by analyzing the characteristics of chain spread. Two models of flight delay propagation prediction based on deep learning methods are presented. Many experiments have verified the effectiveness of the models, and the conclusions are as follows:

(1) Based on the study of flight delay propagation characteristics, a chain model of flight delay propagation effect is established. It can predict the delay level of subsequent departing flights affected by the delay of previous departing flights.

(2) The improved CBAM-CondenseNet overcomes the problem of gradient disappearance in deep network. It also combines spatial and channel attention mechanisms to achieve adaptive weight calibration. After several experiments, the prediction accuracy of the improved network is improved.

(3) According to the space-time characteristics of the flight chain data set, a SimAM-CNN-MLSTM network model integrating attention mechanisms is proposed. The CNN network layer is used to extract spatial information for the first time. Then, the important features are enhanced by the simultaneous attention of space and channel through the SimAM attention mechanism module. Finally, the Mogrifier LSTM is input to further extract the temporal characteristics in flight delay propagation, which effectively improves the accuracy of flight delay propagation prediction.

In summary, two methods of flight delay propagation prediction based on deep learning are presented to realize the prediction of flight delay propagation. In the next stage, we will consider how to use regression models to make predictions on the specific duration of flight delays, and also add more influencing factors to the analysis of flight delay propagation when the data allows.

Author Contributions: Methodology, J.Q.; validation, S.W., J.Z.; investigation, J.Q.; writing—original draft preparation, S.W., J.Z.; writing—review and editing, S.W. All authors have read and agreed to the published version of the manuscript.

Funding: This research was funded by the Scientific Research Project of the Tianjin Educational Committee, grant number XJ2022000301; the National Natural Science Foundation of China, grant number U1833105; and the Fundamental Research Funds for the Central Universities, grant number 3122019185.

Institutional Review Board Statement: Not applicable.

Informed Consent Statement: Not applicable.

Data Availability Statement: Not applicable.

Conflicts of Interest: The authors declare no conflict of interest.

References

1. Ding, J.L.; Chen, T.T.; Liu, Y.J. Colored-timed Petri nets model of flight delays and propagated analysis. *Comput. Integr. Manuf. Syst.* **2008**, *14*, 2334–2340.
2. Liu, Y.; Pilian, H.E.; Liu, C.; Cao, W. Flight delay propagation research based on Bayesian net. *Comput. Eng. Appl.* **2008**, *44*, 242–245.
3. Pyrgiotis, N.; Malone, K.M.; Odoni, A. Modelling delay propagation within an airport network. *Transp. Res. Pt. C Emerg. Technol.* **2013**, *27C*, 60–75. [CrossRef]
4. Shao, Q.; Zhu, Y.; Jia, M.; Zhang, H.J. Analysis of flight delay propagation based on complex network theory. *Aeronaut. Comput. Techn.* **2015**, *45*, 24–28.
5. Campanelli, B.; Fleurquin, P.; Arranz, A.; Etxebarria, I.; Ciruelos, C.; Eguíluz, V.M.; Ramasco, J.J. Comparing the modeling of delay propagation in the US and European air traffic networks. *J. Air Transp. Manag.* **2016**, *56*, 12–18. [CrossRef]
6. Wu, W.; Wu, C.L. Enhanced delay propagation tree model with Bayesian Network for modelling flight delay propagation. *Transp. Plan. Technol.* **2018**, *41*, 319–335. [CrossRef]
7. Baspinar, B.; Ure, N.K.; Koyuncu, E.; Inalhan, G. Analysis of delay characteristics of European air traffic through a data-driven airport-centric queuing network model. *IFAC-PapersOnLine* **2016**, *49*, 359–364. [CrossRef]
8. Khanmohammadi, S.; Tutun, S.; Kucuk, Y. A new multilevel input layer artificial neural network for predicting flight delays at JFK airport. *Procedia Comput. Sci.* **2016**, *95*, 237–244. [CrossRef]

9. Takeichi, N. Prediction of delay due to air traffic control by machine learning. In Proceedings of the AIAA Modeling and Simulation Technologies Conference, Grapevine, TX, USA, 9–13 January 2017; pp. 191–199.
10. Huang, G.; Liu, S.; Laurens, V.; Weinberger, K.Q. CondenseNet: An efficient DenseNet using learned group convolutions. In Proceedings of the IEEE Conference on Computer Vision and Pattern Recognition(CVPR), Salt Lake City, UT, USA, 18–23 June 2018; pp. 2752–2761.
11. Woo, S.; Park, J.; Lee, J.Y.; Kweon, I.S. CBAM: Convolutional block attention module. In Proceedings of the European Conference on Computer Vision (ECCV), Munich, Germany, 8–14 September 2018; pp. 3–19.
12. Rebollo, J.J.; Balakrishnan, H. Characterization and prediction of air traffic delays. *Transp. Res. Pt. C Emerg. Technol.* **2014**, *44*, 234–241. [CrossRef]
13. Graves, A. Long short-term memory. *Neural Comput.* **1997**, *9*, 1735–1780.
14. Melis, G.; Koisk, T.; Blunsom, P. Mogrifier LSTM. *arXiv* **2019**, arXiv:1909.01792.
15. Yang, L.; Zhang, R.Y.; Li, L.; Xie, X. SimAM: A simple, parameter-free attention module for convolutional neural networks. In Proceedings of the International Conference on Machine Learning, PMLR, Online, 18–24 July 2021; pp. 125–137.
16. LeCun, Y.; Bengio, Y.; Hinton, G. Deep learning. *Nature* **2015**, *521*, 436–444. [CrossRef] [PubMed]
17. Wan, R.; Mei, S.; Wang, J.; Liu, M.; Yang, F. Multivariate temporal convolutional network: A deep neural networks approach for multivariate time series forecasting. *Electronics* **2019**, *8*, 876. [CrossRef]
18. Bai, S.; Kolter, J.Z.; Koltun, V. An empirical evaluation of generic convolutional and recurrent networks for sequence modeling. *arXiv* **2018**, arXiv:1803.01271.
19. He, K.; Zhang, X.; Ren, S.; Sun, J. Deep residual learning for image recognition. In Proceedings of the 2016 IEEE Conference on Computer Vision and Pattern Recognition (CVPR), Las Vegas, NV, USA, 27–30 June 2016; pp. 770–778.
20. Jie, H.; Li, S.; Gang, S.; Albanie, S. Squeeze-and-Excitation Networks. In Proceedings of the IEEE Conference on Computer Vision and Pattern Recognition, Honolulu, HI, USA, 21–26 July 2017; p. 99.
21. Arikan, M.; Deshpande, V.; Sohoni, M.G. Building reliable air-travel infrastructure using empirical data and stochastic models of airline networks. *Oper. Res.* **2013**, *61*, 45–64. [CrossRef]
22. Sha, M.Y.; Chi, H.; Gao, M.G. Estimation of flight delays and propagation under the airport capacity constraints. *Math. Pract. Theory.* **2019**, *49*, 96–105.
23. Xu, B.G.; Liu, Q.Q.; Gao, M.G. The flight delay propagation analysis based on airport busy state. *Chin. J. Manag. Sci.* **2019**, *27*, 87–95.
24. Qiu, S.; Wu, W.W.; Hou, M. Correlation analysis of flight delay based on copula function. *J. Wuhan Univ. Technol.* **2015**, *39*, 117–120.
25. Vaswani, A.; Shazeer, N.; Parmar, N.; Uszkoreit, J.; Jones, L.; Gomez, A.N.; Kaiser, L.; Polosukhin, I. Attention is all you need. *arXiv* **2017**, arXiv:1706.03762.
26. Ahmadbeygi, S.; Cohn, A.; Guan, Y.; Belobaba, P. Analysis of the potential for delay propagation in passenger airline networks. *J. Air Transp. Manag.* **2008**, *14*, 221–236. [CrossRef]
27. Ahmadbeygi, S.; Cohn, A.; Lapp, M. Decreasing airline delay propagation by re-allocating scheduled slack. *IIE Trans.* **2010**, *42*, 478–489. [CrossRef]
28. Sternberg, A.; Soares, J.; Carvalho, D.; Ogasawara, E. A review on flight delay prediction. *arXiv* **2017**, arXiv:1703.06118.
29. Shao, W.; Prabowo, A.; Zhao, S.; Tan, S.; Salim, F.D. Flight delay prediction using airport situational awareness map. In Proceedings of the 27th ACM SIGSPATIAL International Conference, Chicago, IL, USA, 5–8 November 2019; pp. 432–435.
30. Yu, B.; Guo, Z.; Asian, S.; Wang, H.Z.; Chen, G. Flight delay prediction for commercial air transport: A deep learning approach. *Transp. Res. Pt. e-Logist. Transp. Rev.* **2019**, *125*, 203–221. [CrossRef]
31. Alvaro, R.S.; Fernando, G.C.; Rosa, A.V.; Javier, P.C.; Rock, B.M.; Sergio, C.S. Assessment of airport arrival congestion and delay: Prediction and reliability. *Transp. Res. Pt. C Emerg. Technol.* **2019**, *98*, 255–283.
32. Khanna, S.; Tan, V. Economy statistical recurrent units for inferring nonlinear granger causality. *arXiv* **2019**, arXiv:1911.09879.
33. Nicholas, G.P.; Vadim, O.S. Deep learning for short-term traffic flow prediction. *Transp. Res. Pt. C-Emerg. Technol.* **2017**, *79*, 1–17.
34. Kim, Y.J.; Sun, C.; Briceno, S.; Mavris, D. A deep learning approach to flight delay prediction. In Proceedings of the Digital Avionics Systems Conference, Sacramento, CA, USA, 25–29 September 2016; pp. 203–221.
35. Tsoi, A.C.; Tan, S. Recurrent neural networks: A constructive algorithm, and its properties. *Neurocomputing* **1997**, *15*, 309–326. [CrossRef]
36. Cornegruta, S.; Bakewell, R.; Withey, S.; Montana, G. Modelling radiological language with bidirectional Long short-term memory networks. *arXiv* **2016**, arXiv:1609.08409.
37. Klein, A.; Craun, C.; Lee, R.S. Airport delay prediction using weather-impacted traffic index (WITI) model. In Proceedings of the Digital Avionics Systems Conference (DASC), 2010 IEEE/AIAA 29th, Salt Lake City, UT, USA, 3–7 October 2010; pp. 2111–2119.
38. Gai, S.; Bao, Z. Banknote recognition research based on improved deep convolutional neural network. *J. Electron. Inf. Technol.* **2019**, *41*, 1992–2000.
39. Wu, R.B.; Zhao, T.; Qu, J.Y. Flight delay prediction model based on deep SE-DenseNet. *J. Electron. Inf. Technol.* **2019**, *41*, 1510–1517.

40. Cheng, H.; Li, Y.M.; Luo, Q.; Li, C. Study on flight delay with C4.5 decision tree based prediction method. *Syst. Eng. Theory Pract.* **2014**, *34*, 239–247.
41. Xu, T.; Ding, J.; Gu, B.; Wang, J. Forecast warning level of flight delays based on incremental ranking support vector machine. *Acta Aeronaut. Et Astronaut. Sin.* **2009**, *30*, 1256–1263.

Disclaimer/Publisher's Note: The statements, opinions and data contained in all publications are solely those of the individual author(s) and contributor(s) and not of MDPI and/or the editor(s). MDPI and/or the editor(s) disclaim responsibility for any injury to people or property resulting from any ideas, methods, instructions or products referred to in the content.

Article

Semantic Similarity-Based Mobile Application Isomorphic Graphical User Interface Identification

Jing Cheng [1], Jiayi Zhao [1], Weidong Xu [1], Tao Zhang [2,*], Feng Xue [2] and Shaoying Liu [3]

[1] School of Computer Science and Engineering, Xi'an Technological University, Xi'an 710064, China
[2] School of Software, Northwestern Polytechnical University, Xi'an 710060, China
[3] School of Informatics and Data Science, Hiroshima University, Hiroshima 739-8525, Japan
* Correspondence: tao_zhang@nwpu.edu.cn; Tel.: +86-18629083628

Abstract: Applying robots to mobile application testing is an emerging approach to automated black-box testing. The key to supporting automated robot testing is the efficient modeling of GUI elements. Since the application under testing often contains a large number of similar GUIs, the GUI model obtained often contains many redundant nodes. This causes the state space explosion of GUI models which has a serious effect on the efficiency of GUI testing. Hence, how to accurately identify isomorphic GUIs and construct quasi-concise GUI models are key challenges faced today. We thus propose a semantic similarity-based approach to identifying isomorphic GUIs for mobile applications. Using this approach, the information of GUI elements is first identified by deep learning network models, then, the GUI structure model feature vector and the semantic model feature vector are extracted and finally merged to generate a GUI embedding vector with semantic information. Finally, the isomorphic GUIs are identified by cosine similarity. Then, three experiments are conducted to verify the generalizability and effectiveness of the method. The experiments demonstrate that the proposed method can accurately identify isomorphic GUIs and shows high compatibility in terms of cross-platform and cross-device applications.

Keywords: isomorphic GUI; semantic similarity; mobile application testing

MSC: 68U10

1. Introduction

The demand for mobile devices has exploded to staggering heights over the past few years. The latest data show that the number of apps on the Google Play Store has grown from 2.1 million to 3.14 million in a year [1]. With intense competition and budget constraints, most developers lack sufficient time to detect bugs and potential crashes in their applications, resulting in frequent application problems that have a dramatic impact on the user experience. The existing manual testing of mobile applications has problems of low efficiency and high cost and cannot meet the needs of mobile application testing [2]. Hence, the cost-effective automated testing of mobile applications has become a potential solution but how to realize it remains a challenge.

The graphical user interface (GUI) is an important medium for users to interact with mobile applications. It is also a key object for mobile application testing. The existing GUI automation testing techniques can be broadly classified into four categories: record and playback method, data-driven method, keyword-driven method, and hybrid framework method. The record and playback method automatically constructs test scripts by recording the sequence of events in the GUI during the use of the software [3]. However, this method has low test coverage and is sensitive to GUI changes, which are not suitable for a large number of tests [4–6]. The data-driven method separates the test script from the data and places the data into a configuration file. This approach can improve the reuse rate of test scripts but cannot cope with GUI's interface transformations [7,8]. The keyword-driven

method is an optimization of the data-driven method which allows separating the test case design from test development. However, these approach test scripts are difficult to maintain [9,10]. The hybrid framework method combines the advantages of multiple methods to form a unified functional tester based on testing requirements [11].

Robotic testing can reduce labor costs in the process of test execution and realize a full black-box testing process [12]. It simulates real users interacting with mobile applications only at the device level, enabling cross-platform, cross-system, and multi-device operations. It effectively realizes the full black-box automated testing of mobile applications and has broad development prospects. Hence, we built a GUI semantic model-based robot test to lay the foundation for the full automated black-box GUI testing of mobile applications. A particular challenge is the presence of isomorphic GUIs in mobile applications which may adversely affect GUI models in terms of redundancy and sufficiency, thereby affecting test efficiency.

GUIs that differ in appearance (images, text, colors, and size) but have the same functionality, structure, and internal logical relationships between interfaces are isomorphic. Figure 1 shows an example of an isomorphic GUI for Eastern Airlines. Figure 1 (W0) shows the flight list interface for a ticket search while (W1a) to (W1d) show a detailed interface with four columns of flights; (W1a) to (W1d) differ only in the specific image and text information.

Figure 1. Example of an isomorphic GUI.

However, solutions to isomorphic GUIs identification are limited. One method is to extract information based on the HTML structure and measure the similarity in the form of a tree or graph. Long Y [13] simplifies the page DOM tree structure by analyzing the page elements formally. REN [14] mines similar codes using a chunking algorithm and similarity calculates and builds a DOM tree by code parsing. This method can quickly obtain the elements and hierarchy of an interface to make similarity judgments. However, it requires source code support and lacks an understanding of interface semantics. Another method is feature extraction based on machine vision which converts images into feature vectors. Zhang [15] used relative entropy to obtain GUI similarity by acquiring the elements and layout features of the interface. However, this method does not capture the textual content of the GUI, which can affect the similarity judgment of different types of mobile application GUIs.

To address the above problems, we propose a semantic-based method for identifying the isomorphic interfaces of mobile applications. The method is based on machine vision to obtain GUI components, texts, and layout information, and construct a GUI semantic model. The GUI structure model feature vector and semantic model feature vector are extracted through deep learning convolutional networks to synthesize the interface similarity metric results. The main contributions of this paper are as follows:

(1) A semantic similarity-based isomorphic GUI identification method is proposed which avoids redundant test cases and mitigates the problem of the state space explosion of GUI models.
(2) Three experiments are conducted to evaluate the performance of our proposed method and the results show its superiority to the related existing techniques.

The rest of the paper is organized as follows: Section 2 provides the background of the research and related work and Section 3 provides the details of the construction process of the model and the isomorphic GUI identification method. In Section 4, we discuss the experimental setup and analyze the results. Finally, the paper is summarized in Section 5.

2. Related Work

In this section, we briefly describe the work related to semantic similarity-based approaches to isomorphic GUI recognition. First, the development status of GUI automation testing is introduced. Second, the problems of current GUI models are discussed. Finally, some application scenarios of homomorphic GUI recognition are presented.

2.1. Automated GUI Testing

The latest generation of automated testing technology is vision-based GUI automation testing (VGT). VGT automates testing by introducing image recognition algorithms and automated scripts to simulate user behavior [16]. This approach enables the black-box testing of mobile applications to a certain extent but limitations and challenges still remain. The test scripts for VGT are vulnerable to GUI graphical changes; graphical changes occur during system development, which makes maintaining test scripts costly. The slow image recognition speed of VGT technology is also a challenge for robot testing. Reinforcement learning has also been attempted for automated GUI testing. David et al. [17] used a Q-learning-based test generation algorithm to select events systematically and explored the GUI of the application under testing without the need for a pre-existing abstract model. This approach evaluates the performance of the technique based only on block coverage and lacks the exploration of the generalizability of the method.

Because of the diversity of mobile application platforms in the market, test migration is also an important direction for automated testing. Xue Qin et al. [18] proposed a new approach, TestMig, which migrates GUI tests from iOS to Android without any migrated code examples. This approach requires the precise mapping of cross-platform UI controls. Some other assertions involve the absolute position and padding size of UI controls, which also present challenges in the technical approach.

2.2. GUI Modeling

Model-based GUI testing is usually chosen to solve the redundancy problem of GUI testing, facilitate the exploration of behavior space, and support effective debugging. GUI models are usually classified into two types: state-based and event-based models. The state-based model uses finite state machines for GUI modeling. Belli et al. [19] reduced the number and cost of test cases by recommending a hierarchy-centric testing approach and an associated test creation system to prevent the system under test from becoming too large. Baek et al. [20] proposed a set of multi-level GUI comparison criteria which provides multiple options for GUI model generation at the abstraction level. These methods can alleviate the space explosion problem to some extent, but the urgent need for a better solution to the space explosion problem faced by state modeling remains.

The event-based model is another common model. Memon et al. [21] proposed the use of event flow graph (EFG) models in the testing of GUIs, which are a later key component of a commonly used GUI testing framework. Belli et al. [22] constructed an event sequence graph (ESG) model, based on directed graphs, which is used to represent legal and illegal behaviors based on GUI events. The event-based model avoids the definition of a system state; the description of the actual system is more abstract, which also reduces the effectiveness of model error detection to a certain extent.

2.3. Isomorphic GUIs Recognition

The study of isomorphic GUIs has been applied to various aspects of the software development process. Farnaz Behrang et al. [23] designed a technique to use sketches of applications as input to help simplify the process of going from drawing a GUI to creating an actual GUI. Open-source applications from public repositories were used to identify sketches with isomorphic GUIs and transformed applications. Leonardo Mariani et al. [24] exploited the semantic similarity between the textual information of GUI widgets to implement a test reuse approach and led to the migration of manually designed GUI tests from a source application to a target application with similar functionality. Almrayat et al. [25] developed an algorithm to automatically extract GUI features and evaluated the effects of GUI similarity on the functional similarity of Android applications.

In summary, numerous GUI modeling approaches have emerged in automated GUI testing but they do not effectively solve the problem of the state space explosion of GUI models. In comparison, our semantic similarity-based approach to identifying isomorphic GUIs avoids redundant test cases by merging redundant isomorphic nodes in the GUI model to prevent the explosive growth of the number of test cases.

2.4. Explainability for Machine Learning Models

Feature engineering can be guided by interpretable analysis. Generally, features are made based on some expertise and experience and the analysis of feature importance can be used to mine more useful features. Hence, deep learning and other black-box models are becoming increasingly popular. Despite their high performance, they may not be ethically or legally acceptable due to their lack of interpretability. Bibal et al. [26] investigated how the legal requirements for interpretability can be interpreted and applied in machine learning. Nadia Burkart et al. [27] provided basic definitions outlining different principles and approaches to interpretable supervised machine learning. The trade-off between completeness and interpretability from the user's perspective was investigated by Wanner et al. [28]. In particular, they evaluated how existing interpretable AI models can be used for transfer and suggested improvements.

3. Proposed Method

We discuss our semantic similarity-based method for identifying isomorphic GUIs in this section. The identification of GUI isomorphic interfaces is a comparison of GUI structure graphs and GUI semantic similarity. Figure 2 shows the overall architecture of the method. The flow of the method can be divided into three steps: extracting GUI information, vectorizing GUI information, and identifying isomorphic GUIs. First, the class and location of GUI elements are identified by the YOLOv5 target detection network [3]. Removing textual information will greatly reduce the difficulty of GUI modeling. However, the skeleton-only GUI model may recognize non-isomorphic GUIs as isomorphic GUIs [15]. The element text is recognized by optical character recognition (OCR). The semantics of the GUI elements are obtained through a comparison of the text recognition results with the created domain application ontology model (DAOM). Then, the GUI structure map is constructed based on the type and location information of the GUI, the interface text noise effect is eliminated, and the GUI structure vector is extracted by an autoencoder [15]. A pre-trained Sentence-BERT language model is used to extract the interface semantic feature vector [29]. Finally, the GUI structure vector and the semantic vector are combined into a GUI interface embedding vector. The isomorphic GUIs are then identified by cosine similarity.

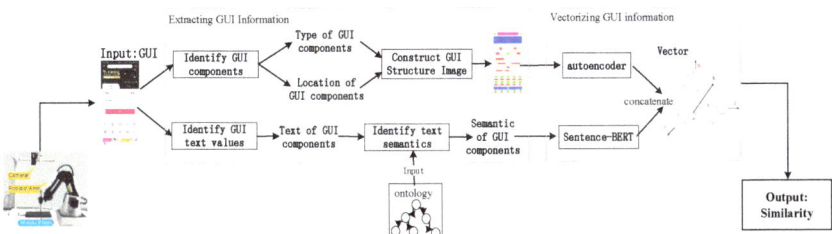

Figure 2. The architecture of the GUI isomorphic recognition method.

3.1. Extracting GUI Information

3.1.1. Identify GUI Components and Obtain the Structure Image

Components are the basic elements that make up a GUI window. Generally, each GUI is composed of multiple types of components. The Finite State Machine (FSM) based GUI modeling includes event-driven state transitions such as clicking on GUI elements. Therefore, the classification and identification of elements are the basis of GUI modeling. Referring to the study of the Rico dataset in [30], the GUI components are divided into basic elements and combined elements by combining the characteristics and layout of the GUI elements. The basic elements include text, icons, images, and input boxes. When the text is a description of an icon or an input box, it is defined as a combination element.

To ensure real-time detection speed for mobile application robot testing, the YOLOv5 target detection model was chosen to identify the GUI elements [31]. The YOLOv5 target detection model sets a set of bounding boxes with a certain width and height in a pre-defined manner. Information about the type and position of the target detection object is returned by extracting image features. The advantage of YOLOv5 is the anchor box mechanism included in the target detection network structure. This mechanism allows the simultaneous detection of multiple objects present in the image. Figure 3b shows an example of recognizing GUI elements. The position and type of this interface element are accurately identified.

The GUI structure image is the feedback of the GUI structure and function. The GUI structure image is constructed by extracting the type and location information of the GUI components. Then, the GUI structure vector is extracted, which can effectively eliminate the interference of interface text noise. The GUI structure image is constructed based on the coloring of GUI component types, as shown in Figure 3c. That is, a color is assigned to each type of component. Rectangular boxes are used to show the size and position of the components, forming a GUI layout that ignores the textual information of the interface.

3.1.2. Obtain the Semantics of GUI Components

The semantics of an element is defined as the content of the element text or the name of the named entity. As shown in Figure 3a, the semantics of "SIA" is the text "SIA", which represents the country Singapore. The complexity of the GUI context poses a great difficulty for text recognition. This paper uses optical character recognition (OCR) for the character recognition of text elements in GUI elements to ensure the accuracy of text element recognition.

Mobile applications in the same domain often contain a large number of GUI elements with similar semantics. The descriptions of these elements are not identical but often have the same functionality. We address this problem by constructing a DAOM which serves as a semantic library to provide unified semantics for GUI models.

Figure 3. Recognition results of GUI elements.

The DAOM is a unified description of the semantics of the GUI elements involved in a mobile application in the same domain. The same domain refers to mobile applications that provide the same or similar services, e.g., the booking software of different airlines belong to the same domain. We combine each airline booking software to manually construct the domain ontology of airline booking software. The domain knowledge is acquired in a common way to provide a common understanding of the relevant concepts in the domain and to realize the sharing and reuse of knowledge among different systems. Some element entities and their attributes in the manually constructed airline booking domain ontology are shown in Figure 4. The results of text recognition are input to the DAOM. The generalized linguistic descriptions are transformed into a unified and standardized element description language through a comparison of the ontology domain knowledge base. A unified description of the main functional elements, for example, flight information, usually includes information such as ID, time, price, etc. Incorporating all this information into the model forms a unified description of the order.

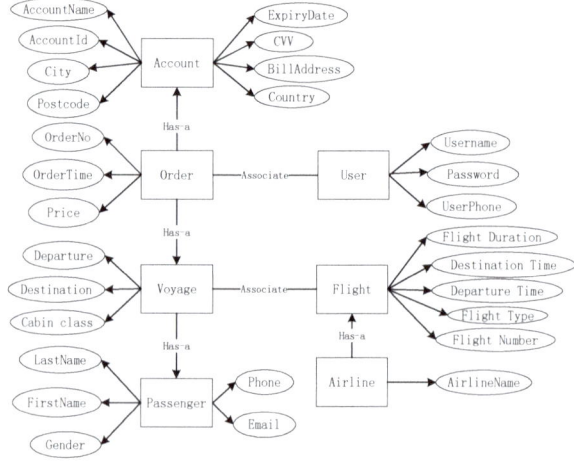

Figure 4. Element entities and their attributes in the airline booking domain ontology.

3.2. Vectorizing GUI Information

The GUI information recognition results are used as the input to extract structure vectors from the type and location information of GUI elements by the autoencoder. The semantic vectors are extracted from the semantic information of the GUI elements by using the Sentence-BERT language model. Then, the two vectors are connected into an embedding vector representing the overall features of the GUI by the concatenate function.

3.2.1. GUI Structure Embeddings

The GUI structure feature vectors are then extracted. To reduce the workload of manually labeling data, an unsupervised learning method autoencoder is selected to extract GUI structure feature vectors [32]. The autoencoder consists of two parts: the encoder encodes and the decoder recovers. The encoder encodes the input x into a learned feature representation. The decoder recovers the original input by decoding the representation.

Autoencoders have certain bottleneck constraints: the compressed encoding must have fewer data dimensions than the original input data. Only important features are kept in the bottleneck stage and noise is ignored to extract isomorphic information from the GUIs.

For the convolutional autoencoder, both the encoder and decoder are modeled as convolutional neural networks. Figure 5 shows the network structure of the autoencoder used in this paper. First, the min-max method is used to normalize the 128×128 GUI structure map to improve the performance of the model. Second, the feature vectors are extracted by auto-encoder. The encoder consists of four convolutional layers and four pooling layers. The input data are compressed by the encoder, and the 512-dimensional GUI structure feature vector is obtained after repeated iterations. The decoder contains four convolutional layers and four upsampling layers. The reconstructed GUI structure is output after iterations.

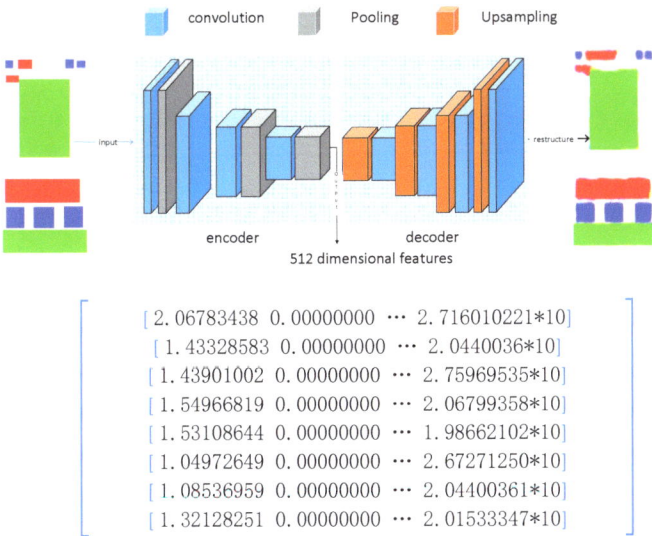

Figure 5. The network structure of the autoencoder.

In our model, the mean-square error (MSE) is used as a loss function to reduce the difference between the input image and the reconstructed image. During the training process of the loss layer, the difference between the original and the reconstructed images will continue decreasing until the model converges.

Taking the GUI skeleton as the input, the encoding process extracts feature vectors through a series of convolution and pooling operations, and the intermediate bottleneck layer outputs the structure vectors of the input GUI skeleton. For high-dimensional GUI information vectors, a certain degree of dimensionality reduction is possible using the autoencoder bottleneck, which will greatly reduce the computational effort.

3.2.2. GUI Semantic Embeddings

The GUI component semantics is encoded into a 386-dimensional semantic vector using a pre-trained Sentence-BERT language model [33]. Sentence-BERT is a modification of the pre-trained Bidirectional Encoder Representations from Transformers (BERT) network. It can map sentences to a vector space out of the box. Sentence-BERT maps each sentence to vector space using concatenation and triadic network structures. Semantically meaningful sentence embeddings with fixed sizes are thus derived. State-of-the-art performance is established through semantic text similarity performance. Semantically similar sentences are very close in vector space, which is usually measured using cosine similarity or Euclidean distance.

3.2.3. Forming the Embedding Vector

The structure vector and feature vector of the GUI are combined to form a single fixed-length embedding vector. Using the concatenate function to join the two vectors to obtain an 898-dimensional fixed-size embedding vector represents the overall GUI features. The concatenate in a neural network is usually used to unite features, which is essentially a union of dimensions. Concatenation functions simply concatenate scattered information. The purpose of this step is to merge the information from the structure vector and the feature vector for the similarity calculation in the next section.

3.3. Identifying Isomorphic GUIs

Finite State Machines (FSM) are used to generate models for GUI model generation. The model consists of nodes representing GUI states and edges representing interactions. Figure 6a shows the jump events from the five pages in Figure 1, ignoring the other buttons and internal components. In Figure 1, the four states jumped by state (W0) have different interfaces, but their logical structures and functions are the same. When constructing the GUI model, (W1a), (W1b), (W1c), and (W1d) transformed by state (W0) can be combined into one state, as shown in Figure 6b. This can reduce the number of states and simplify the GUI model. The key step in this process is the identification of isomorphic GUIs.

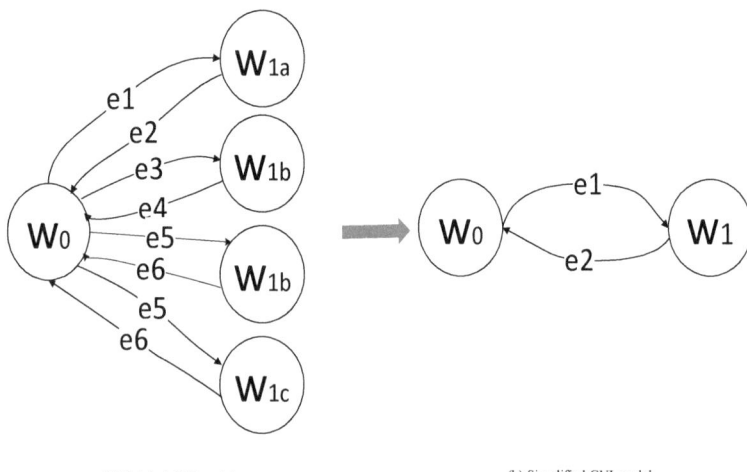

(a) Original GUI model   (b) Simplified GUI model

Figure 6. Simplifying the FSM model.

Cosine similarity is a correlation measure. It measures the similarity between two vectors by measuring the cosine of the angle between them to determine whether the two vectors point in approximately the same direction. Cosine similarity focuses on the difference between two vectors in terms of direction. Hence, cosine similarity is an appropriate measure of the correlation between two vectors for high-dimensional spaces. The cosine similarity between two randomly distributed vectors X and Y can be calculated as follows:

$$consine\_score = \frac{\sum\limits_{i=1}^{n} X_i \times Y_i}{\sqrt{\sum\limits_{i=1}^{n} (X_i)^2} \times \sqrt{\sum\limits_{i=1}^{n} (Y_i)^2}} \quad (1)$$

where $(i = 1, 2, 3, \ldots, n)$ are the properties of vectors X and Y in the i-th dimension. $consine\_score \in [-1, 1]$, a cosine similarity close to 1 indicates that the angle between the two vectors is close to 0, which means that the two vectors are closer. Conversely, the closer to -1 the cosine similarity is, the more dissimilar the two vectors are.

The cosine similarity value is normalized using the min-max method as a basis for determining isomorphic GUIs. The closer to 1 the value is, the more similar the GUI is. The threshold is set to 0.9. When the similarity value is greater than 0.9, it is judged as an isomorphic GUI. In contrast, when the value is less than 0.9, it is judged to be a non-isomorphic GUI.

4. Experimental Analysis and Results

The applicability and effectiveness of our proposed method are evaluated. The current mobile application platforms are diverse. The two most popular mobile application platforms are iOS for Apple and Android. However, because of the variability of platform development, the software GUI can vary greatly from one application platform to another. The differences between the GUI on Android and iOS platforms are shown in Figure 7. Although many approaches have been proposed to support cross-platform compilation and execution of applications [34,35], cross-platform execution is still too inefficient for real-world usage scenarios. The existing test migration methods tend to be highly dependent on software source code, making it difficult to achieve full black-box software testing. Hence, we design the following experiments, accuracy experiment, resolution experiment, and cross-platform experiment, to verify the cross-device and cross-platform properties of the proposed method. In addition, to verify the superiority of the proposed method, we set up two baseline models for each experiment as a comparison.

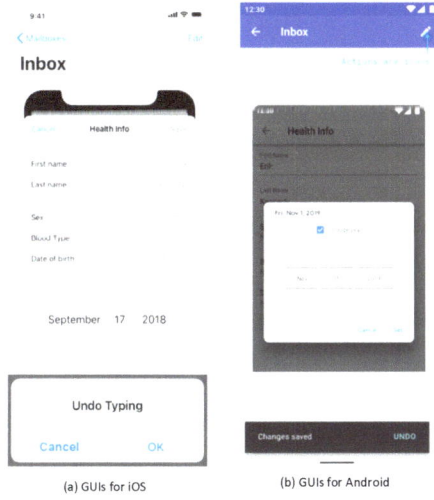

Figure 7. GUI differences on Android and iOS platforms.

4.1. Dataset and Preparation for Experiments

The domain of the airline service mobile application is selected to produce the dataset. The selection of the test set is based on two important factors: representative software, the chosen field needs to have a wide range of applications in daily life, and a distinct and unified interface style, the software interface design in the same field needs to have a similar style. The airline service mobile application fits our needs perfectly. The software has a high degree of functional overlap and the interface style is simple and clear, which means that the element information characteristics are obvious.

For the three experiments set up, we construct the datasets separately. A total of 300 screenshots are taken from six smart devices, four of which have Android as their operating system and the rest have iOS as their operating system. The specific data set is shown in Table 1.

Table 1. The constructed dataset.

Experiment 1: Accuracy Experiment								
Resolution	App No.	Priceline	Kiwi	Wego	Cheap Travel	China Eastern	Spring Airline	Lufthansa	Hainan Airlines
1080*2340		12	12	12	12	12	12	14	14
Experiment 2: Resolution Experiment							
Resolution	App No.	Kiwi	Qatar Airways	Expedia	Priceline	Wego	Kiwi
1080*2270		6	6	6	6	6	6
1440*3200		6	6	6	6	6	6
1080*2340		4	4	4	4	4	4
1080*1920		4	4	4	4	4	4
Experiment 3: Cross-platform Experiment							
System	App No.	Qatar Airways	Expedia	Priceline	Wego	Qatar Airways
Android	1080*2400	6	6	8	6	6
Android	1440*3200	6	6	6	6	6
iOS	1170*2532	6	6	6	8	6
iOS	1242*2208	6	6	6	6	6

During the experiments, the Kera neural network framework for deep learning was mainly used. To maximize the flexibility and speed of the algorithm, we incorporated the Torch framework, which is an open-source framework for machine learning.

4.2. Baselines

The semantic similarity-based isomorphic GUI recognition method is compared with the following baseline models.

1. GUI skeleton vectors only (GSVO) [15]: only GUI visual embedding is considered, improving the approach of screen embedding used in the original RICO paper [36]. The type and location information of GUI components are obtained by end-to-end deep learning. The GUI features are represented with feature vectors extracted by the autoencoder. The isomorphic GUIs are determined by the similarity of the feature vectors.
2. Screen2Vec [29]: the textual content, visual design, and layout patterns of the GUI are considered. The final screen feature vector is derived from a multi-method synthesis.

Screen2Vec requires the support of the underlying framework of the application under testing to obtain the GUI layout pattern embedding vector. Only the textual content of the GUI is considered, i.e., the semantic information contained behind the textual content is not considered.

4.3. Evaluation Metrics

Four evaluation metrics are used to assess the effectiveness of the isomorphic GUI recognition method: accuracy (Acc), precision (P), recall (R), and harmonic mean F1.

- Acc indicates the percentage of correct predictions.
- P is for the predicted outcome, which indicates how many of the samples predicted to be positive are truly positive.
- R is specific to the original sample, which indicates how many positive classes in the sample are correctly predicted.
- F1 is the summed average of precision and recall. F1 combines Acc and R into one metric which evaluates the performance of the model on images where the true value is known.

4.4. Results and Discussion

4.4.1. Accuracy Experiments

One hundred GUI screenshots containing 66 pairs of isomorphic GUIs are selected from eight airline service mobile applications (because some GUIs have more than one isomorphic GUI pair). Then, the first 50 and last 50 GUI feature values are compared sequentially for a total of 2500 times. The recognition results of the isomorphic GUI are represented in the form of a heat map, shown in Figure 8. The similarity measure is represented by the color shade of the heat map; the darker the color, the higher the similarity value.

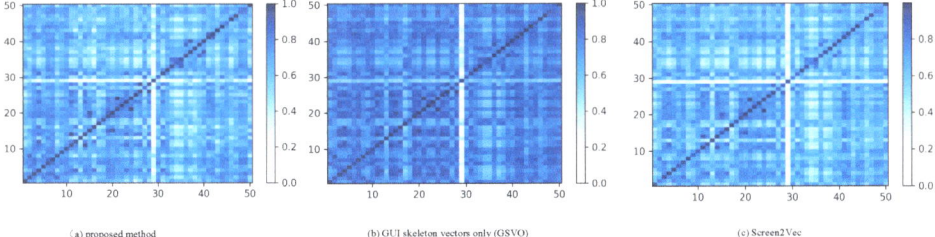

(a) proposed method   (b) GUI skeleton vectors only (GSVO)   (c) Screen2Vec

Figure 8. Results of similarity discriminant matrix for accuracy experiments.

Figure 8 shows that the GSVO method heat map has the darkest color, indicating that the obtained GUI similarity value is high due to the fact that GSVO only constructs the GUI layout structure information vector. While the element text semantic information is ignored, the GUI feature vector acquires incomplete information, leading to the identification of non-isomorphic GUIs as isomorphic GUIs. The Screen2Vec method obtains the structure information along with the GUI text information. However, because of the differences in the textual representation of elements, some isomorphic GUIs are recognized as non-isomorphic GUIs, resulting in low GUI similarity values. Our proposed method shows superiority compared to the first two baseline models. The GUI structure vector is considered and the textual variability is taken into account. The text is transformed into domain ontology semantics, which is universal in the scope of the domain.

The performance metrics of the three methods for identifying isomorphic GUIs are shown in Table 2. The indicator data show that our proposed method has the highest recognition accuracy in 2500 comparative experiments and shows strong superiority in terms of precision and recall, and has an F1 score above 0.8.

Table 2. The proposed method of the accuracy experiment.

	Proposed Method	GUI Skeleton Vectors Only	Screen2Vec
Acc	0.993	0.986	0.989
P	0.853	0.670	0.885
R	0.879	0.894	0.697
F1	0.866	0.766	0.789

We plotted the receiver operating characteristic (ROC) curves of the three methods to compare the recognition results of the three methods for isomorphic GUIs. As shown in Figure 9, the area under the curve (AUC) of the three methods were 0.907, 0.852, and 0.906, respectively. The AUCs of all three methods were above 0.85. Our proposed method has the highest AUC value, which indicates that the proposed method has the highest accuracy value.

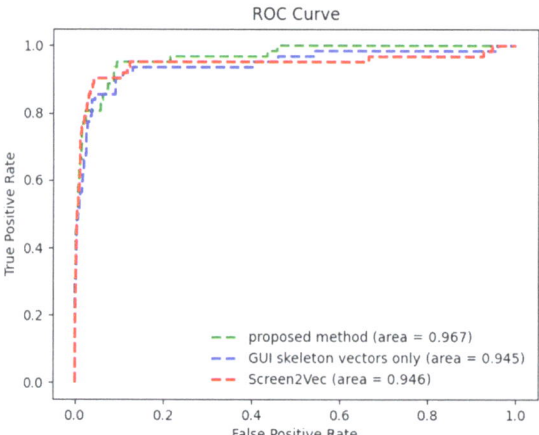

Figure 9. ROC for the accuracy experiments.

4.4.2. Resolution Experiment

Different kinds of smart devices result in GUIs with inconsistent resolutions; the same software will produce different display effects on smart devices with different resolutions, which also affects the screen layout. For example, the same text is displayed as two lines of text on a GUI with a wider screen, but it will be displayed as three lines of text on a GUI with a narrower screen. Hence, resolution can have some effect on isomorphic GUI recognition.

A total of 100 interfaces containing 109 pairs of isomorphic GUIs are intercepted from five pieces of software in the field of airline services selected from four Android smart devices with different resolutions. The heat map of similarity for the three methods for isomorphic GUI recognition at different resolutions is shown in Figure 10. The heat map is lighter in color compared to Figure 8, indicating that the recognition accuracy of the isomorphic GUI has decreased. However, the distribution of the similarity matrix is consistent with Figure 8 as a whole.

An intuitive demonstration of the performance of the three methods in identifying isomorphic GUIs at different resolutions is shown in Table 3. It shows that the resolution has some influence on the recognition results of all three methods. The difference in the resolution of the tested application affects the size of the GUI elements on the screen, resulting in differences in the GUI layout. Some of the isomorphic GUIs are identified as non-isomorphic, which to some extent leads to a decrease in the evaluation score. However, the recognition accuracies of all three methods remain above 0.97, while our proposed method remained at 0.98. Compared with the first two baseline models, the F1 score of the integrated performance index of this method is above 0.8, which demonstrates the stability of the method. It is verified that our proposed method still has good usability in the face of GUIs with different resolutions.

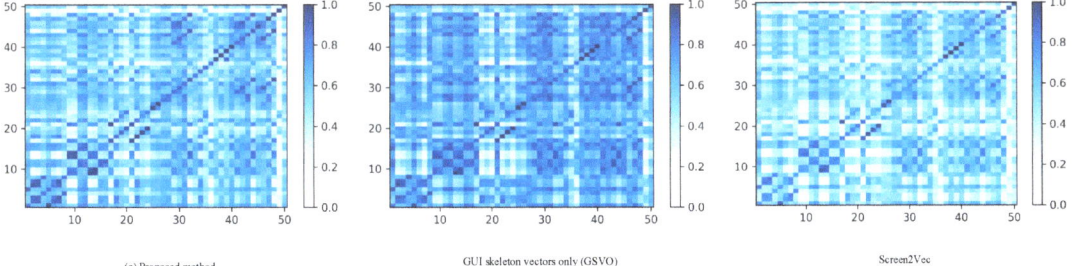

Figure 10. Results of similarity discriminant matrix for resolution experiments.

Table 3. The proposed method of the resolution experiment.

	Proposed Method	GUI Skeleton Vectors Only	Screen2Vec
Acc	0.984	0.979	0.976
P	0.752	0.798	0.853
R	0.872	0.743	0.674
F1	0.808	0.769	0.753

The ROCs of the three methods are plotted according to Table 3. As shown in Figure 11, the area under the curve (AUC) of the three methods are 0.945, 0.926, and 0.906, respectively. The AUCs of all three methods are above 0.9, but our proposed method has the highest AUC value. This indicates that the proposed method still performs well in identifying isomorphic GUIs with different resolutions.

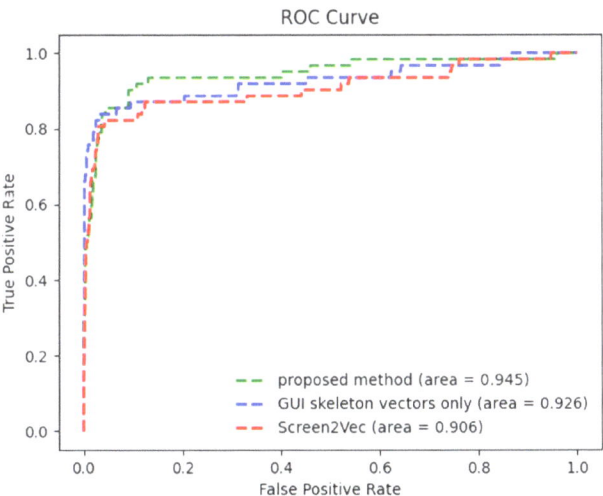

Figure 11. ROC for the resolution experiments.

4.4.3. Cross-Platform Experiment

Smart devices in the market employ various platforms, among which Android and iOS are the mainstream, and the different development methods of Android and IOS are inconvenient for mobile application testing. Our approach is based on robot testing and uses industrial cameras instead of human eyes and robotic arms instead of human arms for click experiments. There is no need to obtain the source code of the mobile application, which is theoretically compatible with different operating systems.

We took 100 GUI screen images of airline service mobile applications including 116 pairs of isomorphic GUIs from two Android OS and two iOS OS smart devices. In the 2500 comparison experiments, isomorphic GUIs were mainly present in the comparison of the 1st to 30th GUI screen images and the 50th to 80th GUI screen images. The heat map of the similarity matrix obtained by the three methods under different operating systems is shown in Figure 12.

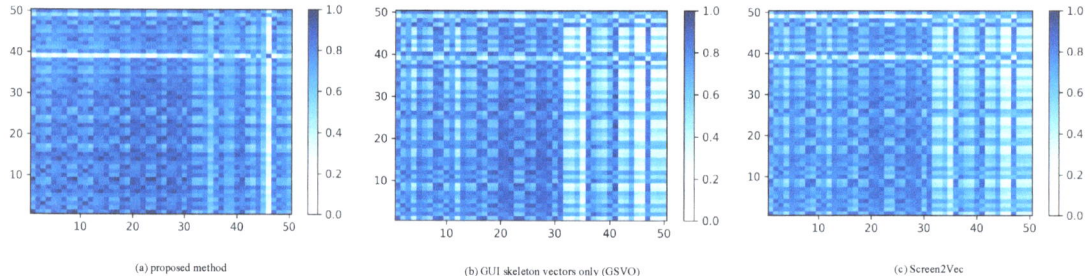

Figure 12. Results of similarity discriminant matrix for cross-platform experiments.

The consistent color of the thermogram in regard to the initial experimental design as a whole can determine the correct direction of the experiment. The performance metrics of the three methods for isomorphic GUI recognition under different operating systems are shown in Table 4. The interface of the same software in different OS platforms has some differences, for example, the resolution of Android and iOS smart devices is not consistent. These factors add many variables to the experiment and cause a decrease in the recognition accuracy of the isomorphic GUI. Table 4. shows the recognition accuracy of our method reached 97.7%, indicating that the method has good stability. The F1 scores are much higher than those of the two baseline methods, highlighting the advantage of the proposed method in performing isomorphic GUI recognition tasks across operating systems.

Table 4. The proposed method of the platform experiment.

	Proposed Method	GUI Skeleton Vectors Only	Screen2Vec
Acc	0.977	0.969	0.975
P	0.736	0.679	0.798
R	0.793	0.655	0.612
F1	0.763	0.667	0.693

The ROCs of the three methods are plotted according to Table 4. As shown in Figure 13, the area under the curve (AUC) for the three methods is 0.967, 0.945, and 0.946, respectively. Our proposed method has the highest AUC value, indicating that our proposed method has good adaptability across platforms.

In summary, the three experiments show that our proposed method maintains an accuracy above 0.97 for isomorphic GUI recognition, which is significantly better than the two baseline models. In terms of the resolution and cross-platform experiments, the proposed method exhibits stability that far exceeds that of the two baseline models. It is shown that the proposed method has a well-performed cross-device and cross-platform compatibility.

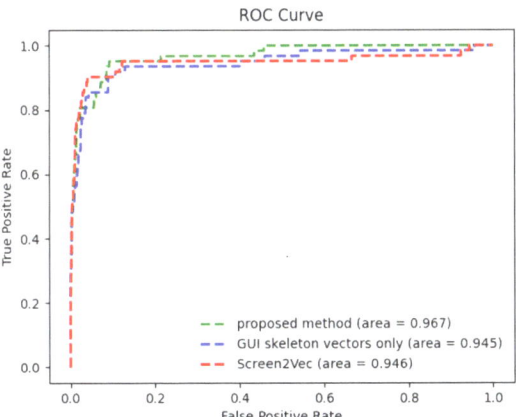

Figure 13. ROC for the cross-platform experiments.

Despite the progress we have made in our method, it still has some limitations. Since our DAOM is built manually, it consumes upfront preparation time to some extent. In addition, if the domain model does not contain enough element semantics, it may result in unresolved element semantics. Hence, our next step is to build more complete domain knowledge to automate the generation of the DAOM. In the future, we will continue to improve the detection efficiency of the method and promote its integration with the testing process of commercial mobile applications.

5. Conclusions

We propose a semantic similarity-based isomorphic GUI identification method to deal with the state space explosion problem of GUI models. The information on GUI elements (type, location, and semantic information) is first obtained through deep learning network models, and then the GUI information is vectorized by extracting GUI structure vectors and semantic vectors. Finally, the isomorphic GUIs are identified through a comparison of cosine similarity. The proposed method can simplify the GUI model and lay the foundation for the full black-box mobile application robot testing. Our experiments prove that the proposed method is compatible with smart devices of different resolutions and platforms.

The proposed approach is fully black-boxed and does not violate users' data and privacy in real-world scenarios. However, there are still some limitations to the method. Since our DAOM is built manually, this consumes upfront preparation time to some extent. Our next step is to build more complete domain knowledge to automate the generation of the DAOM. In addition, a large amount of image information needs to be processed which places high demands on the configuration of the experimental equipment. This poses a considerable challenge for project implementation. Furthermore, we are currently conducting research on isomorphic GUIs in English visual interfaces only and have not conducted experiments in other languages. In the future, we will consider extending the model to full language validation.

Author Contributions: Conceptualization, writing—original, J.C. and S.L.; supervision, J.C.; validation, J.Z., W.X. and T.Z.; propose the new method or methodology, J.C. and T.Z.; formal analysis, investigation, J.C.; resources, F.X. and W.X.; writing—review and editing, J.C., T.Z. and F.X. All authors have read and agreed to the published version of the manuscript.

Funding: This research received no external funding.

Data Availability Statement: The data that support the findings of this study are openly available at https://zenodo.org/record/7519136#.Y7zV6nZBxnI (accessed on 10 January 2023).

Conflicts of Interest: The authors declare no conflict of interest.

References

1. Wimalasooriya, C.; Licorish, S.A.; da Costa, D.A.; MacDonell, S.G. A systematic mapping study addressing the reliability of mobile applications: The need to move beyond testing reliability. *J. Syst. Softw.* **2022**, *186*, 111166. [CrossRef]
2. Contan, A.; Dehelean, C.; Miclea, L. Test automation pyramid from theory to practice. In Proceedings of the 2018 IEEE International Conference on Automation, Quality and Testing, Robotics (AQTR), Cluj-Napoca, Romania, 24–26 May 2018; pp. 1–5.
3. Zhang, T.; Su, Z.; Cheng, J.; Xue, F.; Liu, S. Machine vision-based testing action recognition method for robotic testing of mobile application. *Int. J. Distrib. Sens. Netw.* **2022**, *18*, 15501329221115375. [CrossRef]
4. Pandya, A.; Eslamian, S.; Ying, H.; Nokleby, M.; Reisner, L.A. A Robotic Recording and Playback Platform for Training Surgeons and Learning Autonomous Behaviors Using the da Vinci Surgical System. *Robotics* **2019**, *8*, 9. [CrossRef]
5. Garousi, V.; Elberzhager, F. Test automation: Not just for test execution. *IEEE Softw.* **2017**, *34*, 90–96. [CrossRef]
6. Ilyin, V.K.; Morozova, Y.A.; Usanova, N.A.; Gotovskiy, M.Y.; Roik, O.A.; Matiushin, A.O. Ultra-weak electromagnetic signals: Effects of storing and playback on example of saccharomyces. *Int. J. High Dilution Research* **2018**, *17*, 40. [CrossRef]
7. Huang, T.X.; Ji, J.W.; Shou, Y.X.; Kong, Y. Research and Application of a User Interface Automatic Testing Method Based on Data Driven. In *International Symposium on Software Reliability, Industrial Safety, Cyber Security and Physical Protection for Nuclear Power Plant*; Springer: Singapore, 2019; pp. 202–211.
8. Anbunathan, R.; Basu, A. Data driven architecture based automated test generation for Android mobile. In Proceedings of the 2015 IEEE International Conference on Computational Intelligence and Computing Research (ICCIC), Madurai, India, 10–12 December 2015; pp. 1–5.
9. Pereira, R.B.; Brito, M.A.; Machado, R.J. Architecture Based on Keyword Driven Testing with Domain Specific Language for a Testing System. In *Lecture Notes in Computer Science, ICTSS 2020, Naples, Italy, 9–11 December 2020*; Springer Science & Business Media: Berlin/Heidelberg, Germany, 2020; Volume 12543, pp. 310–316.
10. Divya, R.; Prasad, K.N. Automation of Desktop Applications Using Keyword Driven Approach. In Proceedings of the Second International Conference on Emerging Trends in Science & Technologies For Engineering Systems (ICETSE-2019), Chickballapur, India, 17–18 May 2019.
11. Lenka, R.K.; Nayak, K.M.; Padhi, S. Automated Testing Tool: QTP. In Proceedings of the 2018 International Conference on Advances in Computing, Communication Control and Networking (ICACCCN), Greater Noida, India, 12–13 October 2018; pp. 526–532.
12. Mao, K.; Harman, M.; Jia, Y. Robotic Testing of Mobile Apps for Truly Black-Box Automation. *IEEE Softw.* **2017**, *34*, 11–16. [CrossRef]
13. Long, Y.; Wang, J.L. Picture-text webpage model and pale element feature induction. *Comput. Eng. Sci.* **2013**, *35*, 136–143.
14. Ren, S.; Wang, Z.; Wang, Y. Layout mining and pattern matching algorithm on automatic Web page design. *Comput. Eng. Appl.* **2018**, *54*, 227–232.
15. Zhang, T.; Liu, Y.; Gao, J.; Gao, L.P.; Cheng, J. Deep Learning-Based Mobile Application Isomorphic GUI Identification for Automated Robotic Testing. *IEEE Softw.* **2020**, *37*, 67–74. [CrossRef]
16. Dobslaw, F.; Feldt, R.; Michaëlsson, D.; Haar, P.; de Oliveira Neto, F.G.; Torkar, R. Estimating return on investment for gui test automation frameworks. In Proceedings of the 2019 IEEE 30th International Symposium on Software Reliability Engineering (ISSRE), Berlin, Germany, 28–31 October 2019; pp. 271–282.
17. Adamo, D.; Khan, M.K.; Koppula, S.; Bryce, R. Reinforcement learning for Android GUI testing. In Proceedings of the 9th ACM SIGSOFT International Workshop on Automating TEST Case Design, Selection, and Evaluation, Lake Buena Vista, FL, USA, 5 November 2018; Association for Computing Machinery: New York, NY, USA, 2018; pp. 2–8.
18. Qin, X.; Zhong, H.; Wang, X. Migrating GUI test cases from iOS to Android. In Proceedings of the 28th ACM SIGSOFT International Symposium on Software Testing and Analysis (ISSTA 2019), Beijing, China, 15–19 July 2019; Association for Computing Machinery: New York, NY, USA, 2019; pp. 284–295.
19. Belli, F. Finite state testing and analysis of graphical user interfaces. In Proceedings of the 12th International Symposium on Software Reliability Engineering ISSRE 2001, Hong Kong, China, 27–30 November 2001.
20. Baek, Y.M.; Bae, D.H. Automated model-based Android GUI testing using multi-level GUI comparison criteria. In Proceedings of the 2016 31st IEEE/ACM International Conference on Automated Software Engineering (ASE), Singapore, 3–7 September 2016; pp. 238–249.
21. Memon, A.M.; Soffa, M.L.; Pollack, M.E. Coverage Criteria for GUI Testing. In Proceedings of the 8th European Software Engineering Conference Held Jointly with 9th ACM SIGSOFT International Symposium on Foundations of Software Engineering ESEC/FSE-9, Vienna, Austria, 10–14 September 2001; pp. 256–267.
22. Belli, F.; Hollmann, A.; Nissanke, N. Modeling, Analysis and Testing of Safety Issues—An Event-Based Approach and Case Study. In *Lecture Notes in Computer Science, Proceedings of the International Conference on Computer Safety, Reliability, and Security, SAFECOMP 2007, Nurmberg, Germany, 18–21 September 2007*; Saglietti, F., Oster, N., Eds.; Springer: Berlin/Heidelberg, Germany, 2007; Volume 4680.

23. Behrang, F.; Reiss, S.P.; Orso, A. Supporting app design and development through GUI search. In Proceedings of the 5th International Conference on Mobile Software Engineering and Systems (MOBILESoft '18), Gothenburg, Sweden, 27–28 May 2018; Association for Computing Machinery: New York, NY, USA, 2018; pp. 236–246.
24. Mariani, L.; Mohebbi, A.; Pezzè, M.; Terragni, V. Semantic matching of GUI events for test reuse: Are we there yet? In Proceedings of the 30th ACM SIGSOFT International Symposium on Software Testing and Analysis (ISSTA 2021), Virtual, Denmark, 11–17 July 2021; Association for Computing Machinery: New York, NY, USA, 2021; pp. 177–190.
25. Almrayat, S.; Yousef, R.; Sharieh, A. Evaluating the Impact of GUI Similarity between Android Applications to Measure their Functional Similarity. *Int. J. Comput. Appl.* **2018**, *975*, 8887. [CrossRef]
26. Bibal, A.; Lognoul, M.; De Streel, A.; Frénay, B. Legal requirements on explainability in machine learning. *Artif. Intell. Law* **2021**, *29*, 149–169. [CrossRef]
27. Burkart, N.; Huber, M.F. A Survey on the Explainability of Supervised Machine Learning. *J. Artif. Intell. Res.* **2021**, *70*, 245–317. [CrossRef]
28. Wanner, J.; Herm, L.V.; Janiesch, C. How much is the black box? The value of explainability in machine learning models. In Proceedings of the 2020 European Conference on Information Systems, Marrakech, Morocco, 15–17 June 2020; 2020; Volume 85. Available online: https://aisel.aisnet.org/ecis2020_rip/85 (accessed on 12 May 2020).
29. Li, T.J.J.; Popowski, L.; Mitchell, T.; Myers, B.A. Screen2Vec: Semantic Embedding of GUI Screens and GUI Components. In Proceedings of the 2021 CHI Conference on Human Factors in Computing Systems (CHI '21), Yokohama, Japan, 8–11 May 2021; Association for Computing Machinery: New York, NY, USA, 2021. Article no. 578. pp. 1–15.
30. Liu, T.F.; Craft, M.; Situ, J.; Yumer, E.; Mech, R.; Kumar, R. Learning Design Semantics for Mobile Apps. In Proceedings of the 31st Annual ACM Symposium on User Interface Software and Technology, Berlin, Germany, 14–17 October 2008; Association for Computing Machinery: New York, NY, USA, 2018; pp. 569–579.
31. Cheng, J.; Tan, D.; Zhang, T.; Wei, A.; Chen, J. YOLOv5-MGC: GUI Element Identification for Mobile Applications Based on Improved YOLOv5. *Mob. Inf. Syst.* **2022**, *2022*, 8900734. [CrossRef]
32. Boutarfass, S.; Besserer, B. Convolutional Autoencoder for Discriminating Handwriting Styles. In Proceedings of the 2019 8th European Workshop on Visual Information Processing (EUVIP), Roma, Italy, 28–31 October 2019; pp. 199–204.
33. Reimers, N.; Gurevych, I. Sentence embeddings using siamese bert-networks. *arXiv* **2019**, arXiv:1908.10084.
34. Choi, W.; Sen, K.; Necula, G.; Wang, W. DetReduce: Minimizing Android GUI Test Suites for Regression Testing. In Proceedings of the 2018 ACM/IEEE 40th International Conference on Software Engineering, Gothenburg, Sweden, 27 May–3 June 2018; pp. 445–455.
35. Xue, F.; Wu, J.; Zhang, T. Visual Identification of Mobile App GUI Elements for Automated Robotic Testing. *Comput. Intell. Neurosci.* **2022**, *2022*, 447–455. [CrossRef] [PubMed]
36. Deka, B.; Huang, Z.; Franzen, C.; Hibschman, J.; Afergan, D.; Li, Y.; Nichols, J.; Kumar, R. Rico: A mobile app dataset for building data-driven design applications. In Proceedings of the 30th Annual ACM Symposium on User Interface Software and Technology, Québec City, QC, Canada, 22–25 October 2017; pp. 845–854.

Disclaimer/Publisher's Note: The statements, opinions and data contained in all publications are solely those of the individual author(s) and contributor(s) and not of MDPI and/or the editor(s). MDPI and/or the editor(s) disclaim responsibility for any injury to people or property resulting from any ideas, methods, instructions or products referred to in the content.

Article

Behavior Cloning and Replay of Humanoid Robot via a Depth Camera

Quantao Wang [1], Ziming He [1], Jialiang Zou [2], Haobin Shi [1,*] and Kao-Shing Hwang [3]

[1] School of Computer Science, Northwestern Polytechnical University, Xi'an 710129, China
[2] School of Software, Northwestern Polytechnical University, Xi'an 710129, China
[3] Department of Electrical Engineering, National Sun Yat-sen University, Kaohsiung 80424, Taiwan
* Correspondence: shihaobin@nwpu.edu.cn

Abstract: The technique of behavior cloning is to equip a robot with the capability of learning control skills through observation, which can naturally perform human–robot interaction. Despite many related studies in the context of humanoid robot behavior cloning, the problems of the unnecessary recording of similar actions and more efficient storage forms than recording actions by joint angles or motor counts are still worth discussing. To reduce the storage burden on robots, we implemented an end-to-end humanoid robot behavior cloning system, which consists of three modules, namely action emulation, action memorization, and action replay. With the help of traditional machine learning methods, the system can avoid recording similar actions while storing actions in a more efficient form. A jitter problem in the action replay is also handled. In our system, an action is defined as a sequence of many pose frames. We propose a revised key-pose detection algorithm to keep minimal poses of each action to minimize storage consumption. Subsequently, a clustering algorithm for key poses is implemented to save each action in the form of identifiers series. Finally, a similarity equation is proposed to avoid the unnecessary storage of similar actions, in which the similarity evaluation of actions is defined as an LCS problem. Experiments on different actions have shown that our system greatly reduces the storage burden of the robot while ensuring that the errors are within acceptable limits. The average error of the revised key-pose detection algorithm is reduced by 69% compared to the original and 26% compared to another advanced algorithm. The storage consumption of actions is reduced by 97% eventually. Experimental results demonstrate that the system can efficiently memorize actions to complete behavioral cloning.

Keywords: behavior cloning; humanoid robot; action emulation; action representation; action combination; key-pose

MSC: 68T05

1. Introduction

Nowadays, the role of robots is highlighted due to their great potential, popularity [1] and the social influence [2]. Human–computer interaction is always the focus of robotics research, where safety [3], personalization [4], output complexity [5], and data collection [6] should all be considered. To improve the social identity of human–computer interaction, the primary problem to be solved is adapting the robot to the characteristics of human motion. The action and posture of the humanoid robot are essential manifestations of the robot's ability, which will also have a profound impact on the user. Therefore, how to control the robot's limb movement is a challenging task, and it is also an essential problem in robot research. In this work, human–computer interaction is implemented through behavioral cloning. Behavioral cloning is the most direct human–computer interaction [7]. In behavioral cloning, a human trainer first demonstrates the control task by observing a visualization of sensor data that is available to an autonomous controller and selecting the appropriate action that the controller should perform. Scholars from various countries have conducted research on this topic. Ref. [8] proposed the concept and method of basic motion set that is used to establish the basic motion set of the dynamic system, and study the motion learning problem of the humanoid robot. Refs. [9,10] showed how to evaluate the robots' memory of pose. Ref. [11] achieved human-style locomotion with reinforcement learning methods, Ref. [12] used meta-learning to implement behavioral cloning, Ref. [13] designed neural networks for particular joints to enhance one-to-one mapping imitation. In addition, and Ref. [14] created a robot simulation learning platform that uses a series of evaluation indicators to evaluate the accuracy of robot motion simulation. While some achievements have been made in behavioral cloning, there are still aspects to be improved. First, due to the presence of environmental noise, the sensor has real-time variability when acquiring human joint data, which makes the robot easily cause jitter in action replay. Second, the same or similar actions performed by human demonstrators are often unnecessarily saved by robots. Third, data of partially similar actions are always stored separately in the form of the angles or motor counts of joints, consuming a large storage space. What is more, when the humanoid robot has limited computational performance, it is difficult to implement larger neural networks that allow it to autonomously perform saved actions.

In this work, a key-pose detection algorithm was proposed to keep minimal poses of each action. When the RGB-D camera sends the action data, the value of the rotation speed of the joints and the rotation direction of the joints on the robot will be used to determine whether the corresponding pose is a key pose. The value of each key-pose is assigned by the dissimilarity formula to distinguish them. In addition, we propose to implement a clustering algorithm [15], which documents the data by assigning each pose to its suitable group, and each group is labeled with a different ID. It not only effectively improves the memory efficiency of actions, but also further calculates the similarity between actions.

The remainder of this paper is organized as follows: Section 2 introduces two algorithms that we proposed and the functions of the designed system on the humanoid robot. The implementation of the system and the experimental data are presented in Section 3. In Section 4, the conclusion and future work are given.

2. Our Works

The architecture of the proposed system is shown in Figure 1. The personal computer (PC) in the system implements an inverse-kinematic algorithm and interpolation algorithm to process the data collected by the Kinect, a line of motion sensing input devices, and sends the results to the robot via a wireless network. On the humanoid robot side, three basic functional modules are implemented. Respectively, they serve for action emulation, action replay, and action memorization. When the RGB-D camera observes an action taken by a particular user, it sends the raw data to the PC, which further processes the data to convert them into geometrical information that is compatible with the modules on the robot.

2.1. Key-Pose Detection Algorithm

'Key pose' is a term that originates in the animation field, where an action can be fully reflected by several key poses extracted from the action. It has already been applied in academic research as well. In our system, an action is defined as a sequence of many pose frames. Key poses are defined as the essential poses taken out of the sequence of poses of an action and are capable of composing a new sequence of poses necessary to recreate the action, from which 'essential' means that once one of the key poses is deleted, the action created by the new sequence of key poses will have an unacceptable error value compared to the original action, or will not look similar to the original action at all.

When implementing behavioral cloning on robots, if image frames collected by the RGB-D camera are directly recorded to represent any actions, a large amount of storage space will be consumed. Additionally, it costs huge calculating resources to process and retrieve image data, which may result in lags in the system. Therefore, the key-pose detection algorithm is proposed to identify and record the key poses.

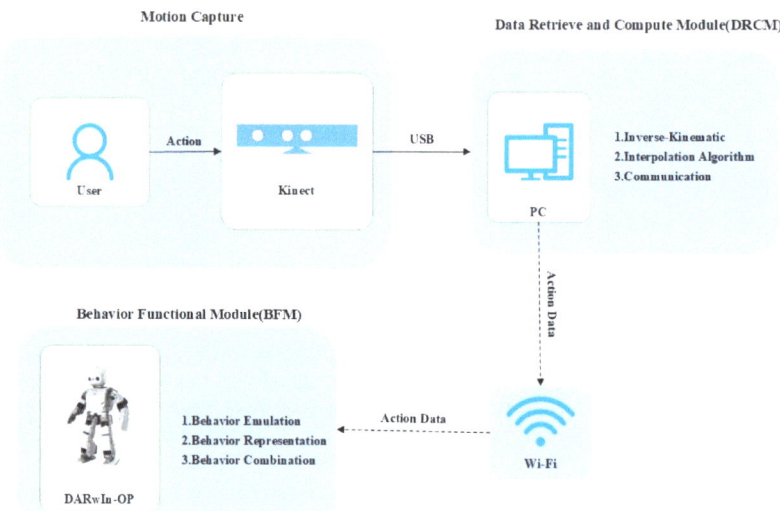

Figure 1. System architecture.

UDP, user datagram protocol, is chosen as the communication protocol in our system since retrieving data from the RGB-D camera only costs about 70 ms each time. Because of the relatively short time intervals, the action emulation can work even if some packets are lost. As is shown in Figure 2, each UDP packet contains motor counts, a bit for conforming key posture, a bit for conforming continuity, the group ID of the key pose, and the time interval needed by the pose.

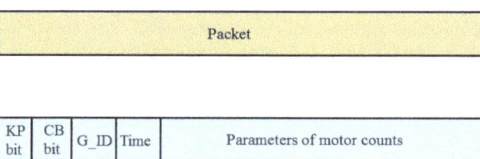

Figure 2. Architecture of packet.

'KP_bit', 'CB_bit', 'G_ID' , and 'Time' in Figure 2 respectively refer to the 'key pose bit' (the bit for conforming key posture), 'continuous bit' (the bit for conforming continuity), the group ID of the key pose and the time interval between the next key pose and the key pose. If the value of 'KP_Bit' is 0, the value of 'Time' will be 0 as well. Otherwise, if the value of 'KP_Bit' is not 0, the value of 'Time' will be exactly the time interval between two key poses.

Algorithm 1 shows how each key pose is identified. Each time the skeleton data are generated, the data are simultaneously determined whether they are a key pose or not by the information about the rotation direction and speed of joints in the skeleton data. In Algorithm 1, two variables recording current and previous states are set to check whether the state in the algorithm changes. Firstly, inverse kinematics is implemented to calculate the rotation angle of each joint. Then, the value of the current angles of the joints is compared with the previous value. The state that the discrepancy between two angles is bigger than a preset threshold is defined as an 'action state'. Otherwise, it is a 'static state'. If the current state differs from the previous, key_pose_bit will be set as 1; otherwise, it is set as 0. After that, if the key_pose_bit is 0, the rotation directions of each joint are checked to be changed or not. If they are changed, the key_pose_bit will be set as 1. Otherwise, it will be designated as 0. All the data in the algorithm will be saved.

In this paper, we modified formula (1) into formula (2) to calculate the dissimilarity of poses so that the errors will be reduced:

$$\rho_{i,i+1} = \left| \frac{(n-1)\sigma_i \sigma_{i+1} - \sum_{j=1}^{12}\left(\beta_{i,j} - \overline{\beta}_j\right)\left(\beta_{i+1,j} - \overline{\beta}_j\right)}{(n-1)\sigma_i \sigma_{i+1}} \right| \quad (1)$$

where $\rho_{i,i+1}$ presents the calculated dissimilarity value, n is the total number of poses, σ is the standard deviation of pose numbered i, $\beta_{i,j}$ presents the angle of the joint j in the pose numbered i, and $\overline{\beta}_j$ is the average value of different angles of the joint numbered j in all poses:

$$\rho_{i-1,i,i+1} = 1 - \frac{\sum_{j=1}^{N}\left(\left|\Delta\phi_{i-1,i,j} - \overline{\Delta\phi_j}\right| \cdot \left|\Delta\phi_{i,i+1,j} - \overline{\Delta\phi_j}\right|\right)}{N(\sigma_{i-1,i})(\sigma_{i,i+1})} \quad (2)$$

where $\rho_{i-1,i,i+1}$ presents the calculated dissimilarity value, N is the total number of joints, $\sigma_{i-1,i}$ is the standard deviation of changes in values of joints angles of poses numbered i and $i-1$. $\Delta\phi_{i-1,i,j}$ is the angle change of poses numbered i and $i-1$ in joint j, and $\overline{\Delta\phi_j}$ represents the average of all the variation in joint numbered j of the poses:

Algorithm 1 Key-pose detection algorithm.

1: **while** not Terminated **do**
2:    Calculate Dissimilarity Between Previous Data Via Inverse-Kinematics
3:    **if** The Dissimilarity≥Threshold **then**
4:       CurrentState = ActionState
5:    **else**
6:       CurrentState = StaticState
7:    **end if**
8:    **if** CurrentState == PreState **then**
9:       key_pose_bit = 1
10:    **else**
11:       **if** the Direction is Changed **then**
12:          key_pose_bit = 1
13:       **else**
14:          key_pose_bit = 0
15:       **end if**
16:    **end if**
17:    Save Data
18: **end while**

2.2. Clustering Algorithm

The concept of grouping is always used in data mining and many other fields. In our work, grouping is defined as similar to clustering in data mining. With a key-pose detection algorithm, raw data from the RGB-D camera are transformed into data symbolizing essential poses, which are stored by way of motor counts and are less storage-consuming. In this paper, the agglomerative hierarchical clustering algorithm [15] is applied to the data of key poses to document them. Each pose will be assigned to a group with the group ID, and in this way, the storage load is reduced, and the similarity between actions can be further calculated with such group IDs. Figure 3 illustrates the changes in groups through the clustering algorithm, where each red dot presents the central point in the group it belongs to. Additionally, due to the geometric position of each red dot, every such dot can represent all the data points in the same group.

The key poses will be divided into several groups after the clustering algorithm, and each group will be assigned a unique group ID. Instead of recording motor counts, each action is stored by recording its group ID. Table 1 shows the storage space status of the humanoid robot. Table 2 compares the storage consumption of saving group ID and the storage consumption of saving motor counts. As Table 2 shows, saving each action by group ID reduces the total storage consumption substantially. In total, 450,000 actions could be saved in the format of group ID, which is over 30 times more than the maximum number of actions saved by recording the motor counts, which is only 13,000, as is shown in Table 2.

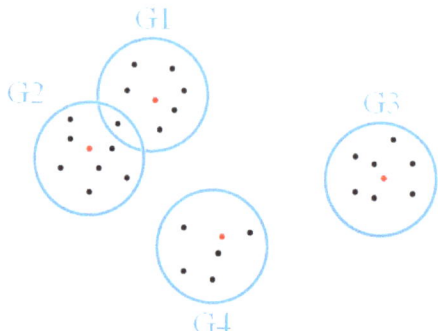

Figure 3. Illustration of group.

Table 1. Storage space of the humanoid robot.

Storage Space	Size
Total	3.6 GB
Used	2.3 GB
Available	1.3 GB

Table 2. Different format comparison.

Item	Group ID	Motor Counts
Action Size	About 3 KB	About 100 KB
Number of Action	About 450,000	About 13,000

2.3. The Humanoid Robot Functions

2.3.1. Action Emulation

The humanoid robot retrieves the built-in library to find and calls for matched data when it receives processed data from the PC via Wi-Fi to synchronously imitate the user's actions. Due to the discrepancy between the DOF, degree of freedom, of the humanoid robots' shoulders, which is 2, and the DOF of the human shoulder, which is 3, humanoid robots cannot achieve complete imitation. In addition, synchronous imitation on the lower body is impossible to be reached due to the following two reasons:
- RGB-D camera has low stability on the lower body skeleton relatively.
- Robots have no ability to balance themselves.

Because of the above two reasons, only upper motors can be applied to synchronous imitation. When imitating lower body poses, some robots' actions may differ from human actions. For instance, it is hard to find a way to process the raw data generated by the RGB-D camera focusing on a standing user to obtain precise knee joint data. Even if the knee joint data are accurate, chances are that the humanoid robot will fall backward or forward when performing emulation in the lower body due to imbalance.

The humanoid robot unpacks the UDP packets after receiving them from the PC. Then, it calls the functions in its local library and runs the emulation that keeps running until the end of the program.

2.3.2. Action Memorization

In our system, an action is defined as a sequence of many pose frames. As mentioned in the previous paragraph, each pose is assigned a unique group ID after the clustering algorithm. Therefore, each action could consist of a series of group IDs. The action can be compared with the groups' IDs it concerns this way. To further reduce the storage cost, we propose a method to determine whether the latest received action data are worth being saved locally in the database. When the humanoid robot receives the action data, it checks whether the same data exist in the local database. If the data already exist, the data will be ignored.

When comparing two actions, the discrepancy in the key poses that they could be split into and the discrepancy in the speed of shifting the key poses from one to the other are noted. In our system, discrepancies in speed between actions are ignored when calculating the similarity between two actions because of the high storage cost of recording all the time variables. However, speed differences between actions will still be active when implementing the system. When calculating the similarity of actions, they are compared by the group IDs of the key poses contained by them. Evaluating the similarity of two series of key poses of two actions is characterized as solving the LCS, longest common subsequence, problem in our system. The longest common subsequence (LCS) problem [16] is the problem of finding the longest subsequence common to all sequences in a set of sequences. A similarity table is established to restore all the similarities. Algorithm 2 is the modified LCS algorithm procedure. The number of the longest common subsequence between two actions will be figured out by the algorithm, and Equation (3) shows how to calculate the similarity rate with the results of the LCS algorithm:

$$Similarity\ Rate = \frac{N(LCS(A_1, A_2))}{n} \quad (3)$$

where $Similarity\ Rate$ presents how similar the two actions are. n is the number of segments of the compared actions; A_1, A_2 respectively represent the data of action numbered 1 and 2; and $N(LCS(A_1, A_2))$ represents the number of LCS.

2.3.3. Action Replay

The robot has to achieve consistency in the representation and speed of the user's actions. Such consistency can be attained with the help of applying and clustering algorithms, which will minimize the error between the representation and the original action. Figure 4 illustrates how to calculate the speech of each action. In Figure 4, 'T' refers to the time consumed. Each elapsed time interval between two key poses is calculated and can be further used to compute the changes in the speed of every joint. As shown in Figure 5, the elapsed time between the Key Pose labeled 1 and the Key Pose labeled 2 is (T1+T2+T3). The speed of the whole action can be calculated with the data from the motor or the number of total key poses.

Algorithm 2 Revised LCS algorithm.
```
 1: function LCS(S₁, S₂)
 2:     for i = 0, 1, ..., m do
 3:         len(i,0) = 0
 4:     end for
 5:     for j = 1, 2, ..., n do
 6:         len(0,j) = 0
 7:     end for
 8:     for i = 1, 2, ..., m do
 9:         for j = 1, 2, ..., n do
10:             Search similarity table
11:             if aᵢ = bⱼ then
12:                 len(i,j)=len(i-1,j-1)+1
13:             end if
14:             if len(i-1,j)≥len(i,j-1) then
15:                 len(i,j)=len(i-1,j)
16:             else
17:                 len(i,j)=len(i,j-1)
18:             end if
19:         end for
20:     end for
21: end function
```

As is shown in Figure 4, after taking data consistency and speed variations into account, there still exist standstills in the progress of imitation because the humanoid robot will directly implement the action data without any optimizing processing. Thus the whole action played by the robot seems to be not natural.

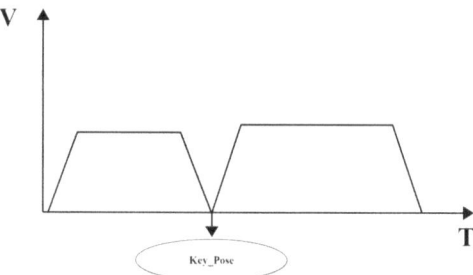

Figure 4. Continuous motion interrupt diagram.

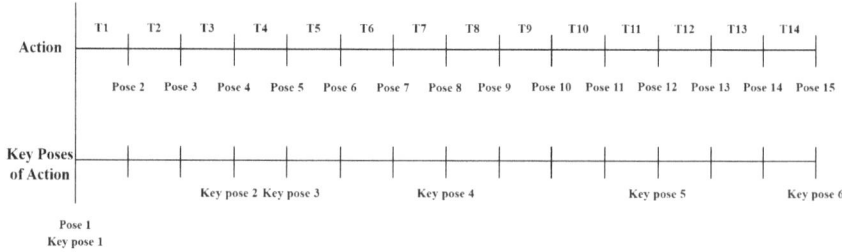

Figure 5. Relation of poses and key poses.

To solve the problem, a 'continuous bit' is added to the program. It is proposed to symbolize whether the state of the robot is active or not. The continuous bit is either 0 or 1. In the program, the speed of each joint is checked. If it is stable, implying that all the velocities of the joints are 0, the continuous bit will be set as 0, meaning that the robot is in a static state; otherwise, if there still exists any joint that is constantly moving, the continuous bit will be set as 1, meaning that the robot is in an active state, as is shown in Figure 6.

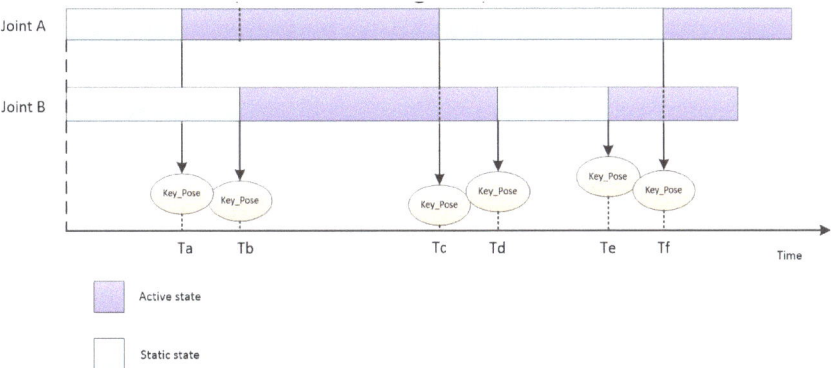

Figure 6. Influence of key-pose detection diagram.

The continuous bit is used to enable the robot to perform the actions smoothly. If the current continuous bit is 1, the number of each motor count will add or remove a constant so that the motor will keep its speed and direction for a while after reaching its original goal position. The current motor count is continuously checked to ensure the accuracy of the action. The actual goal position of each pose may be changed because of the functions of the continuous bit. However, once the check and a particular pose are done, the motors on the robot will return to the original goal position or move to the next goal position. In this way, each motor will not halt when the robot reads the next key pose while the accuracy is ensured, as shown in Figure 7.

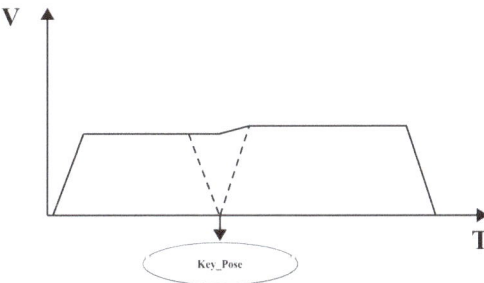

Figure 7. Improved of continuous motion diagram.

3. Implementation
3.1. Implementation of the Key-Pose Detection Algorithm

In this section, the method to identify key poses will be introduced. Two other methods are to be discussed besides the algorithm, which is revised from the key-pose detection algorithm based on dissimilarity, adopted in our study. They are the condition key-pose detection algorithm [17] and key-pose detection algorithm based on dissimilarity [18].

To evaluate the proposed key-pose detection algorithm, several experiments are conducted. Figure 8a is labeled Action I in the experiment; Figure 8b, Action II; Figure 8c, Action III, Figure 8d, Action IV. Action I, Action II, Action III and Action IV explain the research results.

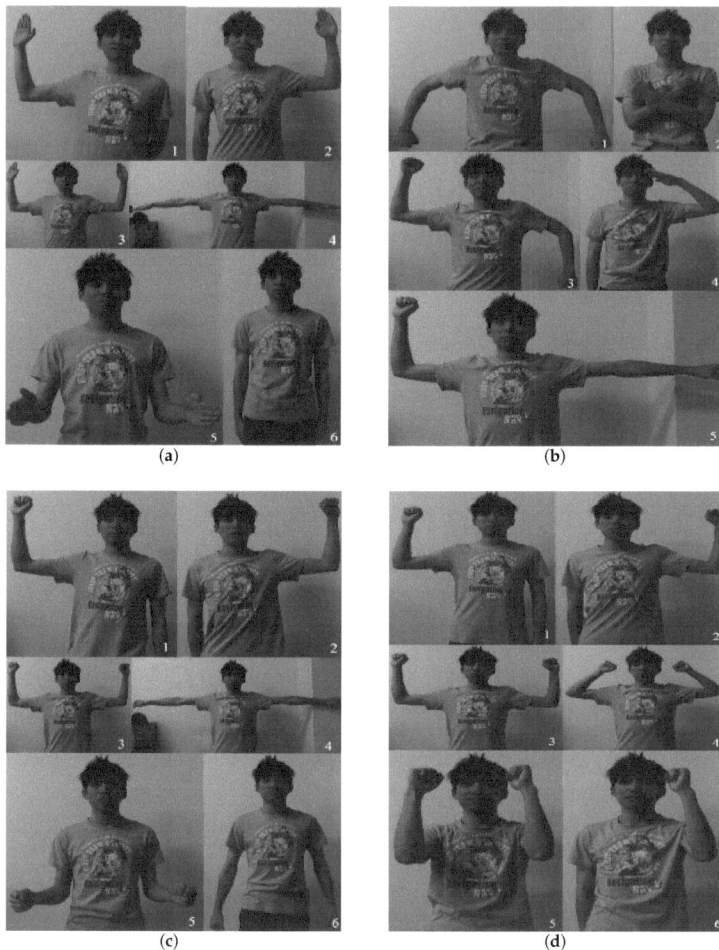

Figure 8. Action I (**a**), Action II (**b**), Action III (**c**) and Action IV (**d**).

To ensure accuracy, each action consists of 250 poses, taking nearly 15 seconds to be executed. Additionally, six joints of the humanoid robot are set to active to perform the action. They are respectively Left_Elbow, Left_Shoulder_Roll, Left_Shoulder_Pitch, Right_Elbow, Right_Shoulder_Roll, Right_Shoulder_Pitch.

After the action (Action I) performed by the user is received and processed by the RGB-D camera, three different algorithms will further process the data. The three corresponding results are shown below. Figures 9–11 show the comparison between these three algorithms. Figure 9 presents the result for the condition key-pose detection algorithm. Figure 10 shows the result for the key-pose detection algorithm based on dissimilarity. Figure 11 is the result for the key-pose detection algorithm revised from the key-pose detection algorithm based on dissimilarity, which is used in our implementation.

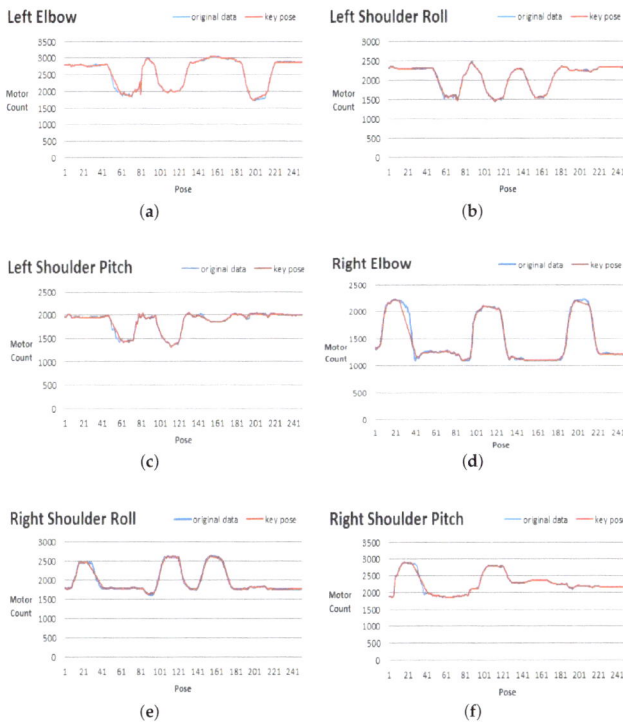

Figure 9. Results of [17] condition key-pose detection algorithm versus original pose data: (**a**) motor counts data on Left Elbow. (**b**) Motor counts data on Left Shoulder Roll. (**c**) Motor counts data on Left Shoulder Pitch. (**d**) Motor counts data on Right Elbow. (**e**) Motor counts data on Right Shoulder Roll. (**f**) Motor counts data on Right Shoulder Pitch.

Table 3 compares the average error values of the three algorithms with the same amount of key poses. As is shown in Table 3, after the modification, the key-pose detection algorithm based on dissimilarity can achieve the lowest error value, reducing 69% error compared to the original, 26% compared to the condition key-pose detection algorithm. The error is defined as the average value of the difference between the angles of each joint of the original poses and the key poses, as Equation (4) shows:

$$Error = \frac{\sum_{j=1}^{6} \sum_{n=1}^{250} |K_n - O_n|}{6 \times 250} \times 0.0878 \qquad (4)$$

where j is the label of the joint, n is the label of the data of the pose, K_n is the angles value of joints in the key pose, and O_n is the angles value of the joints in the original pose.

Table 3. Comparison of the three key-pose detection algorithms.

Algorithm	Average of Error	Amount of Key Poses
Condition Key-Pose Algorithm	1.24146	250 → 100
Original Dissimilarity Key-Pose Algorithm	2.74349	250 → 100
Revised Dissimilarity Key-Pose Algorithm	0.91062	250 → 100

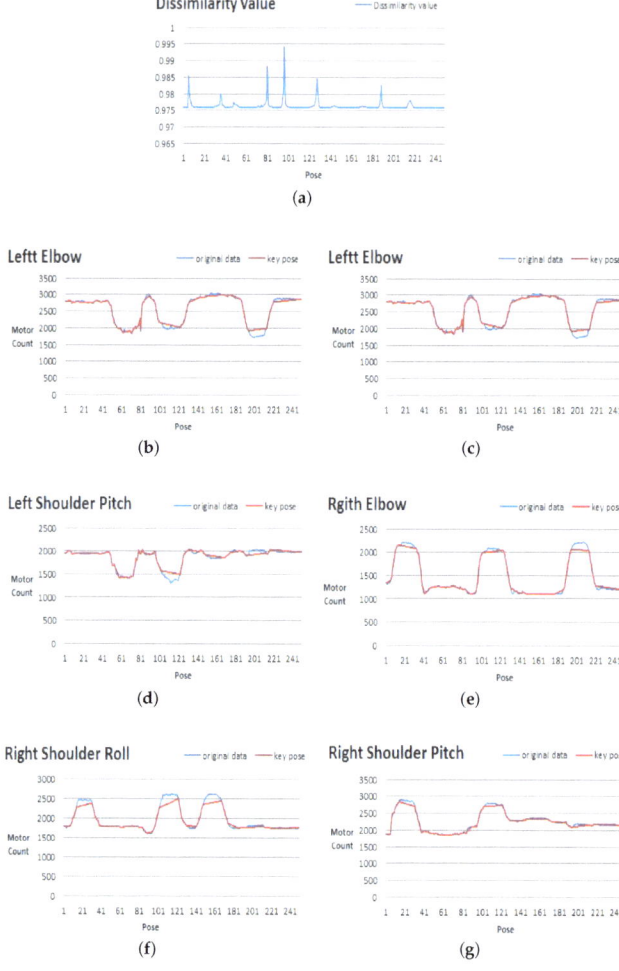

Figure 10. Results of [18] key-pose detection algorithm based on dissimilarity versus original pose data: (**a**) Calculated dissimilarity value. (**b**) Motor counts data on Left Elbow. (**c**) Motor counts data on Left Shoulder Roll. (**d**) Motor counts data on Left Shoulder Pitch. (**e**) Motor counts data on Right Elbow. (**f**) Motor counts data on Right Shoulder Roll. (**g**) Motor counts data on Right Shoulder Pitch.

The number of key poses and the value of the error can be varied with different values of the threshold, so a suitable value of the threshold, which maximizes the number of key poses recorded and minimizes the value of the error, should be established. Experiments are conducted for that, and the results are shown in Table 4, where different values of threshold, error, and numbers of key poses are listed. To facilitate the work, we specified that any threshold with an error of less than 3 is eligible and we eventually chose 0.35 as our final threshold value.

Table 4. Different threshold and its average of error and amount of key poses.

Threshold	Average of Error	Amount of Key Poses
0.21	0.91062	250 → 100
0.25	1.84542	250 → 89
0.3	2.47993	250 → 78
0.35	2.68958	250 → 69
0.4	3.38649	250 → 58

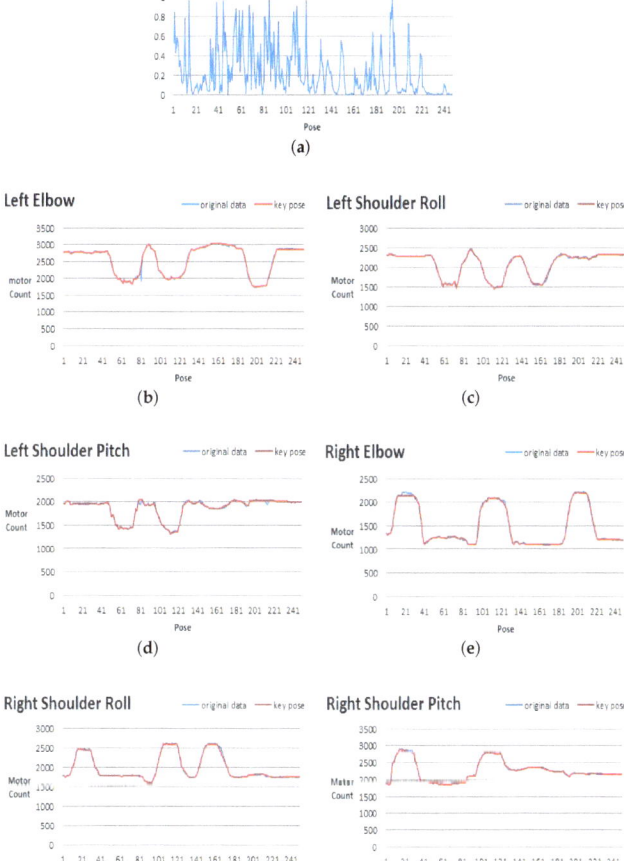

Figure 11. Results of revised key-pose algorithm based on dissimilarity versus original pose data. (**a**) Calculated dissimilarity value. (**b**) Motor counts data on Left Elbow. (**c**) Motor counts data on Left Shoulder Roll. (**d**) Motor counts data on Left Shoulder Pitch. (**e**) Motor counts data on Right Elbow. (**f**) Motor counts data on Right Shoulder Roll. (**g**) Motor counts data on Right Shoulder Pitch.

3.2. Implementation of Clustering Algorithm

In this section, the implementation of the clustering algorithm on the key poses from the key-pose detection algorithm is discussed and shown. Figure 12 compares the pose data of key poses with and without the clustering algorithm.

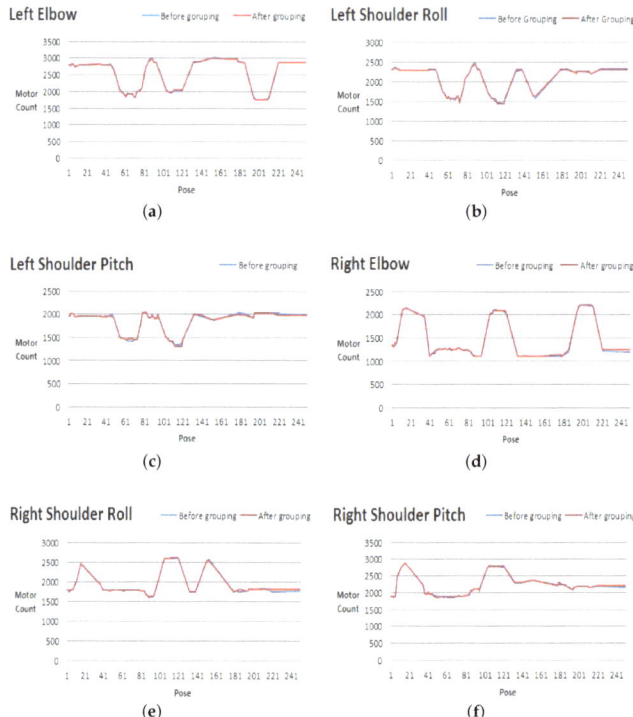

Figure 12. (**a**) Motor counts data on Left Elbow. (**b**) Motor counts data on Left Shoulder Roll. (**c**) Motor counts data on Left Shoulder Pitch. (**d**) Motor counts data on Right Elbow. (**e**) Motor counts data on Right Shoulder Roll . (**f**) Motor counts data on Right Shoulder Pitch.

Table 5 shows the comparison of error values of the key poses processed with and without the clustering algorithm on different parts of the robot. The storage consumption is reduced with the help of the clustering algorithms, while a relatively slight increase in the total error value exists, which is acceptable.

Table 5. Group algorithms comparison table.

Error	on L_E	on L_S_R	on L_S_P	on R_E	on R_S_R	on R_S_P
Without Clustering Algorithm	2.088	2.625	2.159	2.499	4.053	2.711
With Clustering Algorithm	2.263	2.656	2.386	2.695	4.390	3.306

In Table 5, L_E is Left Elbow; L_S_R is Left Shoulder Roll; L_S_P is Left Shoulder Pitch; R_E is Right Elbow , R_S_R is Right Shoulder Roll, R_S_P is Right Shoulder Pitch. All the key poses will be assigned to the suitable group with the group ID after being processed by the clustering algorithm.

3.3. Implementation of Action Emulation, Representation and Memorization

3.3.1. Action Emulation

Figure 13 shows how the humanoid robot replays Action I, which is the result of real-time imitation.

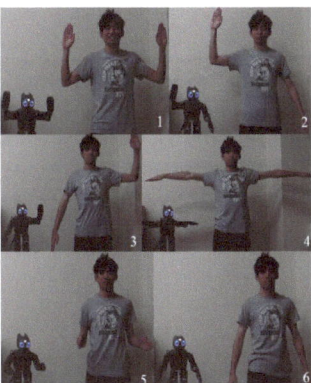

Figure 13. The emulation of humanoid robot.

The motor counts of the motor should be ensured not to damage the motor when implementing synchronous behavior cloning, which means the difference in the structure of different robots must be taken into account. In our experiment, MX-28 is the motor of the humanoid robot, which can rotate in the range of 360 degrees, but it does not ensure that each joint can rotate freely like that, which may cause machinery problems in the robot. Table 6 shows the minimum and maximum scales of the joints on the robot. If such values are not compatible with the number of motor counts, the robot could be damaged.

Table 6. Limited rotation range of the humanoid robot motors.

Name	Minimum	Maximum
L_Elbow	1300	3072
R_Elbow	1024	2700
L_Shoulder_Roll	512	2560
R_Shoulder_Roll	1536	3584
L_Shoulder_Pitch	2048	N/A
R_Shoulder_Pitch	N/A	2048

3.3.2. Action Representation

Figure 14 shows the result of the replay in Action I of the humanoid robot. In the experiment, the action could be entirely duplicated by the robot, and acceptable time consumption was also ensured. In addition, the increase in the error due to the clustering algorithm could be ignored since it is slight enough.

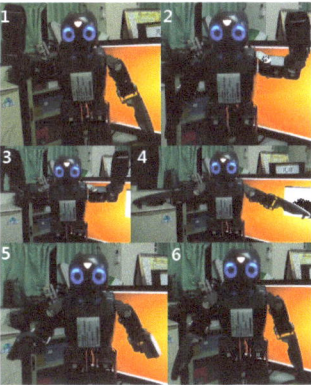

Figure 14. The humanoid robot is replaying action I.

3.3.3. Action Memorization

With the formula calculating the similarity rate of the poses, data processed by the clustering algorithm and the key-pose detection algorithm contain enough information to lead the robot to perform the displayed action, meaning that the function of action memorization is ensured. Table 7 lists the numbers of the original poses and the key poses of Action I to IV. The key poses are the results of the key-pose detection algorithm and the clustering algorithm. As is shown in Table 7, the number of key poses of Action II outnumbers that of Action I by 52, which is great enough to help the algorithm determine that the actions are different. For Actions I to IV, the similarity rates are calculated if the difference of the degree values of joints in key poses falls in a certain range.

Table 7. Amount of the key poses of Actions I, II, III and IV.

Action	Action I	Action II	Action III	Action IV
Number of key poses	250 → 69	250 → 121	250 → 83	250 → 93

After Action I is displayed in front of the RGB-D camera by the user, the data received by the camera will be saved into the database of the robot after being processed by the key-pose detection algorithm and the clustering algorithm. Action II will also be saved into the database because it could be determined to be a new action after being compared to the actions in the database. However, when the Action III is displayed, the data of the action will not be saved because they will be determined as an identical action to Action I. Meanwhile, Action IV will be detected as a new action though it is partially similar to the Action I; for that, the later part of the action is detected as a part of Action IV. In this way, the storage consumption is reduced since no superfluous action will be recorded.

4. Conclusions

In our behavior cloning system, two algorithms are implemented. They are the key-pose detection algorithm and the clustering algorithm. With a fixed limit on the number of key poses that can be stored for different actions, the average error value of the results from the key-pose detection algorithm is nearly 26% lower than [17] and nearly 69% lower than [18]. After assigning each key pose to suitable groups with group IDs, an action can be saved in the form of a series of group IDs, which makes it possible to store nearly 33 times more actions than saving the action in the form of the motor count. Results from the two algorithms ensure acceptable error values while reducing the storage consumption of the action data effectively. In addition, the system implements three basic functions. They are action emulation, action representation, and action memorization. These functions simplify the process of human–computer interaction and expand the user age range of the humanoid robots, which may lend the humanoid robots to become more useful in daily life. Additionally, our system requires less storage space on the robots with the help of the algorithm in the action memorization function.

There still exist problems to be investigated in future work. Currently, the source of the skeleton data is an RGB-D camera in our system, which cannot ensure the accuracy of the processed results, so more advanced multi-view human 3D posture reconstruction methods should be applied in our system to ensure that the original data in our behavior cloning system are not affected by environmental noise or misrecognition. Additionally, if there exist no real-time requirements, then optimization methods, such as genetic algorithms or simulated annealing, can be implemented to find the most suitable threshold parameter in the key-pose detection algorithm with the help of high-performance PCs and robot virtual platforms in order to minimize the error of the recreated action. Furthermore, a module for the equilibrium of the robot should be established to achieve lower body imitation.

Author Contributions: Conceptualization, Q.W., Z.H. and K.-S.H.; Data curation, Q.W. and J.Z.; Formal analysis, Q.W. and H.S.; Funding acquisition, H.S.; Investigation, Q.W. and Z.H.; Methodology, Q.W., Z.H. and H.S.; Project administration, Q.W.; Resources, Q.W.; Supervision, K.-S.H.; Validation, Q.W.; Visualization, Q.W.; Writing—original draft, Q.W., Z.H. and J.Z.; Writing—review and editing, J.Z. All authors have read and agreed to the published version of the manuscript.

Funding: This work is supported in part by National Natural Science Foundation of China under Grant 92267110, 62076202 and 61976178, Open Research Projects of Zhejiang Lab (NO.2022NB0AB07), Shaanxi Province Key Research and Development Program of China under Grant 2023-YBGY-354 and 2022GY-090, and CAAI-Huawei MindSpore Open Fund (NO.CAAIXSJLJJ-2021-041A).

Institutional Review Board Statement: Not applicable.

Informed Consent Statement: Not applicable.

Data Availability Statement: Not applicable.

Conflicts of Interest: The authors declare no conflict of interest.

Abbreviations

The following abbreviations are used in this manuscript:

PC	Personal computer
RGB-D	Red, green, blue plus depth
UDP	User datagram protocol
DOF	Degree of freedom
LCS	Longest common subsequence
$\rho_{i,i+1}$	Calculated dissimilarity value of two poses
$\rho_{i-1,i,j+1}$	Calculated dissimilarity value of three poses
$\beta_{i,j}$	Angle of the joint j in the pose numbered i
$\overline{\beta_j}$	Average value of different angles of the joint numbered j in all poses
σ_{i-1}	Standard deviation of changes in values of joints angles of poses numbered i and $i-1$
$\Delta\phi_{i-1,i,j}$	Angle change of poses numbered i and $i-1$ in joint j
$\overline{\Delta\phi_j}$	Average of all the variation in joint numbered j of the poses
T	Time consumed

References

1. Spenko, M.; Buerger, S. *The DARPA Robotics Challenge Finals: Humanoid Robots To The Rescue*; Springer: Berlin/Heidelberg, Germany, 2018.
2. de Andres-Sanchez, J.; Almahameed, A.A.; Arias-Oliva, M.; Pelegrin-Borondo, J. Correlational and Configurational Analysis of Factors Influencing Potential Patients’ Attitudes toward Surgical Robots: A Study in the Jordan University Community. *Mathematics* **2022**, *10*, 4319. [CrossRef]
3. Quevedo, F.; Muñoz, J.; Castano Pena, J.A.; Monje, C.A. 3D Model Identification of a Soft Robotic Neck. *Mathematics* **2021**, *9*, 1652. [CrossRef]
4. Leonardi, N.; Manca, M.; Paternò, F.; Santoro, C. Trigger-Action Programming for Personalising Humanoid Robot Behaviour. In Proceedings of the 2019 CHI Conference on Human Factors in Computing Systems, Glasgow, UK, 4–9 May 2019; Association for Computing Machinery: New York, NY, USA, 2019; pp. 1–13. [CrossRef]
5. Yang, Q.; Steinfeld, A.; Rosé, C.; Zimmerman, J. Re-Examining Whether, Why, and How Human-AI Interaction Is Uniquely Difficult to Design. In Proceedings of the 2020 CHI Conference on Human Factors in Computing Systems, Honolulu HI USA, 25–30 April 2020; Association for Computing Machinery: New York, NY, USA, 2020; pp. 1–13. [CrossRef]
6. Styling Words: A Simple and Natural Way to Increase Variability in Training Data Collection for Gesture Recognition. In Proceedings of the 2021 CHI Conference on Human Factors in Computing Systems, Yokohama, Japan, 8–13 May 2021; Association for Computing Machinery: New York, NY, USA, 2021. [CrossRef]
7. Torabi, F.; Warnell, G.; Stone, P. Behavioral Cloning from Observation. In Proceedings of the 27th International Joint Conference on Artificial Intelligence, Stockholm Sweden, 13–19 July 2018; pp. 4950–4957.
8. Saponaro, G.; Vicente, P.; Dehban, A.; Jamone, L.; Bernardino, A.; Santos-Victor, J. Learning at the Ends: From Hand to Tool Affordances in Humanoid Robots. In Proceedings of the 2017 Joint IEEE International Conference on Development and Learning and Epigenetic Robotics (ICDL-EpiRob), Lisbon, Portugal, 18–21 September 2017; pp. 331–337. [CrossRef]

9. Kosaka, A.; Katakura, T.; Toyama, S.; Ikeda, F. Evaluation of Posture Memory Retentivity using Coached Humanoid Robot. In Proceedings of the HRI '18: Companion of the 2018 ACM/IEEE International Conference on Human-Robot Interaction, Chicago, IL, USA, 5–8 March 2018.
10. Jie, L.; Song, M.; Li, Z.N.; Chen, C. Whole-body humanoid robot imitation with pose similarity evaluation. *Signal Process.* **2015**, *108*, 136–146.
11. Yang, C.; Yuan, K.; Shuai, H.; Taku, K.; Li, Z. Learning Natural Locomotion Behaviors for Humanoid Robots Using Human Bias. *IEEE Robot. Autom. Lett.* **2020**, *5*, 2610–2617. [CrossRef]
12. Yang, X.; Peng, Y.; Li, W.; Wen, J.Z.; Zhou, D. Vision-Based One-Shot Imitation Learning Supplemented with Target Recognition via Meta Learning. In Proceedings of the 2021 IEEE International Conference on Mechatronics and Automation (ICMA), Takamatsu, Japan, 8–11 August 2021; pp. 1008–1013. [CrossRef]
13. Wang, C.; Liao, G. Real-Time Pose Imitation by Mid-Size Humanoid Robot With Servo-Cradle-Head RGB-D Vision System. *IEEE Trans. Syst. Man, Cybern. Syst.* **2019**, *49*, 181–191. [CrossRef]
14. Duranton, C.; Gaunet, F. Behavioral synchronization and affiliation: Dogs exhibit human-like skills. *Learn. Behav.* **2018**, *46*, 364–373. [CrossRef] [PubMed]
15. Aljumily, R. *Agglomerative Hierarchical Clustering: An Introduction to Essentials. (1) Proximity Coefficients and Creation of a Vector-Distance Matrix and (2) Construction of the Hierarchical Tree and a Selection of Methods*; Social Science Electronic Publishing: New York, NY, USA, 2017.
16. Wang, Q. A Matching Path Constrained Longest Common Subsequence Length Algorithm. *J. Electron. Inf. Technol.* **2017**, *39*, 2615–2619.
17. Zhao, S.; Wu, Y.; Yang, W.; Li, X. Key Pose Frame Extraction Method of Human Motion Based on 3D Framework and X-Means. *J. Beijing Inst. Technol.* **2017**, *26*, 75–83.
18. Overhill, H. Design as Choreography: Information in Action. *Curator Mus. J.* **2015**, *58*, 5C15. [CrossRef]

Disclaimer/Publisher's Note: The statements, opinions and data contained in all publications are solely those of the individual author(s) and contributor(s) and not of MDPI and/or the editor(s). MDPI and/or the editor(s) disclaim responsibility for any injury to people or property resulting from any ideas, methods, instructions or products referred to in the content.

Article

A Multi-Factor Selection and Fusion Method through the CNN-LSTM Network for Dynamic Price Forecasting

Yishun Liu, Chunhua Yang, Keke Huang * and Weiping Liu

School of Automation, Central South University, Changsha 410083, China
* Correspondence: huangkeke@csu.edu.cn

Abstract: Commodity prices are important factors for investment management and policy-making, and price forecasting can help in making better business decisions. Due to the complex and volatile nature of the market, commodity prices tend to change frequently and fluctuate violently, often influenced by many potential factors with strong nonstationary and nonlinear characteristics. Thus, it is difficult to obtain satisfactory prediction effects by only using the historical data of prices individually. To address this problem, a novel dynamic price forecasting method based on multi-factor selection and fusion with CNN-LSTM is proposed. First, the factors related to commodity price are collected, and Granger causality inference is used to identify causal factors that affect the commodity price. Then, XGBoost is used to evaluate the importance of the remaining factors and screen out critical factors to reduce the interference of redundant information. Due to the high amount and complicated changes of the selected factors, a convolutional neural network is employed to fuse the selected factors and extract the hidden features. Finally, a long short-term memory network is adopted to establish a multi-input predictor to obtain the dynamic price. Compared with several advanced approaches, the evaluation results indicate that the proposed method has an excellent performance in dynamic price forecasting.

Keywords: price forecasting; multi-factor selection; information fusion; long short-term memory network

MSC: 68T07

1. Introduction

Commodities are important basic raw materials for industrial and agricultural production, including crude oil, non-ferrous metals, steel, coal, etc. [1]. They have industrial attributes, as well as typical financial attributes. The commodity price is an important basis for investment management, business decision-making, and policy-making [2]. It is usually affected by multiple hidden variables, such as the global economy, supply-demand relationship, exchange rate, and so on [3,4]. With the development of economic globalization, the financial market, as a highly complex nonlinear dynamic system, has become more volatile [5]. Commodity prices usually fluctuate frequently, change widely, and exhibit strong nonstationary and nonlinear characteristics [6]. The inherent volatility and uncertainty of data changes bring many difficulties to high-precision price forecasting [7]. Therefore, accurate and robust price forecasting has become an important issue.

In the past decades, commodity price forecasting, which was focused on price analysis and prediction, has given rise to extensive attention. In general, these methods can be roughly divided into three categories: chaotic economics methods, statistical methods, and artificial intelligence methods. For chaotic economics methods, they use the nonlinear chaos theory to analyze and model price series. Rodríguez et al. adopted the multi-scroll Chua system to identify the Colombian coffee price dynamics, and employed artificial bee colony optimization to fine-tune the model [8]. Yuan et al. proposed an improved multifractal volatility approach to analyze the stock market price [9]. Wang et al. used the partial differential equation of the bitcoin trading network to analyze the changes in the bitcoin price [10]. Frezza assumed that the price followed a multi-fractional process with a random exponent to model the fluctuation of stock price [11]. Chaotic economics can take into account the impact of complex relationships, but it is too sensitive to parameters and initial conditions.

For statistical methods, Krzysztof employed various Bayesian models to predict the spot price of nickel, lead, and zinc together with dynamic model averaging (DMA) [12]. Zhu et al. extended the leverage heterogeneous autoregressive model with continuous volatility and jump (LHAR-CJ) with generalized autoregressive conditional heteroscedasticity (GARCH) to predict the Chinese nonferrous metals futures market volatility [13]. Thomas et al. combined wavelet-based multi-resolution analysis with autoregressive integrated moving average (ARIMA) models to forecast the monthly base metal price [14]. Sahinli adopted Holt–Winters multiplicative and additive methods to explore the future trend of potato prices in Turkey [15]. Hesam and Dejan chose the Brownian motion with mean reversion (BMMR) to estimate the copper price and used the bat algorithm to optimize the parameters [16]. Although the statistics-based methods can accomplish the general task of commodity price prediction, it is hard to deal with sequences with strong nonlinearity and time-varying characteristics.

With the prosperity of artificial intelligence and the advent of the big data era, many data-driven machine learning methods have emerged and are widely applied [17,18]. Astudillo et al. used the support vector regression (SVR) technique to make long-term predictions for copper prices [19]. Diego and Werner developed an adaptive hybrid forecasting model for copper price volatility together with GARCH and the fuzzy inference system (FIS) [20]. Zakaria et al. adopted the adaptive neuro-fuzzy inference system (ANFIS) to predict the volatility of the copper price and optimized the parameters in ANFIS through the genetic algorithm (GA), which effectively improved the prediction accuracy [21]. Machine learning approaches can effectively capture the nonlinearity and irregularity of price series, so they have good prediction performance.

In recent years, deep learning models have proven to be the most promising tools for time series forecasting. A neural network can learn from sample data and approximate any nonlinear function with arbitrary precision, so it usually has satisfactory results [22,23]. Chen et al. combined the residual with the extreme learning machine and proposed a deep residual compensation extreme learning machine model (DRC-ELM), which was used in the regression analysis of gold price [24]. Atsalakis et al. adopted the neuro-fuzzy controller to predict the change direction of daily Bitcoin price for investment trade [25]. Kamdem et al. adopted long short-term memory (LSTM) to predict commodity prices, such as for crude oil, and analyzed the correlation between COVID-19 and commodity price [26]. Wang and Li used the artificial neural network (ANN) to analyze the gold future in the New York Commodity Exchange COMEX [27]. Ugurlu et al. modified the traditional recurrent neural network and proposed a multi-layer gated recurrent unit to predict the Turkish electricity market price [28].

Furthermore, considering the unavoidable shortcomings of a single model in dealing with complex time series, many scholars combined multiple methods to generate synergistic effects and improve the overall forecasting performance. Werner and Esteban introduced ANN into GARCH with regressors to forecast the price of gold, silver, and copper, and the incorporation promoted the forecasting accuracy [29]. Ana et al. adopted a combined model based on the recurrent neural network (RNN) and graph convolutional network (GCN) to predict real-time oil prices [30]. Hu et al. proposed a hybrid deep learning method by integrating the LSTM-ANN network with the GARCH model for copper price volatility prediction [31]. Livieris et al. adopted convolutional layers and the LSTM network to analyze and forecast the daily gold price [32]. Marian employed discrete wavelet transform with support vector regression to predict gold-price dynamics [33]. Hu et al. proposed a hybrid carbon price forecasting method for multimodal carbon emission trading market combining complete ensemble empirical mode decomposition with adaptive noise (CEEMDAN) and a windowed-based XGBoost approach [34]. Zhang and Liao employed the principal component analysis (PCA) and the hybrid fuzzy clustering algorithm to integrate technical indicators and adopted the radial basis function (RBF) neural network as the predictor for gold prices [35]. In general, hybrid models have better performance.

Although the existing methods have achieved good results, most of them only analyze their own historical data. They ignore the very important fact that commodity price is affected by many hidden factors, such as economic situations, transaction statuses, and so on. In the pattern of only using historical data to make forecasting, the information considered is relatively one-sided. In the multivariate forecasting framework, the auxiliary information of multiple factors is effectively used to make it possible to model prices more accurately, so it has a very large development space for improving the prediction performance [36,37]. However, as far as we know, there is relatively little research in the field of multivariate forecasting for commodity prices.

To this end, a novel commodity price forecasting method based on multi-factor selection and fusion together with the convolutional neural network (CNN) and long short-term memory (LSTM) network is proposed. Firstly, the factors that may be related to the change in commodity price were collected, and Granger causality inference was adopted to collect the causal factors. Next, extreme gradient boosting (XGBoost) was used to evaluate the importance of the remaining factors and screen out the most important factors. Then, in order to deeply explore the potential variation characteristics, the CNN was employed for factor fusion and feature extraction to reduce the burden of the predictor. Finally, considering the superiority of LSTM in sequence processing, it was adopted to build a multi-input long-term forecasting model to obtain the future price. Compared with several advanced methods, the proposed forecasting method takes into account the influence of external contributors, carries out screening and fusion processing, and has the best performance in general. In summary, the main contributions of this paper are as follows:

- In order to distinguish the core components of exogenous variables, a two-layer factor selection method based on the Granger causality inference and XGBoost is proposed.
- Utilizing the advantages of a CNN in hidden feature extraction and LSTM in time series processing, a multi-factor hybrid price forecasting model is proposed.
- Through the application of the proposed factor selection method in the SMM 0# zinc price, the conclusion further confirms the impact of the London Metal Exchange (LME) on Shanghai Metals Market (SMM). This provides a strong basis for the prediction and analysis of the zinc price.
- Compared with several advanced approaches, the realistic experiments show the superiority of the proposed method.

The rest of this paper is organized as follows. In Section 2, the methods related to this work are introduced. Section 3 describes the proposed method in detail. The experimental design and comparative analysis are given in Section 4. Finally, Section 5 presents the concluding remarks.

2. Preliminaries

2.1. Granger Causality Inference

The Granger causality inference (GCI) is a classical method that can measure the interaction between different time series [38]. It has been widely used in economics, neuroscience, and other fields in recent decades. For sequences $f(t)$ and $u(t)$, if the prediction effect of $f(t)$ with the past information of $f(t)$ and $u(t)$ is better than that alone with the past information of $f(t)$, sequence $u(t)$ helps to explain the future change of sequence $f(t)$. Therefore, $u(t)$ is considered to be the Granger cause of $f(t)$. The Granger causality is not the relationship between cause and effect as we usually understand it to be; it declares that the previous change of $u(t)$ can effectively explain the future change of $f(t)$. It only tests the chronological order of the variables in statistics.

A precondition of the Granger causality inference is that the time series must be stable, otherwise, there will be pseudo regression. Hence, the stationarity of each time series should be confirmed by the unit root test before the test. To test whether the variable $u(t)$ is a Granger cause of sequence $f(t)$, the original hypothesis "H_0: $f(t)$ is not the Granger cause of $u(t)$ changing" is put forward. The Granger causality inference model is established by estimating the following two regression models:

$$f(t) = \alpha_0 + \sum_{i=1}^{p} \alpha_i f(t-i) + \sum_{i=1}^{q} \beta_i u(t-i) + \varepsilon(t) \quad (1)$$

$$f(t) = \alpha_0 + \sum_{i=1}^{p} \alpha_i f(t-i) + \varepsilon(t) \quad (2)$$

where Equation (1) is an unconstrained regressive model of $f(t)$ and $u(t)$, noted as U. For Equation (2), it is an autoregressive model of $f(t)$, and is a constrained regression model, noted as R. α_0 is the constant term. α_i, β_i are the ratios of $f(t-i)$ and $u(t-i)$, they denote the contribution to $f(t)$. p and q represent the maximum time lag of variables $f(t)$ and $u(t)$, respectively, and $\varepsilon(t)$ is white noise. For p and q, the appropriate values can be determined by the Bayesian information criterion (BIC) or Akaike information criterion (AIC) [39].

The magnitude of Granger causality can be estimated by the logarithm of the corresponding F-statistic [40]. Then, the F-statistics can be constructed by the sum of residual squared RSS_R and RSS_U of the two regression models:

$$F = \frac{(RSS_R - RSS_U)/q}{RSS_U/(n-p-q-1)} \sim F(q, n-p-q-1) \quad (3)$$

where n is the sample size and RSS is calculates as follows:

$$RSS = \sum_{t=1}^{n} \left(f(t) - \hat{f}(t) \right)^2 \quad (4)$$

Finally, the probability ρ of the original hypothesis can be obtained by looking up the table of F-distribution. If $\rho \leq \rho_{\max}$, $\beta_1, \beta_2, \ldots, \beta_q$ significantly do not equal 0, so the original hypothesis should be rejected. In other words, $u(t)$ is the Granger cause of $f(t)$ changing. Otherwise, the original hypothesis should be accepted.

2.2. Extreme Gradient Boosting

Extreme gradient boosting (XGBoost) is an integrated promotion algorithm developed by Chen and Guestrin [41]. It evaluates the influence of different features by constructing the regression problem with gradient boosting. Unlike traditional gradient boosting, XGBoost does not add residuals to construct a stump every time, rather introduces a slightly larger tree with leaves and normalization to avoid high variance and overfitting. Therefore, the XGBoost algorithm can be regarded as an additive model consisting of multiple decision trees, expressed as Formula (5):

$$\hat{f}(t) = \sum_{k=1}^{K} RT_k(u(t)), RT_k \in G \quad (5)$$

Assuming that the dataset has n samples and m features $\Im = \{(u(t), f(t))\}(t = 1, 2, \ldots, n)$, RT stands for a regression tree, the notation K is the number of trees, and $\hat{f}(t)$ is the regression result. $u(t)$ represents the input factor, and G is the space that contains the function of all decision trees.

$$G = \left\{ RT(u) = \omega_{s(u)} \right\} \quad (6)$$

where s denotes the structure of each tree which maps a sample to the corresponding leaf index and ω represents the leaf weights, namely the score of corresponding leaves.

$f_l(t)$ is defined as the regression result of t-th instance at l-th iteration, in order to train the tree structure, the objective function is minimized as Equation (7):

$$J_l = \sum_{t=1}^{n} L\left(f_l(t), \hat{f}_{l-1}(t) + RT_l(u(t))\right) + \Omega(f_l) \tag{7}$$

$$\Omega(f_l) = \gamma \cdot N_l + \frac{1}{2}\lambda \sum_{j=1}^{N_l} \omega_j^2 \tag{8}$$

where L denotes the loss function, N is the number of leaf nodes, and γ and λ are penalty factors. The second term $\Omega(f_l)$ represents the complexity of the tree model to avoid overfitting. Under the regularized objective function, complex models will be penalized, and the model with simple predictive functions will be selected as the best model.

Since the objective is difficult to deal with in Euclidean space by conventional methods, second-order Taylor expansion is employed to optimize the above problem [42]. Then, Equation (7) can be simplified as:

$$J_l = \sum_{t=1}^{n}\left[L\left(f_l(t), \hat{f}_{l-1}(t) + g_t RT_l(u(t)) + \frac{1}{2}g'_t RT_l^2(u(t))\right)\right] + \Omega(f_l) \tag{9}$$

$$g_t = \frac{\partial L\left(f(t), \hat{f}_{l-1}(t)\right)}{\partial \hat{f}_{l-1}(t)} \tag{10}$$

$$g'_t = \frac{\partial^2 L\left(f(t), \hat{f}_{l-1}(t)\right)}{\partial \hat{f}_{l-1}^2(t)} \tag{11}$$

where g_t and g'_t are the first and second-order gradients of loss functions, respectively.

The constant terms can be removed, and the objective is simplified as follow approximate formulation:

$$J_l = \sum_{t=1}^{n}\left[g_t \omega_{s(u(t))} + \frac{1}{2}g'_t \omega_{s(u(t))}^2\right] + \gamma N_l + \frac{1}{2}\lambda \sum_{j=1}^{N_l} \omega_j^2 \tag{12}$$

For a fixed structure $s(u(t))$, the optimal weight ω_j^* of leaf j is obtained.

$$\omega_j^* = -\frac{\sum_{t \in I_j} g_t}{\sum_{t \in I_j} g'_t + \lambda} \tag{13}$$

The corresponding optimal solution is calculated by

$$J_l = -\frac{1}{2}\sum_{j=1}^{T} \frac{\left(\sum_{t \in I_j} g_t\right)^2}{\sum_{t \in I_j} h_t + \lambda} + \gamma N_l \tag{14}$$

where $I_j = \{t \mid s(u(t)) = j\}$ is the instance set of leaf j in the tree structure. The final value J_l is used to evaluate the quality of the tree. The smaller the value, the better the structure.

2.3. Convolutional Neural Network

The convolutional neural network (CNN) is a kind of feedforward neural network, which has a powerful ability on extracting features and has good performance in image vision, natural language processing, and so on [43]. The basic architecture of the CNN is mainly composed of two parts, i.e., the convolutional layer and pooling layer, as shown in Figure 1. In essence, the CNN pursues constructing multiple filters to extract useful potential information through a layer-by-layer convolution and pooling of input data.

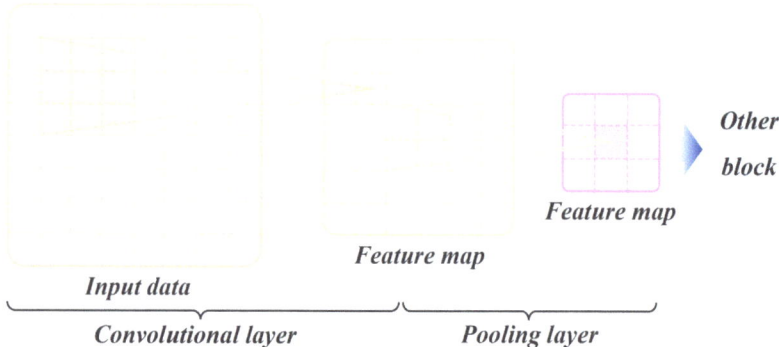

Figure 1. The basic architecture of a typical CNN.

In the convolutional layer, it contains a plurality of convolution kernels, which can be considered tiny windows. Feature maps of the previous layer are convolved with a convolution kernel and the output feature is generated by an activation function. The generated new features are usually more useful than the original features of the input data, which can promote the performance of the model. The operation of the convolutional layer can be described as follows:

$$m_j^l = a\left(\sum_{i \in M_j} m_i^{l-1} * k_{ij}^l + b_j^l\right) \tag{15}$$

where m_j^l represents the jth output feature map of the lth layer, M_j is the selection of input maps, k_{ij}^l denotes the weights between the ith input map and the jth output map, $*$ is the convolution operation, and b_j^l is the bias of the convolution kernel. $a(\cdot)$ represents the activation function such as rectified linear unit (ReLU), and it enables the nonlinear expression of the feature maps to enhance the feature expression capacity.

After the convolution operation, the features of the original data have been extracted, but the dimension of the extracted features is very high, and the application cost is very high in practice. In order to solve this problem, a pooling layer is usually added behind the convolution layer to reduce the dimension of the extracted features, so as to accelerate the convergence of the network. The pooling layer is a sub-sampling technique to extract certain values from convolution features and generate low-dimensional matrices. The pooling layer adopts a process similar to that of the convolution layer, using a small sliding window to take the convoluted features as the input and output a new value. Therefore, the output of the pooling layer can be regarded as a condensed version of the convolution layer's features. There are three pooling operations: maximum, minimum, and average pooling. The operation of the pooling layer can be formulated as Equation (16):

$$m_j^l = a\left(\zeta_j^l mp\left(m_i^{l-1}\right) + b_j^l\right) \tag{16}$$

where $mp(\cdot)$ represents the max pooling sub-sampling function and ζ_j^l is the bias. The pooling operation can ensure that the CNN can obtain a relatively robust feature representation, because small changes in input data will not change the output value of the pooling layer.

2.4. Long Short-Term Memory (LSTM) Network

The recurrent neural network (RNN) is a special kind of neural network; it can circulate the state in its own network and learn a lot of historical information, so it is very suitable for processing time series data [44]. However, with the growth of time, the RNN will not be able to complete the connection of information. LSTM is an improved recurrent neural network that uses cells to store long-term memory and introduces the gating mechanism to control cell states [45]. It avoids the problem that RNN cannot deal with long-distance information dependence, and can also solve the common problems of gradient explosion and gradient disappearance in neural networks. LSTM has been widely used in many fields, such as natural language processing, autonomous driving, weather forecasting, etc.

The infrastructure of LSTM is illustrated in Figure 2. The aforementioned gating mechanism includes an input gate, forget gate, and output gate. LSTM uses the historical data x to predict the output sequence $y = (y_1, y_2, \ldots, y_d)$, where d is the prediction period. The maintenance and update of information follow several steps below. First, the input gate determines how much new information can be stored in the cell state, while calculating the candidate value $\hat{C}_t$ that may be added to the cell state.

$$i_t = \sigma(W_i \cdot [h_{t-1}, x_t] + b_i) \tag{17}$$

$$\hat{C}_t = \tanh(W_c \cdot [h_{t-1}, x_t] + b_c) \tag{18}$$

Next, the forget gate determines how much information should be forgotten.

$$f_t = \sigma\left(W_f \cdot [h_{t-1}, x_t] + b_f\right) \tag{19}$$

The cell state of this block C_t is calculated by discarding partial information of the previous cell state C_{t-1} and adding the cell state candidate of this block $\hat{C}_t$.

$$C_t = f_t \odot C_{t-1} + i_t \odot \hat{C}_t \tag{20}$$

Finally, the output gate decides how much information in the cell state can be passed to the next memory block, and the final output results are as follows:

$$o_t = \sigma(W_o \cdot [h_{t-1}, x_t] + b_o) \tag{21}$$

$$h_t = o_t \odot \tanh(C_t) \tag{22}$$

$$y_t = \Phi(W_y h_t + b_y) \tag{23}$$

where h_t is the hidden layer state. i_t, f_t, o_t are the state of the input gate, forget gate, and output gate, respectively. W_i, W_f, W_c, W_o, and W_y represent the appropriate weight matrices, b_i, b_f, b_c, b_o, and b_y denote the corresponding bias vectors. Moreover, $\sigma()$ and $tanh()$ are sigmoid and hyperbolic tangent function, respectively, $\odot$ is the element-wise product of the vectors and $\Phi()$ is the network output activation function.

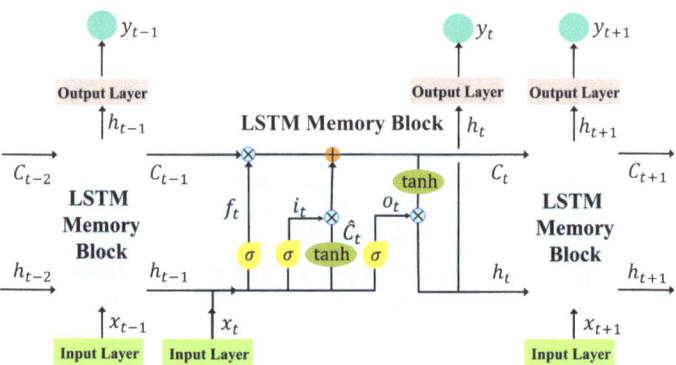

Figure 2. The structure of LSTM memory block.

3. The Proposed Method

This paper establishes a hybrid commodity price forecasting method based on multi-factor selection and fusion with the CNN-LSTM network (MFSFCL), which includes factors selection and price forecasting. Firstly, collect the factors that may affect the change in commodity price, use Granger causality inference to screen out the factors that have a causal relationship with the commodity price, and select the most important factors from the candidate factors by XGBoost. Then, the CNN is used to fuse the selected factors and extract the implicit features, and LSTM is employed to model the sequence to obtain the predicted value of the future price. The schematic diagram of the proposed MFSFCL method is illustrated in Figure 3.

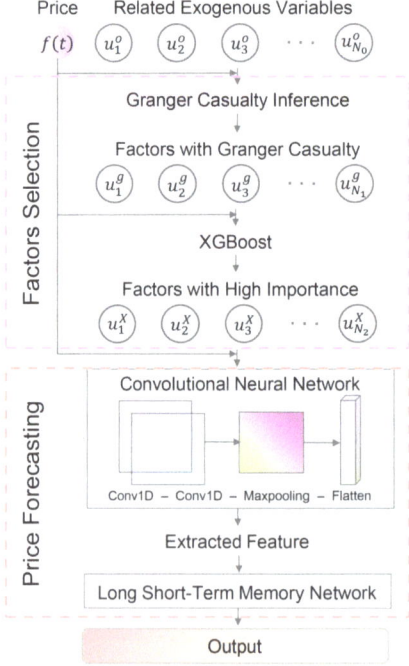

Figure 3. The schematic diagram of the proposed MFSFCL method.

3.1. Factor Selection

In detail, assuming that $f(t), t = 1, 2, \ldots n$ is the original price sequence, and n is the number of samples. $u_i^o(t), i = 1, 2, \ldots, N_0$ are the sequences of collected factors, N_0 is the number of collected factors. For commodity price, the related factors perhaps include the economic situation, international currency exchange rate, the changes in mainstream exchanges, and so on.

First of all, not all of the collected factors are related to the change in commodity price, so we need to find out the factors that have an impact on price. The Granger causality inference is conducted between the collected exogenous factors and the target price sequence. If the probability ρ is less than $\rho_{\max}$, it indicates that the factor is one of the Granger causes of the price sequence $f(t)$. That is, adding this factor together to predict $f(t)$, the performance is better than using only $f(t)$. N_1 factors are screened out through the hypothesis test, defined as $u_j^g(t), j = 1, 2, \ldots, N_1$.

Then, even though the above operation performed a preliminary screening of exogenous factors, there are still many remaining factors. Although the selected factors $u_j^g(t)$ are related to the price series $f(t)$ to a certain extent, different factors have different degrees of influence; that is, different degrees of importance. If all factors are employed to predict price in general, it will bring a great burden to the predictor. At the same time, factors with different influence degrees are mixed together and treated equally, and factors with low influence degrees may directly obscure those with high influence degrees. This overly complex and redundant information may not greatly improve the prediction effect or even have a negative effect. Hence, as the saying goes, "take the essence and discard the dross", it is necessary to analyze and pick out the important factors.

XGBoost is a classic algorithm for feature engineering, which can automatically analyze the importance of each feature. Therefore, XGBoost is adopted to pick out the factors with high importance from $u_j^g(t)$. To assess the importance of each factor, information gain is adopted as Equation (24):

$$imp = \frac{1}{2}\left[\frac{G_L^2}{H_L + \lambda} + \frac{G_R^2}{H_R + \lambda} - \frac{(G_L + G_R)^2}{H_L + H_R + \lambda}\right] - \gamma \quad (24)$$

where $G_L = \sum_{t \in I_L} |g_t|$, $G_R = \sum_{t \in I_R} |g_t|$, $H_L = \sum_{t \in I_L} g_t'$ and $H_R = \sum_{t \in I_R} g_t'$. I_L and I_R are the instances sets of left and right nodes.

After ranking the importance of factors imp, N_2 factors $u_k^X(t), k = 1, 2, \ldots, N_2$ are finally obtained according to the change of importance, where N_2 is the number of factors ultimately selected. These factors also are the core exogenous variables that mainly affect the change in price.

3.2. Price Forecasting

After determining the factors affecting the changes in price, the next task is to make the prediction. Usually, there will be several factors selected by XGBoost, which still seems not so friendly for a single model to complete both feature extraction and prediction. In order to alleviate this problem, the CNN is employed to conduct factors fusion and feature extraction from a total of $N_2 + 1$ time series of the selected factors and price to obtain a higher-level feature representation (HLF) before establishing the predictor.

$$HLF = CNN\left(u_1^X(t), u_2^X(t), \cdots, u_{N_2}^X(t), f(t)\right) \quad (25)$$

Of course, it is necessary to reconstruct the time series data before using the CNN to adapt to the input structure of the CNN [46]. The specific operations will not be repeated due to space limitations.

Finally, a prediction model is established based on the extracted features of the HLF. Due to the existence of memory cells, the LSTM network is very good at extracting sequence characteristics and has a good performance in time series prediction. Therefore, this paper adopts the LSTM network as a predictor to establish a multi-input long-term prediction model to forecast the future price. In detail, the complete procedure of the proposed framework is conducted and given in Algorithm 1.

Algorithm 1: Price forecasting based on multi-factor selection and fusion with the CNN-LSTM network;

Input: The historical zinc price $f(t)$, the collected exogenous variables $u_i^o(t), i = 1, 2, \ldots, N_0$;
Output: The forecasted future price $y(t)$;
1 **#Factors Selection**
2 **for** $i = 1, \ldots, N_0$ **do**
3   Establish regression models according to Equations (1) and (2) for factor $u_i^o(t)$ and price series $f(t)$;
4   On the basis of Equations (3) and (4), the F-statistic is calculated according to the sum resident squared of the regression models;
5   Obtain the corresponding probability by looking up the table of F-distribution;
6   **if** $\rho < \rho_{max}$ **then**
7        $u_i^o(t)$ is a causal factor and is selected;
8   **end**
9 **end**
10 The selected factors $u_j^g(t), j = 1, 2, \ldots, N_1$ and $f(t)$ are combined to establish a decision tree according to XGBoost;
11 Calculate the importance of each factor by Equation (24);
12 Sort imp in descending order, and select the most critical factors $u_k^X(t), k = 1, 2, \ldots, N_2$ based on the inflection point of imp change;
13 **#Price Forecasting**
14 Utilize the CNN to fuse selected factors $u_k^X(t)$ and price series $f(t)$, and extract hidden features $HLF = CNN\left(u_1^X(t), u_2^X(t), \cdots, u_{N_2}^X(t), f(t)\right)$;
15 Take the extracted features as input and establish a long-term forecasting model based on the LSTM network to obtain the future price $y(t)$.

---

4. Case Study

4.1. Experiment Settings

4.1.1. Data Description

This paper uses the classic commodity zinc as an example to verify the excellent performance of the proposed method. The price of 0# zinc in SMM is collected and set as the target. At the same time, 18 possible factors are collected which may affect the change in the zinc price, including the economic situation, international currency exchange rate, and stock, such as the S&P 500 Index, the price of LME zinc, and so on. For the convenience of expression, relevant abbreviations are shown in Table 1. The price series of SMM 0# zinc is illustrated in Figure 4. Due to the influence of many factors, the price fluctuates frequently and changes widely. Specifically, the time span of zinc price is from 3 January 2017 to 2 December 2020, excluding public holidays, with a total of 953 daily observations. The data from 3 January 2017 to 24 February 2020 (763 observations) is used for model training, meanwhile, the remaining data (190 observations) serves as a testing dataset to verify the ability of the forecasting model.

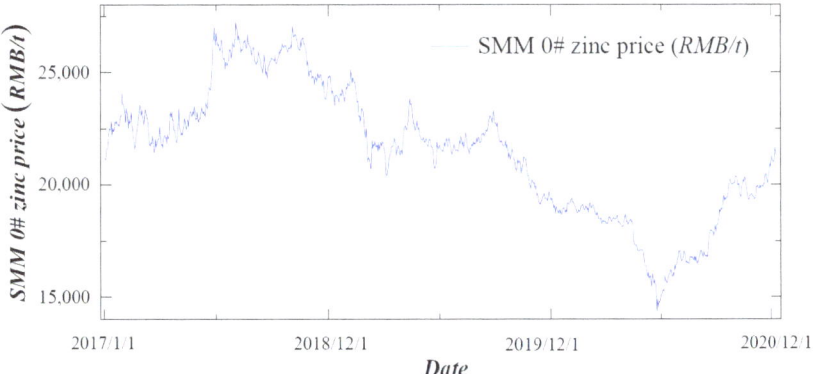

Figure 4. The 0# zinc price of Shanghai Metal Market from 3 January 2017 to 2 December 2020.

Table 1. Abbreviations of collected factors.

Number	Factor	Abbreviation	Number	Factor	Abbreviation
1	Closing price of S&P500	CPSP	10	Cash price of LME zinc	CAPLME
2	Opening price of S&P500	OPSP	11	Settlement price of LME zinc	SPLME
3	High price of S&P500	HPSP	12	Asian Stock of LME zinc	ASLME
4	Low price of S&P500	LPSP	13	Closing price of US dollar index	CPUS
5	Closing price of LME zinc	CPLME	14	Opening price of US dollar index	OPUS
6	Opening price of LME zinc	OPLME	15	High price of US dollar index	HPUS
7	High price of LME zinc	HPLME	16	Low price of US dollar index	LPUS
8	Low price of LME zinc	LPLME	17	Zinc index	ZI
9	Average price of LME zinc for three months	APLME	18	Nonferrous metals index fund	NMIF

4.1.2. Performance Evaluation Criteria

In order to evaluate the performance of the proposed MFSFCL more comprehensively, this paper uses some criteria from two different dimensions, numerical prediction accuracy, and direction prediction accuracy. For numerical prediction accuracy, several commonly used evaluation indexes are adopted, such as mean absolute error (MAE), mean absolute percentage error (MAPE), and root mean squared error (RMSE). The smaller the value of these indexes, the smaller the prediction error. For price series, it is also very important to judge the direction of future change, so the direction prediction accuracy D_{stat} should also be considered. For D_{stat}, a higher value represents a more accurate prediction direction. The specific calculation process of the above indicators can be seen in [47].

4.1.3. Parameters Settings

For a more comprehensive analysis of market changes, long-term forecasts are usually more appropriate. Here, the historical price and the selected exogenous factors of the past 7 days are utilized to predict zinc price in the next 3 days, rather than just a single-step forecast. For Granger causality inference, the maximum lag is naturally set to 7 through the analysis of AIC and BIC, and the significance level ρ_{max} is set to 0.01. For XGBoost, according to experience, the maximum tree depth is set to 3, the learning rate is 1, and the number of decision trees is 100. For the CNN, it contains two convolution layers—a pooling layer and a 'flatten' layer. The number of convolution kernels is 256 and 512, respectively, and the time domain length of the convolution kernel is 3. The activation function is ReLU. Max pooling is used, followed by a flatten layer to facilitate connection with the LSTM predictor. For the LSTM network, the step size of the input layer and output layer are 7 and 3, respectively. The number of neurons in the two hidden layers is set to (512, 64) by trial and error. A reasonable number of neurons is helpful to learn the complex changes of the sequence, while not making the model too complicated. As a rule of thumb, ReLU is used as the activation function, the learning rate is 0.01 and the batch size is 16.

4.2. Factor Selection

To remove the invalid information in the originally collected exogenous variables, the Granger causality inference is employed. Each variable carries out regression modeling with the zinc price, and the hypothesis test is used to judge whether this variable is helpful for price prediction. The concrete results are depicted in Table 2.

Table 2. The results of the Granger causality inference.

Factor	ρ	Factor	ρ
CPSP	**0.0000**	CAPLME	**0.0000**
OPSP	0.2378	SPLME	**0.0000**
HPSP	**0.0022**	ASLME	0.4320
LPSP	**0.0004**	CPUS	**0.0042**
CPLME	**0.0000**	OPUS	0.0319
OPLME	0.3726	HPUS	**0.0070**
HPLME	**0.0000**	LPUS	**0.0043**
LPLME	**0.0000**	ZI	0.7402
APLME	**0.0000**	NMIF	0.0344

In detail, if the hypothesis test probability of a factor is less than $\rho_{\max} = 0.01$, it will be considered to have a causal relationship with the change in the zinc price. In Table 2, there are 12 out of the original 18 factors that are causal to zinc price. They are CPSP, HPSP, LPSP, APLME, CAPLME, SPLME, CPUS, HPUS, LPUS, CPLME, HPLME, and LPLME. Generally speaking, S&P 500 index, the zinc price of the London Metal Exchange and the US dollar index, directly affect the change of the zinc price in the Shanghai Metal Market. In other words, the zinc price is mainly affected by international currency exchange rates and economic conditions. This is roughly consistent with our cognition. Generally, when the economic situation is good, the price of basic raw materials rises, and vice versa. The international price is marked and settled in US dollars. When the US dollar depreciates, the price of metals rises, and vice versa.

After removing the non-causal factors, it can be seen that there are still many factors. In reality, a few influencing factors often play a key role, and redundant information may reduce the prediction effect to a certain extent [48]. Therefore, XGBoost is utilized to evaluate the importance of the remaining factors to select the core elements. Set the zinc price series $f(t)$ as the regression target, and the information gain is adopted to measure the importance of each factor. The larger the information gain, the higher the importance of the factor. Figure 5 depicts the rank of factor importance.

It is clear that the importance of HPLME, CPLME, CAPLME, and APLME is much higher than other factors. Therefore, these four factors are selected as the key factors affecting the change in the zinc price in the Shanghai Metals Market. This does not mean that other factors are not helpful to the SMM zinc price forecasting, but that the selected four factors have a more direct and important influence. In general, the selected factors have a common characteristic. They are the zinc price of the London Metal Exchange, which means that LME has a great impact on SMM. It is gratifying that this conclusion is consistent with Yue's work. Yue et al. used the VAR-DCC-GARCH model to explore the relationship between Chinese nonferrous metals prices and the nonferrous metals prices from LME. The results showed that LME nonferrous metals prices have a great impact on Chinese nonferrous metals prices, and the co-movement of nonferrous metal prices between LME and Chinese markets presents hysteretic nature [49]. This finding directly reflects the effectiveness of the proposed factor selection method.

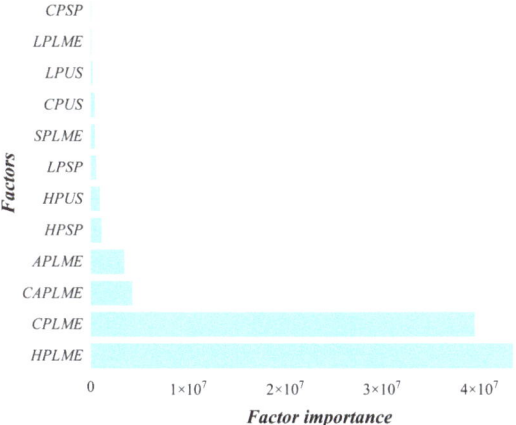

Figure 5. The rank of factor importance.

4.3. Comparative Analysis of Price Forecasting

4.3.1. Compared with Univariate Forecasting Method

In order to explore the performance of the proposed multi-factor forecasting method, MFSFCL is compared with several advanced univariate prediction methods such as ARIMA, multiple-output support vector regression (MSVR), ELM, feedforward neural network (FNN), and LSTM. The parameter (p,d,q) of ARIMA can be determined by AIC and BIC. For MSVR, the kernel function is linear, and the epsilon is set to 1. For the ELM network, the (neuron) number of hidden layers is 110. As for FNN (I-H-H-O), the number of hidden nodes is (64, 16), and the learning rate and batch size are set to 0.01 and 16. For LSTM, the parameter settings are the same as FNN.

The qualitative analysis results are shown in Figure 6. From the perspective of the numerical accuracy of the prediction, the proposed MFSFCL has the smallest MAE, RMSE, and MAPE, which means that it has the smallest prediction error. Compared with other univariate forecasting methods, the prediction error of MFSFCL is greatly reduced, which has obvious advantages. Interestingly, it can be found that except for the poor performance of ELM, the remaining univariate forecasting methods have similar numerical forecasting accuracy at different time steps. This is because the zinc price is affected by many factors. Although these univariate forecasting methods have good prediction capabilities, the single information also determines the upper limit of forecasting performance. The forecasting performance of ARIMA, MSVR, FNN, and LSTM reaches the upper limit for univariate forecasting methods. ELM often usually does not perform well in dealing with such complex prediction tasks due to their stochastic nature. In terms of directional accuracy, MFSFCL has obvious advantages in one-step forecasting and two-step forecasting compared with other univariate methods and also has competitive accuracy in three-step forecasting. In general, MFSFCL has the best overall performance on D_{stat}. At the same time, it can be found that the prediction effect gradually deteriorates with the passage of time, which is an inevitable phenomenon of all methods. After all, the future is full of uncertainty. The more uncertain it is in the future, the more difficult it is to predict.

From a quantitative point of view, MFSFCL significantly reduces the prediction errors compared to other univariate prediction methods, as shown in Table 3. The MAE, RMSE, and MAPE performances of the proposed MFSFCL are 58.66%, 54.22%, and 74.71% lower than those of the best performance of other methods, respectively, for the first day. Moreover, there is a prediction error decrease of 65.77%, 60.72%, and 79.51% for the second day and 70.35%, 65.79%, and 82.39% for the third day. Due to the characteristics of strong noise and violent fluctuation in financial time series, the univariate prediction method only considers one-sided information, which is difficult to obtain satisfactory results. Nevertheless, the proposed MFSFCL reasonably takes into account the influence of exogenous variables on the change in the zinc price, and has strong predictive performance.

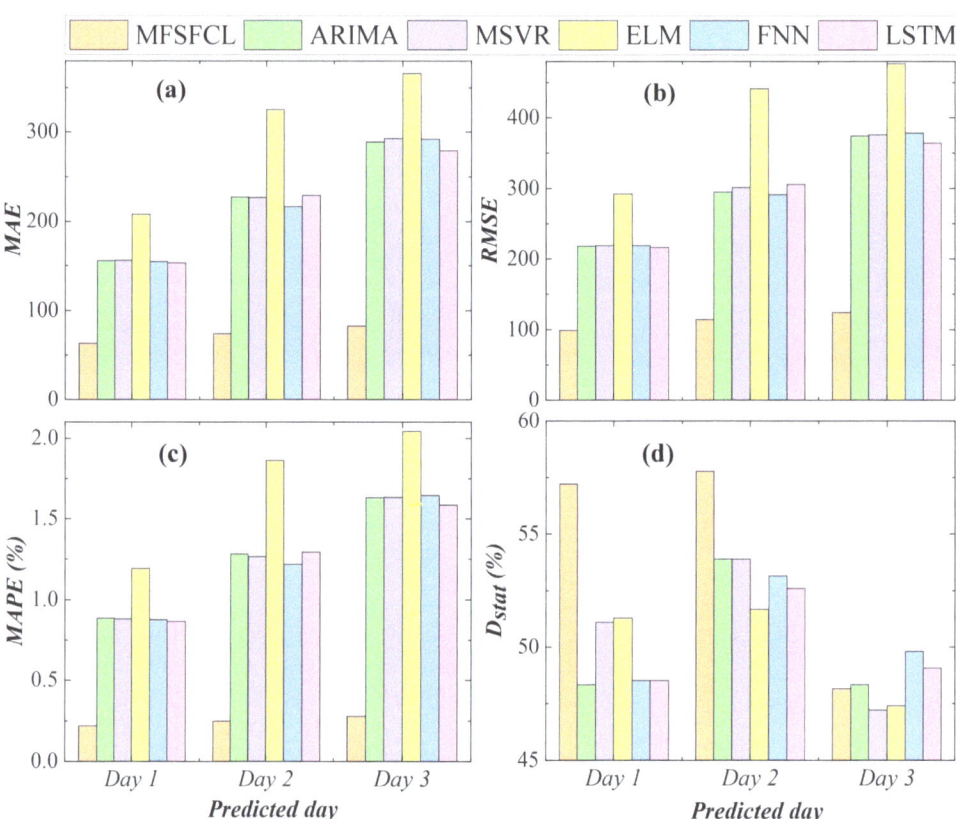

Figure 6. The comparison of different forecasting models for different days. (**a**–**d**) are the results for MAE, RMSE, MAPE, and D_{stat}, respectively.

Table 3. Forecasting performance evaluation metrics of the proposed MFSFCL and other univariate methods.

		MFSFCL	ARIMA	MSVR	ELM	FNN	LSTM
Day1	MAE	**63.33**	155.94	156.32	208.22	154.85	153.19
	RMSE	**99.05**	218.02	218.97	292.32	219.00	216.36
	MAPE (%)	**0.22**	0.89	0.88	1.19	0.88	0.87
	D_{stat}	**57.22**	48.33	51.11	51.30	48.52	48.52
Day2	MAE	**74.13**	227.54	226.96	325.18	216.59	229.23
	RMSE	**114.37**	295.18	301.08	441.41	291.20	305.68
	MAPE (%)	**0.25**	1.28	1.27	1.86	1.22	1.29
	D_{stat}	**57.78**	53.89	53.89	51.67	51.15	52.59
Day3	MAE	**82.82**	288.95	293.11	365.87	292.42	279.38
	RMSE	**124.61**	373.98	375.99	476.86	378.38	364.30
	MAPE (%)	**0.28**	1.63	1.64	2.04	1.65	1.59
	D_{stat}	48.15	48.33	47.22	47.41	**49.81**	49.07

Figure 7 explores the distribution of relative prediction errors for different methods on different days. In order to show the specific changes more clearly, a portion of the view is presented separately. In general, compared with the univariate prediction method, the relative forecasting error value of the proposed MFSFCL is the smallest, and basically fluctuates around 0, which means that MFSFCL has accurate forecasting accuracy and robust performance. This directly reflects that the rational use of exogenous variables can improve the forecasting effect.

Moreover, it also can be found that the performances of deep learning methods, such as FNN and LSTM, seem to be better than those of statistical prediction methods and machine learning methods. This is because the deep neural network has a strong modeling ability and can extract and analyze the variation rules of complex sequences. However, other methods may be difficult to deal with the time series data that fluctuates violently and varies dramatically. It is worth noting that LSTM performs the best among all univariate forecasting methods, which reflects the superiority of the LSTM network for time series processing. It builds the structure of the information cycle through memory cells, which can effectively associate the historical information with the current input, capture the dynamic change characteristics of the sequence, and obtain a better prediction effect.

4.3.2. Compared with the Case with Other Factors

To further clarify the effectiveness of the factors selected by the proposed MFSFCL, we randomly select 4 factors from the original 18 factors to predict the future zinc price. Due to the large number of combinations, 20 sets of non-repetitive factors are randomly selected. For each set of factors, they are sent to the CNN and LSTM for prediction, and the average of 10 interdependent experiments is used for analysis. Finally, the 3 sets with the best results among the 20 sets are selected for comparative analysis. The experimental results are shown in Table 4.

Table 4. Forecasting performance evaluation matrix under different factor combinations.

		The Selected Factors	OPSP-CAPLME-HPUS-SPLME	LPSP-NMIF-LPLME-SPLME	CPSP-ZI-ASLME-OPLME
Day1	MAE	**63.33**	88.53	99.84	104.66
	RMSE	**99.05**	117.05	126.11	137.12
	MAPE (%)	**0.22**	0.29	0.32	0.34
	D_{stat}	**57.22**	49.1	48.33	50.01
Day2	MAE	**74.13**	110.52	114.64	100.68
	RMSE	**114.37**	153.23	145.44	136.81
	MAPE (%)	**0.25**	0.37	0.37	0.33
	D_{stat}	**57.78**	56.94	53.78	56.11
Day3	MAE	**82.82**	135.18	124.68	124.13
	RMSE	**124.61**	189.14	159.55	161.56
	MAPE (%)	**0.28**	0.45	0.40	0.40
	D_{stat}	48.15	49.17	50.55	48.89

For the factors selected by the proposed method based on Granger causality inference and XGBoost, the prediction effect is significantly better than other factor combinations. Further, it can be found that the three best-performing combinations all contain several exogenous variables screened by Granger causality inference. This means that it is really helpful to use the screened factors for prediction. In the proposed MFSFCL, Granger causality inference determines whether the factor can promote the prediction effect of price series from the perspective of econometrics, and XGBoost analyzes and sorts the importance of each factor to the prediction from the perspective of machine learning. It is logical to use valid, critical information to achieve great predictions. For the randomly selected factor combination, the addition of irrelevant factors brings redundant and inappropriate information, which affects the judgment of zinc price to a certain extent. The above results demonstrate the importance and validity of factor selection.

In addition, the multi-factor prediction results in Table 4 are all superior to the tested univariate prediction methods. This indicates that exogenous factors provide more reliable information for prediction and significantly improve the prediction accuracy.

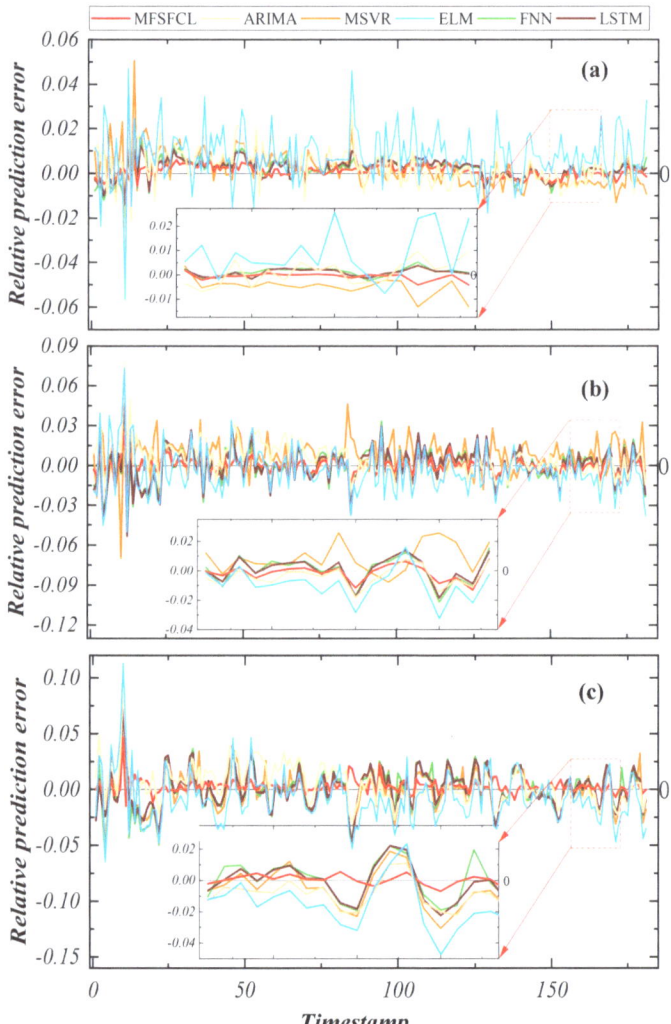

Figure 7. The relative prediction errors of different forecasting models for different days; (**a**–**c**) depict the relative prediction errors of day 1, day 2, and day 3, respectively.

4.3.3. Ablation Experiment

Finally, to verify the necessity and effectiveness of each module, an ablation experiment is performed on the proposed MFSFCL. The relevant results are shown in Table 5. For the convenience of demonstration, the combination of each module's abbreviations represents different scenarios under the ablation experiment. For instance, GCI-CNN-LSTM represents the combination of Granger casualty inference, convolutional neural network, and long short-term memory network.

Table 5. Forecasting performance evaluation matrix under different scenarios in the ablation experiment.

		MFSFCL	GCI-XGBoost-LSTM	GCI-CNN-LSTM	CNN-LSTM	LSTM
Day1	MAE	**63.33**	138.54	170.31	203.45	224.34
	RMSE	**99.05**	171.28	206.38	238.67	264.19
	MAPE (%)	**0.22**	0.45	0.57	0.66	0.71
	D_{stat}	**57.22**	47.47	48.54	46.54	46.98
Day2	MAE	**74.13**	160.25	194.05	210.67	239.32
	RMSE	**114.37**	196.92	233.30	249.45	282.50
	MAPE (%)	**0.25**	0.53	0.65	0.69	0.77
	D_{stat}	**57.78**	54.44	54.03	54.26	54.26
Day3	MAE	**82.82**	178.53	213.86	203.96	271.08
	RMSE	**124.61**	222.04	256.62	246.71	325.43
	MAPE (%)	**0.28**	0.58	0.71	0.67	0.88
	D_{stat}	48.35	48.15	**50.22**	50.06	48.46

Unsurprisingly, MFSFCL has the best performance in all scenarios of the ablation experiment. Compared with GCI-XGBoost-LSTM, the proposed method uses the CNN to fuse factors and price effectively, and learns the internal representation of time series data to extract higher-level features. Advanced knowledge representation can reduce the burden of the prediction model and improve the performance. For GCI-CNN-LSTM, it does not conduct further screening of Granger causality factors, but directly uses a large number of factors for prediction. MFSFCL uses XGBoost to pick out the factors with high importance and screen out the key components that have a great impact on price, avoiding the complex network structure in the predictor. Therefore, it has significant advantages in all kinds of prediction performance. For the CNN-LSTM, it does not perform any factor processing, and its forecasting performance is much worse than the previous methods. This is because some of the factors originally collected only have weak effects or even have no correlation with the change in the zinc price. The complex and redundant information not only brings great interference to the analysis of future changes for zinc price but also creates a complex network structure. With the model, it is difficult to obtain good forecasting performance in this case. For the single LSTM network, it is clear that various complex exogenous variables do not improve the forecasting effects and bring about very heavy burdens. Therefore, the overall performance of the LSTM network is the worst. Furthermore, the prediction performance in this case is far inferior to that of univariate LSTM, which directly reflects the importance of factor selection and processing.

Specifically, for the LSTM and CNN-LSTM, although their performances are not so ideal, it is obvious that the introduction of the CNN can extract hidden information from high-dimensional input and obtain high-level representation. This directly reduces the burden of the predictor LSTM, thus improving the prediction effect. Therefore, the CNN plays a key role in dealing with complex high-dimensional sequences. Compared with CNN-LSTM, GCI-CNN-LSTM adopts Granger causality inference to conduct preliminary processing on the originally collected exogenous variables and removes some invalid information, which directly improves the overall forecasting accuracy. Of course, on this basis, MFSFCL uses XGBoost to screen out the core components of the influencing factors, which greatly reduces the complexity of the prediction model and improves the overall forecasting performance.

In general, the proposed MFSFCL effectively makes use of the advantages of each module, takes into account the influence of external factors on zinc price, and conducts screening, fusion, and modeling for each factor. In general, it has a robust and accurate prediction performance.

5. Conclusions

The change in the commodity price is the key basis of market transactions and economic management, so it is necessary to make an accurate prediction of the dynamic commodity price. However, due to the influences of various hidden factors, the commodity price usually varies frequently and fluctuates violently with obvious nonlinear characteristics. Therefore, it is difficult to obtain accurate and robust prediction results only using the historical data of the price itself. To this end, this paper proposes a hybrid multi-factor price forecasting method based on factor selection and fusion with the CNN-LSTM network. Firstly, the Granger causality inference is used to remove the non-causal factors in the collected exogenous variables. Then, in order to screen out the factors which have a significant impact on the commodity price, XGBoost is adopted to evaluate and sort the importance of the remaining factors. Next, a CNN is employed to fuse the selected factors together and extract hidden features. Finally, a multi-input long-term prediction model is established by using the LSTM network to obtain the future price. The quantitative and qualitative results of comparative experiments indicate that the performance of the proposed MFSFCL outperforms other state-of-the-art methods. The analysis conclusion on the factors affecting the price of SMM also provides strong support for zinc price forecasting. It is a promising multi-factor forecasting method and can be widely used in other fields. Considering that different exogenous variables have different influences on prices, how to effectively use this characteristic to obtain more accurate prediction results is a direction that will be worthy of more research in the future.

Author Contributions: Conceptualization, Y.L.; methodology, Y.L. and C.Y.; software, W.L.; validation, Y.L.; writing—original draft preparation, Y.L.; writing—review and editing, C.Y. and K.H. All authors have read and agreed to the published version of the manuscript.

Funding: This work was supported in part by the National Natural Science Foundation of China (grant nos. 62073340, 61860206014), in part by the National Key R&D Program of China (2019YFB1705300), in part by the Shandong Key Laboratory of Industrial Control Technology (Qingdao University), in part by Fundamental Research Funds from the Central Universities of Central South University (2021zzts0199), and in part by the Science and Technology Innovation Program of Hunan Province (grant nos. 2021RC3018 and 2021RC4054).

Data Availability Statement: Not applicable.

Conflicts of Interest: The authors declare no conflict of interest.

References

1. Bakas, D.; Triantafyllou, A. Commodity price volatility and the economic uncertainty of pandemics. *Econ. Lett.* **2020**, *193*, 109283. [CrossRef]
2. Liu, Y.; Yang, C.; Huang, K.; Gui, W.; Hu, S. A Systematic Procurement Supply Chain Optimization Technique Based on Industrial Internet of Thing and Application. *IEEE Internet Things J.* **2022**, in press. [CrossRef]
3. Ivanova, M.; Dospatliev, L. Effects of Diesel Price on Changes in Agricultural Commodity Prices in Bulgaria. *Mathematics* **2023**, *11*, 559. [CrossRef]
4. Giannerini, S.; Goracci, G. Entropy-Based Tests for Complex Dependence in Economic and Financial Time Series with the R Package tseriesEntropy. *Mathematics* **2023**, *11*, 757. [CrossRef]
5. Huang, K.; Wang, Z.; Jusup, M. Incorporating Latent Constraints to Enhance Inference of Network Structure. *IEEE Trans. Netw. Sci. Eng.* **2020**, *7*, 466–475. [CrossRef]
6. Fister, D.; Perc, M.; Jagrič, T. Two robust long short-term memory frameworks for trading stocks. *Appl. Intell.* **2021**, *51*, 7177–7195. [CrossRef] [PubMed]
7. Liu, W.; Wang, C.; Li, Y.; Liu, Y.; Huang, K. Ensemble forecasting for product futures prices using variational mode decomposition and artificial neural networks. *Chaos Solitons Fractals* **2021**, *146*, 110822. [CrossRef]

8. Rodríguez, A.; Melgarejo, M. Identification of Colombian coffee price dynamics. *Chaos Interdiscip. J. Nonlinear Sci.* **2020**, *30*, 013145. [CrossRef]
9. Yuan, Y.; Zhang, T. Forecasting stock market in high and low volatility periods: a modified multifractal volatility approach. *Chaos Solitons Fractals* **2020**, *140*, 110252. [CrossRef]
10. Wang, Y.; Wang, H. Using networks and partial differential equations to forecast bitcoin price movement. *Chaos Interdiscip. J. Nonlinear Sci.* **2020**, *30*, 073127. [CrossRef]
11. Frezza, M. A fractal-based approach for modeling stock price variations. *Chaos Interdiscip. J. Nonlinear Sci.* **2018**, *28*, 091102. [CrossRef] [PubMed]
12. Drachal, K. Forecasting prices of selected metals with Bayesian data-rich models. *Resour. Policy* **2019**, *64*, 101528. [CrossRef]
13. Zhu, X.H.; Zhang, H.W.; Zhong, M.R. Volatility forecasting in Chinese nonferrous metals futures market. *Trans. Nonferrous Met. Soc. China* **2017**, *27*, 1206–1214. [CrossRef]
14. Kriechbaumer, T.; Angus, A.; Parsons, D.; Casado, M.R. An improved wavelet–ARIMA approach for forecasting metal prices. *Resour. Policy* **2014**, *39*, 32–41. [CrossRef]
15. Şahinli, M.A. Potato price forecasting with Holt-Winters and ARIMA methods: A case study. *Am. J. Potato Res.* **2020**, *97*, 336–346. [CrossRef]
16. Dehghani, H.; Bogdanovic, D. Copper price estimation using bat algorithm. *Resour. Policy* **2018**, *55*, 55–61. [CrossRef]
17. Wang, Z.; Li, Z.; Wang, R.; Nie, F.; Li, X. Large graph clustering with simultaneous spectral embedding and discretization. *IEEE Trans. Pattern Anal. Mach. Intell.* **2021**, *43*, 4426–4440. [CrossRef]
18. Huang, K.; Tao, Z.; Liu, Y.; Sun, B.; Yang, C.; Gui, W.; Hu, S. Adaptive multimode process monitoring based on mode-matching and similarity-preserving dictionary learning. *IEEE Trans. Cybern.* **2022**, in press. [CrossRef]
19. Astudillo, G.; Carrasco, R.; Fernández-Campusano, C.; Chacón, M. Copper Price Prediction Using Support Vector Regression Technique. *Appl. Sci.* **2020**, *10*, 6648. [CrossRef]
20. García, D.; Kristjanpoller, W. An adaptive forecasting approach for copper price volatility through hybrid and non-hybrid models. *Appl. Soft Comput.* **2019**, *74*, 466–478. [CrossRef]
21. Alameer, Z.; Abd Elaziz, M.; Ewees, A.A.; Ye, H.; Jianhua, Z. Forecasting copper prices using hybrid adaptive neuro-fuzzy inference system and genetic algorithms. *Nat. Resour. Res.* **2019**, *28*, 1385–1401. [CrossRef]
22. Liu, C.; Wang, K.; Wang, Y.; Yuan, X. Learning deep multimanifold structure feature representation for quality prediction with an industrial application. *IEEE Trans. Ind. Inform.* **2021**, *18*, 5849–5858. [CrossRef]
23. Wang, S.H.; Nayak, D.R.; Guttery, D.S.; Zhang, X.; Zhang, Y.D. COVID-19 classification by CCSHNet with deep fusion using transfer learning and discriminant correlation analysis. *Inf. Fusion* **2021**, *68*, 131–148. [CrossRef] [PubMed]
24. Chen, Y.; Xie, X.; Zhang, T.; Bai, J.; Hou, M. A deep residual compensation extreme learning machine and applications. *J. Forecast.* **2020**, *39*, 986–999. [CrossRef]
25. Atsalakis, G.S.; Atsalaki, I.G.; Pasiouras, F.; Zopounidis, C. Bitcoin price forecasting with neuro-fuzzy techniques. *Eur. J. Oper. Res.* **2019**, *276*, 770–780. [CrossRef]
26. Kamdem, J.S.; Essomba, R.B.; Berinyuy, J.N. Deep learning models for forecasting and analyzing the implications of COVID-19 spread on some commodities markets volatilities. *Chaos Solitons Fractals* **2020**, *140*, 110215. [CrossRef]
27. Wang, J.; Li, X. A combined neural network model for commodity price forecasting with SSA. *Soft Comput.* **2018**, *22*, 5323–5333. [CrossRef]
28. Ugurlu, U.; Oksuz, I.; Tas, O. Electricity price forecasting using recurrent neural networks. *Energies* **2018**, *11*, 1255. [CrossRef]
29. Kristjanpoller, W.; Hernández, E. Volatility of main metals forecasted by a hybrid ANN-GARCH model with regressors. *Expert Syst. Appl.* **2017**, *84*, 290–300. [CrossRef]
30. Lazcano, A.; Herrera, P.J.; Monge, M. A Combined Model Based on Recurrent Neural Networks and Graph Convolutional Networks for Financial Time Series Forecasting. *Mathematics* **2023**, *11*, 224. [CrossRef]
31. Hu, Y.; Ni, J.; Wen, L. A hybrid deep learning approach by integrating LSTM-ANN networks with GARCH model for copper price volatility prediction. *Phys. A Stat. Mech. Its Appl.* **2020**, *557*, 124907. [CrossRef]
32. Livieris, I.E.; Pintelas, E.; Pintelas, P. A CNN–LSTM model for gold price time-series forecasting. *Neural Comput. Appl.* **2020**, *32*, 17351–17360. [CrossRef]
33. Risse, M. Combining wavelet decomposition with machine learning to forecast gold returns. *Int. J. Forecast.* **2019**, *35*, 601–615. [CrossRef]
34. Zhang, C.; Zhao, Y.; Zhao, H. A Novel Hybrid Price Prediction Model for Multimodal Carbon Emission Trading Market Based on CEEMDAN Algorithm and Window-Based XGBoost Approach. *Mathematics* **2022**, *10*, 4072. [CrossRef]
35. Zhang, F.; Liao, Z. Gold price forecasting based on RBF neural network and hybrid fuzzy clustering algorithm. In *Proceedings the Seventh International Conference on Management Science and Engineering Management*; Springer: Berlin/Heidelberg, Germany, 2014; pp. 73–84.
36. Vakitbilir, N.; Hilal, A.; Direkoğlu, C. Hybrid deep learning models for multivariate forecasting of global horizontal irradiation. *Neural Comput. Appl.* **2022**, *34*, 8005–8026. [CrossRef]
37. Zhang, Y.D.; Dong, Z.; Wang, S.H.; Yu, X.; Yao, X.; Zhou, Q.; Hu, H.; Li, M.; Jiménez-Mesa, C.; Ramirez, J.; et al. Advances in multimodal data fusion in neuroimaging: overview, challenges, and novel orientation. *Inf. Fusion* **2020**, *64*, 149–187. [CrossRef] [PubMed]

38. Bekun, F.V.; Alhassan, A.; Ozturk, I.; Gimba, O.J. Explosivity and Time-Varying Granger Causality: Evidence from the Bubble Contagion Effect of COVID-19-Induced Uncertainty on Manufacturing Job Postings in the United States. *Mathematics* **2022**, *10*, 4780. [CrossRef]
39. Gustavo, P.; O. Durão, F.; Bernardo, P.A.; Silva, M.C.E. Neural network approach based on a bilevel optimization for the prediction of underground blast-induced ground vibration amplitudes. *Neural Comput. Appl.* **2020**, *32*, 5975–5987.
40. Geweke, J. Measurement of linear dependence and feedback between multiple time series. *J. Am. Stat. Assoc.* **1982**, *77*, 304–313. [CrossRef]
41. Chen, T.; Guestrin, C. Xgboost: A scalable tree boosting system. In Proceedings of the 22nd ACM Sigkdd International Conference on Knowledge Discovery and Data Mining, San Francisco, CA, USA, 13–17 August 2016; pp. 785–794.
42. Zhou, Y.; Li, T.; Shi, J.; Qian, Z. A CEEMDAN and XGBOOST-based approach to forecast crude oil prices. *Complexity* **2019**, *2019*, 4392785. [CrossRef]
43. Gao, R.; Xu, J.; Chen, Y.; Cho, K. Heterogeneous Feature Fusion Module Based on CNN and Transformer for Multiview Stereo Reconstruction. *Mathematics* **2023**, *11*, 112. [CrossRef]
44. Mikolov, T.; Karafiát, M.; Burget, L.; Cernocký, J.; Khudanpur, S. Recurrent neural network based language model. In Proceedings of the Interspeech, Makuhari, Chiba, Japan, 26–30 September 2010; Volume 2, pp. 1045–1048.
45. Yu, Y.; Si, X.; Hu, C.; Zhang, J. A review of recurrent neural networks: LSTM cells and network architectures. *Neural Comput.* **2019**, *31*, 1235–1270. [CrossRef]
46. Huang, K.; Wu, S.; Li, F.; Yang, C.; Gui, W. Fault Diagnosis of Hydraulic Systems Based on Deep Learning Model With Multirate Data Samples. *IEEE Trans. Neural Networks Learn. Syst.* **2021**, *33*, 6789–6801. [CrossRef]
47. Liu, Y.; Yang, C.; Huang, K.; Gui, W. Non-ferrous metals price forecasting based on variational mode decomposition and LSTM network. *Knowl.-Based Syst.* **2020**, *188*, 105006. [CrossRef]
48. Wang, S.; Celebi, M.E.; Zhang, Y.D.; Yu, X.; Lu, S.; Yao, X.; Zhou, Q.; Miguel, M.G.; Tian, Y.; Gorriz, J.M.; et al. Advances in data preprocessing for biomedical data fusion: An overview of the methods, challenges, and prospects. *Inf. Fusion* **2021**, *76*, 376–421. [CrossRef]
49. Yue, Y.D.; Liu, D.C.; Shan, X. Price linkage between Chinese and international nonferrous metals commodity markets based on VAR-DCC-GARCH models. *Trans. Nonferrous Met. Soc. China* **2015**, *25*, 1020–1026. [CrossRef]

Disclaimer/Publisher's Note: The statements, opinions and data contained in all publications are solely those of the individual author(s) and contributor(s) and not of MDPI and/or the editor(s). MDPI and/or the editor(s) disclaim responsibility for any injury to people or property resulting from any ideas, methods, instructions or products referred to in the content.

Article

PLDH: Pseudo-Labels Based Deep Hashing

Huawen Liu [1,*], Minhao Yin [2], Zongda Wu [1], Liping Zhao [1], Qi Li [1], Xinzhong Zhu [3] and Zhonglong Zheng [3]

[1] Department of Computer Science, Shaoxing University, Shaoxing 312000, China
[2] School of Information Science and Technology, Northeast Normal University, Changchun 130024, China
[3] School of Computer Science and Technology, Zhejiang Normal University, Jinhua 311231, China
* Correspondence: liu@usx.edu.cn

Abstract: Deep hashing has received a great deal of attraction in large-scale data analysis, due to its high efficiency and effectiveness. The performance of deep hashing models heavily relies on label information, which is very expensive to obtain. In this work, a novel end-to-end deep hashing model based on pseudo-labels for large-scale data without labels is proposed. The proposed hashing model consists of two major stages, where the first stage aims to obtain pseudo-labels based on deep features extracted by a pre-training deep convolution neural network. The second stage generates hash codes with high quality by the same neural network in the previous stage, coupled with an end-to-end hash layer, whose purpose is to encode data into a binary representation. Additionally, a quantization loss is introduced and interwound within these two stages. Evaluation experiments were conducted on two frequently-used image collections, CIFAR-10 and NUS-WIDE, with eight popular shallow and deep hashing models. The experimental results show the superiority of the proposed method in image retrieval.

Keywords: learning to hash; image retrieval; deep learning; nearest neighbor search; unsupervised learning; pseudo-label

MSC: 68T07

1. Introduction

Finding interesting objects from a given data collection is an essential task in information retrieval, data mining and image retrieval. When the given data collection is small and low-dimensional, precisely identifying exactly desired objects from the collection has been extensively studied and a great number of retrieval methods have been developed during the past decades [1]. Taking kNN (k nearest neighbors), which is the most classic and popular neighbor search technique, as an example, it is highly efficient and effective to pick exact neighbors out from a small scale and low dimensional data collection [2]. Along with the modern information technology emerging, the scale of data collected from a variety of domains becomes larger and larger. The large-scale property poses great challenges to traditional retrieval techniques. Even for kNN, its efficiency of finding exact neighbors in a large-scale data collection is very low, hampering its wide applications in practice greatly [3].

Approximate nearest neighbor search (ANNS) derives objects, which are similar or proximate to a given query, from a large-scale data collection [2]. Since it is highly efficient and scales to the large-scale property without degrading retrieval precision and recall slightly, ANNS has received significant attention. Hash learning and vector quantity are two representative approximate search techniques, where hash learning attracts more extraordinary attentions because of its extreme efficiency [4]. Hash learning encodes data objects into a binary representation by linear or non-linear projection functions [5]. With the binary representation, the search process can be turned to bit operations, e.g., XOR and POPCNT, which can be executed straightforwardly by CPU.

Roughly speaking, hash techniques can be grouped into two major categories, i.e., data-independent hashing and data-dependent hashing, according to whether the projection functions are learned from data [5]. Locality sensitive hashing (LSH) and its variants are typical examples of the former, whose projection functions are generated randomly [6]. Generally, LSH has relatively poor performance, because it is independent of data. On the contrary, the data-dependent hashing methods construct hashing functions by virtue of inherent properties of data, so that the structural information of data can be preserved. Emblematic data-dependent methods include spectral hashing (SH) [7], iterative quantization (ITQ) [8] and spherical hashing (SpH) [9]. Compared to the data-independent hashing, the data-dependent hashing is superior in retrieval performance.

A recent trend of hash learning is that hash functions are often learned by deep learning [10]. The underlying motivation is that deep learning can derive deep features from data by exploiting deep neural networks, such as AlexNet, CNN, VGG and ResNet [10]. Since the deep features embed high-order semantic information of data, deep hashing methods usually have competitive performance than the conventional ones. DeepBit [11], SGH [12] and DistillHash [13] are typical deep hashing algorithms. For instance, semantic structure-based deep hashing (SSDH) [14] extracts deep features with rich semantic information to construct data labels by using a pre-training convolution neural network, so that the hashing objective functions can preserve semantic similarities among data [15]. For deep hashing, notwithstanding its popularity, there are several limitations that require more effort to work on. Firstly, the early deep hashing methods usually generate binary codes from hand-crafted features (e.g., GIST and SIFT) [16]. As we know, the hand-crafted features embodies less semantic information, making the performance improvement limitedly. Additionally, most of deep hashing methods exploit label information to learn semantic features of data and further to derive binary codes. However, data labels are often unavailable in real-world applications and obtaining them is expensive and intractable.

With this motivation, in this work we leverage a novel end-to-end deep hashing method, called pseudo-labels-based deep hashing (PLDH), for image retrieval. It mainly consists of two stages: obtaining pseudo-labels and generating binary codes. To be specific, the proposed method first adopts a pre-training deep convolution neural network to obtain the similarity degree for each pair of data objects. Afterwards, the pseudo-labels of data objects are generated based on the similarity degrees. The second stage of PLDH covers three major components, i.e., feature learning, code transformation and loss function. Feature learning aims to extract semantic features from data by using a seven-layer convolution neural network, where the first layers are convolution ones, followed by two full-connection layers. Code transformation encodes the data objects into a binary representation by an end-to-end layer. The loss function is used to control the similarity preservation of data and the quality of binary representation. These components are interwound with each other and obtain feedback information alternately during the whole learning process. Owing to the end-to-end layer, the generated binary codes have higher quality and more powerful capabilities.

In a nutshell, the main contributions of this work are briefly summarized as follows:

- We exploit a pre-training deep convolution neural network to obtain the similarity degrees of data, so that the pseudo-labels of data can be further derived.
- The binary representation of data can be achieved by the end-to-end deep neural network, coupled with the pseudo-labels, where information loss between feature learning and code transformation is considered during the whole learning process.
- We conducted extensive experiments on public datasets, i.e., CIFAR-10 and NUS-WIDE. The experimental results show the superiority of PLDH to the state-of-the-art hashing algorithms.

2. Related Work

Due to its extreme efficiency, hash learning receives a great deal of attention and has now become one of the hot topics in image retrieval and big data analysis. To date, many hash learning methods have been developed. More details can be found in good survey papers, e.g., [4,5], and references therein. Here, we only discuss several typical ones briefly.

As mentioned above, hash techniques include data-independent hashing and data-dependent hashing, according to whether the projection functions are learned from data [5]. Additionally, the hash techniques can also be categorized as supervised hashing and unsupervised hashing, if the label information of data is considered. The former constructs a hashing model with the label information, while the latter does not take data labels into account when constructing a hashing model. For example, ITQ [8] first adopts the technique of principal component analysis to transform data and then take the principal components to generate hash functions. Additionally, SpH [9] employs a hypersphere, instead of hyperplane, to partition data, so that those similar data may fall into closest adjacent regions. As a result, the generated hash functions are more determinative.

Typical supervised hashing algorithms include KSH (Supervised Hashing with Kernels) [17], FastH (Fast Supervised Hashing) [18] and FSDH (Fast Supervised Discrete Hashing) [19], where KSH considers the kernels of binary codes when design hash functions, so that it can effectively handle non-linear data. FastH [18] utilizes boosting trees to cope with the problem raised by the high-dimensional data, while FSDH [19] exploits the strategy of regression of the class labels to binary codes to accelerate hashing process. Note that the performance of supervised hashing is usually better than that of the unsupervised one, because the supervised hashing fully exploits the semantic information of data.

Recently, deep learning has also be widely used in hash learning. The underlying reason is that deep learning can effectively capture the semantic information of data, which may benefit analyzing the inherent properties of data. CNNH (Convolutional Neural Network Hashing) [20] is a representative deep supervised hashing method. It simultaneously derives a feature representation as well as hash functions by using a deep convolutional neural network within two stages. In a similar vein, DPSH (Deep Pairwise-Supervised Hashing) [21] makes use of pairwise labels to learn deep features and hash codes simultaneously. DSDH (Deep Supervised Discrete Hashing) [22] takes both the pairwise label and classification information into consideration within one schema when learning hash codes.

As we know, obtaining class labels for data is a tedious and very expensive thing, especial for large-scale data. Thus, some studies focus on unsupervised deep hashing techniques coupled with inherent properties of data or hash codes. For instance, DeepBit [11] adopts three strategies, i.e., training quantization loss, code even-distributions and bit invariance, to evaluate the quality of generated binary codes. To preserve semantic similarities, SSDH (Semantic Structure Deep Hashing) [14] constructs the semantic structure of data, where data are semantically similar if their distances is obviously smaller than others, to guide the generation of hash codes. Recently, UDPH (Unsupervised Deep Pairwise Hashing) [23] employs anchor-based pairwise similarities to enhance the robustness of binary codes. HashSIM (Hashing via Structural and Intrinsic siMilarity) [24] first constructs structural similarities on highly confident data, and then utilizes them to guide the generation of codes. SPL-UDH (Soft-Pseudo-Label-based Unsupervised Deep Hashing) [25] utilizes a deep auto-encoder network to generate soft pseudo-labels and local similarities of images, and then derive binary codes based on them via the Bayesian theory.

3. Materials and Methods

3.1. Problem Statement

Assume that $\mathbf{X} = \{(\mathbf{x}_i, \mathbf{y}_i)\}_{i=1}^n \in \mathcal{R}^{n \times d}$ is a training data collection consisting of n data objects, each $\mathbf{x}_i$ ($i = 1, \ldots, n$) is the feature vector, represented as d dimensions, of the i-th data object. $\mathbf{y}_i \in \{0,1\}^m$ refers to the label information of $\mathbf{x}_i$. $\mathbf{X}$ is a multi-label data collection when each $\mathbf{y}_i$ ($i = 1, \ldots, n$) is a vector with p values of 0 or 1, i.e., $\mathbf{y}_i \in \{0,1\}^p$; otherwise, it is a normal data collection for supervised learning, where $\mathbf{y} \in \{0,1\}$. Contrastively, as the label information is unavailable, $\mathbf{X} = \{\mathbf{x}_i\}_{i=1}^n \in \mathcal{R}^{n \times d}$ is used for unsupervised learning.

Since obtaining the label information is extremely expensive in reality, here we only discuss the unsupervised case of $\mathbf{X}$.

Learning to hash attempts to implicitly or explicitly derive a series of hash functions $\mathbf{H} = [\mathbf{h}_1, \mathbf{h}_2, \ldots, \mathbf{h}_m] \in \mathcal{R}_d^m$, so that the data objects $\mathbf{X}$ can be encoded as a binary representation such as $\mathbf{B} \in \{0,1\}^{n \times m}$, where m is the length of binary code, i.e., the number of hash bits, and $m < d$ usually. Formally, each hash function $\mathbf{h}$ is defined as

$$\mathbf{h} : \mathbf{x} \mapsto b \in \{0,1\}, \tag{1}$$

that is, each function $\mathbf{h}$ represents the data object $\mathbf{x}$ as a binary value. If m hash functions $\mathbf{h}_i$ ($i = 1, \ldots, m$) are applied, $\mathbf{x}$ can be further denoted as a binary vector $\mathbf{b} = [b_1, b_2, \ldots, b_m]$ by assembling straightly the m binary values generated by $\mathbf{h}_i$ ($i = 1, \ldots, m$). With this context, the hash codes of $\mathbf{X}$ can be shown as the binary representation $\mathbf{B} = \{\mathbf{b}_i\}_{i=1}^n \in \{0,1\}^{n \times m}$, where $\mathbf{b}_i$ is the binary vector of $\mathbf{x}_i$. For the convenience of discussion, hereafter the binary values within $\mathbf{B}$ are denoted as -1 and 1, i.e., $\mathbf{B} \in \{-1,1\}^{n \times m}$.

How to learning efficient and effective hashing functions is still an open and challenging issue. A naive strategy is to generate the hashing functions randomly [6]. Since this kind of generating manner has not taken the property of data into consideration, the quality of generated hash codes is relatively poor. Some shallow hashing techniques exploit the property of data to learn the hashing functions. However, the original features of data are hand-crafted, e.g., GIST or SIFT features of images, and have less semantic information [16]. To address this problem, deep hashing has been introduced. It adopts deep features to construct the hash functions non-linearly. As a result, the generated hash codes are more compact and powerful. Although many deep hashing methods have been developed by now, they pay more attention on the data with label information and less on the data without label information. In this work, we consider the similarities between the data objects as pseudo-labels to address the problem of the deficiency of label information.

3.2. Hashing Model Framework

In this work, we leverage a novel end-to-end deep hashing algorithm, called PLDH (pseudo-labels based deep hashing), for data without label information. The model framework of PLDH is shown as Figure 1. It mainly includes two stages: generating pseudo-labels and deriving hash codes. The first stage first applies a pre-training deep convolution neural network to capture deep features of data, and then calculates the similarity degrees between the data. According to the pairwise similarity degrees, the pseudo-labels of data can be further obtained. The second stage transforms the data into the hash codes via an additional hash layer, with the help of deep features captured by the same deep network. These two stages are interwined to derive the codes and the pseudo-labels in terms of errors estimated by a loss function alternatively.

For the convolution network in PLDH, we take VGGNet (Visual Geometry Group Network) as the architecture of a deep neural network to capture the deep features of data [26]. The architecture of VGGNet was initially designed for large-scale image classification, e.g., ImageNet [27]. Due to its high efficiency and effectiveness, VGGNet has been widely applied in a variety of domains since it was introduced [28]. The VGGNet architecture here is comprised of five convolution layers with different sizes and quantities of sub-layers, and three fully-connected layers. For our purpose, only the first two fully-connected layers are considered and the output of the second layer is used to represent deep features during the first stage of PLDH. In the second stage, the third fully-connected layer, consisting of 1000 units, is taken as the hash layer, whose output is binary.

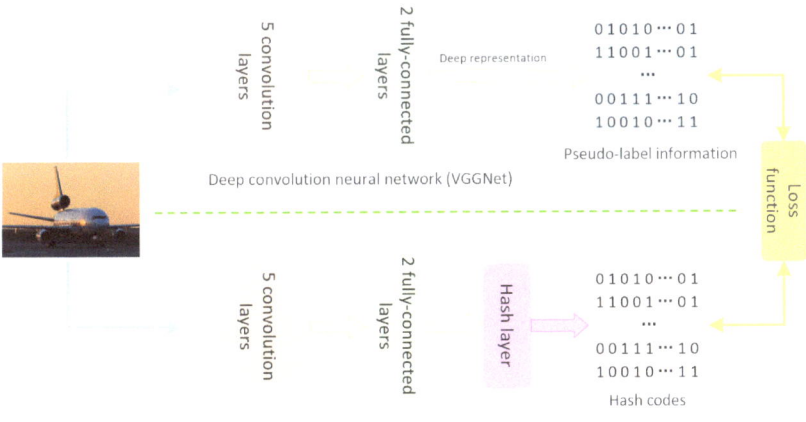

Figure 1. The model framework of PLDH.

3.2.1. Pseudo-Labels

As we know, deep learning is primitively devised for supervised learning, where data labels are available in advance. This implies that the predominant performance of deep learning is heavily dependent on the label information of data. Indeed, data labels are tagged by experienced experts in reality. Thus, they often embody some kind of semantic information and can help to make a decision in data analysis. Unfortunately, tagging data with label information is nontrivial and expensive in the real world, especially for large-scale data collections. To tackle the deficiency problem of label information, several supervised learning techniques utilize Euclidean distance or cosine distance between data objects to take the place of label information. However, the learning performance can be improved limitedly, because there is a large semantic gap between the true semantic of data and the made-up metric space with the hand-crafted features [16].

We exploit deep features of data to mimic the true semantic information, so that the semantic gap can be narrowed further. As a matter of fact, the deep features of graphs extracted by a pre-training deep convolution neural network embody rich semantic information [29]. To verify this statement, we conducted an experiment on two public image collections, i.e., CIFAR-10 and NUS-WIDE, to obtain the similarity degrees of images by a pre-training deep convolution neural network. Specifically, for each image collection, we first picked 1000 images out from the collection randomly, and then extracted deep features for each image by the VGG16 network trained on ImageNet in advance; that is,

$$\mathbf{F} = \{f_i\}_{i=1}^{1000}, \qquad (2)$$

where f_i is the deep features of the i-th image. Based on the deep features, the cosine similarity between two images can be estimated as follows.

$$sim(f_i, f_j) = \frac{f_i \cdot f_j}{\|f_i\|_2 \cdot \|f_j\|_2} \qquad (3)$$

The frequency of cosine similarities of images is given in Figure 2. Observing the frequency, we can find that the higher the pairwise similarity of images, the lower the corresponding frequency. This property is inherent consistent with the structural information of image collections, where the similar images are relatively rarely and sparse. The quantity of dissimilar images is far more than that of similar images in each collection.

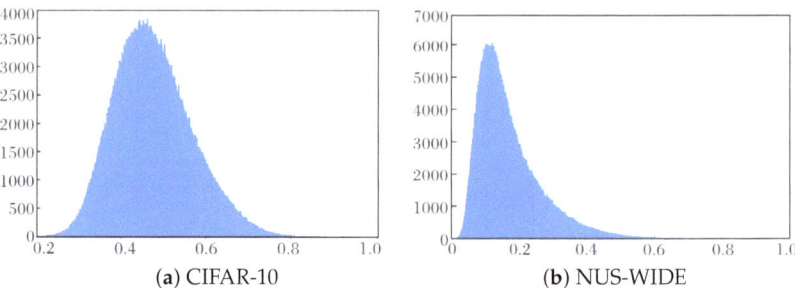

Figure 2. The frequency histogram of cosine similarities of images.

With the observation above, we construct semantic pseudo-labels based on the pairwise similarities of images. Let $sim(f_i, f_j)$ be the similarity of the i-th image to the j-th image. The similarity label, s_{ij}, of f_i to f_j is defined as

$$s_{ij} = \begin{cases} 1, & sim(f_i, f_j) > \alpha \\ 0, & otherwise \end{cases} \quad (4)$$

where α is a threshold value between 0 and 1, i.e., $\alpha \in [0,1]$. From this definition, an image is semantically similar to another one if their cosine similarity is larger than the given threshold; otherwise, they are not considered to be similar to each other. Thus, the semantic labels of images are represented as $S = \{s_{ij}\}_{i,j=1}^{n}$. Since these semantic labels are not true labels, they are pseudo-labels of images.

3.2.2. Deep Hashing

Once the pseudo-labels S are available, the hash codes of data can be derived by the estimation of maximum posterior probability. Let B be the binary representation, i.e., hash codes, of data X. The posterior probability of B with respect to S is

$$\begin{aligned} p(B \mid S) &\propto p(S \mid B)p(B) \\ &= \prod_{s_{ij} \in S} p(s_{ij} \mid b_i, b_j)p(b_i)p(b_j), \end{aligned} \quad (5)$$

where $p(S \mid B)$ is the likelihood function of S under the context of B given, while $p(B)$ is the distribution of prior probability. For $p(s_{ij} \mid b_i, b_j)$, it refers to the conditional probability of the pseudo-label s_{ij}, after the hash codes, b_i and b_j, of the i-th and the j-th data objects are derived. Assume that Φ_{ij} is the inner product of b_i and b_j, i.e.,

$$\Phi_{ij} = \frac{1}{2}\langle b_i, b_j \rangle = \frac{1}{2}b_i^T b_j. \quad (6)$$

The conditional probability function $p(s_{ij} \mid b_i, b_j)$ can be calculated as the following equation.

$$p(s_{ij} \mid b_i, b_j) = \begin{cases} \sigma(\Phi_{ij}), & s_{ij} = 1 \\ 1 - \sigma(\Phi_{ij}), & s_{ij} = 0 \end{cases} \quad (7)$$

where $\sigma(\cdot)$ is an active function. For convenience, here we take Sigmoid function as the active function, i.e.,

$$\sigma(\Phi_{ij}) = (1 + e^{-\Phi_{ij}})^{-1}. \quad (8)$$

Equation (7) is capable of representing the inherent property of data. Let $D_H(b_i, b_j)$ be the Hamming distance of binary codes, b_i and b_j, i.e.,

$$dist_H(b_i, b_j) = \frac{1}{2}(k - b_i^T b_j), \quad (9)$$

where k is the length of binary codes. According to the definition of Equation (7), we know the smaller the Hamming distance $dist_H(b_i, b_j)$, the larger the inner product $b_i^T b_j$, and the larger the conditional probability $p(1 \mid b_i, b_j)$. This indicates that the data objects corresponding to b_i and b_j are more similar to each other than others. On the other hand, a far distance $dist_H(b_i, b_j)$ between b_i and b_j implies that $p(0 \mid b_i, b_j)$ is large, resulting in them being highly dissimilar.

Owing to the semantic property of S, the loss function of PLDH can be defined to maximize the likelihood function of the conditional probability. Formally, it is represented as

$$\min_B \quad L = -\frac{1}{|S|}\Sigma_{s_{ij}\in S}\ln p(s_{ij} \mid b_i, b_j)$$
$$= -\frac{1}{|S|}\Sigma_{s_{ij}\in S}(s_{ij}\Phi_{ij} - \ln(1+e^{\Phi_{ij}})) \quad (10)$$
$$s.t. \quad b_i, b_j \in \{-1,1\}^k, i,j = 1,2,\ldots,n.$$

where $|S|$ denotes the total number of pairwise similarities. Solving straightforwardly the optimization problem of Equation (10) is NP-hard, because its constraint condition is a discrete one; that is, b_i only involves binary values. To cope with this issue, a frequently-used strategy is to relax the discrete constraint into a continuous one. Specifically, we introduce an auxiliary variable u_i for the binary code b_i, i.e., $u_i = b_i$. Hence, the optimization problem of Equation (10) can be transformed as the following formulation.

$$\min_{B,U} \quad L = -\frac{1}{|S|}\Sigma_{s_{ij}\in S}(s_{ij}\Phi_{ij} - \ln(1+e^{\Phi_{ij}})) + \eta\frac{1}{|B|}\Sigma_{i=1}^n \|u_i - b_i\|_2^2$$
$$s.t. \quad \Phi_{ij} = \frac{1}{2}u_i^T u_j. \quad (11)$$

where $u_i \in \mathcal{R}^k$, η is a Lagrange operator, and $|B|$ is the total number of binary codes. For the second penalty term in Equation (11), it aims to narrow the difference of the discrete space to its corresponding continuous one as much as possible.

3.3. Optimization Analysis

For the optimization problem above, it can be solved by an alternative way. Let Θ be the hyper-parameters of deep convolution neural network (i.e., VGGNet) and $F(x_i; \Theta)$ be the output of the last fully-connected layer of VGGNet. The output u_i of hash layer for x_i can be represented as

$$u_i = W^T F(x_i; \Theta) + v, \quad (12)$$

where $W \in \mathcal{R}^{4096 \times k}$ is the weighted matrix of hash layer, and $v \in \mathcal{R}^{k \times 1}$ is a bias. Substituting u_i in Equation (11) with Equation (12), we have the following equivalent form of Equation (11).

$$\min_{B,\Theta,W,v} \quad L = -\frac{1}{|S|}\Sigma_{s_{ij}\in S}(s_{ij}\Phi_{ij} - \ln(1+e^{\Phi_{ij}})) + \eta\frac{1}{|B|}\Sigma_{i=1}^n \|W^T F(x_i;\Theta) + v - b_i\|_2^2. \quad (13)$$

We can iteratively derive the optimization values of B, Θ, W and v alternatively; that is, solving one of them, while fixing others. To be specific, the iteration process of the optimization problem consists of the following steps.

- **Updating B, as Θ, W and v fixed.** In this case, each hash code $b_i \in B$ can be easily obtained by a soft-threshold function. For example, if the sign function is adopted, b_i can be derived as follows.

$$b_i = sgn(W^T F(x_i; \Theta) + v), \quad (14)$$

where $sgn(x)$ is the sign function. If $x > 0$, $sgn(x) = 1$; otherwise, $sgn(x) = 0$.

- **Updating Θ, W and v, as B fixed.** We can apply the strategy of back-propagation to estimate the optimal values as B is fixed. Concretely, let the gradients of Equation (13) with respect to the parameters Θ, W and v, respectively, be zero, and we have the following equations hold.

$$\frac{\partial L}{\partial F(x_i; \Theta)} = W \frac{\partial L}{\partial u_i}, \quad (15)$$

$$\frac{\partial L}{\partial W} = F(x_i; \Theta)(\frac{\partial L}{\partial u_i})^{\mathrm{T}}, \qquad (16)$$

$$\frac{\partial L}{\partial v} = \frac{\partial L}{\partial u_i}, \qquad (17)$$

where

$$\frac{\partial L}{\partial u_i} = \frac{1}{2|S|}\Sigma_{j:s_{ij}\in S}(\sigma(\Phi_{ij}) - s_{ij})u_j + \frac{1}{2|S|}\Sigma_{j:s_{ji}\in S}(\sigma(\Phi_{ji}) - s_{ji})u_j + \eta\frac{2}{|B|}(u_i - b_i). \qquad (18)$$

Based on the aforementioned discussion, the implementation details of PLDH are given as follows (Algorithm 1).

Algorithm 1 PLDH: Pesudo-Labels based Deep Hashing

Input: A data collection $X = \{x_i\}_{i=1}^n$, the code length k, and the hyper-parameter η.
Output: The hash codes B of X.
1: Take the output of the pre-training VGGNet as deep features $F = \{f_i\}_{i=1}^n$;
2: Obtain the pseudo-labels $S = \{s_{ij}\}_{i,j=1}^n$ by virtue of Equations (3) and (4);
3: Initialize Θ with the same parameters of the pre-trained VGGNet;
4: Initialize W and v with random values in $[-\alpha, \alpha]$, where $\alpha = 1/64$;
    Repeat
5:    Select a mini-batch training data $\{x_i\}_{i=1}^t$ ($t \ll n$) from X;
6:    Obtain $\{F(x_i; \Theta)\}_{i=1}^t$ by the back-propagation strategy;
7:    Calculate $\{u_i\}_{i=1}^n$ via Equation (12);
8:    Calculate $\{b_i\}_{i=1}^n$ via Equation (14);
9:    Update W, v and Θ via Equations (15)–(17), respectively;
    Until iteration steps reach a given threshold
10: Return B as the hash codes of X.

---

4. Results

To validate the effectiveness of PLDH, we conducted a series of comparison experiments with eight popular hashing algorithms on two public data collections. In this section, we will discuss the experimental results.

4.1. Experimental Settings

The comparison experiments were conducted on two frequently used benchmark data collections, i.e., CIFAR-10 and NUS-WIDE. The CIFAR data collection contains 60,000 colorful images, each with the size of 32×32 pixels. These images are tagged with ten class labels, such as airplane, truck, ship, car, horse, dog, cat, frog, deer and bird. Each class label involves 6000 colorful images. For each class, 1000 images were randomly picked as queries, and 500 images were taken as training data. NUS-WIDE comprises 269,648 images collected from Flickr, where each image was associated to multiple class labels. There are eighty-one class labels totally, including cars, dogs, airports, birds and earthquake. In the experiments, only the images associated with top-10 frequently-used class labels were considered, and 5000 images were randomly selected as the query, while 10,500 images were taken as training data.

To verify the competitive performance of PLDH, eight popular hashing algorithms were adopted in the comparison experiments. The baselines cover both shallow hashing, such as LSH, SH, ITQ and SpH; and deep hashing, such as DeepBit, SGH, SSDH and DistillHash. They stand for different hash learning techniques. To make a fair comparison, the shallow hashing algorithms were trained on deep features, which were the outputs of the last layer of VGGNet, rather than the original features. Following the routine in the literature, we treated the similarities of images calculated according to their class labels as the ground-truth; that is, two images were considered to be similar, if they were tagged with the same labels. Otherwise, they were dissimilar to each other.

The evaluation protocol used to compare the baselines in our experiments was mean average precision (mAP), which is a widely-used measurement to evaluate the retrieval performance of hashing techniques in information retrieval. Let $Q = \{q_i\}_{i=1}^t$ be a set of query. For each query $q \in Q$, its average precision in retrieval is represented as

$$AP(q) = \frac{\sum_{r=1}^{R} Pre_q(r)\delta(\ell_r = \ell_q)}{\sum_{r=1}^{R} \delta(\ell_r = \ell_q)}, \quad (19)$$

where R is the total number of the retrieval results for the query q, and $Pre_q(r)$ is the retrieval precision for the top r results. ℓ_i refers to the data label of the i-th retrieval result. $\delta(\cdot)$ is an indication function, where $\delta(\ell_r = \ell_q) = 1$ if the r-th retrieval result is truly similar to the query q; otherwise, $\delta(\ell_r = \ell_q) = 0$, that is, they have different class labels. Based on this definition, the mean average precision of the set Q of queries is

$$mAP(Q) = \frac{1}{|Q|} \sum_{q \in Q} AP(q). \quad (20)$$

The proposed hashing algorithm is implemented under the framework of PyTorch. To be specific, the optimizer of PLDH is the mini-batch stochastic gradient descent. During the experiments, the size of batch, the momentum and the weight decay of the optimizer were set to 32, 0.9 and 0.0005, respectively. Additionally, the learning rate on CIFAR-10 and NUS-WIDE was fixed at 0.0003 and 0001, respectively, after the cross-validation manner was performed. All experiments were carried out under the platform of Ubuntu Server 16.04, with Intel i7 8700@3.20GHz CPU, Nvidia GTX 1060 GPU and 32GB main memory.

4.2. Experimental Results

mAP is a widely-used evaluation protocol in information retrieval. We also adopted this evaluation protocol to measure the retrieval performance of PLDH to the baselines. Table 1 provides the comparison results of mAP scores of the baselines with different quantities of hash bits, where the bold values are the best ones among the hashing techniques.

Table 1. The mAP comparison of PLDH to the baselines with different numbers of hash bits.

	CIFAR-10				NUS-WIDE			
	16 bits	32 bits	64 bits	128 bits	16 bits	32 bits	64 bits	128 bits
LSH [6]	0.132	0.158	0.167	0.179	0.432	0.441	0.443	0.482
SH [7]	0.161	0.158	0.151	0.154	0.446	0.454	0.493	0.500
SpH [9]	0.144	0.167	0.178	0.184	0.453	0.460	0.496	0.513
ITQ [8]	0.194	0.209	0.215	0.219	0.528	0.532	0.532	0.542
DeepBit [11]	0.220	0.241	0.252	0.253	0.454	0.463	0.476	0.492
SGH [12]	0.180	0.183	0.189	0.190	0.494	0.483	0.487	0.498
SSDH [14]	0.257	0.256	0.259	0.260	0.623	0.630	0.632	0.649
DistillHash [13]	0.284	0.285	0.287	0.290	0.667	0.675	0.677	0.675
PLDH	**0.459**	**0.495**	**0.509**	**0.500**	**0.685**	**0.701**	**0.702**	**0.703**

From the experimental results in Table 1, one can observe that PLDH has achieved competitive performance in comparing the baselines on these two benchmark image collections. For example, PLDH boosted 28.15% and 16.42% retrieval performance on CIFAR-10 and NUS-WIDE, respectively, in comparing to ITQ, which is the best shallow hashing algorithms. Contrastively, for DistillHash, the best deep hashing algorithms, the retrieval performance was improved 20.43% and 2.42% on CIFAR-10 and NUS-WIDE, respectively, by the proposed hashing method.

For the shallow hashing techniques, the data-dependent algorithms, i.e., ITQ, SH and SpH, achieved better retrieval precision than LSH, which is independent of training data. This fact, however, is consistent with our knowledge, because the data-dependent algorithms can effectively capture the inherent properties of data. It should be pointed out that the performance of the shallow hashing techniques was better than that of deep ones in some cases. For instance, ITQ had higher precision than SGH on these image collections. The underlying reason is that the shallow hashing models were constructed on deep features extracted by VGGNet. Additionally, the performance of deep hashing models heavily rely on label information. The absence of label information may degrade the retrieval precision of deep hashing models, notwithstanding the pseudo-labels that are available.

Generally, SSDH, DistillHash and PLDH achieved comparable performance in comparing the shallow hashing techniques, because they were not only constructed on deep features, but also with the help of semantic information, which is derived from the similarities of images. Note that SSDH also adopted the analogical strategy to derive semantic labels on the similarities of data. However, PLDH involved less hyper-parameters and did not require to calculate the cosine similarities, making it more robust and efficient. Additionally, their learning objective functions were also different, where the objective functions of SSDH and PLDH were the minimum of the mean square errors of similarity matrix and the maximum of the likelihood function of similarity matrix, respectively. Moreover, both SSDH and DistillHash did not take the quantization loss into account during the learning stage. In fact, the quantization loss can further improve the quality of hash codes.

4.3. Ablation Analysis

As discussed above, there are two hyper-parameters, i.e., α and η, for PLDH, where the threshold α is used to derive the pseudo-labels. The Lagrange operator η controls the quantization loss during the hash learning stage. To test how much effect they might have brought to PLDH, we carried out additional experiments with different values of α and η on the benchmark data collections.

Figure 3 illustrates the mAP scores of PLDH with different values of the threshold α, when η was fixed. According to the mAP scores in Figure 3, one can observe that the optimization threshold values of α were 0.6 and 0.2 for CIFAR-10 and NUS-WIDE, respectively, albeit the length of hash codes derived by PLDH was different. This is consistent with the distributions of data; that is, the quantities of the pairwise similarities of images are far less than those of dissimilar ones (see Figure 2).

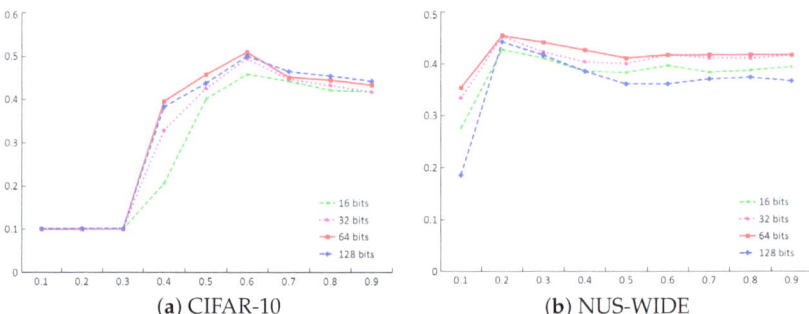

(a) CIFAR-10   (b) NUS-WIDE

Figure 3. The mAP scores of PLDH with different α values.

Figure 4 shows the mAP curves of PLDH with different values of the operator η, when the threshold α was fixed (α was set to 0.6 for CIFAR-10 and 0.2 for NUS-WIDE, respectively). From the experimental results, we know that as the length of hash codes increases, the optimal value of η also turns out to be large. For example, the optimal values of η were 5, 5, 10 and 25 on CIFAR-10, if the hash codes contained 16, 32, 64 and 128 hash bits, respectively. Similar cases can be found for the data collection of NUS-WIDE. Another observation is that the performance of the model was relatively poor if the quantization loss was not considered, i.e., $\eta = 0$. This fact implies that the quantization loss may be beneficial to the performance of the deep model, if it is taken into account during the training stage.

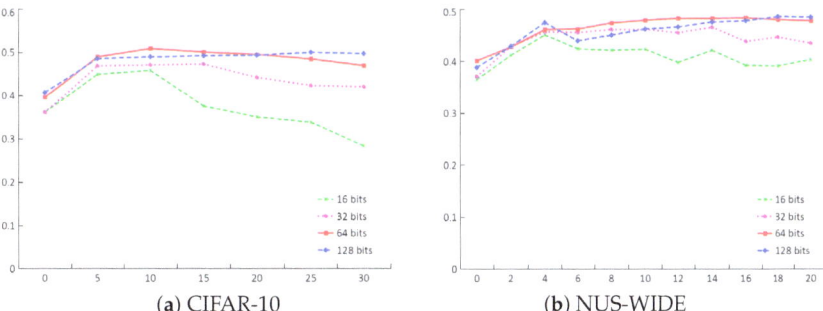

Figure 4. The mAP scores of PLDH with different η values.

5. Conclusions

In this work, we proposed a novel end-to-end deep hashing method, called PLDH, for large-scale data without label information. It constructs pseudo-labels for deep hashing by using the inherent semantic property of data, namely the pairwise similarities of data calculated from deep features, to remedy the absence of label information. Compared to unsupervised hashing models, PLDH takes the semantic information of data into account, so that the similarities of data can be preserved, making the generated hashing codes with higher quality. To validate the effectiveness of PLDH, we conducted a series of experiments on two public benchmark image collections. The experimental results show the superiority of PLDH in comparison to the state-of-the-art hashing models. Since deep features are vital to the pseudo-labels, we will adopt different deep learning architectures with different layers to obtain semantic features in our future work.

Before obtaining the pseudo-labels, the similarities among data should be calculated in advance. This requires a large amount of storage space, resulting in PLDH not being very friendly to particularly large-scale data. Thus, our future work will concentrate on addressing this issue by sampling techniques. Moreover, apart from VGG, there are many architectures, e.g., AlexNet, ResNet and Transformer, developed in deep learning, where the Transformer one has received extraordinary popularity recently. So, we will adopt the Transformer architecture as the backbone of PLDH to further improve its performance. Meanwhile, we will also testify the retrieval performance of PLDH on more large-scale image collections.

Author Contributions: Conceptualization, H.L., M.Y. and Z.Z.; methodology, Z.W. and X.Z.; software, Q.L.; validation, H.L., L.Z. and Z.Z.; formal analysis, H.L. and M.Y.; investigation, L.Z.; resources, Z.W.; data curation, Z.W.; writing—original draft preparation, H.L.; writing—review and editing, H.L. and M.Y.; visualization, Q.L.; supervision, X.Z.; project administration, Q.L.; funding acquisition, H.L., X.Z. and Z.Z. All authors have read and agreed to the published version of the manuscript.

Funding: This work was partially funded by the Natural Science Foundation (NSF) of China (No. 61976195, 62271321, 62272419, 61976196, 62002226) and the Natural Science Foundation of Zhejiang Province (No. LZ23F020003, LR23F020001, LZ22F020010), Outstanding Talents of "Ten Thousand Talents Plan" in Zhejiang Province (No. 2018R51001), and the Science and Technology Plan Project in Basic Public Welfare class of Shaoxing city (No.2022A11002).

Data Availability Statement: Not applicable.

Conflicts of Interest: The authors declare no conflict of interest.

References

1. Manning, C.; Raghavan, P.; Schütze, H. *Introduction to Information Retrieval*; Cambridge University Press: Cambridge, UK, 2008.
2. Liu, H.; Li, X.; Zhang S.; Tian, Q. Adaptive hashing with sparse matrix factorization. *IEEE Trans. Neural Netw. Learn. Syst.* **2020**, *31*, 4318–4329. [CrossRef] [PubMed]
3. Chen, J.; Zhu, X.; Liu, H. A mutual neighbor-based clustering method and its medical applications. *Comput. Biol. Med.* **2022**, *150*, 106184. [CrossRef]
4. Liu, H.; Zhou, W.; Zhang, H.; Li, G.; Zhang, S.; Li, X. Bit Reduction for Locality-Sensitive Hashing. *IEEE Trans. Neural Netw. Learn. Syst.* **2023**, 1–12. [CrossRef] [PubMed]
5. Wang, J.; Zhang, T.; Song, J.; Sebe N.; Shen, H.T. A survey on learning to hash. *IEEE Trans. Pattern Anal. Mach. Intell.* **2018**, *40*, 769–790. [CrossRef] [PubMed]
6. Jafari, O.; Maurya, P.; Nagarkar, P.; Islam, K.M.; Crushev, C. A survey on locality sensitive hashing algorithms and their applications. *arXiv* **2021**, arXiv:2102.08942.
7. Weiss, Y.; Torralba, A.; Fergus, R. Spectral hashing. In Proceedings of the Advances in Neural Information Processing Systems 21 (NIPS 2008), Vancouver, BC, Canada, 8–11 December 2008; pp. 1753–1760.
8. Gong, Y.C.; Lazebnic, S. Iterative Quantization: A procrustean approach to learning binary codes. In Proceedings of the IEEE Conference on Computer Vision and Pattern Recognition (CVPR2011), Washington, DC, USA, 20–25 June 2011; pp. 817–824.
9. Heo, J.-P.; Lee, Y.; He, J.; Chang, S.-F.; Yoon, S.-E. Spherical hashing. In Proceedings of the IEEE Conference on Computer Vision and Pattern Recognition (CVPR2012), Washington, DC, USA, 16–21 June 2012; pp. 2957–2964.
10. Luo, X.; Wang, H.; Wu, D.; Chen, C.; Deng, M.; Huang, J.; Hua, X. A survey on deep hashing methods. *ACM Trans. Knowl. Discov. Data* **2023**, *17*, 50. [CrossRef]
11. Lin, K.; Lu, J.; Chen, C.-S.; Zhou, J.; Sun, M.-T. Unsupervised deep learning of compact binary descriptors. *IEEE Trans. Pattern Analy. Mach. Intell.* **2019**, *41*, 1501–1514. [CrossRef] [PubMed]
12. Dai, B.; Guo, R.; Kumar, S.; He, N.; Song, L. Stochastic generative hashing. In Proceedings of the International Conference om Machine Learning (ICML2017), Sydney, Australia, 6–11 August 2017; pp. 913–922.
13. Yang, E.; Liu, T.; Deng, C.; Liu, W.; Tao, D. DistillHash: Unsupervised deep hashing by distilling data pairs. In Proceedings of the IEEE/CVF Conference on Computer Vision and Pattern Recognition 2019 (CVPR2019), Long Beach, CA, USA, 16–17 June 2019; pp. 2941–2950.
14. Yang, E.; Deng, C.; Liu, T.; Liu, W.; Tao, D. Semantic structure-based unsupervised deep hashing. In Proceedings of the 27th International Joint Conference on Artificial Intelligence 2018 (IJCAI2018), Stockholm, Sweden, 13–19 July 2018; pp. 1064–1070.
15. Zhou, Z.; Liu, H.; Lou, J.; Chen, X. Locality sensitive hashing with bit selection. *Appl. Intell.* **2022**, *52*, 14724–14738. [CrossRef]
16. Malik, S.; Amin, J.; Sharif, M.; Yasmin, M.; Kadry, S.; Anjum S. Fractured elbow classification using hand-crafted and deep feature fusion and selection based on whale optimization approach. *Mathematics* **2022**, *10*, 3291. [CrossRef]
17. Liu, W.; Wang, J.; Ji, R.; Jiang, Y.-G.; Chang, S.-F. Supervised hashing with kernels. In Proceedings of the 2012 IEEE Conference on Computer Vision and Pattern Recognition, Providence, RI, USA, 16–21 June 2012; pp. 2074–2081.
18. Lin, G.; Shen, C.; Shi Q.; Hengel, A.; Suter D. Fast supervised hashing with decision trees for high-dimensional data. In Proceedings of the IEEE Conference on Computer Vision and Pattern Recognition 2014, Washington, DC, USA, 23–28 June 2014; pp. 1971–1978.
19. Gui, J.; Liu, T.; Sun, Z.; Tao, D.; Tan, T. Fast supervised discrete hashing. *IEEE Tran. Pattern Anal. Mach. Intell.* **2018**, *40*, 490–496. [CrossRef] [PubMed]
20. Xia, R.; Pan, Y.; Lai, H.; Liu, C.; Yan, S. Supervised hashing for image retrieval via image representation learning. In Proceedings of the 28th AAAI Conference Artificial Intelligence (AAA14), Quebec City, QC, Canada, 27–31 July 2014; pp. 2156–2162.
21. Li, W.-J.; Wang, S.; Kang, W.-C. Feature learning based deep supervised hashing with pairwise labels. In Proceedings of the 25th International Joint Conference on Artificial Intelligence (IJCAI16), New York, NY, USA, 9–15 July 2016; pp. 1711–1717.
22. Li, Q.; Sun, Z.; He, R.; Tan, T. Deep supervised discrete hashing. In Proceedings of the Advances in Neural Information Processing Systems 30 (NIPS 2017), Long Beach, CA, USA, 4–9 December 2017; pp. 2479–2488.
23. Ma, Y.; Li, Q.; Shi, X.; Guo, Z. Unsupervised deep pairwise hashing. *Electronics* **2022**, *11*, 744. [CrossRef]
24. Luo, X.; Ma, Z.; Cheng, W.; Deng, M. Improve deep unsupervised hashing via structural and intrinsic similarity learning. *IEEE Signal Process. Lett.* **2022**, *29*, 602–606. [CrossRef]
25. Sun, Y.; Ye, Y.; Li, X.; Feng, S.; Zhang, B.; Kang, J.; Dai, K. Unsupervised deep hashing through learning soft pseudo label for remote sensing image retrieval. *Knowl.-Based Syst.* **2022**, *239*, 107807. [CrossRef]
26. Simonyan, K.; Zisserman, A. Very deep convolutional networks for large-scale image recognition. In Proceedings of the 3rd International Conference on Learning Representations, ICLR 2015, San Diego, CA, USA, 7–9 May 2015; pp. 1–14.
27. Russakovsky, O.; Deng, J.; Su, H.; Krause, J.; Satheesh, S.; Ma, S.; Huang, Z.; Karpathy, A.; Khosla, A.; Bernstein, M.; et al. ImageNet large scale visual recognition challenge. *Int. J. Comput. Vis.* **2015**, *115*, 211–252. [CrossRef]

28. Tian, C.; Zhang, Y.; Zuo, W.; Lin, C.-W.; Zhang, D.; Yuan, Y. A Heterogeneous Group CNN for Image Super-Resolution. *IEEE Trans. Neural Netw. Learn. Syst.* **2023**, *115*, 1–13. [CrossRef]
29. Girshick, R.; Donahue, J.; Darrell, T.; Malik, J. Rich feature hierarchies for accurate object detection and semantic segmentation. In Proceedings of the 2014 IEEE Conference on Computer Vision and Pattern Recognition (CVPR14), Columbus, OH, USA, 23–28 June 2014; pp. 580–587.

Disclaimer/Publisher's Note: The statements, opinions and data contained in all publications are solely those of the individual author(s) and contributor(s) and not of MDPI and/or the editor(s). MDPI and/or the editor(s) disclaim responsibility for any injury to people or property resulting from any ideas, methods, instructions or products referred to in the content.

Article

A Kind of Water Surface Multi-Scale Object Detection Method Based on Improved YOLOv5 Network

Zhongli Ma, Yi Wan, Jiajia Liu *, Ruojin An and Lili Wu

College of Automation, Chengdu University of Information Technology, Chengdu 610103, China; mazl@cuit.edu.cn (Z.M.); wy17062920@163.com (Y.W.); an1587601@163.com (R.A.); 15082386704@163.com (L.W.)
* Correspondence: liujj@cuit.edu.cn

Abstract: Visual-based object detection systems are essential components of intelligent equipment for water surface environments. The diversity of water surface target types, uneven distribution of sizes, and difficulties in dataset construction pose significant challenges for water surface object detection. This article proposes an improved YOLOv5 target detection method to address the characteristics of diverse types, large quantities, and multiple scales of actual water surface targets. The improved YOLOv5 model optimizes the extraction of bounding boxes using K-means++ to obtain a broader distribution of predefined bounding boxes, thereby enhancing the detection accuracy for multi-scale targets. We introduce the GAMAttention mechanism into the backbone network of the model to alleviate the significant performance difference between large and small targets caused by their multi-scale nature. The spatial pyramid pooling module in the backbone network is replaced to enhance the perception ability of the model in segmenting targets of different scales. Finally, the Focal loss classification loss function is incorporated to address the issues of overfitting and poor accuracy caused by imbalanced class distribution in the training data. We conduct comparative tests on a self-constructed dataset comprising ten categories of water surface targets using four algorithms: Faster R-CNN, YOLOv4, YOLOv5, and the proposed improved YOLOv5. The experimental results demonstrate that the improved model achieves the best detection accuracy, with an 8% improvement in mAP@0.5 compared to the original YOLOv5 in multi-scale water surface object detection.

Keywords: surface target detection; YOLOv5; multi-scale targets; spatial pyramid pooling; attention mechanism

MSC: 68T07

Citation: Ma, Z.; Wan, Y.; Liu, J.; An, R.; Wu, L. A Kind of Water Surface Multi-Scale Object Detection Method Based on Improved YOLOv5 Network. *Mathematics* **2023**, *11*, 2936. https://doi.org/10.3390/math11132936

Academic Editors: Huawen Liu, Chengyuan Zhang, Weiren Yu and Chunwei Tian

Received: 2 June 2023
Revised: 26 June 2023
Accepted: 28 June 2023
Published: 30 June 2023

Copyright: © 2023 by the authors. Licensee MDPI, Basel, Switzerland. This article is an open access article distributed under the terms and conditions of the Creative Commons Attribution (CC BY) license (https://creativecommons.org/licenses/by/4.0/).

1. Introduction

Visual-based intelligent equipment for water surface object detection plays a crucial role in regulating water environments, ensuring maritime safety, executing military tasks, conducting marine resource exploration, and monitoring unmanned islands and reefs [1,2]. The diversity of water surface target types, uneven distribution of target sizes, and the difficulties in constructing comprehensive datasets significantly increase the challenges associated with water surface object detection. The current multi-scale object detection suffers from uneven detection accuracy, making it a challenging task to improve the overall performance of the current object detector [3].

In 2012, AlexNet [4] achieved breakthrough results in large-scale image classification with the adoption of Convolutional Neural Networks (CNNs) on the ImageNet [5] dataset, which ignited the popularity of deep learning techniques. In 2013, Zuo Jianjun et al. [6] used the background subtraction method for the detection of floating objects on water surfaces. The method involved first establishing a background image without any objects and then subtracting the background image from the input image to detect the objects. In 2016, Xu Peng [7] investigated various motion detection methods, including frame differencing, Gaussian mixture background model, and optical flow. They determined that combining Gaussian differencing with three-frame differencing and utilizing mathematical morphology achieved effective detection of moving objects on the water surface. Wang Fangchao [8] introduced a rapid detection method for water surface ships based on geometric features. They employed an improved Sobel algorithm to enhance the contrast of ships at a coarse resolution. In 2018, Tang Lidan [9] addressed the issue of low detection accuracy for small objects in the Faster R-CNN algorithm. They proposed a detection method that combined the ResNet and DenseNet fusion backbone networks with a recurrent feature pyramid, achieving effective detection of water surface targets. In 2019, Liu Hehe [10] designed a network structure for water surface object detection using the SSD algorithm and made improvements to it. However, the aforementioned methods generally suffer from slow detection speeds. In 2020, Liang Yuexiang [11] presented a deep convolutional neural network-based fine-grained detection method using YOLOv3-tiny. This method could assist ship operators in identifying water surface targets. In 2022, Wang [12] proposed the SPMYOLOv3 algorithm for detecting water surface debris. This algorithm addresses the challenges of varying object shapes and sizes, as well as the difficulty in distinguishing objects from the background in water surface debris detection. The improved algorithm achieves a detection accuracy of 73.32% on a water surface debris dataset. In 2022, Wang Zhiguo [13] proposed an improved YOLOv4 method for water surface object detection. They validated the algorithm on a self-constructed dataset, achieving a detection accuracy of 89.86%. However, due to the limited size of the dataset, further improvements are required to enhance the model's accuracy and robustness.

This study focuses on the demand for accurate multi-scale object detection on water surfaces and combines the strengths and weaknesses of current mainstream object detection algorithms. YOLOv5, which exhibits outstanding performance in terms of speed and detection accuracy, was chosen as the base algorithm [14–16]. However, it was observed that the basic YOLOv5 model suffered from issues such as missed detection and false positives for small objects, as well as overfitting and low accuracy due to imbalanced sample classification. To address these problems, this paper conducts research on the improvement of the YOLOv5 network architecture. In response to the demand for improved accuracy in multi-scale object detection on water surfaces, this study focuses on the research and improvement of the YOLOv5 network model structure. The specific optimization methods employed in this research are described as follows. Firstly, the optimization of object bounding boxes is performed using the K-means++ algorithm. This approach effectively addresses classification errors by refining the localization accuracy of detected objects. Secondly, attention mechanisms are integrated into the backbone network architecture. This inclusion enhances the learning capacity of the object detection network, enabling it to effectively detect and classify multi-scale targets present on water surfaces. Furthermore, the SPPF (Spatial Pyramid Pooling with FPN) layer in the backbone network is enhanced. This modification facilitates faster and stronger learning capabilities of the network for detecting multi-scale targets on water surfaces. To address the issue of imbalanced sample distribution, the loss function is optimized by introducing Focal loss [17]. This adaptation allows for better handling of the uneven distribution of positive and negative samples, thereby improving the model's ability to detect multi-scale water surface objects. By incorporating these enhancements, the proposed model exhibits significant improvements in detecting multi-scale targets on water surfaces. The optimizations contribute to increased detection accuracy, making the model better suited for real-world scenarios involving multi-scale water surface objects. Experimental results demonstrate that the improved YOLOv5 model significantly enhances the detection accuracy and recognition precision of multi-scale water surface targets.

2. Related Work

2.1. YOLOv5 Model Analysis

The model structure of YOLOv5 is shown in Figure 1.

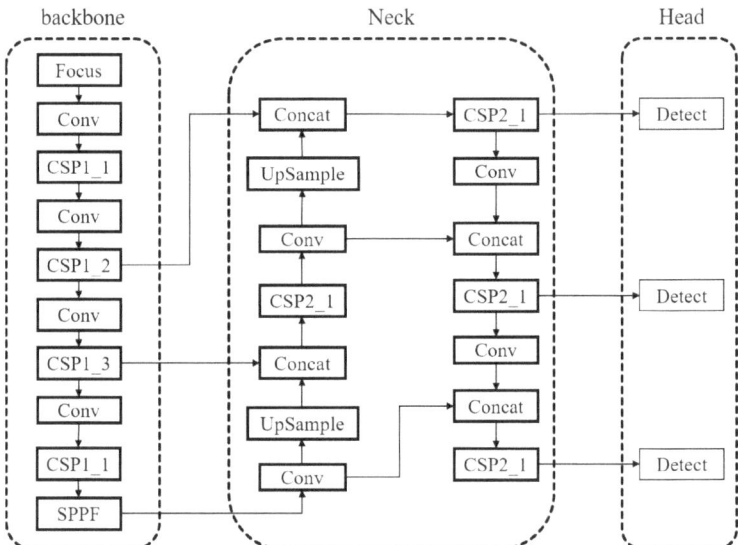

Figure 1. Network structure diagram of YOLO V5.

Model Key Features:
1. Mosaic Data Augmentation: In the training phase, the model utilizes Mosaic data augmentation, which greatly improves the training speed of the network [18,19].
2. Focus Structure and CSPNet-inspired Backbone: The model employs the Focus structure in the backbone network and draws inspiration from the CSPNet [20] architecture. It uses the ReLU activation function [21], which enhances the gradient flow within the network, improves computational speed, and facilitates better extraction of depth information.
3. Feature Fusion and Contextual Information: The model incorporates the "FPN+PAN" structure in the neck layer for feature fusion, allowing for repeated feature extraction. The SPPF module is utilized to effectively capture contextual image features [22,23].
4. GIOU loss and Anchor-based Detection: The YOLOv5 model employs the GIOU loss as the loss function at the output end. It utilizes anchor boxes to predict target boxes [24].

2.2. GAMAttention Attention Mechanism

Filtering out crucial features related to the target objects within the entire feature space is crucial for improving the accuracy of object detection [25]. Inspired by the Convolutional Block Attention Module (CBAM) [26], the GAMAttention attention mechanism [27] enhances the global interaction feature without significant information loss, thereby improving the detection accuracy of the model. The GAMAttention structure consists of two modules: channel attention and spatial attention, as shown in Figure 2.

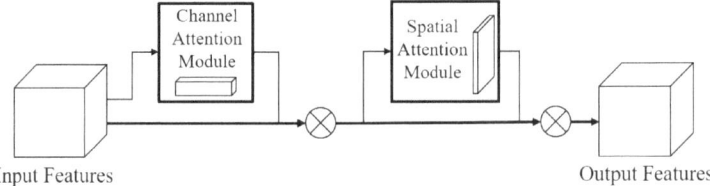

Figure 2. GAMAttention network structure diagram.

The GAM (Global Attention with Multi-scale attention) structure achieves global perception and multi-scale attention through two key components.

Firstly, the global perception module is used to capture the global contextual information of the image. It employs global average pooling and fully connected layers to enable global perception over the entire feature map, generating a global context description.

Secondly, the multi-scale attention module is designed to enhance the focus on objects at different scales. This module utilizes multiple parallel attention branches to independently apply attention weights to feature maps at different scales. Each branch adjusts the scale of the feature map through convolutional and pooling operations and calculates the corresponding attention weights. Subsequently, the feature maps at different scales are multiplied by their corresponding attention weights, resulting in weighted feature representations. This enables the model to better discriminate objects at different scales and enhance the detection capability for small objects.

2.3. SPPFCSPC Spatial Pyramid Pooling Module

In the YOLOv5-6.0 network model, the spatial pyramid pooling is implemented using the SPPF module. The SPPF module is an evolution of the Spatial Pyramid Pooling (SPP) module [28] and enables adaptive-sized output. The SPPF module, as depicted in Figure 3, allows for capturing features at multiple scales and achieving better contextual information representation.

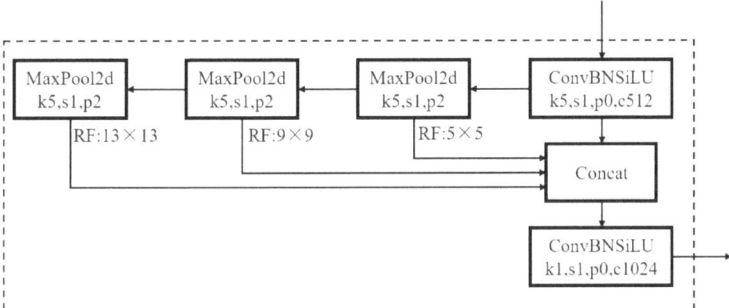

Figure 3. Network structure diagram of SPPF.

The Spatial Pyramid Pooling Fully Connected Spatial Pyramid Convolution (SPPFC-SPC) module is designed based on the Spatial Pyramid Pooling Connected Spatial Pyramid Convolution (SPPCSPC) module and incorporates the design principles of the SPPF module. It is an improved approach that provides better performance. The structure of the SPPFCSPC module is illustrated in Figure 4.

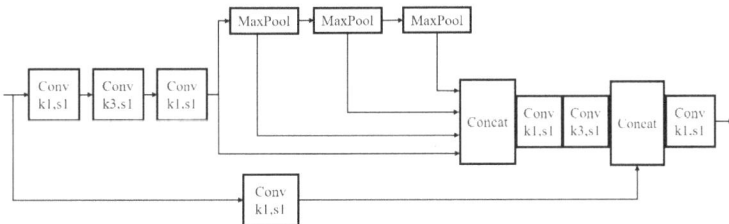

Figure 4. Network structure diagram of SPPFCSPC.

The SPPFCSPC module consists of two key techniques: Spatial Pyramid Pooling (SPP) and Fully Connected Spatial Pyramid Convolution (FCSPC).

First, the SPP component adopts the concept of spatial pyramid pooling, which involves pooling operations on the input feature map at different scales. This enables the capture of object information of varying sizes. The pyramid structure allows the network to process objects of different scales on a single fixed-size feature map, mitigating the impact of scale variations on object detection. The SPP generates fixed-length feature vectors that can serve as inputs to subsequent classifiers.

Secondly, the FCSPC component employs fully connected spatial pyramid convolution to operate on the feature vectors generated by the SPP. This integration and utilization of information at different scales aims to enhance the network's ability to handle multi-scale objects.

2.4. Focal Loss Classified Loss Function

In object detection tasks, the loss functions primarily consist of two categories: classification loss functions and regression loss functions [29]. Here, we focus on discussing the classification loss function. To address the challenges of difficult-to-classify samples and class imbalance, Dr. Kaiming He introduced the Focal loss [11] as a classification loss function. Its mathematical representation is as follows:

$$loss = -y(1-a)^\gamma \log y' - (1-y)a^\gamma \log(1-a) \quad (1)$$

In the equation, y represents the true label of the sample, a represents the predicted output values after applying the SoftMax function, and γ is a factor introduced on top of binary cross-entropy. If $\gamma > 0$, it indicates that the loss for easy samples will be reduced, allowing the network to pay more attention to difficult samples that are prone to misclassification and mitigate the impact of easy samples during network training.

To address the issue of imbalanced distribution of positive and negative samples, a balancing factor β is introduced to Equation (1), resulting in the Focal loss function that can mitigate class imbalance and explore difficult-to-classify samples. The modified Focal loss function is represented as Equation (2):

$$loss = -\beta y(1-a)^\gamma \log y' - (1-\beta)(1-y)a^\gamma \log(1-a) \quad (2)$$

3. Improvement of YOLOv5 Network Model

3.1. Basic Idea of Improving YOLOv5 Model

In multi-scale object detection on water surfaces, the features of small targets tend to become increasingly weak as the network deepens, leading to issues of missed and false detection. To address this issue, incorporating attention mechanisms into the YOLOv5 network can enhance its expressive power by focusing on crucial features in the feature maps while suppressing irrelevant features that contribute less to network training, thereby effectively reducing missed and false detection. The dual attention mechanism considers not only the varying importance of pixels across different feature channels but also the varying importance of pixels at different positions within the same feature channel. Therefore, the GAMAttention mechanism is attempted to be integrated into the YOLOv5 network model. In addition to the aforementioned challenges, water surface object detection is also affected by issues such as low contrast and lighting variations. To mitigate these challenges, image enhancement techniques are applied as a preprocessing step on the dataset. Image enhancement techniques, such as histogram equalization, contrast stretching, and adaptive histogram equalization, are employed to improve the contrast of the images and enhance the visibility of the objects in the water surface scenes.

By incorporating these techniques, the visibility and detectability of water surface objects in challenging lighting conditions and low-contrast scenarios can be significantly improved.

3.2. Optimization of Target Box Based on K-Means++

The traditional YOLO algorithm utilizes the K-means clustering algorithm [30] to obtain anchor boxes for object detection. This algorithm is simple to implement and efficient, but it is sensitive to the initial point selection, outliers, and isolated points. In comparison to K-means, K-means++ [31] improves the selection of initial points and has been shown to effectively enhance the classification error and improve the detection accuracy of multi-scale objects based on testing experiments conducted on public datasets such as PASCAL VOC. It is particularly suitable for scenarios with significant variations in object sizes.

The basic steps of K-means++ for generating anchor boxes are as follows:

1. Initialize the cluster centers by randomly selecting the bounding box regions of certain samples.
2. Calculate the distances from the initial cluster centers to each data sample.
3. Compute the probability for each sample to become the next cluster center using Equation (3).

$$P(x) = \frac{D(x)}{\sum D(x)^2} \quad (3)$$

4. Compare the probabilities and select the next cluster center using the roulette wheel selection method.

Repeat the above steps until the size of the obtained anchor box no longer change.

3.3. Embedding GAMAttention and SPPFCSPC Modules

(1) Embedding of GAMAttention module

The embedding of GAMAttention attention mechanism can introduce complexity and increase computational overhead to the network model. Therefore, it is considered to be added only at one position in the YOLOv5 model.

To incorporate the GAMAttention module into the backbone network for testing, the embedding process is depicted in Figure 5. The algorithm that embeds the GAMAttention module into the backbone network is named YWFA_B.

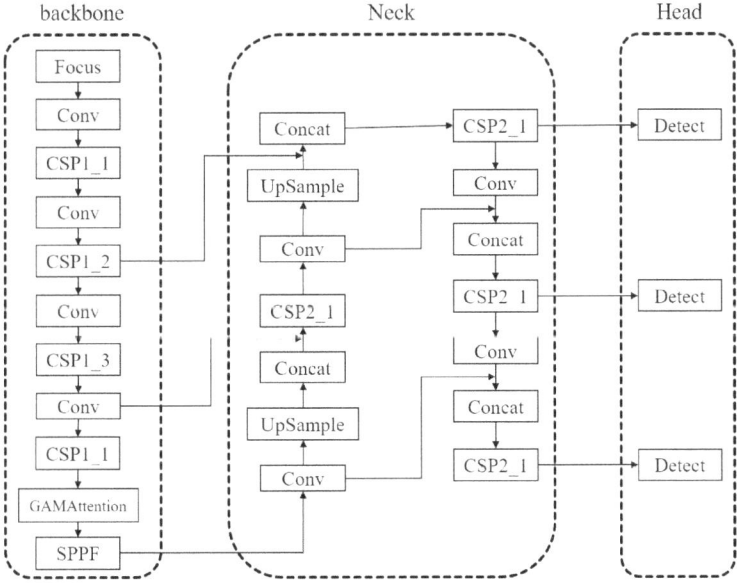

Figure 5. YWFA_B algorithm structure.

(2) Embedding of SPPFCSPC module

The SPPF module in the YOLOv5 backbone network is replaced with the SPPFCSPC module, which is named YWFS_B. The improved model with this modification is illustrated in Figure 6.

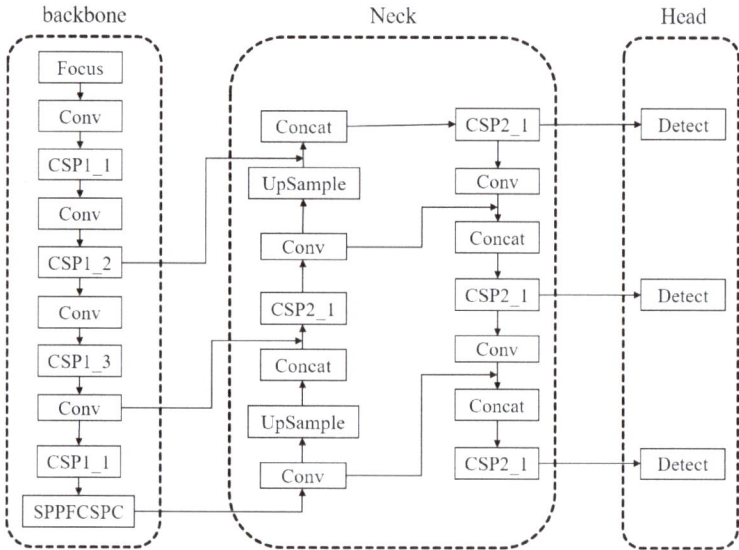

Figure 6. YWFS_B algorithm structure.

(3) GAMAttention and SPPFCSPC module are embedded at the same time

After conducting separate studies on the effects of different embedding approaches for the GAMAttention and SPPFCSPC modules in the network, it is being considered to simultaneously embed both the GAMAttention and SPPFCSPC modules into the network. The specific embedding approach will be chosen based on the results obtained from testing.

3.4. Loss Function Optimization

Due to the existence of class imbalance in the self-built dataset used for water surface object detection, the Mosaic data augmentation technique is applied to the input of YOLOv5. This technique involves randomly scaling, cropping, and placing four images before concatenating them (as shown in Figure 7). This approach helps mitigate the overfitting and low accuracy issues caused by the imbalanced distribution of samples among different classes.

Figure 7. Mosaic Data Enhancement.

In this study, a modified version of YOLOv5 named YOLOv5_F is proposed, which incorporates the Focal loss as part of the classification loss function. This modification further addresses the issue of class imbalance. The improved YOLOv5 model is illustrated in Figure 8.

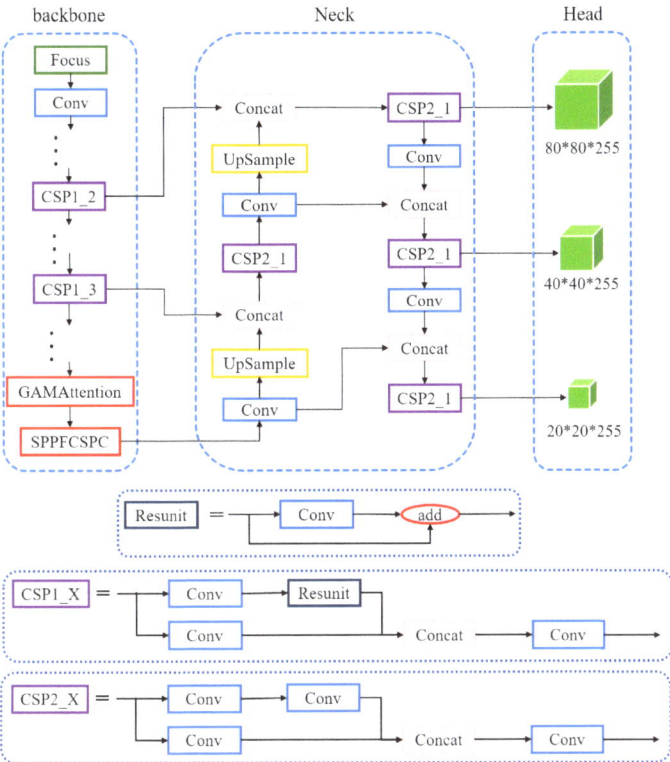

Figure 8. The improved YOLOv5 algorithm model in this paper.

3.5. Pseudocode of the Improved Model

The pseudocode of the improved model is shown in Figure 9.

pseudocode 1: A Method Based on Improved YOLOv5 for Water Surface Multi-scale Target Detection
Input: Number class; Class name;
1: Load images and pre-process data
2: Define the model architecture:
3:　　- Backbone network (e.g., CSPNet, GAMAttention, SPPFCSPC)
4:　　- Neck network (e.g., YOLOv5Neck)
5:　　- Detection head (e.g., YOLOv5Head)
6:　　- Loss function (e.g., Focal Loss)
7: **Train the model:**
8:　　- Compute loss on mini-batch of images
9:　　- Compute gradients and update weights using optimizer (e.g., Adam)
10: **Prediction:**
11:　　- Apply non-maximum suppression to remove overlapping predictions
12:　　- Output final detection results (bounding boxes, class probabilities, confidence scores)

Figure 9. Pseudo code diagram.

The proposed improvements in this study primarily focused on the backbone network and the loss function of the object detection algorithm. The GAMAttention attention mechanism is incorporated into the backbone network, enhancing its ability to capture relevant features. Additionally, the SPPF pooling module is modified to improve the network's capability to handle objects of various scales on the water surface. Furthermore, the loss function is optimized to better balance the uneven distribution of positive and negative samples.

4. Experimental Research and Result Analysis

The experiments were conducted under the following conditions: GeForce RTX 3080 12G GPU model, Windows 10 operating system, CUDA 11.3, and PyTorch 1.10.1 as the deep learning environment and framework. The self-built water surface multi-scale object dataset was used for evaluation and testing.

4.1. Establishment of Water Surface Target Data Set

Currently, there are many open-source datasets available with abundant object categories, such as the ImageNet dataset [5], the PASCAL VOC dataset [32,33], and COCO dataset [34]. However, there is currently no open-source dataset specifically designed for water surface object detection and recognition. Considering that the water surface visual system primarily focuses on monitoring the condition of the current water area, the key target objects for detection and recognition include ships, low-flying airplanes and birds, people on boats, and large fish leaping out of the water. Ships can be further classified into categories such as warships, cruise ships, cargo ships, sailboats, yachts, and other types of boats.

Based on the above considerations, this study has developed a self-built dataset comprising 5 major categories and 10 subcategories. The category labels are as follows: person, Cargoship, yacht, youlun, warship, bird, fish, fanchuan, other boat, and airplane. Some sample images from each category of the dataset are shown in Figure 10.

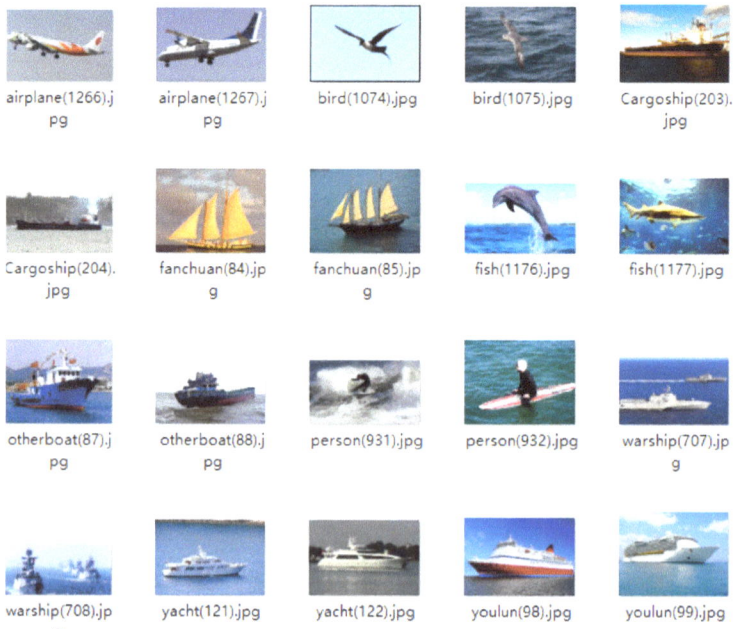

Figure 10. Part of the image of the data set established.

The dataset is divided into training, validation, and testing sets in a ratio of 8:1:1. Following the definition of absolute targets, the dataset is analyzed to determine the distribution of object scales in terms of large, medium, and small objects. Objects occupying less than 0.12% of the total image area are classified as small objects, those occupying more than 0.12% but less than 0.38% are classified as medium objects, and those occupying more than 0.38% are classified as large objects. The distribution of objects based on these criteria is illustrated in Figure 11.

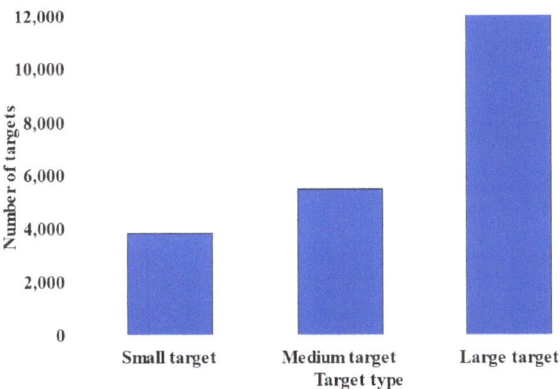

Figure 11. Distribution of large, medium, and small targets.

Due to the varying quantity and quality of images available online, the constructed multi-class object dataset may suffer from class imbalance, where certain classes have more samples than others. This can potentially lead to lower accuracy in algorithms. Figure 11 illustrates the distribution of object categories in the self-built dataset.

From Figure 12, it can be observed that the most frequent category in the self-built dataset is "person," while the least frequent category is "yacht." This indicates a certain degree of class imbalance issue among the samples in the dataset.

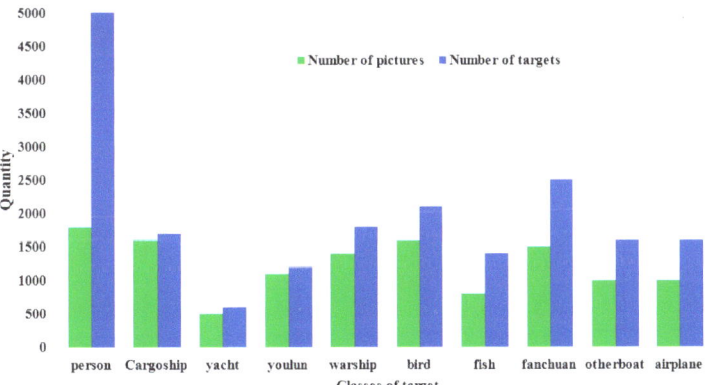

Figure 12. Distribution of target species.

4.2. Target Detection Evaluation Index

The problem of object detection involves locating and classifying objects in an image. Object detection models are typically trained on a fixed set of classes, so the model can only locate and classify those specific classes in the image. Furthermore, the location of the objects is usually represented by bounding boxes. Therefore, object detection requires both the localization of objects in the image and their classification. The accuracy of object detection is commonly measured using Mean Average Precision (mAP). Although mAP is not an absolute measure of the model's output, it is a useful relative measure. When computing this metric on a dataset, it allows for easy comparison between different object detection methods. which is calculated as follows:

$$mAP = \frac{\sum_{i=1}^{c} AP_i}{c} \qquad (4)$$

where $AP = \int_0^1 P(R)dR$ represents the average precision for a specific class in the dataset. The average precision is calculated by plotting the precision-recall curve and calculating the area under the curve (AUC). The calculation of precision (P) and recall (R) involves the following formulas:

$$P = \frac{X_{TP}}{X_{TP} + X_{FP}} \qquad (5)$$

$$R = \frac{X_{TP}}{X_{TP} + X_{FN}} \qquad (6)$$

where X_{TP} represents true positive (correctly classified positive samples), X_{TN} represents true negative (incorrectly classified negative samples), X_{FP} represents false positive (incorrectly classified positive samples), and X_{FN} represents false negative (incorrectly classified negative samples).

In the experiments, mAP@0.5 is used as the performance evaluation metric for the network. mAP@0.5 calculates the average precision by considering the intersection over union (IOU) between the predicted bounding boxes and the ground truth boxes, with an IOU threshold of 0.5. The AP for each class is calculated, and then the average of all class APs is taken, resulting in mAP@0.5.

4.3. Classification and Comparison Experiment

The algorithm in this paper is trained for a total of 100 epochs. The specific parameter settings used in the training process are listed in Table 1.

Table 1. List of Hyperparameters.

Argument	Value
batch_size	−1
Imgsz	640
epochs	100
loss	Focal_loss
classes	10

(1) Comparative experiment of target box optimization

Here is a comparison of the object detection accuracy between YOLOv5 and YOLOv5 with optimized bounding boxes using the K-means++ algorithm (named YKmeans++). In the experiments, the Anchor box cluster centers obtained using the K-means++ algorithm are as follows: (13, 24), (21, 57), (38, 106), (50, 45), (69, 176), (99, 98), (129, 270), (219, 168), (364, 333). The training epochs for both models are set to 100, and the IOU threshold is set to 0.5. The comparison of object detection accuracy before and after bounding box optimization is shown in Table 2.

Table 2. object Detection Accuracy Comparison (before and after bounding box optimization.

Network Model	P/IOU0.5	R/IOU0.5	mAP@0.5
YOLOv5	89.7%	81.6%	86.5%
YKmeans++	90.60%	82.42%	87.37%

From Table 1, it can be visually observed that the YOLOv5 network with optimized bounding boxes (YKmeans++) shows an improvement of 0.87% in mAP@0.5 compared to the network without optimization. This indicates that optimizing the bounding boxes has a certain effect on improving object detection accuracy.

(2) Comparative experiment of GAMAttention embedded in backbone network

The YWFA_B algorithm obtained by embedding the GAMAttention mechanism module into the backbone network of the YOLOv5 network model is tested and compared with the original YOLOv5 algorithm. The results are shown in Table 3.

Table 3. Comparison of Embedded GAMAttention.

Network Model	P/IOU0.5	R/IOU0.5	mAP@0.5
YOLOv5	89.7%	81.6%	86.5%
YWFA_B	83.2%	92.5%	92.2%

From Table 3, it can be observed that when the GAMAttention module is embedded in the backbone of the YOLOv5 network, there is a significant improvement in mAP@0.5, which increased by 5.7% compared to the original network. This suggests that incorporating the GAMAttention attention mechanism enhances the network's ability to train and perform better on the given dataset.

(3) Comparative experiment of replacing SPPFCSPC module with backbone network

The model algorithm YWFS_B (direct replacement of backbone network) formed by replacing SPPF in YOLOv5 network structure with SPPFCSPC module is compared and analyzed with YOLOv5 original network, and the results are shown in Table 4.

Table 4. Comparison of Embedded SPPFCSPC.

Network Model	P/IOU0.5	R/IOU0.5	mAP@0.5
YOLOv5	89.7%	81.6%	86.5%
YWFS_B	90.4%	85.5%	93.4%

From Table 4, it can be observed that replacing the SPPF module with the SPPFCSPC module in the YOLOv5 network (YWFS_B algorithm) improves the detection accuracy on the self-built test dataset. The improved model achieves a 6.9% increase in mAP@0.5 for water surface object detection compared to the original YOLOv5 algorithm.

(4) Comparative experiment before and after adding the loss function Focal loss

Comparing the algorithms before and after the YOLOv5 network is added to the classification loss function Focal loss, training, and testing are carried out on the self-built data set in this paper, and the results are shown in Table 5.

Table 5. Comparison of Focal loss before and after Addition.

Network Model	P/IOU0.5	R/IOU0.5	mAP@0.5
YOLOv5	89.7%	81.6%	86.5%
YWFS_BF	92.3%	88.2%	93.7%

From Table 5, it can be observed that adding the Focal loss as a classification loss function in the YOLOv5 network (YWFS_BF algorithm) helps balance the impact of imbalanced class distribution on the detection accuracy. The addition of Focal loss results in a 7.2% increase in mAP@0.5 for water surface object detection compared to the original YOLOv5 algorithm.

4.4. Comparative Experiment of Improved YOLOv5 Model

Based on the analysis of the comparative experiments in (2) and (3) of Section 4.3, it can be concluded that embedding the GAMAttention attention mechanism in the backbone network and replacing the SPPF module with the SPPFCSPC module in the backbone network can significantly improve the detection accuracy of the YOLOv5 algorithm for water surface objects. By combining these two improvements, a modified YOLOv5 algorithm is proposed, named YOLOv5_WFT.

In YOLOv5_WFT, the classification loss function Focal loss is incorporated, and the optimized bounding boxes obtained through K-means++ are used during network training. This modification results in an improved model referred to as YOLOv5_WFT_KF.

The two modified YOLOv5 models and the original YOLOv5 model are tested on the test set, and the results are shown in Table 6. From Table 6, it can be observed that the improved YOLOv5 models can significantly enhance the accuracy of object detection. Specifically, YOLOv5_WFT_KF achieves an 8.1% improvement in mAP@0.5 compared to YOLOv5.

Table 6. Comparison of target detection quality before and after YOLOv5 improvement.

Network Model	P/IOU0.5	R/IOU0.5	mAP@0.5
YOLOv5	89.7%	81.6%	86.5%
YOLOv5_WFT	93.6%	86.4%	94%
YOLOv5_WFT_KF	93.8%	87.2%	94.6%

Figure 13 lists the training results of YOLOv5 and YOLOv5_WFT_KF for this water surface target data set.

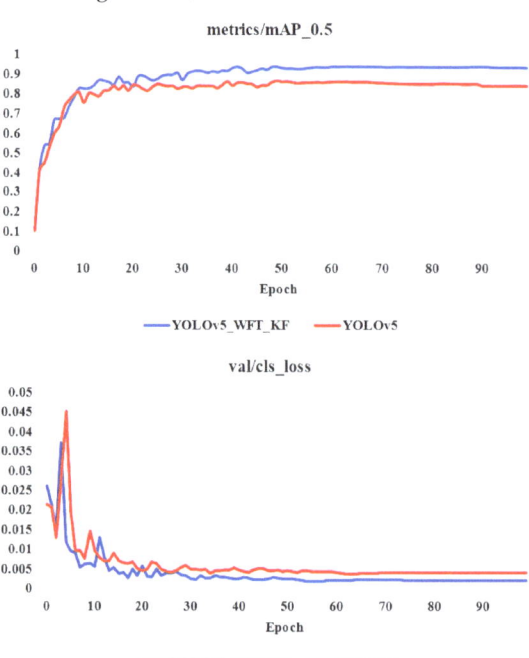

Figure 13. The training results of YOLOv5 model and YOLOv5_WFT_KF model.

From Figure 13, it can be observed that the proposed YOLOv5_WFT_KF model demonstrates good training convergence. The training loss curve shows that the model's training process reaches convergence around epoch = 55. After this point, there is no evidence of overfitting or failure to converge, indicating that the model has effectively learned the underlying patterns and features of the multi-scale water surface objects during training. This indicates the stability and effectiveness of the proposed model in achieving convergence and avoiding training issues.

This paper presents a comparative analysis of detection quality for classification targets among Faster R-CNN, YOLOv4, YOLOv5, and the proposed YOLOv5_WFT_KF algorithm. As shown in Table 7, the YOLOv5_WFT_KF algorithm, which is an improved version of YOLOv5, significantly improves the accuracy of multi-scale target detection on water surface compared to the other three algorithms.

Table 7. FasterR-CNN YOLOv4 YOLOv5 and YOLOv5_WFT_KF Classification target detection quality.

Algorithm Model	Airplane (%)	Bird (%)	Cargoship (%)	Fanchuan (%)	Fish (%)
Faster R-CNN	81.16	88.99	81.09	80.66	60.38
YOLOv4	94.34	80.31	83.10	88.92	35.03
YOLOv5	99.1	95.7	93.9	94.7	85.4
YOLOv5_WFT_KF	95.2	94.4	93.8	98.4	93.9
Otherboat (%)	Person (%)	Youlun (%)	Warship (%)	Yacht (%)	mAP@0.5 (%)
57.51	52.70	90.61	80.84	71.13	74.51
81.79	65.81	85.14	95.99	95.24	80.57
59.3	66.6	91.8	91.4	86.8	86.5
89.9	83.7	99.5	94.3	97.3	94.6

Figure 14 illustrates a comparison of detection performance on three randomly selected images from a self-built water surface target dataset before and after the improvement of the YOLOv5 model. Figure 14a shows the original images, while Figure 14b,c show the detection results of the original YOLOv5 model and the improved YOLOv5_WFT_KF model, respectively.

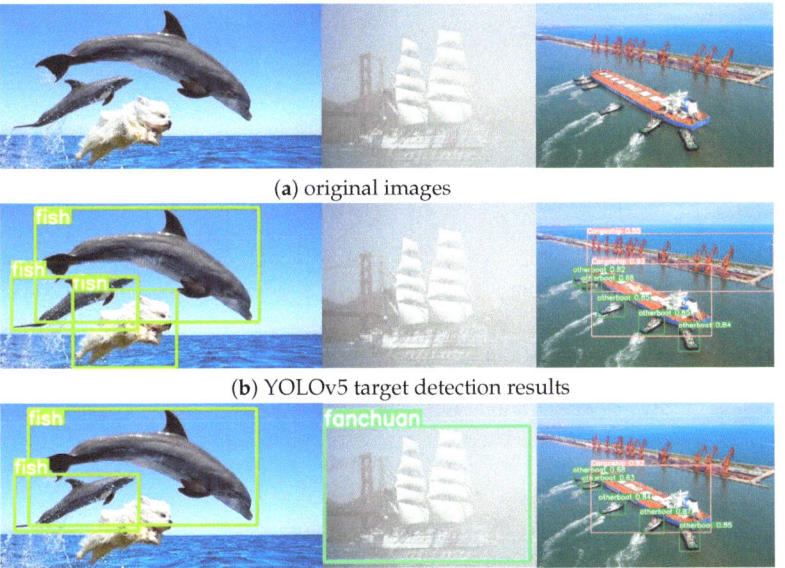

(a) original images

(b) YOLOv5 target detection results

(c) YOLOv5_WFT_KF target detection results

Figure 14. Comparison of target detection results between YOLOv5 and its improved model.

From Figure 15a, it can be observed that the proposed improved YOLOv5 algorithm effectively detects each category in the dataset used in the study without any instances of missed detections or false detections. Figure 15b showcases the detection results for multi-scale objects. It can be seen from the figure that the proposed improved algorithm accurately detects objects of different sizes and categories in an image, including large, medium, and small objects, with high confidence scores. This effectively demonstrates the feasibility of the proposed algorithm improvements presented in this study.

(a) YOLOv5_WFT_KF detection results of 10 kinds of water surface targets

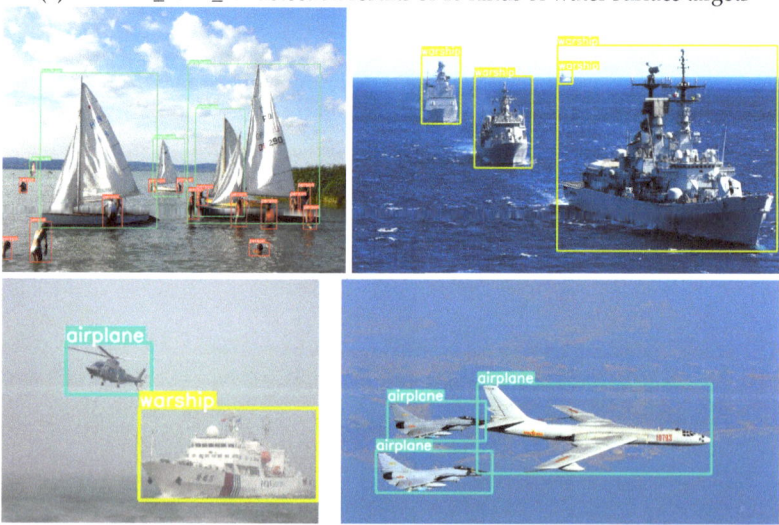

(b) YOLOv5_WFT_KF detection results of multi-scale water surface targets

Figure 15. YOLOv5_WFT_KF target detection results.

From Figures 14 and 15, it can be observed that the improved YOLOv5 model, YOLOv5_WFT_KF, can recognize the ten classes of targets in the self-built dataset as well as multi-scale targets. Compared to the YOLOv5 model, the improved model can provide more accurate bounding boxes for small and occluded targets with high confidence.

In addition to comparing the accuracy of the network models for object detection, this paper also conducted experiments to compare the number of layers, parameters, FLOPs, and FPS between the improved and original YOLOv5 models when inputting an RGB three-channel 640 × 640 color image. The results of the comparison are summarized in Table 8.

Table 8. Comparison of parameters before and after YOLOV5 improvement.

Network Model	Layers	Parameters	Flops	FPS
YOLOv5	213	7 M	15.8 G	203.415
YOLOv5_WFT_KF	239	15.2 M	22.4 G	172.015

According to the experimental results in Table 8, the improved algorithm in this paper achieves an average precision increase of 8.1% compared to YOLOv5 when using the same input resolution. This is due to the addition of attention mechanisms and replacement of the network spatial pyramid module, which leads to an increase in the number of layers and parameters of the network model, with the parameter amount being twice that of the original network. However, this also results in a decrease in the FPS during inference.

5. Conclusions

To address the demand for multi-scale and small target detection on water surfaces, this paper proposes an improved YOLOv5 model based on the characteristics of the deep learning YOLOv5 model. The improved model mainly improves the target box setting, embeds the attention mechanism module in the backbone network, replaces the original spatial pyramid SPPF module, and uses the Focal loss classification loss function to alleviate overfitting and detection accuracy problems caused by multi-scale targets and imbalanced class samples in water surface targets. Tests on a self-built water surface target dataset show that the improved YOLOv5 model has a certain degree of improvement in detection accuracy for most classes of targets and is suitable for multi-scale target detection on water surfaces. However, there are relatively few images of occluded targets in the dataset, and the detection performance of the model for occluded targets still needs to be verified.

Furthermore, the addition of multiple modules increases the computational complexity and the model's complexity, which will affect the real-time performance of the algorithm. Therefore, in future research, the model's lightweight design should be considered to reduce the consumption of unnecessary resources while ensuring a certain level of detection accuracy, thus improving the real-time performance and efficiency of network detection.

Author Contributions: Conceptualization, J.L.; Methodology, Z.M.; Software, Y.W.; Validation, Y.W.; Formal analysis, J.L.; Investigation, R.A.; Data curation, L.W. All authors have read and agreed to the published version of the manuscript.

Funding: The authors are grateful to College of Automation, Chengdu University of Information Technology, this paper is supported by International Cooperation Project of Science and Technology Bureau of Chengdu (No. 2019-GH02-00051-HZ), Sichuan unmanned system and intelligent perception Engineering Laboratory Open Fund, and Research Fund of Chengdu University of information engineering, under Grant (No. WRXT2020-001, No. WRXT2020-002, No. WRXT2021-002 and No. KYTZ202142), and the Sichuan Science and Technology Program China, under Grant (No. 2022YFS0565); This paper is also supported by the Key R&D project of Science and Technology Department of Sichuan Province, under Grant (2023YFG0196 and 2023YFN0077), Science and Technology achievements transformation Project of Science and Technology Department of Sichuan Province, under Grant (2023JDZH0023), Sichuan Provincial Science and Technology Department, Youth Fund project, under Grant (2023NSFSC1429).

Data Availability Statement: Data sharing not applicable. Since this article uses a self-built dataset, the dataset is not shared.

Conflicts of Interest: The authors declare no conflict of interest.

References

1. Li, H. Research on Multi-Target Recognition and Tracking Technology of Ship Vision System for Sea-Air Targets. Master's Thesis, Harbin Engineering University, Harbin, China, 2019.
2. Yin, K.; Wang, X.; Wu, Y.; Qin, M.; Zhang, J.; Chu, Z. Water Surface Garbage Detection Based on YOLOv5. *Comput. Knowl. Technol.* **2022**, *18*, 28–30.
3. Chen, K.; Zhu, Z.; Deng, X.; Ma, C.; Wang, H. A Survey on Deep Learning for Multi-Scale Object Detection. *J. Softw.* **2021**, *32*, 1201–1227.
4. Krizhevsky, A.; Sutskever, I.; Hinton, G.E. ImageNet classification with deep convolutional neural networks. *Commun. ACM* **2017**, *60*, 84–90. [CrossRef]
5. Russakovsky, O.; Deng, J.; Su, H.; Krause, J.; Satheesh, S.; Ma, S.; Huang, Z.; Karpathy, A.; Khosla, A.; Bernstein, M.; et al. ImageNet large scale visual recognition challenge. *Int. J. Comput. Vis.* **2015**, *115*, 211–252. [CrossRef]
6. Zuo, J.; Wu, Y. Intelligent Monitoring Technology of Water Floating Objects. *Softw. Guide* **2013**, *12*, 150–152.
7. Xu, P. Research on Dynamic Obstacle Detection Technology of Water Surface Unmanned Vessels. Master's Thesis, Shenyang Li Gong University, Shenyang, China, 2016.
8. Wang, F.; Zhang, M.; Gong, L. A Rapid Detection Algorithm for Surface Ships Based on Geometric Features. *J. Nav. Univ. Eng.* **2016**, *28*, 57–63.
9. Tang, L. Research on Image-Based Object Detection of Unmanned Surface Vehicles. Master's Thesis, Harbin Institute of Technology, Harbin, China, 2018.
10. Liu, H. Research on Detection of Water Surface Target Images Based on SSD Algorithm. Master's Thesis, Dalian Maritime University, Dalian, China, 2019.
11. Liang, Y.; Feng, H.; Xu, H. Fine-grained Detection of Ship Visible Light Images Based on YOLOv3-tiny. *J. Wuhan Univ. Technol. (Transp. Sci. Eng.)* **2020**, *44*, 1041–1045+1051.
12. Wang, Y.L.; Ma, J.; Luo, X.;Wang, S. Surface garbage target detection based on SPMYOLOv3. *Comput. Syst. Appl.* **2023**, *32*, 163–170.
13. Wang, Z.; Wang, Y.; Tan, X.; Zhang, H. Rapid Detection of Water Surface Targets Based on YOLOv4. *Ship Electron. Eng.* **2022**, *42*, 110–113.
14. Li, Y.; Fan, Y.; Wang, S.; Bai, J.; Li, K. Application of YOLOv5 Based on Attention Mechanism and Receptive Field in Identifying Defects of Thangka Images. *IEEE Access* **2022**, *10*, 81597–81611. [CrossRef]
15. Wang, J.; Chen, Y.; Dong, Z.; Gao, M. Improved YOLOv5 network for real-time multi-scale traffic sign detection. *Neural Comput. Appl.* **2023**, *35*, 7853–7865. [CrossRef]
16. Zhu, X.; Lyu, S.; Wang, X.; Zhao, Q. TPH-YOLOv5: Improved YOLOv5 Based on Transformer Prediction Head for Object Detection on Drone-captured Scenarios. In Proceedings of the 2021 IEEE/CVF International Conference on Computer Vision Workshops (ICCVW), Montreal, BC, Canada, 24 October 2022; IEEE: Piscataway, NJ, USA, 2021; pp. 2778–2788.
17. Lin, T.Y.; Goyal, P.; Girshick, R.; He, K.; Dollár, P. Focal loss for dense object detection. In Proceedings of the 2017 IEEE International Conference on Computer Vision, Venice, Italy, 22–29 October 2017; pp. 2999–3007.
18. Yun, S.; Han, D.; Oh, S.J.; Chun, S.; Choe, J.; Yoo, Y. Cutmix: Regularization strategy to train strong classifiers with localizable features. In Proceedings of the IEEE/CVF International Conference on Computer Vision, Seoul, Republic of Korea, 27 October–2 November 2019; pp. 6023–6032.
19. Dulal, R.; Zheng, L.; Kabir, M.A.; McGrath, S.; Medway, J.; Swain, D.; Swain, W. Automatic Cattle Identification using YOLOv5 and Mosaic Augmentation: A Comparative Analysis. *arXiv* **2022**, arXiv:2210.11939.
20. Wang, C.Y.; Liao, H.Y.; Wu, Y.H.; Chen, P.Y.; Hsieh, J.W.; Yeh, I.H. CSPNet: A new backbone that can enhance learning capability of CNN. *arXiv* **2019**, arXiv:1911.11929.
21. Glorot, X.; Bordes, A.; Bengio, Y. Deep Sparse Rectifier Neural Networks. In Proceedings of the Fourteenth International Conference on Artificial Intelligence and Statistics, Lauderdale, FL, USA, 14 June 2011.
22. Lin, T.Y.; Dollár, P.; Girshick, R.; He, K.; Hariharan, B.; Belongie, S. Feature Pyramid Networks for Object Detection. *arXiv* **2017**, arXiv:1612.03144.
23. Liu, S.; Qi, L.; Qin, H.; Shi, J.; Jia, J. Path Aggregation Network for Instance Segmentation. *arXiv* **2018**, arXiv:1803.01534.
24. Rezatofighi, H.; Tsoi, N.; Gwak, J. Generalized Intersection over Union: A Metric and A Loss for Bounding Box Regression. *arXiv* **2019**, arXiv:1902.09630.
25. Zhang, X.; Sun, C.; Han, H.; Wang, H.; Sun, H.; Zheng, N. Object-fabrication Targeted Attack for Object Detection. *arXiv* **2022**, arXiv:2212.06431.
26. Woo, S.; Park, J.; Lee, J.Y.; Kweon, I.S. Cbam: Convolutional block attention module. In Proceedings of the European Conference on Computer Vision (ECCV), Munich, Germany, 8–14 September 2018; pp. 3–19.
27. Liu, Y.; Shao, Z.; Hoffmann, N. Global Attention Mechanism: Retain Information to Enhance Channel-Spatial Interactions. *arXiv* **2021**, arXiv:2112.05561.
28. He, K.; Zhang, X.; Ren, S.; Sun, J. Spatial Pyramid Pooling in Deep Convolutional Networks for Visual Recognition. *IEEE Trans. Pattern Anal. Mach. Intell.* **2014**, *37*, 1904–1916. [CrossRef]
29. Yang, Q.; Zhang, C.; He, Q.; Wang, H. Research Progress on Loss Functions for Object Detection. *Comput. Sci. Appl.* **2021**, *11*, 2836–2844.

30. MacQueen, J. Some methods for classification and analysis of multivariate observations. In Proceedings of the Fifth Berkeley Symposium on Mathematical Statistics and Probability, Los Angeles, CA, USA, 21 June 1967; Volume 1, pp. 281–297.
31. Arthur, D. Vassilvitskii S. k-means++: The advantages of careful seeding. In Proceedings of the Eighteenth annual ACM-SIAM Symposium on Discrete Algorithms, New Orleans, LA, USA, 7 January 2007.
32. Everingham, M.; Van Gool, L.; Williams, C.K.; Winn, J.; Zisserman, A. The pascal visual object classes challenge. *Int. J. Comput. Vis.* **2010**, *88*, 303–338. [CrossRef]
33. Everingham, M.; Eslami, S.A.; Van Gool, L.; Williams, C.K.; Winn, J.; Zisserman, A. The pascal visual object classes challenge: A retrospective. *Int. J. Comput. Vis.* **2015**, *111*, 98–136. [CrossRef]
34. Lin, T.Y.; Maire, M.; Belongie, S.; Hays, J.; Perona, P.; Ramanan, D.; Dollár, P.; Zitnick, C.L. Microsoft coco: Common objects in context. In Proceedings of the Computer Vision—ECCV 2014: 13th European Conference, Zurich, Switzerland, 6–12 September 2014; Springer: Cham, Switzerland, 2014; pp. 740–755.

Disclaimer/Publisher's Note: The statements, opinions and data contained in all publications are solely those of the individual author(s) and contributor(s) and not of MDPI and/or the editor(s). MDPI and/or the editor(s) disclaim responsibility for any injury to people or property resulting from any ideas, methods, instructions or products referred to in the content.

Article

FDDS: Feature Disentangling and Domain Shifting for Domain Adaptation

Huan Chen [1], Farong Gao [1,2,*] and Qizhong Zhang [1,2]

1. HDU-ITMO Joint Institute, Hangzhou Dianzi University, Hangzhou 310018, China; 202320035@hdu.edu.cn (H.C.); zqz@hdu.edu.cn (Q.Z.)
2. School of Automation, Hangzhou Dianzi University, Hangzhou 310018, China
* Correspondence: frgao@hdu.edu.cn

Abstract: Domain adaptation is a learning strategy that aims to improve the performance of models in the current field by leveraging similar domain information. In order to analyze the effects of feature disentangling on domain adaptation and evaluate a model's suitability in the original scene, we present a method called feature disentangling and domain shifting (FDDS) for domain adaptation. FDDS utilizes sample information from both the source and target domains, employing a nonlinear disentangling approach and incorporating learnable weights to dynamically separate content and style features. Additionally, we introduce a lightweight component known as the domain shifter into the network architecture. This component allows for classification performance to be maintained in both the source and target domains while consuming moderate overhead. The domain shifter uses the attention mechanism to enhance the ability to extract network features. Extensive experiments demonstrated that FDDS can effectively disentangle features with clear feature separation boundaries while maintaining the classification ability of the model in the source domain. Under the same conditions, we evaluated FDDS and advanced algorithms on digital and road scene datasets. In the 19 classification tasks for road scenes, FDDS outperformed the competition in 11 categories, particularly showcasing a remarkable 2.7% enhancement in the accuracy of the bicycle label. These comparative results highlight the advantages of FDDS in achieving high accuracy in the target domain.

Keywords: feature disentangling; domain adaptation; attention mechanism; adaptation separation; domain shifting

MSC: 68T05

1. Introduction

Compared with traditional machine learning methods, deep learning has powerful feature-extraction and feature-processing capabilities for solving big data problems and has achieved remarkable results [1,2]. Nevertheless, when neural networks attempt to generalize across domains, domain shifting will lead to decreases in performance. It is challenging to solve this problem [3]. Researchers have made extensive efforts in domain adaptation, exploring various approaches to facilitate cross-domain generalization [4,5]. Among these strategies, the feature domain adaptation and pixel-level domain adaptation methods are two of the most prominent.

Feature domain adaptation methods [6,7] learn domain-invariant features by applying a feature-extraction model in a feature space [8] or a generative adversarial network model [9]. However, the training process of these methods is difficult to visualize, and there may be difficulties in capturing domain shifting at the pixel level and some edge information. In addition, pixel-level domain adaptation methods [10,11] utilize generative adversarial networks (GANs) [12] to adjust the source domain image in the original pixel space, making it resemble an image drawn from the target domain. Both feature- and pixel-level domain adaptation methods have advantages, and they operate in different ways [13]. As a result, some methods [14,15] combine feature domain adaptation with pixel-level domain adaptation to enhance the performance of domain adaptation from different aspects and achieve significant results.

In recent years, some methods [16,17] have attempted to separate image features into a potential feature space and extract shared and private components from source and target domain image samples. The results have shown that feature disentangling has a positive effect on extracting domain-shared features to a certain extent, thereby improving the classification accuracy of the target domain's model [16]. However, these methods often focus on the shared features of the two domains while overlooking the private features that may limit performance improvement to some degree [15]. In this context, one method [18] introduced a state-of-the-art separation methodology that linearly divided features into content and style components, albeit with a fixed 1:1 ratio for disentangling content and style features. This fixed ratio may reduce the adaptability of models across diverse scenes. Oppositely, another model proposed in method [15] incorporated a non-linear disentangling manifold allowing for flexible determination of the proportion of content and style features during model training. Therefore, it is crucial to study feature disentanglement comprehensively.

In a specific scenario, one model needs to fulfill the requirements of the target domain while maintaining a relatively accurate recognition ability in the source domain. For instance, when a network model operates on a server, it should use its functions from the source domain while serving clients in the target domain. To tackle this challenge, a traditional approach is to train the network model exclusively for the target domain and then transfer it back to the source domain when necessary. However, this iterative process results in a significant waste of training resources and fails to meet the needs of both domains adequately. It remains challenging for a compressed or service-providing model to simultaneously address the services of both domains [14].

To address the aforementioned issues, we propose a Feature Disentangling and Domain Shifting (FDDS) method for domain adaptation. This approach utilizes a non-linear disentangling technique to separate features from two domains into content and style components. The proportion of content features in different domains is determined by learnable weights, allowing for more accurate feature separation based on the specified proportion. Furthermore, in addition to providing additional information for feature disentangling, our method incorporates a domain shifter that enhances the performance of the target domain while ensuring the performance of the source domain to the maximum extent possible. Unlike the data calibrator proposed in previous methods [14], our domain shifter incorporates a dual-attention mechanism, involving both spatial and channel attention [19]. This mechanism enables the model to focus on key points within the scene, capture more valuable image information, and disregard irrelevant details, thereby improving the efficiency of image-processing.

The contributions of our approach are summarized as follows:

1. We proposed a new non-linear feature disentangling method, which determines the proportion of content features and style features in source and target domains through learnable weights. This approach enables the precise separation of content and style features based on their corresponding proportions;
2. We integrated a dual-attention mechanism involving both spatial and channel attention into the domain shifter network, which preserves the performance of the source domain after domain shifting. As a result, our model can seamlessly transition between serving the source and target domains;
3. To evaluate our approach, we conducted experiments in the digit classification and semantic segmentation tasks. Our method exhibited superior performance compared to competing approaches, particularly in the semantic segmentation tasks. Specifically,

our FDDS method outperformed the competition in 11 out of 19 classification labels and achieves optimal or suboptimal results in 16 categories.

This paper is structured as follows. In Section 1, we introduce the background of the research, which led to our work. And in Section 2, we introduce the related work in the field. Section 3 presents the method details of FDDS. Moving on to Sections 4 and 5, we demonstrate and analyze the numerical results of FDDS on public datasets and discussed ablation experiments. Finally, we conclude by summarizing the text in full.

2. Related Work

2.1. Deep Domain Adaptation

Transfer learning is a methodology that utilizes known information to learn new knowledge in unknown fields. Domain adaptation is a type of transfer learning and serves as a prevalent technique for addressing the transferability of diverse datasets. After Yosinski et al. [20] explored how to transfer features in neural networks, many feature domain adaptation methods have emerged. Tzeng et al. [21] built upon this by incorporating an adaptation layer into the AlexNet, proposing the deep domain confusion (DDC) method. Long et al. [22] expanded upon DDC, arguing that multi-layer adaptation was superior to single-layer adaptation, and created the deep adaptation network (DAN). Sun et al. [23] used the feature scale factor to express the relative importance of features, and captured the internal manifold structure of data in the low-dimensional manifold subspace, thus reducing the probability distribution between different domains. Recently, GANs [12] has become more and more popular. Ganin et al. [24] first combined domain adaptation with GANs, proposing the domain-adversary neural network (DANN) which leverages GANs to improve the network's feature extraction capability. Akada et al. [25] used GANs to learn the domain invariant features of the network by self-supervised learning, and complete the transfer from synthetic images to real images.

In order to enhance the interpretability of neural networks, scholars have conducted a series of studies on pixel-level domain adaptation. Bousmalis et al. [26] utilized a generative adversarial network to align the distribution of the source domain with the target domain in pixel space. Pixel-level domain adaptation is beneficial for both assigning labels to images and improving feature-level domain adaptation. Hence, researchers have attempted to integrate these two methods. Hoffman et al. [13] were the first to incorporate feature and pixel-level domain adaptation, introducing cycle-consistent loss to augment the model's semantic consistency. Ye et al. [14] further improved the network's accuracy in the target domain by introducing a data calibrator, while at the same time ensuring that the classifier retains its ability to accurately classify the source domain. In this paper, we sought to improve upon the data calibration mechanism by embedding an attention mechanism into the network. The attention mechanism [27] enables the network to focus on key features in the scene, thereby further enhancing the model's classification accuracy in the source domain.

2.2. Attention Mechanism in Image Generation

The attention mechanism (AM) was initially applied in the domain of machine translation. With the development of AM in recent years, AM has emerged as an important solution for addressing the issue of information overload in the field of image generation. Chen et al. [28] proposed attention-GAN, which leverages the AM to transform the specific position of an image while leaving the background unaffected, thus demonstrating the feasibility of cooperative functioning between the AM and the GAN. Emami et al. [29] introduced self-attention generative adversarial networks (SAGAN) that capture long-distance dependencies via the AM, enabling the generated image to represent global features, resulting in significant success in the field of image generation. Daras et al. [30] proposed the design of a two-dimensional local attention mechanism to generate the model. By reducing the attention feature map, operation efficiency was accelerated, and the model became lightweight. Woo et al. [31] proposed CBAM, which combined the channel and spatial attention mechanisms on features, and achieved better results than the single attention mechanism. Following this, many methods [32] incorporated the attention mechanism into the network as a component to improve image generation performance. In this paper, we incorporate the AM into the domain shifter network, effectively rendering it lightweight and better-equipped to extract key features from the scene.

2.3. Feature Disentangling

In the field of domain adaptation, the research on feature separation methods has recently aroused people's interest. Bousmalis et al. [16] learned to divided features into two components: private and shared features, and demonstrated that the modeling of private features is helpful to extract domain-invariant features. Gonzalez-Garcia et al. [33] attempted to separate the private factors in both fields from those that were shared across fields. Liu et al. [17] proposed a cross-domain feature disentangling, which can connect information and transmit attributes across data domains. Zou et al. [34] proposed a joint learning framework to separate identity-related/irrelevant features for personnel re-identification tasks.

Feature disentangling can also decompose features into style features and content features. This disentangling method was initially employed in the domain of style transfer and was extensively investigated in the context of artistic styles. Tenebaum et al. [35] demonstrated how perceptual systems separate content and style and proposed a bilinear model to address these two factors. Elgammal et al. [36] introduced a method for separating style and content on the manifold that represents dynamic objects. Gatys et al. [37] presented a way to manipulate the content and style of natural images by leveraging the universal feature representation of convolutional neural networks (CNN) learning. Zhang et al. [18] linearly separated features into content components and style components. However, Lee et al. [15] argued that features are not necessarily linearly separable in real-life scenarios and proposed a non-linear disentangling method to isolate potential variables on non-linear manifolds. In this paper, we also employ a non-linear disentangling method to determine the proportion of content features in different fields using learnable weights, leading to more accurate feature separation based on the content proportion.

3. Materials and Methods

3.1. Model Description

The network architecture of our method is shown in Figure 1. The FDDS network consists of a domain shifter DS, an encoder E, a feature separator S, a generator G, two discriminators of source and target domains D_A, D_B and a perceptual network P.

In the FDDS network, source and target images I_A, I_B are fed into the model and initially processed by the domain shifter DS, which is processed I_A, I_B into I_{DSA}, I_{DSB} and captures and stores critical information necessary to preserve the model's classification ability for the source domain. The images are then passed through the encoder E to extract their features $F_A, F_B, F_{DSA}, F_{DSB}$, respectively. The feature separator utilizes feature merging factors λ_1, λ_2 to merge features and decompose the merged features F_A', F_B' into content and style components, where content features are represented by C_A, C_B and style features are represented by S_A, S_B. The generator G maps the original features F_A, F_B and transfers features $F_{A \to B}, F_{B \to A}$ into the image space. In addition, a pre-trained perceptual network P is employed to extract perceptual features and enforce constraints on content and style similarities. In the training phase, two discriminators D_A, D_B are utilized to impose adversarial loss constraints on both source and target domains.

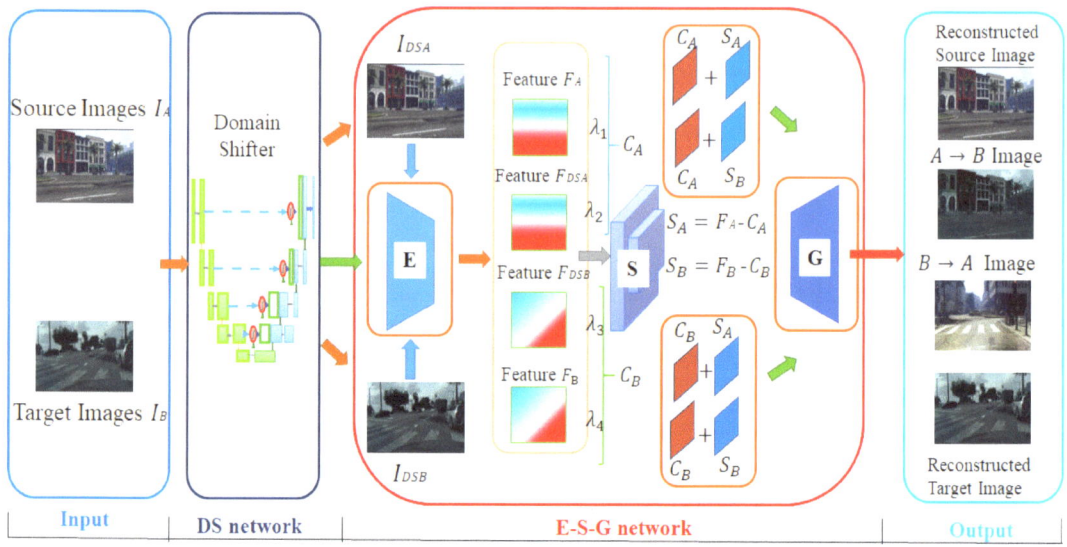
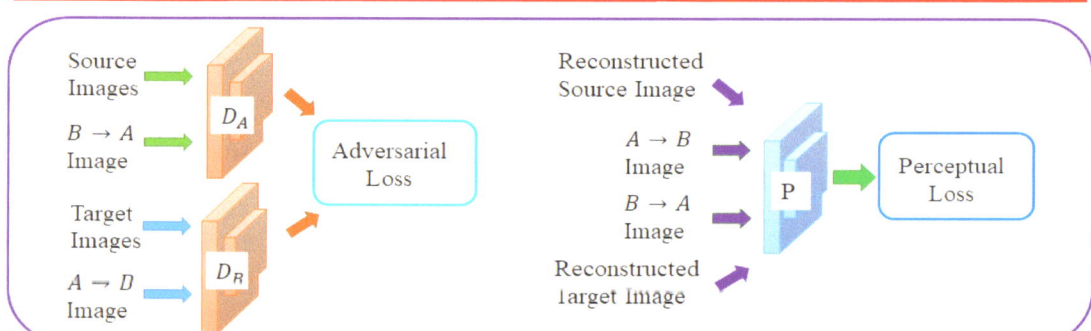

Figure 1. The network architecture of FDDS: (**up**) The network is composed of a domain shifter, an encoder, a feature separator, a generator, and the input and output of the model; and (**down**) the adversarial loss and perceptual loss of the network.

3.2. Domain Shifter Network

The first step of our method involves utilizing the domain shifter to process the input image. The network structure of domain shifter is composed of U-Net [38], with the dual attention mechanism of spatial and channel added during each up-sampling to capture the inter-channel dependencies and intra-pixel spatial relationships, respectively. This design enables more effective feature extraction and ultimately leads to superior performance results [19]. The network architecture of the domain shifter is shown in Figure 2.

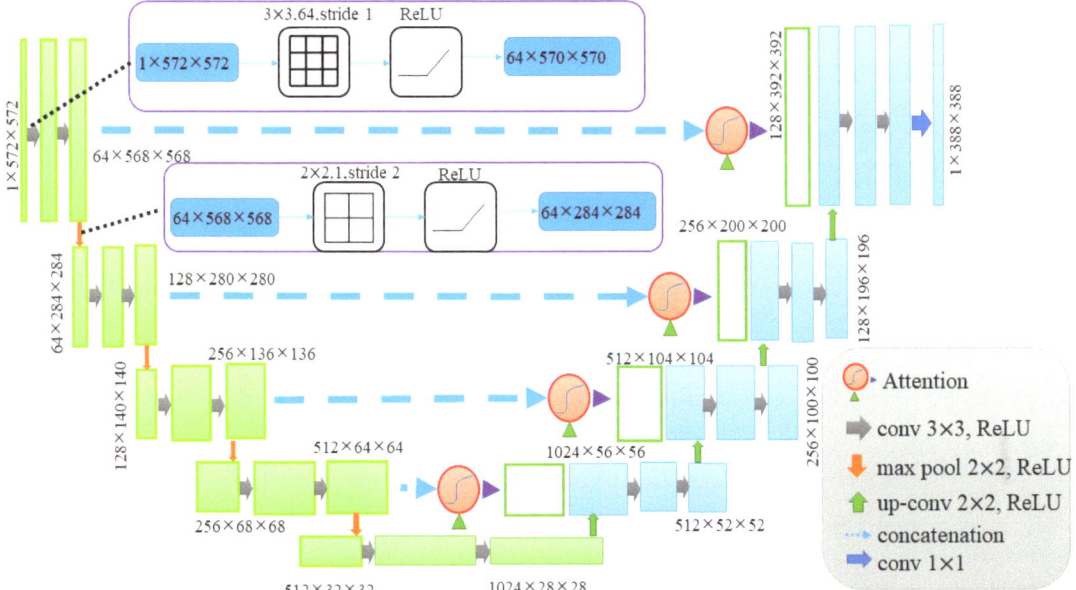

Figure 2. Domain shifter network architecture. (The two purple boxes in the figure represent two network structures in first layer, and the number of channels and step sizes of other modules not shown may be slightly different, which can be inferred by using the feature numbers of different dimensions of the results).

As shown in Figure 2, our domain shifter adopts the U-Net with an attention mechanism and two features to extract the network and uses ReLU as the activation function. The right three and the corresponding feature map are shown on the left. The features on the left require attention-mechanism processing and fusion.

The structure of the attention mechanism is shown in Figure 3.

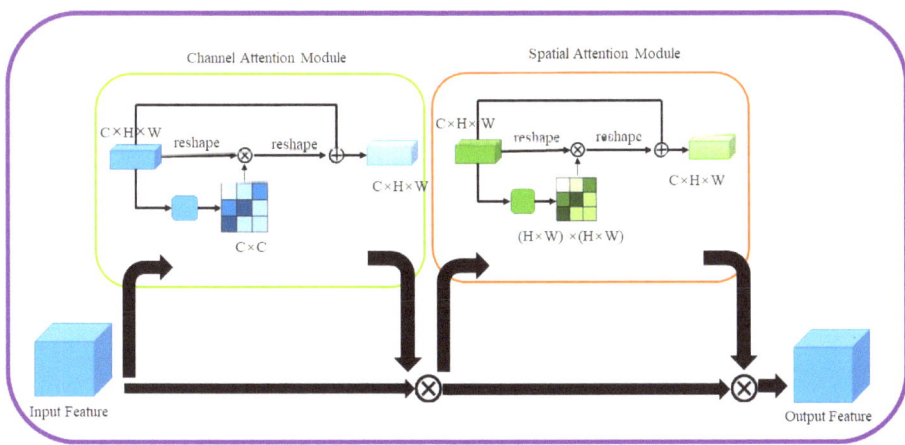

Figure 3. The structure of the attention mechanism ($\otimes$ represents matrix multiplication element by element, while $\oplus$ represents feature fusion).

As shown in Figure 3, we adopted a dual-attention mechanism with channel and spatial concatenation to complete feature extraction and fusion. In Figure 3, the solution of the channel and spatial attention mechanism is as follows.

$$\begin{aligned} F' &= M_c(F_{in}) \otimes F_{in}, \\ F'' &= M_s(F') \otimes F', \\ F_{out} &= F' \oplus F'' \end{aligned} \tag{1}$$

where F_{in} is the input feature, F' is the feature after channel attention processing, F'' is the image after spatial attention processing, and F_{out} is the output feature; $\otimes$ represents the matrix multiplication element by element, and $\oplus$ represents feature fusion.

The primary aim of introducing the domain shifter into the network is to ensure the accuracy of the target domain while preserving the classification accuracy of the source domain. Specifically, the domain shifter tries to produce analogous results for both the processed target domain image and the unprocessed source domain image when fed into the final classifier. This approach effectively preserves the classifier's classification ability for the source domain, thereby ensuring its accuracy. To achieve this outcome, the domain shift must satisfy certain conditions, including but not limited to,

$$Y(I_{DSB}) \sim Y(I_A), Y(I_{DSA}) \sim Y(I_A) \tag{2}$$

where $Y(I_A)$ represents the classification result obtained by the final classifier when the input I_A, and the same is true for others.

In order to make the classification result better, the domain shifter's constraints are as follows,

$$I_{DSA} \sim I_A, I_{DSB} \sim I_A \tag{3}$$

The domain shifter deceives the discriminator D_d in the model by the following loss function,

$$\mathcal{L}_{DS}^d = \mathbb{E}[y_a \log(D(x_a)) + y_b \log(D(x_b))] \tag{4}$$

where x_a, x_b represent the sample of the source and the target domain, respectively, and y_a, y_b represent the label of the source and the target domain, respectively. $\mathbb{E}$ represents mathematical expectation.

The domain shifter component in the network is trained to adhere to Equation (3). During the training process, the domain shifter captures and stores specific perturbations between source and target domain images, while disregarding other irrelevant information. When training with the source domain, the loss brought by the domain shifter is minimal, resulting in an almost identical mapping. Conversely, when training with the target domain, the domain shifter is required to facilitate a transformation that makes the target domain image more closely resemble the source domain image to deceive the discriminator and achieve optimal performance.

$$I_{DSB} = I_B + j \tag{5}$$

where j represents the perturbation learned by the domain shifter in the target domain.

3.3. Feature Disentangling Module

The generalization ability of deep adaptation domain network model largely depends on the quality of feature disentangling. Therefore, we enhanced the functionality of the feature disentangling module.

Subsequent to the domain shifter processing the image, the input images I_A, I_B of both the source and target domains, along with the image I_{DSA}, I_{DSB} that has been processed by the domain shifter, are fed into the encoder E for encoding. This conversion process translates image information into feature information,

$$
\begin{aligned}
F_A &= E(I_A), F_{DSA} = E(I_{DSA}) \\
F_B &= E(I_B), F_{DSB} = E(I_{DSB})
\end{aligned}
\tag{6}
$$

where $E(I_A)$ represents features of encoding the image I_A with the encoder E, and the same is true for others. F_A, F_B represented the features of source and target domains, respectively.

Subsequent to obtaining the features $F_A, F_B, F_{DSA}, F_{DSB}$ through the encoder, the feature separator S will partition these features into two distinct categories, namely content features C_A, C_B and style features S_A, S_B. Content features C_A, C_B are achieved via processing features by S and multiplying ω_A, ω_B separately. In contrast, style features S_A, S_B are generated by subtracting content features C_A, C_B from two-domain features F_A, F_B. This non-linear method of disentangling serves to completely separate content and style features. In separator S, non-linear mapping is also used to ensure the accuracy of content features [36]. As a result, Equation (7) accurately represents the methods used for processing image samples in both the source and target domains,

$$
\begin{aligned}
C_A &= \omega_A S(\lambda_1 F_A + \lambda_2 F_{DSA}), S_A = F_A - C_A, \text{where } \lambda_1 + \lambda_2 = 1. \\
C_B &= \omega_B S(\lambda_3 F_B + \lambda_4 F_{DSB}), S_B = F_B - C_B, \text{where } \lambda_3 + \lambda_4 = 1.
\end{aligned}
\tag{7}
$$

where ω_A, ω_B represent the weight parameters for the distribution of the source and target domains in the content space that has been standardized. The purpose of these parameters is to minimize feature deviation. λ_1, λ_2 are balance coefficients for source features F_A and features F_{DSA}, respectively. These coefficients play a critical role in proportionately integrating features F_A, F_{DSA}. Meanwhile, λ_3, λ_4 serve as balance coefficients for the target features F_B and features F_{DSB}. During training, the value of these coefficients is determined. The content feature is attained by applying a non-linear function and the learnable feature-scale parameter ω_A, ω_B. On the other hand, the style feature is calculated by subtracting content components from the entire feature.

Feature disentangling is used to transfer features across domains [18], and the specific combination method is as follows,

$$
\begin{aligned}
F_{A \to B} &= \omega_{A \to B} C_A + S_B, F_{B \to A} = \omega_{B \to A} C_B + S_A, \\
\text{where } \omega_{A \to B} &= \frac{\omega_B}{\omega_A}, \omega_{B \to A} = \frac{\omega_A}{\omega_B}
\end{aligned}
\tag{8}
$$

where $\omega_{A \to B}, \omega_{B \to A}$ are the weight parameters for the distribution of domain-transfer images $I_{A \to B}, I_{B \to A}$ in the standardized content space, and the transfer domain features $F_{A \to B}, F_{B \to A}$ are synthesized using learnable scale parameters $\omega_{A \to B}, \omega_{B \to A}$.

During the processing of FDDS, the model can learn all the parameters of Equation (8). Upon undergoing S processing, content features C_A, C_B and style features S_A, S_B are recombined to produce novel domain transfer features $F_{A \to B}, F_{B \to A}$. Then, these transferred features $F_{A \to B}, F_{B \to A}$, along with the features F_A, F_B in Equation (6) are projected into image space through the generator G. This leads to the creation of new images $I_{A \to B}, I_{B \to A}, I'_A, I'_B$ that offer greater value when utilized with a loss function [15]. The image generation method is as follows,

$$
\begin{aligned}
I_{A \to B} &= G(F_{A \to B}), I_{B \to A} = G(F_{B \to A}), \\
I'_A &= G(F_A), I'_B = G(F_B),
\end{aligned}
\tag{9}
$$

where $I_{A \to B}, I_{B \to A}$ is the domain adaptation image and I'_A, I'_B is the reconstructed image.

3.4. Training Loss

FDDS uses domain shifter DS, encoders E, feature separators S and generators G to train the network by minimizing the overall network's loss function $\mathcal{L}^d$, while the discriminator D_d tries to maximize it,

$$\min_{DS,E,S,G} \left(\sum_{d \in \{A,B\}} \max_{D_d} \mathcal{L}^d \right) \tag{10}$$

where the domain d is the source domain A or the target domain B.

The overall loss of the model includes reconstruction loss $\mathcal{L}_{Rec}$ with balance factor α_i, consistency loss $\mathcal{L}_{Con}$, perceptual loss $\mathcal{L}_{Per}$ and adversarial loss $\mathcal{L}_{GAN}$ and domain shifter loss $\mathcal{L}_{DS}^d$,

$$\mathcal{L}^d = \alpha_1 \mathcal{L}_{Rec}^d + \alpha_2 \mathcal{L}_{GAN}^d + \alpha_3 \mathcal{L}_{Con}^d + \alpha_4 \mathcal{L}_{Per}^d + \alpha_5 \mathcal{L}_{DS}^d \tag{11}$$

where $\mathcal{L}_{DS}^d$ has been discussed in Equation (4), and the following are the details of the remaining losses.

(a) Reconstruction loss: Loss $\mathcal{L}_R$ is used to represent that the difference between the input image I_d and the reconstructed image I'_d is minimized after E and G training,

$$\mathcal{L}_{Rec}^d = \mathcal{L}_R(I_d, I'_d), \text{ where } I'_d = \underset{i \in \{1,3\}, j \in \{2,4\}}{G} (E(\lambda_i I_d + \lambda_j I_{DSd})) \tag{12}$$

(b) Adversarial loss: Two discriminators $D_{d \in \{A,B\}}$ are used to evaluate the countermeasure loss on the source and the target domain, respectively [13]. The following is the countermeasure loss of source domain A to target domain adaptation B,

$$\mathcal{L}_{GAN}^B = \mathbb{E}_{x_b \sim P_{data(X_b)}}[\log D_B(x_b)] \\ + \mathbb{E}_{(x_a,y_a) \sim P_{data(X_a,Y_a)}}[\log(1 - D_B(I_{A \to B}(x_a, y_a)))] \tag{13}$$

where x_b represents the sample of the target domain, and (x_a, y_a) represents the sample and label of the source domain.

For the adaptation from the target domain B to the source domain A, the same adversarial loss is also imposed. And the standardization is applied to all layers in G and D, and the discriminator is used for complex scenes, such as road-scene adaptation, together with adversarial loss.

(c) Consistency loss: Consistency loss [13] attempts to preserve content and style modules after re-projecting the domain-transfer image into a representation space represented by,

$$\mathcal{L}_{Con}^A = \mathcal{L}_R(C_A, C_{A \to B}) + \mathcal{L}_R(S_A, S_{B \to A}) \tag{14}$$

where $\mathcal{L}_R$ means to minimize the difference between the input image I_d and the reconstructed image I'_d after training in E and G, and the content factor $C_{A \to B}$ and style factor $S_{B \to A}$ are extracted from the domain-transfer image $I_{A \to B}, I_{B \to A}$ through the same encoder E and separator S, respectively. This loss function serves as a clear incentive to maintain consistency in scene structure during the process of domain adaptation.

(d) Perceptual loss: In traditional semi-supervised training, the class labels are utilized as semantic indicators that guide feature disentangling. Conversely, frame training is capable of disentangling features without the requirement of labeled data. To facilitate the unsupervised learning of feature disentanglement, we implemented a perceptual loss [39] in the network, which is a widely employed framework in style transfer. This is defined as follows,

$$\mathcal{L}_{Per}^A = \mathcal{L}_{Content}^A + \lambda \mathcal{L}_{Style}^A \\ \mathcal{L}_{Per}^B = \mathcal{L}_{Content}^B + \lambda \mathcal{L}_{Style}^B \tag{15}$$

where $\mathcal{L}_{Content}^{A}$, $\mathcal{L}_{Content}^{B}$ are content loss and style loss $\mathcal{L}_{Style}^{A}$, $\mathcal{L}_{Style}^{B}$ [15]. Defined as follows,

$$\mathcal{L}_{Content}^{B} = \sum_{l \in L_c} \|P_l(I_A) - P_l(I_{A \to B})\|_2^2$$
$$\mathcal{L}_{Style}^{B} = \sum_{l \in L_s} \|G_1(P_l(I_B)) - G_1(P_l(I_{A \to B}))\|_F^2 \quad (16)$$

where the set of layers L_c, L_s is a subset of the perceptual network P. The weight parameter λ balances two losses, and G_1 is a function of the matrix, given each layer's feature l. We also applied batch normalization to better-stylize the process.

4. Results

4.1. Digit Classification

4.1.1. Dataset

The MNIST dataset [40] is widely employed for handwritten digit recognition, including 60,000 training images and 10,000 test images. The SVHN dataset [41] consists of a vast collection of house number images that have been extracted from Google Street View. Given that the images in SVHN are real-world images of house numbers taken from street-level, they present greater difficulty with varying styles and backgrounds. With 73,257 training images and 26,032 testing images, SVHN is a sizeable dataset. Yet another typical handwritten digit recognition dataset is the USPS dataset [42], featuring over 20,000 pictures.

4.1.2. Baselines and Implementation Details

- Source Only: The classifier trained in the source domain is directly used in the target domain;
- DANN [24]: GAN is used to improve the feature extraction ability of the network;
- DSN [16]: Decouple features from private features and common features, and identify the target domain through common features;
- ADDA [9]: GAN method based on discriminative model;
- CyCADA [13]: Combine features from features and pixels, and introduce cyclic loss into domain adaptive learning;
- GTA [43]: Using the ideas of generation and discrimination, learning similar features by using GAN;
- LC [14]: It is equally important to put forward the lightweight calibrator component and start to pay attention to the performance of the source domain;
- DRANet [15]: Decouple features into style and content features, and propose nonlinear decoupling;
- CDA [44]: Using two-stage comparison to learn good feature separation boundary;
- Target Only: Training directly in the target domain and testing in the target domain is equivalent to supervised learning.

In the digit classification task, our initial network adopted LeNet; used the training set of the source domain to train the network under supervision; and used the task loss to make it a classifier of the source domain. In order to evaluate the above model, we used the source code provided by the author and some experimental data provided by LC [14]. The FDDS model was implemented in Pytorch. All the models in this paper were trained on a single NVIDIA GTX 2080 GPU using CUDA11.7. The running time of our method is about 4~6 h.

FDDS sets hyper-parameters as follows. In order to train the source domain classifier, we added adversarial loss and perceptual loss to the network. During the source domain classifier's training, we set the learning rate to 1×10^{-4} and the batch size to 128, then trained 200 epochs to add to the network. In the process of domain shifting, we refer to the training parameter setting of LC [14], and set the learning rate to 1×10^{-5}, the batch size to 128, and trained 200 epochs. The reason why the learning rate decreases in the domain shifting process is that we do not want to update the generator parameters too early, which would result in a poor training effect.

4.1.3. Experimental Process

We evaluated the performance of the FDDS model on three prevalent digit datasets: MNIST [40], SVHN [41], and USPS [42]. The network training used the identical data-processing and LeNet architecture as [13], and performed three unsupervised domain adaptation tasks: MNIST to USPS, USPS to MNIST and SVHN to MNIST.

We set up two experimental groups: MNIST to USPS and USPS to MNIST. We wanted to train a classification model that performed well on both USPS and MNIST tasks. In this context, MNIST and USPS are each other's source and target domains, and the experiments aimed to investigate the effect of domain exchange between the two domains.

In the SVHN to MNIST task, while the SVHN samples differed significantly in background and scale from those of the MNIST, the digital shape of the primary content remained relatively unchanged. In contrast, the digital shape of handwritten digits in the MNIST was subject to significant variability due to handwriting, thereby presenting a well-defined yet challenging domain adaptation scene. Lastly, the model was assessed using 1000 MNIST samples to gauge its performance.

Therefore, we conducted three groups of experiments, MNIST to USPS, USPS to MNIST and SVHN to MNIST, and compared FDDS with other competitive methods, in which the source only and target only were used as the control group, which, respectively, represented the results of training only using the source/target domain; DANN [24], DSN [16], ADDA [9] and GTA [43] use traditional feature separation methods to separate features into private and shared parts; CyCADA [13] and DRANet [15] separate features into style and content; and LC [14] and CDA [44] both use lightweight components and confrontation generation networks to realize domain adaptation. The numerical results of these methods are shown in Table 1.

Table 1. Accuracy comparison of FDDS to state-of-the-art methods on domain adaptation for digit classification (%).

Method	MNIST to USPS	USPS to MNIST	SVHN to MNIST
Source Only	80.2	44.9	67.1
DANN (2014) [24]	85.1	73.0	70.7
DSN (2016) [16]	85.1	-	82.7
ADDA (2017) [9]	90.1	95.2	80.1
CyCADA (2018) [13]	95.6	96.5	90.4
GTA (2018) [43]	93.4	91.9	93.5
LC (2020) [14]	95.6	97.1	**97.1**
DRANet (2021) [15]	<u>97.6</u>	96.9	-
CDA (2023) [44]	96.6	<u>97.4</u>	96.8
Ours	**98.1**	**97.6**	<u>96.9</u>
Target Only	97.8	99.1	99.5

The optimal performance is bold, and the suboptimal performance is underlined.

As shown in Table 1, FDDS, as an unsupervised learning algorithm, achieved the same performance as directly applying labeled target domain training in the MNIST to USPS task. This is due to the network structure's ability to increase the number of source domain images to match the quantity of target domain samples. By comparing results from MNIST to USPS and USPS to MNIST, it becomes clear that FDDS maintains its efficacy even when the source and target domains are interchanged. The adaptation learning data augmentation in depth domain, which is based on feature disentangling, brings the classifier closer to target-only model training. Additionally, the attention mechanism incorporated into the network aids in generating images during training and helps to differentiate features into content and style components. The results reveal that the model effectively separates the representation of content and style while preserving key features of each domain, thereby achieving outstanding results in digital classification that surpass those of most competing methods. Notably, in the MNIST to USPS task, FDDS's unsupervised digit recognition accuracy was 0.3% higher than that of supervised training using only the target domain.

4.2. Semantic Segmentation Task

4.2.1. Dataset

Compared with digit classification, semantic segmentation tasks are more complex. In order to compare with baselines and explore FDDS's domain adaptation performance in complex scenes, we used GTA5 [45] to Cityscapes [46] to complete the semantic segmentation task. The GTA5 and Cityscapes are 19 classes of classic public datasets, which have high-quality labeled images at the pixel level. Many methods (such as LC [14] and DRANet [15]) use GTA5 and Cityscapes as source and target domain, respectively, for unsupervised domain adaptation tasks. Compared with some methods, such as [47,48] which completed 13 classes of SYNTHIA [49] to the Cityscapes [46] task, our 19 classes task was more complex and better reflected the performance of domain adaptation.

The GTA5 [45] dataset is a computer-generated dataset of driving scenes, while the Cityscapes [46] dataset comprises genuine driving scenes captured in real-world environments. The GTA5 dataset contains 24,966 labeled RGB image samples sized at 1914×1052 pixels, with each image depicting an object or entity that commonly appears within 19 distinct classes. The Cityscapes dataset consists of 5000 labeled RGB images sized at 2040×1016 pixels, gathered from 50 different cities. Our next experiment used these two road scene datasets to explore the domain shift from synthetic images to real images.

4.2.2. Baselines and Implementation Details

- Source Only: The classifier trained in the source domain is directly used in the target domain;
- FCNs [50]: A classical pixel-level method for semantic segmentation using full convolution networks;
- CyCADA [13]: Combine features from features and pixels, and introduce cyclic loss into domain adaptive learning;
- SIBAN [51]: Classify by extracting shared features;
- LC [14]: It is equally important to put forward the lightweight calibrator component and start to pay attention to the performance of the source domain;
- DRANet [15]: Decouple features into style and content features, and propose nonlinear decoupling;
- Target Only: Training directly in the target domain and testing in the target domain is equivalent to supervised learning.

In the task of semantic segmentation, the initial network of FCN uses VVG-16-FCNS, and the rest of the methods use DRN-26 [52]. The training set of the source domain was used to train the network under supervision, and the task loss was used to make it a classifier of the source domain. In order to evaluate the above model, we used the source code provided by the author and some experimental data provided by SIBAN [51]. Our model, FDDS, was implemented in Pytorch. All the models in this paper were trained on an NVIDIA GTX 2080 GPU using CUDA11.7.

During the source domain classifier's training, we set the learning rate to 1×10^{-3}, SGD momentum to 0.9, and the batch size to 8. Under these conditions, 120 iterations were trained. Because semantic segmentation requires higher-quality images, we preprocessed the images in the dataset, adjusted the image size to 1024×1024 pixels, and used $400 * 400$ random pixel blocks for training. Due to memory limitations, we could only train one group of images at a time (a source domain image and a target domain image, the size of which is the same as the input size of domain shifter, which is 572×572). During the process of domain shifting, due to the large scale of the dataset and the complex task of semantic segmentation, we only trained 20 epochs in our experiment, and the running time was 8–10 h.

4.2.3. Experimental Process

In order to demonstrate the practicality of our model in complex real-world scenarios, we employed the GTA5 and Cityscapes datasets, which contain driving-scene images with dense annotations, representing a significantly more challenging task than the previous digit classification task. Training our model on 24,966 images from the GTA5 dataset and 2975 images from the Cityscapes, we employed 19 common classes to facilitate adaptation from synthetic to real-world settings. Figure 4 depicts the mutual transformation between the source and target domains.

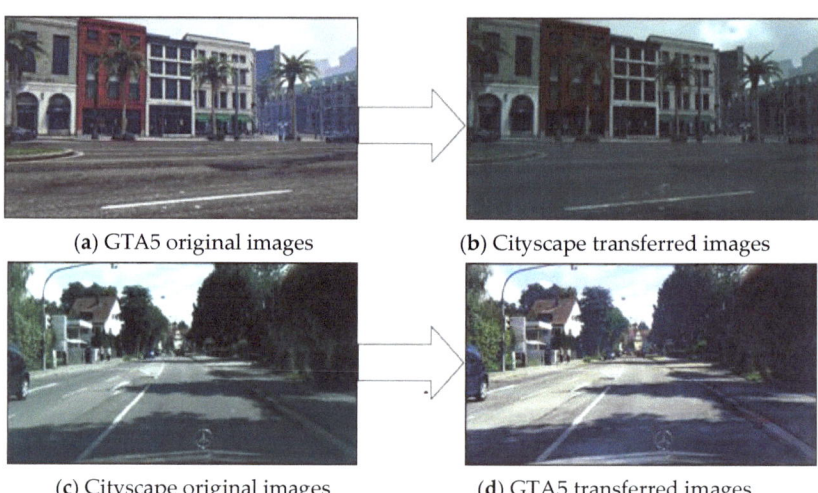

(a) GTA5 original images   (b) Cityscape transferred images

(c) Cityscape original images   (d) GTA5 transferred images

Figure 4. Image transfer between source and target domains.

To evaluate the semantic segmentation performance, we used three metrics: mean intersection-over-union (mIoU), frequency weighted intersection-over-union (fwIoU), and pixel accuracy (PixelAcc). We used the DRN-26 model [52] in CyCADA [13] as our source classifier, which was trained in stylized GTA5 images. To achieve adaptation from synthetic to real-world settings, we trained the DRN-26 model on 19 common classes.

In the task of GTA5 to Cityscape, we identified 19 classes, and compared FDDS with other competitive methods. Among them, FCN [50] is a classical semantic segmentation method, SIBAN [51] is a classification method that extracts shared features, and the linear/non-linear disentangling method was adopted from CyCADA [13], LC [14] and DRANet [15], which was the closest to our method. Numerical results reflecting the accuracy between FDDS and the competing methods under identical conditions are presented in Table 2.

Table 2 shows that our proposed method achieves superior results across all three main semantic segmentation metrics: mIoU, fwIoU and pixel accuracy PixelAcc. Among them, the pixel accuracy improved by 0.8%. There were 19 classes in the dataset, FDDS achieved optimal performance in 11 classes and optimal or suboptimal performance in 16 classes. Specifically, the accuracy of FDDS for the terrain label was improved by 1.1%, and that of the bicycle label was improved by 2.7%. In the case of single source domains and single target domains, our method performed well in the classes with obvious features (such as roads and buildings). This is because we used non-linear adaptation disentangling for feature comparison, which effectively reduces the differences between domains and improves the recognition accuracy of these classes. In contrast, although the domain shifter increased the number of samples compared with other methods, we also found the limitations of the FDDS method, which is that for classes with less training data or relatively changeable appearances, such as poles and trains, the classification performance lacks advantages.

Table 2. Accuracy comparison of FDDS to state-of-the-art methods for the semantic segmentation task on the road scene (%).

	Road	Sidewalk	Building	Wall	Fence	Pole	Traffic Light	Traffic Sign	Vegetation	Terrain	Sky
Source Only	42.7	26.3	51.7	5.5	6.8	13.8	23.6	6.9	75.5	11.5	36.8
FCNs (2015) [50]	70.5	32.3	62.2	14.8	5.4	10.8	14.3	2.7	79.3	21.2	64.6
CyCADA (2018) [13]	79.1	33.1	77.9	23.4	17.3	32.1	33.3	31.8	81.5	26.7	69.0
SIBAN (2019) [51]	83.4	13.1	77.8	20.3	17.6	24.5	22.8	9.7	81.4	29.5	77.3
LC (2020) [14]	83.5	35.2	79.9	**24.6**	16.2	**32.8**	33.1	31.8	81.7	29.2	66.3
DRANet (2021) [15]	83.5	33.7	**80.7**	22.7	19.2	25.2	28.6	25.8	84.1	32.8	84.4
Ours	**84.1**	**35.7**	80.9	23.5	**20.7**	26.7	29.0	27.5	**84.5**	**33.9**	79.6
Target Only	97.3	79.8	88.6	32.5	48.2	56.3	63.6	73.3	89.0	58.9	93.0
	Person	Rider	Car	Truck	Bus	Train	Motorbike	Bicycle	mIoU	fwIoU	Pixel Acc.
Source Only	49.3	0.9	46.7	3.4	5.0	0.0	5.0	1.4	21.7	47.4	62.5
FCNs (2015) [50]	44.1	4.3	70.3	8.0	7.2	0.0	3.6	0.1	27.1	-	-
CyCADA (2018) [13]	62.8	14.7	74.5	20.9	25.6	6.9	18.8	20.4	39.5	72.4	82.3
SIBAN (2019) [51]	42.7	10.8	75.8	21.8	18.9	5.7	14.1	2.1	34.2	-	-
LC (2020) [14]	**63.0**	14.3	**81.8**	21.0	26.5	8.5	16.7	24.0	40.5	75.1	84.0
DRANet (2021) [15]	53.3	13.6	75.7	21.7	30.6	**15.8**	20.3	19.5	40.6	75.6	84.9
Ours	52.9	**15.3**	75.8	21.8	**31.3**	9.7	**20.9**	**26.7**	**41.1**	**76.2**	**85.7**
Target only	78.2	55.2	92.2	45.0	67.3	39.6	49.9	73.6	67.4	89.6	94.3

The optimal performance is bold, and the suboptimal performance is underlined.

5. Discussion

5.1. Feature and Pixel-Level Domain Adaptation

Initially, we conducted an evaluation of transfer in both pixel and feature spaces. Our empirical investigations led us to the conclusion that when migrating USPS and MNIST datasets—two domains exhibiting a relatively small range of transfer learning in pixel space— utilizing images translated by CycleGAN proves highly effective. Indeed, this approach outperforms prior standard domain adaptation methods in terms of both performance and accuracy, and it is comparable to state-of-the-art domain adaptation approaches. Under these circumstances, pixel-level domain adaptation has proven highly advantageous. Conversely, when migrating from the source domain SVHN to the target domain MNIST, we found that feature-level domain adaptation significantly outperformed pixel-level domain adaptation. Consequently, it becomes beneficial to combine the two approaches, leveraging their respective strengths to produce a novel model with high performance across diverse domains.

5.2. Feature Disentangling Method

We propose a new feature separator that is non-linear and distinct from previous linear disentangling approaches. Our separator leverages the domain normalization factor to achieve separation. To demonstrate the effectiveness of our approach, we conducted various combination experiments in the framework, controlling variables and assessing network structure performance and classification results for domain adaptation tasks. The experimental results reveal showed that combining non-linear feature disentangling with the normalization factor yielded superior results than other experiments.

In the process of deep learning, normalization and standardization allow the data to better respond to the activation function and improve the expressiveness of the data. In our method, we set the normalization factor to 255, and map the RGB image [0, 255] to the [0, 1] interval during image preprocessing, so as to complete the normalization. Then, the mean and standard deviations of the RGB images were used to complete the standardization.

After this processing, the average value of the sample is 0 and the standard deviation is 1, which makes the model converge more easily.

In the domain adaptation task involving MNIST and MNIST-M datasets, since both datasets comprise identical content representations, all models exhibited reasonable performance even in the absence of non-linear and normalization factors. It is worth mentioning that MNIST-M denotes a variant of MNIST utilized for unsupervised domain adaptation, wherein background images are replaced, yet each MNIST number is preserved. Conversely, for MNIST and USPS adaptation, there is a significant divergence in content representation. In this case, models without these two components exhibited inadequate classification performance on one side, indicating that the model can only accommodate orientation domain adaptation (e.g., MNIST to USPS or USPS to MNIST) in the same manner as existing approaches. The numerical results are presented in Table 3.

Table 3. The effect of non-linear disentangling and normalization of our method (%).

Non-Linear Disentangling	Normalization	USPS to MNIST	MNIST to USPS	SVHN to MNIST
		86.2	12.7	70.4
	√	90.5	91.6	83.5
√		91.1	97.3	90.6
√	√	97.6	98.1	96.9

As shown in Table 3, our model introduced non-linear disentangling and normalization, which outperformed all the experimental conditions in three tasks. In the three tasks, nonlinear disentangling and normalization both improved the accuracy of domain adaptation. Our experiments indicate that non-linear mapping improves feature disentangling, leading to a significant enhancement in performance. As mentioned in [15], the non-linear mapping of features provides an advantage for clear separation and representation to a greater extent. Moreover, our findings showed that the normalization factor further enhances domain adaptation performance beyond the original experimental setup. Thus, we conclude that both factors play a crucial role in feature disentangling and unsupervised adaptation.

5.3. Domain Shifter Component

As previously discussed, one of the primary constraints of existing domain adaptation approaches is the inability of the same model to serve both the source and target domains. Typically, when confronted with a new target domain, most current domain adaptation methods require fine-tuning of the deployed model parameters [53,54]. However, the model running on the server operates within a specific environment and modifying parameters is not always feasible. Undoubtedly, adapting the running model to the new domain is a time-consuming and costly process unsuitable for time-sensitive applications. In comparison, our proposed method achieves adaptability without updating the running model but merely by integrating a domain shifter, offering greater flexibility when facing novel fields.

While some existing methods enhance target domain performance, they typically do so at the expense of source domain performance. In contrast, our approach maintains strong performance across both domains. To demonstrate the efficacy of our method, we assessed its performance against that of ADDA [9], CyCADA [13], and LC [14] before and after domain adaptation in the SVHN to MNIST task, as illustrated in Table 4.

Table 4. Comparison of some methods in SVHN to MNIST tasks (%).

Method	Source Acc. (Before Adapt)	Source Acc. (After Adapt)	TargetAcc. (After Adapt)
ADDA (2017) [9]	90.5	67.1	80.1
CyCADA (2018) [13]	92.3	31.4	90.4
LC (2020) [14]	93.9	90.8	97.1
Ours	94.1	92.6	96.9

Table 4 shows that ADDA [9] and CyCADA [13] fail to account for the source domain performance following domain adaptation. In addition, LC [14] utilizes a data calibrator to significantly enhance the source domain performance post-adaptation. In contrast, FDDS achieved nearly equivalent source domain performance post-adaptation relative to its performance prior to adaptation. Thus, FDDS offers clear advantages over competing methods.

In Section 3.1, we noted that domain adaptation methods face limitations in their ability to switch flexibly between source and target domains in certain instances. For models providing services, switching between the two domains demands significant resources, which may not be sufficient in time-sensitive applications. However, our proposed method circumvents this issue as it does not necessitate modifications to the model being served. By incorporating a domain shifter, our approach boasts greater versatility in adapting to new fields. Notably, our model is capable of operating in both source and target domains, which is made possible by the inclusion of the domain shifter.

Furthermore, the incorporation of a domain shifter results in moderate overhead. As a component of the network, the introduction of domain shifter into any neural network will inevitably increase the overhead. By comparing the number of parameters between the original network and the domain shifter, we can roughly estimate the overhead of adding the domain shifter. We tested the number of parameters of the classifier and the domain shifter. In the case of digit classification, LeNet comprises 3.1 million parameters, whereas the domain shifter accounts for only 0.19 million parameters, representing a mere 6.12% of the model's total parameters [14]. The relationship between domain shifters and the number of parameters in the original network are shown in Table 5.

Table 5. The number of parameters comparison of domain shifter to original network on two tasks.

	Original Network (ON)	Num of Param. in ON (M)	Num of Param. in DS (M)	Radio of DS to ON (%)
Digit Classification	LeNet	3.1	0.19	6.12
Semantic Segmentation	DRN-26	20.6	0.06	0.29

DS represents domain shift, M represents million.

Table 5 shows the radio of the number of parameters of domain shifter in the original network. Due to different networks, the number of parameters of domain shifter is also different, but from our experimental results, the overhead of the domain shifter is indeed moderate compared with today's large network model. We therefore conclude that, when compared to the larger model being served, the domain shifter, a lightweight component, bolsters the model's ability to identify the source domain without imposing significant overhead on the network.

6. Conclusions

In this paper, we proposed a method of the feature disentangling and domain shifting (FDDS) for domain adaptation. We adopted a lightweight domain shifter component which stored the relevant information of the source domain by adding perturbation to the target domain and generated an image close to the source domain. We added a dual-attention mechanism from the spatial and channel levels in the domain shifter to fuse features. In the feature disentangling, we used learnable weights to nonlinearly decompose a single feature into two parts, namely content and style, and recombined the two parts in different domains to generate domain-transfer images. In the process of domain transfer, FDDS utilized synthetic images to generate realistic domain-transfer images, and achieved performance in various visual recognition tasks, such as image classification and semantic segmentation. The domain shifter with the attention mechanism demonstrated the excellent network performance in the target domain while preserving the classification ability of the source domain, which verified the effectiveness of the attention mechanism in feature extraction in the image-generation field. The results showed that FDDS not only performed well in the digit classification task, but also had higher accuracy than previous methods in the complex cityscapes task. As an unsupervised domain adaptation method, the performance of FDDS was close to that of supervised learning using the target domain. In addition, FDDS is currently suitable for domain adaptation in both single source and single target domains; the limitation is that in the case of less training data, there is no advantage in the transfer effect and classification performance. In the future, this framework can be extended to domain adaptation across three or more domains and can use data augmentation to generate more data to achieve multi-directional transfer from the source domain to multiple target domains. Our work has research significance for domain adaptation methods in complex scenes, as well as in potential applications such as autonomous driving technology in automobile industry tasks.

Author Contributions: Conceptualization, H.C.; methodology, H.C. and H.C.; software, H.C.; validation, H.C. and F.G.; writing—original draft preparation, H.C.; writing—review and editing, F.G. and Q.Z.; project administration, F.G. and Q.Z. All authors have read and agreed to the published version of the manuscript.

Funding: This research was funded by the Zhejiang Provincial Natural Science Foundation of China (ZJNSF), grant numbers LY20E050011.

Informed Consent Statement: Informed consent was obtained from all subjects involved in the study.

Data Availability Statement: Not applicable.

Conflicts of Interest: The authors declare no conflict of interest.

References

1. Zhuang, B.H.; Tan, M.K.; Liu, J.; Liu, L.Q.; Reid, I.; Shen, C.H. Effective Training of Convolutional Neural Networks With Low-Bitwidth Weights and Activations. *IEEE Transations Pattern Anal. Mach. Intell.* **2022**, *44*, 6140–6152. [CrossRef] [PubMed]
2. Matsuo, Y.; LeCun, Y.; Sahani, M.; Precup, D.; Silver, D.; Sugiyama, M.; Uchibe, E.; Morimoto, J. Deep learning, reinforcement learning, and world models. *Neural Netw.* **2022**, *152*, 267–275. [CrossRef] [PubMed]
3. Recht, B.; Roelofs, R.; Schmidt, L.; Shankar, V. Do imagenet classifiers generalize to imagenet? In Proceedings of the International Conference on Machine Learning (ICML), Long Beach, CA, USA, 9–15 June 2019; pp. 5389–5400.
4. Liang, J.; Hu, D.; Feng, J. Domain adaptation with auxiliary target domain-oriented classifier. In Proceedings of the IEEE Conference on Computer Vision and Pattern Recognition (CVPR), Nashvile, TN, USA, 19–25 June 2021; pp. 16632–16642.
5. Mao, C.; Jiang, L.; Dehghani, M.; Vondrick, C.; Sukthankar, R.; Essa, I. Discrete representations strengthen vision transformer robustness. *arXiv* **2021**, arXiv:2111.10493.
6. Chadha, A.; Andreopoulos, Y. Improved techniques for adversarial discriminative domain adaptation. *IEEE Trans. Image Process.* **2020**, *29*, 2622–2637. [CrossRef]
7. Noa, J.; Soto, P.J.; Costa, G.; Wittich, D.; Feitosa, R.Q.; Rottensteiner, F. Adversarial discriminative domain adaptation for deforestation detection. *ISPRS Ann. Photogramm. Remote Sens. Spat. Inf. Sci.* **2021**, *3*, 151–158. [CrossRef]
8. Long, M.; Cao, Y.; Wang, J. Learning transferable features with deep adaptation networks. In Proceedings of the International Conference on Machine Learning (ICML), Lile, France, 6–11 July 2015; pp. 97–105.
9. Tzeng, E.; Hoffman, J.; Saenko, K.; Darrell, T. Adversarial discriminative domain adaptation. In Proceedings of the IEEE Conference on Computer Vision and Pattern Recognition (CVPR), Honolulu, HI, USA, 21–26 July 2017; pp. 7167–7176.
10. Xu, Y.; Fan, H.; Pan, H.; Wu, L.; Tang, Y. Unsupervised Domain Adaptive Object Detection Based on Frequency Domain Adjustment and Pixel-Level Feature Fusion. In Proceedings of the 2022 12th International Conference on CYBER Technology in Automation, Control, and Intelligent Systems (CYBER), Baishan, China, 27–31 July 2022; pp. 196–201.

11. Li, Z.; Togo, R.; Ogawa, T.; Haseyama, M. Improving Model Adaptation for Semantic Segmentation by Learning Model-Invariant Features with Multiple Source-Domain Models. In Proceedings of the 2022 IEEE International Conference on Image Processing (ICIP), Bordeaux, France, 16–19 October 2022; pp. 421–425.
12. Goodfellow, I.; Pouget-Abadie, J.; Mirza, M.; Xu, B.; Warde-Farley, D.; Ozair, S.; Courville, A.; Bengio, Y. Generative adversarial nets. In Proceedings of the Advances in Neural Information Processing Systems (NIPS), Montreal, QC, Canada, 8–13 December 2014; pp. 2672–2680.
13. Hoffman, J.; Tzeng, E.; Park, T.; Zhu, J.Y.; Darrell, T. CyCADA: Cycle-consistent adversarial domain adaptation. In Proceedings of the International Conference on Machine Learning (ICML), Stockholm, Sweden, 10–15 July 2018; pp. 1989–1998.
14. Ye, S.; Wu, K.; Zhou, M.; Yang, Y.; Tan, S.H.; Xu, K.; Song, J.; Bao, C.; Ma, K. Light-weight calibrator: A separable component for unsupervised domain adaptation. In Proceedings of the IEEE Conference on Computer Vision and Pattern Recognition (CVPR), Seattle, WA, USA, 14–19 June 2020; pp. 13736–13745.
15. Lee, S.; Cho, S.; Im, S. Dranet: Disentangling representation and adaptation networks for unsupervised cross-domain adaptation. In Proceedings of the IEEE Conference on Computer Vision and Pattern Recognition (CVPR), Nashville, TN, USA, 19–25 June 2021; pp. 15252–15261.
16. Bousmalis, K.; Trigeorgis, G.; Silberman, N.; Krishnan, D.; Erhan, D. Domain separation networks. *Adv. Neural Inf. Process. Syst.* **2016**, *29*, 343–351.
17. Liu, Y.C.; Yeh, Y.Y.; Fu, T.C.; Wang, S.D.; Chiu, W.C.; Wang, Y. Detach and adapt: Learning cross-domain disentangled deep representation. In Proceedings of the IEEE Conference on Computer Vision and Pattern Recognition (CVPR), Salt Lake City, UT, USA, 18–22 June 2018; pp. 8867–8876.
18. Zhang, R.; Tang, S.; Li, Y.; Guo, J.; Zhang, Y.; Li, J.; Yan, S. Style separation and synthesis via generative adversarial networks. In Proceedings of the 26th ACM International Conference on Multimedia, Seoul, Republic of Korea, 22–26 October 2018; pp. 183–191.
19. Li, C.; Tan, Y.; Chen, W.; Luo, X.; Wang, Z. Attention unet++: A nested attention-aware u-net for liver ct image segmentation. In Proceedings of the IEEE International Conference on Image Processing (ICIP), Virtual Conference, 25–28 October 2020; pp. 345–349.
20. Yosinski, J.; Clune, J.; Bengio, Y.; Lipson, H. How transferable are features in deep neural networks? *Adv. Neural Inf. Process. Syst.* **2014**, *27*, 3320–3328.
21. Tzeng, E.; Hoffman, J.; Zhang, N.; Saenko, K.; Darrell, T. Deep domain confusion: Maximizing for domain invariance. *arXiv* **2014**, arXiv:1412.3474.
22. Long, M.; Wang, J.; Jordan, M.I. Unsupervised domain adaptation with residual transfer networks. *Adv. Neural Inf. Process. Syst.* **2016**, *29*, 136–144.
23. Sun, J.; Wang, Z.H.; Wang, W.; Li, H.J.; Sun, F.M.; Ding, Z.M. Joint Adaptive Dual Graph and Feature Selection for Domain Adaptation. *IEEE Trans. Circuits Syst. Video Technol.* **2022**, *32*, 1453–1466. [CrossRef]
24. Ganin, Y.; Ustinova, E.; Ajakan, H.; Germain, P.; Larochelle, H.; Laviolette, F.O.; Marchand, M.; Lempitsky, V. Domain-adversarial neural networks. *arXiv* **2014**, arXiv:1412.4446.
25. Akada, H.; Bhat, S.F.; Alhashim, I.; Wonka, P. Self-Supervised Learning of Domain Invariant Features for Depth Estimation. In Proceedings of the 2022 IEEE/CVF Winter Conference on Applications of Computer Vision (WACV), Waikoloa, HI, USA, 4–7 January 2022; pp. 997–1007.
26. Bousmalis, K.; Silberman, N.; Dohan, D.; Erhan, D.; Krishnan, D. Unsupervised pixel-level domain adaptation with generative adversarial networks. In Proceedings of the IEEE Conference on Computer Vision and Pattern Recognition (CVPR), Honolulu, HI, USA, 21–26 July 2017; pp. 3722–3731.
27. Guo, M.H.; Xu, T.X.; Liu, J.J.; Liu, Z.N. Attention mechanisms in computer vision: A survey. *Comput. Vis. Media* **2022**, *8*, 331–368. [CrossRef]
28. Chen, X.; Xu, C.; Yang, X.; Tao, D. Attention-gan for object transfiguration in wild images. In Proceedings of the European Conference on Computer Vision (ECCV), Munich, Germany, 8–14 September 2018; pp. 164–180.
29. Emami, H.; Aliabadi, M.M.; Dong, M.; Chinnam, R.B. Spa-gan: Spatial attention gan for image-to-image translation. *IEEE Trans. Multimed.* **2020**, *23*, 391–401. [CrossRef]
30. Daras, G.; Odena, A.; Zhang, H.; Dimakis, A.G. Your local GAN: Designing two dimensional local attention mechanisms for generative models. In Proceedings of the IEEE Conference on Computer Vision and Pattern Recognition (CVPR), Seattle, WA, USA, 14–19 June 2020; pp. 14531–14539.
31. Woo, S.; Park, J.; Lee, J.-Y.; Kweon, I.S. Cbam: Convolutional block attention module. In Proceedings of the European Conference on Computer Vision (ECCV), Munich, Germany, 8–14 September 2018; pp. 3–19.
32. Wang, D.L.; Xiang, S.L.; Zhou, Y.; Mu, J.Z.; Zhou, H.B.; Irampaye, R. Multiple-Attention Mechanism Network for Semantic Segmentation. *Sensors* **2022**, *22*, 4377. [CrossRef] [PubMed]
33. Gonzalez-Garcia, A.; Joost, V.; Bengio, Y. Image-to-image translation for cross-domain disentanglement. *arXiv* **2018**, arXiv:1805.09730.
34. Zou, Y.; Yang, X.; Yu, Z.; Kumar, B.V.; Kautz, J. Joint disentangling and adaptation for cross-domain person re-identification. In Proceedings of the European Conference on Computer Vision (ECCV), Virtual Coference, 23–28 August 2020; pp. 87–104.
35. Tenenbaum, J.B.; Freeman, W.T. Separating style and content with bilinear models. *Neural Comput.* **2000**, *12*, 1247–1283. [CrossRef]

36. Elgammal, A.; Lee, C.S. Separating style and content on a nonlinear manifold. In Proceedings of the IEEE Conference on Computer Vision and Pattern Recognition (CVPR), Washington, DC, USA, 27 June–2 July 2004; pp. 478–485.
37. Gatys, L.A.; Ecker, A.S.; Bethge, M. Image style transfer using convolutional neural networks. In Proceedings of the IEEE Conference on Computer Vision and Pattern Recognition (CVPR), Las Vegas, NV, USA, 27–30 June 2016; pp. 2414–2423.
38. Ronneberger, O.; Fischer, P.; Brox, T. U-net: Convolutional networks for biomedical image segmentation. In Proceedings of the Medical Image Computing and Computer-Assisted Intervention (MICCAI), Munich, Germany, 5–9 October 2015; pp. 234–241.
39. Johnson, J.; Alahi, A.; Fei-Fei, L. Perceptual losses for real-time style transfer and super-resolution. In Proceedings of the European Conference on Computer Vision (ECCV), Amsterdam, The Netherlands, 8–16 October 2016; pp. 694–711.
40. Lecun, Y.; Bottou, L. Gradient-based learning applied to document recognition. *Proc. IEEE* **1998**, *86*, 2278–2324. [CrossRef]
41. Hull, J.J. A database for handwritten text recognition research. *IEEE Trans. Pattern Anal. Mach. Intell.* **2002**, *16*, 550–554. [CrossRef]
42. Netzer, Y.; Wang, T.; Coates, A.; Bissacco, A.; Ng, A.Y. Reading digits in natural images with unsupervised feature learning. In Proceedings of the NIPS Workshop on Deep Learning and Unsupervised Feature Learning, Sierra Nevada, Spain, 16–17 December 2011; pp. 1–9.
43. Sankaranarayanan, S.; Balaji, Y.; Castillo, C.D.; Chellappa, R. Generate to adapt: Aligning domains using generative adversarial networks. In Proceedings of the IEEE Conference on Computer Vision and Pattern Recognition (CVPR), Salt Lake City, UT, USA, 18–22 June 2018; pp. 8503–8512.
44. Yadav, N.; Alam, M.; Farahat, A.; Ghosh, D.; Gupta, C.; Ganguly, A.R. CDA: Contrastive-adversarial domain adaptation. *arXiv* **2023**, arXiv:2301.03826.
45. Richter, S.R.; Vineet, V.; Roth, S.; Koltun, V. Playing for data: Ground truth from computer games. In Proceedings of the European Conference on Computer Vision (ECCV), Amsterdam, The Netherlands, 8–16 October 2016; pp. 102–118.
46. Cordts, M.; Omran, M.; Ramos, S.; Rehfeld, T.; Schiele, B. The cityscapes dataset for semantic urban scene understanding. In Proceedings of the IEEE Conference on Computer Vision and Pattern Recognition (CVPR), Las Vegas, NV, USA, 27–30 June 2016; pp. 3213–3223.
47. Zheng, Z.; Yang, Y. Rectifying Pseudo Label Learning via Uncertainty Estimation for Domain Adaptive Semantic Segmentation. *Int. J. Comput. Vis.* **2021**, *129*, 1106–1120. [CrossRef]
48. Guan, L.; Yuan, X. Iterative Loop Method Combining Active and Semi-Supervised Learning for Domain Adaptive Semantic Segmentation. *arXiv* **2023**, arXiv:2301.13361.
49. Ros, G.; Sellart, L.; Materzynska, J.; Vazquez, D.; Lopez, A.M. The SYNTHIA Dataset: A Large Collection of Synthetic Images for Semantic Segmentation of Urban Scenes. In Proceedings of the IEEE Conference on Computer Vision and Pattern Recognition (CVPR), Las Vegas, NV, USA, 27–30 June 2016.
50. Long, J.; Shelhamer, E.; Darrell, T. Fully Convolutional Networks for Semantic Segmentation. *IEEE Trans. Pattern Anal. Mach. Intell.* **2015**, *39*, 640–651.
51. Luo, Y.; Liu, P.; Guan, T.; Yu, J.; Yang, Y. Significance-Aware Information Bottleneck for Domain Adaptive Semantic Segmentation. In Proceedings of the 2019 IEEE/CVF International Conference on Computer Vision (ICCV), Seoul, Republic of Korea, 27 October–2 November 2019; pp. 6777–6786.
52. Yu, F.; Koltun, V.; Funkhouser, T. Dilated residual networks. In Proceedings of the IEEE Conference on Computer Vision and Pattern Recognition (CVPR), Honolulu, HI, USA, 21–26 July 2017; pp. 472–480.
53. Hu, S.X.; Li, D.; Stühmer, J.; Kim, M.; Hospedales, T.M. Pushing the Limits of Simple Pipelines for Few-Shot Learning: External Data and Fine-Tuning Make a Difference. In Proceedings of the IEEE Conference on Computer Vision and Pattern Recognition (CVPR), New Oreans, LA, USA, 18–24 June 2022; pp. 9058–9067.
54. Zhong, H.Y.; Yu, S.M.; Trinh, H.; Lv, Y.; Yuan, R.; Wang, Y.A. Fine-tuning transfer learning based on DCGAN integrated with self-attention and spectral normalization for bearing fault diagnosis. *Measurement* **2023**, *210*, 112421. [CrossRef]

Disclaimer/Publisher's Note: The statements, opinions and data contained in all publications are solely those of the individual author(s) and contributor(s) and not of MDPI and/or the editor(s). MDPI and/or the editor(s) disclaim responsibility for any injury to people or property resulting from any ideas, methods, instructions or products referred to in the content.

Article

A Hybrid Medium and Long-Term Relative Humidity Point and Interval Prediction Method for Intensive Poultry Farming

Hang Yin [1,2,*], Zeyu Wu [2], Junchao Wu [3], Junjie Jiang [2], Yalin Chen [2], Mingxuan Chen [2], Shixuan Luo [2] and Lijun Gao [4,*]

[1] College of Big Data and Internet, Shenzhen Technology University, Shenzhen 518118, China
[2] College of Information Science and Technology, Zhongkai University of Agriculture and Engineering, Guangzhou 510225, China; wuzeyu0929@163.com (Z.W.); jjj021021@163.com (J.J.); 18148881808@163.com (Y.C.); a13662513987@126.com (M.C.); sx1819395734@163.com (S.L.)
[3] Institute of Collaborative Innovation, University of Macau, Macao 999078, China; junchao.wu@connect.um.edu.mo
[4] College of Computer Science, Shenyang Aerospace University, Shenyang 110136, China
* Correspondence: yinhang@sau.edu.cn (H.Y.); gaolijun@sau.edu.cn (L.G.)

Abstract: The accurate and reliable relative humidity (RH) prediction holds immense significance in effectively controlling the breeding cycle health and optimizing egg production performance in intensive poultry farming environments. However, current RH prediction research mainly focuses on short-term point predictions, which cannot meet the demand for accurate RH control in poultry houses in intensive farming. To compensate for this deficiency, a hybrid medium and long-term RH prediction model capable of precise point and interval prediction is proposed in this study. Firstly, the complexity of RH is reduced using a data denoising method that combines complete ensemble empirical mode decomposition with adaptive noise (CEEMDAN) and permutation entropy. Secondly, important environmental factors are selected from feature correlation and change trends. Thirdly, based on the results of data denoising and feature selection, a BiGRU-Attention model incorporating an attention mechanism is established for medium and long-term RH point prediction. Finally, the Gaussian kernel density estimation (KDE-Gaussian) method is used to fit the point prediction error, and the RH prediction interval at different confidence levels is estimated. This method was applied to analyze the actual collection of waterfowl (Magang geese) environmental datasets from October 2022 to March 2023. The results indicate that the CEEMDAN-FS-BiGRU-Attention model proposed in this study has excellent medium and long-term point prediction performance. In comparison to LSTM, the mean absolute error (MAE), root mean square error (RMSE), and mean absolute percentage error (MAPE) are reduced by 57.7%, 48.2%, and 56.6%, respectively. Furthermore, at different confidence levels, the prediction interval formed by the KDE-Gaussian method is reliable and stable, which meets the need for accurate RH control in intensive farming environments.

Keywords: medium and long-term point prediction; interval prediction; data denoising; feature selection; BiGRU; attention mechanism; KDE-Gaussian

MSC: 68T07

1. Introduction

Poultry are highly sensitive to environmental changes and have poor adaptability to adverse conditions [1]. Environmental control is a critical part of intensive poultry farming [2]. In intensive poultry farming, the high density of production leads to problems such as temperature and humidity imbalances in the rearing environment and excessive emissions of pollutants, which have a negative impact on poultry health and breeding [3,4].

Relative humidity (RH) is one of the key factors in measuring the poultry-rearing environment, and the optimal range for RH is approximately between 50% and 80%. Low RH increases the risk of virus transmission, while high RH accelerates feed mold growth, reduces poultry evaporation rate, increases heat stress, and affects the physiological function and egg production performance of poultry [5–7]. In addition, RH and temperature inside the poultry house are coupled [8], and their changes affect each other. However, compared with temperature, the change in RH is larger and has a shorter period, making it more unstable [9]. Therefore, continuous monitoring of RH in the poultry house with the necessary regulation and intervention are beneficial for ensuring poultry health and improving laying rates [10].

In recent years, various machine learning (ML) and deep learning (DL) based time-series prediction models have been applied to environmental monitoring in livestock and poultry breeding. Arulmozhi et al. [11] compared the performance of different ML models in predicting pigsty humidity and found that the random forest regression (RFR) had the best predictive performance. Liu et al. [12] used an extreme gradient boosting tree (XGBoost) to predict and regulate the concentration of odor in chicken coops, ensuring a clean environment. Lee et al. [13] utilized a recurrent neural network (RNN) to predict and control the temperature and RH of duck houses. Wang et al. [14] proposed a pigsty ammonia concentration prediction model based on a convolutional neural network (CNN) and gate recurrent unit (GRU), which can timely grasp the trend of ammonia concentration changes. Environmental data collected by sensors are complex and nonlinear and are affected by irregular noise. Hybrid prediction methods can achieve better predictive performance [15]. Existing hybrid prediction methods mainly include feature selection, data denoising or decomposition, and selection and optimization of prediction models. Shen et al. [16] employed empirical mode decomposition (EMD) to decompose environmental parameters and used an Elman neural network to predict the ammonia concentration in pigsties. Data decomposition simplifies a complex time series. Song et al. [17] employed kernel principal component analysis (KPCA) to extract the main component information from multiple environmental factors and established a QPSO-RBF combination prediction algorithm to predict ammonia concentration levels in cowsheds. Yin et al. [18] employed LightGBM and the Recursive Feature Elimination (RFE) method to screen out environmental factors with high correlation with carbon dioxide in sheep houses and established an SSA-ELM model to predict carbon dioxide concentration. Feature selection reduces model training time, while optimization algorithms reduce the time required to determine prediction model initialization parameters. Huang et al. [19] used wavelet transformation (WT) to remove noise from environmental data and used a time convolutional network (TCN) to predict the pollution index in waterfowl breeding farms, effectively improving data quality.

Although there has been a certain research foundation regarding the environmental prediction of animal husbandry, it is insufficient to meet the needs for predicting RH within poultry houses. Current research mainly focuses on the one-step-ahead prediction stage, which estimates the next predicted value using partial past observations [20]. Poultry is sensitive and responsive to environmental changes. Due to their biological characteristics, changes in environmental conditions do not immediately affect the egg production and health indicators of poultry, and it will take a certain amount of time to reflect, showing a certain lagging effect. Short-term point prediction is not conducive to resource scheduling and management regulation in intensive poultry farming and is even less conducive to accurate regulation of breeding period variables and assessment of the whole life cycle health status of poultry. Therefore, achieving RH multi-step-ahead prediction is particularly urgent and necessary. However, as the prediction time steps increase, the predictive performance of the model will inevitably decrease, resulting in more errors and risks and making it difficult for regulators to make decisions. Interval prediction can effectively quantify the risk brought by multi-step point predictions. Unlike point prediction, it ensures that future observation values fall within the specified range by constructing prediction intervals (PI) at different confidence levels. For regulators, it can provide more useful information than point prediction and assist in decision-making and management [21].

Synthesizing the aforementioned research, this study proposes a comprehensive and practical hybrid medium and long-term prediction model that can predict point and interval ranges of RH in intensive poultry farming environments. The main contributions and innovations of this study are as follows:

- Exploring methods to enhance the quality of input data for the model. Spearman rank correlation analysis and gray relation analysis (GRA) are used to eliminate redundant environmental factors, and complete ensemble empirical mode decomposition with adaptive noise (CEEMDAN) and permutation entropy are combined to reduce the noise of RH data. Feature selection and data denoising eliminate interference from redundant data.
- Proposing a deep learning model based on BiGRU and an attention mechanism to achieve effective medium and long-term point prediction of poultry house RH. Compared with common models, the BiGRU-Attention model can improve the utilization rate of multi-dimensional and long-term data, fully extract causal relationships between variables and targets, and enhance the accuracy of medium and long-term RH prediction.
- Demonstrating measures to reduce decision-making risks caused by point prediction errors. Kernel density estimation (KDE) is used to fit the errors generated by point prediction, and PI at different confidence levels is calculated to quantify the risk brought by point prediction errors. This provides regulators with more useful information.

2. Materials and Methods

The proposed architecture of the hybrid medium and long-term RH prediction model mainly consists of five modules: data preprocessing, data denoising, feature selection, RH point prediction, and interval prediction. The data preprocessing module involves linear interpolation to fill in missing data in the sensor-collected Internet of Things (IoT) datasets and ensure data completeness. The data denoising module primarily employs CEEMDAN to decompose RH data and removes the intrinsic mode functions (IMFs) located in the high-frequency region of permutation entropy, thus achieving noise reduction of RH data. In the feature selection module, Spearman rank correlation analysis and GRA are used in feature selection to select out environmental factors with low correlation and similar to RH, simplifying the model training process and enhancing prediction performance. In the RH point prediction module, data is separated into training, validation, and test sets, and a BiGRU-Attention model is built to train on the training set, adjust model parameters using the validation set, and prevent overfitting, finally conducting testing on the test set. In the RH interval prediction module, a KDE and Gaussian kernel function is used to fit the distribution of point prediction errors in the validation set, ultimately achieving medium and long-term point and interval predictions for future RH. The methodological framework is shown in Figure 1.

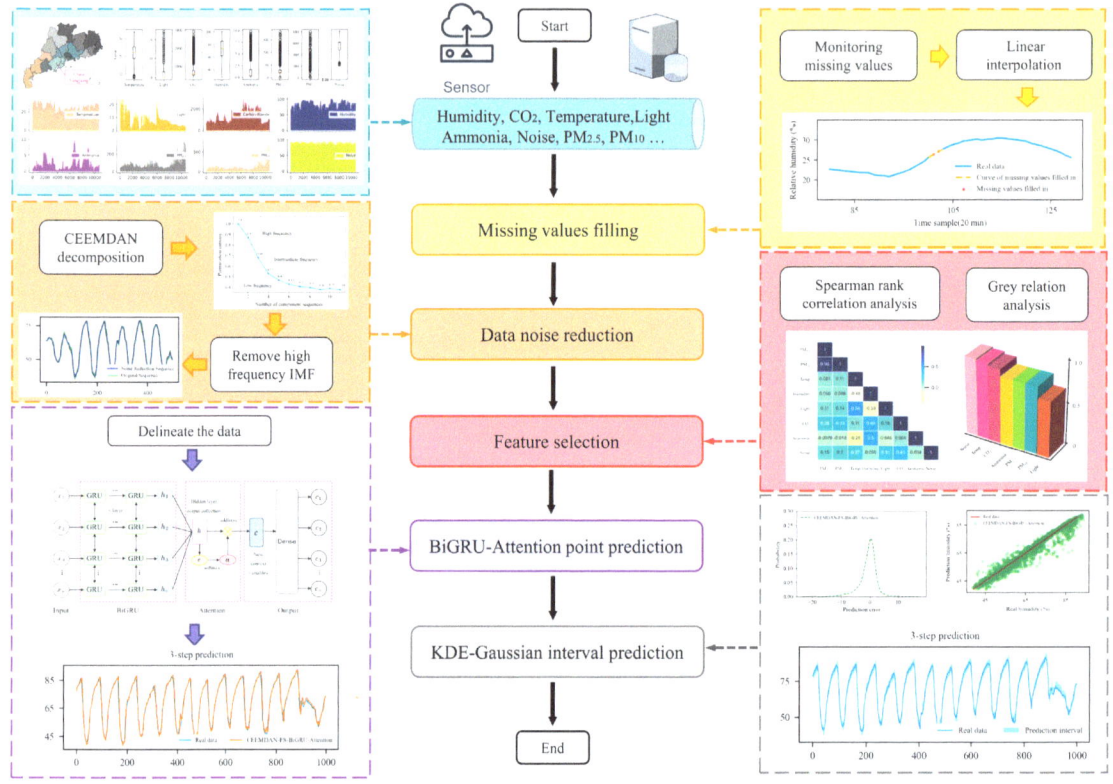

Figure 1. Methodological framework for medium and long-term prediction of humidity.

2.1. Experimental Area

In this study, the Magang Goose Intensive Breeding Base, situated in Jiangmen City, Guangdong Province, China, served as the designated area for collecting experimental data. We have constructed an IoT-based remote monitoring platform for waterfowl-intensive farming environments, as shown in Figure 2. We used eight IoT sensors to collect real-time $PM_{2.5}$, PM_{10}, CO_2, humidity, light, ammonia, temperature, and noise in poultry houses at intervals of 20 min. To ensure the rigor and consistency of the experiment, this study selected the integrated environmental monitoring device from Guangzhou Hairui Information Technology Co., Ltd. (Guangzhou, China). The specific parameters are shown in Table 1. The sensors were chosen to be installed in the goose house, with the CO_2 concentration sensor and total suspended particulate matter sensor positioned 2.4 m above the ground, while the other sensors were positioned at a height of 3.0 to 3.1 m above the ground. As shown in Figure 3, the gateway is used to transmit the IoT-collected data to the database of the remote cloud service center, which can be accessed by the user through a computer browser or smartphone application for easy use.

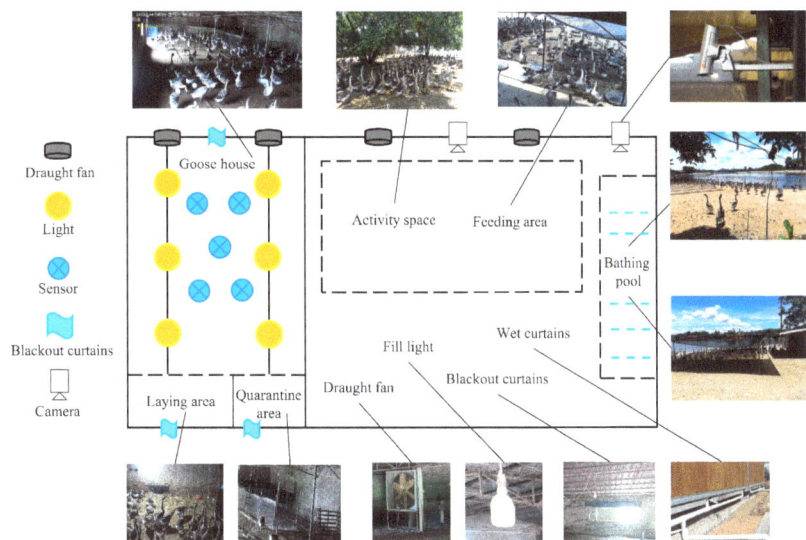

Figure 2. Waterfowl Intensive Farming Site Plan.

Table 1. Technical data of sensors.

Environmental Variables	Measurement Range	Precision	Agreement
Humidity (%)	0~100	±5	IIC
Temperature (°C)	−40~105	±0.4	IIC
Carbon dioxide (ppm)	0~50,000	±20	PWM
Ammonia (ppm)	0~100	±5%	Modbus
Light (lx)	0~65,535	±5	IIC
$PM_{2.5}$ (ug/m^3)	0~999.9	±7%	Modbus
PM_{10} (ug/m^3)	0~999.9	±7%	Modbus
Noise (db)	35~120	±0.5	Modbus

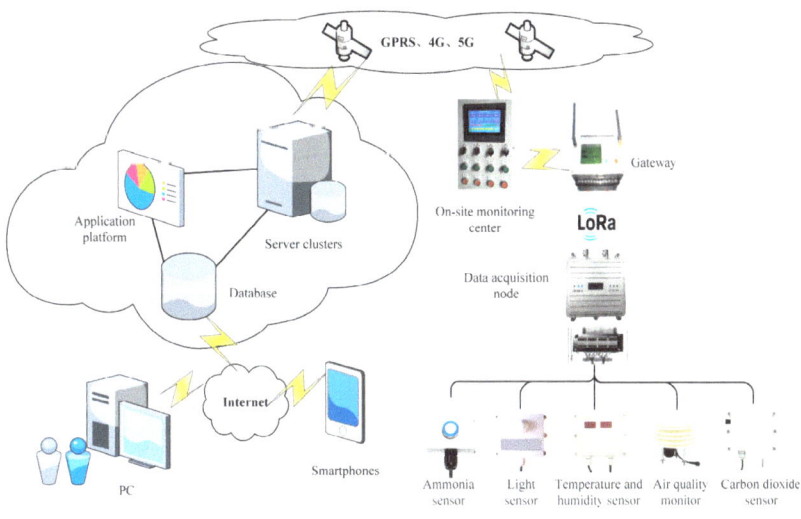

Figure 3. Network structure topology diagram.

2.2. Preprocessing of Data

2.2.1. Missing Data Repair

As a result of factors such as sensor aging, line faults, network delays, and adverse weather conditions, data loss may occur during the IoT sensor online collection of environmental data. Therefore, it is necessary to monitor the collected data and fill in missing data using linear interpolation to maintain data integrity and ensure the normal progress of subsequent experiments. Assuming the coordinates (x_0, y_0) and (x_1, y_1) are known, and x is between x_0 and x_1. The y at position x can be obtained by linear interpolation formula as follows:

$$y = y_0 + (x - x_0)\frac{y_1 - y_0}{x_1 - x_0} \quad (1)$$

2.2.2. Data Outlier Repair and Processing

The environmental data is a typical time series data that exhibits periodicity and trend. Under normal circumstances, there should not be drastic changes in the data between adjacent time points. If the change at a certain moment exceeds 10% of the preceding and succeeding monitored values, it is considered an outlier and is smoothed using a smoothing method. The formula is as follows:

$$x_k = \frac{x_{k-1} + x_{k+1}}{2} \quad (2)$$

2.2.3. Data Set Division

The data sampling for this study took place between 10 October 2022 and 13 March 2023, during which period there was a relatively higher poultry egg production rate [22]. After filling in missing data values, the total number of samples included amounted to 11,021. The data was divided into training, validation, and testing sets in a ratio of 7:3:3. Specifically, the training set was utilized to train the model, while the validation set acted as an effective component in averting overfitting and assisting in fitting the point prediction error distribution. Ultimately, the model's predictive efficacy was assessed on the testing dataset.

2.2.4. Data Normalization

Significant scale differences between different environmental factors may lead to train models that lack robustness or fall into overfitting. Therefore, there is a need to transform the data to a uniform scale. In this study, mapping the data to the interval [0, 1] using the Max-Min normalization formula:

$$X_{new} = \frac{X - X_{min}}{X_{max} - X_{min}} \quad (3)$$

2.3. Data Noise Reduction Method

2.3.1. Complete Ensemble Empirical Mode Decomposition with Adaptive Noise

CEEMDAN is a novel signal time–frequency analysis and processing method suitable for non-stationary signals [23]. By adding specific white noise during each step of the mode decomposition and then averaging them, it can effectively address the issue of IMF mode mixing produced by Empirical Mode Decomposition (EMD) while overcoming the noise residue problem in Ensemble Empirical Mode Decomposition (EEMD), resulting in a reconstruction error essentially equaling to zero with fewer averaging times and higher computational efficiency. Additionally, CEEMDAN introduces the complete ensemble strategy, which improves the stability and reliability of the decomposition results by performing multiple random samplings and decompositions on the signal. This method has been used for the decomposition and denoising of time series in various fields [24–26].

2.3.2. Permutation Entropy

Permutation Entropy [27] is a metric used to measure the randomness and abrupt changes in time series, characterized by its fast calculation speed and strong anti-interference ability. Meanwhile, it has found extensive applications across various domains for calculating the complexity of time series [28–30], owing to its high sensitivity and robustness towards mutation-type time series.

2.4. Feature Selection Method

2.4.1. Spearman Rank Correlation Analysis

Spearman rank correlation analysis [31] is a measure applied to quantify the degree of correlation between variables. Its calculation method is as follows:

$$r^s = 1 - \frac{6\sum_{r=1}^{n} d_r^2}{n(n^2-1)} \quad (4)$$

where n is the sample size and d_r is the positional difference between the two data pairs at the r-th index in the sequence. The Spearman rank correlation coefficient, denoted by r^s, has a value between 1 and -1, with a larger absolute value indicating a stronger correlation.

2.4.2. Grey Relational Analysis

Grey Relational Analysis (GRA) [32] evaluates the level of correlation between variables by calculating the similarity in sequence among their respective factors. GRA uses Grey Relational Degree (GRD) as a quantitative index to measure the extent of the input feature impact on the output, which ranges between 0 and 1. A higher association score indicates greater similarity between input and output.

2.5. BiGRU-Attention Point Prediction Model

2.5.1. Gate Recurrent Unit

Gate Recurrent Unit (GRU) is an RNN-based improved model [33]. By introducing gating devices and a cyclic structure, GRU effectively overcomes the problems of long dependencies and gradient vanishing in RNN. Compared with LSTM, GRU selects information only through updating gate and resetting gate, which results in a shorter runtime. Figure 4a illustrates the architecture of the GRU neural network. Here, the updating gate selectively forgets the unimportant information in the previous moment hidden layer state, while the resetting gate implements selective memory of current and historical information. The formula is expressed as:

$$r_t = \sigma(W_r \cdot [h_{t-1}, x_t]) \quad (5)$$

$$z_t = \sigma(W_z \cdot [h_{t-1}, x_t]) \quad (6)$$

$$\tilde{h}_t = \tanh(W_h \cdot [r_t * h_{t-1}, x_t]) \quad (7)$$

$$h_t = (1 - z_t) * h_{t-1} + z_t * \tilde{h}_t \quad (8)$$

where r_t is the reset gate, z_t is the update gate; x_t is the current input, $\tilde{h}_t$ represents the summary of the current input and preceding hidden state, and h_t is the updated output of the hidden layer. W_r and W_z are the weight matrices for the reset gate and update gate, W_h is the weight matrix for the hidden layer, and σ and $\tanh$ are the sigmoid activation function and hyperbolic tangent activation function, respectively.

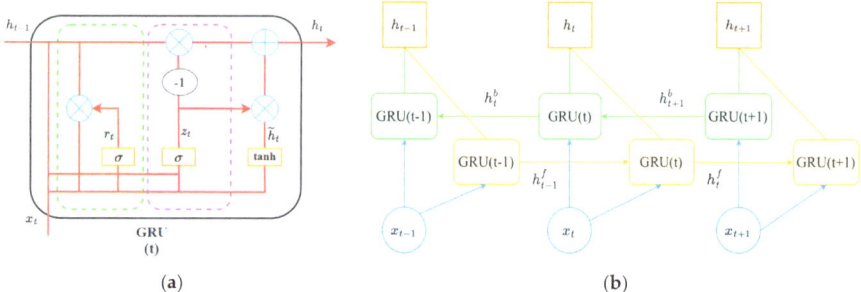

Figure 4. GRU and BiGRU structure. (**a**) GRU structure. (**b**) BiGRU structure.

2.5.2. Bi-Directional Gate Recurrent Unit

Bi-directional Gate Recurrent Unit (BiGRU) consists of two layers of GRU. One layer handles the forward propagation of the input sequence, while the other layer handles the reverse propagation of the input sequence. The final prediction is obtained by fitting the output results of the two layers. Compared with a single-layer GRU, BiGRU can better utilize both past and future information of the input sequence data. The network structure of BiGRU is illustrated in Figure 4b.

$$C^f_t = GRU\left(x_t, h^f_{t-1}, C^f_{t-1}\right) \quad (9)$$

$$C^b_t = GRU\left(x_t, h^b_{t-1}, C^b_{t-1}\right) \quad (10)$$

$$C_t = W^T C^f_{t-1} + W^V C^b_{t-1} \quad (11)$$

where C^f_{t-1} and C^b_{t-1} represent the memory cell state of the forward and backward GRU at time t, and W^T and W^V represent weight coefficients of the forward and backward matrix units.

2.5.3. BiGRU-Attention

The attention mechanism simulates the way human brains think. When processing received information, the brain focuses on important information and ignores irrelevant things. By incorporating the attention mechanism into the time series prediction process, correlations between multiple dimensions of the time series can be effectively explored, and the utilization rate of historically important information can be improved, thereby enhancing the predictive performance of the model [34]. We add an attention mechanism layer behind the BiGRU neural network to prevent the model from losing significant information due to long time series.

Figure 5 illustrates the architecture of the BiGRU-Attention model. The hidden layer output h_t of the BiGRU is fed into the attention layer, and the importance degree of each historical moment is calculated and scored using the softmax activation function to acquire the attention weights. Finally, the attention weights corresponding to each historical state are assigned to obtain the output c_t optimized by the attention mechanism. The formulas are:

$$e_t = \tanh(W_s h_t + b_s) \quad (12)$$

$$a_t = softmax(e_t) \quad (13)$$

$$c_t = \sum_{t=1}^{T} a_t h_t \quad (14)$$

where e_t is the matching degree score, which represents the correlation between the historical state and the output state; W_s and b_s are matrix weight and bias terms. a_t is the attention weight of h_t, indicating the importance of this historical state.

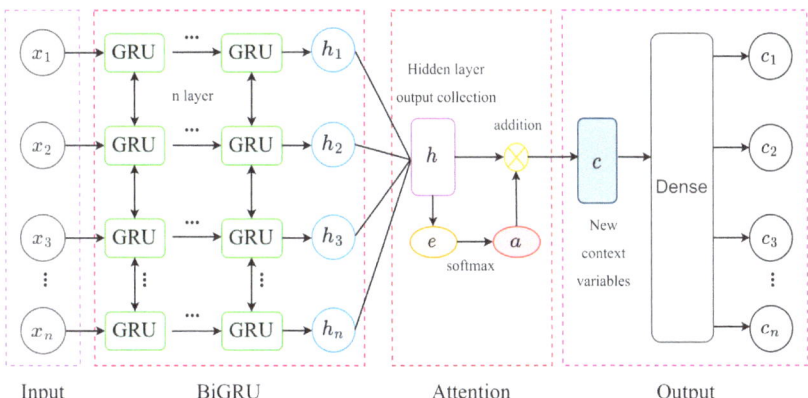

Figure 5. BiGRU-Attention architecture.

2.6. Kernel Density Estimation

Interval prediction aims to output upper and lower bounds and obtain PI under a given confidence interval. Based on Kernel Density Estimation (KDE) [35] method, which is a non-parametric probability density estimation method, this study analyzes and estimates the errors of point prediction on the model test set. Non-parametric estimation does not require any distribution assumptions when fitting unknown distributions of observed data. Instead, it models the probability density function based on the observed data itself, with lower usage requirements and good performance. Currently, KDE has been applied to interval prediction of time series across multiple fields and achieved good results [36–38]. However, it has not yet been applied in livestock and poultry environmental monitoring. The process of KDE is as follows:

Assuming $y = \{y_1, y_2, \cdots, y_n\}$ is the sample data of n continuous distributions f (y) and the function $\hat{f}(y)$ is the kernel density estimate of f (y), the expression of $\hat{f}(y)$ is:

$$\hat{f}(y) = \frac{1}{nh} \sum_{i=1}^{n} K\left(\frac{y - y_i}{h}\right) \tag{15}$$

where n denotes the sample count within the prediction error interval, h denotes the bandwidth factor, and K represents the kernel function. Different kernel functions result in different distributions. A Gaussian kernel function is applied in this study, whose equation expression is expressed as follows:

$$K(x) = \frac{1}{\sqrt{2\pi}} \exp\left(-\frac{1}{2}(x)^2\right) \tag{16}$$

2.7. Model Performance Evaluation Metrics

2.7.1. Metrics for Evaluating Point Prediction

In this study, the performance of point predictions was assessed using evaluation metrics, including Root Mean Squared Error (RMSE), Mean Absolute Error (MAE), and Mean Absolute Percentage Error (MAPE). Assuming there are n prediction samples, where

Y_i represents the predicted results, and y_i represents the actual values. The formulas for the selected evaluation metrics are as follows:

$$\text{RMSE} = \sqrt{\frac{1}{n}\sum_{i=1}^{n}(Y_i - y_i)^2} \tag{17}$$

$$\text{MAE} = \frac{1}{n}\sum_{i=1}^{n}|Y_i - y_i| \tag{18}$$

$$\text{MAPE} = \frac{100\%}{n}\sum_{i=1}^{n}\left|\frac{Y_i - y_i}{y_i}\right| \tag{19}$$

2.7.2. Metrics for Evaluating Interval Prediction

In this study, the performance of the interval predictions was evaluated using the metrics of Prediction Interval Coverage Probability (PICP), Percentage of Incorrectly Narrowed Intervals Average Width (PINAW), and Coverage Weighted Confidence (CWC). Among them, PICP is used to indicate the probability of observation values falling inside the predicted interval. The closer to 1 the value of PICP is, the higher the probability that the predicted interval covers the actual observed values. PINAW mainly calculates the percentage of the average width between the predicted interval and the actual observation values, preventing the model from pursuing high PICP at the cost of a too-wide interval width, which makes the predicted interval unable to effectively describe the uncertain information of the observation values. The CWC metric simultaneously considers the coverage and width of the model-predicted interval, providing a comprehensive evaluation of interval prediction.

$$\text{PICP} = \frac{1}{N}\left(\sum_{i=1}^{N} C_i\right)$$

$$C_i = \begin{cases} 1, & y_i \in [y_i^U, y_i^L] \\ 0, & y_i \notin [y_i^U, y_i^L] \end{cases} \tag{20}$$

$$\text{PINAW} = \frac{1}{NA}\sum_{i=1}^{N}\left|y_i^U - y_i^L\right| \tag{21}$$

$$\text{CWC} = \text{PINAW}\left(1 + \gamma e^{-\eta(\text{PICP}-\mu)}\right)$$

$$\gamma = \begin{cases} 0, & \text{PICP} \geq \mu \\ 1, & \text{PICP} < \mu \end{cases} \tag{22}$$

where y_i^U, y_i^L are the upper and lower bounds of prediction, y_i represents the true value, A is the range of target value; μ is the minimum confidence level for qualified PICP; η donates the penalty factor for unqualified PICP, which is set to 1 here. Therefore, when PICP is lower than the confidence level, PICP is the main influencing factor of CWC, and vice versa for PINAW.

3. Results

3.1. Experimental Environment and Parameter Selection

The experimental setup consisted of an Intel(R) I7-13700H 5.0 GHz CPU, an Nvidia Geforce RTX3060 graphics card, and 24 GB of memory, with Python 3.8.5 as the programming language. The ML and DL frameworks were constructed using Scikit-learn 1.1.1 and Tensorflow 2.10.0.

This study compared commonly used baseline models Random Forest (RF), Long Short-Term Memory (LSTM), Bidirectional Long Short-Term Memory (BiLSTM), GRU, BiGRU, and the BiGRU-Attention point prediction model used in this research. During the model training process, we first utilized the Adam optimizer and MSE loss function, in combination with a grid search algorithm, to acquire the preliminary optimal parameters for the models. Subsequently, we manually fine-tuned the critical parameters within the models while applying learning rate reduction and early stop mechanisms to prevent over-fitting and acquire the optimal parameter combinations. The best results of the grid search for the BiGRU-Attention model are presented in Table 2. The key parameter settings for LSTM, GRU, BiLSTM, and BiGRU were identical to those of the BiGRU-Attention model, while the RF parameters were determined using a trial-and-error approach.

Table 2. Grid Search Scope and Results.

Hyperparameters	Optimal Parameters
Learning rate	0.01
Batch size	64
Hidden units	100
Attention units	64

3.2. Data Denoising Based on CEEMDAN and Permutation Entropy

Due to various factors such as weather, human activities, and monitoring methods, the RH data collected by IoT sensors are inevitably subject to certain interference, resulting in instability, volatility, and noise. Noise increases the difficulty for models to discover important information, leading to poor performance during model training or overfitting, affecting the accuracy and robustness of the model [39]. To reduce the random interference caused by noise, this study employed the CEEMDAN method, in combination with permutation entropy, to denoise the data. Firstly, the CEEMDAN was used to decompose the RH data into multiple IMFs, and the permutation entropy of each IMF was calculated, respectively, as shown in Figure 6.

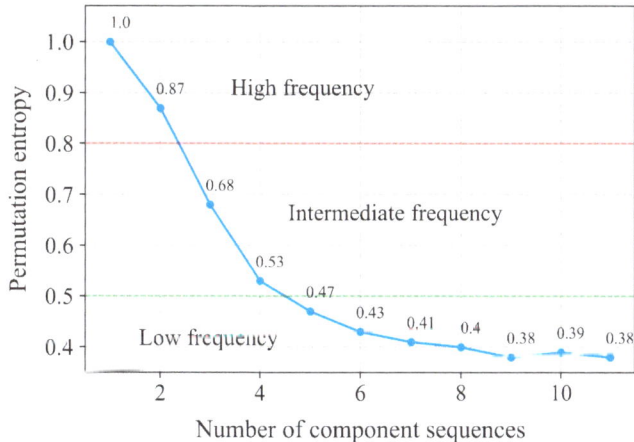

Figure 6. The permutation entropy of each IMF after decomposition.

We can observe that the permutation entropies of IMF1 and IMF2 are in the high-frequency area, indicating that these two IMFs are relatively complex and irregular compared to other IMFs. Therefore, they were regarded as noise and removed. After the denoising process was complete, we extracted the first 1000 pieces of data to observe the denoising effect. As shown in Figure 7, the RH sequence after denoising is smoother and more stable than the original data, indicating that the denoising method can significantly extract non-stationary features and reduce the volatility and complexity of the RH sequence.

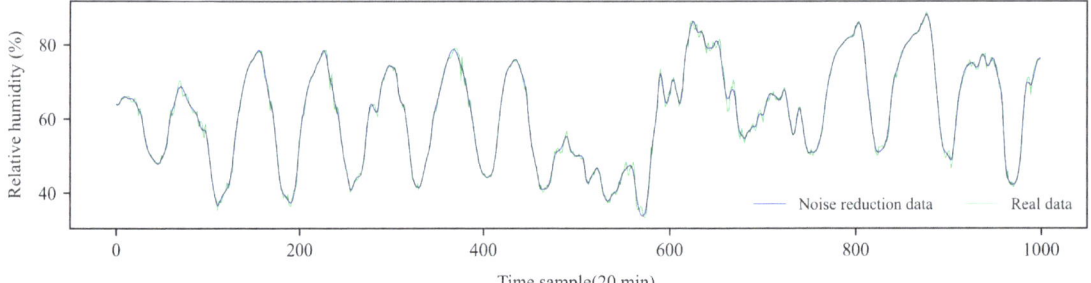

Figure 7. Comparison before and after data denoising.

3.3. Selecting Important Environmental Factors

The environmental factors within poultry sheds are interrelated and coupled, requiring careful consideration of the impacts of different environmental factors on RH. This study conducted experimental comparisons of multiple feature selection methods and ultimately found that utilizing Spearman rank correlation analysis and grey relational analysis (GRA) yielded the optimal results in selecting important environmental factors. The former mainly considers the degree of correlation between RH and different environmental factors, while the latter considers the similarity of the curve changes between RH and different environments, and the calculation results are presented in Figure 8. According to Figure 8a, it can be seen that temperature, carbon dioxide, ammonia, and light have a higher correlation with RH than other environmental factors. However, the GBD between light and RH is relatively low in Figure 8b, only 0.672, indicating that the curve change pattern of light and RH has some differences, and their similarity is not very high. Therefore, considering the results of both the Spearman rank correlation analysis and GRA, temperature, carbon dioxide, and ammonia are further selected as the input factors for the prediction model.

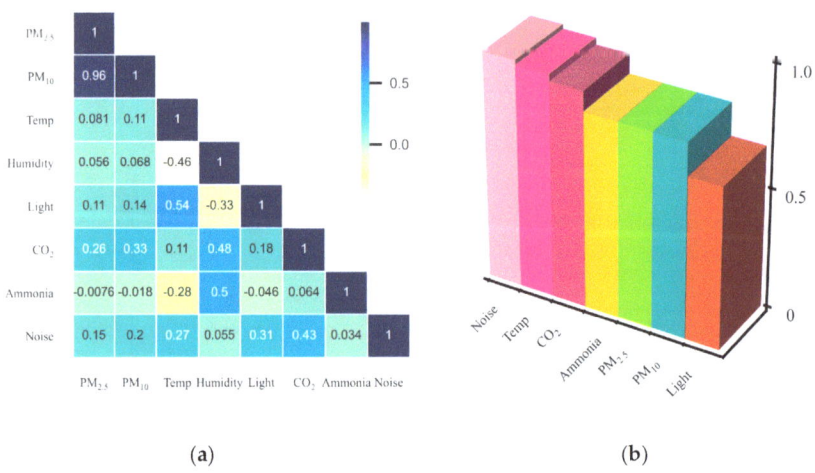

Figure 8. Feature selection process. (**a**) Spearman rank correlation heatmap. (**b**) GBD with different environmental factors.

3.4. Medium and Long-Term RH Point Prediction Based on BiGRU-Attention

With the specified parameter settings, different prediction models were trained for different prediction frameworks and baseline models, and the point prediction performance indicators were calculated. As shown in Table 3 and Figure 9, the proposed CEEMDAN-FS-BiGRU-Attention prediction model has higher stability and accuracy, with a close-fitting prediction curve to the observed values and lower fluctuation, indicating that its fitting effect is superior to other models. Furthermore, we can also observe that an increase in the prediction time step will exacerbate the fluctuation of the prediction curve. Specifically, when the prediction step length is 3, most models exhibit a trend of over-prediction or under-prediction, with large deviations from the observed values, which is worthy of further comparison and discussion.

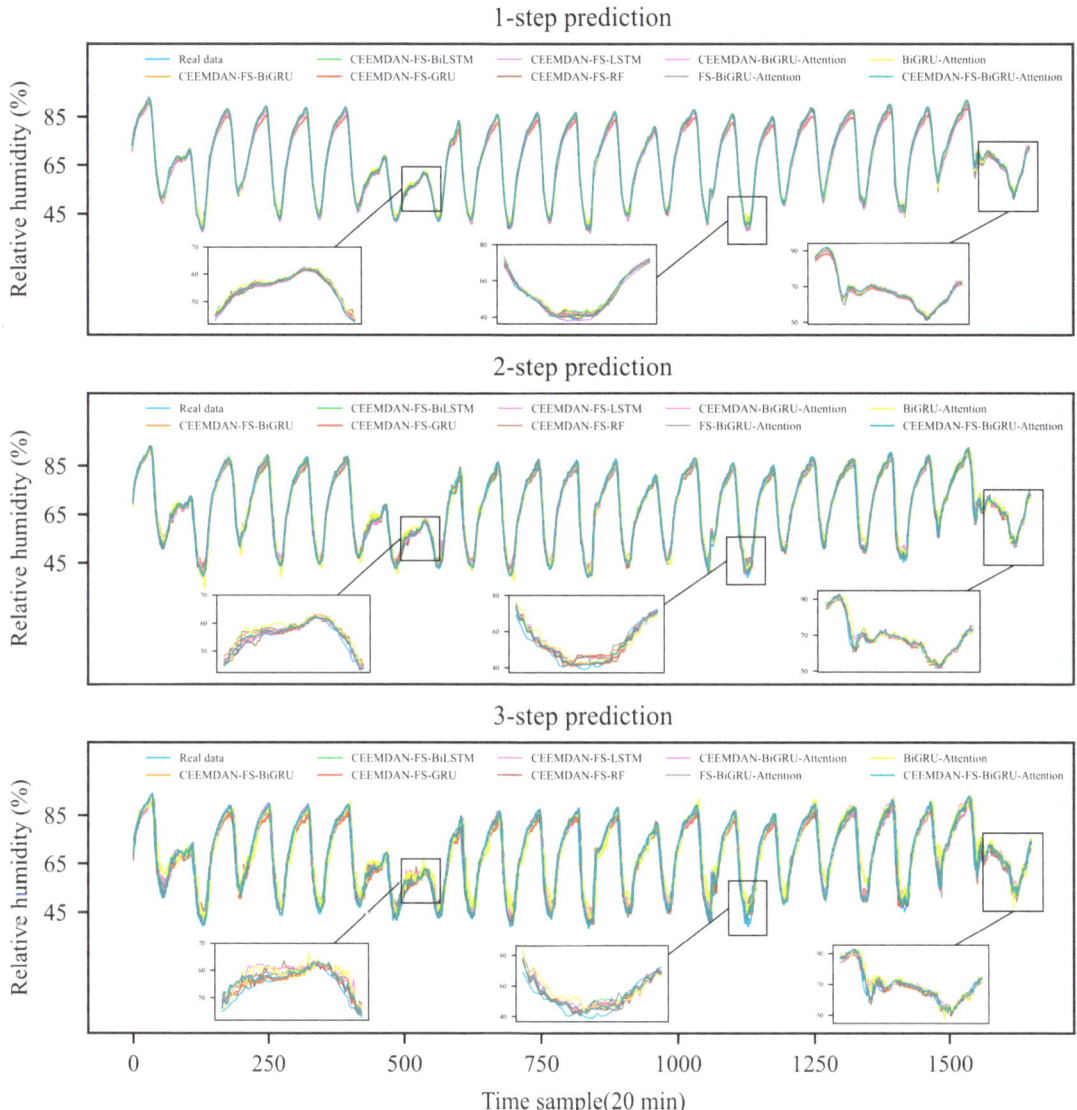

Figure 9. Different model point prediction experimental results.

Table 3. Different baseline model point prediction comparison results.

Model	MAE			RMSE			MAPE		
	1-Step	2-Step	3-Step	1-Step	2-Step	3-Step	1-Step	2-Step	3-Step
RF	1.544	2.327	4.317	2.185	3.257	5.885	2.446	3.710	6.728
FS-RF	1.182	1.974	3.828	1.732	2.789	5.263	1.894	3.123	5.904
CEEMDAN-RF	0.799	1.629	3.388	1.121	2.274	4.610	1.316	2.638	5.327
CEEMDAN-FS-RF	0.709	1.254	2.744	0.989	1.773	3.908	1.153	2.020	4.280
LSTM	1.499	2.910	5.096	1.813	3.441	5.975	2.340	4.508	7.745
FS-LSTM	1.162	1.890	3.362	1.516	2.443	4.831	1.816	2.923	5.060
CEEMDAN-LSTM	1.166	1.899	4.150	1.507	2.600	5.176	1.830	3.060	6.330
CEEMDAN-FS-LSTM	1.044	1.372	3.039	1.231	1.920	4.202	1.636	2.188	4.596
GRU	1.188	2.475	4.584	1.518	3.385	5.693	1.908	4.011	6.965
FS-GRU	1.196	1.850	3.901	1.456	2.418	4.931	1.833	2.907	5.854
CEEMDAN-GRU	0.884	1.954	4.060	1.254	2.629	4.999	1.485	3.187	6.243
CEEMDAN-FS-GRU	0.802	1.482	2.952	1.034	1.916	3.681	1.309	2.380	4.494
BiLSTM	1.238	2.234	4.159	1.653	3.100	5.763	1.978	3.538	6.351
FS-BiLSTM	1.240	2.067	3.235	1.520	2.847	4.476	1.995	3.331	4.916
CEEMDAN-BiLSTM	0.863	2.328	3.944	1.211	2.787	4.813	0.014	3.514	5.905
CEEMDAN-FS-BiLSTM	0.870	1.316	2.647	1.106	1.691	3.813	1.346	2.099	4.067
BiGRU	1.025	2.458	4.367	1.362	3.089	5.533	1.696	3.845	6.613
FS-BiGRU	0.916	1.548	3.575	1.161	2.092	4.602	1.450	2.456	5.419
CEEMDAN-BiGRU	0.499	2.030	3.791	0.693	2.467	4.651	0.804	3.061	5.792
CEEMDAN-FS-BiGRU	0.763	1.388	2.565	0.912	1.675	3.421	1.147	2.103	3.825
BiGRU-Attention	0.867	1.668	3.687	1.252	2.362	5.283	1.411	2.682	5.701
FS-BiGRU-Attention	0.854	1.427	2.842	1.214	2.034	3.929	1.410	2.271	4.397
CEEMDAN-BiGRU-Attention	0.838	1.453	3.179	1.210	2.092	4.453	1.337	2.319	4.983
CEEMDAN-FS-BiGRU-Attention	0.557	0.932	2.154	0.781	1.344	3.094	0.896	1.470	3.355

3.5. Medium and Long-Term RH Interval Prediction Based on KDE-Gaussian

Through point prediction comparative analysis, we demonstrated that the CEEMDAN-FS-BiGRU-Attention prediction model has outstanding point prediction performance. However, as shown in Table 3 and Figure 9, many unavoidable errors still occur during the prediction process, and the errors accumulate as the prediction length increases. Hence, it is imperative to implement interval prediction of RH to overcome the risk associated with point prediction bias and offer more useful information.

In this study, the Gaussian kernel density estimation (KDE-Gaussian) method was used to realize the interval prediction of RH. First, the point prediction error distribution generated by the validation set during model training was statistically analyzed to obtain the error distribution. Then, the KDE-Gaussian method was used to fit the error distribution curve to acquire the probability distribution function. Finally, the prediction interval formed under different confidence distribution levels was calculated and compared.

Figure 10 and Table 4 show the interval prediction results based on CEEMDAN-FS-BiGRU-Attention-KDE-Gaussian. We can observe that the prediction intervals are within the specified confidence level for different prediction time steps, indicating that the method can stably measure the uncertain risks of RH sequence changes. At the same time, the low PINAW indicates that the formed prediction intervals are generally narrow and can well describe the irregular variation information of the RH sequence.

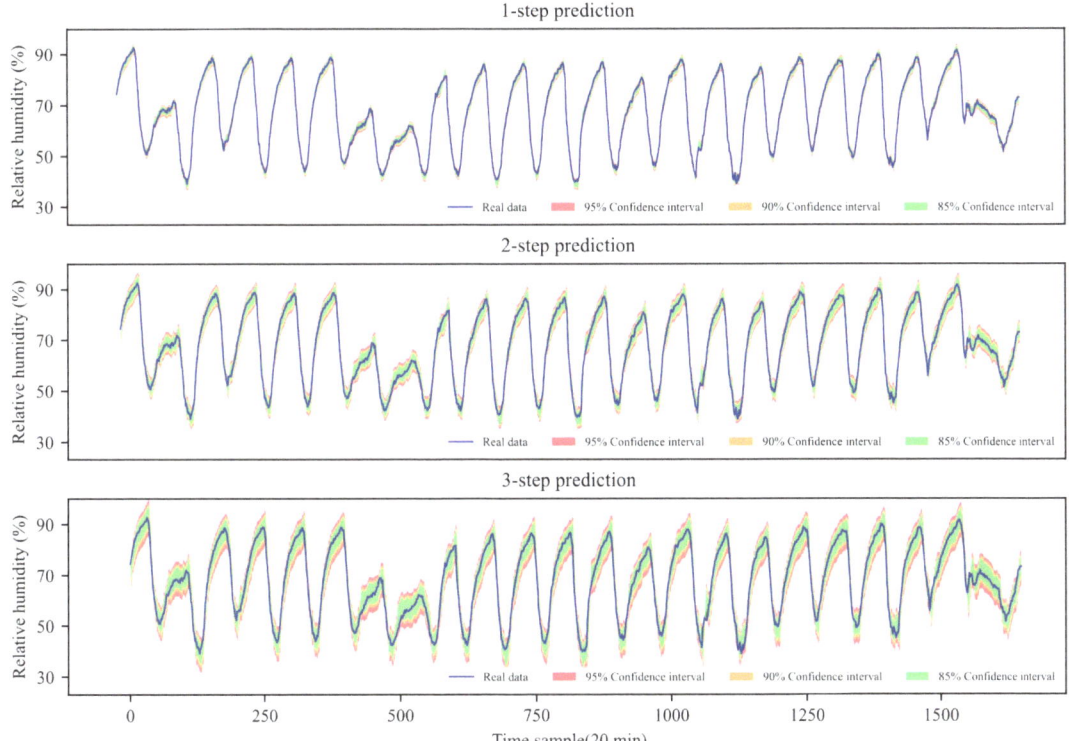

Figure 10. Interval prediction results of CEEMDAN-FS-BiGRU-Attention-KDE-Gaussian.

Table 4. Interval prediction results of CEEMDAN-FS-BiGRU-Attention-KDE-Gaussian.

Prediction Step	Confidence Level	PICP	PINAW	CWC
1-step prediction	95%	0.964	0.082	0.082
	90%	0.929	0.064	0.064
	85%	0.881	0.051	0.051
2-step prediction	95%	0.950	0.144	0.144
	90%	0.908	0.114	0.114
	85%	0.868	0.095	0.095
3-step prediction	95%	0.953	0.201	0.201
	90%	0.914	0.159	0.159
	85%	0.875	0.129	0.129

4. Discussion

4.1. Analysis of Model Results in Comparison Based on Feature Selection

After feature selection, the MAE of FS-BiGRU-Attention and FS-BiGRU models for predicting the future 3 steps decreased by 23.0% and 18.1%, respectively, and their RMSE decreased by 25.6% and 32.2%, respectively. Additionally, the MAPE also decreased by 22.8% and 18.1%. As shown in Figure 11, other baseline models' predictive errors were reduced, and their prediction performance significantly improved after the feature selection process. This indicates that the feature selection method based on Spearman rank correlation analysis and GRA can effectively select out environmental factors that have a high correlation with RH and similar trend changes. By eliminating redundant environmental factors, feature selection can help models focus on relevant and useful covariates, making it easier to uncover causal relationships between input and output data and thereby improve the predictive performance.

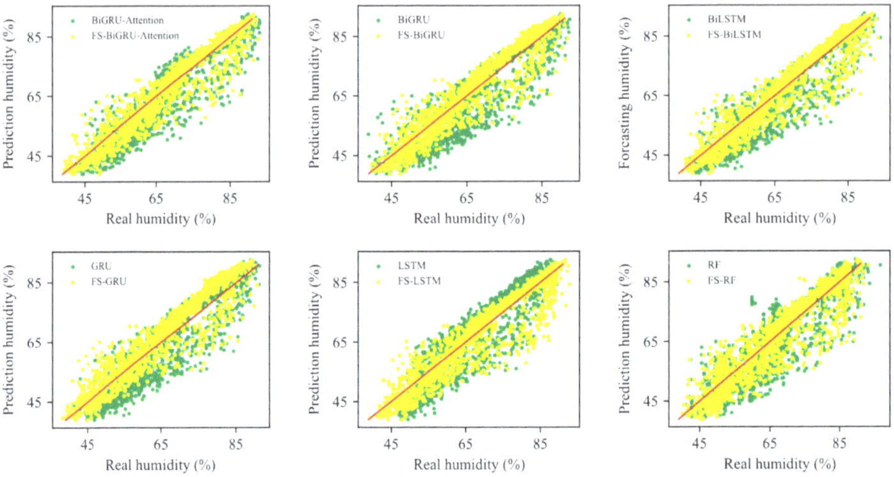

Figure 11. The performance impact of feature selection on predicting the future 3 steps for different baseline models.

4.2. Analysis of Model Results in Comparison Based on CEEMDAN-Based Denoising

After data denoising, the MAE of CEEMDAN-BiGRU-Attention and CEEMDAN-BiGRU models for predicting the future 3 steps decreased by 13.7% and 5.2%, respectively. The RMSE also decreased by 15.7% and 20.1%, while the MAPE decreased by 12.5% and 12.4%, respectively. As shown in Figure 12, other baseline models had reduced errors and improved predictive performance after data denoising. This demonstrates that the CEEMDAN-based method combined with permutation entropy can effectively extract irregular noise from RH, resulting in a more regular and stable RH curve. After denoising, the predictive models can extract useful information more simply and efficiently and eliminate the interference of redundant information, thereby enhancing robustness and accuracy.

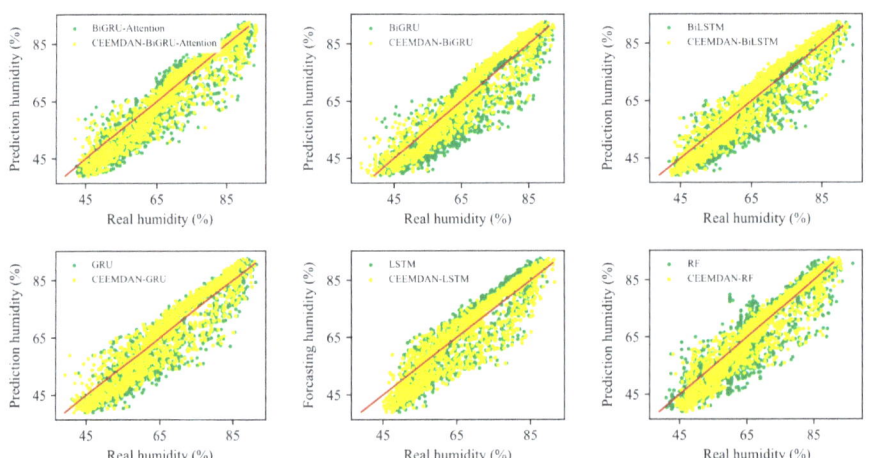

Figure 12. The performance impact of data denoising on predicting the future 3 steps for different baseline models.

4.3. Analysis of Results Based on the CEEMDAN-FS-BiGRU-Attention Model

To substantiate the excellence of the proposed CEEMDAN-FS-BiGRU-Attention hybrid prediction model, it was compared and analyzed with multiple models. As shown in Table 5, under the same prediction framework, BiGRU-Attention outperformed other baseline models in terms of predictive performance. Compared to CEEMDAN-FS-LSTM, CEEMDAN-FS-BiGRU-Attention reduced the MAE, RMSE, and MAPE for predicting the future 3 steps by 29.1%, 26.4%, and 27.0%, respectively.

Table 5. Comparison of prediction performance of different baseline models under the same prediction framework.

Model	MAE			RMSE			MAPE		
	1-Step	2-Step	3-Step	1-Step	2-Step	3-Step	1-Step	2-Step	3-Step
CEEMDAN-FS-BiGRU-Attention vs. CEEMDAN-FS-BiGRU	27.0%	29.2%	16.0%	14.3%	19.8%	9.6%	21.9%	30.1%	12.2%
CEEMDAN-FS-BiGRU-Attention vs. CEEMDAN-FS-BiLSTM	36.0%	29.1%	18.6%	29.4%	20.5%	18.9%	33.4%	30.0%	17.5%
CEEMDAN-FS-BiGRU-Attention vs. CEEMDAN-FS-GRU	30.5%	37.1%	27.0%	24.5%	29.9%	15.9%	31.5%	38.2%	25.3%
CEEMDAN-FS-BiGRU-Attention vs. CEEMDAN-FS-LSTM	46.6%	32.0%	29.1%	36.6%	30.0%	26.4%	45.2%	32.8%	27.0%
CEEMDAN-FS-BiGRU-Attention vs. CEEMDAN-FS-RF	21.4%	25.7%	21.5%	21.0%	22.4%	20.8%	22.3%	27.2%	21.6%
CEEMDAN-FS-BiGRU-Attention vs. LSTM	62.8%	70.0%	57.7%	60.0%	61.0%	48.2%	61.7%	67.4%	56.6%

From the perspective of the prediction framework, feature selection and data denoising can fully extract features highly correlated with RH, remove noise, and eliminate the influence of redundant factors, thereby enhancing the quality of the model input. From the perspective of the baseline model, BiGRU can fully explore the correlation between model inputs and outputs and has good fitting ability. The introduction of an attention mechanism enables capturing the long-term dependence of the RH sequence and effectively improves the situation where important information is lost due to excessive data during BiGRU training. Compared with LSTM, CEEMDAN-FS-BiGRU-Attention reduced the MAE, RMSE, and MAPE for predicting the future 3 steps by 57.7%, 48.2%, and 56.6%, respectively, demonstrating outstanding predictive performance.

4.4. Comparative Analysis of Interval Prediction Performance

To compare and access the interval prediction performance of different models, this study conducted a comparative analysis using BiGRU and BiLSTM as baseline models. Figure 13 shows the error probability distribution function curves of different baseline model validation sets fitted by KDE-Gaussian. It can be observed that the error distribution of CEEMDAN-FS-BiGRU-Attention is relatively concentrated, mainly between [−7, 7]. The error distribution of CEEMDAN-FS-BiGRU and CEEMDAN-FS-BiLSTM are more dispersed, mainly between [−9, 9]. This indicates that CEEMDAN-FS-BiGRU-Attention has smaller errors on the validation set and better predictive performance than the other two models.

To further substantiate the efficacy of the KDE-Gaussian method, we compare its performance in constructing prediction intervals for the future 3 steps using the commonly used normal distribution estimation (NDE) method and Bootstrap method. NDE is a parameter estimation method that assumes a sample follows a normal distribution, while Bootstrap is an estimation method based on a random sampling of error distributions. As shown in Table 6, we can observe that the KDE-Gaussian method has the best and most stable interval prediction performance. Compared with the KDE-Gaussian method, both the NDE and Bootstrap methods have the disadvantage of forming prediction intervals with PICP lower than the confidence level. A lower PICP indicates that the formed prediction intervals do not cover the true RH data well and may lead to incorrect decisions by regulators. The KDE-Gaussian method can output suitable prediction intervals stably, meeting the requirement of the lowest confidence level without producing excessively wide prediction intervals, which is more reliable and practical.

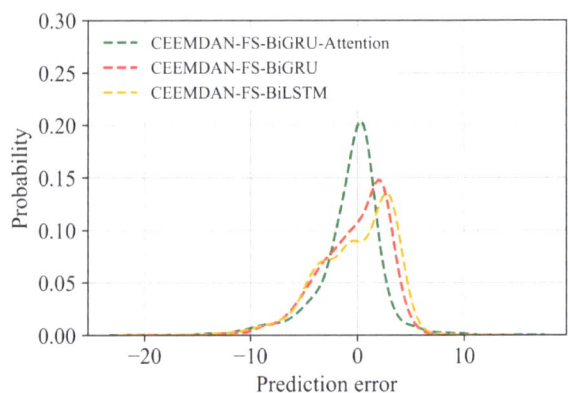

Figure 13. Error distribution of KDE-Gaussian under different baseline models.

Table 6. Comparison of different baseline models and interval prediction methods.

Prediction Model	Interval Prediction Method	Confidence Level	PICP	PINAW	CWC
CEEMDAN-FS-BiLSTM	KDE-Gaussian	95%	0.964	0.236	0.236
		90%	0.934	0.194	0.194
		85%	0.883	0.165	0.165
	NDE	95%	0.933	0.195	0.394
		90%	0.867	0.161	0.328
		85%	0.751	0.137	0.288
	Bootstrap	95%	0.899	0.183	0.377
		90%	0.799	0.148	0.313
		85%	0.699	0.129	0.280
CEEMDAN-FS-BiGRU	KDE-Gaussian	95%	0.970	0.230	0.230
		90%	0.935	0.189	0.189
		85%	0.873	0.156	0.156
	NDE	95%	0.931	0.185	0.375
		90%	0.855	0.150	0.308
		85%	0.767	0.126	0.264
	Bootstrap	95%	0.899	0.171	0.351
		90%	0.801	0.139	0.293
		85%	0.699	0.118	0.256
CEEMDAN-FS-BiGRU-Attention	KDE-Gaussian	95%	0.953	0.201	0.201
		90%	0.914	0.159	0.159
		85%	0.875	0.129	0.129
	NDE	95%	0.915	0.161	0.328
		90%	0.874	0.128	0.260
		85%	0.823	0.107	0.217
	Bootstrap	95%	0.900	0.149	0.306
		90%	0.801	0.103	0.222
		85%	0.799	0.099	0.203

From the perspective of baseline models, since under the same prediction framework, the errors of the BiGRU-Attention model on the validation set are lower than the other two models, even though the PICP of the prediction interval formed by the BiGRU-Attention model is lower than that of BiGRU and BiLSTM, it still meets the requirement of the confidence level. It is worth mentioning that compared with BiGRU and BiLSTM, BiGRU-Attention can maintain a narrower interval width while fulfilling the requirement of the confidence level, accurately describing the uncertainty information of RH variations, which makes it perform better in practical applications.

In conclusion, the prediction interval formed by the proposed CEEMDAN-FS -BiGRU-Attention-KDE-Gaussian model is capable of closely monitoring the trend of changes in RH sequences, forming well-confident prediction intervals while ensuring narrow interval width. The model can provide more accurate and useful information for regulators and is suitable for precise prediction and control of RH in poultry houses.

5. Conclusions

This study proposes an effective hybrid point and interval prediction framework for RH, which significantly improves the accuracy and stability of medium and long-term RH prediction. Through comparison with multiple models, CEEMDAN-FS-BiGRU-Attention has been proven to be a reliable and efficient RH prediction model. Additionally, using the KDE-Gaussian method to form prediction intervals based on point prediction error distribution has demonstrated excellent interval prediction performance under different confidence levels and prediction steps.

The specific conclusions are as follows:

(1) Due to the influence of various factors, the RH data collected by the sensor will inevitably produce noise, which will cause random interference for model training and prediction. After data denoising, the MAE of BiGRU-Attention, BiGRU, and BiLSTM future 3 steps prediction was reduced by 13.8%, 13.2%, and 5.2%, respectively. This indicates that the data denoising method based on CEEMDAN and permutation entropy effectively extracts irregular noise from RH, making it easier for the model to learn useful information while suppressing overfitting.

(2) Environmental factors in poultry houses impact each other. The comprehensive analysis and selection of environmental factors with high correlation and similar trend changes are important to improve the accuracy of RH prediction. After feature selection, the MAE of BiGRU-Attention, BiGRU, and BiLSTM future 3 steps prediction were reduced by 23.0%, 18.1%, and 22.2%, respectively. This indicates that the feature selection method based on Spearman rank correlation analysis and GRA can select important environmental factors, reduce input dimensions, and improve prediction accuracy.

(3) Common baseline models in existing research have the disadvantage of losing important information due to sequences being too long, which is not conducive to predicting long time series. Self-attention mechanism is an efficient solution. Compared with BiGRU and BiLSTM, BiGRU-Attention MAE for predicting future 3 steps decreased by 15.6% and 11.3%, respectively, illustrating that the attention mechanism can improve the utilization of past data, suppress useful information loss, and effectively improve model prediction performance.

(4) Point prediction outputs only a single datum, providing relatively less information. At the same time, as the prediction step length increases, point prediction will have inevitable fluctuations and larger errors. Therefore, it is necessary to implement interval prediction for RH. Compared with commonly used PI construction methods NDE and Bootstrap, KDE-Gaussian has better interval construction performance, outputting reliable and narrow prediction intervals. This method can provide more useful information for producers to make decisions and warnings.

(5) In terms of the overall prediction framework, the CEEMDAN-FS-BiGRU-Attention model proposed in this paper has the best point prediction performance. The MAE, RMSE, and MAPE of predicting future 3 steps were reduced by 57.7%, 48.2%, and 56.6%,

respectively, compared with LSTM. Moreover, the CEEMDAN-FS-BiGRU-Attention -KDE-Gaussian method can form the most appropriate prediction interval at different confidence levels.

This study guides predicting and controlling RH or other environmental factors in livestock breeding from multiple environmental factors and is of great significance for achieving intelligent breeding. However, there are still some limitations in this study, including subjectivity in the feature selection process and high time cost in parameter optimization. In the future, our focus will be on finding more objective and effective feature selection methods and using heuristic optimization algorithms to initialize model parameters.

Author Contributions: Conception, H.Y. and Z.W.; methodology, H.Y., Z.W. and J.W.; software, Z.W. and J.J.; validation, H.Y., Z.W., J.W., Y.C. and M.C.; formal analysis, H.Y., M.C. and S.L.; investigation, H.Y., Z.W. and J.W.; resource, H.Y. and L.G.; data, H.Y. and Z.W.; writing—original draft preparation, H.Y. and Z.W.; writing—review and editing, H.Y., Z.W. and L.G.; projection administration, H.Y. All authors have read and agreed to the published version of the manuscript.

Funding: The work was supported by the National Natural Science Foundation of China (61871475); Guangdong Natural Science Foundation (2021A1515011605); Opening Foundation of Xinjiang Production and Construction Corps Key Laboratory of Modem Agricultural Machinery (BTNJ2021002); Guangzhou Innovation Platform Construction Project (201905010006); Guangdong Province Science and Technology Plan Project (2019B020215003); Yunfu Science and Technology Plan Project (2022020302) and Key R & D projects of Guangzhou (202103000033).

Institutional Review Board Statement: Not applicable.

Data Availability Statement: The data presented in this study are available upon request from the corresponding author.

Conflicts of Interest: The authors declare no conflict of interest.

References

1. Wu, D.; Cui, D.; Zhou, M.; Ying, Y. Information perception in modern poultry farming: A review. *Comput. Electron. Agric.* **2022**, *199*, 107131. [CrossRef]
2. Zheng, H.; Zhang, T.; Fang, C.; Zeng, J.; Yang, X. Design and implementation of poultry farming information management system based on cloud database. *Animals* **2021**, *11*, 900. [CrossRef]
3. Gržinić, G.; Piotrowicz-Cieślak, A.; Klimkowicz-Pawlas, A.; Górny, R.L.; Ławniczek-Wałczyk, A.; Piechowicz, L.; Olkowska, E.; Potrykus, M.; Tankiewicz, M.; Krupka, M.; et al. Intensive poultry farming: A review of the impact on the environment and human health. *Sci. Total Environ.* **2022**, *858 Pt 3*, 160014. [CrossRef]
4. Li, Y.; Arulnathan, V.; Heidari, M.D.; Pelletier, N. Design considerations for net zero energy buildings for intensive, confined poultry production: A review of current insights, knowledge gaps, and future directions. *Renew. Sustain. Energy Rev.* **2022**, *154*, 111874. [CrossRef]
5. El-Hanoun, A.M.; Rizk, R.E.; Shahein, E.H.; Hassan, N.S.; Brake, J. Effect of incubation humidity and flock age on hatchability traits and growth in Pekin ducks. *Poult. Sci.* **2012**, *91*, 2390–2397. [CrossRef] [PubMed]
6. Xiong, Y.; Meng, Q.S.; Gao, J.; Tang, X.F.; Zhang, H.F. Effects of relative humidity on animal health and welfare. *J. Integr. Agric.* **2017**, *16*, 1653–1658. [CrossRef]
7. Saeed, M.; Abbas, G.; Alagawany, M.; Kamboh, A.A.; Abd El-Hack, M.E.; Khafaga, A.F.; Chao, S. Heat stress management in poultry farms: A comprehensive overview. *J. Therm. Biol.* **2019**, *84*, 414–425. [CrossRef] [PubMed]
8. Chang, Y.; Wang, X.J.; Feng, J.H.; Zhang, M.H.; Diao, H.J.; Zhang, S.S.; Peng, Q.Q.; Zhou, Y.; Li, M.; Li, X. Real-time variations in body temperature of laying hens with increasing ambient temperature at different relative humidity levels. *Poult. Sci.* **2018**, *97*, 3119–3125. [CrossRef] [PubMed]
9. Gao, L.; Er, M.; Li, L.; Wen, P.; Jia, Y.; Huo, L. Microclimate environment model construction and control strategy of enclosed laying brooder house. *Poult. Sci.* **2022**, *101*, 101843. [CrossRef]
10. Pereira, W.F.; da Silva Fonseca, L.; Putti, F.F.; Góes, B.C.; de Paula Naves, L. Environmental monitoring in a poultry farm using an instrument developed with the internet of things concept. *Comput. Electron. Agric.* **2020**, *170*, 105257. [CrossRef]
11. Arulmozhi, E.; Basak, J.K.; Sihalath, T.; Park, J.; Kim, H.T.; Moon, B.E. Machine learning-based microclimate model for indoor air temperature and relative humidity prediction in a swine building. *Animals* **2021**, *11*, 222. [CrossRef]
12. Liu, Y.; Zhuang, Y.; Ji, B.; Zhang, G.; Rong, L.; Teng, G.; Wang, C. Prediction of laying hen house odor concentrations using machine learning models based on small sample data. *Comput. Electron. Agric.* **2022**, *195*, 106849. [CrossRef]

13. Lee, S.-Y.; Lee, I.-B.; Yeo, U.-H.; Kim, J.-G.; Kim, R.-W. Machine Learning Approach to Predict Air Temperature and Relative Humidity inside Mechanically and Naturally Ventilated Duck Houses: Application of Recurrent Neural Network. *Agriculture* **2022**, *12*, 318. [CrossRef]
14. Wang, K.; Liu, C.; Duan, Q. Piggery Ammonia Concentration Prediction Method Based on CNN-GRU. *J. Phys. Conf. Ser.* **2020**, *1624*, 042055. [CrossRef]
15. Hajirahimi, Z.; Khashei, M. Hybrid structures in time series modeling and forecasting: A review. *Eng. Appl. Artif. Intell.* **2019**, *86*, 83–106. [CrossRef]
16. Shen, W.; Fu, X.; Wang, R.; Yin, Y.; Zhang, Y.; Singh, U.; Lkhagva, B.; Sun, J. A prediction model of NH3 concentration for swine house in cold region based on Empirical Mode Decomposition and Elman neural network. *Inf. Process. Agric.* **2019**, *6*, 297–305. [CrossRef]
17. Song, L.; Wang, Y.; Zhao, B.; Liu, Y.; Mei, L.; Luo, J.; Zuo, Z.; Yi, J.; Guo, X. Research on prediction of ammonia concentration in QPSO-RBF cattle house based on KPCA nuclear principal component analysis. *Procedia Comput. Sci.* **2021**, *188*, 103–113. [CrossRef]
18. Cen, H.; Yu, L.; Pu, Y.; Li, J.; Liu, Z.; Cai, Q.; Liu, S.; Nie, J.; Ge, J.; Guo, J.; et al. Prediction of CO_2 concentration in sheep sheds in Xinjiang based on LightGBM-SSA-ELM. *J. Agric. Mach.* **2022**, *53*, 261–270.
19. Huang, J.; Liu, S.; Hassan, S.G.; Xu, L. Pollution index of waterfowl farm assessment and prediction based on temporal convoluted network. *PLoS ONE* **2021**, *16*, e0254179. [CrossRef] [PubMed]
20. Du, S.; Li, T.; Horng, S.J. Time series forecasting using sequence-to-sequence deep learning framework. In Proceedings of the 2018 9th International Symposium on Parallel Architectures, Algorithms and Programming (PAAP), Taipei, China, 26–28 December 2018; IEEE: Washington, DC, USA, 2018; pp. 171–176.
21. Khosravi, A.; Nahavandi, S.; Creighton, D.; Atiya, A.F. Comprehensive review of neural network-based prediction intervals and new advances. *IEEE Trans. Neural Netw.* **2011**, *22*, 1341–1356. [CrossRef]
22. Li, Q.; Ma, H.P.; Liu, A.F.; Li, M.Y.; Guo, Z.H. Research progress on the effects of light on goose reproductive performance and hormone levels. *Chin. J. Anim. Sci.* **2015**, *51*, 88–92. [CrossRef]
23. Torres, M.E.; Colominas, M.A.; Schlotthauer, G.; Flandrin, P. A complete ensemble empirical mode decomposition with adaptive noise. In Proceedings of the 2011 IEEE International Conference on Acoustics, Speech and Signal Processing (ICASSP), Prague, Czech Republic, 22–27 May 2011; pp. 4144–4147.
24. Zhou, F.; Huang, Z.; Zhang, C. Carbon price forecasting based on CEEMDAN and LSTM. *Appl. Energy* **2022**, *311*, 118601. [CrossRef]
25. Dai, S.; Niu, D.; Li, Y. Daily peak load forecasting based on complete ensemble empirical mode decomposition with adaptive noise and support vector machine optimized by modified grey wolf optimization algorithm. *Energies* **2018**, *11*, 163. [CrossRef]
26. Li, K.; Huang, W.; Hu, G.; Li, J. Ultra-short term power load forecasting based on CEEMDAN-SE and LSTM neural network. *Energy Build.* **2023**, *279*, 112666. [CrossRef]
27. Bandt, C.; Pompe, B. Permutation entropy: A natural complexity measure for time series. *Phys. Rev. Lett.* **2002**, *88*, 174102. [CrossRef] [PubMed]
28. Li, Y.; Li, Y.; Chen, X.; Yu, J.; Yang, H.; Wang, L. A new underwater acoustic signal denoising technique based on CEEMDAN, mutual information, permutation entropy, and wavelet threshold denoising. *Entropy* **2018**, *20*, 563. [CrossRef]
29. Zhao, C.; Sun, J.; Lin, S.; Peng, Y. Rolling mill bearings fault diagnosis based on improved multivariate variational mode decomposition and multivariate composite multiscale weighted permutation entropy. *Measurement* **2022**, *195*, 111190. [CrossRef]
30. Chen, Z.; Li, Y.; Cao, R.; Ali, W.; Yu, J.; Liang, H. A new feature extraction method for ship-radiated noise based on improved CEEMDAN, normalized mutual information and multiscale improved permutation entropy. *Entropy* **2019**, *21*, 624. [CrossRef]
31. Schober, P.; Boer, C.; Schwarte, L.A. Correlation coefficients: Appropriate use and interpretation. *Anesth. Analg.* **2018**, *126*, 1763–1768. [CrossRef]
32. Kuo, Y.; Yang, T.; Huang, G.W. The use of grey relational analysis in solving multiple attribute decision-making problems. *Comput. Ind. Eng.* **2008**, *55*, 80–93. [CrossRef]
33. Chung, J.; Gulcehre, C.; Cho, K.; Bengio, Y. Empirical evaluation of gated recurrent neural networks on sequence modeling. *arXiv* **2014**, arXiv:1412.3555.
34. Węglarczyk, S. Kernel density estimation and its application. *ITM Web Conf. EDP Sci.* **2018**, *23*, 00037. [CrossRef]
35. Niu, Z.; Zhong, G.; Yu, H. A review on the attention mechanism of deep learning. *Neurocomputing* **2021**, *452*, 48–62. [CrossRef]
36. Du, B.; Huang, S.; Guo, J.; Tang, H.; Wang, L.; Zhou, S. Interval forecasting for urban water demand using PSO optimized KDE distribution and LSTM neural networks. *Appl. Soft Comput.* **2022**, *122*, 108875. [CrossRef]
37. Niu, D.; Sun, L.; Yu, M.; Wang, K. Point and interval forecasting of ultra-short-term wind power based on a data-driven method and hybrid deep learning model. *Energy* **2022**, *254*, 124384. [CrossRef]

38. Pan, C.; Tan, J.; Feng, D. Prediction intervals estimation of solar generation based on gated recurrent unit and kernel density estimation. *Neurocomputing* **2021**, *453*, 552–562. [CrossRef]
39. Maharana, K.; Mondal, S.; Nemade, B. A review: Data pre-processing and data augmentation techniques. *Glob. Transit. Proc.* **2022**, *3*, 91–99. [CrossRef]

Disclaimer/Publisher's Note: The statements, opinions and data contained in all publications are solely those of the individual author(s) and contributor(s) and not of MDPI and/or the editor(s). MDPI and/or the editor(s) disclaim responsibility for any injury to people or property resulting from any ideas, methods, instructions or products referred to in the content.

Article

Lightweight Image Denoising Network for Multimedia Teaching System

Xuanyu Zhang [1], Chunwei Tian [1,2,*], Qi Zhang [3,4], Hong-Seng Gan [5] and Tongtong Cheng [6] and Mohd Asrul Hery Ibrahim [4]

[1] School of Software, Northwestern Polytechnical University, Xi'an 710129, China; xuanyuzhang@mail.nwpu.edu.cn
[2] Research & Development Institute, Northwestern Polytechnical University, Shenzhen 518057, China
[3] School of Economics and Management, Harbin Institute of Technology at Weihai, Weihai 264209, China; hit_zq910057@163.com
[4] Faculty of Entrepreneurship and Business, Universiti Malaysia Kelantan, Kota Bharu 16100, Malaysia
[5] School of AI and Advanced Computing, XJTLU Entrepreneurship College (Taicang), Xi'an Jiaotong-Liverpool University, Suzhou 215400, China
[6] School of Power and Energy, Northwestern Polytechnical University, Xi'an 710129, China
* Correspondence: chunweitian@nwpu.edu.cn

Abstract: Due to COVID-19, online education has become an important tool for teachers to teach students. Also, teachers depend on a multimedia teaching system (platform) to finish online education. However, interacted images from a multimedia teaching system may suffer from noise. To address this issue, we propose a lightweight image denoising network (LIDNet) for multimedia teaching systems. A parallel network can be used to mine complementary information. To achieve an adaptive CNN, an omni-dimensional dynamic convolution fused into an upper network can automatically adjust parameters to achieve a robust CNN, according to different input noisy images. That also enlarges the difference in network architecture, which can improve the denoising effect. To refine obtained structural information, a serial network is set behind a parallel network. To extract more salient information, an adaptively parametric rectifier linear unit composed of an attention mechanism and a ReLU is used into LIDNet. Experiments show that our proposed method is effective in image denoising, which can also provide assistance for multimedia teaching systems.

Keywords: lightweight CNN; dynamic convolution; adaptive activation function; image denoising; multimedia teaching system

MSC: 68T45

1. Introduction

Traditional teaching requires students to learn knowledge through face-to-face methods. Although it has good effects, it has higher requirements for students in terms of time and space. To break these limitations, online education has been developed. It mainly depends on a multimedia system (platform) to complete teaching tasks. Also, obtained images in the multimedia system constitute important media for human-to-human interaction. However, these images often suffer from some challenges from noise caused by camera shake, hardware quality, weather [1], etc. After analyzing the process of collecting and disseminating relevant teaching resources, teaching images often suffer from challenges, i.e., noise from collection equipment. To address these mentioned drawbacks, image denoising techniques are also applied.

An image denoising technique is a classical low-level technique and has been applied in various fields, i.e., activities recognition [2] and remote sensing [3]. For instance, an expected patch log likelihood (EPLL) [4] used a mixed Gaussian model to learn prior knowledge from many natural image blocks for image denoising. Also, block matching and three-dimensional filtering (BM3D) [5] utilized collaborative filtering on similar two-dimensional image blocks to remove noise. A weighted nuclear norm minimization (WNNM) algorithm can exploit an image's non-local self-similarity to extract more information for image denoising [6]. Although these methods can restore images, they face some challenges. That is, they excessively rely on manual adjustment of parameters and complex parameters. Due to strong expressive ability, convolutional neural networks (CNNs) have obtained abilities of feature extraction. Thus, CNNs have been applied in the field of image denoising. For instance, a denoising convolutional neural network (DnCNN) first utilized convolution and residual learning operations to complete denoising work [7]. To suppress the influence of the background on noise, an attention mechanism is fused in a CNN to separate background and foreground to suppress noise [8]. To address image denoising under complex scenes, a dynamic convolution is used in a CNN to achieve an adaptive denoiser, according to different noisy images [9]. To obtain a better denoising effect, a combination of an omni-dimensional dynamic convolution and attention mechanisms is integrated into a CNN to enhance the expressive ability of a denoising network, which can enhance interaction quality of the multimedia teaching system between students and teachers. Le et al. uses two phases, i.e., a feature augmentation stage and a feature refinement stage, to design a CNN to extract more accurate structural information for image denoising [10]. To reduce the complexity of a denoiser, Lin et al. simplified the residual spatial–spectral module and knowledge distillation to achieve a lightweight method to accelerate noise removal [11] Alternatively, a combination of a non-local algorithm and a residual CNN achieves a lightweight CNN to suppress noise [12]. That is, we present a lightweight image denoising network as well as LIDNet for multimedia teaching systems. LIDNet uses a parallel sub-network to mine complementary information for image denoising. To achieve an adaptive CNN, a dynamic convolution based on kernel information and input channel number and output channel number fused into an upper network can automatically adjust parameters to achieve a robust CNN, according to different input noisy images. That also enlarges differences in network architecture, which can improve the denoising effect. To refine the obtained structural information, a serial network is set behind a parallel network. To extract more salient information, an adaptively parametric rectifier linear unit composed of an attention mechanism and a ReLU is used in LIDNet. Experiments show that our proposed method is effective in image denoising, which may also provide assistance for multimedia teaching systems.

The contributions of the proposed method can be summarized as follows:

1. A dynamic convolution based on kernel information and input channel number and output channel number is used to adaptively mine more useful information, according to different input images.
2. A combination of attention mechanism and ReLU is set behind each convolutional layer in addition to the final convolutional layer to enhance the same distributions of training samples for pursuing better denoising performance.
3. Our denoising method is useful for enhancing the interaction quality of a multimedia teaching system between teacher and student.

The remainder of this paper is organized as follows. Section 2 lists related work about image denoising based on dual networks and dynamic networks. Section 3 provides detailed information of the proposed method. Section 4 presents analysis of our proposed method and results. Section 5 gives the conclusion of this paper.

2. Related Work
2.1. A Dual Network for Image Denoising

To extract complementary information, dual networks are developed in image denoising [13]. For instance, Tian et al. [13] presented a dual denoising network with sparse mechanism as well as DudeNet to extract complementary information to enhance denoising effects. Alternatively, Bai et al. [14] achieved a dual network via encoder–decoder and channel attention architecture to extract local and non-local information for image denoising, where image spatial details and semantic information can be obtained by a criss-cross attention. To extract more information, Holla et al. [15] used edge information to design a CNN to capture high-frequency information in image denoising. Zhang et al. fused different masks into a CNN to facilitate complementary information to suppress noise [16]. To mine more high-frequency information, Qiao et al. combined two different networks and a sharpening loss function to improve the quality of visual denoising images [17]. Liu et al. used a wavelet decomposition technique to achieve a wide CNN to prevent vanishing and exploding gradient problems [18]. To extract salient noise information, Chen et al. fused a CNN and a transformer to implement a parallel network to extract structural information and key information based on pixel relations for improving denoising effects [19]. For medical noisy image denoising, Jiang et al. [20] used residual connections and dilated convolutions to achieve a heterogeneous dual network to mine more complementary information to suppress noise. According to the mentioned illustrations, we can see that dual networks are useful for image denoising. Inspired by that, we design a dual network architecture for image denoising in this paper.

2.2. Dynamic Networks for Image Denoising

To enhance the robustness of the image denoiser, a dynamic network is created [21]. For instance, Song et al. [21] combined dynamic convolutions and residual learning operations into a CNN to dynamically adjust parameters to obtain a robust denoising network, according to different input images. Du et al. [22] exploited a dynamic attention mechanism to better extract salient information for image denoising. Alternatively, Shen et al. [23] fused a spatial module and dynamic convolution to obtain more spatial context information to obtain better denoising performance. Tian et al. [9] used dynamic convolution and wavelet transform to extract more useful information to improve denoising effects. According to the mentioned descriptions, we can see that dynamic convolution is effective in image denoising. Motivated by that, we use a dynamic convolution in this paper, according to different kernel and channel information.

3. Proposed Method

3.1. Network Architecture

The proposed 17-layer LIDNet combines a parallel and series architecture. The parallel architecture is composed of a 6-layer block called the dynamic feature extraction block (DFEB) and a 6-layer block named complementary feature extraction block (CFEB). The series architecture contains an 11-layer block called the cascaded purification block (CPB), which is shown in Figure 1. DFEB uses a dynamic convolutional layer to adaptively extract structural information, including kernel information and channel information. To extract complementary information, CFEB use several stacked convolutional layers, BN and a combination of attention mechanism and activation function to extract complementary salient information. Also, a residual learning operation is used to connect the obtained information from a parallel network. To prevent over enhancement, a 11-layer CPB is designed behind the parallel network. To construct a clean image, a residual learning operation is used to act between an input image and output image of LIDNet. This process can be shown as Equation (1).

$$\begin{aligned} I_C &= LIDNet(I_N) \\ &= CPB(DFEB(I_N) + CFEB(I_N)) + (I_N), \end{aligned} \quad (1)$$

where I_C represents an output of LIDNet, which is regraded to a denoised image. I_N denotes the input noisy image, and $LIDNet()$ expresses a function of LIDNet. $DFEB$, $CFEB$, and CPB stand for functions of DFEB, CFEB, and CPB, respectively. $+$ is a residual learning operation, which is also shown as $\oplus$ in Figure 1. Furthermore, the MSE loss function of LIDNet is introduced in Section 3.2.

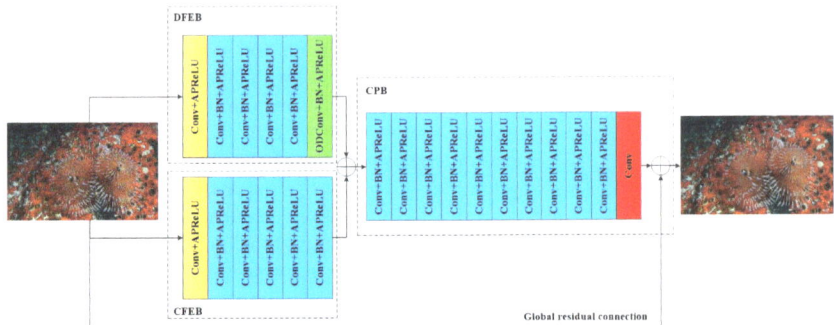

Figure 1. Network architecture of LIDNet.

3.2. Loss Function

To fairly compare with the famous denoising benchmark of DnCNN, a mean squared error (MSE) [24] is chosen as the loss function to train LIDNet. Specifically, MSE uses pairs of $\{I_N^i, I_C^i\}$ ($1 \leq i \leq n$) to train our LIDNet in a supervised way, where I_N^i and I_C^i are defined as the i-th noisy and clean image, respectively. n represents the number of image pairs in the training dataset. LIDNet also uses the popular Adam [25] to obtain reasonable parameters. The mathematical expression of the loss function is as follows:

$$L(\theta) = \frac{1}{2n} \sum_{i=1}^{n} \left\| LIDNet(I_N^i) - I_C^i \right\|^2, \qquad (2)$$

where L is a loss function of MSE and θ stands for learned parameters.

3.3. Dynamic Feature Extraction Block

The first layer in DFEB consists of a convolutional and a rectified linear unit (ReLU) [26] operation. The following 4 layers are composed of a convolutional, a batch normalization (BN) operation and an adaptively parametric rectified linear unit (APReLU) [27]. And the final layer has an omni-dimensional dynamic convolution (ODConv) [28], BN and APReLU. In terms of parameter setting, the input channel number of the first convolutional operation is the same with the channel of the input images. If the input image is color, input channel number of LIDNet is 3. otherwise, input channel number of LIDNet is 1. Other numbers of input and output channels of all the layers are 64. Every size of convolutional kernels in LIDNet is set to 3×3. And the output of the DFEB is fused with the output of the CFEB via a concatenation connection. Mathematical expression of the DFEB is shown as follows:

$$\begin{aligned}O_{DFEB} &= DFEB(I_N) \\ &= Conv_6(4Conv_2(Conv_1(I_N))) \\ &= APReLU(BN(ODConv(4APReLU(4BN(4Conv(ReLU(Conv(I_N)))))))), \end{aligned} \qquad (3)$$

where O_{DFEB} is the output of DFEB. $DFEB()$ expresses a function of DFEB. $Conv_1$ means the first layer of the DFEB, $4Conv_2$ means 4 stacked layers in DFEB, which form the second layer to the fifth layer, and $Conv_6$ means the last layer of the DFEB. $Conv$ stands for a function of a convolutional operation, $ReLU$ stands for an activation function of ReLU, BN stands for the batch normalization operation, $APReLU$ stands for another activation function of APReLU, and $ODConv$ stands for ODConv operation. $4APReLU(4BN(4Conv()))$ is the equation for the $4Conv_2$.

3.4. Complementary Feature Extraction Block

The lower branch in a parallel architecture is CFEB, which is responsible for extracting complementary features by a different network architecture. The first layer in CFEB consists of a convolutional and a ReLU operation. And the following 5 layers are composed of a stacked combination of convolutional, BN, and APReLU operations. As shown in Figure 1, the difference between DFEB and CFEB is mainly reflected on the last convolutional layer. Specifically, the CFEB uses a common convolution operation to replace the ODConv as the final layer in the DFEB. Input and output channel numbers of the final convolutional layer are both 64. The mathematical expression of CFEB is as follows:

$$\begin{aligned} O_{CFEB} &= CFEB(I_N) \\ &= 5Conv_2(Conv_1(I_N)) \\ &= 5APReLU(5BN(5Conv(ReLU(Conv(I_N))))), \end{aligned} \quad (4)$$

where O_{CFEB} is the output of CFEB. $CFEB()$ expresses a function of CFEB. $Conv_1$ means the first layer of the CFEB and $5Conv_2$ means 5 stacked layers in the DFEB, which is as the second layer to the sixth layer in the CFEB. $5APReLU(5BN(5Conv()))$ is equal to $5Conv_2$.

3.5. Concatenated Purification Block

To refine fused structural information from DFEB and CFEB, CPB is set as the last part of LIDNet. Specifically, its first 10 layers in CPB are composed of convolutional, BN, and APReLU operations. And its last layer is simply a common convolutional operation, which is used to construct clean images. To construct a clean image, a residual learning operation is used to act between an input image and output image of LIDNet. The numbers of input and output channels are 64 except the output channel number of the final convolutional layer, which is the same as the channel of the input image. The mathematical expression of CPB is as follows:

$$\begin{aligned} O_{CPB} &= CPB(O_{DFEB} + O_{CFEB}) \\ &= Conv_{11}(10Conv_1(O_{DFEB} + O_{CFEB})) \\ &= Conv(10APReLU(10BN(10Conv(O_{DFEB} + O_{CFEB})))), \end{aligned} \quad (5)$$

$$I_C = I_N - O_{CPB}, \quad (6)$$

where O_{CPB} is the output of CPB. $CPB()$ expresses a function of CPB. $10Conv_1$ means the 10 stacked layers in CPB, which form the first layer to the tenth layer, and $Conv_{11}$ means the last layer of the CPB. $10APReLU(10BN(10Conv()))$ is equal to $10Conv_1$.

4. Experiments

4.1. Datasets

The video quality of many courses inevitably declines due to the impact of the environment and equipment during shooting. To achieve better performance in multimedia, we propose LIDNet to denoise these teaching images. The architecture of our LIDNet is shown in Figure 1.

For image denoising with Gaussian noise, 400 images with sizes of 180×180 from Ref. [29] are used to train a denoising model. Three different denoising models with noise levels of 15 and 25 can be trained, respectively. To train a blind denoising model with noise levels from 0 to 55, a blind model is trained. Specifically, patch sizes are set to 40×40.

To fairly test denoising performance, public BSD68 [30], Set 12 [31], Kodak24 [32], and collected educational images from the Internet are used as test datasets. Guassian noise with noise levels of 15 and 25 is added on BSD68, Set12, Kodak24, and collected educational images from the Internet to test the denoising performance of the proposed method.

4.2. Parameter Setting

This paper has the following experimental settings. The number of training epochs is 180. The original learning rate is 1×10^{-3} and it will decline to 0.2 times when the epoch is 30, 60, and 90, respectively. Batch size is set to 128. Adam is used to optimize parameters [25], where β_1 is 0.9 and β_2 is 0.999. More parameters can be found in Ref. [13].

The LIDNet can be trained on a PC with Intel Xeon Gold 6330 Processor and one Nvidia GeForce RTX 3090. Furthermore, all the codes run on Ubuntu 20.04 with Python 3.8, PyTorch 1.11.0, and CUDA 11.7.

4.3. Network Analysis

This paper uses a parallel network architecture to extract complementary information for image denoising, where a parallel network consists of an upper network (also regarded as dynamic feature extraction block, DFEB) and lower network (also regarded as complementary feature extraction block, CFEB). It connects a serial architecture (concatenated purification block, CPB) to extract more hierarchical structural information. Also, each branch in the parallel network is composed of six layers of stacked architecture. The upper network is composed of a Conv + APReLU, four Conv + BN + APReLU, and a ODConv + BN + APReLU, where APReLU [27] is composed of an attention mechanism and a ReLU is used to extract salient information and nonlinear information. Also, OD-Conv [28] utilizes convolutional kernel information and channel information to dynamically learn parameters to adaptively train a denoising model for different given noisy images. 'LIDNet without global residual connection and ODConv + BN + APReLU' has an improvement of 0.013dB compared to 'LIDNet with only Conv + APReLU in the upper network' in Table 1, which describes the effectiveness of four Conv + BN + APReLU in the upper network for image denoising. Also, the denoising effect of 'Conv + APReLU' in the upper network is verified by 'The combination of lower network and CPB' and 'LIDNet with only Conv + APReLU in upper network and without global residual connection' in Table 1. To test the denoising performance of DFEB, we use 'The combination of lower network and CPB' and 'LIDNet without global residual connection' to conduct comparative experiments. As shown in Table 1, we can see that 'LIDNet without global residual connection' exceeds 'The combination of lower network and CPB' in terms of PSNR. That shows that DFEB in the parallel network is effective for image denoising. Additionally, to test complementarity of two sub-networks, 'The combination of lower network and CPB' is superior to 'CPB' in terms of image denoising in Table 1, which shows the superiority of a parallel network for image denoising. To prevent the interference of upper and lower networks, a serial network is set behind a parallel network to refine the obtained structural information for image denoising. Finally, a global residual connection is employed between outputs of the first layer in a lower network and the last layer in the CPB to construct clean images.

Table 1. Denoising results (average PSNR (dB)) of several networks on BSD68 for noise level of 25.

Different Networks	PSNR(dB)
CPB	28.937
The combination of lower network and CPB	28.944
LIDNet with only Conv + APReLU in upper network and without global residual connection	29.219
LIDNet without global residual connection and ODConv + BN + APReLU	29.232
LIDNet without global residual connection	29.237
LIDNet (Ours)	29.247

4.4. Comparisons with State of the Art

To test the effectiveness of proposed method, we choose several popular denoising methods, i.e., EPLL, BM3D, WNNM, DnCNN, image restoration CNN (IRCNN) [33], fast and flexible denoising network (FFDNet) [34], and a cascade of shrinkage fields (CSF) [35] as comparative methods on the BSD68 and Set12 to conduct experiments. As shown in Table 2, we can see that our LIDNet has obtained the best denoising result on the BSD68 for $\sigma = 15$ and $\sigma = 25$. For instance, our LIDNet has an improvement of 0.11 dB compared to

IRCNN for $\sigma = 15$. That shows that our method is effective for gray noisy image denoising. To verify good denoising performance for a single gray noisy image, different methods on Set12 are used to conduct denoising effects. As illustrated in Table 3, we can see that our LIDNet has obtained the best denoising effect for single noisy image denoising. For instance, our LIDNet has obtained an improvement of 0.09 dB compared to a popular denoising method, i.e., WNNM for a noise level of 15. That shows that our method is a good denoising tool for low-frequency noisy image denoising. Our LIDNet has obtained an improvement of 0.06 dB compared to a popular denoising method, i.e., IRCNN for noise level of 25. That shows that our method is a good denoising tool for high-frequency noisy image denoising. According to that, we can see that our method is effective for single noisy image denoising. Furthermore, to further demonstrate the denoising performance of our LIDNet on color images, Table 4 records the denoising results from different models with different noise levels. Compared with popular methods, i.e., IRCNN, FFDNet, D-BSN, FL(NLM), and FL(BM3D), our LIDNet has also achieved improvements in denoising performance for color noisy images. This also proved the effectiveness of LIDNet in processing color noisy images.

Table 2. Average PSNR (dB) results of several networks on BSD68 for noise levels of 15 and 25.

Methods	EPLL [4]	BM3D [5]	WNNM [6]	DnCNN [7]	IRCNN [23]	FFDNet [34]	CSF [35]	LIDNet (Ours)
$\sigma = 15$	31.21	31.07	31.37	31.73	31.63	31.62	31.24	31.74
$\sigma = 25$	28.68	28.57	28.83	29.23	29.15	29.19	28.74	29.25

Table 3. PSNR (dB) results of different methods on Set12 with noise levels of 15 and 25.

Images	C.man	House	Peppers	Starfish	Monarch	Airplane	Parrot	Lena	Barbara	Boat	Man	Couple	Average
Noise level						15							
EPLL [4]	31.8	34.17	32.64	31.13	32.10	31.19	31.42	33.92	31.38	31.93	32.00	31.93	32.14
BM3D [5]	31.91	34.93	32.69	31.14	31.85	31.07	31.37	34.26	33.10	32.13	31.92	32.10	32.37
WNNM [6]	32.17	35.13	32.99	31.82	32.71	31.39	31.62	34.27	33.60	32.27	32.11	32.17	32.70
IRCNN [33]	32.55	34.89	33.31	32.02	32.82	31.70	31.84	34.53	32.43	32.34	32.40	32.40	32.77
FFDNet [34]	32.43	35.07	33.25	31.99	32.66	31.57	31.81	34.62	32.54	32.38	32.41	32.46	32.77
CSF [35]	31.95	34.39	32.85	31.55	32.33	31.33	31.37	34.06	31.92	32.01	32.08	31.98	32.32
LIDNet (Ours)	31.93	35.03	33.24	32.21	33.09	31.73	31.93	34.54	32.57	32.40	32.29	32.46	32.79
Noise level						25							
EPLL [4]	29.26	32.17	30.17	28.51	29.39	28.61	28.95	31.73	28.61	29.74	29.66	29.53	29.69
BM3D [5]	29.45	32.85	30.16	28.56	29.25	28.42	28.93	32.07	30.71	29.90	29.61	29.71	29.97
WNNM [6]	29.64	33.22	30.42	29.03	29.84	28.69	29.15	32.24	31.24	30.03	29.76	29.82	30.26
IRCNN [33]	30.08	33.06	30.88	29.27	30.09	29.12	29.47	32.43	29.92	30.17	30.04	30.08	30.38
FFDNet [34]	30.10	33.28	30.93	29.32	30.08	29.04	29.44	32.57	30.01	30.25	30.11	30.20	30.44
CSF [35]	29.48	32.39	30.32	28.80	29.62	28.72	28.90	31.79	29.03	29.76	29.71	29.53	29.84
LIDNet (Ours)	30.20	33.10	30.83	29.39	30.40	29.09	29.52	32.39	30.04	30.18	30.04	30.08	30.44

To comprehensively test the denoising effect of our proposed method, we use qualitative analysis to measure the effects of visual images. Specifically, we choose one area of denoising images from BM3D, FFDNet, IRCNN, and LIDNet as observation areas. If the observation area is clearer, its corresponding method shows better denoising performance. As shown in Figures 2–4, we can see that our LIDNet is clearer than the results of other methods. In Figure 3, other methods can obtain more incorrect texture information. Because real noisy images are difficult to obtain in the world, we choose Guassian noise added on educational images to test the performance of the proposed method for educational image denoising. In Figure 4, we can see that our method can obtain clearer detailed information for noisy educational image denoising. Thus, that not only shows that our method is superior to other methods in terms of qualitative analysis, but also that it is robust for different scenes in terms of image denoising.

Table 4. Average PSNR (dB) results of different methods on CBSD68 and Kodak24 datasets with noise levels of 15 and 25.

Datasets	Models	$\sigma = 15$	$\sigma = 25$
CBSD68	CBM3D [5]	33.52	30.71
	DnCNN [7]	33.98	31.31
	IRCNN [33]	33.86	31.16
	FFDNet [34]	33.80	31.18
	D-BSN [30]	33.56	30.61
	FL (NLM) [12]	-	31.01
	FL (BM3D) [12]	-	31.13
	LIDNet (Ours)	33.99	31.37
Kodak24	CBM3D [5]	34.28	31.68
	DnCNN [7]	34.73	32.23
	IRCNN [33]	34.56	32.03
	FFDNet [34]	34.55	32.11
	D-BSN [30]	33.74	31.64
	FL (NLM) [12]	-	32.11
	FL (BM3D) [12]	-	32.26
	LIDNet (Ours)	34.57	32.12

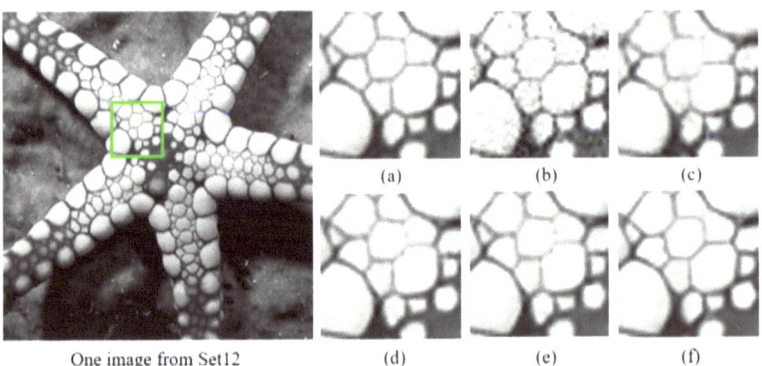

Figure 2. Visual effects of several denoising methods on an image from Set12 for noise level of 15. (**a**) Original image, (**b**) noisy image (24.60 dB), (**c**) BM3D [4] (30.98 dB), (**d**) FFDNet [34] (31.99 dB), (**e**) IRCNN [33] (32.02 dB), and (**f**) LIDNet (Ours) (32.21 dB).

Figure 3. Visual effects of several denoising methods on an image from BSD68 for noise level of 25. (**a**) Original image, (**b**) noisy image (20.19 dB), (**c**) BM3D [4] (29.49 dB), (**d**) FFDNet [34] (30.04 dB), (**e**) IRCNN [33] (30.07 dB), and (**f**) LIDNet (Ours) (30.14 dB).

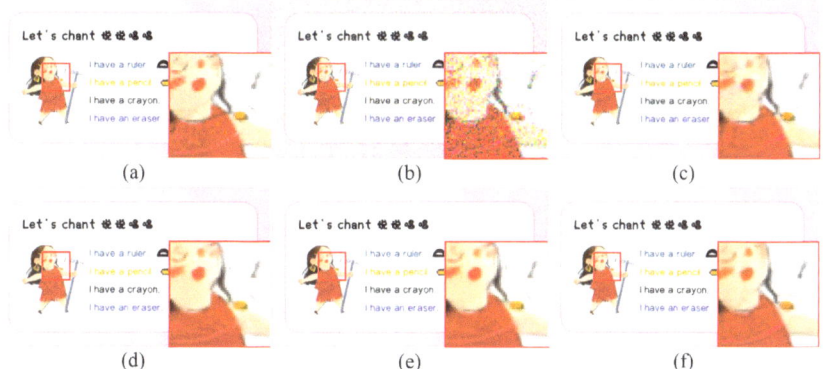

Figure 4. Visual results of several denoising methods on a real teaching image for noise level of 25. (**a**) Original image, (**b**) noisy image (20.18 dB), (**c**) BM3D [4] (36.22 dB), (**d**) IRCNN [33] (36.50 dB), (**e**) FFDNet [34] (36.73 dB) and (**f**) LIDNet (Ours) (36.82 dB).

5. Conclusions

Multimedia teaching systems have become a popular tool for online education. However, interacted images from a multimedia teaching system may suffer from noise. In this paper, we present a lightweight image denoising network as well as LIDNet for multimedia teaching systems. LIDNet uses a parallel network to mine complementary information. To improve robustness of the obtained denoiser, an omni-dimensional dynamic convolution is designed in one sub-network from the parallel network to automatically adjust parameters to achieve an adaptive CNN. That also enlarges the differences in network architecture, which can improve the denoising effect. To refine the obtained structural information, a serial network is set behind a parallel network. To extract more salient information, an adaptively parametric rectifier linear unit composed of an attention mechanism and a ReLU is used in LIDNet. Experiments show that our LIDNet is effective in image denoising, which can also provide assistance for multimedia teaching systems.

Author Contributions: Methodology, X.Z. and C.T.; software, X.Z., Q.Z. and H.-S.G.; validation, X.Z., C.T., Q.Z. and H.-S.G.; formal analysis, X.Z., C.T., Q.Z. and T.C.; writing—original draft, X.Z.; writing—review & editing, X.Z., C.T., Q.Z., T.C. and M.A.H.I.; supervision, Q.Z.; project administration, C.T.; funding acquisition, C.T. All authors have read and agreed to the published version of the manuscript.

Funding: This research was funded by the Guangdong Basic and Applied Basic Research Foundation Grant under 2021A1515110079, in part by Shandong Natural Science Foundation under ZR2023OG074, in part by the Ideological and Political Education of Financial Decision Support System under KVSZZZ202315, in part by Collaborative Education by the Ministry of Education under 220501210164954, in part by Teaching Education Reform of NPU under 06410-23GZ230106.

Data Availability Statement: No new data were created or analyzed in this study. Data sharing is not applicable to this article.

Acknowledgments: The authors would like to thank the Guangdong Basic and Applied Basic Research Foundation, Shandong Natural Science Foundation, Ideological and Political Education of Financial Decision Support System, Collaborative Education by the Ministry of Education and Teaching Education Reform for supporting this work.

Conflicts of Interest: The authors declare no conflict of interest.

References

1. Khorov, E.; Kureev, A.; Levitsky, I.; Akyildiz, I.F. A phase noise resistant constellation rotation method and its experimental validation for NOMA Wi-Fi. *IEEE J. Sel. Areas Commun.* **2022**, *40*, 1346–1354. [CrossRef]
2. Gu, F.; Khoshelham, K.; Valaee, S.; Shang, J.; Zhang, R. Locomotion activity recognition using stacked denoising autoencoders. *IEEE Internet Things J.* **2018**, *5*, 2085–2093. [CrossRef]
3. Liu, P.; Huang, F.; Li, G.; Liu, Z. Remote-sensing image denoising using partial differential equations and auxiliary images as priors. *IEEE Geosci. Remote Sens. Lett.* **2011**, *9*, 358–362. [CrossRef]
4. Zoran, D.; Weiss, Y. From learning models of natural image patches to whole image restoration. In Proceedings of the 2011 International Conference on Computer Vision, Barcelona, Spain, 6–13 November 2011; pp. 479–486.
5. Dabov, K.; Foi, A.; Katkovnik, V.; Egiazarian, K. Image denoising by sparse 3-D transform-domain collaborative filtering. *IEEE Trans. Image Process.* **2007**, *16*, 2080–2095. [CrossRef]
6. Gu, S.; Zhang, L.; Zuo, W.; Feng, X. Weighted nuclear norm minimization with application to image denoising. In Proceedings of the IEEE Conference on Computer Vision and Pattern Recognition, Columbus, OH, USA, 23–28 June 2014; pp. 2862–2869.
7. Zhang, K.; Zuo, W.; Chen, Y.; Meng, D.; Zhang, L. Beyond a gaussian denoiser: Residual learning of deep cnn for image denoising. *IEEE Trans. Image Process.* **2017**, *26*, 3142–3155. [CrossRef]
8. Tian, C.; Xu, Y.; Li, Z.; Zuo, W.; Fei, L.; Liu, H. Attention-guided CNN for image denoising. *Neural Netw.* **2020**, *124*, 117–129. [CrossRef] [PubMed]
9. Tian, C.; Zheng, M.; Zuo, W.; Zhang, B.; Zhang, Y.; Zhang, D. Multi-stage image denoising with the wavelet transform. *Pattern Recognit.* **2023**, *134*, 109050. [CrossRef]
10. Le T.H.; Lin, P.H.; Huang, S.C. LD-Net: An efficient lightweight denoising model based on convolutional neural network. *IEEE Open J. Comput. Soc.* **2020**, *1*, 173–181. [CrossRef]
11. Lin, Y.; Cai, Z.; Li, J.; Zhang, J. Lightweight Remote Sensing Image Denoising via Knowledge Distillation. In Proceedings of the 2022 IEEE 24th International Workshop on Multimedia Signal Processing (MMSP), Shanghai, China, 26–28 September 2022; pp. 1–7.
12. Guo, Y.; Davy, A.; Facciolo, G.; Morel, J.-M.; Jin, Q. Fast, nonlocal and neural: A lightweight high quality solution to image denoising. *IEEE Signal Process. Lett.* **2021**, *28*, 1515–1519. [CrossRef]
13. Tian, C.; Xu, Y.; Zuo, W.; Du, B.; Lin, C.-W.; Zhang, D. Designing and training of a dual CNN for image denoising. *Knowl.-Based Syst.* **2021**, *226*, 106949. [CrossRef]
14. Bai, Y.; Liu, M.; Yao, C.; Lin, C.; Zhao, Y. MSPNet: Multi-stage progressive network for image denoising. *Neurocomputing* **2023**, *517*, 71–80. [CrossRef]
15. Holla, S.; Park, N.; Lee, B. EFID: Edge-Focused Image Denoising Using a Convolutional Neural Network. *IEEE Access* **2023**, *11*, 9613–9626.
16. Zhang, D.; Zhou, F.; Jiang, Y.; Fu, Z. Mm-bsn: Self-supervised image denoising for real-world with multi-mask based on blind-spot network. In Proceedings of the IEEE/CVF Conference on Computer Vision and Pattern Recognition, Vancouver, BC, Canada, 24–31 January 2023; pp. 4188–4197.
17. Qiao, S.; Yang, J.; Zhang, T.; Zhao, C. Layered input GradiNet for image denoising. *Knowl.-Based Syst.* **2022**, *254*, 109587. [CrossRef]
18. Liu, G.; Dang, M.; Liu, J.; Xiang, R.; Tian, Y.; Luo, N. True wide convolutional neural network for image denoising. *Inf. Sci.* **2022**, *610*, 171–184. [CrossRef]
19. Chen, Y.; Yin, M.; Li, Y.; Cai, Q. CSU-Net: A CNN-Transformer parallel network for multimodal brain tumour segmentation. *Electronics* **2022**, *11*, 2226. [CrossRef]
20. Jiang, X.; Jin, Y.; Yao, Y. Low-dose CT lung images denoising based on multiscale parallel convolution neural network. *Vis. Comput.* **2021**, *37*, 2419–2431. [CrossRef]
21. Song, Y.; Zhu, Y.; Du, X. Dynamic residual dense network for image denoising. *Sensors* **2019**, *19*, 3809. [CrossRef]

22. Du, Y.; Han, G.; Tan, Y.; Xiao, C.; He, S. Blind image denoising via dynamic dual learning. *IEEE Trans. Multimed.* **2020**, *23*, 2139–2152. [CrossRef]
23. Shen, H.; Zhao, Z.-Q.; Zhang, W. Adaptive Dynamic Filtering Network for Image Denoising. In Proceedings of the AAAI Conference on Artificial Intelligence, Washington, DC, USA, 7–14 February 2023; pp. 2227–2235.
24. Douillard, C.; Jézéquel, M.; Berrou, C.; Electronique, D.; Picart, A.; Didier, P.; Glavieux, A. Iterative correction of intersymbol interference: Turbo-equalization. *Eur. Trans. Telecommun.* **1995**, *6*, 507–511. [CrossRef]
25. Kingma, D.P.; Ba, J. Adam: A method for stochastic optimization. *arXiv* **2014**, arXiv:1412.6980.
26. Krizhevsky, A.; Sutskever, I.; Hinton, G.E. Imagenet classification with deep convolutional neural networks. In Proceedings of the Advances in Neural Information Processing Systems 2012: 26th Annual Conference on Neural Information Processing Systems 2012, Lake Tahoe, NV, USA, 3–6 December 2012; Volume 25.
27. Zhao, M.; Zhong, S.; Fu, X.; Tang, B.; Dong, S.; Pecht, M. Deep residual networks with adaptively parametric rectifier linear units for fault diagnosis. *IEEE Trans. Ind. Electron.* **2020**, *68*, 2587–2597. [CrossRef]
28. Li, C.; Zhou, A.; Yao, A. Omni-dimensional dynamic convolution. *arXiv* **2022**, arXiv:2209.07947.
29. Chen, Y.; Pock, T. Trainable nonlinear reaction diffusion: A flexible framework for fast and effective image restoration. *IEEE Trans. Pattern Anal. Mach. Intell.* **2016**, *39*, 1256–1272. [CrossRef] [PubMed]
30. Wu, X.; Liu, M.; Cao, Y.; Ren, D.; Zuo, W. Unpaired learning of deep image denoising. In Proceedings of the European Conference on Computer Vision, Glasgow, UK, 23–28 August 2020; pp. 352–368.
31. Mairal, J.; Bach, F.; Ponce, J.; Sapiro, G.; Zisserman, A. Non-local sparse models for image restoration. In Proceedings of the 2009 IEEE 12th International Conference on Computer Vision, Kyoto, Japan, 29 September–2 October 2009; pp. 2272–2279.
32. Franzen, R. Kodak Lossless True Color Image Suite. 1999. Available online: https://r0k.us/graphics/kodak/ (accessed on 15 November 1999).
33. Zhang, K.; Zuo, W.; Gu, S.; Zhang, L. Learning deep CNN denoiser prior for image restoration. In Proceedings of IEEE the Conference on Computer Vision and Pattern Recognition, Honolulu, HI, USA, 21–26 July 2017; pp. 3929–3938.
34. Zhang, K.; Zuo, W.; Zhang, L. FFDNet: Toward a fast and flexible solution for CNN-based image denoising. *IEEE Trans. Image Process.* **2018**, *27*, 4608–4622. [CrossRef] [PubMed]
35. Schmidt, U.; Roth, S. Shrinkage fields for effective image restoration. In Proceedings of the IEEE Conference on Computer Vision and Pattern Recognition, Columbus, OH, USA, 23–28 June 2014; pp. 2774–2781.

Disclaimer/Publisher's Note: The statements, opinions and data contained in all publications are solely those of the individual author(s) and contributor(s) and not of MDPI and/or the editor(s). MDPI and/or the editor(s) disclaim responsibility for any injury to people or property resulting from any ideas, methods, instructions or products referred to in the content.

MDPI AG
Grosspeteranlage 5
4052 Basel
Switzerland
Tel.: +41 61 683 77 34

Mathematics Editorial Office
E-mail: mathematics@mdpi.com
www.mdpi.com/journal/mathematics

Disclaimer/Publisher's Note: The title and front matter of this reprint are at the discretion of the Guest Editors. The publisher is not responsible for their content or any associated concerns. The statements, opinions and data contained in all individual articles are solely those of the individual Editors and contributors and not of MDPI. MDPI disclaims responsibility for any injury to people or property resulting from any ideas, methods, instructions or products referred to in the content.

www.ingramcontent.com/pod-product-compliance
Lightning Source LLC
LaVergne TN
LVHW072320090526
838202LV00019B/2316